Over 10 Million Copies in Print!

COMPREHENSIVE
CURRICULUM
of Basic Skills

GRADE 5

Math

Reading

Reading Comprehension

English

Writing

Thinking Kids®
Carson-Dellosa Publishing LLC
Greensboro, North Carolina

Thinking Kids®
Carson-Dellosa Publishing LLC
P.O. Box 35665
Greensboro, NC 27425 USA

ISBN 978-1-4838-2414-7

Reading

Reading Comprehension

English

*Comprehensive Curriculum - **Grade 5***

TABLE OF CONTENTS

READING

Spelling: Digraphs

A **digraph** is two consonants pronounced as one sound.

Examples: sh as in **shell**, **ch** as in **chew**, **th** as in **thin**

Directions: Write **sh**, **ch**, or **th** to complete each word below.

1. _Th_ reaten

2. _Ch_ ill

3. _Sh_ ock

4. _Sh_ iver

5. _th_ aw

6. _Ch_ allenge

7. peri _Ch_

8. _ch_ ield

9. _Ch_ art

10. _th_ rive

Directions: Complete these sentences with a word, or form of the word, from the list above.

1. A trip to the South Pole would really be a (**ch**) _challengh_ .

2. The ice there never (**th**) _thaw_ because the temperature averages –50°C.

3. How can any living thing (**th**) _thrive_ or even live when it's so cold?

4. With 6 months of total darkness and those icy temperatures, any plants would soon (**sh**) _shiver_ .

5. Even the thought of that numbing cold makes me (**sh**) _shiver_ .

6. The cold and darkness (**th**) _thrive_ the lives of explorers.

7. The explorers take along maps and (**ch**) _chart_ to help them find their way.

8. Special clothing helps protect and (**sh**) _shiver_ them from the cold.

9. Still, the weather must be a (**sh**) _shock_ at first.

10. Did someone leave a door open? Suddenly, I feel a (**ch**) _c___ .

Spelling: Listening for Sounds

Not every word spelled with **ow** is pronounced **ou** as in **powder** and **however**. In the same way, not every word spelled with **ou** is pronounced **ou** as in **amount** and **announce**. The letters **ou** can be pronounced a number of ways.

Directions: Write the word from the box that rhymes with each of the words or phrases below. Some words are used twice.

| doubt | amount | avoid | annoy | announce |
| choice | poison | powder | soil | however |

joys in — Choice

shout — amount

a boy — annoy

employed — annoy

now never — however

voice — choice

a bounce — announce

enjoyed — avoid

two counts — amount

loyal — soil

crowd her — powder

Joyce — choice

a count — announce

employ — annoy

louder — however

trout — amount

Name _____

Spelling: The *J* and *Ch* Sounds

The **j** sound can be spelled with a **j** as in **jump**, with a **g** before **e** or **i** as in **agent** and **giant**, or with **ge** at the end of a word as in **page**.

The **ch** sound is often spelled with the letters **ch** but can also be spelled with a **t** before **u**, as in **nature**.

Directions: Use words from the box to complete the exercises below.

statue	imagination	jealous	future	arrangements
furniture	stranger	project	justice	capture

1. Say each word, and then write it in the correct row, depending on whether it has the **j** or **ch** sound.

j _imagination stranger_ _Jealos_
arrangements Project _Justis arrangmen_

ch _Statue_ _Furniture Future_ _capture_

2. Write a word from the box that belongs to the same word family as each word below.

imagine _imagination_   arranging _arrangment_

strangely _Stranger_   furnish _Furniture_

just _Justice_   jealousy _Jealous_

Directions: Complete each sentence with a word containing the given sound.

1. What is your group's (**j**) _Joke_ this week?

2. There is a (**ch**) _Stachue_ of George Washington in front of our school.

3. She used her (**j**) _Joke_ to solve the problem.

4. My sister keeps rearranging the (**ch**) _Chare_ in our room.

Spelling: Words with Silent Letters

Some letters in words are not pronounced, such as the **s** in **island**, the **t** in **listen**, the **k** in **knee**, the **h** in **hour**, and the **w** in **write**.

Directions: Use words from the box to complete the exercises below.

wrinkled	honest	aisle	knife	wrist
rhyme	exhaust	glisten	knowledge	wrestle

1. Write each word beside its silent letter. Two words have two silent letters—write them twice.

s _aisle_

t _glisten_

h _rhyme_   _exHaust_   _____

w _wrinkled_   _honest_   _wrist_   _wrestle_

k _knife_   _knowledg_   _____

2. Write in the missing letter or letters for each word.

_W_ res _t_ le   ex _g_ aust   _k_ nife   glis _t_ en   ai _s_ le

_k_ nowledge   _W_ rinkle   r _H_ yme   _H_ onest   _W_ rist

Directions: Complete each sentence with a word that has the given silent letter. Use each word only once.

1. He always tells the truth. He's very **(h)** _honest_ .

2. I like **(s)** _aisle_ seats in airplanes.

3. I need a sharper **(k)** _knife_ to cut this bread.

4. I think a long hike might **(h)** _exhaust_ me.

5. Did you sleep in that shirt? It is so **(w)** _wrinkled_ !

6. The snow seemed to **(t)** _glisten_ in the sunlight.

7. To play tennis, you need a strong **(w)** _wrinkled_ .

Name _____

Spelling: Syllables

A **syllable** is a part of a word with only one vowel sound. Some words have only one syllable, like **cat**, **leaf**, and **ship**. Some words have two or more syllables. **Be-lief** and **trac-tor** have two syllables, **to-ge-ther** and **ex-cel-lent** have three syllables, and **con-ver-sa-tion** has four syllables. Some words can have six or more syllables! The word **ex-tra-ter-res-tri-al**, for example, has six syllables.

Directions: Follow the instructions below.

1. Count the syllables in each word below, and write the number of syllables on the line.

    a. badger _____2_____

    b. location _____2_____

    c. award _____2_____

    d. national _____3_____

    e. necessary _____4_____

    f. grease _____4_____

    g. relationship _____5_____

    h. communication ___7___

    i. government _____4_____

    j. Braille _____2_____

2. Write four words with four syllables each in the blanks.

    a. ___Baskitbullhope___

    b. ___ricecrispytrts___ *treats*

    c. ___mississippi___

    d. ___arizona___

3. Write one word with five syllables and one with six syllables. If you need help, use a dictionary.

    Five syllables: ___nitroglycerin___

    Six syllables: ___Azithromycin___

Writing: Sounding Out Syllables

Directions: Use words from the box to complete the exercises below.

decision	division	pressure	addition	ancient
subtraction	confusion	multiplication	social	correction

1. Write each word in the row showing the correct number of syllables.

Two: _Pressure_ _ancient_ _social_

Three: _decision_ _division_ _addition_

Subtraction _confusion_ _correction_

Five: _multiplication_

2. Write in the missing syllables for each word.

_So_ cial   sub _trac_ tion   mul _ult_ pli _ca_ tion   pres _sure_

di _vi_ sion   an _cient_   deci _sion_   ad _di_ tion

con fusion   cor _rec_ tion

3. Beside each word below, write a word with the same number of syllables. Use each word from the box only once.

daily _Social_   challenging _division_

syllable _decision_   election _confusion_

decreasing _addition_   threaten _correction_

advantage _Subtraction_   shivering _ancient_

title _pressure_   experimenting _multiplication_

Writing: Word Families

A **word family** is a group of words based on the same word. For example, **playful**, **playground**, and **playing** are all based on the word **play**.

Directions: Use words from the box to complete the exercises below.

decision	division	pressure	addition	create
subtraction	confusion	multiplication	social	correction

1. Write the word that belongs to the same word family as each word below.

correctly _____correction_____   confused _____confusion_____

divide _____divsion_____   subtracting _____subtraction_____

pressing _____Pressure_____   society _____Social_____

multiply _____Multiplication_____   decide _____decision_____

added _____Addition_____   creativity _____create_____

2. Complete each sentence by writing the correct form of the given word.

   Example: Have you (decide) <u>decided</u> what to do? Did you make a (decide) <u>decision</u> yet?

I am (add) _____adding_____ the numbers right now. Would you check my

(add) _____addition_____ ?

This problem has me (confuse) _____confused_____ . Can you clear up my

(confuse) _____ ?

This is a (press) _____pressuring_____ problem. We feel (press) _____

to solve it right away.

Is he (divide) _____dividing_____ by the right number? Will you help him with his

(divide) _____ ?

Try to answer (correct) _____correctlee_____ . Then, you won't have to make any

(correct) _____ on your paper later on.

Writing: Word Families

Directions: Write the word that belongs to the same word family as each word below.

doubt	amount	avoid	annoy	announce
choice	poison	powder	soil	however

avoidance   _avoied_

doubtful   _doubtti_

announcement   _announce_

choose   _chose_

powdery   _powder_

annoyance   _annoy_

soiled   _soiling_

poisonous   _poison_

amounted   _amoun_

whenever   _when_

Directions: Complete each sentence by writing the correct form of the given word.

Example: Are you (doubt) <u>doubting</u> my word? You never (doubt) <u>doubted</u> it before.

1. The teacher is (announce) ___annouñcing___ the next test. Did you hear what he (announce) ___announced___ ?

2. This stream was (poison) ___Poisoned___ by a chemical from a factory nearby.

3. Is the chemical (poison) ___Poisoning___ any other water supply? How many (poison) ___poisons.___ does the factory produce?

4. My cat always (annoy) ___annoys___ our dog.

5. Last night, Camie (annoy) ___annoyed___ Lucas for hours.

6. I think Carrie is (avoid) ___avoiding___ me. Yesterday, she (avoid) ___avoid___ walking home with me.

Spelling: Double Consonants

When adding endings such as **ing** and **ed** to verbs, use the following rule: Double the final consonant of verbs that have short vowel sounds and end with only one consonant. For example, **rip** becomes **ripped**, and **beg** becomes **begging**. However, do not double the final consonant in words that end in double consonants. For example, **rock** ends with two consonants, **ck**. So even though it has a short vowel sound, **rock** becomes **rocked**.

Directions: Add **ed** to the verbs below. Remember, when a verb ends with **e**, drop the **e** before adding an ending (**taste**, **tasting**). The first one has been done for you.

top	**topped**	rip	RiPiNg
pet	Petting	punch	Punching
sob	Sobbing	rinse	rinseing
brag	Braging	stock	stocking
scrub	Scrubbing	lack	Lacking
flip	Fliping	dent	dent

Directions: Add **ing** to the verbs below. The first one has been done for you.

flap	**flapping**	snack	Snack
scrub	scrubing	flip	Fliping
stock	Stocking	rinse	rinseing
dent	denting	brag	Braging
pet	Peting	lack	Lacking
sob	Sobing	punch	Punching

Writing: Verb Forms

Directions: In the following story, some of the verbs are missing. Write the proper form of the verbs shown, adding **ed** or **ing** when necessary.

What's Your Verb Form?

Yesterday, I was (brag) _bragging_ to my brother

about how much I (help) _helped_ our mother

around the house. I had (scrub) _scrubbed_ the

kitchen floor, (wipe) _wiped_ off all the counters,

and (rinse) _rinsed_ out the sink. I was (pour)

pouring the dirty water out of the bucket when

our mother came in. She looked around the kitchen and

(smile) _smiled_ . "Who did all this work?" she (ask)_asked_ .

I was (get) _getting_ ready to tell her what I had done when my

brother (interrupt) _interrupted_ me. "We both did! We've been

(work) _working_ very hard!" he said. "He's not (tell) _tellig_ the

truth!" I said to Mom. "I did everything!" My brother (glare) _glared_ at me.

"Is that true?" asked Mom. My brother (look) _looked_ at the floor

and (nod) _nodded_ . He was (think) _thikng_ about all the trouble

he would get into. Instead, Mom smiled again. "Well, that's okay," she said. "The rest

of the house needs to be (clean) _cleaned_ , too. You can get (start)

started right away!"

Name _____

Spelling: Math Plurals

To make most nouns plural, add **s**. When a noun ends with **s**, **ss**, **sh**, **ch**, or **x**, add **es**: bus—bus**es**, cross—cross**es**, brush—brush**es**, church—church**es**, box—box**es**. When a noun ends with a consonant and **y**, change the **y** to **i** and add **es**: berry—berr**ies**. For some words, insteading of adding **s** or **es**, the spelling of the word changes: man—men, mouse—mice.

Directions: Write the correct plural or singular form of the words in these math problems. Write whether the problem requires addition (**A**), subtraction (**S**), multiplication (**M**), or division (**D**). The first one has been done for you.

1. 3 (box) __boxes__ – 2 (box) __boxes__ = __1 box__ **S**

2. 2 (supply) __supplies__ + 5 (supply) __suplies__ = __5__ __S__

3. 4 (copy) __copies__ x 2 (copy) __copies__ = __8__ __S__

4. 6 (class) __classes__ ÷ 2 (class) __classes__ = __2__ __S__

5. 5 (factory) __factories__ – 3 (factory) __factories__ = __3__ __S__

6. 3 (daisy) __daisies__ x 3 (daisy) __daisies__ = __30__ __S__

7. 8 (sandwich) __sandwiches__ – 4 (sandwich) __sandwiches__ = __4__ __S__

8. 3 (child) __childs__ – 1 (child) __childs__ = __1__ __S__

9. 10 (brush) __Brushes__ ÷ 5 (brush) __Brushes__ = __5__ __S__

10. 4 (goose) __geese__ + 1 (goose) __goose__ = __1__

11. 3 (mouse) __mice__ + 1 (mouse) __mouse__ = __1__

Spelling: More Plurals

Remember, in some words, an **f** changes to a **v** to make the plural form.

Examples: life — li**v**es   wife — wi**v**es   knife — kni**v**es   leaf — lea**v**es

Directions: Complete these sentences by writing the correct plural form of the given word. Also, circle the spelling errors, and write the words correctly on the lines to the right.

1. The (leaf) __leaves__ are dry and rinkled. _____

2. The (knife) __knife__ glisened in the sun. _____

3. I think the (child) __Children__ in this school are honist. _____

4. The (supply) __sluppies__ were stacked in the isle. _____

5. (mouse) __Mice__ rimes with **twice**. _____

6. Some people feel exausted all their (life) __Lives__. _____

7. The (class) __Glasses__ were trying to gain more knowlege about Olympic athletes. _____

8. The kittens were wresling in the (bush) __bushes__. _____

9. Jamie nearly broke his rist trying to carry all those

   (box) __Boxes__. _____

10. Some kings had several (wife) __Wives__ who new about each other. _____

11. (Daisy) __Daisies__ are knot expensive. _____

12. Right your name on both (copy) __copies__. _____

13. We watched the (monkey) __Monkeies__ play on the swings for ours. _____

14. Do you like (strawberry) __staberries__ hole or sliced? _____

Name _____

Spelling: Finding Mistakes

Directions: Circle the four spelling mistakes in each paragraph. Then, write the words correctly on the lines below.

Last nite, our family went to a nice restaurant. As we were lookking at the menus, a waiter walked in from the kichen carrying a large tray of food. As he walked by us, he triped, and the tray went flying! The food flew all over our table and all over us, too!

_____ _____

_____ _____

Last week, while my dad was washing the car, our dog Jack dicided to help. He stuck his nose in the pale of soapy water, and it tiped over and soaked him! As he shook himself off, the water from his fur went all over the car. "Look!" Dad laffed. "Jack is doing his part!"

_____ _____

_____ _____

For our next feild trip, my class is going to the zoo. We have been studying about animals in sceince class. I'm very eksited to see the elephants, but my freind Tasha really wants to see the monkeys. She has been to the zoo before, and she says the monkeys are the most fun to watch.

_____ _____

_____ _____

It seems the rain will never stop! It has been rainning for seven days now, and the sky is always dark and clowdy. Everyone at school is in a bad mood, because we have to stay inside during resess. Will we ever see the son again?

_____ _____

_____ _____

Spelling: Finding Mistakes

Directions: Circle the four spelling mistakes in each paragraph. Then, write the misspelled words correctly on the lines below.

According to the newspaper, a man came into the store and stood near a clerk. The clerk was stockking the shelves with watches. Then, the man suddenly grabed several watches and raced out of the store. The clerk shouted, "Stop him! He's robing us!" The police searched for the man, but they still lak a suspect.

_____   _____

_____   _____

Tony always braged about the tricks he could do with his skateboard. One day, he tried to skate up a ramp and jump over three bikes. Well, he landed on the last bike and dentted it. The last I saw Tony, he was runing down the street. The owner of the bike was chassing him.

_____   _____

_____   _____

One day, I was peting my dog when I felt something sticky in his fur. It was time for a bath! I put him in a tub of water and scrubed as best I could. Then, I rinced the soap out of his fur. He jumped out of the tub, soaking wet, and rolled in some dirt. I sighed and draged him back into the tub. This dog makes me tired sometimes!

_____   _____

_____   _____

Last night, my little sister started braging about how fast she could wash the dishes. I told her to prove it. (It was my turn to do the dishes.) She started fliping the dishes around in the sink, washing them as fast as she could. I noticed she was rinseing only about half of them. Finally, it happened. She droped a cup on the floor. Dad made me finish the dishes, but at least she did some of them.

_____   _____

_____   _____

Name _____

Spelling: Finding Mistakes

Spelling Mistake

Directions: Circle the spelling mistakes in each paragraph. Write the words correctly on the lines below.

Some poisions that kill insects can also threten people. Often these pouders and sprays are used on corn, beans, and other plants we eat. Unless these plants are well scrubed, we may eat a small amount of the poison.

_____ _____ _____ _____

Sometimes the poison is put into the soyl and moves into the plant through its roots. Then, it stays in the plant in spyte of all our rinseing. All we can do is avoyd eating food that has been grown this way. Howver, that also means we have to expect more insects in our food. Its a hard chioce! Some people dout that a little bit of poision will hurt them, while others have made a dicision to grow their own food.

_____ _____ _____ _____

_____ _____ _____ _____

_____ _____

Yesterday, the teacher anownced a new projict. She chalenged us to think of a new arangement for the furnichure in the room. We voated to put the chairs in groups. Then, Brian said it would be easier to cheet that way. I was annoyd. I told him we had more pryde than that!

_____ _____ _____

_____ _____ _____

_____ _____

Spelling: Proofreading Practice

Directions: Circle the six spelling and pronoun mistakes in each paragraph. Write the words correctly on the lines below.

Jenna always braged about being ready to meet any chalenge or reach any gole. When it was time for our class to elekt it's new officers, Jenna said we should voat for her to be president.

_____   _____   _____

_____   _____   _____

Simon wanted to be ours president, too. He tried to coaks everyone to vote for his. He even lowned kids money to get their votes! Well, Jenna may have too much pryde in herself, but I like her in spit of that. At least she didn't try to buy our votes!

_____   _____   _____

_____   _____   _____

Its true that Jenna tried other ways to get us to vote for hers. She scrubed the chalkboards even though it was my dayly job for that week. One day, I saw her rinseing out the paintbrushes when it was Peter's turn to do it. Then, she made sure we knew about her good deeds so we would praize her.

_____   _____   _____

_____   _____   _____

We held the election, but I was shalked when the teacher releesed the results. Simon won! I wondered if he cheeted somehow. I feel like our class was robed! Now, Simon is the one who's braging about how great he is. I wish he knew the titel of president doesn't mean anything if no one wants to be around you!

_____   _____   _____

_____   _____   _____

Name _____

Adding Suffixes

A **suffix** is a syllable at the end of a word that changes its meaning.
The suffixes **ant** and **ent** mean "a person or thing that does something."

Examples:

A person who occupies a place is an **occupant**.
A person who obeys is **obedient**.

A **root word** is the common stem that gives related words their basic meanings.

When a word ends in silent **e**, keep the **e** before adding a suffix beginning with a consonant. Drop the **e** before adding a suffix beginning with a vowel.

Examples:

announce + ment = **announcement**
announce + ing = **announcing**

Announce is the root word in this example.

Directions: Combine each root word and suffix to make a new word. The first one has been done for you.

Root word	Suffix	New word
observe	ant	observant
contest	ant	_____
please	ant	_____
preside	ent	_____
differ	ent	_____

Directions: Use the meanings in parentheses to complete the sentences with one of the above new words. The first one has been done for you.

1. To be a good scientist, you must be very __observant__ . (pay careful attention)

2. Her perfume had a strong but very _____ smell. (nice)

3. Because the bridge was out, we had to find a _____ route home. (not the same)

4. The game show _____ jumped up and down when she won the grand prize. (person who competes)

5. Next week, we will elect a new student council _____ . (highest officer)

Adding Suffixes

The suffix **less** means "without"; **ative** means "having the nature of" or "relating to";
ive means "having" or "tending to be."

Examples:
    Faultless means "without fault or blame."
    Formative means "something that can be formed or molded."
    Corrective means "something that fixes a problem."

Directions: Combine each root word and suffix to form a new word. The first one has
been done for you.

Root word	Suffix	New word
sleep	less	sleepless
imagine	ative	_____
talk	ative	_____
impress	ive	_____
attract	ive	_____

Directions: Use the meanings in parentheses to complete the sentences with one of the
above new words.

1. The night before his birthday, Michael spent a _____ night. (wide awake)

2. Our history teacher is a rather _____man who likes to tell jokes and
   stories. (fond of speaking)

3. That book has such an _____ plot! (showing creativity)

4. Monica thought the dress in the store window was very_____ . (pleasing)

5. The high school basketball team was _____ in its Friday night game,
   beating its rivals by 30 points. (making an impact on the mind or emotions)

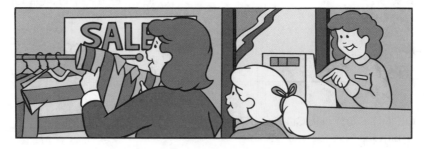

Comprehensive Curriculum - **Grade 5**

Name _____

Adding Prefixes

A **prefix** is a syllable at the beginning of a word that changes its meaning. The prefixes **il**, **im**, **in**, and **ir** all mean "not."

Examples:
   Illogical means "not logical or practical."
   Impossible means "not possible."
   Invisible means "not visible."
   Irrelevant means "not relevant or practical."

Directions: Divide each word into its prefix and root word. The first one has been done for you.

	Prefix	Root Word
illogical	il	logical
impatient	_____	_____
immature	_____	_____
incomplete	_____	_____
insincere	_____	_____
irresponsible	_____	_____
irregular	_____	_____

Directions: Use the meanings in parentheses to complete the sentences with one of the above words.

1. I had to turn in my assignment _____ because I was sick last night. (not finished)

2. It was _____ for Jimmy to give me his keys because he can't get into his house without them. (not practical)

3. Yoko and Joel were _____ to leave their bikes out in the rain. (not doing the right thing)

4. I sometimes get _____ waiting for my ride to school. (restless)

5. The boys sounded _____ when they said they were sorry. (not honest)

6. These towels didn't cost much because they are _____. (not straight or even)

Adding Prefixes

The prefix **pre** means "before." The prefix **re** means "again."

Examples:
  Preview means "to see in advance."
  Redo means "to do again."

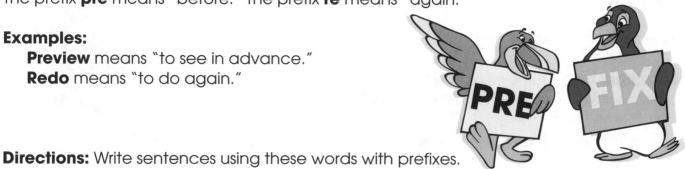

Directions: Write sentences using these words with prefixes.

1. prefix _____

_____

2. redirect _____

_____

3. regain _____

_____

4. predetermine _____

_____

5. reorganize _____

_____

6. prepackage _____

_____

7. redistribute _____

_____

8. precook _____

_____

Name _____

Synonyms

A **synonym** is a word with the same or similar meaning as another word.

Examples: bucket — pail   happy — cheerful   dirty — messy

Directions: Match the words on the left with their synonyms on the right. The first one has been done for you.

tired	beverage
start	notice
get	boring
fire	busy
dull	sleepy
big	couch
noisy	receive
crowded	begin
sofa	loud
drink	halt
sign	large
stop	flames

Directions: Rewrite the sentences below using synonyms for the bold words.

1. Because the road was **rough**, we had a **hard** time riding our bikes on it.

    _____

2. After the accident, the driver appeared to be **hurt**, so someone **ran** to call an ambulance.

    _____

3. Yesterday, everyone stayed after school to pick up litter, and now the school yard is **nice** and **clean**.

    _____

Synonyms

Directions: Circle a word or a phrase in each sentence that is a synonym for a word in the box. Write the synonym on the line.

challenged	shocked	thaw	chart	frighten
perish	chill	shivering	thrive	shield

Example: The writing was in an (old) code.   _ancient_

1. A fish out of water will quickly die.   _____

2. The ice carving is beginning to melt.   _____

3. I was amazed when I saw how he looked.   _____

4. The puppy was trembling with excitement.   _____

5. Ferns need moisture to grow well.   _____

6. Are you trying to scare me?   _____

7. Let the salad get cold in the refrigerator.   _____

8. She tried to protect him from the truth.   _____

9. He made a list of different kinds of birds.   _____

10. They dared us to enter the contest.   _____

Directions: Write your own sentences using five words from the box. If you're not sure what a word means, look it up in a dictionary.

_____

_____

_____

_____

_____

Name _____

Finding Synonyms

Directions: Circle a word, or group of words, in each sentence that is a synonym for a word in the box. Write the synonym on the line.

statue	imagination	jealous	future	arrangements
furniture	stranger	project	justice	capture

Example: She will (lend) me her book. _____loan_____

1. He tried to catch the butterfly. _____

2. No one knows what will happen in the time to come. _____

3. They are loading the chairs, tables, and beds into the moving van. _____

4. We almost finished our team assignment. _____

5. They made plans to have a class party. _____

6. Penny made a model of a horse. _____

7. The accused man asked the judge for fairness. _____

Directions: Write your own sentences for these words: **stranger, imagination, jealous**. Then, choose one other word from the box, and use it in a sentence. Make each sentence at least 10 words long. The sentences should show that you know what the word means.

1. _____

_____

2. _____

_____

3. _____

_____

4. _____

_____

Synonyms

Synonyms are words that mean the same or nearly the same.

Examples:
    small and **little**
    big and **large**
    bright and **shiny**
    unhappy and **sad**

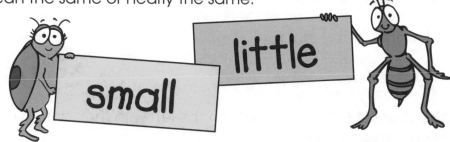

Directions: Write a synonym for each word. Then, use it in a sentence. Use a dictionary if you are unsure of the meaning of a word.

1. cup _____
   _____

2. book _____
   _____

3. looking glass _____
   _____

4. hop _____
   _____

5. discover _____
   _____

6. plan _____
   _____

7. lamp _____
   _____

8. friend _____
   _____

9. discuss _____
   _____

10. rotate _____
    _____

Name _____

Antonyms

An **antonym** is a word with the opposite meaning of another word.

Examples: hot — cold
up — down
start — stop

Directions: Match the words on the left with their antonyms on the right. The first one has been done for you.

asleep	sloppy
sit	shut
excited	full
north	awake
wild	tame
hairy	stand
open	bored
quick	bald
neat	south
hungry	slow

Directions: In the sentences below, replace each bold word with a synonym or an antonym so that the sentence makes sense. Write the word on the line. Then, write either **synonym** or **antonym** to show its relationship to the given word. The first one has been done for you.

1. If the weather stays warm, all the plants will **perish**.   _live — antonym_

2. Last night, Mom made my favorite meal, and it was **delicious**. _____

3. The test was **difficult**, and everyone in the class passed it. _____

4. The music from the concert was so **loud** we could hear it in the parking lot! _____

5. The bunks at camp were **comfortable**, and I didn't sleep very well. _____

Finding Antonyms

Directions: Write a word that is an antonym for each bold word in the sentences below.

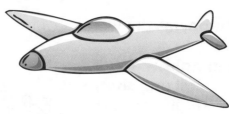

1. Jared made his way **quickly** through the crowd. _____

2. My friends and I arrived **late** to the party. _____

3. My sister loves to watch airplanes **take off**. _____

4. The teacher seems especially **cheerful** this morning. _____

5. When are you going to **begin** your project? _____

Directions: Write antonyms for the following words on the lines. Then, write a short paragraph using all the words you wrote.

dirty _____   whisper _____

old _____   carefully _____

down _____   night _____

sit _____   happy _____

_____

_____

_____

_____

_____

_____

_____

_____

_____

Name _____

Antonyms

Antonyms are words that mean the opposite.

Examples:
    tall and **short**
    high and **low**
    top and **bottom**

Directions: Write an antonym for each word. Then, use it in a sentence. Use a dictionary if you are unsure of the meaning of a word.

1. tired _____

    _____

2. bright _____

    _____

3. sparkling _____

    _____

4. tame _____

    _____

5. fresh _____

    _____

6. elegant _____

    _____

7. real _____

    _____

8. odd _____

    _____

9. unruly _____

    _____

10. valor _____

    _____

Homophones

Homophones are words that sound alike but have different spellings and meanings. The words **no** and **know** are homophones. They sound alike, but their spellings and meanings are very different.

Directions: Use words from the box to complete the exercises below.

hour	wring	knot	whole	knew
wrap	knight	piece	write	

1. Write each word beside its homophone.

peace _____   new _____   ring _____

hole _____   rap _____   night _____

not _____   right _____   our _____

2. Write three words that have a silent **k**. _____ _____ _____

3. Write one word that has a silent **h**. _____

Directions: Circle the misused homophones in each sentence. Then, rewrite the sentences, using the correct homophones.

1. By the time knight fell, I new she was knot coming.

_____

2. I would never have any piece until I new the hole story.

_____

3. He spent an our righting down what had happened.

_____

4. I could see write through the whole in the night's armor.

_____

Homophones

Homophones are words that are pronounced the same but are spelled differently and have different meanings.

Example: to, two, too

Directions: Use these homophones in sentences of your own.

1. forth _____
   _____

2. fourth _____
   _____

3. shown _____
   _____

4. shone _____
   _____

5. they're _____
   _____

6. their _____
   _____

7. there _____
   _____

8. not _____
   _____

9. knot _____
   _____

Homophones

Directions: Complete the story below by writing the correct homophones for the words in parentheses.

Last Saturday, I went to (meat) _____ my friend, Andrea, at the mall.

When I got there, I noticed she looked a little (pail) _____ .

"What's wrong?" I asked her.

She (side) _____ . "I'm (knot) _____ feeling so (grate) _____ ," she said. "I don't (no) _____ what's wrong with me."

"Maybe you (knead) _____ to drink some water or some juice," I said. "Let's go to the drugstore. It's this (weigh) _____ ."

As we were walking, we passed a (flour) _____ shop, and I bought (sum) _____ roses for my mother. Then, we found the drugstore, and Andrea bought some juice. An (our) _____ later, she felt much better.

That (knight) _____ , I gave the roses to my mother. "You shouldn't (waist) _____ your money on (presence) _____ for me!" she said, but she was smiling. I (new) _____ she was pleased.

"That's okay, Mom, I wanted to buy them for you," I said. "But now I'm broke. How about a (lone) _____ ?"

Name _____

Homographs

Homographs are words that have the same spelling but different meanings and pronunciations.

pres´ent	**n.**	a gift
pre sent´	**v.**	to introduce or offer to view
rec´ord	**n.**	written or official evidence
re cord´	**v.**	to keep an account of
wind	**n.**	air in motion
wind	**v.**	to tighten the spring by turning a key
wound	**n.**	an injury in which the skin is broken
wound	**v.**	past tense of **wind**

Directions: Write the definition for the bold word in each sentence.

1. I would like to **present** our new student council president, Olivia Hall.

   _____

2. The store made a **record** of all my payments.

   _____

3. **Wind** the music box to hear the song.

   _____

4. His **wound** was healing quickly.

   _____

5. The **wind** knocked over my bicycle.

   _____

6. I bought her a birthday **present** with my allowance.

   _____

Similes

A **simile** uses the words **like** or **as** to compare two things.

Examples:
 The snow glittered **like** diamonds.
 He was **as** slow **as** a turtle.

Directions: Circle the two objects being compared in each sentence.

1. The kittens were like gymnasts performing tricks.

2. My old computer is as slow as molasses.

3. When the lights went out in the basement, it was as dark as night.

4. The sun was like a fire, heating up the earth.

5. The young girl was as graceful as a ballerina.

6. The puppy cried like a baby all night.

7. He flies that airplane like a daredevil.

8. The girl was as pretty as a picture.

9. The snow on the mountaintops was like whipped cream.

10. The tiger's eyes were like emeralds.

Directions: Complete the simile in each sentence.

11. My cat is as _____ as _____ .

12. He was as _____ as _____ .

13. Melissa's eyes shone like _____ .

14. The paints were like _____ .

15. The opera singer's voice was as _____ as _____ .

16. My friend is as _____ as _____ .

Metaphors

A **metaphor** is a direct comparison between two things. The words **like** or **as** are not used in a metaphor.

Example: The **sun** is a **yellow ball** in the sky.

Directions: Underline the metaphor in each sentence. Write the two objects being compared on the line.

1. As it bounded toward me, the dog was a quivering furball of excitement.

   _____

2. The snow we skied on was mashed potatoes.

   _____

3. Diego is a mountain goat when it comes to rock climbing.

   _____

4. The light is a beacon shining into the dark basement.

   _____

5. The famished child was a wolf, eating for the first time in days.

   _____

6. The man's arm was a tireless lever as he fought to win the wrestling contest.

   _____

7. The flowers were colorful polkadots against the green of the yard.

   _____

Idioms

An **idiom** is a phrase that says one thing but actually means something quite different.

Example: A **horse of a different color** means something quite unusual.

Directions: Write the letter of the correct meaning for each bold phrase. The first one has been done for you.

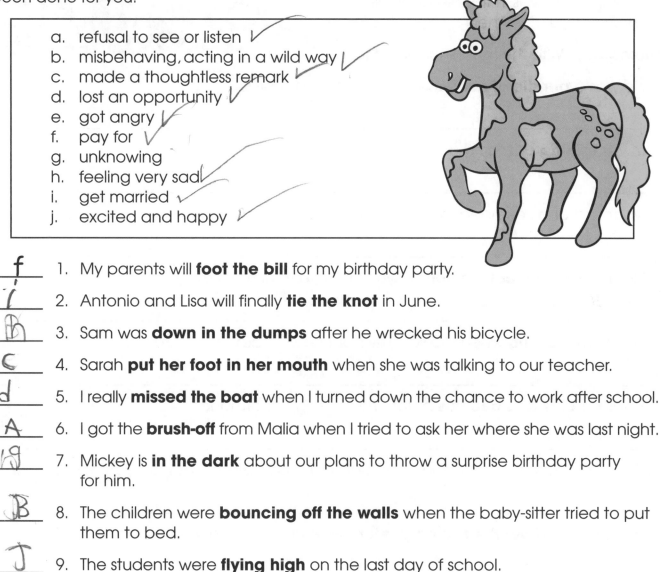

a. refusal to see or listen
b. misbehaving, acting in a wild way
c. made a thoughtless remark
d. lost an opportunity
e. got angry
f. pay for
g. unknowing
h. feeling very sad
i. get married
j. excited and happy

_f_ 1. My parents will **foot the bill** for my birthday party.

_i_ 2. Antonio and Lisa will finally **tie the knot** in June.

_B_ 3. Sam was **down in the dumps** after he wrecked his bicycle.

_C_ 4. Sarah **put her foot in her mouth** when she was talking to our teacher.

_d_ 5. I really **missed the boat** when I turned down the chance to work after school.

_A_ 6. I got the **brush-off** from Malia when I tried to ask her where she was last night.

_g_ 7. Mickey is **in the dark** about our plans to throw a surprise birthday party for him.

_B_ 8. The children were **bouncing off the walls** when the baby-sitter tried to put them to bed.

_J_ 9. The students were **flying high** on the last day of school.

_e_ 10. My sister **lost her cool** when she discovered I had spilled chocolate milk on her new sweater.

Name _____

Idioms

An **idiom** is a figure of speech that has a meaning different from the literal one.

Example:

Dad is **in the doghouse** because he was late for dinner.

Meaning: Dad is in trouble because he was late for dinner.

Directions: Write the meanings of the idioms in bold.

1. He was a **bundle of nerves** waiting for his test scores.

_____

2. It was **raining cats and dogs**.

_____

3. My friend and I decided to **bury the hatchet** after our argument.

_____

4. He gave me the **cold shoulder** when I spoke to him.

_____

5. My mom **blew up** when she saw my poor report card.

_____

6. I was **on pins and needles** before my skating performance.

_____

7. When the student didn't answer, the teacher asked, "**Did the cat get your tongue**?"

_____

8. The city **rolled out the red carpet** for the returning Olympic champion.

_____

9. They hired a clown for the young boy's birthday party to help **break the ice**.

_____

Name _____

Review

Directions: Circle the word or phrase that best defines the bold words.

1. The woman has a very **pleasant** voice.

   loud   nice   strange

2. He had a very **imaginative** excuse for not turning in his homework.

   creative   difficult to believe   acceptable

3. I didn't get credit for my answer on the test because it was **incomplete**.

   not correct   too short   not finished

4. Will you **wind** the music box for the baby?

   air in motion   injury in which the skin is broken

   tighten the spring by turning a key

5. To enroll in the school, you must bring your birth certificate or some other legal **record** for identification.

   to keep an account   a flat disk that plays music

   written or official evidence

6. We use the crystal **pitcher** when we have company.

   printed likeness of a person or object

   baseball team member   container for pouring

7. This block is as **light as a feather**!

   very heavy   not heavy at all   bright

8. The whole family was there when Bill and Lynn **tied the knot** last weekend.

   were caught in a trap   bought a house   got married

9. I will have to **foot the bill** for the damage you caused.

   kick   pay for   seek payment

10. Madison **lost her cool** when the party was called off.

    got angry   had a fever   went home

11. The kite **soared like an eagle**.

    flapped and fluttered   glided along high in the air

    crashed to the ground

Review

Directions: Write a synonym for each word.

1. amusing _____   3. terrifying _____

2. prison _____   4. flee _____

Directions: Write an antonym for each word.

5. insult _____   7. discourage _____

6. famine _____   8. generous _____

Directions: Write a homophone pair.

9. _____   _____

Directions: Write a sentence containing a simile.

10. _____

Directions: Write a sentence containing a metaphor.

11. _____

Directions: Write the letter of the correct meaning for the idiom in each sentence.

a. made a thoughtless remark
b. lost an opportunity
c. pay for
d. feeling very sad
e. excited and happy

_____ 12. My uncle promised to foot the bill for a new computer if I got terrific grades this year.

_____ 13. Takeo was down in the dumps when his team lost the game.

_____ 14. The opposing team was flying high after the win.

_____ 15. Jonah put his foot in his mouth when he told his mother what he really thought of her new hairdo.

_____ 16. Sean really missed the boat when he turned down the chance to travel to England.

Using a Dictionary

Directions: Read about dictionaries. Then, answer the questions.

Dictionaries are books that give definitions of words. Dictionaries list words in alphabetical order. **Guide words** at the top of each page show the first and last words listed on the page. All other words on the page are listed in alphabetical order between the guide words. This helps you locate the word you want quickly and easily.

In addition to definitions, dictionaries also show the following: how to pronounce, or say, each word; the individual syllables found in each word; the part of speech for each word; and the plural form or verb forms if the base word changes.

Some dictionaries provide considerably more information. For example, The Tormont Webster's Illustrated Encyclopedic Dictionary includes many color illustrations of terms, a pronunciation key on every other page and two pages of introductory information on how to use the dictionary effectively.

Other highlights of the Tormont Webster are **historical labels** that tell the history of words no longer in common use; **geographic labels** that tell in what part of the world uncommon words are used; **stylistic labels** that tell whether a word is formal, informal, humorous or a slang term; and **field labels** that tell what field of knowledge—such as medicine—the word is used in.

1. Where are guide words found? _____

   _____

2. What is the purpose of guide words? _____

   _____

3. Which label tells if a word is a slang term? _____

4. Which label tells the history of a word? _____

5. Which type of information is not provided for each word in the dictionary?

   ☐ definition

   ☐ part of speech

   ☐ picture

Using a Dictionary

Directions: Use the dictionary entry below to answer the questions.

ad-he-sive (ad-he´-siv) adj. 1. Tending to adhere; sticky. 2. Gummed so as to adhere. n. 3. An adhesive substance such as paste or glue. **ad-he-sive-ly** adv. **ad-he-sive-ness** n.

1. Based on the first definition of **adhesive**, what do you think **adhere** means?

   _____

   _____

2. Which definition of **adhesive** is used in this sentence?
   The tape was so adhesive that we couldn't peel it loose. _____

   _____

3. Which part of speech is **adhesive** used as in this sentence?
   We put a strong adhesive on the package to keep it sealed. _____

4. How many syllables does **adhesive** have? _____

5. Is **adhesive** used as a noun or an adjective in this sentence?
   The adhesive we chose to use was not very gummy. _____

6. **Adhesive** and variations of the word can be used as what parts of speech? _____

   _____

Directions: Write sentences using these words.

7. adhesiveness _____

   _____

8. adhesively _____

   _____

9. adhere _____

   _____

Using a Dictionary

Guide words are the words that appear at the top of dictionary pages. They show the first and last words on each page.

Directions: Read the guide words on each dictionary page below. Then, look around for objects whose names come between the guide words. Write the names of the objects, and then number them in alphabetical order.

babble	buzz
___ ___	
___ ___	
___ ___	

magic	myself
___ ___	
___ ___	
___ ___	

cabin	cycle
___ ___	
___ ___	
___ ___	

pea	puzzle
___ ___	
___ ___	
___ ___	

dairy	dwarf
___ ___	
___ ___	
___ ___	

scar	sword
___ ___	
___ ___	
___ ___	

feast	future
___ ___	
___ ___	

tack	truth
___ ___	
___ ___	

Name _____

Using a Dictionary: Guide Words

Directions: Use the guide words and page numbers shown on the top of the dictionary pages below. Write the page number where each word would be found.

156 blur — boatmanship   boat neck — body 157

158 body check — boisterous

1. boast _____

2. bodkin _____

3. body language _____

4. board _____

5. bodice _____

6. bobbin _____

7. boar fish _____

8. boatload _____

9. boilermaker _____

10. body clock _____

11. bogie _____

12. bode _____

13. bodily _____

14. blurt _____

15. blusher _____

16. bodiless _____

17. boardroom _____

18. blurb _____

19. boggle _____

20. boccie _____

Using a Dictionary: Multiple Meanings

If a word has more than one meaning, you will find that information in a dictionary.

Directions: Use the dictionary entry below to answer the questions about the word **record**.

re-cord v. (ri kord') **1.** a) to put in writing, print, etc. for future use; draw up an account of (to record the day's events); b) to make a permanent or official note of (to record a vote) **2.** a) to indicate automatically or permanently, as on a graph or chart (a seismograph records earthquakes); b) to show, as on a dial (a thermometer records temperatures) **3.** to remain as evidence of (metal tools record a superior civilization) **4.** a) to register (sound or visual images) in some permanent form, such as digitally or on a phonograph disc, magnetic tape, etc. for reproduction on a playback device; b) to register the performance of (a musician, actor, composition, etc.) in this way. (for n. & adj. rek' erd) **5.** an account of facts or events preserved, esp. in writing **6.** information or knowledge about a person's achievements or performances **7.** standing with respect to contests won, lost, and tied **8.** the best performance of its kind to date **9.** something, as in a disk, on which sound or images have been recorded **10.** adj. surpassing all others.

1. How many and which parts of speech are listed for all definitions of **record**? _____

_____

2. Including all the subheadings, how many definitions are listed? _____

3. Which definition uses the example of a thermometer recording a temperature? _____

4. Which definition describes a record you might play to listen to music? _____

5. Is **record** used as a noun or a verb in this sentence?
   She held the all-time record for most wins.   _____

6. Is **record** used as a noun or a verb in this sentence?
   I will record our conversation.   _____

Name _____

Multiple Meanings

Directions: Circle the correct definition of the bold word in each sentence. The first one has been done for you.

1. Try to **flag** down a car to get us some help!

   (to signal to stop)
   cloth used as symbol

2. We listened to the **band** play the National Anthem.

   group of musicians
   a binding or tie

3. He was the **sole** survivor of the plane crash.

   bottom of the foot
   one and only

4. I am going to **pound** the nail with this hammer.

   to hit hard
   a unit of weight

5. He lived on what little **game** he could find in the woods.

   animals for hunting
   form of entertainment

6. We are going to **book** the midnight flight from Miami.

   to reserve in advance
   a written work

7. The **pitcher** looked toward first base before throwing the ball.

   baseball team member
   container for pouring

8. My grandfather and I played a **game** of checkers last night.

   animals for hunting
   form of entertainment

9. They raise the **flag** over City Hall every morning.

   to signal to stop
   cloth used as symbol

Using a Dictionary: Choosing the Correct Word

Directions: Use a dictionary to look up the words in parentheses. Then, write the correct word in the blanks.

_____ 1. Our class visited an art (galley/gallery) last week to learn about paintings and sculptures.

_____ 2. He didn't (scrutinize/scruple) his essay very carefully before handing it in.

_____ 3. She squeezed the clay in her hands until it became (plentiful/pliable).

_____ 4. The quarterback's (laudable/laughable) performance helped his team win the game.

_____ 5. The science that deals with the universe beyond Earth's atmosphere is known as (astronomy/astrology).

_____ 6. My mother was (grateful/graphic) that I helped her with the dishes.

_____ 7. The police did not have any (tantamount/tangible) evidence that the man was guilty.

_____ 8. It was very (unfortunate/unfamiliar) that she broke her arm right before the big game.

_____ 9. The gardener was using a (trough/trowel) to dig up the flowers.

_____ 10. That company manufactures men's and women's (appendage/apparel).

_____ 11. After vegetable scraps (decompose/decongest), you can put them on your garden as fertilizer.

_____ 12. Most bats are (nocturnal/noble) and sleep during the day.

_____ 13. We bought some (venerable/venetian) blinds for our windows instead of curtains.

_____ 14. The noisy class (exasperated/exaggerated) the teacher.

_____ 15. The prisoner was released on (parody/parole).

Learning New Words

Directions: Write a word from the box to complete each sentence. Use a dictionary to look up words you are unsure of.

bouquet	unconscious	inspire	disability
inherit	hovering	assault	enclosure
commotion	criticize		

1. He was knocked _____ by the blow to his head.

2. Megan never let her _____ stand in the way of accomplishing what she wanted.

3. The teacher burst into the noisy room and demanded to know what all the _____ was about.

4. He offered her a _____ of flowers as a truce after their argument.

5. The zoo was in the process of building a new _____ for the elephants.

6. The mother was _____ over her sick child.

7. The movie was meant to _____ people to do good deeds.

8. My friend will eventually _____ a fortune from his grandmother.

9. Not many people enjoy having someone _____ their work.

10. The female leopard led the _____ on the herd of zebras.

Learning New Words

Directions: Use a dictionary. Define the following words. Then, use each word in a sentence.

1. mechanical _____

_____

2. cashmere _____

_____

3. deplorable _____

_____

4. illusion _____

_____

5. rivalry _____

_____

6. traction _____

_____

7. whittle _____

_____

8. pageant _____

_____

9. nectarine _____

_____

10. javelin _____

_____

Comprehensive Curriculum - **Grade 5**

Name _____

Using a Thesaurus

A **thesaurus** is a type of reference book that lists words in alphabetical order followed by their synonyms and antonyms. **Synonyms** are words that mean the same. **Antonyms** are words that mean the opposite.

A thesaurus is an excellent tool for finding just the right word. It is also a valuable resource for finding a variety of synonyms and/or antonyms to make your writing livelier.

Each main entry in a thesaurus consists of a word followed by the word's part of speech, its definition, an example, a list of related words, and other information. You can also find several thesauruses online.

Here is a typical entry in a thesaurus, with an explanation of terms below:

SLOW
ADJ **SYN** deliberate, dilatory, laggard, leisurely, unhasty, unhurried
REL lateness, limited, measured, slowish, steady, unhurrying, slowfooted, plodding, pokey, straggling, snail-like **IDIOM** as slow as molasses in January; as slow as a turtle **CON** blitz, quick, rapid, swift **ANT** fast

ADJ means "adjective"

CON means "contrasted words"

SYN means "synonym"

ANT means "antonym"

REL means "related words"

idiom means "a common phrase that is not literal"

Directions: Use the thesaurus entry to answer the questions.

1. What is the antonym listed for **slow**? _____

2. How many contrasting words are listed for **slow**? _____

3. How many synonyms are listed for **slow**? _____

4. What is **slow** compared to in the two idioms listed? _____

5. What is the last related word listed for **slow**? _____

Using a Thesaurus to Find Synonyms

A thesaurus can help you find synonyms.
Example:
FIND: VERB **SYN** locate, discover, detect, uncover, see, etc.

Directions: Use a thesaurus. Replace each word
in bold with a synonym.

1. My father does not like our **artificial** Christmas tree.

_____

2. The **fabulous** home sat on a large hill overlooking a wooded ravine.

_____

3. My dog is allowed to be **loose** if someone is home.

_____

4. A **peaceful** rally was held to bring attention to the needs of the homeless.

_____

5. The artist completed his **sketch** of the girl.

_____

6. The **timid** boy could not bring himself to speak to the man at the counter.

_____

7. My family is cutting down the **timber** at the back of our property

_____

8. Her necklace was very **attractive**.

_____

9. The girl looked hopelessly at her **clothes** and moaned that she had nothing to wear.

_____

10. The team's **feat** of winning 20 games in a row was amazing.

_____

Name _____

Using a Thesaurus

Directions: Use a thesaurus to list as many synonyms as possible for the following words.

1. calm _____

2. hunt _____

3. quilt _____

4. tender _____

5. vacate _____

Directions: Use a thesaurus to list as many related words as possible for the following words.

6. value _____

7. difference _____

8. enable _____

Directions: Use a thesaurus to list one idiom for each of the following words.

9. beauty _____

10. cake _____

Using a Thesaurus to Find Antonyms

Antonyms are words that mean the opposite. Antonyms can be found in some thesauruses. They are identified by the abbreviation **ANT**.

Examples:

FOUND:
VERB **ANT** misplaced, gone, lost, missing, mislaid, etc.

RIDDLE:
NOUN **ANT** key, solution, answer, etc.

ANCIENT:
ADJECTIVE **ANT** new, recent, current, etc.

Directions: Use a thesaurus to replace each word in bold with an antonym.

_____ 1. Today's weather will undoubtedly be very **humid**.

_____ 2. Can you **give** my sister a napkin?

_____ 3. The man **insulted** me by laughing at my artwork.

_____ 4. I thought the rules for the classroom were too **lax**.

_____ 5. The broken leg was quite **painful**.

_____ 6. We made great **progress** last night on the parade float.

_____ 7. The girl received a **reward** for returning the lost wallet.

_____ 8. The teacher asked us to **separate** the types of art brushes.

_____ 9. The home was decorated in a **simple** manner.

_____ 10. They became very **tense** during the earthquake.

_____ 11. Mr. Kurtzman gave us a math test **today**.

_____ 12. My father loves hiking in the **hills**.

_____ 13. Stephen ran over my **new** red bike.

Comprehension: Word Origins

Did you ever wonder why we call our midday meal "lunch"? Or where the name "Abraham" came from? Or why one of our lovely eastern states is called "Vermont"?

These and other words have a history. The study of where words came from and how they began is called **etymology** (ett-a-mol-o-gee).

The word **lunch** comes from the Spanish word **longja** which means "a slice of ham." Long ago, Spanish people ate a slice of ham for their midday meal. Eventually, what they ate became the word for the meal itself. Still later, it came to be pronounced "lunch" in English.

Abraham also has an interesting history. Originally, it came from the Hebrew word **avarahem**. Abraham means "father of many."

City and state names are often based on the names of Native American tribes or describe the geography of the area. **Vermont** is actually made from two French words. **Vert** is French for "green." **Mont** is French for "mountain."

Directions: Answer these questions about word origins.

1. What is the study of the history and origin of words? _____

2. From which language did the word **lunch** come? _____

3. What is the French word for "green"? _____

4. **Vermont** comes from two words of what language?

☐ Spanish   ☐ English   ☐ French

5. Which is not correct about the origin of names of cities and states?

☐ They describe geography.

☐ They name Native American tribes.

☐ They are mostly French in origin.

Comprehension and Context

Comprehension is understanding what is seen, heard, or read.

Context is the rest of the words in a sentence or the sentences before or after a word. Context can help with comprehension.

Context clues help you figure out the meaning of a word by relating it to other words in the sentence.

Directions: Use the context clues in the sentences to find the meanings of the bold words.

1. Ana was a **wizard** at games. She mastered them in no time and seldom lost.

   ☒ evil magician   ☒ gifted person   ☐ average player

2. The holiday was so special that she was sure she'd never forget it. The memory would be **imprinted** forever on her mind.

   ☐ found   ☒ weighed   ☒ fixed

3. "John will believe anything anyone tells him," his teacher said. "He's a very **impressionable** young man."

   ☒ easily influenced   ☐ unhappy   ☐ unintelligent

4. "Do you really think it's **prudent** to spend all your money on clothes?" his mother asked crossly.

   ☐ foolish   ☒ wise   ☐ funny

5. "Your plan has **merit**," Elizabeth's father said. "Let me give it some thought."

   ☒ value   ☐ awards   ☐ kindness

6. Isaiah was very **gregarious** and loved being around people.

   ☐ shy   ☒ outgoing   ☐ unfriendly

Name _____

Name _____

Classifying

Classifying means putting items into categories based on similar characteristics.

Example: Tag, hide-and-seek, and tic-tac-toe could be classified as games.

Directions: Cross out the word in each group that does not belong. Then, add a word of your own that does belong. The first one has been done for you.

1. wren   robin   ~~feather~~
   sparrow   eagle   __bluebird__

2. sofa   stool   chair
   carpet   bench   _____

3. lettuce   salad   corn
   broccoli   spinach   _____

4. pencil   chalk   crayon
   pen   drawing   _____

5. perch   shark   penguin
   bass   tuna   _____

6. rapid   quick   unhurried
   swift   speedy   _____

7. lemon   daisy   melon
   lime   grapefruit _____

Directions: Write a category name above each group of words. Then, write a word of your own that belongs in each group.

_____   _____
blizzard   ankle
hurricane   shin
thunder   thigh

_____   _____

_____   _____
engine   hockey
horn   ice skating
steering wheel   bobsledding

_____   _____

Classifying

Directions: Write three objects that could belong in each category.

1. whales _____ _____ _____

2. songs _____ _____ _____

3. sports stars _____ _____ _____

4. fruit _____ _____ _____

5. schools _____ _____ _____

6. teachers _____ _____ _____

7. tools _____ _____ _____

8. friends _____ _____ _____

9. books _____ _____ _____

10. mammals _____ _____ _____

11. fish _____ _____ _____

12. snacks _____ _____ _____

13. cars _____ _____ _____

14. hobbies _____ _____ _____

15. vegetables _____ _____ _____

16. insects _____ _____ _____

Classifying: Regional Forecast

Directions: Read the forecast. Then, write words in the correct categories.

The very warm, early spring weather will continue to spread along the East Coast today. With some sunshine, afternoon temperatures will climb to 90 degrees in many places. Columbia, South Carolina, and neighboring areas could reach 100 degrees. Showers are expected from Washington, D.C., to New York City. Severe thunderstorms are likely in Virginia and North Carolina. Central South Carolina will be under a tornado watch during the afternoon.

Cities

_____

_____

_____

States

_____

_____

_____

Weather Conditions

_____

_____

_____

_____

Analogies

An **analogy** is a way of comparing objects to show how they are related.

Example: Nose is to **smell** as **tongue** is to **taste**.

Directions: Write the correct word in the blank to fill in the missing part of each analogy. The first one has been done for you.

1. <u>Scissors</u> are to **paper** as saw is to **wood**.　　fold　　scissors　　thin

2. **Man** is to **boy** as **woman** is to _____girle_____.　　mother　　~~girl~~　　lady

3. _____allise_____ is to **cellar** as **sky** is to **ground**.　　down　　~~attic~~　　up

4. **Rag** is to **dust** as _____Broom_____ is to **sweep**.　　floor　　straw　　broom

5. **Freezer** is to **cold** as **stove** is to _____hot_____.　　cook　　~~hot~~　　recipe

6. **Car** is to _____ride_____ as **book** is to **bookshelf**.　　~~ride~~　　gas　　garage

7. **Window** is to _____glass_____ as **car** is to **metal**.　　~~glass~~　　clear　　house

8. **Eyes** are to **seeing** as **feet** are to _____walking_____　　legs　　~~walking~~　　shoes

9. **Gas** is to **car** as _____electricity_____ is to **lamp**.　　~~electricity~~　　plug　　cord

10. **Refrigerator** is to **food** as _____closet_____ is to **clothes**.　　fold　　material　　~~closet~~

11. **Floor** is to **down** as **ceiling** is to _____high_____.　　high　　over　　up

12. **Pillow** is to **soft** as **rock** is to _____hard_____.　　dirt　　~~hard~~　　hurt

13. **Carpenter** is to **house** as **poet** is to _____writing_____verse　　novel　　~~writing~~

14. **Lamp** is to **light** as **clock** is to _____time_____.　　~~time~~　　hands　　numbers

15. _____Palm_____ is to **hand** as **sole** is to **foot**.　　wrist　　finger　　~~palm~~

Analogies

Directions: Write your own words on the blanks to complete each analogy. The first one has been done for you.

1. **Fuse** is to **firecracker** as **wick** is to <u>candle</u> .

2. **Wheel** is to **steering** as <u>Break</u> is to **stopping**.

3. **Scissors** are to <u>Cut</u> as **needles** are to **sew**.

4. **Water** is to **skiing** as **rink** is to <u>Skat</u> .

5. **Steam shovel** is to **dig** as **tractor** is to <u>P</u> .

6. **Stick** is to **hockey** as <u>Bat</u> is to **baseball**.

7. **Watch** is to **television** as <u>Lisen</u> is to **radio**.

8. <u>gees</u> are to **goose** as **children** are to **child**.

9. **Multiply** is to **multiplication** as <u>Subtrakt</u> is to **subtraction**.

10. **Milk** is to **cow** as **egg** is to <u>chin</u> .

11. **Yellow** is to **banana** as <u>Red</u> is to **tomato**.

12. <u>Fast</u> is to **slow** as **day** is to **night**.

13. **Pine** is to **tree** as <u>Stem</u> is to **flower**.

14. **Zipper** is to **jacket** as <u>Butens</u> is to **shirt**.

15. **Museum** is to **painting** as **library** is to <u>Book</u> .

16. **Petal** is to **flower** as **branch** is to <u>tree</u> .

17. **Cow** is to **barn** as **car** is to <u>Grog</u> .

18. **Dresser** is to **bedroom** as <u>cupBoart</u> is to **kitchen**.

19. **Teacher** is to <u>stoodent</u> as **doctor** is to **patient**.

20. **Ice** is to **cold** as **fire** is to <u>hot</u> .

Synonym and Antonym Analogies

Analogies are a way of comparing items to show how they are related. Analogies can show different types of relationships. Two relationships analogies might show are synonyms or antonyms.

Examples:
   Antonyms: hot is to **cold** as **happy** is to **sad**
   Synonyms: happy is to **glad** as **run** is to **jog**

You can write an analogy this way:
   slow : fast :: up : down
You read it this way:
   Slow is to **fast** as **up** is to **down**.

Directions: Write **S** for synonym or **A** for antonym in the blanks in front of each analogy. Then, complete the analogies by choosing a word from the box.

life	run	comforter	fail	photograph
above	feline	play	drape	different

_____ 1. dog : canine :: cat : _____

_____ 2. coat : parka :: curtain : _____

_____ 3. asleep : awake :: work : _____

_____ 4. ground : sky :: below : _____

_____ 5. freeze : thaw :: stroll : _____

_____ 6. dangerous : treacherous :: picture : _____

_____ 7. ancient : old :: bedspread : _____

_____ 8. win : lose :: succeed : _____

_____ 9. manmade : artificial :: unique : _____

_____ 10. wealthy : poor :: death : _____

Name _____

Part/Whole and Cause/Effect Analogies

Other types of analogies are part to whole and cause and effect.

Example:
Part to whole: fingers : hand :: toes : foot
Cause and effect: rain : flood :: matches : fire

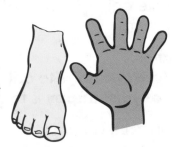

Directions: Write **P** for part to whole or **C** for cause and effect in the blanks in front of each analogy. Then, complete the analogies by choosing a word from the box.

tree	bike	punishment	stomachache
beach	laugh	fingers	hawk
pencil	blizzard		

_____ 1. hair : head :: fingernails : _____

_____ 2. germ : virus :: misbehavior : _____

_____ 3. fall : injury :: overeating : _____

_____ 4. keyboard : computer :: wheels : _____

_____ 5. tongue : shoe :: sand : _____

_____ 6. practice : win :: joke : _____

_____ 7. read : learn :: snow : _____

_____ 8. pouch : kangaroo :: beak : _____

_____ 9. leaf : plant :: bark :

_____

_____ 10. ink : pen :: lead :

_____

Facts and Opinions

A **fact** is information that can be proved.

Example: Hawaii is a state.

An **opinion** is a belief. It tells what someone thinks. It cannot be proved.

Example: Hawaii is the prettiest state.

Directions: Write **F** (fact) or **O** (opinion) on the line by each sentence. The first one has been done for you.

___F___ 1. Hawaii is the only island state.

_____ 2. The best fishing is in Michigan.

_____ 3. It is easy to find a job in Wyoming.

_____ 4. Trenton is the capital of New Jersey.

_____ 5. Kentucky is nicknamed the Bluegrass State.

_____ 6. The friendliest people in the United States live in Georgia.

_____ 7. The cleanest beaches are in California.

_____ 8. Summers are most beautiful in Arizona.

_____ 9. Only one percent of North Dakota is forest or woodland.

_____ 10. New Mexico produces almost half of the nation's uranium.

_____ 11. The first shots of the Civil War were fired in South Carolina on April 12, 1861.

_____ 12. The varied geographical features of Washington include mountains, deserts, a rainforest, and a volcano.

_____ 13. In 1959, Alaska and Hawaii became the 49th and 50th states admitted to the Union.

_____ 14. Wyandotte Cave, one of the largest caves in the United States, is in Indiana.

Directions: Write one fact and one opinion about your own state.

Fact: _____

_____

Opinion: _____

_____

Name _____

Facts and Opinions

A **fact** is a statement based on truth. It can be proven. **Opinions** are the beliefs of an individual that may or may not be true.

Examples:
    Fact: Alaska is a state.
    Opinion: Alaska is the most magnificent state.

Directions: Write **F** if the statement is a fact. Write **O** if the statement is an opinion.

1. _____ The Grand Canyon is the most scenic site in the United States.

2. _____ Dinosaurs roamed Earth millions of years ago.

3. _____ Scientists have discovered how to clone sheep.

4. _____ All people should attend this fair.

5. _____ Purebreds are the best dogs to own because they are intelligent.

6. _____ Nobody likes being bald.

7. _____ Students should be required to get straight A's to participate in extracurricular activities.

8. _____ Reading is an important skill that is vital in many careers.

9. _____ Snakes do not make good pets.

10. _____ Many books have been written about animals.

11. _____ Thomas Edison invented the lightbulb.

12. _____ Most people like to read science fiction.

13. _____ Insects have three body parts.

Facts and Opinions

Directions: Read the articles about cats. List the facts and opinions.

Cats make the best pets. Domestic or house cats were originally produced by crossbreeding several varieties of wild cats. They were used in ancient Egypt to catch rats and mice, which were overrunning bins of stored grain. Today, they are still the most useful domestic animal.

Facts:

_____

_____

_____

Opinions:

_____

_____

It is bad luck for a black cat to cross your path. This is one of the many legends about cats. In ancient Egypt, for example, cats were considered sacred and often were buried with their masters. During the Middle Ages, cats often were killed for taking part in what people thought were evil deeds. Certainly, cats sometimes do bring misfortune.

Facts:

_____

_____

_____

Opinions:

_____

_____

Facts and Opinions

Directions: Write nine statements that are facts and nine statements that are opinions.

FACTS

1. _____

2. _____

3. _____

4. _____

5. _____

6. _____

7. _____

8. _____

9. _____

OPINIONS

1. _____

2. _____

3. _____

4. _____

5. _____

6. _____

7. _____

8. _____

9. _____

Cause and Effect

A **cause** is an event or reason that has an effect on something else.

Example:
The heavy rains produced flooding in Chicago.
Heavy rains were the **cause** of the flooding in Chicago.

An **effect** is an event that results from a cause.

Example:
Flooding in Chicago was due to the heavy rains.
Flooding was the **effect** caused by the heavy rains.

Directions: Read the paragraphs. Complete the charts by writing the missing cause (reason) or effect (result).

Club-footed toads are small toads that live in the rainforests of Central and South America. Because they give off a poisonous substance on their skins, other animals cannot eat them.

Cause:

They give off a poisonous substance.

Effect:

_____

Civets (siv its) are weasel-like animals. The best known of the civets is the mongoose, which eats rats and snakes. For this reason, it is welcome around homes in its native India.

Cause:

_____

Effect:

It is welcome around homes in its native India.

Bluebirds can be found in most areas of the United States. Like other members of the thrush family of birds, young bluebirds have speckled breasts. This makes them difficult to see and helps them hide from their enemies. The Pilgrims called them "blue robins" because they are much like the English robin. They are the same size and have the same red breast and friendly song as the English robin.

Cause:

Young bluebirds have speckled breasts.

_____

Effect:

_____

The Pilgrims called them "blue robins."

Name _____

Review

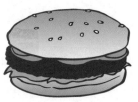

Directions: Write the answers.

1. Define classifying.

   _____

2. Add words to these classifications:

   meat:
   hamburger
   steak
   sirloin tip
   _____
   _____

   music groups:
   the Backstreet Boys
   the Beatles
   _____
   _____
   _____

   breakfast drinks:
   orange juice
   cranberry juice
   grapefruit juice
   _____
   _____
   _____

   colors:
   blue
   fuschia
   melon
   _____
   _____
   _____

3. What is an analogy? _____

4. Give an example of an analogy. _____

5. Write two sentences that are facts.

   _____
   _____

6. Write two sentences that are opinions.

   _____
   _____

7. Write an example of cause and effect. Underline the cause. Circle the effect.

   _____
   _____

Review

Directions: Write three statements about yourself that are facts.

1. _____

2. _____

3. _____

Directions: Write three statements about yourself that are opinions.

4. _____

5. _____

6. _____

Directions: Write a category name for each set of words.

7. Arizona, Wisconsin, Texas _____

8. mouse, rat, squirrel _____

9. saddle, reins, halter _____

Directions: Finish the analogies with words from the box.
Not all words will be used.

10. look : see :: kind :

_____

11. bald : hairy :: difficult :

_____

12. insomnia : nightmares :: crumbs :

_____

13. engine : car :: heart :

_____

| friend |
| nice |
| ants |
| pretzels |
| human |
| hard |
| easy |
| alone |

Main Idea

The **main idea** is the most important idea, or main point, in a sentence, paragraph, or story.

Directions: Read the paragraphs below. For each paragraph, underline the sentence that tells the main idea.

Sometimes, people think they have to choose between exercise and fun. For many people, it is more fun to watch television than to run 5 miles. Yet, if you don't exercise, your body gets soft and out of shape. You move more slowly. You may even think more slowly. But why do something that isn't fun? Well, there are many ways to exercise and have fun.

One family solved the exercise problem by using their TV. They hooked up the television to an electric generator. The generator was operated by an exercise bike. Anyone who wanted to watch TV had to ride the bike. The room with their television in it must have been quite a sight!

Think of the times when you are just hanging out with your friends. You go outside and jump rope, play ball, run races, and so on. Soon, you are all laughing and having a good time. Many group activities can provide you with exercise and be fun, too.

Maybe there aren't enough kids around after school for group games. Perhaps you are by yourself. Then what? You can get plenty of exercise just by walking, biking, or even dancing. In the morning, walk the long way to the bus. Ride your bike to and from school. Practice the newest dance by yourself. Before you know it, you will be the fittest dancer of all your friends!

Directions: Write other ideas you have for combining fun and exercise below.

_____

_____

_____

_____

_____

_____

Reading Skills: Skimming

Skimming an article means to read quickly, looking for headings and key words to give an overall idea of the content of an article or to find a particular fact. When skimming for answers, read the questions first. Then, look for specific words that will help locate the answers.

Directions: Skim the paragraph to answer this question.

1. What "marvel" is the paragraph about?_____

   In America, there is so much magnificent scenery. Perhaps the most stunning sight of all is the Grand Canyon. This canyon is in northern Arizona. It is the deepest, widest canyon on Earth. The Grand Canyon is 217 miles long, 4 to 18 miles wide and, in some places, more than a mile deep. The rocks at the bottom of the steep walls are at least 500 million years old. Most of the rocks are sandstone, limestone, and shale. By studying these rocks, scientists know that this part of the world was once under the sea.

Directions: Skim the paragraph again to find the answers to these questions.

1. How deep are the lowest points in the Grand Canyon?

   _____

2. How old are the rocks at the bottom of the Grand Canyon?

   _____

3. What kinds of rocks would you find in the Grand Canyon?

   _____

4. What do these rocks tell us?

   _____

Comprehensive Curriculum - **Grade 5**

Reading Skills: Maps

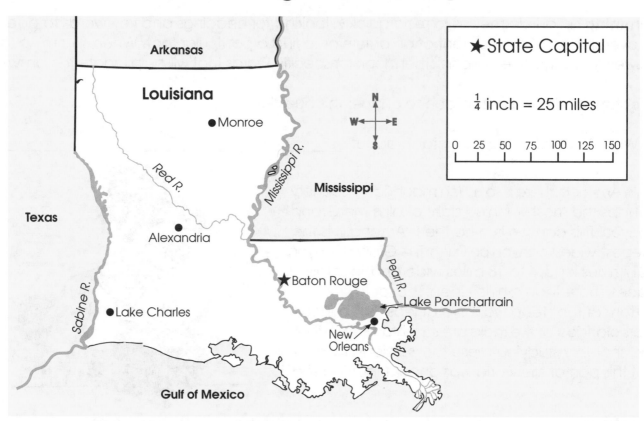

Directions: Use this map to answer the questions.

1. What state borders Louisiana to the north?

   _____

2. What is the state capital of Louisiana?

   _____

3. What cities are located near Lake Pontchartrain?

   _____

4. In which direction would you be traveling if you drove from Monroe to Alexandria?

   _____

5. About how far is it from Alexandria to Lake Charles?

   _____

6. Besides Arkansas, name one other state that borders Louisiana.

   _____

Reading Skills: Maps

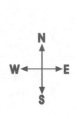

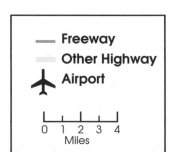

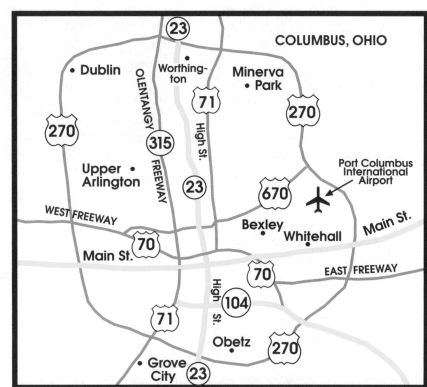

Directions: Use this map of Columbus, Ohio, to answer the questions.

1. Does Highway 104 run east and west or north and south?

_____

2. What is the name of the freeway numbered 315?

_____

3. Which is farther south, Bexley or Whitehall?

_____

4. What two freeways join near the Port Columbus International Airport?

_____

5. Which two suburbs are farther apart, Dublin and Upper Arlington, or Dublin and Worthington?

_____

6. In which direction would you be traveling if you drove from Grove City to Worthington?

_____

Name _____

Sequencing: Maps

Directions: Read the information about planning a map.

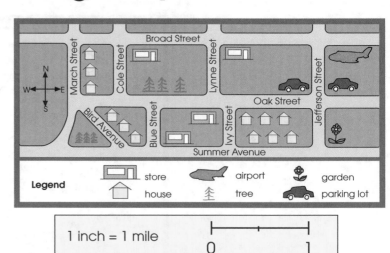

Maps have certain features that help you to read them. A **compass rose** points out directions. Color is often used so you can easily see where one area (such as a county, state, or country) stops and the next starts.

To be accurate, a map must be drawn to scale. The **scale** of a map shows how much area is represented by a given measurement. The scale can be small: 1 inch = 1 mile; or large: 1 inch = 1,000 miles.

Symbols are another map tool. An airplane may represent an airport. Sometimes, a symbol does not look like what it represents. Cities are often represented by dots. A map **legend** tells what each symbol means.

One of the best ways to learn about maps is to make one of your own. You may be surprised at how much you learn about your neighborhood, too. You will need a large piece of paper, a ruler, a pencil, and colored pencils.

You will need to choose the area you want to map out. It is important to decide on the scale for your map. It could be small: 1 inch = 3 feet, if you are mapping out your own backyard. Be sure to include symbols, like a picnic table to represent a park or a flag to represent a school. Don't forget to include the symbols and other important information in your legend.

Directions: Number in order the steps to making your own map.

_____ Figure out the scale that will work best for your map.

_____ Obtain a large piece of paper, ruler, pencil, and colored pencils.

_____ Make a legend explaining the symbols you used.

_____ Draw your map!

_____ Draw symbols to represent features of the area you are mapping.

_____ Decide on the area you want to map out.

Creating a Map

Directions: In the space below, draw a map of your street or town. Be sure to include a compass rose, scale, symbols, and a map legend.

Name _____

Following Directions

Directions: Read and follow the directions.

1. Draw a vertical line from the top mid-point of the square to the bottom mid-point of the square.
2. Draw a diagonal line from top left to bottom right of the square.
3. In each of the two triangles, draw a heart.
4. Draw a picture of a cat's face below the square.
5. Draw a horizontal line from the left mid-point to the right mid-point of the square.
6. Draw two intersecting lines in each of the two smaller squares so they are equally divided into four quadrants.
7. Draw a triangle-shaped roof on the square.
8. Draw a circle next to each heart.
9. Write your name in the roof section of your drawing.

Following Directions: Continents

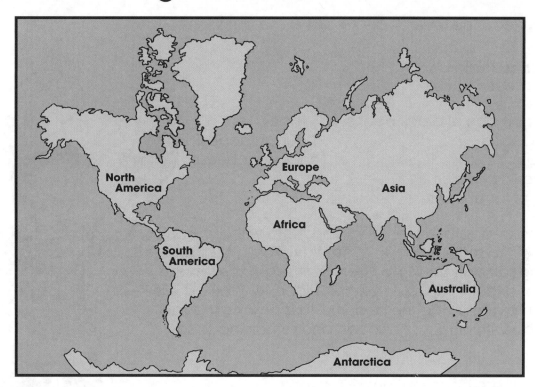

Directions: Read the facts about the seven continents, and follow the directions.

1. Asia is the largest continent. It has the largest land mass and the largest population. Draw a star on Asia.
2. Africa is the second largest continent. Write a **2** on Africa.
3. Australia is the smallest continent in area: 3 million square miles, compared to 17 million square miles for Asia. Write **3,000,000** on Australia.
4. Australia is not a very crowded continent, but it does not rank lowest in population. That honor goes to Antarctica, which has no permanent population at all! This ice-covered continent is too cold for life. Write **zero** on Antarctica.
5. Australia and Antarctica are the only continents entirely separated by water. Draw circles around Australia and Antarctica.
6. North America and South America are joined together by a narrow strip of land. It is called Central America. Write an **N** on North America, an **S** on South America, and a **C** on Central America.
7. Asia and Europe are joined together over such a great distance that they are sometimes called one continent. The name given to it is Eurasia. Draw lines under the names of the two continents in Eurasia.

Name _____

Reading a Recipe

Directions: Read the recipe. Then, answer the questions.

**Black Bean and
Cheese Tacos**

1 15-ounce can of black beans   8 taco shells
$\frac{3}{4}$ c. mild salsa   1 cup shredded
$\frac{1}{4}$ tsp. salt   cheddar cheese
$\frac{1}{4}$ tsp. garlic powder
1 head of lettuce

Drain the beans, and then combine them with $\frac{1}{4}$ cup of the salsa in a medium bowl. Microwave for 1 to 2 minutes. Stir in the salt and garlic powder. Next, wash the lettuce, and tear or cut it into small pieces. Place two taco shells on each plate. Divide the bean mixture among the taco shells. Top with lettuce, cheddar, and remaining salsa.

1. What do these abbreviations stand for?

   tsp. _____

   c. _____

2. Number the steps in the correct order.

   ___ Wash the lettuce.

   ___ Place two taco shells on each plate.

   ___ Microwave the beans and salsa.

   ___ Drain the beans.

   ___ Combine the beans with a quarter cup of the salsa.

3. Why is it important to follow the correct sequence when cooking?

   _____

Reading Skills: Labels

Labels provide information about products.

Directions: Read the label on the medicine bottle. Answer the questions.

> **Remember:** Children should never take medicines without their parents' knowledge and consent.

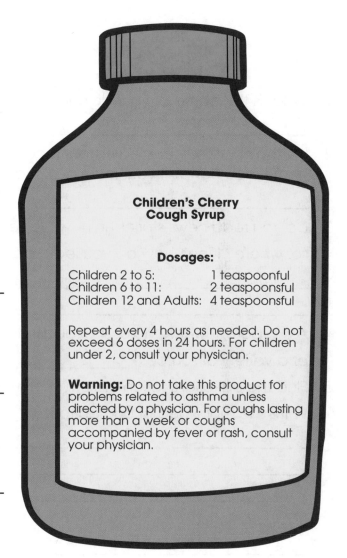

Children's Cherry
Cough Syrup

Dosages:

Children 2 to 5:   1 teaspoonful
Children 6 to 11:   2 teaspoonsful
Children 12 and Adults: 4 teaspoonsful

Repeat every 4 hours as needed. Do not exceed 6 doses in 24 hours. For children under 2, consult your physician.

Warning: Do not take this product for problems related to asthma unless directed by a physician. For coughs lasting more than a week or coughs accompanied by fever or rash, consult your physician.

1. What is the dosage, or amount to be taken, for a three-year-old child?

   _____

2. How often can you take this medicine if it is needed?

   _____

3. How many times a day can you take this medicine?

   _____

4. What should you do before taking the medicine if you have a rash in addition to your cough?

   _____

5. Will this medicine help you if you are sneezing?

   _____

6. What is the dosage for an adult?

   _____

Name _____

Reading Skills: News Stories

Directions: Write the answers.

1. What is the name of your daily local newspaper?

   _____

2. List the sections included in your local newspaper. If you do not get a newspaper at home, you can visit your local newspaper's Web site or look for a copy at a library.

   _____

3. Do you read news stories (in newspapers, magazines, or online) on a regular basis? If so, where? If not, how do you learn about current events? _____

   _____

   _____

4. Ask a parent where he or she reads the news. Is it a newspaper, an online news site, or a variety of sources? _____

5. Find the editorial section of your newspaper. An editorial is the opinion of one person. Write the main idea of one editorial. _____

   _____

   _____

   _____

6. If you could work as a news reporter, what sorts of stories would you like to report on?

   _____

   _____

   _____

7. Go online, and search for a news source intended for kids. (Some options are www.timeforkids.com, www.dogonews.com, and www.magazines.scholastic.com.) Write down two headlines that interest you.

   _____

   _____

Reading Skills: A Newspaper Index

An **index** is a listing in a book, magazine, or newspaper that tells where to find items or information.

Newspapers provide many kinds of information. You can read about national events, local news, the weather, and sports. You will also find opinions, feature stories, advice columns, comics, entertainment, recipes, advertisements, and more. A guide that tells you where to find different types of information in a newspaper is called a **newspaper index**. An index of the newspaper usually appears on the front page. In an online version of a newspaper, the index appears on the paper's home page. There are usually drop-down menus that allow you to chose more specific topics within a section.

Directions: Use the newspaper index to answer the questions.

Business	8	Local News	5–7
Classified Ads	18–19	National News	1–4
Comics	20	Television	17
Editorials	9	Sports	11–13
Entertainment	14–16	Weather	10

1. Where would you look for results of last night's basketball games?

   Section: _____ Page(s) _____

2. Where would you find your favorite cartoon strip?

   Section: _____ Page(s) _____

3. Where would you find opinions of upcoming elections?

   Section: _____ Page(s) _____

4. Where would you look to locate a used bicycle to buy?

   Section: _____ Page(s) _____

5. Where would you find out if you need to wear your raincoat tomorrow?

   Section: _____ Page(s) _____

6. Which would be first, a story about the president's trip to Europe or a review of the newest movie?

   _____

Name _____

Reading Skills: Classified Ads

A **classified ad** is an advertisement found in a newspaper, online, or in a magazine offering a product or service for sale or rent.

Example: For Sale: Used 26" 30-speed bike. $100.
Call 555-5555.

Directions: Read these advertisements. Answer the questions.

1.

**Yard Work
Breaking Your Back?**
Give Mike and Jane a crack!
Mowing, raking, trash hauled.
References provided.
Call 555-9581 or
email yrdwrk@linknet.com.

2.

Pet Sitter:
Going on vacation?
Away for the weekend?
I am 14 years old and
have experience caring
for dogs and cats.
Your home or mine.
Excellent references.
Call Riley Trent.
Phone: 999-8250

3.

**Singing Lessons
for All Ages!**
Be popular at parties!
Fulfill your dreams!
20 years coaching
experience.
Madame Rinaud . . .
Coach to the Stars.
Call 555-5331 or
email songbird@
global.com.

1. What is promised in the third ad? _____

2. Is it fact or opinion? _____

3. What fact is offered in the third ad? _____

4. Give an example of a slogan, or easy-to-remember phrase, that appears in one of

   the ads. _____

5. Which ad gives the most facts? _____

6. Which ad is based mostly on opinion? _____

Reading Skills: Classified Ads

Directions: Write a classified ad for these topics. Include information about the item, a phone number or email address, and an eye-catching title.

1. An ad to wash cars

_____

_____

_____

2. An ad for free puppies

_____

_____

_____

3. An ad for something you would like to sell

_____

_____

_____

4. An ad to sell your house

_____

_____

_____

_____

Reading Skills: Schedules

A **schedule** lists events or programs by time, date, and place or channel.

Example:

Packer Preseason Games

August 14	7 P.M.	NY Jets at Green Bay
August 23	7 P.M.	Denver Broncos at Madison
August 28	3 P.M.	Saints at New Orleans
September 2	Noon	Miami Dolphins at Green Bay

Directions: Use this television schedule to answer the questions.

Evening

6:00	ANM	Let's Talk! Guest: Animal expert Jim Porter
	CAR	Cartoons
	NTV	News
	WMU	News
7:00	FRM	Farm Report
	COM	Movie. *A Laugh a Minute* (1955) James Rayburn. Comedy about a boy who wants to join the circus.
	GMS	Spin for Dollars!
	CKG	Cooking with Cathy. Tonight: Chicken with mushrooms
7:30	COM	Double Trouble (comedy). The twins disrupt the high school dance.
	WST	Wall Street Today: Stock Market Report
8:00	STS	NBA Basketball. Teams to be announced.
	WMU	News Special. "Saving Our Waterways: Pollution in the Mississippi."
	THT	Movie. *At Day's End* (2009). Michael Collier, Julie Romer. Drama set in World War II.

1. What two stations have the news at 6:00? _____

2. What time would you turn on the television to watch a funny movie?_____
   What channel?_____

3. What could you watch if you are a sports fan? _____
   What time and channel is it on?_____

4. Which show title sounds like it could be a game show?_____

5. What show might you want to watch if you are interested in the environment?

   _____

   What time and channel is it on?_____

Review

Directions: Write the answers.

1. What is the purpose of a classified ad? _____

2. Skim a paper or digital version of your local newspaper. List at least six categories of classified ads.

_____   _____

_____   _____

_____   _____

3. What sections are included in the index of your local newspaper?

_____

4. What four pieces of information should a television program schedule contain?

_____   _____

_____   _____

5. What information is present on a medicine bottle?

_____   _____

_____   _____

6. Why is it important for medicine labels to include warnings?

_____

_____

_____

Name _____

Using Prior Knowledge: Books

Directions: Before reading about books in the following section, answer these questions.

1. What books have you read recently?

_____

_____

2. Write a summary of one of the books you listed above.

_____

_____

_____

_____

_____

_____

3. Define the following types of books and, if possible, give an example of each.

biography: _____

_____

fiction: _____

_____

mystery: _____

_____

nonfiction: _____

_____

Context Clues: Remember Who You Are

Directions: Read each paragraph. Then, use context clues to figure out the meanings of the bold words.

During the 1940s, Esther Hautzig lived in the town of Vilna, which was then part of Poland. Shortly after the **outbreak** of World War II, she and her family were **deported** to Siberia by Russian communists who hated Jews. She told what happened to her and other Polish Jews in a book. The book is called *Remember Who You Are: Stories About Being Jewish.*

1. Choose the correct definition of **deported**.

☒ sent away   ☐ asked to go   ☐ invited to visit

2. Choose the correct definition of **outbreak**.

☒ a sudden occurrence   ☐ to leave suddenly

Remember Who You Are: Stories About Being Jewish is a nonfiction book that tells true stories. An interesting **fiction** book is *Wonder* by R.J. Palacio. It tells the story of a boy named August Pullman who was born with a facial difference. He begins fifth grade at a new school, and all he wants is to fit in. However, his classmates have a hard time showing **empathy** and getting past what he looks like on the outside.

3. Choose the correct definition of **fiction**.

☐ stories that are true   ☒ stories that are not true

4. Choose the correct definition of **empathy**.

☐ interesting   ☒ understanding   ☐ rejection

Comprehension: Books and More Books!

Variety is said to be the spice of life. Where books are concerned, variety is the key to reading pleasure. There is a type of book that appeals to every reader.

Each year, hundreds of new books are published for children. A popular series for girls between the ages of 8 and 12 is *Dear America*. Each book focuses on a different time period or event in American history. The stories are told through the fictional diary entries of a girl living in that period.

If you like legends, an interesting book is *Dream Wolf* by Paul Goble. *Dream Wolf* is a retelling of an old Native American legend. Legends are stories passed down from one generation to another that may or may not be true. Some of them are scary! *The Legend of Sleepy Hollow*, for example, is about a headless horseman. Other legends are about a person's brave or amazing deeds. For example, there are many legends about Robin Hood, who stole from the rich and gave to the poor.

Many children like to read nonfiction books, which are about things that really exist or really happened. Those interested in information about Native Americans might like to read these books: *North American Indian* by David S. Murdoch, *Native American History for Kids* by Karen Bush Gibson, and *If You Lived with the Indians of the Northwest Coast* by Anne Kamma.

Directions: Answer these questions about different types of books.

1. What is the name of a book series that takes place in different periods of American

   history? _____

2. What legend is about a headless horseman? _____

3. Which of the following is not correct about legends?

   ☐ Legends are passed down through the generations.

   ☐ All legends are scary.

   ☐ Some legends are about people who did brave things.

Comprehension: Shel Silverstein

Who is your favorite author? For many young people, the answer is Shel Silverstein. Shel's first book was published in the 1960s, and since then, his children's books have sold more than 20 million copies!

Shel Silverstein was born in Chicago, Illinois, in 1932. Although he was best known for writing children's poetry, Shel was creative in many ways. He was a talented singer, songwriter, composer, and illustrator. In fact, Shel illustrated all of his children's books himself. That is one reason the pictures seem to accompany the poetry so perfectly.

Shel's *Where the Sidewalk Ends*, first published in 1984, is one of the most beloved children's books of all time. What makes Shel's poetry so timeless and popular? His poems are often hilarious, with exaggerated situations, funny characters, and clever language. Shel's poems often rhyme and have a good rhythm, making them easy and interesting to read.

Shel Silverstein died in 1999 at his home in Key West, Florida. However, his quirky humor and incredible imagination will live on in his work, bringing joy to young readers for many generations to come.

Directions: Answer these questions about Shel Silverstein.

1. What is Shel Silverstein best known for? _____

2. Who illustrated Shel Silverstein's books? _____

3. In what year was *Where the Sidewalk Ends* published? _____

4. Which two words best describe Shel Silverstein's writing?

☐ hilarious   ☐ rhythmic   ☐ serious

5. Where was Shel Silverstein born?

☐ London, England

☐ Key West, Florida

☐ Chicago, Illinois

Name _____

Fact or Opinion?

Directions: Read the paragraphs below. Then, in the corresponding numbered blanks, write whether each numbered sentence is a fact or an opinion.

Have you ever seen the show *Reading Rainbow*? **(1)** It's a show about books, and its host is LeVar Burton. **(2)** *Reading Rainbow* was broadcast for more than 20 years on PBS stations across the country.

Some books that have been featured on the show are *I Can Be an Oceanographer* by Paul Sipiera, *Soccer Sam* by Jean Marzolla, *Redbird* by Patrick Fort, and *Miss Nelson Has a Field Day* by Harry Allard. **(3)** *Miss Nelson Has a Field Day* sounds like the most interesting book of all!

(4) On *Reading Rainbow*, children give informal book reports about books they have read. **(5)** All the children are adorable! In about 1 minute, each child describes his or her book. **(6)** While the child is talking, pictures of some of the pages from the book are shown. **(7)** Seeing the pictures will make you want to read the book. A few books are described on each show. **(8)** Other activities include trips with LeVar to places the books tell about. **(9)** Every child should make time to watch *Reading Rainbow*! **(10)** It's a fabulous show!

1. _____

2. _____

3. _____

4. _____

5. _____

6. _____

7. _____

8. _____

9. _____

10. _____

Context Clues: Kids' Books Are Big Business

Between 1978 and 1988, the number of children's books published in the United States doubled. The publishing industry, which prints, promotes, and sells books, does not usually move this fast. Why? Because if publishers print too many books that don't sell, they lose money. They like to wait, if they can, to see what the demand is for certain types of books. Then, they accept manuscripts from writers who have written the types of books the public seems to want. More than 4,600 children's books were published in 1988, because publishers thought they could sell that many titles. Many copies of each title were printed and sold to bookstores and libraries. The publishers made good profits and, since then, the number of children's books published each year has continued to grow. Today, more than 30,000 children's books are published each year!

Some people are worried that old-fashioned books will soon be a thing of the past. More and more information is available for free on the Internet. In addition, many people choose to read their books in digital form, on a tablet or computer screen. There is something special about reading an actual book with paper pages. Humans may have entered the digital age, but I'm sure that old-fashioned books are here to stay!

Directions: Answer these questions about how interest in writing, reading, and selling children's books has grown.

1. Use context clues to choose the correct definition of **industry**.

☐ booksellers   ☐ writers   ☐ entire business

2. If 4,600 books were sold in 1988, how many books were sold in 1978? _____

3. The number of children's books published
in the United States doubled between 1978 and 1988.   Fact   Opinion

4. More and more information is available for free on
the Internet.   Fact   Opinion

5. Many people choose to read their books in digital form,
on a tablet or computer screen.   Fact   Opinion

6. There is something special about reading an actual book
with paper pages.   Fact   Opinion

Name _____

Review

Directions: Follow the instructions below.

1. Write a summary of the selection "Shel Silverstein" (page 91).

_____

_____

_____

2. What skills must a writer have in order to produce a book?

_____

_____

_____

3. Define the following words from this section.

appeal: _____

legend: _____

deed: _____

generation: _____

profit: _____

distribute: _____

suspense: _____

manuscript: _____

4. Interview the members of your family. Ask each person his or her favorite book title and the reason he or she enjoyed it. Then, summarize your findings in a paragraph.

_____

_____

_____

_____

READING COMPREHENSION

Using Prior Knowledge: Music

Using **prior knowledge** means being able to use what one already knows to find an answer or get information.

Directions: Before reading about music in the following section, answer these questions.

1. In your opinion, why is music important to people?

_____

_____

_____

2. Name as many styles of music as you can.

_____

_____

_____

3. What is your favorite type of music? Why?

_____

_____

_____

4. If you could choose a musical instrument to play, what would it be? Why?

_____

_____

_____

5. Name a famous musician, and describe what you know about him or her.

_____

_____

_____

_____

Main Idea: Where Did Songs Come From?

Historians say the earliest music was probably connected to religion. Long ago, people believed the world was controlled by a variety of gods. Singing was among the first things humans did to show respect to the gods.

Singing is still an important part of most religions. Buddhists (bood-ists), Christians, Muslims, and Jews all use chants and/or songs in their religious ceremonies. If you have ever sung a song—religious or otherwise—you know that singing is fun. The feeling of joy that comes from singing must have also made ancient people feel happy.

Another time people sang was when they worked. Egyptian slaves sang as they carried the heavy stones to build the pyramids. Soldiers sang as they marched into battle. Farmers sang one song as they planted and another when they harvested. Singing made the work less burdensome. People used the tunes to pace themselves. Sometimes, they followed instructions through songs. For example, "Yo-oh, heave ho!/Yo-oh, heave ho!" was sung when sailors pulled on a ship's ropes to lift the sails. **Heave** means "to lift," and that is what they did as they sang the song. The song helped sailors work together and pull at the same time. This made the task easier.

Directions: Answer these questions about music.

1. Circle the main idea:

   Singing is fun, and that is why early people liked it so much.

   Singing began as a way to show respect to the gods and is still an important part of most religious ceremonies.

   Traditionally, singing has been important as a part of religious ceremonies and as inspiration for workers.

2. Besides religious ceremonies, what other activity fostered singing? _____

   _____

3. When did farmers sing two different songs? _____

4. How did singing "Yo-oh, heave ho!" help sailors work? _____

   _____

Comprehension: Facts About Folk Music

Folk music literally means music "of the folks," and it belongs to everyone. The names of the musicians who composed most folk music have long been forgotten. Even so, folk music has remained popular because it tells about the lives of people. Usually, the tune is simple, and even though folk songs often have many verses, the words are easy to remember. Do you know the words to "She'll Be Comin' 'Round the Mountain"?

Although no one ever says who "she" is, the verses tell you that she will be "riding six white horses" and that "we'll go out to greet her." The song also describes what will be eaten when she comes (chicken and dumplings) and what those singing will be wearing (red pajamas).

"Clementine" is a song that came out of the California gold rush in the mid-1800s. It tells the story of a woman who was "lost and gone forever" when she was killed. ("In a cavern, in a canyon, excavating for a mine/Met a miner '49er and his daughter, Clementine.")

Another famous folk song is "Swing Low, Sweet Chariot." This song was sung by slaves in the United States and today is sung by people of all races. The words "Swing low, sweet chariot, coming for to carry me home . . . " describe the soul being united with God after death. Like other folk songs that sprang from slaves, "Swing Low, Sweet Chariot" is simple, moving, and powerful.

Directions: Answer these questions about folk music.

1. What is the purpose of folk music? _____

_____

2. What food is sung about in "She'll Be Comin' 'Round the Mountain"? _____

_____

3. Where did Clementine live?

☐ Florida   ☐ Mississippi   ☐ California

4. Where in the United States do you think "Swing Low, Sweet Chariot" was first sung?

☐ the North   ☐ the West   ☐ the South

Recalling Details: Woodwinds

There are four kinds of woodwind instruments in modern bands. They are flutes, oboes, clarinets, and bassoons. They are called "woodwind" instruments for two sensible reasons. In the beginning, they were all made of wood. Also, the musician's breath, or "wind," was required to play them.

Although they are all woodwinds, these instruments look different and are played differently. To play an oboe, the musician blows through a mouthpiece on the front of the instrument. The mouthpiece, called a reed, is made of two flat pieces of a kind of wood called cane. Clarinet players also blow into a reed mouthpiece. The clarinet has only one reed in its mouthpiece.

To play the flute, the musician blows across a hole near one end of the instrument. The way the breath is aimed helps to make the flute's different sounds. The bassoon is the largest woodwind instrument. Bassoon players blow through a mouthpiece that goes through a short metal pipe before it goes into the body of the bassoon. It makes a very different sound from the clarinet or the oboe.

Woodwind instruments also have keys—but not the kind of keys that open locks. These keys are more like levers that the musician pushes up and down. The levers cover holes. When the musician pushes down on a lever, it closes that hole. When he or she lifts his or her finger, it opens the hole. Different sounds are produced by controlling the amount of breath, or "wind," that goes through the holes.

Directions: Answer these questions about woodwind instruments.

1. What instruments are in the woodwind section? _____

2. Why are some instruments called woodwinds? _____

_____

3. How is a flute different from the other woodwinds? _____

4. What happens when a musician pushes down on a woodwind key? _____

_____

5. How would a woodwind musician open the holes on his/her instrument?

_____

Comprehensive Curriculum - **Grade 5**

Comprehension: Harp Happenings

If you have ever heard a harpist play, you know what a lovely sound a harp makes. Music experts say the harp is among the oldest of instruments. It probably was invented several thousand years ago in or near Egypt.

The first harps are believed to have been made by stretching a string tightly between an empty tortoise shell and a curved pole. The empty shell magnified the sound the string made when it was plucked. More strings were added later so that more sounds could be made. Over the centuries, the shape of the harp gradually was changed into that of the large, graceful instruments we recognize today.

Here is how a harpist plays a harp. First, he or she leans the harp against his or her right shoulder. Then, the harpist puts his or her hands on either side of the harp and plucks its strings with both hands.

A harp has seven pedals on the bottom back. The audience usually cannot see these pedals. Most people are surprised to learn about them. The pedals are connected to the strings. Stepping on a particular pedal causes certain strings to tighten. The tightening and loosening of the strings makes different sounds; so does the way the strings are plucked with the hands.

At first glance, harps look like simple instruments. Actually, they are rather complicated and difficult to keep in tune. A harpist often spends as long as half an hour before a performance tuning his or her harp's strings so it produces the correct sounds.

Directions: Answer these questions about harps.

1. When were harps invented? _____

2. Where were harps invented? _____

3. What is a person called who plays the harp? _____

4. The harpist leans the harp against his or her

☐ right shoulder.   ☐ left shoulder.   ☐ left knee.

5. How many pedals does a harp have?

☐ five   ☐ six   ☐ seven

6. Harps are easy to play.

☐ yes   ☐ no

Comprehension: Brass Shows Class

If you like band music, you probably love the music made by brass instruments. Bright, loud, moving, and magnificent—all these words describe the sounds made by brass.

Some of the earliest instruments were horns. Made from hollowed-out animal horns, these primitive instruments could not possibly have made the rich sounds of modern horns that are made of brass.

Most modern brass bands have three instruments—tubas, trombones, and trumpets. Combined, these instruments can produce stirring marches, as well as haunting melodies. The most famous composer for brass instruments was John Philip Sousa. Born in Washington, D.C., in 1854, Sousa was a military band conductor and composer. He died in 1932, but his music is still very popular today. One of Sousa's most famous tunes for military bands is "Stars and Stripes Forever."

Besides composing band music, Sousa also invented a practical band instrument—the sousaphone. The sousaphone is a huge tuba that makes very low noises. Because of the way it curls around the body, a sousaphone is easier to carry than a tuba, especially when the musician must march. This is exactly why John Philip Sousa invented it!

Directions: Answer these questions about brass instruments.

1. Who invented the sousaphone? _____

2. What were the first horns made from? _____

3. Where was John Philip Sousa bor n? _____

4. When did John Philip Sousa die? _____

5. Why did Sousa invent the sousaphone? _____

_____

6. What types of instruments make up a modern brass band? _____

_____

Comprehension: Violins

If you know anything about violin music, chances are you have heard the word **Stradivarius** (Strad-uh-vary-us). Stradivarius is the name for the world's most magnificent violins. They are named after their creator, Antonio Stradivari.

Stradivari was born in northern Italy and lived from 1644 to 1737. Cremona, the town he lived in, was a place where violins were manufactured. Stradivari was very young when he learned to play the violin. He grew to love the instrument so much that he began to make them himself.

Violins were new instruments during Stradivari's time. People made them in different sizes and shapes and of different types of wood. Stradivari is said to have been very particular about the wood he selected for his violins. He took long walks alone in the forest to find just the right tree. He is also said to have used a secret and special type of varnish to put on the wood. Whatever the reasons, his violins are the best in the world.

Stradivari put such care and love into his violins that they are still used today. Many of them are in museums. But some wealthy musicians, who can afford the thousands and thousands of dollars they cost, own Stradivarius violins.

Stradivari passed his methods on to his sons. But the secrets of making Stradivarius violins seem to have died out with the family. Their rarity, as well as their mellow sound, make Stradivarius violins among the most prized instruments in the world.

Directions: Answer these questions about Stradivarius violins.

1. Where did Stradivari live? _____

2. Why did he begin making violins? _____

3. Why are Stradivarius violins special? _____

_____

4. Where can Stradivarius violins be found today? _____

_____

5. How did Stradivari select the wood for his violins? _____

_____

6. Who else knew Stradivari's secrets for making such superior violins?_____

Review

Directions: Complete the following exercises.

1. Write a four-sentence summary of the selection "Where Did Songs Come From?" (page 97).

_____

_____

_____

_____

2. Describe the main difference between a clarinet and an oboe.

_____

_____

3. How do the keys of woodwind instruments work?

_____

_____

4. Write a summary of the history of the harp.

_____

_____

_____

5. Define the following words from the selection "Facts About Folk Music" (page 98).

verses: _____

excavating: _____

chariot: _____

composed: _____

Using Prior Knowledge: Art

Directions: Before reading about art in the following section, answer these questions.

1. Write a short paragraph about a famous artist of your choice.

   _____

   _____

   _____

2. Many artists paint realistic scenes. Other artists paint imaginary scenes. Which do you prefer? Why?

   _____

   _____

3. Although we often think of art as painting and drawing, art also includes sculpture, fabric weavings, and metalwork. Are you talented at a particular type of art? If so, what type? If not, what would you like to learn?

   _____

   _____

   _____

4. Why are art museums important to society?

   _____

   _____

   _____

5. Why do you think some artwork is worth so much money? Would you pay several thousand dollars for a piece of artwork? Why or why not?

   _____

   _____

   _____

Main Idea: Creating Art

No one knows exactly when the first human created the first painting. Crude drawings and paintings on the walls of caves show that humans have probably always expressed themselves through art. These early cave pictures show animals being hunted, people dancing, and other events of daily life. The simplicity of the paintings reflect the simple lifestyles of these primitive people.

The subjects of early paintings also help to make another important point. Art is not created out of nothing. The subjects an artist chooses to paint reflect the history, politics, and culture of the time and place in which he or she lives. An artist born and raised in New York City, for example, is not likely to paint scenes of the Rocky Mountains. An artist living in the Rockies is not likely to paint pictures of city life.

Of course, not all paintings are realistic. Many artists choose to paint pictures that show their own "inner vision" as opposed to what they see with their eyes. Many religious paintings of earlier centuries look realistic but contain figures of angels. These paintings combine the artist's inner vision of angels with other things, such as church buildings, that can be seen.

Directions: Answer these questions about creating art.

1. Circle the main idea:

   Art was important to primitive people because it showed hunting and dancing scenes, and it is still important today.

   Through the ages, artists have created paintings that reflect the culture, history, and politics of the times, as well as their own inner visions.

2. Why is an artist living in the Rocky Mountains less likely to paint city scenes?

   _____

   _____

3. In addition to what the artists see with their eyes, what do some paintings also show?

   _____

   _____

Comprehension: Leonardo da Vinci

Many people believe that Leonardo da Vinci, an Italian artist and inventor who lived from 1452 to 1519, was the most brilliant person ever born. He was certainly a man ahead of his time! Records show that da Vinci loved the world and was curious about everything in it.

To learn about the human body, he dissected corpses to find out what was inside. In the 15th and 16th centuries, dissecting the dead was against the laws of the Catholic Church. Leonardo was a brave man!

He was also an inventor. Leonardo invented a parachute and designed a type of helicopter—five centuries before airplanes were invented! Another of da Vinci's major talents was painting. You have probably seen a print, or copy, of one of his most famous paintings. It is called *The Last Supper*, and it shows Jesus eating his final meal with his disciples. It took da Vinci three years to paint *The Last Supper*. The man who hired da Vinci to do the painting was upset. He went to da Vinci to ask why it was taking so long. The problem, said da Vinci, was that in the painting, Jesus has just told the disciples that one of them would betray me. He wanted to get their expressions exactly right as each one cried out, "Lord, am I the one?"

Another famous painting by da Vinci is called the *Mona Lisa*. Have you seen a print of this painting? Maybe you have been lucky enough to see the original hanging in a Paris art museum called the Louvre (loov). If so, you know that Mona Lisa has a wistful expression on her face. The painting is of a real woman, the wife of an Italian merchant. Art historians believe she looks wistful because one of her children had recently died.

Directions: Answer these questions about Leonardo da Vinci.

1. How old was da Vinci when he died? _____

2. Name two of da Vinci's inventions. _____

3. Name two famous paintings by da Vinci. _____

4. In which Paris museum does *Mona Lisa* hang? ☐ Lourre ☐ Loure ☐ Louvre

Context Clues: Leonardo da Vinci

Directions: Read the sentences below. Use context clues to figure out the meaning of the bold words.

1. Some people are **perplexed** when they look at *The Last Supper*, but others understand it immediately.

   ☐ unhappy   ☐ happy   ☐ puzzled

2. Because his model felt **melancholy** about the death of her child, da Vinci had music played to lift her spirits as he painted the *Mona Lisa*.

   ☐ sad   ☐ unfriendly   ☐ hostile

3. Because da Vinci's work is so famous, many people **erroneously** assume that he left behind many paintings. In fact, he left only 20.

   ☐ rightly   ☐ correctly   ☐ wrongly

4. Leonardo da Vinci was not like most other people. He didn't care what others thought of him—he led an interesting and **unconventional** life.

   ☐ dull   ☐ not ordinary   ☐ ordinary

5. The **composition** of *The Last Supper* is superb. All the parts of the painting seem to fit together beautifully.

   ☐ the picture frame   ☐ parts of the picture

6. Leonardo's **genius** set him apart from people with ordinary minds. He never married, he had few friends, and he spent much of his time alone.

   ☐ great mental abilities   ☐ great physical abilities

   ☐ improper way to do things   ☐ proper way to do things

7. Because he was a loner, da Vinci worried no one would come to his funeral when he died. In his will, he set aside 70 cents each to hire 60 **mourners** to accompany his body to his grave.

   ☐ friends   ☐ people who grieve   ☐ people who smile

Comprehension: Michelangelo

Another famous painter of the late 14th and early 15th centuries was Michelangelo Buonarroti. Michelangelo, who lived from 1475 to 1564, was also an Italian. Like da Vinci, his genius was apparent at a young age. When he was 13, the ruler of his hometown of Florence, Lorenzo Medici (muh-dee-chee), befriended Michelangelo and asked him to live in the palace. There, Michelangelo studied sculpture and met many artists.

By the time he was 18, Michelangelo was a respected sculptor. He created one of his most famous religious sculptures, the *Pieta* (pee-ay-tah), when he was only 21. Then, the Medici family abruptly fell from power and Michelangelo had to leave Florence.

Still, his work was well known, and he was able to make a living. In 1503, Pope Julius II called Michelangelo to Rome. He wanted Michelangelo to paint the tomb where he would someday be buried. Michelangelo preferred sculpting to painting, but no one turned down the pope! Before Michelangelo finished his painting, however, the pope ordered Michelangelo to begin painting the ceiling of the Sistine Chapel inside the Vatican. (The Vatican is the palace and surrounding area where the pope lives in Rome.)

Michelangelo was very angry! He did not like to paint. He wanted to create sculptures. But no one turns down the pope. After much complaining, Michelangelo began work on what would be his most famous project.

Directions: Answer these questions about Michelangelo.

1. How old was Michelangelo when he died? _____

2. What was the first project Pope Julius II asked Michelangelo to paint?

_____

3. What is the Vatican? _____

4. What was the second project the pope asked Michelangelo to do?

☐ paint his tomb's ceiling   ☐ paint the Sistine Chapel's ceiling

Comprehension: Rembrandt

Most art critics agree that Rembrandt (Rem-brant) was one of the greatest painters of all time. This Dutch artist, who lived from 1606 to 1669, painted some of the world's finest portraits.

Rembrandt, whose full name was Rembrandt van Rijn, was born in Holland to a wealthy family. He was sent to a fine university, but he did not like his studies. He only wanted to paint. He sketched the faces of people around him. During his lifetime, Rembrandt painted 11 portraits of his father and nearly as many of his mother. From the beginning, the faces of old people fascinated him.

When he was 25, Rembrandt went to paint in Amsterdam, a large city in Holland where he lived for the rest of his life. There, he married a wealthy woman named Saskia, whom he loved deeply. She died from a disease called tuberculosis (ta-bur-ku-lo-sis) after only eight years, leaving behind a young son named Titus (Ty-tuss).

Rembrandt was heartbroken over his wife's death. He began to spend all his time painting. But instead of painting what his customers wanted, he painted exactly the way he wanted. Unsold pictures filled his house. They were wonderful paintings, but they were not the type of portraits people wanted. Rembrandt could not pay his debts. He and his son were thrown into the streets. The creditors took his home, his possessions, and his paintings. One of the finest painters on Earth was treated like a criminal.

Directions: Answer these questions about Rembrandt.

1. How old was Rembrandt when he died? _____

2. In what city did he spend most of his life? _____

3. How many children did Rembrandt have? _____

4. Rembrandt's wife was named

☐ Sasha.   ☐ Saskia.   ☐ Saksia.

5. These filled his house after his wife's death.

☐ friends   ☐ customers   ☐ unsold paintings

Review

Directions: Follow the instructions below.

1. Write a one-sentence main idea for the selection "Leonardo da Vinci" (page 106).

   _____

   _____

2. Write a summary of the selection "Leonardo da Vinci" (page 106).

   _____

   _____

   _____

3. Complete the sequence of events from the selection "Michelangelo" (page 108).

   1) Michelangelo was born in 1475 in Italy.

   2) _____

   3) _____

   4) _____

   5) _____

   6) _____

   7) _____

4. Define the following words from this section.

   crude: _____

   dissect: _____

   disciples: _____

   merchant: _____

   wistful: _____

Using Prior Knowledge: Big Cats

Directions: Before reading about big cats in the following section, answer these questions.

1. Name at least four big wild cats.

_____   _____

_____   _____

2. Compare and contrast a house cat with a wild cat.

_____

_____

_____

_____

3. What impact might the expansion of human population and housing have on big cats?

_____

_____

_____

4. Do you have a cat? What are the special qualities of this pet? Write about your cat's name and its personality traits. If you don't have a cat, write about a cat you would like to have.

_____

_____

_____

_____

Comprehension: Jaguars

The jaguar is a large cat, standing up to 2 feet tall at the shoulder. Its body can reach 73 inches long, and the tail can be another 30 inches long. The jaguar is characterized by its yellowish-red coat covered with black spots. The spots themselves are made up of a central spot surrounded by a circle of spots.

Jaguars are not known to attack humans, but some ranchers claim that jaguars attack their cattle. This claim has given jaguars a bad reputation.

The jaguar can be found in southern North America, but is most populous in Central and South America. Jaguars are capable climbers and swimmers, and they eat a wide range of animals.

Female jaguars have between one and four cubs after a gestation of 93 to 105 days. Cubs stay with the mother for two years. Jaguars are known to have a life expectancy of at least 22 years.

Directions: Use context clues for these definitions.

1. populous: _____

2. reputation: _____

3. gestation: _____

Directions: Answer these questions about jaguars.

4. Describe the spots on a jaguar's coat.

_____

_____

5. Why would it be to a jaguar's advantage to have spots on its coat?

_____

_____

Comprehension: Leopards

The leopard is a talented nocturnal hunter and can see very well in the dark. Because of its excellent climbing ability, the leopard is able to stalk and kill monkeys and baboons. Leopards are also known to consume mice, porcupines, and fruit.

LEOPARD

Although the true leopard is characterized by a light beige coat with black spots, some leopards can be entirely black. These leopards are called black panthers. Many people refer to other cat species as leopards. Cheetahs are sometimes referred to as hunting leopards. The clouded leopard lives in southeastern Asia and has a grayish spotted coat. The snow leopard, which has a white coat, lives in Central Asia. A leopard's spots help to camouflage (cam-o-floj) it as it hunts.

True leopards can grow to over 6 feet long, not including their 3-foot-long tail. Leopards can be found in Africa and Asia.

Directions: Use context clues for these definitions.

1. consume: _____

2. ability: _____

3. nocturnal: _____

Directions: Answer these questions about leopards.

4. List three differences between the leopard and the jaguar.

_____

_____

_____

_____

_____

_____

5. What makes a leopard able to hunt monkeys and baboons?

_____

Comprehension: Lynxes

Lynxes are strange-looking cats with very long legs and large paws. Their bodies are a mere 51 inches in length, and they have short little tails. Most lynxes have a clump of hair that extends past the tip of their ears.

Lynxes are known to chase down their prey and also to leap on them from a perch above the ground. They eat small mammals and birds, as well as an occasional deer.

There are four types of lynxes. Bobcats can be found in all areas of the United States except the Midwest. The Spanish lynx is an endangered species. The Eurasian lynx, also known as the northern lynx, and the Canadian lynx are two other kinds of lynxes.

Directions: Use context clues for these definitions.

1. prey: _____

2. perch: _____

Directions: Answer these questions about lynxes.

3. What are the four types of lynxes? _____

_____

4. Use the following words in a sentence of your own.

   mammal _____

   endangered _____

5. Do you believe it is important to classify animals as "endangered" to protect a species that is low in population? Explain your answer.

_____

_____

_____

Comprehension: Pumas

The puma is a cat most recognized by the more popular names of "cougar" or "mountain lion." Just like other large cats, the puma is a carnivore. It feeds on deer, elk, and other mammals. It can be found in both North and South America.

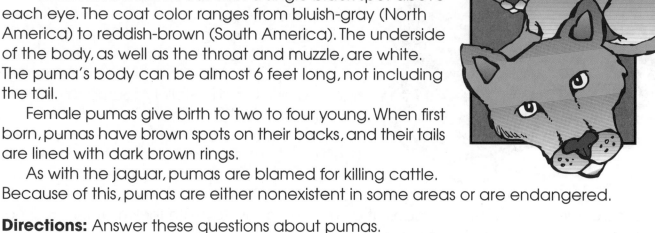

Pumas have small heads with a single black spot above each eye. The coat color ranges from bluish-gray (North America) to reddish-brown (South America). The underside of the body, as well as the throat and muzzle, are white. The puma's body can be almost 6 feet long, not including the tail.

Female pumas give birth to two to four young. When first born, pumas have brown spots on their backs, and their tails are lined with dark brown rings.

As with the jaguar, pumas are blamed for killing cattle. Because of this, pumas are either nonexistent in some areas or are endangered.

Directions: Answer these questions about pumas.

1. What is a muzzle? _____

2. As the population increases in North America, predict what might happen to pumas.

   _____

   _____

   _____

3. What are two other popular names for the puma? _____

4. What other cat besides the puma is blamed for killing cattle? _____

5. Reviewing the sizes of cats discussed so far, write their names in order, from smallest to largest.

   1)_____   2)_____

   3)_____   4)_____

Comprehension: Tigers

Tigers live on the continent of Asia. The tiger is the largest cat, often weighing over 500 pounds. Its body can grow to be 9 feet long and the tail can be up to 36 inches in length.

There are three types of tigers. The Siberian tiger is very rare and has a yellow coat with dark stripes. The Bengal tiger can be found in southeastern Asia and central India. Its coat is more orange, and its stripes are darker. There is a tiger that lives on the island of Sumatra as well. It is smaller and darker in color than the Bengal tiger.

Tigers lead solitary lives. They meet with other tigers only to mate and share food or water. Tigers feed primarily on deer and cattle but are also known to eat fish and frogs. If necessary, tigers will also eat dead animals.

Female tigers bear one to six cubs at a time. The cubs stay with their mother for almost two years before going out on their own.

Because tiger parts are in high demand for use in Chinese medicine and recipes, tigers have been hunted almost to extinction. All tigers are currently listed as endangered.

Directions: Use context clues for these definitions.

1. rare: _____

2. solitary: _____

3. extinction: _____

Directions: Answer these questions about tigers.

4. Why have tigers been hunted almost to extinction?

_____

_____

5. Name the three types of tigers.

_____

Comprehension: Lions

The lion, often referred to as the king of beasts, once commanded a large territory. Today, lions' territory is very limited. Lions are savanna-dwelling animals, which has made them easy targets for hunters. The increasing population of humans and their livestock has also contributed to the lion's decreased population.

Lions are heavy cats. Males weigh over 500 pounds and can grow to be over 8 feet in length, with a tail over 36 inches long. Males are characterized by a long, full mane that covers the neck and most of the head and shoulders. Females do not have a mane and are slightly smaller in size. Both males and females have beige coats, hooked claws, and powerful jaws. Their roars can be heard up to 5 miles away!

Lions tend to hunt in the evening and spend the day sleeping. They prefer hunting zebra or giraffe but will eat almost anything. A lion is capable of eating over 75 pounds of meat at a single kill and then going a week without eating again. Generally, female lions do the hunting, and the males come to share the kill.

Lions live in groups called prides. Each pride has between four and 37 lions. Females bear one to four cubs approximately every two years.

Directions: Answer these questions about lions.

1. What are the differences between male and female lions? _____

_____

2. Why would living on a savanna make the lion an "easy target"? _____

_____

Directions: Use context clues for these definitions.

3. pride: _____

4. territory: _____

5. savanna: _____

6. capable: _____

Review

Directions: Follow the instructions below.

1. Choose any two big cats from this section, and compare them.

_____

_____

_____

_____

2. Why are each of these big cats endangered or decreasing in number?

_____

_____

_____

3. What can be done to get these big cats off the endangered list?

_____

_____

_____

4. Now that you have read about big cats, compare and contrast them with a house cat. What do you know now that you didn't know before reading this section?

_____

_____

_____

_____

Using Prior Knowledge: Farm Animals

Directions: Before reading about farm animals in the following section, answer these questions.

1. List at least nine types of farm animals by mother and baby names.

   Example: sow—piglet

   _____   _____   _____

   _____   _____   _____

   _____   _____   _____

2. If you owned a large ranch, what type of livestock would you enjoy keeping? Why?

   _____

   _____

3. Some animals routinely give birth to twins, triplets, or larger litters. Which animals give birth to more than one baby at a time?

   _____

   _____

4. Would you enjoy living on a farm? Why or why not?

   _____

   _____

   _____

5. What is the importance of raising livestock today?

   _____

   _____

   _____

Comprehension: All About Sheep

Did you ever wonder what really happened to the tails of Little Bo-Peep's sheep? Here's the real story.

When sheep are born, they are called lambs. Lambs are born with long tails. A few days after lambs are born, the shepherd cuts off their tails. Because they get dirty, the lambs' long tails can pick up lots of germs. Cutting them off helps to prevent disease. The procedure is called "docking." This is probably what happened to Bo-Peep's sheep! Another shepherd must have cut their tails off without telling her.

Little lambs are cute. A lamb grows inside its mother for 150 days before it is born. This is called the "gestation period." Some types of sheep, such as hill sheep, give birth to one lamb at a time. Other types of sheep, such as lowland sheep, give birth to two or three lambs at a time.

After it is born, it takes a lamb three or four days to recognize its mother. Once it does, it stays close to her until it is about 3 weeks old. After that, the lamb becomes friendly toward other lambs.

Young lambs then form play groups. They chase each other in circles. They butt into each other. Like children, they pretend to fight. When play gets too rough, the lambs run back to their mothers for protection.

Lambs follow their mothers as they graze on grass. Usually, sheep move in single file behind an older female sheep. Female sheep are called ewes. The ewes teach their lambs how to keep themselves clean. This is called "grooming." Sheep groom only their faces. Here is how they do it: They lick one of their front legs, and then they rub their faces against the spot they have licked.

Directions: Follow the instructions below.

1. Define the word **docking**. _____

2. Name a type of sheep that gives birth to one lamb at a time. _____

3. Name a type of sheep that gives birth to two or three lambs at a time.

_____

4. Female sheep are called

☐ grazers.   ☐ ewes.   ☐ dockers.

5. Lambs begin playing in groups when they are

☐ 2 weeks old.   ☐ 3 weeks old.   ☐ 4 weeks old.

Comprehension: Pigs Are Particular

Have you ever wondered why pigs wallow in the mud? It's not because they are dirty animals. Pigs have no sweat glands. They can't sweat, so they roll in the mud to cool themselves. When people who are hot say, "I'm sweating like a pig!" that's not really true. Humans can sweat, but pigs cannot.

Actually, pigs are particular about their pens. They are very clean animals. They prefer to sleep in clean, dry places. They move their bowels and empty their bladders in another area. They do not want to get their homes dirty.

Another misconception about pigs is that they are smooth. Only cartoon pigs are pink, smooth, and shiny-looking. The skin of real pigs is covered with bristles—small, stiff hairs. Their bristles protect their tender skin.

Female pigs are called sows. Sows have babies twice a year and give birth to 10 to 14 piglets at a time. The babies have a gestation period of 16 weeks before they are born.

All the piglets together are called a litter. Newborn piglets are on their tiny feet within a few minutes after birth. Can you guess why? They are hungrily looking for their mother's teats so they can get milk. As they nurse, piglets snuggle in close to their mother's belly to keep warm.

Directions: Answer these questions about pigs.

1. Why do pigs wallow in mud? _____

2. How long is the gestation period for pigs? _____

3. What is one misconception about pigs? _____

4. Tell two reasons pigs are on their feet soon after they are born.

a.) _____   b.) _____

5. A female pig is called a

☐ bristle.   ☐ piglet.   ☐ sow.

6. Together, the newborn piglets are called a

☐ group.   ☐ family.   ☐ litter.

Context Clues: No Kidding About Goats

Goats are independent creatures. Unlike sheep, which move easily in herds, goats cannot be driven along by a goatherd. They must be moved one or two at a time. Moving a big herd of goats can take a long time, so goatherds must be patient people.

Both male and female goats can have horns, but some goats don't have them at all. Male goats have longer and bushier beards than females. Males goats also have thicker and shaggier coats than females. During breeding season, when goats mate, male goats have a very strong smell.

Goats are kept in paddocks with high fences. The fences are high because goats are good jumpers. They like to nibble on hedges and on the tips of young trees. They can cause a lot of damage this way! That is why many farmers keep their goats in a paddock.

Baby goats are called "kids," and two or three at a time are born to the mother goat. Farmers usually begin to bottle-feed kids when they are a few days old. They milk the mother goat and keep the milk. Goat's milk is much easier to digest than cow's milk, and many people think it tastes delicious.

Directions: Answer these questions about goats.

1. Use context clues to choose the correct definition of **goatherd**.

   ☐ person who herds goats   ☐ goats in a herd   ☐ person who has heard of goats

2. Use context clues to choose the correct definition of **paddock**.

   ☐ pad   ☐ fence   ☐ pen

3. Use context clues to choose the correct definition of **nibble**.

   ☐ take small bites   ☐ take small drinks   ☐ take little sniffs

4. Use context clues to choose the correct definition of **delicious**.

   ☐ delicate   ☐ tasty   ☐ terrible

Comprehension: Cows Are Complicated

Would you believe cows have four stomachs? It sounds incredible, but it's true.

Here are the "hows" and "whys" of a cow's digestive system. First, it's important to know that cows do not have front teeth. They eat grass by wrapping their tongues around it and pulling it from the ground. They do have back teeth, but still they cannot properly chew the grass.

Cows swallow grass without chewing it. When it's swallowed, the grass goes into the cow's first stomach, called a **rumen** (roo-mun). There, it is broken up by the digestive juices and forms into a ball of grass. This ball is called cud. The cow is able to bring the cud back up into its mouth. Then, the cow chews the cud into a pulp with its back teeth and re-swallows it.

After it is swallowed the second time, the cud goes into the cow's second stomach. This second stomach is called the **reticulum** (re-tick-u-lum). The reticulum filters the food to sort out any small stones or other non-food matter. Then, it passes the food onto the cow's third stomach. The third stomach is called the **omasum** (oh-mass-um).

From there, any food that is still undigested is sent back to the first stomach so the cow can bring it back up into her mouth and chew it some more. The rest goes into the cow's fourth stomach. The fourth stomach is called the **abomasum** (ab-oh-ma-sum). Digesting food that can be turned into milk is a full-time job for cows!

Directions: Answer these questions about cows.

1. List in order the names of a cow's four stomachs.

a) _____ b) _____ c) _____ d) _____

2. What is the name of the ball of grass a cow chews on? _____

3. A cow has no

☐ front teeth.   ☐ back teeth.   ☐ fourth stomach.

4. Which stomach acts as a filter for digestion?

☐ reticulum   ☐ rumen   ☐ abomasum

Context Clues: Dairy Cows

Some cows are raised for their beef. Other cows, called dairy cows, are raised for their milk. A dairy cow cannot produce any milk until after its first calf is born. Cows are not mature enough to give birth until they are 2 years old. A cow's gestation period is 40 weeks long, and she usually gives birth to one calf. Then, she produces a lot of milk to feed it. When the calf is 2 days old, the dairy farmer takes the calf away from its mother. After that, the cow is milked twice a day.

The dairy cow's milk comes from the large, smooth udder beneath her body. The udder has four openings called teats. To milk the cow, the farmer grasps a teat and squeezes it with his thumb and forefinger. Then, he gently but firmly pulls his hand down the teat to squeeze the milk out. Milking machines that are hooked to the cow's teats duplicate this action and can milk many cows quickly.

A dairy cow's milk production is not at the same level all the time. When the cow is pregnant, milk production gradually decreases. For two months before her calf is born, a cow is said to be "dry" and is not milked. This happens because, like humans, much of the cow's food is actually being used to nourish the unborn calf.

Farmers give the cow extra food at this time to make sure the mother and unborn calf are well nourished. Again, like humans, well-nourished mothers are more likely to produce healthy babies.

Directions: Answer these questions about dairy cows.

1. Use context clues to choose the correct definition of **grasp**.

   ☐ pull firmly   ☐ hold firmly   ☐ hold gently

2. Use context clues to choose the correct definition of **duplicate**.

   ☐ correct   ☐ make   ☐ copy

3. Use context clues to choose the correct definition of **decrease**.

   ☐ become more   ☐ become less   ☐ become quicker

4. Use context clues to choose the correct definition of **nourish**.

   ☐ to be happy   ☐ to be friendly   ☐ to feed

Comprehension: Chickens

Have you ever heard the expression "pecking order"? In the pecking order of a school, the principal is at the top of the order. Next comes the assistant principal, then the teachers and students.

In the pecking order of chickens, the most aggressive chicken is the leader. The leader is the hen that uses her beak most often to peck the chickens she bosses. These chickens, in turn, boss other chickens by pecking them, and so on. Chickens can peck all others who are "below" them in the pecking order. They never peck "above" themselves by pecking their bosses.

Directions: Answer these questions about chickens.

1. Put this pecking order of four chickens in order.

_____ This chicken pecks numbers 3 and 4 but never 1.

_____ No one pecks this chicken. She's the top boss.

_____ This chicken can't peck anyone.

_____ This chicken pecks chicken number 4.

2. Use context clues to figure out the definition of **aggressive**. _____

_____

_____

3. Who is at the top of the pecking order in a school? _____

_____

Review

Directions: Follow the instructions for each section.

1. Write a summary of the selection "All About Sheep" (page 120).

_____

_____

_____

2. What is the purpose of a pig's bristles?

_____

_____

_____

3. Write a summary of the selection "No Kidding About Goats" (page 122).

_____

_____

_____

4. What is the purpose of a cow's four stomachs?

_____

_____

_____

5. How do chickens establish leaders and followers?

_____

_____

_____

6. What is cud?

_____

_____

Using Prior Knowledge: Stamp Collecting

Directions: Before reading about stamp collecting in the following section, answer these questions.

1. Why do you think people collect stamps?

_____

_____

_____

2. What hobby do you most enjoy? Why?

_____

_____

_____

3. Name at least six famous people who have been pictured on a stamp.

_____   _____

_____   _____

_____   _____

4. Why do you think the postal service issues many different stamps each year? Why not just issue one stamp?

_____

_____

_____

5. Most stamps today are self-stick stamps. What are the benefits of these stamps? Do you think these create any drawbacks for collectors?

_____

_____

_____

Fact or Opinion?

Directions: Read the paragraphs below. Then, in the corresponding numbered blanks, write whether each numbered sentence is a fact or an opinion.

   (1) An important rule for stamp collectors to follow is never to handle stamps with their fingers. **(2)** Instead, to keep the stamps clean, collectors use stamp tongs to pick up stamps. **(3)** Stamps are stored by being placed on mounts. **(4)** Stamp mounts are plastic holders that fit around the stamp and keep it clean. **(5)** The backs of the mounts are sticky, so they can be stuck onto a stamp album page. **(6)** What a great idea!
   (7) The stamps are mounted in stamp albums that have either white or black pages. **(8)** Some people prefer black pages, claiming that the stamps "show" better. **(9)** Some people prefer white pages, claiming that they give the album a cleaner look. **(10)** I think this foolish bickering over page colors is ridiculous!

1. _____

2. _____

3. _____

4. _____

5. _____

6. _____

7. _____

8. _____

9. _____

10. _____

Comprehension: More Stamp Collecting

Many people collect stamps in blocks of four. Each stamp in the block is stuck to the other stamps along the edges. Collectors do not tear the stamps apart from one another. They buy blocks of stamps bearing new designs directly from the post office. Then, they mount the blocks of stamps and place them in their albums.

Collectors also get their stamps off of envelopes. This is a bit tricky, because the stamps are glued on. Usually, collectors soak the stamps in warm water to loosen the glue. Then, they gently pull the stamps from the paper and let them dry before mounting them.

Some beginners start their collections by buying a packet of mixed stamps. The packets, or bags, contain a variety of different stamps. Beginners buy these packets from companies that supply stamps to philatelists (fuh-lay-tell-lists). Philately (fuh-lay-tell-lee) is the collection and study of postage stamps. Philatelists are the people who collect and study them.

Packets of stamps usually contain stamps from many different countries. Often, they contain duplicates of some of the stamps. Suppliers usually don't sort the stamps that go into the packets for beginners. They leave that for beginning philatelists to enjoy!

Directions: Answer these questions about stamp collecting.

1. Name three places some people get stamps. _____

_____

2. What is the word that describes the collection and study of stamps? _____

3. What are people called who collect and study stamps? _____

4. The bag that a mixture of stamps comes in is called a

☐ postal bag.   ☐ packet.   ☐ philatelist.

5. Do stamp mixtures usually include only U.S. stamps?

☐ Yes   ☐ No

Recalling Details: Philately Abbreviations

Like other hobbies, philately has its own jargon and symbols. Collectors and dealers know what they mean, but outsiders would be puzzled if they saw the following abbreviations without their definitions. Read them carefully, and then refer to them when answering the questions below.

Avg. — average condition

blk. — block of four stamps

C — cancelled (used) stamp

OG — original gum
   (glue on back of stamp)

G — good condition

M — mint (excellent and unused) condition

s — single stamp

U — used stamp

VF — very fine condition

Wmk — watermark (can occur when water
   is used to remove stamp from envelope)

Directions: Answer these questions about the abbreviations used by stamp dealers and collectors.

1. If a philatelist wrote the following description, what would he or she mean?

   I have a blk. in VF. _____

   _____

2. What does this mean? **s with OG, condition M** _____

   _____

3. What other abbreviation would most likely be used do describe a used (U) stamp?

   _____

4. What does this mean? **s in Avg. with Wmk** _____

   _____

5. Which is more valuable, a rare stamp in **M** or **VF** condition? _____

6. Would you rather own a single U stamp or a blk. in M? _____

Comprehension: Faces on Stamps

Most faces that appear on postage stamps are of famous people who are no longer alive. Until 2011, the U.S. Postal Service had a rule that no living people could be featured on stamps. In fact, a person had to be deceased for five years before appearing on a stamp. The Postal Service changed the rule in 2011. The actors from the Harry Potter movies were among the first to be honored on a series of stamps.

Many U.S. presidents' faces have been on postage stamps, as have pictures of the faces of other important people in U.S. history. Some people's faces have been on many different stamps. Through the years, George Washington and Benjamin Franklin have been on dozens of different types of stamps!

Other people whose pictures have been on stamps include John Quincy Adams, the sixth president of the United States; Jane Addams, a U.S. social worker and writer; Louisa May Alcott, author of *Little Women* and many other books; Clara Barton, nurse and founder of the American Red Cross; Alexander Graham Bell, inventor of the telephone; and poet, Emily Dickinson. These are only a few of the hundreds of famous Americans whose faces have appeared on U.S. postage stamps.

Directions: Answer these questions about some of the people whose faces have appeared on U.S. stamps.

1. Name six occupations of people whose faces have appeared on postage stamps.

   GeorgeWashington and BenjaminFranklin

   Jan JohnAdams Alexander Bell Jane addams
       President   Phone   social worker

2. What two people's pictures have appeared on more stamps than on any others?

   Georg washington and Bengmin Frunkiin

3. What living person do you think should appear on a stamp? Why does he or she deserve this honor? __my BFF Daina because she is righing epilepsy__

4. Which person featured on a postage stamp was a social worker?

   ☐ Clara Barton   ☐ Louisa May Alcott   ☑ Jane Addams

5. Which person featured on a postage stamp was an inventor?

   ☐ Emily Dickinson   ☑ Alexander Graham Bell   ☐ John Quincy Adams

Comprehension: Valuable Stamps

Most people collect stamps as a hobby. They spend small sums of money to get the stamps they want, or they trade stamps with other collectors. They rarely make what could be considered "big money" from their philately hobby.

A few collectors are in the business of philately as opposed to the hobby. To the people who can afford it, some stamps are very valuable. For example, a U.S. airmail stamp with a face value of 24 cents when it was issued in 1918 is now worth more than $35,000 if a certain design appears on the stamp. Another stamp, the British Guiana, an ugly stamp that cost only a penny when it was issued, later sold for $280,000!

The *Graf Zeppelin* is another example of an ugly stamp that became valuable. *Graf Zeppelin* is the name of a type of airship, similar to what we now call a blimp, invented around the turn of the century. Stamps were issued to mark the first roundtrip flight the *Zeppelin* made between two continents. A set of three of these stamps cost $4.55 when they were issued. The stamps were ugly, and few of them sold. The Postal Service destroyed the rest. Now, because they are rare, each set of the *Graf Zeppelin* stamps is worth hundreds of dollars.

Directions: Answer these questions about valuable stamps.

1. What is the most valuable stamp described? _____

2. For how much did this stamp originally sell? _____

3. What did a collector later pay for it? _____

4. The *Graf Zeppelin* stamps originally sold for $4.55 for a set of

    ☐ four.   ☐ six.   ☐ three.

5. Which stamp did the Postal Service destroy because it didn't sell?

    ☐ British Guiana   ☐ *Graf Zeppelin*   ☐ *British Zeppelin*

Fact or Opinion?

Directions: Read the paragraphs below. Then, in the corresponding numbered blanks, write whether each numbered sentence is a fact or an opinion.

(1) Nearly every valuable stamp on Earth has been counterfeited (coun-ter-fit-tid) at one time or another. **(2)** A counterfeit is a fake that looks nearly identical to the original. **(3)** It takes a lot of nerve to try to pass off counterfeits as the real thing. **(4)** Counterfeiting is big business, especially with stamps from overseas. **(5)** Because a collector often has no original for comparison, he or she can be easily fooled by a good counterfeit!

(6) One way people can make sure a stamp is real is to have it checked by a company that authenticates (aw-then-ti-kates) stamps. **(7)** To authenticate means to prove the stamp is real. **(8)** Of course, there is a fee for this service. **(9)** But I think paying a reasonable fee is worth what collectors get in return. **(10)** Those counterfeiters should be locked up forever!

1. _____

2. _____

3. _____

4. _____

5. _____

6. _____

7. _____

8. _____

9. _____

10. _____

Comprehensive Curriculum - **Grade 5**

Comprehension: Stamp Value

It's nearly impossible to predict which stamps will rise in value. Why? Because the value is based on the law of supply and demand. How much does someone or a group of "someones" want a particular stamp? If many people want a stamp, the value will increase, especially if few of the stamps exist.

However, collectors are also always on the lookout for things that can lower the value of a stamp. Are the stamp's perforations (per-four-ay-shuns) torn along the edges? (Perforations are ragged edges where stamps tear apart.) Is there a watermark on the stamp? Has the gum worn off the back? All these things can make a stamp less valuable.

Directions: Answer these questions about determining the value of stamps.

1. Name three things that can lower the value of a stamp.

   _____

   _____

2. Collecting stamps is a fascinating hobby.   Fact   Opinion

3. What is one thing the value of stamps is based upon? _____

4. What will happen if many people want a rare stamp? _____

   _____

5. Explain how to spot a stamp that will become valuable. _____

   _____

   _____

   _____

Review

Directions: Follow the instructions below.

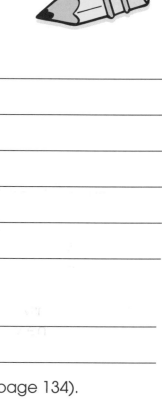

1. Define the following words from this section.

   mount: _____

   bickering: _____

   philately: _____

   counterfeit: _____

   authenticate: _____

   perforations: _____

2. Choose two of the words above, and use each in a sentence.

   a)_____

   b)_____

3. Write a one-sentence main idea for the selection "Stamp Value" (page 134).

   _____

   _____

4. Write a summary of the selection "Faces on Stamps" (page 131).

   _____

   _____

   _____

5. Write a summary of the selection "More Stamp Collecting" (page 129).

   _____

   _____

   _____

Comprehensive Curriculum - **Grade 5**

Using Prior Knowledge: Cooking

Directions: Before reading about cooking in the following section, answer these questions.

1. What is your favorite recipe? Why?

_____

_____

_____

2. What do you most like to cook? Why?

_____

_____

_____

3. Have you tried food from cultures other than your own? If so, which type of food do you like most? Why?

_____

_____

_____

4. Why is it important to follow the correct sequence when preparing a recipe?

_____

_____

_____

5. What safety precautions must be followed when working in a kitchen?

_____

_____

_____

Following Directions: Chunky Tomato and Green Onion Sauce

Following directions means to do what the directions say to do, step by step, in the correct order.

Directions: Read the recipe for chunky tomato and green onion sauce. Answer the questions below.

Ingredients:

- 2 tablespoons corn oil
- 2 cloves of garlic, finely chopped
- $1\frac{1}{2}$ pounds plum tomatoes, cored, peeled, seeded, then coarsely chopped
- 3 green onions, cut in half lengthwise, then thinly sliced
- salt
- freshly ground pepper

Heat oil in a heavy skillet over medium heat. Add garlic, and cook until yellow, about 1 minute. Stir in tomatoes. Season with salt and pepper. Cook until thickened, about 10 minutes. Stir in green onions and serve.

1. What is the last thing the cook does to prepare the tomatoes before cooking them?

_____

2. What kind of oil does the cook heat in the heavy skillet? _____

3. How long should the garlic be cooked? _____

4. What does the cook do to the tomatoes right before removing the seeds?

_____

5. Is the sauce served hot or cold? _____

Comprehension: Cooking with Care

People are so busy these days that many have no time to cook. This creates a problem, because most families love home cooking! The food tastes good and warm, and a family meal brings everyone together. In some families, meals are often the only times everyone sees one another at the same time.

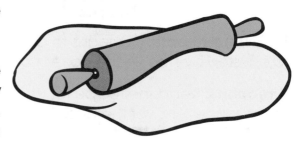

Another reason people enjoy home cooking is that it is often more nutritious than prepared foods. Restaurant meals and prepared foods are often much higher in fat, salt, and preservatives. At home, people tend to make more wholesome foods. You know what every ingredient in a meal is when you cook from home!

There's also something about the smell of good cooking that appeals to people of all ages. It makes most of us feel secure and loved—even if we are the ones doing the cooking! Next time you smell muffins baking, stop for a moment and pay attention to your mood. Chances are, the good smell is making you feel happy.

Real estate agents know that good cooking smells are important. They sometimes advise people whose homes are for sale to bake cookies or bread if prospective buyers are coming to see the house. The good smells make the place "feel like home." These pleasant smells help convince potential buyers that the house would make a good home for their family, too!

Directions: Answer these questions about good cooking.

1. Why do fewer people cook nowadays? _____

2. Why are family meals important? _____

3. Why are home-cooked meals usually more nutritious than prepared foods?

_____

4. Real estate agents often advise home sellers holding open houses to

   ☐ clean the garage.   ☐ bake cookies or bread.

5. The smell of baking at open houses may encourage buyers to

   ☐ bake cookies.   ☐ buy the house.   ☐ bake bread.

Sequencing: Pumpkin-Nut Muffins

$2\frac{1}{4}$ cups flour

2 teaspoons pumpkin pie spice

$1\frac{1}{2}$ teaspoons baking soda

1 teaspoon ground ginger

$\frac{1}{4}$ teaspoon salt

$\frac{1}{2}$ cup chopped pecans

1 cup packed brown sugar

1 cup canned pumpkin

$\frac{1}{3}$ cup buttermilk

$\frac{1}{3}$ cup canola oil

$\frac{1}{4}$ cup maple syrup

1 teaspoon vanilla extract

2 large eggs

Before you begin, preheat the oven to 400°. Combine the flour, pumpkin pie spice, baking soda, ginger, and salt in a medium bowl. Stir the dry ingredients with a whisk. Stir in the nuts. Next, make a well in the center of the mixture. In a separate bowl, combine the brown sugar, canned pumpkin, buttermilk, canola oil, maple syrup, vanilla extract, and eggs. Stir well with a whisk. Now, add the sugar mixture to the flour mixture, and stir just until moist.

Scoop the batter into 18 muffin cups coated with cooking spray. Bake at 400° for about 15 minutes, or until a wooden pick inserted in the center of a muffin comes out clean. Cool the muffins on a wire rack. Eat and enjoy!

Directions: Number in correct order the steps for making pumpkin-nut muffins.

_____ Combine the dry ingredients.

_____ Stir in the nuts.

_____ Whisk together the wet ingredients.

_____ Cool the muffins on a wire rack.

_____ Preheat the oven to 400°.

_____ Add the sugar mixture to the flour mixture.

_____ Eat and enjoy!

_____ Make a well in the center of the mixture.

Comprehension: Eating High-Fiber Foods

Have you heard your parents or other adults talk about "high-fiber" diets? Foods that are high in fiber, like oats and other grains, are believed to be very healthy. Here's why: The fiber adds bulk to the food the body digests and helps keep the large intestines working properly. Corn, oatmeal, apples, celery, nuts, and other chewy foods also contain fiber that helps the body's systems for digesting and eliminating food keep working properly.

Researchers at the University of Minnesota have found another good reason to eat high-fiber food, especially at breakfast. Because fiber is bulky, it absorbs a lot of liquid in the stomach. As it absorbs the liquid, it swells. This fools the stomach into thinking it's full. As a result, when lunchtime comes, those who have eaten a high-fiber breakfast are not as hungry. They eat less food at lunch. Without much effort on their parts, dieters eating a high-fiber breakfast can lose weight.

The university researchers say a person could lose 10 pounds in a year just by eating a high-fiber breakfast! This is good news to people who are only slightly overweight and want an easy method for losing that extra 10 pounds.

Directions: Answer these questions about eating high-fiber foods.

1. Why is fiber healthy? _____

_____

2. How does fiber fool the stomach? _____

_____

3. Name four examples of healthy, fiber-rich foods. _____

_____

4. How many pounds could a dieter eating a high-fiber breakfast lose in a year?

☐ 20 pounds   ☐ 30 pounds   ☐ 10 pounds

5. The university that did the research is in which state?

☐ Michigan   ☐ Minnesota   ☐ Montana

Name _____

Main Idea: New Corn

I will clothe myself in spring clothing

And visit the slopes of the eastern hill.

By the mountain stream, a mist hovers,

Hovers a moment and then scatters.

Then comes a wind blowing from the south

That brushes the fields of new corn.

Directions: Answer these questions about this ancient poem, which is translated from Chinese.

1. Circle the main idea:

   The poet will dress comfortably and go to where the corn grows so he or she can enjoy the beauty of nature.

   The poet will dress comfortably and visit the slopes of the eastern hill, where he or she will plant corn.

2. From which direction does the wind blow? _____

3. Where does the mist hover? _____

4. What do you think the poet means by "spring clothing"? _____

_____

Comprehension: The French Eat Differently

Many people believe that French people are very different from Americans. This is certainly true where eating habits are concerned! Obesity rates are about three times higher in America than they are in France. And yet, the French are known for their rich cheeses and delicious pastries. So how do the French manage to stay fit and healthy? There are several differences between the eating habits of Americans and the French.

One difference has to do with quality versus quantity. In America, portion sizes are known for being very large. In France, portions are much smaller, which means the French consume fewer calories. Also, when the foods are high quality, a small amount can be very satisfying.

In general, the French also really savor and enjoy their food. Americans are often in a hurry and rush through meals. Eating quickly or mindlessly can lead to overeating. The French take their time with meals. They eat more slowly, which gives the body a chance to recognize when it is full.

Finally, the French tend to cook at home more often than Americans do. In the United States, eating out is a popular pastime. It is convenient, and it's also enjoyable. The problem is that restaurant foods and processed foods are higher in fat and calories. Eating at home, like the French tend to do, results in healthier meals.

French meals are high in quality and flavor, and the French leave a meal feeling satisfied. Their eating habits keep them fit and healthy. Eating like the French could make America healthier, too!

Directions: Answer these questions about the eating habits of French and American people

1. Why is it surprising that the French tend to be healthy and have low rates of obesity?

   _____

2. Are Americans or the French more likely to rush through meals?

   _____

3. Why is eating at home generally a better idea than eating out or eating processed

   foods? _____

4. What is the difference between portion sizes in France and America?

   _____

5. What is a benefit of eating slowly?

   _____

Comprehension: Chinese Cabbage

Many Americans enjoy Chinese food. It's a popular take-out meal in cities across the United States. Because it tastes so good, many people are curious about the ingredients in Chinese food. Siu choy and choy sum are two types of Chinese cabbage that many people enjoy eating. Siu choy grows to be 2 to 3 feet! Of course, it is chopped into small pieces before it is cooked and served. Its leaves are light green and soft. It is not crunchy like American cabbage. Siu choy is used in soups and stews. Sometimes, it is pickled with vinegar and other ingredients and served as a side dish to other courses.

Choy sum looks and tastes different from siu choy. Choy sum grows to be only 8 to 10 inches. It is a flowering cabbage that grows small yellow flowers, which are edible. Its leaves are long and bright green. After its leaves are boiled for four minutes, choy sum is often served as a salad. Oil and oyster sauce are mixed together and poured over choy sum as a salad dressing.

Directions: Answer these questions about Chinese cabbage.

1. Which Chinese cabbage grows small yellow flowers?_____

2. Which Chinese cabbage is served as a salad?_____

3. Is siu choy crunchy? _____

4. What ingredients are in the salad dressing used on choy sum?

   _____

5. To what size does siu choy grow? _____

6. Name two main dishes in which siu choy is used. _____

Review

Here's a recipe for a special mashed potato treat that serves two people. The recipe is fast and easy to follow, and the results are delicious!

Begin by peeling two large potatoes and cooking them in a pot of boiling water. When a fork or knife inserted into them pulls out easily, you will know they are done. Then, take them from the pot, and drain them well. Place them in a large mixing bowl, and add 2 tablespoons of milk and 2 tablespoons of butter. Mash with a potato masher until the lumps are gone.

In a skillet, melt a tablespoon of butter, and add one bunch of chopped green onions. Cook them about 1 minute. Add them to the potatoes, and mix gently. Season with salt and pepper. Serve and eat!

Directions: Answer these questions about how to make mashed potatoes with green onions.

1. Circle the main idea:

   This recipe is fast and easy, and the potatoes are delicious.

   This recipe has only four ingredients (plus salt and pepper).

2. Name the main ingredients in this recipe (not including salt and pepper).

   _____

3. How many people does this recipe serve? _____

4. Number in order the steps for making mashed potatoes with green onions.

   _____ Cook the chopped green onions for 1 minute.

   _____ Peel two potatoes.

   _____ Season with salt and pepper and serve.

   _____ Put the cooked potatoes in a bowl with milk and butter, then mash.

   _____ Add the onions to the mashed potatoes.

   _____ Boil the potatoes until they are done.

Using Prior Knowledge: Greek and Roman Mythology

Directions: Before reading about Greek and Roman mythology in the following section, answer these questions.

1. Hercules is a man from Greek and Roman mythology. Write a short paragraph describing what you know about Hercules.

_____

_____

_____

2. Can you think of anything today that derived its name from a Greek or Roman myth?

_____

_____

_____

3. Compare and contrast what you know of Greek and Roman beliefs about mythology with your beliefs.

_____

_____

_____

_____

_____

_____

4. Many constellations are named after gods, goddesses, and mythical creatures. Name at least six.

_____   _____   _____

_____   _____   _____

Comprehension: Roman Legends

Long ago, people did not know as much about science and astronomy as they do today. When they did not understand something, they thought the gods were responsible. The ancient Romans believed there were many gods and that each god or goddess (a female god) was responsible for certain things.

For example, the Romans believed Ceres (Sir-eez) was the goddess who made flowers, plants, trees, and other things grow. She was a lot like what people today refer to as Mother Nature. Ceres was also responsible for the good weather that made crops grow. You can see why Ceres was such an important goddess to the ancient Romans.

Apollo was the god of the sun. People believed he used his chariot to pull the sun up each day and take it down at night. Apollo was extremely good-looking. His home was a golden palace near the sun surrounded by fluffy white clouds. Apollo had to work every single day, but he lived a wonderful life.

Jupiter was the most important god of all. He was the god who ruled all of the other gods, as well as the people. Jupiter was also called Jove. Maybe you have heard someone use the exclamation, "By Jove!" That person is talking about Jupiter! The word **father** is derived from the word **Jupiter**. Although he did not really exist, Jupiter influenced our language.

Directions: Answer these questions about Roman legends.

1. What imaginary figure is Ceres compared to today? _____

2. Where did Apollo live? _____

3. The word **father** is derived from the name of this god:

   ☐ Ceres   ☐ Apollo   ☐ Jupiter

4. Which is not true of Apollo?   ☐ He had to work every day.

   ☐ He lived in a mountain cave.

   ☐ He was very handsome.

Comprehension: Apollo and Phaethon

Apollo, the sun god, had a son named Phaethon (Fay-a-thun). Like most boys, Phaethon was proud of his father. He liked to brag to his friends about Apollo's important job, but no one believed that the great Apollo was his father.

Phaethon thought of a way to prove to his friends that he was telling the truth. He went to Apollo and asked if he could drive the chariot of the sun. If his friends saw him making the sun rise and set, they would be awestruck!

Apollo did not want to let Phaethon drive the chariot. He was afraid Phaethon was not strong enough to control the horses. But Phaethon begged until Apollo gave in. "Stay on the path," Apollo said. "If you dip too low, the sun will catch Earth on fire. If you go too high, people will freeze."

Unfortunately, Apollo's worst fears came true. Phaethon could not control the horses. He let them pull the chariot of the sun too close to Earth. To keep Earth from burning, Jupiter, father of the gods, sent a thunderbolt that hit Phaethon and knocked him from the driver's seat. When Phaethon let go of the reins, the horses pulled the chariot back up onto the proper path. Phaethon was killed as he fell to Earth. His body fell and became a shooting star.

Directions: Answer these questions about the Roman legend of Apollo and his son.

1. Who did not believe Apollo was Phaethon's father? _____

2. What did Phaethon do to prove Apollo was his father? _____

_____

3. Why did Jupiter send a lightning bolt? _____

_____

4. Which was not a warning from Apollo to Phaethon?

☐ Don't go too close to Earth. It will burn up.

☐ Don't pet the horses. They will run wild.

☐ Don't go too far from Earth. It will freeze.

Context Clues: Mighty Hercules

Some people lift weights to build their strength. But Hercules (Her-cu-lees) had a different idea. He carried a calf on his shoulders every day. As the calf grew, it got heavier, and Hercules got stronger. Eventually, Hercules could carry a full-grown bull!

Hercules used his enormous strength to do many kind things. He became famous. Even the king had heard of Hercules! He called for Hercules to kill a lion that had killed many people in his kingdom. Hercules tracked the lion to its den and strangled it. Then, Hercules made clothes for himself from the lion's skin. This kind of apparel was unusual, and soon Hercules was recognized everywhere he went. Hercules was big, and his clothes made it easy to pick him out in a crowd!

The king asked Hercules to stay in his kingdom and help protect the people who lived there. Hercules performed many feats of strength and bravery. He caught a golden deer for the king. The deer had outrun everyone else. Then, Hercules killed a giant, a dragon, and other dangerous creatures. Hercules became a hero and was known throughout the kingdom.

Directions: Answer these questions about Hercules.

1. Use context clues to choose the correct definition of **enormous**.

☐ huge   ☐ tiny   ☐ smart

2. Use context clues to choose the correct definition of **strangle**.

☐ beat   ☐ choke   ☐ tickle

3. Use context clues to choose the correct definition of **den**.

☐ pond   ☐ hutch   ☐ home

4. Use context clues to choose the correct definition of **apparel**.

☐ appearance   ☐ clothing   ☐ personality

5. Use context clues to choose the correct definition of **feat**.

☐ trick   ☐ treat   ☐ act

Comprehension: Ceres and Venus

Remember Ceres? She was like Mother Nature to the ancient Romans.

Ceres made the flowers, plants, and trees grow. She made crops come up and rain fall. Ceres was a very important goddess. The ancient Romans depended on her for many things.

Although the gods and goddesses were important, they had faults like ordinary people. They argued with one another. Sometimes they got mad and lost their tempers. This is what happened to Ceres and another goddess named Venus (Veen-us). Venus, who was the goddess of love and beauty, got mad at Ceres. She decided to hurt Ceres by causing Pluto, gloomy god of the underworld, to fall in love with Cere's daughter, Proserpine (Pro-sur-pin-ay).

To accomplish this, Venus sent her son Cupid to shoot Pluto with his bow and arrow. Venus told Cupid that the man shot by this arrow would then fall in love with the first woman he saw. Venus instructed Cupid to make sure that woman was Ceres's daughter. Cupid waited with his bow and arrow until Pluto drove by Ceres's garden in his chariot. In the garden was Proserpine. Just as Pluto's chariot got near her, Cupid shot his arrow.

Ping! The arrow hit Pluto. It did not hurt, but it did its job well. Pluto fell instantly in love with poor Proserpine, who was quietly planting flowers. Pluto was not a gentleman. He did not even introduce himself! Pluto swooped down and carried Proserpine off in his chariot before she could call for help.

Directions: Answer these questions about Ceres and Venus.

1. With whom was Venus angry? _____

2. How did Venus decide to get even? _____

_____

3. Ceres's daughter's name was

☐ Persperpine.   ☐ Prosperline.   ☐ Proserpine.

4. Venus's son's name was

☐ Apollo.   ☐ Cupid.   ☐ Persperpine.

Comprehension: Proserpine and Pluto

Proserpine was terrified in Pluto's palace in the underworld. She missed her mother, Ceres, and would not stop crying.

When Ceres discovered her daughter was missing, she searched the whole Earth looking for her. Of course, she did not find her. Ceres was so unhappy about Proserpine's disappearance that she refused to do her job, which was to make things grow. When Ceres did not work, rain could not fall and crops could not grow. Finally, Ceres went to Jupiter for help.

Jupiter was powerful, but so was Pluto. Jupiter told Ceres he could get Proserpine back from Pluto if she had not eaten any of Pluto's food. As it turned out, Proserpine had eaten something. She had swallowed six seeds from a piece of fruit. Because he felt sorry for the people on Earth who were suffering, Pluto told Jupiter that Proserpine could return temporarily to Ceres so she would cheer up and make crops grow again. But Pluto later came back for Proserpine and forced her to spend six months each year with him in the underworld—one month for each seed she had eaten. Every time she returned to the underworld, Ceres mourned and refused to do her job. This is how the Romans explained the seasons—when Proserpine is on Earth with Ceres, it is spring and summer; when Proserpine goes to the underworld, it is fall and winter.

Directions: Answer these questions about Proserpine and Pluto.

1. What happened to Ceres when Pluto took her daughter? _____

_____

2. Whom did Ceres ask for help to get her daughter back? _____

3. Why did Proserpine have to return to Pluto's underworld? _____

_____

4. How long did Proserpine have to stay in the underworld each time she returned?

_____

Comprehension: Orpheus Saves the Day

Orpheus (Or-fee-us) was a talented Greek musician. Once, by playing beautiful music on his lyre (ly-er), he caused a ship that was stuck in the sand to move into the water. (A lyre is a stringed instrument that looks like a small harp and fits in the musician's lap.) The song was about how wonderful it was to sail upon the sea. The ship itself must have thought the song was wonderful, too, because it slipped into the water and sailed away!

There was a reason the ship understood Orpheus's song. Inside the ship was a piece of wood that a goddess had given to the captain of the ship. The captain's name was Jason. Once, Jason had helped an old woman across a deep river. He later learned that the old woman was a goddess. To thank him, the goddess gave Jason a piece of wood that could talk. She told him to use the wood when he built a new ship. If he ever got stuck while building the ship and did not know what to do, the goddess told Jason to ask the wood.

Several times, Jason and his crew got instructions from the wood. Finally, the ship was finished. It was beautiful and very large. Because it was so big, Jason and his men were unable to move it into the water. They called on Hercules for help, and even he could not make it budge. That's when Orpheus saved the day with his lyre.

Directions: Answer these questions about Orpheus's amazing talent.

1. Who owned the ship that was stuck? _____

2. Where was the ship stuck? _____

3. Why did the ship get stuck? _____

4. A lyre looks like what other instrument?

☐ harmonica   ☐ guitar   ☐ harp

5. Who did Jason first ask for help to move the ship?

☐ Orpheus   ☐ Hercules   ☐ Jupiter

Review

Directions: Follow the instructions below.

1. Define the following words from this section.

   astronomy: _____

   reins: _____

   lyre: _____

   centaur: _____

   minotaur: _____

   myth: _____

2. Choose two words from above, and use each in a sentence.

   a)_____

   b)_____

3. Write a summary of the selection "Mighty Hercules" (page 148).

   _____

   _____

   _____

   _____

4. Complete the sequence of events from the selection "Proserpine and Pluto" (page 150).

   a) Pluto fell in love with Proserpine and kidnapped her in his chariot.

   b) _____

   c) _____

   d) _____

   e) _____

Using Prior Knowledge: Famous Ships

Directions: Before reading about famous ships in the following section, answer these questions.

1. Look up the following terms in a dictionary, and write their definitions.

   vessel: _____

   bow: _____

   stern: _____

   poop deck: _____

   hull: _____

   caravel: _____

   mast: _____

   frigate: _____

   lateen: _____

   spar: _____

   fore: _____

   aft: _____

2. Have you ever been on a large ship? If so, describe the experience. If not, on what kind of ship or boat would you like to ride? Why?

   _____

   _____

   _____

3. Name at least one famous ship, and write what you know about it.

   _____

   _____

   _____

Comprehensive Curriculum - **Grade 5**

Comprehension: The *Constitution*

The *Constitution*, or "Old Ironsides," was built by the United States Navy in 1798. Its success in battle made it one of the most famous vessels in the United States. The *Constitution*'s naval career began with the war with Tripoli from 1803 to 1804. Later, it was also used in the War of 1812. During this war, it was commanded by Isaac Hull. The *Constitution* won a 30-minute battle with the British ship, *Guerriere*, in August of 1812. The *Guerriere* was nearly demolished. Later that same year, the *Constitution* was used to capture a British frigate near Brazil.

The *Constitution* was taken out of service in 1829 and was rebuilt many times over the years. Today, it is on display at the Boston Navy Yard.

Directions: Answer these questions about the *Constitution*.

1. What is the main idea of the selection? _____

_____

2. Which ship was almost demolished by the *Constitution*? _____

3. In which two wars was the *Constitution* used? _____

4. Where is the *Constitution* now on display? _____

5. Complete the following time line with dates and events described above.

_____   _____   _____   _____   _____

|———|————|————|————|————|———|

Comprehension: The *Santa Maria, Niña,* and *Pinta*

When Christopher Columbus decided to attempt a voyage across the ocean, the ships he depended upon to take him there were called "caravels." A caravel is a small sailing ship built by Spain and Portugal in the 15th and 16th centuries. The caravels Columbus used to sail to the New World were named the *Santa Maria, Niña,* and *Pinta.*

The ships were not very large. It is believed the *Santa Maria* was only 75 to 90 feet long, and the *Niña* and *Pinta* were only about 70 feet long. Caravels typically had three to four masts with sails attached. The foremast carried a square sail, while the others were more triangular in shape. These triangular-shaped sails were called "lateen sails."

These three small ships were quite seaworthy and proved excellent ships for Columbus. They carried him safely to the other side of the world!

Directions: Answer these questions about the *Santa Maria, Niña,* and *Pinta.*

1. What is a lateen sail? _____

2. What is the main idea of the selection? _____

_____

_____

3. What is a caravel? _____

4. Where did Columbus sail in his caravels? _____

5. Do some research, and compare a 15th-century caravel with a ship built in the 20th century.

_____

_____

_____

_____

Comprehensive Curriculum - **Grade 5**

Comprehension: The *Lusitania*

The *Lusitania* was a British passenger steamship. It became famous when it was torpedoed and sunk by the Germans during World War I. On May 7, 1915, the *Lusitania* was traveling off the coast of Ireland when a German submarine fired on it without warning. The ship stood no chance of surviving the attack and sunk in an astonishing 20 minutes. Of the 1,198 people who perished, 128 were American citizens. At the time the ship was torpedoed, the United States was not yet involved in the war. Public opinion over the attack put pressure on President Woodrow Wilson to declare war on Germany. The Germans proclaimed that the *Lusitania* was carrying weapons for the allies.

This claim was later proven to be true. President Wilson demanded that the German government apologize for the sinking and make amends. Germany did not accept responsibility but did promise to avoid sinking any more passenger ships without first giving a warning.

Directions: Answer these questions about the *Lusitania*.

1. What does **proclaimed** mean? _____

2. What does **perished** mean? _____

3. What does **amends** mean? _____

4. What does **allies** mean? _____

5. If the *Lusitania* was carrying arms, do you think the Germans had a right to sink it? Why or why not?

_____

_____

_____

_____

Comprehension: The *Titanic*

The British passenger ship, *Titanic*, debuted in the spring of 1912. It was billed as an unsinkable ship due to its construction. It had 16 watertight compartments that would hold the ship afloat even in the event that four of the compartments were damaged.

But on the evening of April 14, 1912, during *Titanic*'s first voyage, its design proved unworthy. Just before midnight, *Titanic* struck an iceberg, which punctured 5 of the 16 compartments. The ship sunk in a little under 3 hours. Approximately 1,513 of the over 2,220 people onboard died. Most of these people died because there weren't enough lifeboats to accommodate everyone onboard. These people were left floating in the water. Many died from exposure, since the Atlantic Ocean was near freezing in temperature. It was one of the worst ocean disasters in history.

Because of the investigations that followed the *Titanic* disaster, the passenger ship industry instituted many reforms. It is now required that there is ample lifeboat space for all passengers and crew. An international ice patrol and full-time radio coverage were also instituted to prevent such disasters in the future.

Directions: Answer these questions about the *Titanic*.

1. How did most of the 1,513 people onboard the *Titanic* die? _____

2. Why did this "unsinkable" ship sink? _____

_____

3. What changes have been made in ship safety as a result of the *Titanic* tragedy?

_____

_____

4. There have been many attempts to rescue artifacts from the *Titanic*. But many families of the dead wish the site to be left alone, as it is the final resting place of their relatives. They feel burial sites should not be disrupted. Do you agree or disagree? Why?

_____

_____

_____

Name _____

Venn Diagram: *Lusitania* and *Titanic*

A **Venn diagram** is used to chart information that shows similarities and differences between two things.

Example:	**Dogs**	**Both**	**Cats**
	bark	good pets	one size
	dependent	can live inside or outside	kill mice
	large and small breeds	have fur	can use litterbox
	protect the home	four legs	independent

Directions: Complete the Venn diagram for the *Lusitania* and the *Titanic*.

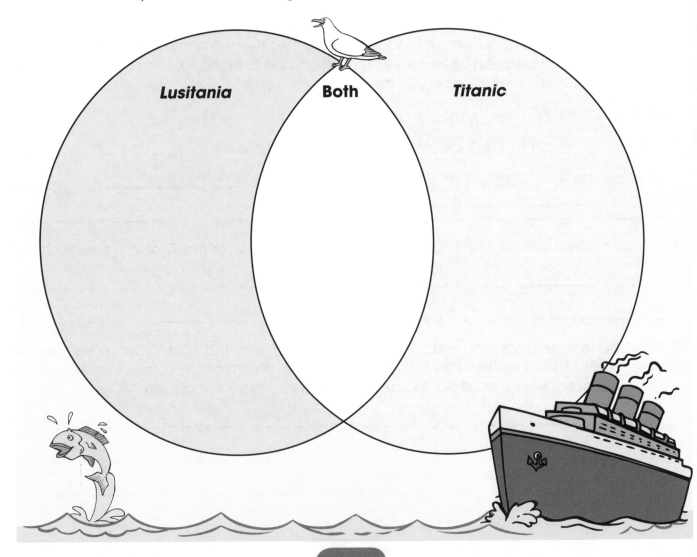

Lusitania   Both   Titanic

Comprehension: The *Monitor* and the *Virginia*

During the Civil War, it became customary to cover wooden warships with iron. This increased their durability and made them more difficult to sink. Two such ships were built using iron. They were the *Monitor* and the *Virginia*.

Most people are more familiar with the name the *Merrimack*. The *Merrimack* was a U.S. steam frigate that had been burnt and sunk by Union forces when the Confederates were forced to abandon their navy yard. The Confederate Navy raised the hull of the *Merrimack* and rebuilt her as the ironclad *Virginia*.

Both the *Monitor* and the *Virginia* engaged in battle on March 9, 1862. After several hours of battle, the bulky *Virginia* had no choice but to withdraw in order to avoid the lowering tides. This battle, called Hampton Roads, was considered to be a tie between the two ships.

Although both ships survived the battle, they were later destroyed. Two months later, the *Virginia* was sunk by her crew to avoid capture. The *Monitor* sunk on December 31, 1862, during a storm off the coast of North Carolina.

Directions: Use context clues for these definitions.

1. customary: _____

2. durability: _____

3. ironclad: _____

Directions: Answer these questions about the *Monitor* and the *Virginia*.

4. Who won the battle between the *Virginia* and the *Monitor*? _____

5. Why would lowering tides present danger to a ship? _____

_____

6. Describe how each ship was finally destroyed. _____

_____

_____

_____

Review

1. Use the Venn diagram you completed comparing the *Lusitania* and the *Titanic* (page 158) to write a two-paragraph compare/contrast essay about the two ships. Describe their similarities in the first paragraph and their differences in the second

_____

_____

_____

_____

_____

_____

_____

_____

2. Describe the differences in the structure of the following ships: *Santa Maria*, *Monitor*, and *Titanic*.

_____

_____

_____

_____

3. Why did people think the *Titanic* was unsinkable? After the ship actually did sink, how do you think this affected the way people thought about new technology?

_____

_____

_____

_____

_____

Reading Comprehension: Railroads

Directions: Read the information about railroads. Then, answer the questions.

As early as the 1550s, a rough form of railroad was already being used in parts of Europe. Miners in England and other areas of western Europe used horse- or mule-drawn wagons on wooden tracks to pull loads out of mines. With these tracks, the horses could pull twice as much weight as they could without them. No one could have known then that one day this simple idea would change the world.

There were many developments along the way that helped make railroads a practical and valuable form of transportation. Two of the most important were the iron track and the "flanged" wheel, which has a rim around it to hold it onto the track. The most important invention was the steam engine by James Watt in 1765.

The first railroads in the United States were built during the late 1820s and caused a lot of excitement. They were faster than other forms of travel, and they could provide service year-round, unlike boats and stagecoaches. Trains were soon the main means of travel in the U.S.

Railroads played a major part in the Industrial Revolution—the years of change when machines were first used to do work that had been done by hand for many centuries. Trains provided cheaper rates and quicker service for transporting goods. Because manufacturers could ship their goods over long distances, they could sell their products all over the nation instead of only in the surrounding cities and towns. This meant greater profits for the companies. Trains also brought people into the cities to work in factories.

1. What was the source of power for the earliest railroads? _____

   _____

2. What were three important developments that made railroads a practical means of transportation?

   _____

   _____

   _____

3. What is meant by the Industrial Revolution? _____

   _____

4. What were two ways that railroads changed life in America?_____

   _____

Comprehensive Curriculum - **Grade 5**

Main Idea: Locomotives

Directions: Read the information about locomotives. Then, answer the questions.

In the 1800s, the steam locomotive was considered by many to be a symbol of the new Industrial Age. It was, indeed, one of the most important inventions of the time. Over the years, there have been many changes to the locomotive. One of the most important has been its source of power. During its history, the locomotive has gone from steam to electric to diesel power.

The first railroads used horses or mules for power, but the development of the steam locomotive made railroads a practical means of transportation. The first steam locomotive was built in 1804 in Great Britain by Richard Trevithick. It could haul 50,000 pounds, but it was not very successful because it was so heavy it caused the tracks to fall apart. However, it encouraged other engineers to try to build steam locomotives. Two of the most important men to accept the challenge were George Stephenson and his son, Robert. Robert once won a contest to build the best locomotive. The *Rocket*, as he called it, had a top speed of 29 miles per hour.

In America, developments in steam engines were close behind those of the British. In 1830, Peter Cooper's tiny locomotive, called Tom Thumb, lost a famous race against a horse-drawn coach. In spite of the loss, it still convinced railroad officials that steam power was more practical than horsepower.

Just before the turn of the century, the electric locomotive was widely used. At its peak in the 1940s, U.S. railroads had 2,400 miles of electric routes.

The diesel locomotive was invented in the 1890s by Rudolf Diesel, a German engineer. The power of this locomotive was supplied by a diesel fuel engine. The diesel locomotive is still used today. It costs about twice as much as a steam locomotive to build, but it is much cheaper to operate.

1. What is the main idea of this selection?
   ___ The steam locomotive was considered a symbol of the Industrial Age.
   ___ Over the years, there have been many changes to the locomotive.

2. Who built the first steam locomotive in 1804?

   _____

3. How fast could the *Rocket* travel?

   _____

4. Who built the locomotive called Tom Thumb?

   _____

5. Tom Thumb was in a race against a horse-drawn coach. Which won?

   _____

6. What kind of fuel does a diesel engine use?

   _____

Review

Directions: Define these words as used in the selections "Railroads" and "Locomotives."

1. flanged wheel _____

_____

2. transportation _____

3. profit _____

4. locomotive _____

5. diesel _____

6. engineer _____

Directions: Use information from the selection "Locomotives" to create a time line of the invention of locomotives.

7. _____

Directions: Write your answer in a complete sentence.

8. The world is going through another "revolution" in industry today. What new technology is leading this change, and how might it affect workers in the future?

_____

_____

_____

Reading Comprehension: Railroad Pioneer

Directions: Read the information about railroad pioneers. Then, answer the questions by circling **Yes** or **No**.

George Stephenson was born in Wylam, England, in 1781. His family was extremely poor. When he was young, he didn't go to school but worked in the coal mines. In his spare time, he taught himself to read and write. After a series of explosions in the coal pits, Stephenson built a miner's safety lamp. This helped bring him to the attention of the owners of the coal mines. They put him in charge of all the machinery.

In 1812, Stephenson became an engine builder for the mines. The owners were interested in locomotives because the cost of horse feed was so high. They wanted Stephenson to build a locomotive to pull the coal cars from the mines. His first locomotive, the *Blucher*, was put on the rails in 1814.

Stephenson was a good engineer, and he was fortunate to work for a rich employer. Between 1814 and 1826, Stephenson was the only man in Great Britain building locomotives.

When the Stockholm and Darlington Railway, the first public railroad system, was planned, Stephenson was named company engineer. He convinced the owners to use steam power instead of horses. He built the first locomotive on the line. The *Locomotion*, as it was called, was the best locomotive that had been built anywhere in the world up to that time. Over the years, Stephenson was responsible for many other important developments in locomotive design, such as improved cast-iron rails and wheels, and the first steel springs strong enough to carry several tons.

Stephenson was convinced that the future of railroads lay in steam power. His great vision of what the railroad system could become was a driving force in the early years of its development.

1. George Stephenson was an excellent student in school.   Yes   No

2. Stephenson's first invention was a miner's safety lamp.   Yes   No

3. Between 1814 and 1826, Stephenson was one of many engineers building locomotives in Great Britain.   Yes   No

4. The Stockholm and Darlington Railway was the first public railroad system.   Yes   No

5. The first locomotive on the Stockholm and Darlington line was the *Locomotion*, built by Stephenson.   Yes   No

6. Stephenson's ideas did not influence the development of the railroad system.   Yes   No

Tall Tales

A **tall tale** is a fictional story with exaggerated details and a "super" hero. The main character in a tall tale is much larger, stronger, smarter, or better than a real person. Tall tales may be unbelievable, but they are fun to hear.

America had nearly 200,000 miles of railroad track by 1900. Because of the rapid growth and the excitement over the railroads, many colorful tall tales about railroad heroes and their adventures were told.

Directions: Read the story about John Henry. Then, answer the questions.

A Steel-Driving Man

On the night John Henry was born, forked lightning split the air and the earth shook. He weighed 44 pounds at birth, and the first thing he did was reach for a hammer hanging on the wall. "He's going to be a steel-driving man," his father told his mother.

One night, John Henry dreamed he was working on a railroad. Every time his hammer hit a spike, the sky lit up with the sparks. "I dreamed that the railroad was going to be the end of me, and I'd die with a hammer in my hand," he said. When John Henry grew up, he did work for the railroad. He was the fastest, most powerful steel-driving man in the world.

In about 1870, the steam drill was invented. One day, the company at the far end of a tunnel tried it out. John Henry's company, working at the other end, continued to use men to do the drilling. There was much bragging from both companies as to which was faster. Finally, they decided to have a contest. John Henry was matched against the best man with a steam drill.

John Henry swung a 20-pound hammer in each hand. The sparks flew so fast and hot that they burned his face. At the end of the day, the judges said John Henry had beaten the steam drill by 4 feet!

That night, John Henry said, "I was a steel-driving man." Then, he laid down and closed his eyes forever.

1. How much was John Henry said to have weighed at birth? _____
2. Why did his father think he would be a steel-driving man? _____
3. What invention was John Henry in a contest against? _____
4. Why was the contest held? _____
5. What tools did John Henry use in the contest? _____
6. Who won the contest? _____
7. What happened to John Henry after the contest? _____

Tall Tales

Directions: Write a tall tale about yourself. Be sure to make it a fantastic and incredible story!

I am gging on a trip in my favorite rocket ship and i'm bringing ... m.m, Mc'D.G? B.t. a.D, and we landed on the moon and thats the ent.

Directions: Reread your tall tale. Does it make sense? Check and correct spelling and grammar mistakes. Does your story fit the category of tall tale?

Context Clues: Passenger Cars

Directions: Read the information about passenger cars. Use context clues to determine the meaning of words in bold. Check the correct answers.

Early railroad passenger cars were little more than stagecoaches fitted with special wheels to help them stay on the tracks. They didn't hold many passengers, and because they were made out of wood, they were fire **hazards**. They also did not hold up very well if the train came off the track or had a **collision** with another train.

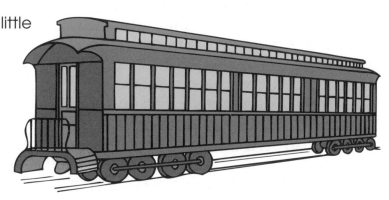

In the United States, it wasn't long before passenger cars were lengthened to hold more people. Late in the 1830s, Americans were riding in **elongated** cars with double seats on either side of a center aisle. By the early 1900s, most cars were made of metal instead of wood.

Sleeping and dining cars were introduced in the United States by the early 1860s. Over the next 25 years, other improvements were made, including electric lighting, steam heat, and covered **vestibules** that allowed passengers to walk between cars. All of these **luxuries** helped make railroad travel much more comfortable.

1. Based on the other words in the sentence, what is the correct definition of **hazards**?

   ____ engines   ____ risks   ____ stations

2. Based on the other words in the sentence, what is the correct definition of **collision**?

   ____ crash   ____ race   ____ track

3. Based on the other words in the sentence, what is the correct definition of **elongated**?

   ____ wooden   ____ new   ____ lengthened

4. Based on the other words in the sentence, what is the correct definition of **vestibules**?

   ____ passageways   ____ cars   ____ depots

5. Based on the other words in the sentence, what is the correct definition of **luxuries**?

   ____ additions   ____ things offering the greatest comfort   ____ inventions

Reading Skills: Railroads

Directions: Read the information about railroads. Then, answer the questions.

When railroads became the major means of transportation, they replaced earlier forms of travel, like the stagecoach. Railroads remained the unchallenged leader for a hundred years. Beginning in the early 1900s, railroads faced **competition** from newer forms of transportation.

Today, millions of people have their own automobiles. Buses offer inexpensive travel between cities. Large trucks haul goods across the country. Airplanes provide quick transportation over long distances. The result has been a sharp drop in the use of trains.

Today, nearly all railroads face serious problems that threaten to drive them out of business. But railroads still provide low-cost, fuel-saving transportation that will remain important. One gallon of diesel fuel will haul about four times as much by railroad as by truck. In a time when the world is concerned about saving fuel, this is but one area in which the railroads still have much to offer.

1. What is the main idea of this selection?

____ When railroads became the major means of transportation, they replaced earlier forms of travel.

____ Beginning in the early 1900s, railroads have faced competition from newer forms of transportation.

2. Based on the other words in the sentence, what is the correct definition of **competition**?

____ businesses trying to get the same customers

____ problems

____ support

3. What are four newer forms of transportation that have challenged railroads?

_____

4. One gallon of diesel fuel will haul about twice as much by railroad as by truck.   Yes   No

Reading Comprehension: Printing

Directions: Read the information about printing. Then, answer the questions.

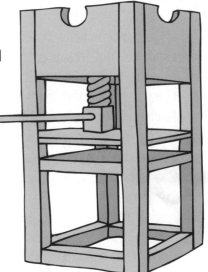

When people talk about printing, they usually mean making exact copies of an original document, such as a newspaper, magazine, or an entire book. The inventions that have allowed us to do this are some of the most important developments in history. Look around you at the many examples of printed materials. Can you imagine life without them?

Until the thirteenth century, all material had to be printed by hand, one copy at a time. To make a copy of a book took much time and effort.

The oldest known example of a printed book was made in China in 848 A.D. by Wang Chieh, who carved each page of a book by hand onto a block of wood. He then put ink on the wood and pressed it on paper. The idea of printing with wood blocks spread to Europe. The letters in these block books were made to look handwritten.

In about 1440, a German goldsmith named Johann Gutenberg developed the idea of movable type. He invented separate letters made of metal for printing. The letters could be joined together to make words and sentences. Ink was applied to the letters to print many copies of the same material. Because they were made of metal, the letters could be used over and over. This wonderful invention made it possible to have more printed material at a lower cost.

Gutenberg had other ideas that were important to printing. He developed a special type of ink that would stick to the new metal letters. Gutenberg's ideas were so successful that the process of printing went almost unchanged for more than 300 years.

1. In what country was the oldest known printed book made?

_____

2. Who made the first printed book?

_____

3. What is "movable type"?

_____

4. Who developed the idea of movable type?

_____

5. What was another one of Gutenberg's important inventions?

_____

Comprehensive Curriculum - **Grade 5**

Reading Comprehension: Newspapers

Directions: Read the information about newspapers. Then, answer the questions.

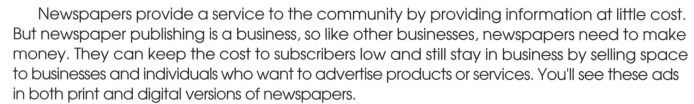

Newspapers keep us informed about what is going on in the world. They entertain, educate, and examine the events of the day. For millions of people worldwide, newspapers are an important part of daily life.

Newspapers are published at various intervals, but they usually come out daily or weekly. The number of newspapers has fallen in recent years. As more and more people have access to the Internet, there are many more ways for them to receive their news.

Some newspapers have many subscribers—people who pay to have each edition delivered to them. While some people choose to receive a paper copy of the newspaper, others use an online subscription and read the paper on a computer screen.

Newspapers provide a service to the community by providing information at little cost. But newspaper publishing is a business, so like other businesses, newspapers need to make money. They can keep the cost to subscribers low and still stay in business by selling space to businesses and individuals who want to advertise products or services. You'll see these ads in both print and digital versions of newspapers.

1. Why has the number of newspapers published fallen in recent years?

   _____

2. What services do newspapers provide?

   _____

3. What are subscribers?

   _____

4. How often are most newspapers published?

   _____

5. What do newspapers do to keep the cost to the reader low, but still make money?

   _____

6. What is the name of the newspaper in the town or city where you live?

   _____

Reading Comprehension: Newspapers

Directions: Read the information about the first newspapers. Then, answer the questions.

Long ago, town criers walked through cities reading important news to the people. The earliest newspapers were probably handwritten notices posted in towns for the public to read.

The first true newspaper was a weekly paper started in Germany in 1609. It was called *The Strassburg Relation*. The Germans were pioneers in newspaper publishing. Johann Gutenberg, the man who developed movable type, was German.

One of the first English-language newspapers, *The London Gazette*, was first printed in England in 1665. **Gazette** is an old English word that means "official publication." Many newspapers today still use the word **gazette** in their names.

In America, several papers began during colonial days. The first successful one, *The Boston News-Letter*, began printing in 1704. It was very small—about the size of a sheet of notebook paper with printing on both sides.

An important date in newspaper publishing was 1833. In that year, *The New York Sun* became the first penny newspaper. The paper actually did cost only a penny. The penny newspapers were similar to today's papers: they printed news while it was still new, they were the first to print advertisements and to sell papers in newsstands, and they were the first to be delivered to homes.

1. How were the earliest newspapers different from today's newspapers?

   _____

2. In what year and where was the first true newspaper printed?

   _____

3. What was the name of the first successful newspaper in America?

   _____

4. Why was 1833 important in newspaper publishing?

   _____

5. List four ways penny newspapers were like the newspapers of today.

   _____

   _____

   _____

   _____

Reading Comprehension: News Stories

Directions: Read the information about news stories. Then, draw an **X** on the line to show the correct meaning of the bold word.

Here is an example of how a news story gets published:

Let's imagine that a city bus has turned over in a ditch, injuring some of the passengers. An **eyewitness** might call the newspaper, or an editor might hear a report on the police scanner. The editor assigns a reporter to go to the scene. The reporter talks to the passengers, driver, and witnesses who saw the accident. She finds out what they saw and how they feel, recording their answers electronically. At the same time, a photographer is busy taking pictures.

Today, many reporters write the story on the spot and then send it back to the office via the Internet. Things moved a lot more slowly in the news world just a few decades ago!

Next, an editor reads the story, checking facts, grammar, and spelling. Meanwhile, the photographer submits his or her digital photos electronically, and a picture is chosen to represent the story.

It's now the job of other editors to build the various newspaper pages on a computer, using specialized software. Finally, the presses begin to run, and the printing process can begin.

Miles of paper are turned into thousands of printed, cut, and folded newspapers. They are counted, put into bundles, and placed in waiting trucks. The paper is also posted online, so people everywhere have access to it. No matter how people receive their news, it's only a matter of hours before they can read an account of the bus accident in their local newspaper.

1. Based on the other words in the sentence, what is the correct definition of **eyewitness**?

_____ a reporter

_____ a person who saw what happened

_____ a lawyer

2. How is the way that reporters send in stories different today than it was in the past?

_____

_____

Reading Comprehension: Nellie Bly

Directions: Read the information about Nellie Bly. Then, answer the questions.

A hundred years ago, journalism and reporting were usually seen as a man's job. A young woman named Elizabeth Cochran changed that idea in ways that people would never forget. Nellie Bly, (Elizabeth's pen name) was curious and courageous. She did not take no for an answer, and she was intent on finding the real story. She wanted to give a voice to people who could not speak for themselves.

Investigative reporting is common today, but it was new in Bly's time. After she took a job with a newspaper called *The World* in New York, Bly accepted an assignment for an unusual story. She pretended to be mentally ill so that she would be admitted to an insane asylum. Her goal was to report on abuses going on at the asylum. Bly spent ten days working undercover as a patient. *The World* published Bly's story with satisfying results. The city investigated the asylum, and treatment of the mentally ill improved.

In 1889, Bly came up with an interesting idea for a story. She would travel around the world in 80 days. In 1873, writer Jules Verne had published a fictional book called *Around the World in 80 Days*. Bly decided to see if the trip could really be made and to write about it. It was unusual for women to travel alone, but that didn't stop Nellie Bly. She returned triumphantly to New York 72 days later. People all around the country bought copies of *The World* to track Bly's progress. More than a century later, Bly is still remembered for her trailblazing writing and adventurous spirit.

1. What does it mean "to give a voice to people who could not speak for themselves"?

   _____

   _____

2. Was *Around the World in 80 Days* a work of fiction or nonfiction?_____

3. The name of the New York newspaper Bly wrote for was _____.

4. What was the result of Bly's story about the insane asylum?

   _____

   _____

5. Investigative reporting is no longer a common practice.   **True**   **False**

Comprehensive Curriculum - **Grade 5**

Reading Comprehension: Samuel Clemens

Directions: Read the information about Samuel Clemens.

Samuel Langhorne Clemens was born in Florida, Missouri, in 1835. In his lifetime, he gained worldwide fame as a writer, lecturer, and humorist.

Clemens first worked for a printer when he was only 12 years old. Soon after that, he worked on his brother's newspaper.

Clemens traveled frequently and worked as a printer in New York, Philadelphia, St. Louis, and Cincinnati. On a trip to New Orleans in 1857, he learned the difficult art of steamboat **piloting**. Clemens loved piloting and later used it as a background for some of his books, including *Life on the Mississippi*.

A few years later, Clemens went to Nevada with his brother and tried gold mining. When this proved unsuccessful, he went back to writing for newspapers. At first, he signed his humorous pieces with the name "Josh." In 1863, he began signing them Mark Twain. The words **mark twain** were used by riverboat pilots to mean two fathoms (12 feet) deep, water deep enough for steamboats. From then on, Clemens used this now-famous **pseudonym** for all his writing.

As Mark Twain, he received attention from readers all over the world. His best-known works include *The Adventures of Tom Sawyer* and *The Adventures of Huckleberry Finn*. These two books about boyhood adventures remain popular with readers of all ages.

Directions: Check the correct answer.

1. Based on the other words in the sentence, what is the correct definition of **pseudonym**?
   _____ book title
   _____ a made-up name used by an author
   _____ a humorous article

2. Based on the other words in the sentence, what is the correct definition of **piloting**?
   _____ driving an airplane
   _____ steering a steamboat on a river
   _____ being a train engineer

Directions: Write the answers.

3. Under what name did Samuel Clemens write his books?
   _____

4. What do the words **mark twain** mean?
   _____

5. Besides author, list two other jobs held by Mark Twain.
   _____

6. List two of the best-known books written by Mark Twain.
   _____

Review

Directions: Write the answers.

1. What are two ways newspapers earn money?

   _____

   _____

2. What was Mark Twain's real name?

   _____

3. Explain how newspaper reporting is different today than it was in the past.

   _____

   _____

   _____

   _____

   _____

   _____

4. How has social media changed the way stories are discovered and reported?

   _____

   _____

   _____

   _____

   _____

Directions: Use dates from the articles "Printing" and "Newspapers" to create a time line of the development of newspapers.

Recognizing Details: The Coldest Continent

Directions: Read the information about Antarctica. Then, answer the questions.

Antarctica lies at the South Pole and is the coldest continent. It is without sunlight for months at a time. Even when the sun does shine, its angle is so slanted that the land receives little warmth. Temperatures often drop to 100 degrees below zero, and a fierce wind blows almost endlessly. Most of the land is covered by snow heaped thousands of feet deep. The snow is so heavy and tightly packed that it forms a great ice cap covering more than 95 percent of the continent.

Considering the conditions, it is no wonder there are no towns or cities in Antarctica. There is no permanent population at all, only small scientific research stations. Many teams of explorers and scientists have braved the freezing cold since Antarctica was sighted in 1820. Some have died in their effort, but a great deal of information has been learned about the continent.

From fossils, pieces of coal, and bone samples, we know that Antarctica was not always an ice-covered land. Scientists believe that 200 million years ago it was connected to southern Africa, South America, Australia, and India. Forests grew in warm swamps, and insects and reptiles thrived there. Today, there are animals that live in and around the waters that border the continent. In fact, the waters surrounding Antarctica contain more life than oceans in warmer areas of the world.

1. Where is Antarctica?_____

2. How much of the continent is covered by an ice cap?_____

3. When was Antarctica first sighted by explorers?_____

4. What clues indicate that Antarctica was not always an ice-covered land?

_____

5. Is Antarctica another name for the North Pole?   Yes   No

Reading Comprehension: The Arctic Circle

Directions: Read the article about the Arctic Circle. Then, answer the questions.

On the other side of the globe from Antarctica, at the northernmost part of Earth, is another icy land. This is the Arctic Circle. It includes the North Pole itself and the northern fringes of three continents—Europe, Asia, and North America, including the state of Alaska—as well as Greenland and other islands.

The seasons are opposite at the two ends of Earth. When it is summer in Antarctica, it is winter in the Arctic Circle. In both places, there are very long periods of sunlight in summer and very long nights in the winter. On the poles themselves, there are six full months of sunlight and six full months of darkness each year.

Compared to Antarctica, the summers are surprisingly mild in some areas of the Arctic Circle. Much of the snow cover may melt, and temperatures often reach 50 degrees in July. Antarctica is covered by water—frozen water, of course—so nothing can grow there. Plant growth is limited in the polar regions, not only by the cold, but also by wind, lack of water, and the long winter darkness.

In the far north, willow trees grow but only become a few inches high! The annual rings, the circles within the trunk of a tree that show its age and how fast it grows, are so narrow in those trees that you need a microscope to see them.

A permanently frozen layer of soil, called permafrost, keeps roots from growing deep enough into the ground to anchor a plant. Even if a plant could survive the cold temperatures, it could not grow roots deep enough or strong enough to allow the plant to get very big.

1. What three continents have land included in the Arctic Circle?

   _____   _____   _____

2. Is the Arctic Circle generally warmer or colder than Antarctica?

   _____

3. What is permafrost? _____

4. Many tall pine trees grow in the Arctic Circle.   Yes   No

Reading Comprehension: Undersea Harvest

Directions: Read the selection. Then, answer the questions that follow.

A group of Inuit in Arctic Canada are known for an extremely dangerous type of harvesting **expedition**. You may be surprised to learn that what they are looking for are mussels on the seabed floor. The reason that this is so dangerous is that the mussel hunters must go beneath the icy surface of the Arctic Sea in winter. The mussels provide a welcome relief from a diet that consists mostly of seal meat. During extreme low tides, the level of sea ice drops enough to create caverns below the ice. It exposes the seabed floor—and hundreds of mussels.

Kangiqsujuaq, Quebec

The brave hunters lower themselves as much as 40 feet below the surface to gather mussels. It is dark and cold in the icy caverns. The thick layer of ice creaks eerily overhead. Without the water to support it, it isn't nearly as stable. The Inuit must work quickly. They have only about an hour before the tide starts to move back in and the water level begins to rise. Imagine how scary it would be to hear the water rushing in around you in an icy undersea cavern!

The locals all know stories of mussel hunter who didn't make it out in time. It's a dangerous **expedition**, but the rewards are sweet: plenty of fresh mussels to eat!

1. What group of people is known for harvesting mussels under the ice?

    _____

2. The seabed floor is only exposed at a certain time. When does this occur?

    _____

3. Why are there caverns under the ice?

    _____

4. Why is mussel gathering so risky for the Inuit?

    _____

5. What does the word **expedition** mean?

    ☐ harvest   ☐ mussels   ☐ journey

Main Idea: The Polar Trail

Directions: Read the information about explorers to Antarctica.

A recorded sighting of Antarctica, the last continent to be discovered, was not made until the early nineteenth century. Since then, many brave explorers and adventurers have sailed south to conquer the icy land. Their achievements once gained as much world attention as those of the first astronauts.

Long before the continent was first spotted, the ancient Greeks suspected there was a continent at the bottom of the world. Over the centuries, legends of the undiscovered land spread. Some of the world's greatest seamen tried to find it, including Captain James Cook in 1772.

Cook was the first to sail all the way to the solid field of ice that surrounds Antarctica every winter. In fact, he sailed all the way around the continent but never saw it. Cook went farther south than anyone had ever gone. His record lasted 50 years.

Forty years after Cook, a new kind of seamen sailed the icy waters. They were hunters of seals and whales. Sailing through unknown waters in search of their prey, these men became explorers as well as hunters. The first person known to sight Antarctica was an American hunter, 21-year-old Nathaniel Brown Palmer, in 1820.

Directions: Draw an **X** on the blank for the correct answer.

1. The main idea is:
   _____ Antarctica was not sighted until the early nineteenth century.
   _____ Many brave explorers and adventurers have sailed south to conquer the icy land.

2. The first person to sail to the ice field that surrounds Antarctica was:
   _____ Nathaniel Brown Palmer.
   _____ Captain James Cook.
   _____ Neil Armstrong.

3. His record for sailing the farthest south stood for:
   _____ 40 years.
   _____ 50 years.
   _____ 500 years.

4. The first person known to sight Antarctica was:
   _____ an unknown ancient Greek.
   _____ Captain James Cook.
   _____ Nathaniel Brown Palmer.

5. His profession was:
   _____ hunter.
   _____ ship captain.
   _____ explorer.

Recognizing Details: The Frozen Continent

Directions: Read the information about explorers. Then, answer the questions.

By the mid-1800s, most of the seals of Antarctica had been killed. The seal hunters no longer sailed the icy waters. The next group of explorers who took an interest in Antarctica were scientists. Of these, the man who took the most daring chances and made the most amazing discoveries was British Captain James Clark Ross.

Ross first made a name for himself sailing to the north. In 1831, he discovered the North Magnetic Pole—one of two places on Earth toward which a compass needle points. In 1840, Ross set out to find the South Magnetic Pole. He made many marvelous discoveries, including the Ross Sea, a great open sea beyond the ice packs that stopped other explorers, and the Ross Ice Shelf, a great floating sheet of ice bigger than all of France!

The next man to make his mark exploring Antarctica was British explorer Robert Falcon Scott. Scott set out in 1902 to find the South Pole. He and his team suffered greatly, but they were able to make it a third of the way to the pole. Back in England, Scott was a great hero. In 1910, he again attempted to become the first man to reach the South Pole. But this time, he had competition: an explorer from Norway, Roald Amundsen, was also leading a team to the South Pole.

It was a brutal race. Both teams faced many hardships, but they pressed on. Finally, on December 14, 1911, Amundsen became the first man to reach the South Pole. Scott arrived on January 17, 1912. He was bitterly disappointed at not being first. The trip back was even more horrible. None of the five men in the Scott expedition survived.

1. After the seal hunters, who were the next group of explorers interested in Antarctica?

   _____

2. What great discovery did James Ross make before ever sailing to Antarctica?

   _____

3. What were two other great discoveries made by James Ross?

   _____   _____

4. How close did Scott and his team come to the South Pole in 1902?

   _____

5. Who was the first person to reach the South Pole?_____

Reading Skills: Research

To learn more about the explorers of Antarctica, reference sources like encyclopedias, CD-ROMs, the Internet, and history books are excellent sources for finding more information.

Directions: Use reference sources to learn more about Captain James Cook and Captain James Clark Ross. Write an informational paragraph about each man.

1. Captain James Cook

_____

_____

_____

_____

_____

_____

2. Captain James Clark Ross

_____

_____

_____

_____

_____

_____

3. What dangers did both of these men and their teams face in their attempts to reach the South Pole?

_____

_____

_____

_____

_____

Reading Comprehension: Polar Bears

Directions: Read the information about polar bears. Then, answer the questions by circling **Yes** or **No**.

Some animals are able to survive the cold weather and difficult conditions of the snow and ice fields in the Arctic polar regions. One of the best known is the polar bear.

Polar bears live on the land and in the sea. They may drift hundreds of miles from land on huge sheets of floating ice. They use their great paws to paddle the ice along. Polar bears are excellent swimmers, too. They can cross great distances of open water. While in the water, they feed mostly on fish and seals.

On land, these huge animals, which measure 10 feet long and weigh about 1,000 pounds, can run 25 miles an hour. Surprisingly, polar bears live as plant-eaters rather than hunters while on land. Unlike many kinds of bears, polar bears do not hibernate. They are active the whole year.

Baby polar bears are born during the winter. At birth, they are pink and almost hairless. These helpless cubs weigh only two pounds—less than one-third the size of most human infants. The mother bears raise their young in dens dug in snowbanks. By the time they are 10 weeks old, polar bear cubs are about the size of puppies and have enough white fur to protect them in the open air. The mothers give their cubs swimming, hunting, and fishing lessons. By the time autumn comes, the cubs are left to survive on their own.

1. Polar bears can live on the land and the sea.   Yes   No

2. Polar bears are excellent swimmers.   Yes   No

3. Polar bears hibernate in the winter.   Yes   No

4. A newborn polar bear weighs more than a newborn human baby.   Yes   No

5. Mother polar bears raise their babies in caves.   Yes   No

6. Father polar bears give the cubs swimming lessons.   Yes   No

Context Clues: Seals

Directions: Read the information about seals. Use context clues to determine the meaning of the bold words. Check the correct answers.

Seals are **aquatic** mammals that also live on land at times. Some seals stay in the sea for weeks or months at a time, even sleeping in the water. When seals go on land, they usually choose **secluded** spots to avoid people and other animals.

The 31 different kinds of seals belong to a group of animals often called pinnipeds meaning "fin-footed." Their fins, or flippers, make them very good swimmers and divers. Their nostrils close tightly when they dive. They have been known to stay **submerged** for as long as a half-hour at a time!

Seals are warm-blooded animals that can adjust to various temperatures. They live in both **temperate** and cold climates. Besides their fur to keep them warm, seals have a thick layer of fat, called blubber, to protect them against the cold. It is harder for seals to cool themselves in hot weather than to warm themselves in cold weather. They can sometimes become so overheated that they die.

1. Based on other words in the sentence, what is the correct definition of **aquatic**?

_____ living on the land

_____ living on or in the sea

_____ living in large groups

2. Based on other words in the sentence, what is the correct definition of **submerged**?

_____ under the water

_____ on top of the water

_____ in groups

3. Based on other words in the sentence, what is the correct definition of **secluded**?

_____ rocky

_____ private or hidden

_____ near other animals

4. Based on other words in the sentence, what is the correct definition of **temperate**?

_____ rainy

_____ measured on a thermometer

_____ warm

Reading Comprehension: Walruses

Directions: Read the information about walruses. Then answer the questions.

A walrus is actually a type of seal that lives only in the Arctic Circle. It has two huge upper teeth, or tusks, which it uses to pull itself out of the water or to move over the rocks on land. It also uses its tusks to dig clams, one of its favorite foods, from the bottom of the sea. On an adult male walrus, the tusks may be three and a half feet long!

A walrus has an unusual face. Besides its long tusks, it has a big, bushy mustache made up of hundreds of movable, stiff bristles. These bristles also help the walrus push food into its mouth. Except for small wrinkles in the skin, a walrus has no outer ears.

Like a seal, the walrus uses its flippers to help it swim. Its front flippers serve as paddles, and while swimming, it swings the back of its huge body from side to side. A walrus looks awkward using its flippers to walk on land, but don't be fooled! A walrus can run as fast as a human.

Baby walruses are born in the early spring. They stay with their mothers until they are two years old. There is a good reason for this—they must grow little tusks, at least three or four inches long, before they can catch their own food from the bottom of the sea. Until then, they must stay close to their mothers to eat. A young walrus that is tired from swimming will climb onto its mother's back for a ride, holding onto her with its front flippers.

1. The walrus is a type of seal found only _____ .

2. List two ways the walrus uses its tusks.

    _____   _____

3. A walrus cannot move quickly on land.   Yes   No

4. A walrus has a large, bushy mustache.   Yes   No

5. A baby walrus stays very close to
    its mother until it is two years old.   Yes   No

6. Baby walruses are born late in fall.   Yes   No

Main Idea: Penguins

Directions: Read the information about penguins.

People are amused by the funny, duck-like waddle of penguins and by their appearance, because they seem to be wearing little tuxedos. Penguins are among the best-liked animals on Earth, but they are also a most misunderstood animal. People may have more inaccurate ideas about penguins than any other animal.

For example, many people are surprised to learn that penguins are really birds, not mammals. Penguins do not fly, but they do have feathers, and only birds have feathers. Also, like other birds, penguins build nests and their young hatch from eggs. Because of their unusual looks, though, you would never confuse them with any other bird!

Penguins are also thought of as symbols of the polar regions, but penguins do not live north of the equator, so you would not find a penguin near the North Pole. Penguins don't live at the South Pole, either. Only two of the seventeen **species** of penguins spend all of their lives on the frozen continent of Antarctica. You would be just as likely to see a penguin living on an island in a warm climate as in a cold area.

Directions: Draw an **X** on the blank for the correct answer.

1. The main idea is:

   ____ Penguins are among the best-liked animals on Earth.

   ____ The penguin is a much misunderstood animal.

2. Penguins live

   ____ only at the North Pole.

   ____ only at the South Pole.

   ____ only south of the equator.

3. Based on the other words in the sentence, what is the correct definition of the word **species**?

   ____ number

   ____ bird

   ____ a distinct kind

Directions: List three ways penguins are like other birds.

_____

Review

Directions: Write your answers on the lines.

1. Which contains the South Pole—the Arctic or Antarctica?

   _____

2. Would you like to live in either the Arctic or Antarctica?
   Why or why not?

   _____

   _____

3. What adaptations would people who live (even for a short time) in these areas have
   to make?

   _____

   _____

4. What characteristics are common to animals who live in the polar regions?

   _____

   _____

5. Name two animals that live in the polar regions.

   _____   _____

6. Write three facts you learned about one of the animals that live in the polar regions.

   _____

   _____

   _____

7. On each of the poles, there are six months of sunlight and six months of darkness each
   year. How do you think this would affect you?

   _____

   _____

8. Write three facts you learned about explorers to the North or South Pole regions.

   _____

   _____

   _____

Reading Comprehension: The Desert

Directions: Read the information about the desert. Then, answer the questions by circling **Yes** or **No**.

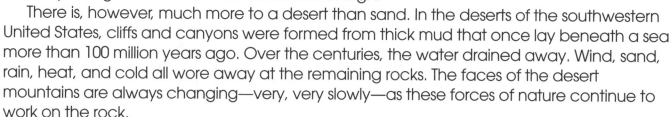

Deserts are found where there is little rainfall or where the rainfall for a whole year occurs in only a few weeks' time. Ten inches of rain may be enough for many plants to survive if the rain is spread throughout the year. If the 10 inches of rain falls during one or two months and the rest of the year is dry, those plants may not be able to survive, and a desert may form.

When people think of deserts, they may think of long stretches of sand. Sand begins as tiny pieces of rock that get smaller and smaller as wind and weather wear them down. Sand dunes, or hills of drifting sand, are formed as winds move the sand across the desert. Grain by grain, the dunes grow over the years, always shifting with the winds and changing shape. Most dunes are only a few feet tall, but they can grow to be several hundred feet high.

There is, however, much more to a desert than sand. In the deserts of the southwestern United States, cliffs and canyons were formed from thick mud that once lay beneath a sea more than 100 million years ago. Over the centuries, the water drained away. Wind, sand, rain, heat, and cold all wore away at the remaining rocks. The faces of the desert mountains are always changing—very, very slowly—as these forces of nature continue to work on the rock.

Most deserts have a surprising variety of life. There are plants, animals, and insects that have adapted to life in the desert. During the heat of the day, a visitor may see very few signs of living things, but as the air begins to cool in the evening, the desert comes to life. As the sun begins to rise again in the sky, the desert once again becomes quiet and lonely.

1. Deserts are found where there is little rainfall or where the rainfall for a whole year falls in only a few weeks.   Yes   No

2. Sand begins as tiny pieces of rock that get smaller and smaller as wind and weather wear them down.   Yes   No

3. Sand dunes were formed from thick mud that once lay beneath a sea more than 100 million years ago.   Yes   No

4. The faces of the desert mountains can never change.   Yes   No

Reading Comprehension: Desert Weather

Directions: Read the information about desert weather. Then, answer the questions.

One definition of a desert is an area that has, on average, less than 10 inches of rain a year. Many deserts have far less than that. Death Valley in California and Nevada, for example, averages fewer than 2 inches of rain each year. The driest of all deserts is the Atacoma Desert in Chile. This desert averages less than 1 inch of rainfall a year. In some parts, no rain fell for 400 years!

Some deserts have a regular rainy season each year, but usually desert rainfall is totally unpredictable. An area may have no rainfall for many years. Sometimes a passing cloud may look like it will send relief to the waiting land, but only a "ghost rain" falls. This means that the hot, dry air dries up the raindrops long before they ever reach the ground.

The temperature in the desert varies greatly. The daytime temperatures in the desert frequently top 120 degrees. In Death Valley, temperatures have been known to reach 190 degrees! In most parts of the world, moisture in the air works like a blanket to hold the heat of the day close to the earth at night. But, because it has so little moisture, the desert has no such blanket. As a result, nighttime temperatures are very chilly. Temperatures have been known to drop 50 or even 100 degrees at night in the desert.

1. On the average, how much rainfall is there in a year in a desert?

    _____

2. Where is the driest desert in the world? _____

3. What is a ghost rain? _____

4. In other parts of the world, what works as a blanket to hold the heat of the day close

    to the earth at night? _____

5. What happens to the temperature in the desert at night?

    _____

Review

Directions: Write a three-sentence summary of each of these selections. Include the main idea in your summaries.

1. "The Desert"

_____

_____

_____

_____

2. "Desert Weather"

_____

_____

_____

_____

Directions: Define these words. Then, use them in sentences of your own.

3. dunes _____

_____

4. canyon _____

_____

5. adapt _____

_____

6. average _____

_____

7. unpredictable _____

_____

Context Clues: Desert Plants

Directions: Read the information about desert plants. Use context clues to determine the meaning of the bold words. Check the correct answers.

Desert plants have special features, or adaptations, that allow them to **survive** the harsh conditions of the desert. A cactus stores water in its tissues when it rains. It then uses this supply of water during the long dry season. The tiny needles on some kinds of **cacti** may number in the tens of thousands. These sharp thorns protect the cactus. They also form tiny shadows in the sunlight that help keep the plant from getting too hot.

Other plants are able to live by dropping their leaves. This cuts down on the **evaporation** of their water supply in the hot sun. Still other plants survive as seeds, protected from the sun and heat by tough seed coats. When it rains, the seeds **sprout** quickly, bloom, and produce more seeds that can **withstand** long dry spells.

Some plants spread their roots close to Earth's surface to quickly gather water when it does rain. Other plants, such as the mesquite, have roots that grow 50 or 60 feet below the ground to reach underground water supplies.

1. Based on the other words in the sentence, what is the correct definition of **survive**?

   _____ continue to live
   _____ bloom in the desert
   _____ flower

2. Based on the other words in the sentence, what is the correct definition of **evaporation**?

   _____ water loss from heat
   _____ much-needed rainfall
   _____ boiling

3. Based on the other words in the sentence, what is the correct definition of **withstand**?

   _____ put up with
   _____ stand with another
   _____ take from

4. Based on the other words in the sentence, what is the correct definition of **cacti**?

   _____ a type of sand dune
   _____ more than one cactus
   _____ a caravan of camels

5. Based on the other words in the sentence, what is the correct definition of **sprout**?

   _____ a type of bean that grows only in the desert
   _____ begin to grow
   _____ a small flower

Name _____

Recognizing Details: The Cactus Family

Directions: Read the information about cacti. Pay close attention to details. Answer the questions.

Although cacti are the best-known desert plants, they don't live only in hot, dry places. While cacti are most likely to be found in the desert areas of Mexico and the southwestern United States, they can by seen as far north as Nova Scotia, Canada. Certain types of cacti can live even in the snow!

Desert cacti are particularly good at surviving very long dry spells. Most cacti have a very long root system so they can absorb as much water as possible. Every available drop of water is taken into the cactus and held in its fleshy stem. A cactus stem can hold enough water to last for two years or longer.

A cactus may be best known for its spines. Although a few kinds of cacti don't have spines, the stems of most types are covered with these sharp needles. The spines have many uses for a cactus. They keep animals from eating the cactus. They collect raindrops and dew. The spines also help keep the plant cool by forming shadows in the sun and by trapping a layer of air close to the plant. They break up the desert winds that dry out the cactus.

Cacti come in all sizes and shapes. The biggest type in North America is the saguaro. It can weigh 12,000 to 14,000 pounds and grow to be 50 feet tall. A saguaro can last several years without water, but it will grow only after summer rains. In May and June, white blossoms appear. Many kinds of birds nest in these enormous cacti: white-winged doves, woodpeckers, small owls, thrashers, and wrens all build nests in the saguaro.

1. Where are you most likely to find a cactus growing?
   _desert of mexo_____

2. How long can most cacti survive without water?
   _2 yers_____

3. What are two ways the spines help a cactus?
   _#1   protexchion_____

4. What is the biggest cactus in North America?
   _sAguaro_____

5. What animals live in a saguaro cactus?
   _Birds_____

Review

Directions: Write a three-sentence summary of these selections. Refer to the reading selections for review if necessary.

1. "Desert Plants"

   _____

   _____

   _____

2. "The Cactus Family"

   _____

   _____

   _____

Directions: Describe the adaptations these plants have made to survive in the desert.

3. cacti _____

   _____

4. mesquite _____

   _____

5. saguaro cactus _____

Directions: Answer these questions.

6. What is the purpose of cactus spines? _____

   _____

7. Why does the mesquite have long roots? _____

   _____

Directions: Define these words. Then, use them in sentences of your own.

8. evaporation _____

   _____

9. spine _____

   _____

Reading Comprehension: Lizards

Directions: Read the information about lizards. Then, answer the questions.

Lizards are reptiles, related to snakes, turtles, alligators, and crocodiles. Like other reptiles, lizards are cold-blooded. This means that their body temperature changes with that of their surroundings. However, by changing their behavior throughout the day, they can keep their temperature fairly constant.

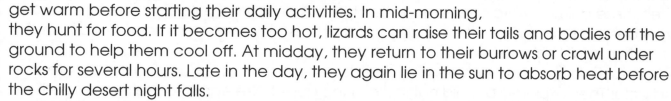

Lizards are among the many animals that live in deserts. They usually come out of their burrows early in the morning. Most lizards lie in the sun to get warm before starting their daily activities. In mid-morning, they hunt for food. If it becomes too hot, lizards can raise their tails and bodies off the ground to help them cool off. At midday, they return to their burrows or crawl under rocks for several hours. Late in the day, they again lie in the sun to absorb heat before the chilly desert night falls.

Like all animals, lizards have ways of protecting themselves. Some types of lizards have developed a most unusual defense. If a hawk or other animal grabs one of these lizards by its tail, the tail will break off. The tail will continue to wiggle around to distract the attacker while the lizard runs away. A month or two later, the lizard grows a new tail.

There are about 3,000 kinds of lizards, and all of them can bite, but only two types of lizards are poisonous: the Gila monster of the southwestern United States and the Mexican bearded lizard. Both are short-legged, thick-bodied reptiles with fat tails. These lizards do not attack people and will not bite them unless they are attacked.

1. What can a lizard do if it becomes too hot? _____

   _____

2. What is an unusual defense some lizards have developed to protect themselves?

   _____

3. What two types of lizards are poisonous? _____

   _____

Main Idea: People in the Desert

Directions: Read the information about people in the desert. Then, answer the questions.

Long before Europeans came to live in America, Native Americans had discovered ways of living in the desert. Some of these Native Americans were hunters or belonged to wandering tribes that stayed in the desert for only short periods of time. Others learned to farm and live in villages. They made their houses of trees, clay, and brush.

The desert met all of their needs for life: food, water, skins for clothing, materials for tools, weapons, and shelter. For meat, the desert offered deer, birds, and rabbits for hunting. When these animals were hard to find, the Native Americans would eat mice and lizards. Many desert plants, such as the prickly pear and mesquite, provided moisture, fruit, and seeds that could be eaten.

The first Europeans in the American deserts were searching for furs and metals, like silver and gold. They explored but did not settle in the desert. The early pioneers were usually unsuccessful at living in the desert. They found the great heat and long dry periods too difficult. When they moved away, they left behind empty mining camps, houses, and sheds that slowly fell apart in the sun and wind.

1. What is the main idea of this selection?

   _____ Before Europeans came to live in America, Native Americans had discovered ways of successfully living in the desert.

   _____ Some Native Americans were hunters or belonged to wandering tribes who stayed in the desert for only short periods of time.

2. Who were the first people to live in the deserts of North America?

   _____

3. What did the Native Americans use to make their houses in the desert?

   _____

4. What kinds of food did the Native Americans find in the desert?

   _____

5. What were the first Europeans who came to the desert looking for?

   _____

Main Idea: Camels

Directions: Read the information about camels. Then, answer the questions.

Camels are well suited to desert life. They can cope with infrequent supplies of food and water, blazing heat during the day, low temperatures at night, and sand blown by high winds.

There are two kinds of camels: the two-humped bactrian and the one-humped dromedary. The dromedary is the larger of the two. It has coarse fur on its back that helps protect it from the sun's rays. The hair on its stomach and legs is short to prevent overheating. When camels **molt** in the spring, their wool can be collected in tufts from the bushes and ground.

The legs of the dromedary are much longer than those of the bactrian. Animals that live in very hot countries tend to have longer legs. This gives them a larger area of body surface from which heat can escape. Bactrian camels live in the deserts of central Asia where winters are bitterly cold, so they are not as tall as dromedaries.

Both kinds of camels have pads on their feet that keep them from sinking into the sand as they walk. A camel's long neck allows it to reach the ground to drink water and eat grass without having to bend its legs. It also can reach up to eat leaves from trees.

Camels do not store water in their humps as many people believe. The hump is for fat storage. When there is plenty of food, the camel's hump swells and feels firm. During the dry season when there is little food, the fat is used up, and the hump shrinks and becomes soft.

1. What is the main idea of this selection?

   _____ Camels are well suited to desert life.

   _____ There are two kinds of camels.

2. Based on the other words in the sentence, what is the correct definition of **molt**?

   _____ turns into a butterfly

   _____ sheds its hair

   _____ becomes overheated

3. What are the two kinds of camels? _____

4. Why don't camels sink into the sand when they walk? _____

_____

5. What is the purpose of a camel's hump? _____

Comprehensive Curriculum - **Grade 5**

Review

Directions: Write your answers in complete sentences.

1. Describe how the cold-blooded lizard regulates its body temperature.

   _____

   _____

   _____

   _____

2. What is the main idea of the selection "Lizards"?

   _____

   _____

3. Describe how Native Americans adapted to life in the desert.

   _____

   _____

   _____

   _____

4. Why do you think early pioneers were unsuccessful at desert living?

   _____

   _____

   _____

   _____

5. Describe the adaptations of camels for successful desert habitation.

   _____

   _____

   _____

Reading Comprehension: Desert Lakes

Directions: Read the information about lakes in the desert. Then, answer the questions.

A few deserts have small permanent lakes. While they may be a welcome sight in the desert, the water in them is not fit for drinking. They are salt lakes. Rain from nearby higher land keeps these lakes supplied with water, but the lakes are blocked in with nowhere to drain. Over the years, mineral salts collect in the water and build up to a high level, making the water undrinkable.

Most desert lakes are only temporary. Occasional rains may fill them to depths of several feet, but in a matter of weeks or months, all the water has been dried up by the heat and sun. The dried lake beds that remain are called **playas**. Some playas are simply areas of sun-baked mud; others are covered with a sparkling layer of salt.

Perhaps the most unusual desert lake is in central Australia. It is called Lake Eyre. It is a huge lake—nearly 3,600 square miles in area—but it is almost totally dry most of the time. Since it was discovered in 1840, it has been filled only two times. Both times, the lake completely dried up again within a few years.

1. Why is the water in a desert lake not fit for drinking?

   _____

2. Why are the lakes in the desert salt lakes?

   _____

3. Why are most desert lakes only temporary?

   _____

4. What is a **playa**? _____

5. What is the name of the unusual desert lake in central Australia?

   _____

6. How big is this desert lake? _____

Review

Directions: Write your answers in complete sentences.

1. What is a desert?

   _____

   _____

2. Name a desert in the United States, and tell where it is.

   _____

   _____

3. What special characteristics must an animal have to survive in the desert?

   _____

   _____

   _____

4. What special characteristics must a plant have to survive in the desert?

   _____

   _____

   _____

5. What differences exist between animals whose habitat is the polar regions and animals whose habitat is the desert regions?

   _____

   _____

   _____

   _____

   _____

6. Would you like to visit the desert? Why or why not?

   _____

   _____

   _____

   _____

Name _____

Nouns

A **noun** is a word that names a person, place, or thing.

Examples:
    person — friend
    place — home
    thing — desk

Nouns are used many ways in sentences. They can be the subjects of sentences.

Example: Noun as subject: Your high-topped **sneakers** look great with that outfit.

Nouns can be direct objects of a sentence. The **direct object** follows the verb and completes its meaning. It answers the question **who** or **what**.

Example: Noun as direct object: Shelly's family bought a new **car**.

Nouns can be indirect objects. An **indirect object** comes between the verb and the direct object and tells **to whom** or **for whom** something was done.

Example: Noun as indirect object: She gave **Vijay** a big hug.

Directions: Underline all the nouns. Write **S** above the noun if it is a subject, **DO** if it is a direct object, or **IO** if it is an indirect object. The first one has been done for you.

1. Do <u>alligators</u> eat <u>people</u>?
    (S above alligators, DO above people)

2. James hit a home run, and our team won the game.

3. The famous actor gave Marissa his autograph.

4. Eric loaned Keith his bicycle.

5. The kindergarten children painted cute pictures.

6. Robin sold David a magazine subscription.

7. The neighbors planned a going-away party and bought a gift.

8. The party and gift surprised Kurt and his family.

9. My scout leader told our group a funny joke.

10. Catalina made her little sister a clown costume.

Nouns B B B

Directions: Write 10 nouns for each category.

People

1. Blaze
2. Dana
3. viv
4. Ava
5. nolan
6. emma
7. Jack
8. Jill
9. tom
10. Jerry

Places

1. home
2. Khols
3. Walmart
4. homedpot
5. Portexion
6. poters
7. Povtters
8. ny
9. ymca
10. corning

Things

1. Lamp
2. stove
3. Plant
4. table
5. LoL Dall
6. tree
7. Phone
8. car
9. window
10. Light

PERSON PLACE THING

Name _____

Proper and Common Nouns

Common nouns name nonspecific people, places, or things.

Examples: man, fortress, dog

Proper nouns name specific people, places, or things.

Examples: Washington, D.C., Thomas Jefferson, Red Sea

Directions: Underline the proper nouns, and circle the common nouns in each sentence.

1. My friend, Josephine, loves to go to the docks to watch the boats sail into the harbor.

2. Josephine is especially interested in the boat named *Maiden Voyage*.

3. This boat is painted red with yellow stripes and has several large masts.

4. Its sails are white and billow in the wind.

5. At Misty Harbor, many boats are always sailing in and out.

6. The crews on the boats rush from bow to stern working diligently to keep the sailboats moving.

7. Josephine has been invited aboard *Maiden Voyage* by its captain.

8. Captain Ferdinand knew of her interest in sailboats, so he offered a tour.

9. Josephine was amazed at the gear aboard the boat and the skills of the crew.

10. It is Josephine's dream to sail the Atlantic Ocean on a boat similar to *Maiden Voyage*.

11. Her mother is not sure about this dangerous dream and urges Josephine to consider safer dreams.

12. Josephine thinks of early explorers like Christopher Columbus, Amerigo Vespucci, and Leif Ericson.

13. She thinks these men must have been brave to set out into the unknown waters of the world.

14. Their boats were often small and provided little protection from major ocean storms.

15. Josephine believes that if early explorers could challenge the rough ocean waters, she can, too.

Abstract and Concrete Nouns

Concrete nouns name something that can be touched or seen.
Abstract nouns name an idea, a thought, or a feeling that cannot be touched or seen.

Examples:
   concrete nouns: house, puppy, chair
   abstract nouns: love, happiness, fear

Directions: Write **concrete** or **abstract** in the blank after each noun.

1. loyalty_____

2. light bulb _____

3. quarter _____

4. hope _____

5. satellite _____

6. ability _____

7. patio _____

8. door _____

9. allegiance _____

10. Cuba _____

11. Michael Jordan _____

12. friendship _____

13. telephone _____

14. computer _____

Directions: Write eight nouns for each category.

Concrete	Abstract
1. _____	1. _____
2. _____	2. _____
3. _____	3. _____
4. _____	4. _____
5. _____	5. _____
6. _____	6. _____
7. _____	7. _____
8. _____	8. _____

Name _____

Verbs

A **verb** tells what something does or that something exists.

Examples:
Tim **has shared** his apples with us.
Those apples **were** delicious.
I hope Tim **is bringing** more apples tomorrow.
Tim **picked** the apples himself.

Directions: Underline the verbs.

1. Gene moved here from Philadelphia.

2. Now, he is living in a house on my street.

3. His house is three houses away from mine.

4. I have lived in this house all my life.

5. I hope Gene will like this town.

6. I am helping Gene with his room.

7. He has a lot of stuff!

8. We are painting his walls green.

9. He picked the color himself.

10. His parents are glad we are helping out.

Directions: Write verbs to complete these sentences.

11. We _____ some paintbrushes.

12. Gene already _____ the paint.

13. I _____ my old clothes.

14. There _____ no furniture in his room right now.

15. It _____ several hours to paint his whole room.

Verbs

A **verb** is the action word in a sentence. It tells what the subject does (**build**, **laugh**, **express**, **fasten**) or that it exists (**is**, **are**, **was**, **were**).

Examples: Randy **raked** the leaves into a pile.
         I **was** late to school today.

Directions: In the following sentences, write verbs that make sense.

1. The quarterback _____ the ball to the receiver.

2. My mother _____ some soup yesterday.

3. John _____ newspapers to make extra money.

4. The teacher _____ the instructions on the board.

5. Last summer, our family _____ a trip to Florida to visit relatives.

Sometimes, a verb can be two or more words. Verbs used to support other verbs are called **helping verbs**.

Examples: We **were** listening to music in my room.
         Chris **has been** studying for over 2 hours.

Directions: In the following sentences, write helping verbs along with the correct form of the given verbs. The first one has been done for you.

1. Michelle (write) ___**is writing**___ a letter to her grandmother right now.

2. My brother (have) _____ trouble with his math homework.

3. When we arrived, the movie (start) _____ already.

4. My aunt (live) _____ in the same house for 30 years.

5. Our football team (go) _____ to win the national championship this year.

6. My sister (talk) _____ on the phone all afternoon!

7. I couldn't sleep last night because the wind (blow) _____ so hard.

8. Last week, Owen was sick, but now he (feel) _____ much better.

9. Tomorrow, our class (have) _____ a bake sale.

10. Mr. Rivera (collect) _____ stamps for 20 years.

Comprehensive Curriculum - **Grade 5**

Name _____

Verb Tenses

Verbs have different forms to show whether something already happened, is happening right now, or will happen.

Examples:
   Present tense: I walk
   Past tense: I walked
   Future tense: I will walk

Directions: Write **PAST** if the verb is past tense, **PRES** for present tense, or **FUT** for future tense. The first one has been done for you.

PRES 1. My sister Sara works at the grocery store.

_____ 2. Last year, she worked in an office.

_____ 3. Sara is going to college, too.

_____ 4. She will be a dentist some day.

_____ 5. She says studying is difficult.

_____ 6. Sara studied pretty hard in high school, too.

_____ 7. I will be ready for college in a few years.

_____ 8. Last night, I read my history book for two hours.

Directions: Complete these sentences using verbs in the tenses listed. The first one has been done for you.

9. take: future tense   My friends and I **will take** a trip.

10. talk: past tense   We _____ for a long time about where to go.

11. want: present tense   Brianna _____ to go to the lake.

12. want: past tense   Jake _____ to go with us.

13. say: past tense   His parents _____ no.

14. ride: future tense   We _____ our bikes.

15. pack: past tense   Dante and Jared already _____ lunches for us.

Verb Tenses

The past tense of many verbs is formed by adding **ed**.

Examples:
remember + **ed** = remembered
climb + **ed** = climbed

If a verb ends in **e**, drop the **e** before adding **ed**.

Examples:

Present	Past
phone	phoned
arrive	arrived

If a verb ends in **y**, change the **y** to **i** before adding **ed**.

Examples:

Present	Past
carry	carried
try	tried

If a verb ends in a short vowel followed by a single consonant, double the final consonant.

Examples:

Present	Past
trip	tripped
pop	popped

Directions: Circle the misspelled verb in each sentence, and write it correctly in the blank.

1. They stopped at our house and then hurryed home. _____

2. I scrubed and mopped the floor. _____

3. The coach nameed the five starting players. _____

4. He popped the potatoes into the oil and fryed them. _____

5. I accidentally droped my papers on the floor. _____

6. I had hopeed you could go climbing with me. _____

7. He triped on the rug. _____

8. The baby cryed and screamed all night. _____

9. I moped the mess up after the glass dropped on the floor. _____

10. First, she frowned, and then she smileed. _____

Writing: Verb Forms

Present-tense verbs tell what is happening right now. To form present-tense verbs, use the "plain" verbs or use **is** or **are** before the verb and add **ing** to the verb.

Examples: We **eat**. We **are eating**.
He **serves**. He **is serving**.

Directions: Complete each sentence with the correct verb form, telling what is happening right now. Read carefully, as some sentences already have **is** or **are**.

Examples: Scott is (loan) <u>loaning</u> Jenny his math book.
Jenny (study) <u>is studying</u> for a big math test.

1. The court is (release) _____ the prisoner early.

2. Jonah and Jill (write) _____ their notes in code.

3. Are you (vote) _____ for Baxter?

4. The girls are (coax) _____ the dog into the bathtub.

5. The leaves (begin) _____ to fall from the trees.

6. My little brother (stay) _____ at his friend's house tonight.

7. Is she (hide) _____ behind the screen?

To change a verb to the **past tense**, or tell what already happened, add **ed**, or use **was** or **were** and add **ing** to the verb.

Example: I **watched**. I **was watching**.

Directions: Complete each sentence with the correct verb form. This time, tell what already happened.

Examples: We (walk) <u>walked</u> there yesterday.
They were (talk) <u>talking</u>.

1. The government was (decrease) _____ our taxes.

2. Was anyone (cheat) _____ in this game?

3. We were (try) _____ to set goals for the project.

Writing: Future-Tense Verbs

Future-tense verbs tell about things that will happen in the future. To form future-tense verbs, use **will** before the verb.

Example: Tomorrow, I **will walk** to school.

When you use **will**, you may also have to add a helping verb and the ending **ing**.

Example: Tomorrow, I **will be walking** to school.

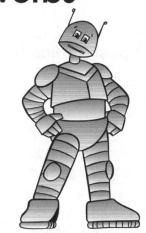

Directions: Imagine what the world will be like 100 years from now. Maybe you think robots will be doing our work for us, or that people will be living on the moon. What will our houses look like? What will school be like? Write a paragraph describing what you imagine. Be sure to use future-tense verbs.

_____

_____

_____

_____

_____

_____

_____

_____

_____

_____

Principal Parts of Verbs

Verbs have three principal parts. They are **present**, **past**, and **past participle**.

Form the past tense of regular verbs by adding **ed** to the present tense.

Form the past participle by using the past tense verb with a helping verb: **has**, **have**, or **had**.

has
have
had

Directions: Write the correct form of each verb. The first one has been done for you.

Present	Past	Past Participle
1. look	looked	have/has/had looked
2. _____	planned	_____
3. _____	_____	has/have/had closed
4. wash	_____	_____
5. _____	prepared	_____
6. _____	_____	has/have/had provided
7. invite	_____	_____
8. _____	discovered	_____
9. approve	_____	_____
10. _____	searched	_____
11. establish	_____	_____
12. _____	_____	has/have/had formed
13. _____	pushed	_____
14. travel	_____	_____

Irregular Verbs

Irregular verbs change completely in the past tense. Unlike regular verbs, the past tense of irregular verbs is not formed by adding **ed**.

Examples:
    Chung **eats** the grapes.
    Chung **ate** them yesterday.
    Chung **has eaten** them for weeks.

Present Tense	Past Tense	Past Participle
begin	began	has/have/had begun
speak	spoke	has/have/had spoken
drink	drank	has/have/had drunk
know	knew	has/have/had known
eat	ate	has/have/had eaten
wear	wore	has/have/had worn

Directions: Rewrite these sentences once using the past tense and again using the past participle of each verb.

1. Todd begins football practice this week.

_____

_____

2. She wears her hair in braids.

_____

_____

3. I drink two glasses of milk.

_____

_____

4. The man is speaking to us.

_____

_____

5. The dogs are eating.

_____

_____

Name _____

Irregular Verbs

The past participle form of an irregular verb needs a helping verb.

present, past, and past participle

Examples:

Present	Past	Past Participle
begin	began	has/have/had begun
drive	drove	has/have/had driven

Directions: Write the past and past participle form of these irregular verbs. Use a dictionary if you need help.

Present	Past	Past Participle
1. speak	_____	_____
2. break	_____	_____
3. beat	_____	_____
4. dream	_____	_____
5. tear	_____	_____
6. forget	_____	_____
7. lead	_____	_____
8. stand	_____	_____
9. sting	_____	_____
10. freeze	_____	_____
11. grow	_____	_____
12. lose	_____	_____
13. run	_____	_____
14. meet	_____	_____
15. sit	_____	_____
16. do	_____	_____

Be as a Helping Verb

A **helping verb** tells when the action of a sentence takes place. The helping verb **be** has several forms: **am**, **is**, **are**, **was**, **were**, and **will**. These helping verbs can be used in all three tenses.

Examples:
Past tense: Kenji **was** talking. We **were** eating.
Present tense: I **am** coming. Simon **is** walking. They **are** singing.
Future tense: I **will** work. The puppies **will** eat.

In the present and past tense, many verbs can be written with or without the helping verb **be**. When the verb is written with a form of **be**, add **ing**. **Was** and **is** are used with singular subjects. **Were** and **are** are used with plural subjects.

Examples:
Present tense: Angela **sings**. Angela **is singing**. The children **sing**. They **are singing**.
Past tense: I **studied**. I **was studying**. They **studied**. They **were studying**.

The helping verb **will** is always needed for the future tense, but the **ing** ending is not used with **will**. **Will** is both singular and plural.

Examples:
Future tense: I **will eat**. We **will watch**.

Directions: Underline the helping verbs.

1. Brian is helping me with this project.
2. We are working together on it.
3. Tess was painting the background yesterday.
4. Matt and Malik were cleaning up.
5. Tomorrow, we will present our project to the class.

Directions: Rewrite the verbs using a helping verb. The first one has been done for you.

6. Our neighborhood plans a garage sale.   *is planning*

7. The sale starts tomorrow.   _____

8. My brother Doug and I think about things we sell.   _____

9. My grandfather cleans out the garage.   _____

10. Doug and I help him.   _____

Name _____

Be as a Linking Verb

A **linking verb** links a noun or adjective in the predicate to the subject. Forms of the verb **be** are the most common linking verbs. Linking verbs can be used in all three tenses.

Examples:
    Present: My father **is** a salesman.
    Past: The store **was** very busy last night.
    Future: Tomorrow **will be** my birthday.

In the first sentence, **is** links the subject (father) with a noun (salesman). In the second sentence, **was** links the subject (store) with an adjective (busy). In the third sentence, **will be** links the subject (tomorrow) with a noun (birthday).

Directions: Circle the linking verbs. Underline the two words that are linked by the verb. The first one has been done for you.

1. Columbus (is) the capital of Ohio.

2. By bedtime, Nicole was bored.

3. Andy will be the captain of our team.

4. Tuesday is the first day of the month.

5. I hate to say this, but we are lost.

6. Ask him if the water is cold.

7. By the time I finished my paper, it was late.

8. Spaghetti is my favorite dinner.

9. The children were afraid of the big truck.

10. Aliyah will be a good president of our class.

11. These lessons are helpful.

12. Was that report due today?

Be as a Linking or Helping Verb

Directions: Write **H** if the form of **be** is used as a helping verb or **L** if it is used as a linking verb.

_____ 1. Bella was watching for the mail.

_____ 2. The mail was late, as usual.

_____ 3. Her friends were calling her to come to the park.

_____ 4. "We will be missed by everyone at the park," they said.

_____ 5. Still, Bella was hopeful as she waited.

_____ 6. She knew her brother was sending her a letter.

_____ 7. He was a soldier in the army.

_____ 8. He was homesick for his family, so he wrote every day.

Directions: Write two sentences using a form of **be** as a helping verb.

9. _____

_____

10. _____

_____

Directions: Write two sentences using a form of **be** as a linking verb.

11. _____

_____

12. _____

_____

Name _____

Transitive and Intransitive Verbs

An **intransitive verb** can stand alone in the predicate because its meaning is complete. In the examples below, notice that each short sentence is a complete thought.

Examples: Intransitive verbs: The tree **grows**. The mouse **squeaked**. The deer **will run**.

A **transitive verb** needs a direct object to complete its meaning. The meaning of a sentence with a transitive verb is not complete without a direct object.

Examples: Transitive verbs: The mouse **wants** seeds. The deer **saw** the hunter. The tree **will lose** its leaves.

The direct object **seeds** tells what the mouse wants. **Leaves** tells what the tree will lose and **hunter** tells what the deer saw.

Both transitive and intransitive verbs can be in the past, present, or future tense.

Directions: Underline the verb in each sentence. Write **I** if the sentence has an intransitive verb or **T** if it has a transitive verb.

_____ 1. The snake slid quietly along the ground.

_____ 2. The snake scared a rabbit.

_____ 3. The rabbit hopped quickly back to its hole.

_____ 4. Safe from the snake, the rabbit shivered with fear.

_____ 5. In the meantime, the snake caught a frog.

_____ 6. The frog was watching flies and didn't see the snake.

Directions: Complete these sentences with intransitive verbs.

7. Our friends _____

8. The movie _____

Directions: Complete these sentences with transitive verbs and direct objects.

9. My family _____

10. The lightning _____

Subjects and Predicates

The **subject** tells who or what a sentence is about. The **predicate** tells what the subject does, did, or is doing. All complete sentences must have a subject and a predicate.

Examples:

Subject	Predicate
Hamsters	are common pets.
Pets	need special care.

Directions: Circle the subjects, and underline the predicates.

1. Many children keep hamsters as pets.

2. Mice are good pets, too.

3. Hamsters collect food in their cheeks.

4. My sister sneezes around furry animals.

5. My brother wants a dog instead of a hamster.

Directions: Write subjects to complete these sentences.

6. _____ has two pet hamsters.

7. _____ got a new pet last week.

8. _____ keeps forgetting to feed his goldfish.

Directions: Write predicates to complete these sentences.

9. Baby hamsters _____.

10. Pet mice _____.

11. I _____.

Directions: Write **S** if the group of words is a sentence or **NS** if the group of words is not a sentence.

12. _____ A new cage for our hamster.

13. _____ Picked the cutest one.

14. _____ We started out with two.

15. _____ Liking every one in the store.

Which Noun Is the Subject?

A **noun** is a word that names a person, place, or thing.

Examples: Andy, Mrs. Henderson, doctor, child, house, shirt, dog, freedom, country

Often, a noun is the subject of a sentence. The **subject** tells who or what the sentence is about. In this sentence, the subject is **Sara**: Sara drank some punch. A sentence can have several nouns, but they are not all subjects.

Directions: Underline each noun in the sentences below. Then, circle the noun that is the subject of the sentence.

Example: (Benny) caught a huge <u>fish</u> in a small <u>net</u>.

1. Anna bragged about her big brother.

2. The car has a dent in the fender.

3. Our school won the city spirit award.

4. The cook scrubbed the pots and pans.

5. The quarter flipped onto the floor.

6. My sister rinsed her hair in the sink.

7. Our neighbor has 12 pets.

8. The cross country team ran 5 miles at practice.

9. Syd walked to the store on the corner.

10. A farmer stocks this pond with fish.

Directions: Each sentence below has two subjects. Underline all the nouns, as you did above. Then, circle both subjects.

Example: (Joe) and (Peter) walked to <u>school</u>.

1. Apples and peaches grow in different seasons.

2. The chair and table matched the other furniture.

Which Noun Is the Subject?

Usually, the noun that is the subject will come at the beginning of the sentence.

Examples: The ⌈truck⌉ turned quickly around the corner.
⌈Kevin⌉ stayed home from school yesterday.

Sometimes, other words will come before the subject.
When this happens, remember to look for who or
what the sentence is about.

Example: After school, ⌈Katie⌉ usually walks to the library.

The sentence is about Katie, not school.

Directions: In the sentences below, circle the nouns that are subjects. Some sentences have more than one subject, and they will not always be at the beginning of the sentence.

1. Mark and I helped the teacher clean the classroom.

2. In the morning, my mother cooks breakfast for the whole family.

3. To finish the project, Keiko had to stay up very late last night.

4. After the storm, power lines were down all over the city.

5. Oranges and grapefruits grow very well in Florida.

6. During the summer, squirrels work hard to gather nuts for the winter.

7. While skiing last weekend, my neighbor fell and broke his leg.

8. Pictures and posters cover all the walls of our classroom.

9. To save gas, my father takes the bus to work instead of driving.

10. In my opinion, dogs and cats make the best pets.

Name _____

Subjects and Verbs

Directions: Underline the subject and verb in each sentence below. Write **S** over the subject and **V** over the verb. If the verb is two words, mark them both.

                 S   V   V

Examples: <u>Dennis</u> <u>was drinking</u> some punch.

                    S   V

         The <u>punch</u> <u>was</u> too sweet.

1. Hayley talks about her dog all the time.

2. Mrs. Thomas scrubbed the dirt off her car.

3. Then, her son rinsed off the soap.

4. The teacher was flipping through the cards.

5. Sophia's rabbit was hungry and thirsty.

6. Your science report lacks a little detail.

7. Chris is stocking the shelves with cans of soup.

8. The accident caused a huge dent in our car.

Just as sentences can have two subjects, they can also have two verbs.

               S   S   V   V

Example: <u>Gabriela</u> and <u>Amie</u> <u>fed</u> the dog and <u>gave</u> him clean water.

Directions: Underline all the subjects and verbs in these sentences. Write **S** over the subjects and **V** over the verbs.

1. Mom and Dad scrubbed and rinsed the basement floor.

2. The men came and stocked the lake with fish.

3. Someone broke the window and ran away.

4. Carrie punched a hole in the paper and threaded yarn through the hole.

5. Julie and Ahmad turned their bikes around and went home.

Writing: Subjects and Verbs

Directions: Make each group of words below into a sentence by adding a subject, a verb, or a subject and a verb. Then, write **S** over each subject and **V** over each verb.

Example: the dishes in the sink

       S   V

The dishes in the sink were dirty.

1. a leash for your pet

_____

2. dented the table

_____

3. a bowl of punch for the party

_____

4. rinsed the soap out

_____

5. a lack of chairs

_____

6. bragging about his sister

_____

7. the cans on the shelf

_____

8. with a flip of the wrist

_____

Name _____

Writing: Subjects and Verbs

Directions: Decide which words in the box are subjects (nouns) and which are verbs. Write each word under the correct heading. Then, match each subject with a verb to make a sentence. Use each subject and verb only once. The first one has been done for you.

dog	~~girls~~	~~walked~~	barked	honked
flew	car	played	neighbor	teacher
wrote	mowed	Marcus	birds	

Subjects	**Verbs**
girls	walked
_____	_____
_____	_____
_____	_____
_____	_____
_____	_____
_____	_____

1. <u>The tired girls walked slowly home from school.</u>

2. _____

3. _____

4. _____

5. _____

6. _____

7. _____

Complete Sentences

A sentence that does not contain both a subject and a predicate is called a **fragment**.

Directions: Write **C** if the sentence is complete or **F** if it is a fragment.

1. _____ My mother and I hope to go to the mall this afternoon.

2. _____ To get shoes.

3. _____ We both need a new pair of tennis shoes.

4. _____ Maybe blue and white.

5. _____ Mom wants a pair of white shoes.

6. _____ That seems rather boring to me.

7. _____ There are many shoe stores in the mall.

8. _____ Sure to be a large selection.

9. _____ Tennis shoes are very expensive.

10. _____ I wore my last pair almost every day.

Directions: Write the missing subject or predicate for these sentences.

11. _____ decided to go for hamburgers.

12. We _____.

13. My parents _____.

14. One day soon, I _____.

15. My favorite subject in school _____.

16. _____ went fishing on Sunday.

Name _____

Direct Objects

A **direct object** is a word or words that follow a transitive verb and complete its meaning. It answers the question **whom** or **what**. Direct objects are always nouns or pronouns.

Examples:

We built a **doghouse**. **Doghouse** is the direct object. It tells **what** we built.
I called **Elena**. **Elena** is the direct object. It tells **whom** I called.

Directions: Underline the direct objects.

1. Maggy drew a picture of the doghouse.

2. Then, we bought some wood at the store.

3. Erin measured each board.

4. Who will saw the wood into boards?

5. Thad hammered nails into the boards.

6. He accidentally hit his thumb with the hammer.

7. Kirsten found some paint in the basement.

8. Should we paint the roof?

9. Will you write Sparky's name above the door?

10. Spell his name correctly.

Directions: Write direct objects to complete these sentences.

11. Will Sparky like _____?

12. When we were finished, we put away _____

13. We washed out _____.

14. We threw away _____.

15. Then, to celebrate, we ate _____.

Indirect Objects

An **indirect object** is a word or words that come between the verb and the direct object. An indirect object tells **to whom** or **for whom** something has been done. Indirect objects are always nouns or pronouns.

Examples:

She cooked **me** a great dinner. **Me** is the indirect object. It tells **for whom** something was cooked.

Give the **photographer** a smile. **Photographer** is the indirect object. It tells **to whom** the smile should be given.

Directions: Circle the indirect objects. Underline the direct objects.

1. Grace showed me her drawing.

2. The committee had given her an award for it.

3. The principal offered Grace a special place to put her drawing.

4. While babysitting, I read Xavier a story.

5. He told me the end of the story.

6. Then, I fixed him some hot chocolate.

7. Xavier gave me a funny look.

8. Why didn't his mother tell me?

9. Hot chocolate gives Xavier a rash.

10. Will his mom still pay me for watching him?

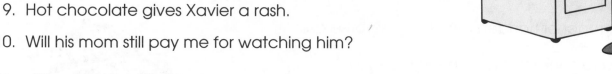

Directions: Write indirect objects to complete these sentences.

11. I will write _____ a letter.

12. I'll give _____ part of my lunch.

13. Show _____ your model.

14. Did you send _____ a card?

15. Don't tell _____ my secret.

Direct and Indirect Objects

Directions: Underline the direct objects. Circle the indirect objects.

1. Please give him a note card.

2. My father told me a secret.

3. I carefully examined the dinosaur bones.

4. Joseph decorated the banquet hall for the wedding.

5. Every night, I telephone my grandmother.

6. The head of the company offered my father a new position.

7. Too much pizza can give you a stomachache.

8. Will you draw me a picture?

9. This new computer gives me a headache!

10. Thomas discovered a new entrance to the cave.

11. He showed me the rare penny.

12. While watching television, I wrote Maria a letter.

13. Mrs. Fetters will pay me ten dollars for shoveling her sidewalk this winter.

14. The teacher handed her class a surprise quiz.

15. I like to drink iced tea on summer days.

16. Mom bought Linh new school supplies for kindergarten.

17. I had to pay the library a fine for overdue books.

18. My family enjoys playing football.

19. Each night my mom reads me one chapter of a novel.

20. The teacher gave us our report cards.

Prepositions

A **preposition** is a word that comes before a noun or pronoun and shows the relationship of that noun or pronoun to other words in the sentence.

The **object of a preposition** is a noun or pronoun that follows a preposition and completes its meaning. A **prepositional phrase** includes a preposition and the object(s) of the preposition.

Examples:

The girl **with red hair** spoke first.
With is the preposition.
Hair is the object of the preposition.
With red hair is a prepositional phrase.

In addition to being subjects, direct objects, and indirect objects, nouns and pronouns can also be objects of prepositions.

Prepositions						
across	behind	from	near	over	to	on
by	through	in	around	off	with	of
after	before	for	between	beyond	at	into

Directions: Underline the prepositional phrases in these sentences. Circle the prepositions. The first sentence has been done for you.

1. The name (of) our street is Redsail Court.
2. We have lived in our house for three years.
3. In our family, we eat a lot of hamburgers.
4. We like hamburgers on toasted buns with mustard.
5. Sometimes we eat in the living room in front of the TV.
6. In the summer, we have picnics in the backyard.
7. The ants crawl into our food and into our clothes.
8. Behind our house is a park with swings.
9. Kids from the neighborhood walk through our yard to the park.
10. Sometimes they cut across Mom's garden and stomp on her beans.
11. Mom says we need a tall fence without a gate.
12. With a fence around our yard, we could get a dog!

Pronouns

A **pronoun** is a word used in place of a noun. Instead of repeating a noun again and again, use a pronoun.

Examples: I   you   he   she   them   us
              me   your   him   her   they   it
              my   our   his   we   their   its

Each pronoun takes the place of a certain noun. If the noun is singular, the pronoun should be singular. If the noun is plural, the pronoun should be plural.

Examples: John told **his** parents **he** would be late.
              The girls said **they** would ride **their** bikes.

Directions: In the sentences below, draw an arrow from each pronoun to the noun it replaces.

Example: Addy needs the salt. Please pass it to her.

1. The workers had faith they would finish the house in time.

2. Jana fell and scraped her knees. She put bandages on them.

3. The teacher told the students he wanted to see their papers.

Directions: Cross out some nouns and write pronouns to replace them.

his
Example: Dan needed a book for ~~Dan's~~ book report.

1. Brian doesn't care about the style of Brian's clothes.

2. Omar dyed Omar's jeans to make the jeans dark blue.

3. Faith said Faith was tired of sharing a bedroom with Faith's two sisters. Faith wanted a
   room of Faith's own.

4. Bathe babies carefully so the soap doesn't get in the babies' eyes and make the babies cry.

5. When the children held up the children's pictures, we could see the pride in the
   children's eyes.

Singular and Plural Pronouns

Directions: Rewrite the sentences so the pronouns match the nouns they replace in gender and number. Change the verb form if necessary. The first one has been done for you.

1. Canada geese are the best-known geese in North America. It was here when the first settlers came from Europe.

   <u>Canada geese are the best-known geese in North America.</u>
   <u>They were here when the first settlers came from Europe.</u>

2. A Canada goose has a white patch from their chin to a spot behind their eyes.

   _____

   _____

3. Canada geese can harm farmland when it grazes in fields.

   _____

   _____

4. Geese have favorite fields where it likes to stop and eat.

   _____

   _____

5. While most of the flock eats, some geese stand guard. He warns if there is any danger.

   _____

   _____

6. Each guard gets their turn to eat, too.

   _____

   _____

7. Female geese usually lay five or six eggs, but she may lay as many as eleven.

   _____

   _____

8. While the female goose sits on the eggs, the male goose guards their mate.

   _____

   _____

Name _____

Possessive Pronouns

A **possessive pronoun** shows ownership. A possessive pronoun can be used with the name of what is owned or by itself.

Examples:
> This is **my** book. The book is **mine**.
> This is **your** sandwich. It is **yours**.
> This is **our** room. The room is **ours**.

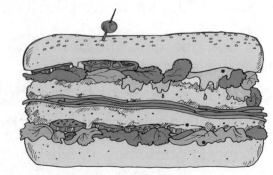

The possessive pronouns are **my**, **your**, **our**, **his**, **her**, **their**, **its**, **mine**, **yours**, **ours**, **hers**, and **theirs**. Possessive pronouns do not have apostrophes.

Directions: Complete the sentences with the correct possessive pronouns.

1. I entered _____ picture in the contest. That farm scene is _____.

2. Shelby entered _____ picture, too. Do you see _____?

3. Hal didn't finish _____ drawing. He left _____ at home.

4. Did you enter _____ clay pot? That looks like _____.

5. One picture has fallen off _____ stand.

6. Brian and Kendell worked together on a chalk drawing. That sketch by the doorway

   is _____.

7. The judges have made _____ choices.

8. We both won! They picked both of _____!

9. Here come the judges with our ribbons in _____ hands.

10. Your ribbon is the same as _____.

Writing: Possessive Pronouns

A **possessive pronoun** shows ownership. Instead of writing "That is Jill's book," write "That is her book" or "That is hers." Instead of "I lost my pencil," write "I lost mine." Use possessive pronouns to name what is owned or possessed.

Examples: my (book)   our (car)   your (hat)   his (leg)
             her (hair)   their (group)   its (team)

Use **mine**, **ours**, **yours**, **his**, **hers**, and **theirs** when you do not name what is possessed. Notice that possessive pronouns don't use apostrophes.

Directions: Complete these sentences with the correct possessive pronoun.

Example: This book belongs to Jon. It is _____ his _____.

1. I brought my lunch. Did you bring _____ ?

2. I can't do my homework. I wonder if Audrey figured out _____ .

3. Deepak saved his pretzels, but I ate _____ .

4. Our team finished our project, but the other team didn't finish _____.

5. They already have their assignment. When will we get _____?

It's easy to confuse the possessive pronoun **its** with the contraction for **it is**, which is spelled **it's**. The apostrophe in **it's** shows that the **i** in **is** has been left out.

Directions: Write **its** or **it's** in each sentence below.

Examples: The book has lost <u>its</u> cover. <u>It's</u> going to rain soon.

1. _____ nearly time to go.

2. The horse hurt _____ leg.

3. Every nation has _____ share of problems.

4. What is _____ name?

5. I think _____ too warm to snow.

6. The teacher said _____ up to us.

Indefinite Pronouns

Indefinite pronouns often end with **body**, **one**, or **thing**.

Examples:
  Everybody is going to be there.
  No one wants to miss it.

Indefinite pronouns do not change form when used as subjects or objects. They are always singular.

Example:
  Incorrect: **Everyone** must bring **their** own lunches.
  Correct: **All students** must bring **their** own lunches.
    Everyone must bring **his or her** own lunch.
    Everyone must bring **a** lunch.

Directions: Write twelve indefinite pronouns by matching a word from column A with a word from column B.

Column A	Column B
any	thing
every	one
no	body
some	

1. _____   7. _____

2. _____   8. _____

3. _____   9. _____

4. _____   10. _____

5. _____   11. _____

6. _____   12. _____

Directions: Write all the indefinite pronouns that would make sense in the sentence below.
_____ can come.

13. _____

Directions: Rewrite this sentence correctly.

14. Everybody has their books.

_____

Interrogative and Relative Pronouns

An **interrogative pronoun** is used when asking a question. The interrogative pronouns are **who**, **what**, and **which**. Use **who** when referring to people. Use **what** when referring to things. **Which** can be used to refer to people or things.

Directions: Circle the interrogative pronouns. Write whether the pronoun refers to people or things.

1. Who brought this salad for the picnic?

    _____

2. Which car will we drive to the movies?

    _____

3. Which girl asked the question?

    _____

4. What time is it?

    _____

5. What will we do with the leftover food?

    _____

6. Who is going to the swim meet?

    _____

Relative pronouns refer to the noun or pronoun that comes before them. The noun or pronoun to which it refers is called the **antecedent**. The relative pronouns are **who**, **whom**, **which**, and **that**. **Who** and **whom** refer to people. **Which** refers to things or animals. **That** can refer to people, animals, or things.

Directions: Circle the relative pronouns, and underline the antecedents.

1. My dog, which is very well-behaved, never barks.

2. The story was about a girl who wanted a horse of her own.

3. The bookcase, which was full, toppled over during the night.

4. The man to whom I spoke gave me complicated directions.

5. The book that I wanted had already been checked out of the library.

Comprehensive Curriculum - **Grade 5**

Name _____

Gender and Number of Pronouns

Pronouns that identify males are **masculine**. The masculine pronouns are **he**, **his**, and **him**. Pronouns that identify females are feminine. The **feminine** pronouns are **she**, **her**, and **hers**. Pronouns that identify something as neither male nor female are **gender**-**neutral**. The gender-neutral pronouns are **it** and **its**.

The plural pronouns **they** and **them** are used to replace masculine, feminine, or gender-neutral nouns.

Examples:

Noun	Pronoun	Noun	Pronoun
boot	it	woman	she
man	he	John's	his
travelers	they	dog's	its

Directions: List four nouns that each pronoun could replace in a sentence. The first one has been done for you.

1. she   <u>mother</u>   <u>doctor</u>   <u>girl</u>   <u>friend</u>

2. he   _____   _____   _____   _____

3. it   _____   _____   _____   _____

4. they   _____   _____   _____   _____

5. hers   _____   _____   _____   _____

6. its   _____   _____   _____   _____

Singular pronouns take the place of singular nouns. Plural pronouns take the place of plural nouns. The singular pronouns are **I**, **me**, **mine**, **he**, **she**, **it**, **its**, **hers**, **his**, **him**, **her**, **you**, and **yours**. The plural pronouns are **we**, **you**, **yours**, **they**, **theirs**, **ours**, **them**, and **us**.

Directions: Write five sentences. Include a singular and a plural pronoun in each sentence.

1. _____

2. _____

3. _____

4. _____

5. _____

Writing: Pronouns

Sometimes, matching nouns and pronouns can be difficult.

Example: A **teacher** should always be fair to **their** students.

Teacher is singular, but **their** is plural, so they don't match. Still, we can't say "A teacher should always be fair to his students," because teachers are both men and women. "His or her students" sounds awkward. One easy way to handle this is to make **teacher** plural so it will match **their**.

Example: Teachers should always be fair to **their** students.

Directions: Correct the problems in the following sentences by crossing out the incorrect words and writing in the correct nouns and pronouns. (If you make the noun plural, make the verb plural, too.)

its
Examples: Ron's school won ~~their~~ basketball game.

cats are
You can tell if ~~a cat is~~ angry by watching their tails.

1. A student should try to praise their friends' strong points.

2. The group finished their work on time in spite of the deadline.

3. A parent usually has a lot of faith in their children.

4. The company paid their workers once a week.

5. The train made their daily run from Chicago to Detroit.

6. Each student should have a title on their papers.

Directions: Complete these sentences with the correct pronouns.

1. Simon fell out of the tree and scraped _____ arm.

2. The citizens felt a deep pride in _____ community.

3. Abby and Leah wear _____ hair in the same style.

4. I dyed some shirts, but _____ didn't turn out right.

5. The nurse showed the mother how to bathe _____ baby.

6. Our school made $75 from _____ carnival.

Name _____

Pronouns as Subjects

A **pronoun** is a word that takes the place of a noun. The pronouns **I**, **we**, **he**, **she**, **it**, **you**, and **they** can be the subjects of a sentence.

Examples:
    I left the house early.
    You need to be more careful.
    She dances well.

A pronoun must be singular if the noun it replaces is singular. A pronoun must be plural if the noun it replaces is plural. **He**, **she**, and **it** are singular pronouns. **We** and **they** are plural pronouns. **You** is both singular and plural.

Examples:
    Jazmin practiced playing the piano. **She** plays well.
    Andre and I are studying Africa. **We** made a map of it.
    The children clapped loudly. **They** liked the clown.

Directions: Write the correct pronouns.

1. Bobcats hunt at night. _____ are not seen during the day.

2. The mother bobcat usually has babies during February or March. _____ may have two litters a year.

3. The father bobcat stays away when the babies are first born. Later, _____ helps find food for them.

4. We have a new assignment. _____ is a project about bobcats.

5. My group gathered pictures of bobcats. _____ made a display.

6. Stella wrote our report. _____ used my notes.

Directions: Circle the pronouns that do not match the nouns they replace. Then, write the correct pronouns on the lines.

7. Two boys saw a bobcat. He told us what happened. _____

8. Then, we saw a film. They showed bobcats climbing trees. _____

Name _____

Pronouns as Direct Objects

The pronouns **me**, **you**, **him**, **her**, **it**, **us**, and **them** can be used as direct objects.

Examples:

I heard Grant. Grant heard **me**.
We like the teacher. The teacher likes **us**.
He saw the dog. The dog saw **him**.

A pronoun used as a direct object must be plural if the noun is plural and singular if the noun is singular.

Directions: Write the correct pronouns.

1. Goldfish come from China. The Chinese used to eat ____them____ like trout.

2. The prettiest goldfish were kept as pets. The Chinese put ____them____ in small bowls and ponds.

3. My sister, brother, and I have goldfish. Grandpa took ____us____ to the store to get them.

4. They come to the top when I am around. I think they like ____me____ .

5. My sister's fish was white. She kept ____it____ for three weeks.

6. She claimed the fish splashed ____you____ when she fed it.

Directions: Circle pronouns that do not match the nouns they replace. Rewrite the sentences using the correct pronouns. Change the verbs after the pronouns if necessary.

7. Goldfish often die because kids don't feed it.

   GoldFish die cuz kids dont Feed it right.

8. Some goldfish live a long time because it is well cared for.

   _____

9. A wild goldfish will eat anything they think looks good.

   _____

10. Birds eat wild goldfish. It likes the young ones best.

   _____

Comprehensive Curriculum - Grade 5

Pronouns as Indirect Objects and Objects of Prepositions

The pronouns **me**, **you**, **him**, **her**, **it**, **us**, and **them** can be used as indirect objects and objects of prepositions.

Examples:
 Pronouns as indirect objects: Shawn showed **me** his new bike. The teacher gave **us** two more days to finish our reports.
 Pronouns as objects of prepositions: It's your turn after **her**. I can't do it without **them**.

A pronoun used as an indirect object or an object of a preposition must be singular if the noun it replaces is singular and plural if the noun it replaces is plural.

Directions: Write the correct pronouns. Above the pronoun, write **S** if it is the subject, **DO** if it is the direct object, **IO** if it is the indirect object, or **OP** if it is the object of a preposition.

1. Markos is coming to our party. I gave _____ the directions.

2. Janelle and Eldon used to be his friends. Is he still friends with _____?

3. Kevin and I like playing soccer, but _____ are not on the same team.

4. We listened closely while she told _____ what happened to _____.

5. My brother hurt his hand, but I took care of _____.

6. A piece of glass cut him when _____ dropped _____.

7. When Annalisa won the race, the coach gave _____ a trophy.

8. We were hot and sweaty, but a breeze cooled _____ off.

Pronouns

Subjects:	he	she	it	you	I	they	we
Objects:	him	her	it	you	me	them	us
Possessive:	his	her	its	your	my	their	our
Possessive:	his	hers	its	yours	mine	theirs	ours
Indefinite:	everyone	nobody	something	(and others)			

Directions: Complete these sentences with the correct pronouns from the box. Above each pronoun, write how it is used: **S** for subject, **DO** for direct object, **IO** for indirect object, **OP** for object of a preposition, **PP** for possessive pronoun, or **IP** for indefinite pronoun.

1. Last week, we had a food drive at _____ church.

2. _____ in our Sunday school class helped collect food.

3. I walked down my street and asked _____ neighbors for food.

4. They gave _____ cans and boxes of food.

5. Kelly came with _____ and helped _____ carry all of _____.

6. Tomas had brought his old red wagon from _____ house.

7. When I saw it, _____ wished I had brought _____.

8. Kelly and _____ had to put _____ cans in grocery bags.

9. Those bags were really heavy when _____ were full.

10. When I picked one up, _____ tore and the cans fell out!

11. Jeremy's sister gave _____ a ride around the neighborhood.

12. Walking made Kelly and _____ hungry.

Review

Directions: Write a noun for each possessive pronoun.

1. my _____   5. our _____

2. his _____   6. her _____

3. your _____   7. its _____

4. their _____

Directions: Use these indefinite pronouns in sentences.

8. everyone _____

9. nobody _____

10. something _____

Directions: Use these interrogative pronouns in sentences.

11. who _____

12. what _____

13. which _____

Directions: Use these relative pronouns in sentences.

14. who _____

15. whom _____

16. which _____

17. that _____

Adjectives

An **adjective** describes a noun or pronoun. There are three types of adjectives. They are **positive**, **comparative**, and **superlative**.

Examples:

Positive	Comparative	Superlative
big	bigger	biggest
beautiful	more beautiful	most beautiful
likely	less likely	least likely

Directions: Write the comparative and superlative forms of these adjectives.

Positive	Comparative	Superlative
1. happy	_____	_____
2. kind	_____	_____
3. sad	_____	_____
4. slow	_____	_____
5. low	_____	_____
6. delicious	_____	_____
7. strong	_____	_____
8. straight	_____	_____
9. tall	_____	_____
10. humble	_____	_____
11. hard	_____	_____
12. clear	_____	_____
13. loud	_____	_____
14. clever	_____	_____

Name _____

Writing: Comparatives

Comparatives are forms of adjectives or adverbs used to compare different things. With adjectives, you usually add **er** to the end to make a comparative. If the adjective ends in **y**, drop the **y** and add **ier**.

Examples: **Adjective** **Comparative**
   tall   taller
   easy   easier

With adverbs, you usually add **more** before the word to make a comparative.

Examples: **Adverb**   **Comparative**
   quickly   more quickly
   softly   more softly

Directions: Using the given adjective or adverb, write a sentence comparing the two nouns.

Example: clean   my room   my sister's room
My room is always cleaner than my sister's room.
_____

1. cold   Alaska   Florida

    _____

2. neatly   Maria   her brother

    _____

3. easy   English   math

    _____

4. scary   book   movie

    _____

5. loudly   the drummer   the guitarist

    _____

6. pretty   autumn   winter

    _____

Good and *Bad*

When the adjectives **good** and **bad** are used to compare things, the entire word changes.

Examples:

	Comparative	**Superlative**
good	better	best
bad	worse	worst

Use the comparative form of an adjective to compare two people or objects. Use the superlative form to compare three or more people or objects.

Examples:

This is a **good** day.
Tomorrow will be **better** than today.
My birthday is the **best** day of the year.

This hamburger tastes **bad**.
Does it taste **worse** than the one your brother cooked?
It's the **worst** hamburger I have ever eaten.

Directions: Write the correct words in the blanks to complete these sentences.

_____ 1. Our team just had its bad/worse/worst season ever.

_____ 2. Not everything about our team was bad/worse/worst, though.

_____ 3. Our pitcher was good/better/best than last year.

_____ 4. Our catcher is the good/better/best in the league.

_____ 5. We had good/better/best uniforms, like we do every year.

_____ 6. I think we just needed good/better/best fielders.

_____ 7. Next season we'll do good/better/best than this one.

_____ 8. We can't do bad/worse/worst than we did this year.

_____ 9. I guess everyone has one bad/worse/worst year.

_____ 10. Now that ours is over, we'll get good/better/best.

Demonstrative and Indefinite Adjectives

A **demonstrative adjective** identifies a particular person, place, or thing. **This**, **these**, **that**, and **those** are demonstrative adjectives.

Examples:
> **this** pen
> **that** chair

> **these** earrings
> **those** books

An **indefinite adjective** does not identify a particular person, place, or thing, but rather a group or number. **All**, **any**, **both**, **many**, **another**, **several**, **such**, **some**, **few**, and **more** are indefinite adjectives.

Examples:
> **all** teachers
> **both** girls
> **another** man

> **any** person
> **many** flowers
> **more** marbles

Directions: Use each noun in a sentence with a demonstrative adjective.

1. dishes _____

2. clothes _____

3. cats _____

4. team _____

5. apples _____

6. stereo _____

7. mountain _____

Directions: Use each noun in a sentence with an indefinite adjective.

8. reporters _____

9. decisions _____

10. papers _____

11. pears _____

12. occupations _____

13. friends _____

Interrogative and Possessive Adjectives

An **interrogative adjective** is used when asking a question. The interrogative adjectives are **what** and **which**.

Examples:

> **What** kind of haircut will you get?
> **Which** dog snarled at you?

A **possessive adjective** shows ownership. The possessive adjectives are **our**, **your**, **her**, **his**, **its**, **my**, and **their**.

Examples:

> That is **my** dog.
> He washed **his** jeans.
> **Our** pictures turned out great.

Directions: Write six sentences containing interrogative adjectives and six sentences containing possessive adjectives.

Interrogative Adjectives

1. _____
2. _____
3. _____
4. _____
5. _____
6. _____

Possessive Adjectives

1. _____
2. _____
3. _____
4. _____
5. _____
6. _____

Prepositional Phrases as Adjectives

An adjective can be one word or an entire prepositional phrase.

Examples:
The **new** boy **with red hair**
The **tall** man **in the raincoat**
The **white** house **with green shutters**

Directions: Underline the prepositional phrases used as adjectives.

1. The boy in the blue cap is the captain.

2. The house across the street is 100 years old.

3. Jo and Ty love muffins with nuts.

4. I lost the book with the green cover.

5. Do you know the girl in the front row?

6. I like the pony with the long tail.

7. The dog in that yard is not friendly.

8. The picture in this magazine looks like you.

Directions: Complete these sentences with prepositional phrases used as adjectives.

9. I'd like a sandwich _____.

10. Did you read the book _____?

11. The dog _____ is my favorite.

12. The woman _____ is calling you.

13. I bought a shirt _____.

14. I'm wearing socks _____.

15. I found a box _____.

Adverbs

Adverbs modify verbs. Adverbs tell **when**, **where**, or **how**. Many, but not all adverbs, end in **ly**.

Adverbs of time answer the questions **how often** or **when**.

Examples:
The dog escapes its pen **frequently**.
Smart travelers **eventually** will learn to use travelers' checks.

Adverbs of place answer the question **where**.

Example: The police pushed bystanders **away** from the accident scene.

Adverbs of manner answer the questions **how** or **in what manner**.

Example: He **carefully** replaced the delicate vase.

Directions: Underline the verb in each sentence. Circle the adverb. Write the question each adverb answers on the line.

1. My grandmother walks gingerly to avoid falls.

   _____

2. The mice darted everywhere to escape the cat.

   _____

3. He decisively moved the chess piece.

   _____

4. Our family frequently enjoys a night at the movies.

   _____

5. Later, we will discuss the consequences of your behavior.

   _____

6. The audience glanced up at the balcony where the noise originated.

   _____

7. The bleachers are already built for the concert.

   _____

8. My friend and I study daily for the upcoming exams.

   _____

Adverbs

Like adjectives, adverbs have types of comparison. They are positive, comparative, and superlative.

Examples:

Positive	**Comparative**	**Superlative**
expertly	more expertly	most expertly
soon	sooner	soonest

Directions: Underline the adverb in each sentence. Then, write the type of comparison on the line.

1. The car easily won the race. _____

2. Our class most eagerly awaited the return of our test. _____

3. My ice cream melted more quickly than yours. _____

4. Frances awoke early on the first day of school. _____

5. He knows well the punishment for disobeying his parents. _____

6. There is much work to be done on the stadium project. _____

7. The child played most happily with the building blocks. _____

8. This article appeared more recently than the other. _____

Directions: Write the comparative and superlative forms of these adverbs.

Positive	Comparative	Superlative
9. hard	_____	_____
10. impatiently	_____	_____
11. anxiously	_____	_____
12. suddenly	_____	_____
13. far	_____	_____
14. long	_____	_____

Prepositional Phrases as Adverbs

An adverb can be one word or an entire prepositional phrase.

Examples:
They'll be here **tomorrow**.
They always come **on time**.
Move it **down**.
Put it **under the picture**.
Drive **carefully**.
He drove **with care**.

Directions: Underline the adverb or prepositional phrase used as an adverb in each sentence. In the blank, write **how**, **when**, or **where** to tell what the adverb or prepositional phrase explains.

1. Don't go swimming without a buddy. _____

2. Don't go swimming alone. _____

3. I wish you still lived here. _____

4. I wish you still lived on our street. _____

5. I will eat lunch soon. _____

6. I will eat lunch in a few minutes. _____

7. He will be here in a few hours. _____

8. He will be here later. _____

9. I'm going outside. _____

10. I'm going in the backyard. _____

11. She smiled happily. _____

12. She smiled with happiness. _____

Writing: Adjectives and Adverbs

An **adjective** is a describing word. It describes nouns. Adjectives can tell:
- Which one or what kind — the dog's **floppy** ears, the **lost** child
- How many — **three** wagons, **four** drawers

An **adverb** is also a describing word. It describes verbs, adjectives, or other adverbs. Adverbs can tell:
- How — ran **quickly**, talked **quietly**
- When — finished **prompty**, came **yesterday**
- Where — lived **there**, drove **backward**
- How often — sneezed **twice**, **always** wins

Directions: The adjectives and adverbs are bold in the sentences below. Above each, write **ADJ** for adjective or **ADV** for adverb. Then, draw an arrow to the noun the adjective describes or to the verb the adverb describes.

Example: A girl in a **green** jacket **quickly** released the birds into the sky.

1. An **old** mayor was elected **twice**.

2. He **carefully** put the **tall** screen between our desks.

3. The **new** boy in our class moved **here** from Phoenix.

4. **Today**, our **soccer** team **finally** made its **first** goal.

5. The woman **gently** coaxed the **frightened** kitten out of the tree.

Directions: Use adjectives and adverbs to answer the questions below.

Example: The boy talked. (Which boy? How?)
The nervous boy talked loudly.

1. The plant grew. (Which plant? How?)

_____

2. The birds flew. (How many? What kind? Where?)

_____

Writing: Adjectives and Adverbs

Adjectives and adverbs make sentences more interesting. Often, we can make adverbs from adjectives by adding **ly** to the end.

Examples:

Adjectives	Adverbs
quick	quickly
brief	briefly

If an adjective ends with a **y**, change the **y** to an **i** before adding **ly**.

Examples:

Adjectives	Adverbs
messy	messily
noisy	noisily

Directions: Write a new sentence using each subject and adjective below. Then, add **ly** to the adjective, and write a new sentence using the adverb.

Example: teacher — brief

    a. The teacher gave a **brief** talk about using lab equipment.
    b. The teacher spoke **briefly** about using lab equipment.

1. sister — quiet

    a. _____

    b. _____

2. children — excited

    a. _____

    b. _____

3. players — tired

    a. _____

    b. _____

4. snow — soft

    a. _____

    b. _____

Placement of Adjective and Adverb Phrases

Adjectives and adverbs, including prepositional phrases, should be placed as close as possible to the words they describe to avoid confusion.

Example:
    Confusing: The boy under the pile of leaves looked for the ball.
                (Is the boy or the ball under the pile of leaves?)
    Clear: The boy looked under the pile of leaves for the ball.

Directions: Rewrite each sentence by moving the prepositional phrase closer to the word or words it describes. The first one has been done for you.

1. A bird at the pet store bit me in the mall.
   A bird at the pet store in the mall bit me.

2. The woman was looking for her dog in the large hat.
   _____

3. This yard would be great for a dog with a fence.
   _____

4. The car hit the stop sign with the silver stripe.
   _____

5. My cousin with a big bow gave me a present.
   _____

6. The house was near some woods with a pond.
   _____

7. I'll be back to wash the dishes in a minute.
   _____

8. We like to eat eggs in the morning with toast.
   _____

9. He bought a shirt at the new store with short sleeves.
   _____

10. We live in the house down the street with tall windows.
    _____

Writing: Parts of Speech Story

Directions: Play the following game with a partner. In the story below, some of the words are missing. Without letting your partner see the story, ask him or her to provide a word for each blank. Each word should be a noun, verb, adjective, or adverb, as shown. Then, read the story aloud. It might not make sense, but it will make you laugh!

Last night, as I was _____ through the _____ , a
                              (verb + ing)   (noun)

_____ _____ fell from the ceiling and landed on my
(adjective)   (noun)

head! "Yikes!" I shrieked. I _____ _____ through the
                              (past-tense verb)   (adverb)

_____ , trying to get rid of the thing. Finally, it fell off, and it started
(noun)

_____ around the _____ . I tried to hit it with a _____ ,
(verb + ing)   (noun)   (noun)

but it was too _____ . I _____ managed to _____
                (adjective)   (adverb)   (verb)

it out of the house, where it quickly climbed the nearest _____ .
                                                            (noun)

Name _____

Writing: Parts of Speech

Directions: Write each word from the box in the column that names its part of speech. Some words can be listed in two columns.

VERB
Example: Smile for the the camera.

NOUN
Hanna has a nice **smile**.

code	young	slowly	today	finally	screen
thirsty	praise	loan	broken	decrease	slowly
nearby	twenty	Monday	town	faithful	red
coax	goal	bathe	release	cheat	there

Noun	Verb	Adjective	Adverb
_____	_____	_____	_____
_____	_____	_____	_____
_____	_____	_____	_____
_____	_____	_____	_____
_____	_____	_____	_____
_____	_____	_____	_____

Directions: Write four sentences, using at least three words from the box in each one. Mark each word as a noun (**N**), verb (**V**), adjective (**ADJ**), or adverb (**ADV**).

     ADJ   ADV   N
Example: Twenty people **slowly** walked through the **town**.

_____

_____

_____

_____

Name _____

Conjunctions

A **conjunction** joins words or groups of words in a sentence. The most commonly used conjunctions are **and**, **but**, and **or**.

Examples: My brother **and** I both want to win the trophy.
Tonight, it will rain **or** sleet.
I wanted to go to the party, **but** I got sick.

Directions: Circle the conjunctions.

1. Dolphins and whales are mammals.

2. They must rise to the surface of the water to breathe, or they will die.

3. Dolphins resemble fish, but they are not fish.

4. Sightseeing boats are often entertained by groups of dolphins or whales.

5. Whales appear to effortlessly leap out of the water and execute flips.

6. Both whale and dolphin babies are born alive.

7. The babies are called calves and are born in the water, but they must breathe air within a few minutes of birth.

8. Sometimes an entire pod of whales will help a mother and calf reach the surface to breathe.

9. Scientists and marine biologists have long been intrigued by these ocean animals.

10. Whales and dolphins do not seem to be afraid of humans or boats.

Directions: Write six sentences using conjunctions.

11. _____

12. _____

13. _____

14. _____

15. _____

16. _____

Writing: Conjunctions

Too many short sentences make writing seem choppy. Short sentences can be combined to make writing flow better. Words used to combine sentences are called **conjunctions**.

Examples: but, before, after, because, when, or, so, and

Directions: Use **or**, **but**, **before**, **after**, **because**, **when**, **and**, or **so** to combine each pair of sentences. The first one has been done for you.

1. I was wearing my winter coat. I started to shiver.

   <u>I was wearing my winter coat, but I started to shiver.</u>

2. Animals all need water. They may perish without it.

   _____

3. The sun came out. The ice began to thaw.

   _____

4. The sun came out. The day was still chilly.

   _____

5. Will the flowers perish? Will they thrive?

   _____

6. The bear came closer. We began to feel threatened.

   _____

7. Winning was a challenge. Our team didn't have much experience.

   _____

8. Winning was a challenge. Our team was up to it.

   _____

Directions: Write three sentences of your own. Use a conjunction in each sentence.

_____

_____

_____

Statements and Questions

A **statement** is a sentence that tells something. It ends with a period (.).

A **question** is a sentence that asks something. It ends with a question mark (?).

Examples:
Statement: Shari is walking to school today.
Question: Is Shari walking to school today?

In some questions, the subject comes between two parts of the verb. In the examples below, the subjects are underlined. The verbs and the rest of the predicates are bold.

Examples:
Is <u>Miguel</u> **coming with us**?
<u>Who</u> **will be there**?
Which one did <u>you</u> **select**?

To find the predicate, turn a question into a statement.

Example: Is Miguel coming with us? Miguel is coming with us.

Directions: Write **S** for statement or **Q** for question. Put a period after the statements and a question mark after the questions.

_____ 1. Today is the day for our field trip

_____ 2. How are we going to get there

_____ 3. The bus will take us

_____ 4. Is there room for everyone

_____ 5. Who forgot to bring a lunch

_____ 6. I'll save you a seat

Directions: Circle the subjects, and underline all parts of the predicates.

7. Do you like field trips?

8. Did you bring your coat?

9. Will it be cold there?

10. Do you see my gloves anywhere?

11. Is anyone sitting with you?

12. Does the bus driver have a map?

13. Are all the roads this bumpy?

Name _____

Statements and Questions

Directions: Write 10 statements and 10 questions.

Statements

1. _____
2. _____
3. _____
4. _____
5. _____
6. _____
7. _____
8. _____
9. _____
10. _____

Questions

1. _____
2. _____
3. _____
4. _____
5. _____
6. _____
7. _____
8. _____
9. _____
10. _____

Commands, Requests, and Exclamations

A **command** is a sentence that orders someone to do something. It ends with a period or an exclamation mark (!).

A **request** is a sentence that asks someone to do something. It ends with a period or a question mark (?).

An **exclamation** is a sentence that shows strong feeling. It ends with an exclamation mark (!).

Examples:
Command: Stay in your seat.
Request: Would you please pass the salt?
Please pass the salt.
Exclamation: Call the police!

In the first and last two sentences in the examples, the subject is not stated. The subject is understood to be **you**.

Directions: Write **C** if the sentence is a command, **R** if it is a request, and **E** if it is an exclamation. Put the correct punctuation at the end of each sentence.

_____ 1. Look both ways before you cross the street

_____ 2. Please go to the store and buy some bread for us

_____ 3. The house is on fire

_____ 4. Would you hand me the glue

_____ 5. Don't step there

_____ 6. Write your name at the top of the page

_____ 7. Please close the door

_____ 8. Would you answer the phone

_____ 9. Watch out

_____ 10. Take one card from each pile

Commands, Requests, and Exclamations

Directions: Write six sentences for each type listed.

Command

1. _____
2. _____
3. _____
4. _____
5. _____
6. _____

Request

1. _____
2. _____
3. _____
4. _____
5. _____
6. _____

Exclamation

1. _____
2. _____
3. _____
4. _____
5. _____
6. _____

Name _____

Writing: Four Kinds of Sentences

There are four kinds of sentences used in writing. Different punctuation is used for different kinds of sentences.

A **statement** tells something. A period is used after statements.

Examples: I jogged five miles yesterday.
We are going to have a spelling test on Friday.

A **question** asks something. A question mark is used after questions.

Examples: What are you wearing to the dance?
Will it ever stop raining?

An **exclamation** shows strong feeling or excitement. An exclamation mark is used after exclamations.

Examples: Boy, am I tired!
What a beautiful painting!

A **command** tells someone to do something. A period or an exclamation mark is used after a command, depending on how strong it is.

Examples: Please hand me that pen. Don't touch the stove!

Directions: Write the correct punctuation mark at the end of each sentence below. Then, write whether the sentence is a statement, question, exclamation, or command.

Example: I didn't have time to finish my homework last night**.** <u>statement</u>

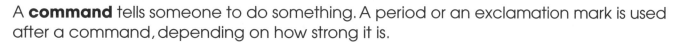

1. Why didn't she come shopping with us _____

2. Somebody call an ambulance _____

3. He's been watching TV all morning _____

4. How did you do on the quiz _____

5. Go sit in the third row _____

6. I have to go to the dentist tomorrow _____

7. I've never been so hungry _____

8. Who tracked mud all over the house _____

9. That restaurant is too expensive _____

Comprehensive Curriculum - **Grade 5**

Compound Subjects/Compound Predicates

A **compound subject** has two or more nouns or pronouns joined by a conjunction. Compound subjects share the same predicate.

Examples:

Suki and Spot walked to the park in the rain.
Cars, buses, and **trucks** splashed water on them.
He and I were glad we had our umbrella.

A **compound predicate** has two or more verbs joined by a conjunction. Compound predicates share the same subject.

Examples:

Suki **went** in the restroom **and wiped** off her shoes.
Chloe **followed** Suki **and waited** for her.

A sentence can have a compound subject and a compound predicate.

Example: Amelia and Maria went to the mall **and shopped** for an hour.

Directions: Circle the compound subjects. Underline the compound predicates.

1. Luke and Kanye went to the store and bought some gum.
2. Police and firefighters worked together and put out the fire.
3. Makayla and Ellie did their homework and checked it twice.
4. In preschool, the boys and girls drew pictures and colored them.

Directions: Write compound subjects to go with these predicates.

5. _____ ate peanut butter sandwiches.
6. _____ left early.
7. _____ don't make good pets.
8. _____ found their way home.
9. _____ are moving to Denver.

Directions: Write compound predicates to go with these subjects.

10. A scary book _____
11. My friend's sister _____
12. The shadow _____
13. The wind _____
14. The runaway car _____

Combining Subjects

Too many short sentences make writing sound choppy. Often, we can combine sentences with different subjects and the same predicate to make one sentence with a compound subject.

Example:
Katrina tried out for the play. Austin tried out for the play.
Compound subject: Katrina and Austin tried out for the play.

When sentences have different subjects and different predicates, we cannot combine them this way. Each subject and predicate must stay together. Two short sentences can be combined with a conjunction.

Examples:
Katrina got a part in the play. Austin will help make scenery.
Katrina got a part in the play, and Austin will help make scenery.

Directions: If a pair of sentences share the same predicate, combine them with compound subjects. If the sentences have different subjects and predicates, combine them using **and**.

1. Rachel read a book about explorers. Eric read the same book about explorers.

_____

2. Rachel really liked the book. Eric agreed with her.

_____

3. Aiko went to the basketball game last night. Dan went to the basketball game, too.

_____

4. Aiko lost her coat. Dan missed his ride home.

_____

5. My uncle planted corn in the garden. My mother planted corn in the garden.

_____

6. Isaac helped with the food drive last week. Amy helped with the food drive, too.

_____

Name _____

Combining Predicates

If short sentences have the same subject and different predicates, we can combine them into one sentence with a compound predicate.

Example:
Andy got up late this morning.
He nearly missed the school bus.
Compound predicate: Andy got up late this morning and nearly missed the school bus.

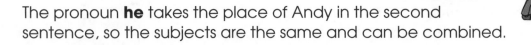

The pronoun **he** takes the place of Andy in the second sentence, so the subjects are the same and can be combined.

When two sentences have different subjects and different predicates, we cannot combine them this way. Two short sentences can be combined with a conjunction.

Examples:
Andy got up late this morning. Pilar woke up early.
Andy got up late this morning, but Pilar woke up early.

Directions: If the pair of sentences share the same subject, combine them with compound predicates. If the sentences have different subjects and predicates, combine them using **and** or **but**.

1. Kyle practiced pitching all winter. Kyle became the pitcher for his team.

_____

2. Kisha studied for her history test for two hours. Angela watched TV.

_____

3. Ethan had an earache. He took medicine four times a day.

_____

4. Nikki found a new hairstyle. Lily didn't like that style.

_____

5. Kirby buys his lunch every day. Sean brings his lunch from home.

_____

Writing: Using Commas Correctly

A **comma** tells a reader where to pause when reading a sentence. Use commas when combining two or more *complete* sentences with a joining word.

Examples: We raked the leaves, and **we put them into bags**.
Brian dressed quickly, but **he still missed the school bus**.

Do not use commas if you are not combining complete sentences.

Examples: We raked the leaves and put them into bags.
Brian dressed quickly but still missed the school bus.

If either part of the sentence does not have both a subject and a verb, do not use a comma.

Directions: Read each sentence below, and decide whether or not it needs a comma. If it does, rewrite the sentence, placing the comma correctly. If it doesn't, write **OK** on the line.

1. The cat stretched lazily and walked out of the room.

   _____

2. I could use the money to buy a new shirt or I could go to the movies.

   _____

3. My sister likes pizza but she doesn't like spaghetti.

   _____

4. Mom mixed the batter and poured it into the pan.

   _____

5. The teacher passed out the tests and she told us to write our names on them.

   _____

6. The car squealed its tires and took off out of the parking lot.

   _____

7. The snow fell heavily and we knew the schools would be closed the next day.

   _____

8. The batter hit the ball and it flew over the fence.

   _____

Run-On Sentences

A **run-on sentence** occurs when two or more sentences are joined together without the correct punctuation. A run-on sentence must be divided into two or more separate sentences.

Example:

Run-on: On Tuesday my family went to the amusement park but unfortunately it rained and we got wet and it took hours for our clothes to dry.

Correct: On Tuesday, my family went to the amusement park. Unfortunately, it rained and we got wet. It took hours for our clothes to dry.

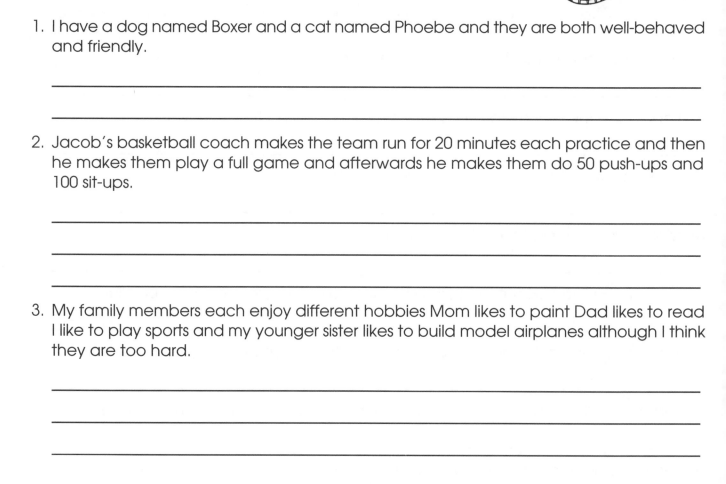

Directions: Rewrite these run-on sentences correctly.

1. I have a dog named Boxer and a cat named Phoebe and they are both well-behaved and friendly.

   _____

   _____

2. Jacob's basketball coach makes the team run for 20 minutes each practice and then he makes them play a full game and afterwards he makes them do 50 push-ups and 100 sit-ups.

   _____

   _____

   _____

3. My family members each enjoy different hobbies Mom likes to paint Dad likes to read I like to play sports and my younger sister likes to build model airplanes although I think they are too hard.

   _____

   _____

   _____

   _____

Commas

Commas are used to separate items in a series.

Example:
   The fruit bowl contains oranges, peaches, pears, and apples.

Commas are also used to separate geographical names and dates.

Examples:
   Today's date is January 13, 2015.
   My grandfather lives in Tallahassee, Florida.
   I would like to visit Paris, France.

Directions: Place commas where needed in these sentences.

1. I was born on September 21 2006.
2. Mateo's favorite sports include basketball football hockey and soccer.
3. The ship will sail on November 16 2016.
4. My family and I vacationed in Salt Lake City Utah.
5. I like to plant beans beets corn and radishes in my garden.
6. Xander's party will be held in Youngstown Ohio.
7. Periods commas colons and exclamation marks are types of punctuation.
8. Cardinals juncos blue jays finches and sparrows frequent our birdfeeder.
9. My grandfather graduated from high school on June 4 1962.
10. The race will take place in Burlington Vermont.

Directions: Write a sentence using commas to separate words in a series.

11. _____

Directions: Write a sentence using commas to separate geographical names.

12. _____

Directions: Write a sentence using commas to separate dates.

13. _____

Commas

Commas are used to separate a noun or pronoun in a direct address from the rest of the sentence. A noun or pronoun in a **direct address** is one that names or refers to the person addressed.

Examples:
> **John,** this room is a mess!
> This room**, John,** is a disgrace!
> Your room needs to be more organized**, John**.

Commas are used to separate an appositive from the rest of the sentence. An **appositive** is a word or words that give the reader more information about a previous noun or pronoun.

Examples:
> My teacher, **Ms. Wright**, gave us a test.
> Thomas Edison, **the inventor of the lightbulb**, was an interesting man.

Directions: Place commas where needed in these sentences. Then, write **appositive** or **direct address** on the line to explain why the commas were used.

1. Li do you know the answer?_____

2. Jackson the local football hero led the parade through town._____

3. Cancun a Mexican city is a favorite vacation destination._____

4. Please help me move the chair Isobel._____

5. My great-grandfather an octogenarian has witnessed many events._____

6. The president of the company Madison Fagan addressed his workers._____

7. My favorite book *Anne of Green Gables* is a joy to read._____

8. Your painting Andre shows great talent._____

Combining Sentences

When the subjects are the same, sentences can be combined by using appositives.

Examples:

Tony likes to play basketball. Tony is my neighbor.
Tony, **my neighbor**, likes to play basketball.

Ms. Herman was sick today. Ms. Herman is our math teacher.
Ms. Herman, **our math teacher**, was sick today.

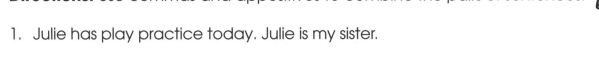

Appositives are set off from the rest of the sentence with commas.

Directions: Use commas and appositives to combine the pairs of sentences.

1. Julie has play practice today. Julie is my sister.

   _____

2. Greg fixed my bicycle. Greg is my cousin.

   _____

3. Mr. Cruz told us where to meet. Mr. Cruz is our coach.

   _____

4. Tiffany is moving to Detroit. Tiffany is my neighbor.

   _____

5. Kyle has the flu. Kyle is my brother.

   _____

6. My favorite football team is playing tonight. Houston is my favorite team.

   _____

7. Bonnie Pryor will be at our school next week. Bonnie Pryor is a famous author.

   _____

8. Our neighborhood is having a garage sale. Our neighborhood is the North End.

   _____

Combining Sentences

Directions: Combine these sentences. Some of them can be combined using commas and appositives. Some can be combined using compound subjects or predicates. Others can be combined using conjunctions.

1. Alana enjoyed playing on the beach. Ty did not like the sand.

_____

2. Jelani studied hard for the math test. Kim studied hard for the math test.

_____

3. Ryan got sick. Ryan had to visit his family doctor.

_____

4. Jeni is my study partner. Jeni is always running late for class.

_____

5. Drake scored the game-winning touchdown. Drake is the team's star quarterback.

_____

6. We were ready to leave. The car wouldn't start.

_____

7. Vanessa ran outside. Vanessa rode her bicycle to the park.

_____

8. The fierce wind ruined our family picnic. The pouring rain ruined our family picnic.

_____

9. Mrs. Raposa handed me a new book about dinosaurs. Mrs. Raposa is the school librarian.

_____

10. School was out for the summer. Amira was ready for new adventures.

_____

Punctuation

Directions: Add commas where needed.
Put the correct punctuation at the end
of each sentence.

1. My friend Jamie loves to snowboard

2. Winter sports such as hockey skiing and skating are fun

3. Oh what a lovely view

4. The map shows the continents of Asia Africa Australia and Antarctica

5. My mother a ballet dancer will perform tonight

6. What will you do tomorrow

7. When will the plane arrive at the airport

8. Jason do you know what time it is

9. Friends of ours the Watsons are coming for dinner

10. Margo look out for that falling rock

11. The young child sat reading a book

12. Who wrote this letter

13. My sister Jill is very neat

14. The trampoline is in our backyard

15. We will have chicken peas rice and salad for dinner

16. That dog a Saint Bernard looks dangerous

Quotation Marks

When a person's exact words are used in a sentence, **quotation marks** (" ") are used to identify those words. Commas are used to set off the quotation from the rest of the sentence. End punctuation is placed inside the final quotation mark.

Examples:

"When are we leaving?" Joe asked.
Jada shouted, **"Go, team!"**

When a sentence is interrupted by words that are not part of the quotation (he said, she answered, etc.), they are not included in the quotation marks. Note how commas are used in the next example.

Example: **"**I am sorry,**"** the man announced, **"**for my rude behavior.**"**

Directions: Place quotation marks, commas, and other punctuation where needed in the sentences below.

1. Watch out yelled Dad.
2. Angela said I don't know how you can eat Brussels sprouts, Ted
3. Put on your coats said Mom. We'll be leaving in 10 minutes
4. Did you hear the assignment asked Salima.
5. Dominic shouted This game is driving me up the wall
6. After examining our dog, the veterinarian said He looks healthy and strong
7. The toddlers both wailed We want a snack
8. The judge announced to the swimmers Take your places
9. Upon receiving the award, the actor said I'd like to thank my friends and family
10. These are my favorite granola bars said Becca
11. This test is too hard moaned the class.
12. When their relay team came in first place, the runners shouted, Hooray
13. Where shall we go on vacation this year Dad asked.
14. As we walked past the machinery, the noise was deafening. Cover your ears said Mom.
15. Fire yelled the chef as his pan ignited.
16. I love basketball my little brother stated.

Capitalization/Punctuation

Directions: Rewrite the paragraphs below, adding punctuation where it is needed. Capitalize the first word of each sentence and all other words that should be capitalized.

my mom is a geologist so she has the opportunity to travel often for work last year she visited england scotland and ireland dad says that he hopes the whole family can come when she goes to the netherlands next year would you like to have a job where you travel or are you a homebody

_____

_____

_____

_____

my cousin jeff is starting college this fall he wants to be a medical doctor, so he's going to central university the mayor of our town went there mayor stevens told jeff all about the university our town is so small that everyone knows what everyone else is doing is your town like that

_____

_____

_____

_____

my grandparents took a long vacation last year grandma really likes to go to the atlantic ocean and watch the dolphins my grandfather likes to fish in the ocean my aunt went with them last summer they all had a party on the fourth of july

_____

_____

_____

_____

Capitalization

Directions: Write **C** if capital letters are used correctly or **X** if they are used incorrectly.

_____ 1. Who will win the election for Mayor in November?

_____ 2. Tom Johnson used to be a police officer.

_____ 3. He announced on monday that he wants to be mayor.

_____ 4. My father said he would vote for Tom.

_____ 5. Mom and my sister Mia haven't decided yet.

_____ 6. They will vote at our school.

_____ 7. Every Fall and Spring they put up voting booths there.

_____ 8. I hope the new mayor will do something about our river.

_____ 9. That River is full of chemicals.

_____ 10. I'm glad our water doesn't come from Raven River.

_____ 11. In late Summer, the river actually stinks.

_____ 12. Is every river in our State so dirty?

_____ 13. Scientists check the water every so often.

_____ 14. Some professors from the college even examined it.

_____ 15. That is getting to be a very educated River!

★ ★ ★ Vote ★ ★ ★
TOM JOHNSON
for Mayor

Directions: Write sentences that include:

16. A person's title that should be capitalized.

_____

17. The name of a place that should be capitalized.

_____

18. The name of a time (day, month, holiday) that should be capitalized.

_____

Who Clauses

A **clause** is a group of words with a subject and a verb. When the subject of two sentences is the same person or people, the sentences can sometimes be combined with a "who" clause.

Examples:

Layla likes animals. Layla feeds the squirrels.
Layla, **who likes animals**, feeds the squirrels.

A "who" clause is set off from the rest of the sentence with commas.

Directions: Combine the pairs of sentences using "who" clauses.

1. Teddy was late to school. Teddy was sorry later.

   _____

2. Our principal is retiring. Our principal will be 65 this year.

   _____

3. Michael won the contest. Michael will receive an award.

   _____

4. Aisha lives next door. Aisha has three cats.

   _____

5. Devon drew that picture. Devon takes art lessons.

   _____

6. Marta was elected class president. Marta gave a speech.

   _____

7. Amy broke her arm. Amy has to wear a cast for six weeks.

   _____

8. Dr. Chandra fixed my tooth. He said it would feel better soon.

   _____

Which Clauses

When the subject of two sentences is the same thing or things, the sentences can sometimes be combined with a "which" clause.

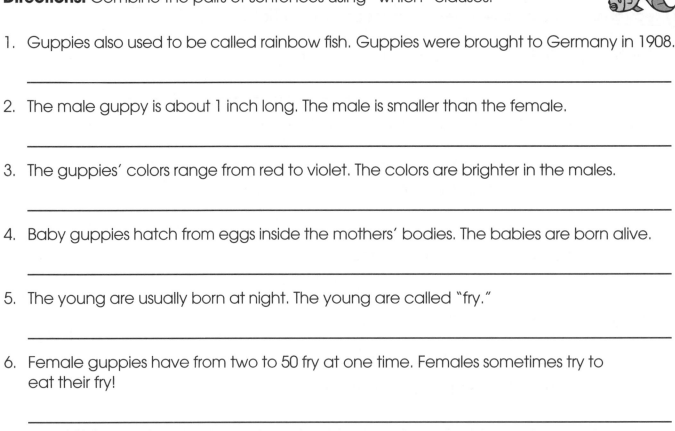

Examples:

The guppy was first called "the millions fish." The guppy was later named after Reverend Robert Guppy in 1866. The guppy, **which was first called "the millions fish,"** was later named after Reverend Robert Guppy in 1866.

A "which" clause is set off from the rest of the sentence with commas.

Directions: Combine the pairs of sentences using "which" clauses.

1. Guppies also used to be called rainbow fish. Guppies were brought to Germany in 1908.

   _____

2. The male guppy is about 1 inch long. The male is smaller than the female.

   _____

3. The guppies' colors range from red to violet. The colors are brighter in the males.

   _____

4. Baby guppies hatch from eggs inside the mothers' bodies. The babies are born alive.

   _____

5. The young are usually born at night. The young are called "fry."

   _____

6. Female guppies have from two to 50 fry at one time. Females sometimes try to eat their fry!

   _____

7. These fish have been studied by scientists. The fish actually like dirty water.

   _____

8. Wild guppies eat mosquito eggs. Wild guppies help control the mosquito population.

   _____

Who and Which Clauses

Directions: Combine the pairs of sentences using "who" or "which" clauses.

1. Bullfrogs are rarely found out of the water. They live near ponds and streams.

   _____

   _____

2. These frogs grow to be about 8 inches long. These frogs can jump 3 feet.

   _____

   _____

3. Mark Twain was a famous writer. He wrote a story about a frog-jumping contest.

   _____

   _____

4. This story took place in California. This story started an annual frog-jumping contest there.

   _____

   _____

5. The contest has rules and judges. The contest allows each frog to make three leaps.

   _____

   _____

6. The judges watch carefully. They measure each frog's leap.

   _____

   _____

7. Bullfrogs eat many insects. Bullfrogs also eat small snakes.

   _____

   _____

8. Scientists study what frogs eat. Scientists know bullfrogs can catch birds.

   _____

   _____

That Clauses

When the subject of two sentences is the same thing or things, the sentences can sometimes be combined with a "that" clause. Use **that** instead of **which** when the clause is very important in the sentence.

Examples:

The store is near our house. The store was closed.
The store **that is near our house** was closed.

The words **that is near our house** are very important in the combined sentence. They tell the reader which store was closed. A "that" clause is not set off from the rest of the sentence with commas.

Examples:

Pete's store is near our house. Pete's store was closed.
Pete's store, which is near our house, was closed.

The words **which is near our house** are not important to the meaning of the combined sentence. The words **Pete's store** already told us which store was closed.

Directions: Combine the pairs of sentences using "that" clauses.

1. The dog lives next door. The dog chased me.

   _____

2. The bus was taking us to the game. The bus had a flat tire.

   _____

3. The fence is around the school. The fence is painted yellow.

   _____

4. The notebook had my homework in it. The notebook is lost.

   _____

5. A letter came today. The letter was from Mary.

   _____

6. The lamp was fixed yesterday. The lamp doesn't work today.

   _____

7. The lake is by our cabin. The lake is filled with fish.

   _____

That and *Which* Clauses

Directions: Combine the pairs of sentences using either a "that" or a "which" clause.

1. The TV show was on at 8:00 last night. The TV show was funny.

_____

2. *The Snappy Show* was on at 8:00 last night. *The Snappy Show* was funny.

_____

3. The Main Bank is on the corner. The Main Bank is closed today.

_____

4. The bank is on the corner. The bank is closed today.

_____

5. The bus takes Dad to work. The bus broke down.

_____

6. The Broad Street bus takes Dad to work. The Broad Street bus broke down.

_____

Combining Sentences

Not every pair of sentences can be combined with "who,"
"which," or "that" clauses. These sentences can be
combined in other ways, either with a conjunction
or by renaming the subject.

Examples:

Tim couldn't go to sleep. Todd was sleeping soundly.
Tim couldn't go to sleep, **but** Todd was sleeping soundly.

The zoo keeper fed the baby ape. A crowd gathered to watch.
When the zoo keeper fed the baby ape, a crowd gathered to watch.

Directions: Combine each pair of sentences using "who," "which," or "that" clauses,
by using a conjunction, or by renaming the subject.

1. The box slipped off the truck. The box was filled with bottles.

    _____

2. Carolyn is our scout leader. Carolyn taught us a new game.

    _____

3. The girl is 8 years old. The girl called the emergency number when her
    grandmother fell.

    _____

4. The meatloaf is ready to eat. The salad isn't made yet.

    _____

5. The rain poured down. The rain canceled our picnic.

    _____

6. The sixth-grade class went on a field trip. The school was much quieter.

    _____

Who's and Whose

Who's is a contraction for **who is**.

Whose is a possessive pronoun.

Examples:
    Who's going to come?
    Whose shirt is this?

To know which word to use, substitute the words "who is." If the sentence makes sense, use **who's**.

Directions: Write the correct words to complete these sentences.

_____ 1. Do you know who's/whose invited to the party?

_____ 2. I don't even know who's/whose house it will be at.

_____ 3. Who's/Whose towel is on the floor?

_____ 4. Who's/Whose going to drive us?

_____ 5. Who's/Whose ice cream is melting?

_____ 6. I'm the person who's/whose gloves are lost.

_____ 7. Who's/Whose in your group?

_____ 8. Who's/Whose group is first?

_____ 9. Can you tell who's/whose at the door?

_____ 10. Who's/Whose friend are you?

_____ 11. Who's/Whose cooking tonight?

_____ 12. Who's/Whose cooking do you like best?

Their, There, and *They're*

Their is a possessive pronoun meaning "belonging to them."

There is an adverb that indicates place.

They're is a contraction for **they are**.

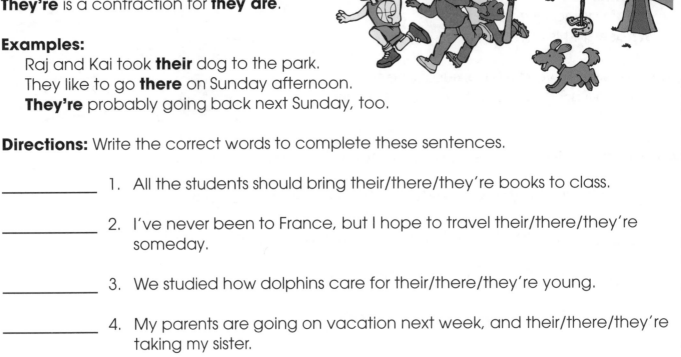

Examples:
Raj and Kai took **their** dog to the park.
They like to go **there** on Sunday afternoon.
They're probably going back next Sunday, too.

Directions: Write the correct words to complete these sentences.

_____ 1. All the students should bring their/there/they're books to class.

_____ 2. I've never been to France, but I hope to travel their/there/they're someday.

_____ 3. We studied how dolphins care for their/there/they're young.

_____ 4. My parents are going on vacation next week, and their/there/they're taking my sister.

_____ 5. Their/There/They're was a lot of food at the party.

_____ 6. My favorite baseball team lost their/there/they're star pitcher this year.

_____ 7. Those peaches look good, but their/there/they're not ripe yet.

_____ 8. The book is right their/there/they're on the table.

Teach and *Learn*

Teach is a verb meaning "to explain something." **Teach** is an irregular verb. Its past tense is **taught**.

Learn is a verb meaning "to gain information."

Examples:
Carrie will **teach** me how to play the piano.
Yesterday, she **taught** me "Chopsticks."

I will **learn** a new song every week.
Yesterday, I **learned** to play "Chopsticks."

Directions: Write the correct words to complete these sentences.

_____ 1. My brother taught/learned me how to ice skate.

_____ 2. With his help, I taught/learned in three days.

_____ 3. First, I tried to teach/learn skating from a book.

_____ 4. I couldn't teach/learn that way.

_____ 5. You have to try it before you can really teach/learn how to do it.

_____ 6. Now, I'm going to teach/learn my cousin.

_____ 7. My cousin already taught/learned how to roller skate.

_____ 8. I shouldn't have any trouble teaching/learning her how to ice skate.

_____ 9. Who taught/learned you how to skate?

_____ 10. My brother taught/learned Mom how to skate, too.

_____ 11. My mother took longer to teach/learn it than I did.

_____ 12. Who will he teach/learn next?

_____ 13. Do you know anyone who wants to teach/learn
how to ice skate?

_____ 14. My brother will teach/learn you for free.

_____ 15. You should teach/learn how to ice skate in the wintertime, though.
The ice is a little thin in the summer!

Lie and *Lay*

Lie is a verb meaning "to rest." **Lie** is an intransitive verb that doesn't need a direct object.

Lay is a verb meaning "to place or put something down." **Lay** is a transitive verb that requires a direct object.

Examples:
    Lie here for a while. (**Lie** has no direct object; **here** is an adverb.)
    Lay the book here. (**Lay** has a direct object: **book**.)

Lie and **lay** are especially tricky because they are both irregular verbs. Notice the past tense of **lie** is **lay**!

Present tense	ing form	Past tense	Past participle
lie	lying	lay	has/have/had lain
lay	laying	laid	has/have/had laid

Examples:
    I **lie** here today.
    I **lay** here yesterday.
    I **was lying** there for three hours.

    I **lay** the baby in her bed.
    I will be **laying** her down in a minute.
    I **laid** her in her bed last night, too.

Directions: Write the correct words to complete these sentences.

_____ 1. Shelly lies/lays a blanket on the grass.

_____ 2. Then, she lies/lays down in the sun.

_____ 3. Her dog lies/lays there with her.

_____ 4. Yesterday, Shelly lay/laid in the sun for an hour.

_____ 5. The workers are lying/laying bricks for a house.

_____ 6. Yesterday, they lay/laid a ton of them.

_____ 7. They lie/lay one brick on top of the other.

_____ 8. The bricks just lie/lay in a pile until the workers are ready for them.

_____ 9. At lunchtime, some workers lie/lay down for a nap.

_____ 10. Would you like to lie/lay bricks?

_____ 11. Last year, my uncle lay/laid bricks for his new house.

_____ 12. He was so tired every day that he lay/laid down as soon as he finished.

Rise and *Raise*

Rise is a verb meaning "to get up" or "to go up." **Rise** is an intransitive verb that doesn't need a direct object.

Raise is a verb meaning "to lift" or "to grow." **Raise** is a transitive verb that requires a direct object.

Examples:
The curtain **rises**.
The girl **raises** her hand.

Raise is a regular verb. **Rise** is irregular.

Present tense	Past tense	Past participle
rise	rose	has/have/had risen
raise	raised	has/have/had raised

Examples:
The sun **rose** this morning.
The boy **raised** the window higher.

Directions: Write the correct words to complete these sentences.

_____ 1. This bread dough rises/raises in an hour.

_____ 2. The landlord will rise/raise the rent.

_____ 3. The balloon rose/raised into the sky.

_____ 4. My sister rose/raised the seat on my bike.

_____ 5. The baby rose/raised the spoon to his mouth.

_____ 6. The eagle rose/raised out of sight.

_____ 7. The farmer rises/raises pigs.

_____ 8. The scouts rose/raised the flag.

_____ 9. When the fog rose/raised, we could see better.

_____ 10. The price of gasoline rose/raised again.

_____ 11. The king rose/raised the glass to his lips.

_____ 12. Rise/Raise the picture on that wall higher.

Name _____

All Right, All Ready, and Already

All right means "well enough" or "very well." Sometimes, you may see **all right** spelled **alright**. This is not the preferred spelling and is considered very informal.

Example:
    Correct: We'll be all right when the rain stops.
    Incorrect: Are you feeling **alright** today?

All ready is an adjective meaning "completely ready."

Already is an adverb meaning "before this time" or "by this time."

Examples:
    Are you **all ready** to go?
    He was **already** there when I arrived.

Directions: Write the correct words to complete these sentences.

_____ 1. The children are all ready/already for the picnic.

_____ 2. Ted was all ready/already late for the show.

_____ 3. Is your sister going to be all right/alright?

_____ 4. I was all ready/already tired before the race began.

_____ 5. Nadia has all ready/already left for the dance.

_____ 6. Will you be all right/alright by yourself?

_____ 7. We are all ready/already for our talent show.

_____ 8. I all ready/already read that book.

_____ 9. I want to be all ready/already when they get here.

_____ 10. Dad was sick, but he's all right/alright now.

_____ 11. The dinner is all ready/already to eat.

_____ 12. Brooklyn all ready/already wrote her report.

Accept and Except / Affect and Effect

Accept is a verb meaning "to receive."

Except can be used as a verb or a preposition. As a verb, it means "to leave out." As a preposition, it means "excluding."

Examples:

I will **accept** the invitation to the dinner dance.
No one **except** Robert will receive an award.

Affect is a verb meaning "to impress one's thoughts or feelings."

Effect can be used as a noun or a verb. As a verb, it means "to accomplish." As a noun, it means "the result of an action."

Examples:

Her attitude may **affect** her performance on the test.
He **effected** several changes during his first few months as governor.
The **effects** of the storm will be felt for some time.

Directions: Write the correct words to complete these sentences.

_____ 1. My partner and I will work to affect/effect attitudes toward rainforest renewal.

_____ 2. He courageously accepted/excepted the challenge of a chess duel.

_____ 3. The affect/effect of the strike by truck drivers was felt nationwide.

_____ 4. The new CEO of the company sought to affect/effect a change in company morale.

_____ 5. Everyone accept/except Zola will attend the game.

_____ 6. My grandmother will never accept/except the fact that she can no longer drive.

_____ 7. Accept/Except for this chewing incident, my puppy has been well-behaved.

_____ 8. The sights of the war affected/effected soldiers for the rest of their lives.

_____ 9. What affect/effect will the drop in the stock market have on the average person?

_____ 10. The affect/effect of the wind was devastating.

_____ 11. How will cheating on a test affect/effect your reputation?

_____ 12. I would like to go to the park on any day accept/except Monday.

Review

Directions: Use each of these words correctly in a sentence of your own.

1. good _____

2. bad _____

3. who's _____

4. whose _____

5. their _____

6. there _____

7. they're _____

8. teach _____

9. learn _____

10. lie _____

11. lay _____

12. rise _____

13. raise _____

14. all ready _____

15. already _____

16. all right _____

17. accept _____

18. except _____

19. affect _____

20. effect _____

Writing: Topic Sentences

The topic sentence in a paragraph usually comes first. Sometimes, however, the topic sentence can come at the end or even in the middle of a paragraph. When looking for the topic sentence, try to find the one that tells the main idea of a paragraph.

Directions: Read the following paragraphs, and underline the topic sentence in each.

The maple tree sheds its leaves every year. The oak and elm trees shed their leaves, too. Every autumn, the leaves on these trees begin changing color. Then, as the leaves gradually begin to die, they fall from the trees. Trees that shed their leaves annually are called deciduous trees.

When our family goes skiing, my brother enjoys the thrill of going down the steepest hill as fast as he can. Mom and Dad like to ski because it gets them out of the house and into the fresh air. I enjoy looking at the trees and birds and the sun shining on the snow. There is something about skiing that appeals to everyone in my family. Even the dog came along on our last skiing trip!

If you are outdoors at night and there is traffic around, you should always wear bright clothing so that cars can see you. White is a good color to wear at night. If you are riding a bicycle, be sure it has plenty of reflectors, and if possible, headlamps as well. Be especially careful when crossing the street, because sometimes drivers cannot see you in the glare of their headlights. Being outdoors at night can be dangerous, and it is best to be prepared!

Writing: Supporting Sentences

A **paragraph** is a group of sentences that tell about one topic. The **topic sentence** in a paragraph usually comes first and tells the main idea of the paragraph. **Supporting sentences** follow the topic sentence and provide details about the topic.

Directions: Write at least three supporting sentences for each topic sentence below.

Example: Topic Sentence: Carly had an accident on her bike.
Supporting Sentences: She was on her way to the store to buy some bread. A car came weaving down the road and scared her. She rode her bike off the road so the car wouldn't hit her. Now, her knee is scraped, but she's all right.

1. I've been thinking of ways I could make some more money after school.

_____

_____

_____

2. In my opinion, cats (dogs, fish, etc.) make the best pets.

_____

_____

_____

3. My life would be better if I had a(n) (younger sister, younger brother, older sister, older brother).

_____

_____

_____

4. I'd like to live next door to a (swimming pool, library, movie theater, etc.).

_____

_____

_____

Writing: Building Paragraphs

Directions: Read the groups of topic sentences and questions below. On another sheet of paper, write supporting sentences that answer the questions. Use your imagination! Write the supporting sentences in order, and copy them on this page after the topic sentence.

1. On her way home from school, Mariko made a difficult decision.

   Questions: What was Mariko's decision? Why did she decide that? Why was the decision hard to make?

   _____

   _____

   _____

   _____

2. Suddenly, Conrad thought of a way to clear up all the confusion.

   Questions: What was the confusion about? How was Conrad involved in it? What did he do to clear it up?

   _____

   _____

   _____

   _____

3. Bethany used to feel awkward at the school social activities.

   Questions: Why did Bethany feel awkward before? How does she feel now? What happened to change the way she feels?

   _____

   _____

   _____

   _____

Writing: Sequencing

When writing paragraphs, it is important to write events in the correct order. Think about what happens first, next, later, and last.

Directions: The following sentences tell about Chandra's day, but they are all mixed up. Read the sentences, and number them in the order in which they happened.

_____ She arrived at school and went to her locker to get her books.

_____ After dinner, she did the dishes, and then read for a while.

_____ Chandra brushed her teeth and put on her pajamas.

_____ She rode the bus home, and then she ate a snack.

_____ She ate breakfast and went out to wait for the bus.

_____ Chandra woke up and picked out her clothes for school.

_____ She met her friend Sarah on the way to the cafeteria.

_____ She worked on homework and watched TV until her mom called her for dinner.

Directions: Write a short paragraph about what you did today. Use words like **first**, **next**, **then**, **later**, and **finally** to indicate the order in which you did things.

_____

_____

_____

_____

_____

_____

_____

_____

_____

_____

_____

Sequencing

Sequencing means to place events in order from beginning to end or first to last.

Example:
   To send a letter, you must:
   Get paper, pencil or pen, an envelope, and a stamp.
   Write the letter.
   Fold the letter, and put it in the envelope.
   Address the envelope correctly.
   Put a stamp on the envelope.
   Put the envelope in the mailbox or take
      it to the post office.

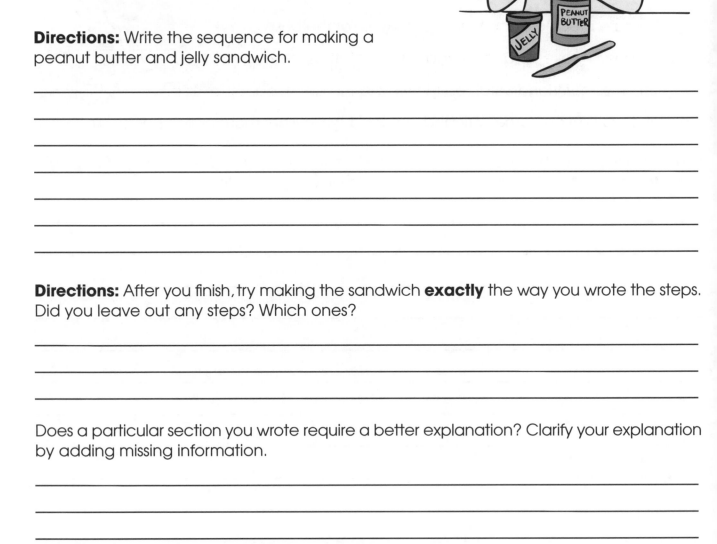

Directions: Write the sequence for making a peanut butter and jelly sandwich.

_____

_____

_____

_____

_____

_____

_____

Directions: After you finish, try making the sandwich **exactly** the way you wrote the steps. Did you leave out any steps? Which ones?

_____

_____

_____

Does a particular section you wrote require a better explanation? Clarify your explanation by adding missing information.

_____

_____

_____

Author's Purpose

Authors write to fulfill one of three purposes: to **inform**, to **entertain**, or to **persuade**.

Authors who write to inform are providing facts for the reader in an informational context.
Examples: Encyclopedia entries and educational websites

Authors who write to entertain are hoping to provide enjoyment for the reader.
Examples: Funny stories and comics

Authors who write to persuade are trying to convince the reader to believe what they believe.
Examples: Editorials and opinion essays

Directions: Read each paragraph. Write **inform**, **entertain**, or **persuade** on the line to show the author's purpose.

1. The whooping crane is a migratory bird. At one time, this endangered bird was almost extinct. These large white cranes are characterized by red faces and trumpeting calls. Through protection of both the birds and their habitats, the whooping crane is slowly increasing in number.

   _____

2. It is extremely important that all citizens place bird feeders in their yards and keep them full for the winter. Birds that spend the winter in this area are in danger of starving due to lack of food. It is every citizen's responsibility to ensure the survival of the birds.

   _____

3. Imagine being able to hibernate like a bear each winter! Wouldn't it be great to eat to your heart's content all fall? Then, sometime in late November, inform your teacher that you will not be attending school for the next few months because you'll be resting and living off your fat? Now, that would be the life!

   _____

4. Bears, woodchucks, and chipmunks are not the only animals that hibernate. The queen bumblebee also hibernates in winter. All the other bees die before winter arrives. The queen hibernates under leaves in a small hole. She is cold-blooded and therefore is able to survive slightly frozen.

   _____

Author's Purpose

Directions: Write a paragraph of your own for each purpose. The paragraph can be about any topic.

1. to inform

   _____

   _____

   _____

   _____

2. to persuade

   _____

   _____

   _____

   _____

3. to entertain

   _____

   _____

   _____

   _____

Directions: Reread your paragraphs. Do they make sense? Check for grammar, spelling, and punctuation errors, and make corrections where needed.

Descriptive Sentences

Descriptive sentences give readers a vivid image and enable them to imagine a scene clearly.

Example:
> **Nondescriptive sentence:** There were grapes in the bowl.
> **Descriptive sentence:** The plump purple grapes in the bowl looked tantalizing.

Directions: Rewrite these sentences using descriptive language.

1. The dog walked in its pen.

   _____

2. The turkey was almost done.

   _____

3. I became upset when my computer wouldn't work.

   _____

4. Jared and Michelle went to the ice-cream parlor.

   _____

5. The telephone kept ringing.

   _____

6. I wrote a story.

   _____

7. The movie was excellent.

   _____

8. Dominique was upset that her friend was ill.

   _____

Writing: Descriptive Details

A writer creates pictures in a reader's mind by telling him/her how something looks, sounds, feels, smells, or tastes. For example, compare **A** and **B** below. Notice how the description in **B** makes you imagine how the heavy door and the cobweb would feel and how the broken glass would look and sound as someone walked on it.

A. I walked into the house.

B. I pushed open the heavy wooden door of the old house. A cobweb brushed my face, and broken glass, sparkling like ice, crackled under my feet.

Directions: Write one or two sentences about each topic below. Add details that will help your reader see, hear, feel, smell, or taste what you are describing.

1. Your favorite dinner cooking

_____

_____

2. Old furniture

_____

_____

3. Wind blowing in the trees

_____

_____

4. A tired stranger

_____

_____

5. Wearing wet clothes

_____

_____

6. A strange noise somewhere in the house

_____

_____

Writing: Descriptive Details

Directions: For each topic sentence below, write three or four supporting sentences. Include details about how things look, sound, smell, taste, or feel. Don't forget to use adjectives, adverbs, similes, and metaphors.

Example: After my dog had his bath, I couldn't believe how much better he looked. His fur, which used to be all matted and dirty, was as clean as new snow. He still felt a little damp when I scratched behind his ears. The smell from rolling in our garbage was gone, too. The shampoo made him smell like apples.

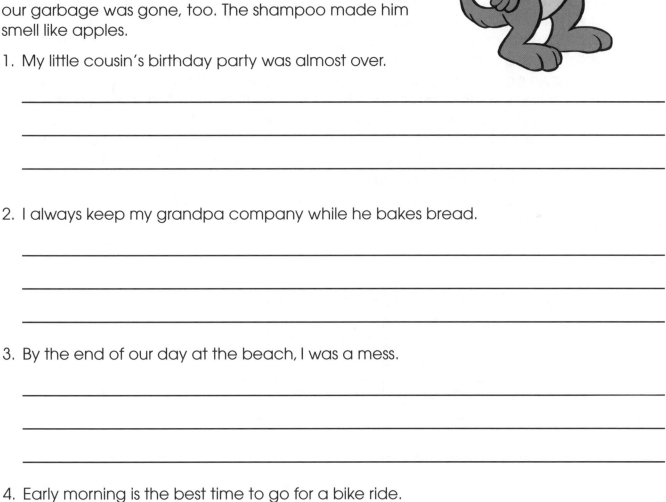

1. My little cousin's birthday party was almost over.

   _____

   _____

   _____

2. I always keep my grandpa company while he bakes bread.

   _____

   _____

   _____

3. By the end of our day at the beach, I was a mess.

   _____

   _____

   _____

4. Early morning is the best time to go for a bike ride.

   _____

   _____

   _____

Personal Narratives

A **personal narrative** tells about a person's own experiences.

Directions: Read the example of a personal narrative. Write your answers in complete sentences.

My Worst Year

When I look back on that year, I can hardly believe that one person could have such terrible luck for a whole year. But then again, I should have realized that if things could begin to go wrong in January, it didn't bode well for the rest of the year.

It was the night of January 26. One of my best friends was celebrating her birthday at the local roller-skating rink, and I had been invited. The evening began well enough with pizza and laughs. I admit I have never been an excellent roller skater, but I could hold my own. After a few minutes of skating, I decided to exit the rink to get a drink of water.

Unfortunately, I did not notice the trailing ribbons of carpet that wrapped around the wheel of my skate, yanking my left leg from under me. My leg was broken. It wasn't just broken in one place but in four places! At the hospital, the doctor set the bone and put a cast on my leg. Three months later, I felt like a new person.

Sadly, the happiness wasn't meant to last. Five short months after the final cast was removed, I fell and broke the same leg again. Not only did it rebreak, but it broke in the same four places! We found out later that it hadn't healed correctly. Three months later, it was early December and the end of a year I did not wish to repeat.

1. List the sequence of events in this personal narrative.

   _____

   _____

   _____

   _____

2. From reading the personal narrative, what do you think were the author's feelings toward the events that occurred?

   _____

   _____

Personal Narratives

A **narrative** is a spoken or written account of an actual event. A **personal narrative** tells about your own experience. It can be written about any event in your life and may be serious or comical.

When writing a personal narrative, remember to use correct sentence structure and punctuation. Include important dates, sights, sounds, smells, tastes, and feelings to give your reader a clear picture of the event.

Directions: Write a personal narrative about an event in your life that was funny.

_____

_____

_____

_____

_____

_____

_____

_____

_____

_____

_____

_____

_____

_____

_____

_____

Complete the Story

Directions: Read the beginning of this story. Then, complete the story with your own ideas.

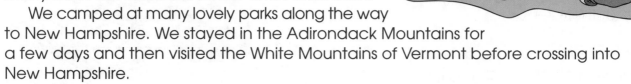

It was a beautiful summer day in June when my family and I set off on vacation. We were headed for Portsmouth, New Hampshire. There, we planned to go on a whale-watching ship and perhaps spy a humpback whale or two. However, there were many miles between our home and Portsmouth.

We camped at many lovely parks along the way to New Hampshire. We stayed in the Adirondack Mountains for a few days and then visited the White Mountains of Vermont before crossing into New Hampshire.

My family enjoys tent camping. My dad says you can't really get a taste of the great outdoors in a pop-up camper or RV. I love sitting by the fire at night, gazing at the stars, and listening to the animal noises.

The trip was going well, and everyone was enjoying our vacation. We made it to Portsmouth and were looking forward to the whale-watching adventure. We arrived at the dock a few minutes early. The ocean looked rough, but we had taken seasickness medication. We thought we were prepared for any kind of weather.

_____

_____

_____

_____

_____

_____

_____

_____

_____

Writing Fiction

Directions: Use descriptive writing to complete each story. Write at least five sentences.

1.   It was a cold, wintry morning in January. Snow had fallen steadily for four days. I was staring out my bedroom window when I saw the bedraggled dog staggering through the snow.

_____

_____

_____

_____

_____

_____

2.   Alyssa was home Saturday studying for a big science test. Report cards were due next Friday, and the test on Monday would be on the report card. Alyssa needed to do well on the test to get an A in Science. The phone rang. It was her best friend, Tierra.

_____

_____

_____

_____

_____

_____

3.   Martin works every weekend delivering newspapers. He wakes up at 5:30 A.M. and begins his route at 6:00 A.M. He delivers 150 newspapers on his bike. He enjoys his weekend job because he is working toward a goal.

_____

_____

_____

_____

_____

_____

Writing: Point of View

People often have different opinions about the same thing. This is because each of us has a different "point of view." **Point of view** is the attitude someone has about a particular topic as a result of his or her personal experience or knowledge.

Directions: Read the topic sentence below about the outcome of a basketball game. Then, write two short paragraphs, one from the point of view of a player for the Reds and one from the point of view of a player for the Cowboys. Be sure to give each person's opinion of the outcome of the game.

Topic Sentence: In the last second of the basketball game between the Reds and the Cowboys, the Reds scored and won the game.

Terry, a player for the Reds . . . _____

_____

_____

Chris, a player for the Cowboys . . . _____

_____

_____

Directions: Here's a different situation. Read the topic sentence, and then write three short paragraphs from the points of view of Katie, her dad, and her brother.

Topic Sentence: Katie's dog had chewed up another one of her father's shoes.

Katie . . . _____

_____

Katie's father . . . _____

_____

Katie's brother, Mark, who would rather have a cat . . . _____

_____

Friendly Letters

A **friendly letter** has these parts: return address, date, greeting, body, closing, and signature.

Directions: Read this letter. Then, label the parts of the letter.

_____ ——→ 222 West Middle Street
Boise, Idaho 33444
May 17, 2015 ←—— _____

Dear Blaine, ←—— _____

    Hello! I know I haven't written in several weeks, but I've been very busy with school and baseball practice. How have you been? How is the weather in Boston? It is finally getting warm in Boise.
    As I mentioned, I am playing baseball this year. My team is called the Rockets, and we are really good. We have a terrific coach. We practice two nights a week and play games on the weekends. Are you playing baseball?
    I can hardly wait to visit you this summer. I can't believe I'll be flying on an airplane and staying with you and your family for 2 weeks! There is probably a lot to do in Boston. When you write, tell me some ideas you have for the 2 weeks.

_____ ——→ Your friend,

_____ ——→ Mason

Envelopes should follow this format:

Mason Fitch
222 West Middle Street
Boise, ID 33444

                    Blaine Morgan
                    111 E. 9th Street, Apt 22B
                    Boston, MA 00011

Friendly Letters

Directions: Write a friendly letter. Then, address the envelope.

Writing: Supporting Your Opinion

Directions: Decide what your opinion is on each topic below. Then, write a paragraph supporting your opinion. Begin with a topic sentence that tells the reader what you think. Add details in the next three or four sentences that show why you are right.

Example: Whether kids should listen to music while they do homework

Kids do a better job on their homework if they listen to music. The music makes the time more enjoyable. It also drowns out the sounds of the rest of the family. If things are too quiet while kids do homework, every little sound distracts them.

1. Whether young people should have a choice about going to school, no matter how old they are

   _____

   _____

   _____

2. Whether all parents should give their children the same amount of money for an allowance

   _____

   _____

   _____

3. Whether you should tell someone if you doubt he or she is telling the truth

   _____

   _____

   _____

Writing from a Prompt: An Opinion Essay

Directions: Write an opinion essay in response to the prompt.

Writing Prompt: Think about rainforests. What is the importance of preserving the rainforests of the world? What problems could arise if there were no longer any rainforest areas? What problems could arise for humans due to the preservation of rainforests? How do rainforests affect you?

_____

_____

_____

_____

_____

_____

_____

_____

_____

Directions: When you finish writing, reread your essay. Use this checklist to help make corrections.

☐ I have used correct spelling, grammar, and punctuation.

☐ I have no sentence fragments.

☐ My essay makes sense.

☐ I wrote complete sentences.

☐ I have no run-on sentences.

☐ I answered the prompt.

Writing a Summary

A **summary** is a short description of what a selection or book is about.

Directions: Read the following selection and the example summary.

Fads of the 1950s

A fad is a practice or an object that becomes very popular for a period of time. Recent popular fads include shaped rubber band bracelets, interactive toy hamsters, and Beanie Babies®. In the 1950s, there were many different fads, including coonskin caps, hula hoops, and 3-D movies.

Coonskin caps were made popular by the weekly television show about Davy Crockett, which began in December of 1954. Not only did Davy's hat itself become popular, but anything with Davy Crockett on it was in hot demand.

Also popular were hula hoops. They were produced by the Wham-O company in 1958. The company had seen similar toys in Australia. Hula hoops were priced at $1.98, and over 30 million hoops were sold within 6 months.

Another fad was the 3-D movie. When television sets began to appear in every American home, the movie industry began to suffer financially. Movie companies rushed to produce 3-D movies, and movie-goers once more flocked to theaters. The first 3-D movie was shown in Los Angeles on November 26, 1952. People loved the special Polaroid® glasses and scenes in the movie that seemed to jump out at them. As with the hula hoop and Davy Crockett, people soon tired of 3-D movies, and they became old news as they were replaced by new fads.

Summary

Over the years, many fads have become popular with the American public. During the 1950s, three popular fads were the hula hoop, Davy Crockett, and 3-D movies. Davy Crockett's coonskin cap became a fad with the beginning of the weekly television show. Hula hoops were sold by the millions, and 3-D movies were enjoyed by people everywhere. However, like all fads, interest in these items soon died out.

Writing a Summary

Directions: Read the following selection. Using page 309 as a guide, write a summary of the selection.

First Flights

In the first few years of the 20th century, most people strongly believed that humans would never be able to fly. However, a few daring individuals worked to prove the public wrong.

On December 8, 1903, Samuel Langley attempted to fly his version of an airplane from the roof of a houseboat on the Potomac River. Langley happened to be the secretary of the Smithsonian Institution, so his flight was covered not only by news reporters but also by government officials. Unfortunately, his trip met with sudden disaster when his aircraft did a nose dive into the river.

Nine days later, brothers Orville and Wilbur Wright attempted a flight. They had assembled their aircraft at their home in Dayton, Ohio, and shipped it to Kitty Hawk, North Carolina. On December 17, the Wright brothers made several flights, the longest one lasting an incredible 59 seconds. Since the Wright brothers had kept their flight attempts secret, their miraculous flight was only reported by two newspapers in the United States.

_____

_____

_____

_____

_____

_____

Comparing and Contrasting

When writing comparison/contrast essays, it is helpful to write one paragraph which contains all the similarities and another paragraph which contains all the differences.

Directions: Write an essay in response to the prompt.

Writing Prompt: Think of your brother, sister, or a friend. What similarities are there between you and this person? What differences are there?

_____

_____

_____

_____

_____

_____

_____

_____

_____

_____

_____

_____

Directions: When you finish writing, reread your essay. Use this checklist to help make corrections.

- ☐ My essay makes sense.

- ☐ I listed at least two similarities and two differences.

- ☐ My sentences are correctly written.

- ☐ I used correct spelling, grammar, and punctuation.

Advantages and Disadvantages

As in the comparison/contrast essay, it is easiest to put all of the advantages in one paragraph and the disadvantages in another paragraph.

Directions: Write an essay in response to the prompt.

Writing Prompt: Think about what a society would be like if all people had the same skin tone, hair color, eye color, height, and weight. What would the benefits of living in such a society be? Would there be any disadvantages? What would they be?

_____

_____

_____

_____

_____

_____

_____

_____

_____

_____

_____

_____

_____

Directions: When you finish writing, reread your essay. Use this checklist to help make corrections.

- [ ] My essay makes sense.

- [ ] I used correct spelling, grammar, and punctuation.

- [ ] I answered the writing prompt.

- [ ] I have varied sentence length.

Newswriting

Newswriting is a style of writing used by news reporters and other journalists who write for periodicals. **Periodicals** are newspapers, magazines, and newsletters that are published regularly either as hard copies or digitally.

Magazine and news writers organize their ideas and their writing around what is called "the five W's and the H" — who, what, when, where, why, and how. As they conduct research and interview people for articles, journalists keep these questions in mind.

Directions: Read a news article of your choice. Use the information you read to answer the questions.

Who

Who is involved? _____

Who is affected? _____

Who is responsible? _____

What

What is the event or subject? _____

What exactly has happened? _____

_____

When

When did this happen?_____

Where

Where did it happen? _____

_____

Why

Why did it happen? _____

Why will readers care? _____

_____

How

How did it happen? _____

_____

Newswriting: Inverted Pyramid Style

Reporters organize their news stories in what is called the **inverted pyramid** style. The inverted pyramid places the most important facts at the beginning of the story—called the lead (LEED)—and the least important facts at the end.

There are two practical reasons for this approach:

1) If the story must be shortened by an editor, he or she can simply cut paragraphs from the end of the story rather than rewriting the entire story.

2) Because so much news and information is available to the public, few people read every word of every story. Instead, many readers skim headlines and opening paragraphs. The inverted pyramid style of writing enables readers to quickly get the basics of what the story is about without reading the entire story.

Directions: Read the news story. Then, answer the questions.

Introducing children to peanuts when they are young helps reduce the risk of peanut allergies, a new study has found.

The study, published in *The New England Journal of Medicine*, could change doctors' recommendations to parents of young babies and children. Instead of telling parents to avoid peanuts in their children's diets, doctors may now recommend that peanuts be introduced in small amounts at an early age. This frequent and early exposure has been shown to cut the risk of peanut allergies in children.

Peanut allergies have become more common among children in recent years. Peanuts are banned from many schools and daycare centers, in hopes of preventing severe reactions. Peanuts are a delicious and nutritious source of protein. In addition to being used as a sandwich spread, they make a nice addition to dips and smoothies.

---

1. What is this news story about? _____

2. Where was the study about peanuts published? _____

3. How have doctors' views about peanuts changed? _____

4. Name two groups of people who might be interested in reading this article.

    _____

5. What two sentences could you cut from this article if you were an editor?

    _____

Writing: Just the Facts

Some forms of writing, such as reports and essays, contain opinions that are supported by the writer. In other kinds of writing, however, it is important to stick to the facts. News reporters, for example, must use only facts when they write their stories.

Directions: Read the following news story about a fire, and underline the sentences or parts of sentences that are opinions. Then, rewrite the story in your own words, giving only the facts.

At around 10:30 P.M. last night, a fire broke out in a house at 413 Wilshire Boulevard. The house is in a very nice neighborhood, surrounded by beautiful trees. The family of four who lives in the house was alerted by smoke alarms, and they all exited the house safely, although they must have been very frightened. Firefighters arrived on the scene at approximately 10:45 P.M., and it took them over 3 hours to extinguish the blaze. The firefighters were very courageous. The cause of the fire has not yet been determined, although faulty electric wiring is suspected. People should have their electric wiring checked regularly. The family is staying with relatives until repairs to their home can be made, and they are probably very anxious to move back into their house.

_____

_____

_____

_____

_____

_____

_____

_____

_____

_____

_____

Writing: You're the Reporter

Directions: Now, write your own short news story about an interesting event that occurred at your school or in your neighborhood. Find out who and what the story is about, where and when it happened, and why and how it happened. Take some notes, interview some of the people involved, and write your story. Give your story a title, and remember to stick to the facts! In the box, draw a picture (or "photo") to go with your story.

_____

_____

_____

_____

_____

_____

_____

_____

_____

_____

_____

_____

_____

_____

Writing: Personification

Sometimes writers use descriptions such as "The fire engine **screamed** as it rushed down the street," or "The sun **crawled** slowly across the sky." We know that fire engines do not really scream, and the sun does not really crawl. Writers use descriptions like these to make their writing more interesting and vivid. When a writer gives an object or animal human qualities, it is called **personification**.

Directions: For each object below, write a sentence using personification. The first one has been done for you.

1. the barn door

   <u>The old, rusty barn door groaned loudly when I pushed it open.</u>

2. the rain

   _____

3. the pickup truck

   _____

4. the radiator

   _____

5. the leaves

   _____

6. the television

   _____

7. the kite

   _____

8. the river

   _____

Comprehensive Curriculum - Grade 5

Similes

A **simile** is a comparison of two things that have something in common but are really very different. The words **like** and **as** are used in similes.

Examples:
> The baby was **as** happy **as** a lark.
> She is **like** a ray of sunshine to my tired eyes.

Directions: Choose a word from the box to complete each comparison. The first one has been done for you.

tack	grass	fish	mule	ox	rail	hornet	monkey

1. as stubborn as a _mule_
2. as strong as an _____
3. swims like a _____
4. as sharp as a _____
5. as thin as a _____
6. as mad as a _____
7. climbs like a _____
8. as green as _____

Directions: Use your own words to complete these similes.

9. as _____ as a tack
10. _____ like a bird
11. as hungry as a _____
12. as white as _____

13. as light as a _____
14. as _____ as honey
15. _____ like a snake
16. as cold as _____

Directions: Use your own similes to complete these sentences.

17. Our new puppy sounded _____.
18. The clouds were _____.
19. Our new car is _____.
20. The watermelon tasted _____.

Writing: Common Similes

There are many similes that are used often in the English language. For example, "as frightened as a mouse" is a very common simile. Can you think of others?

Directions: Match the first part of each common simile to the second part. The first one has been done for you.

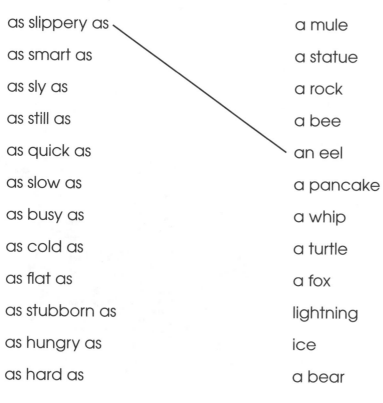

as slippery as	a mule
as smart as	a statue
as sly as	a rock
as still as	a bee
as quick as	an eel
as slow as	a pancake
as busy as	a whip
as cold as	a turtle
as flat as	a fox
as stubborn as	lightning
as hungry as	ice
as hard as	a bear

Directions: Write sentences using these common similes.

1. eats like a bird

_____

2. fits like a glove

_____

3. sits there like a bump on a log

_____

4. like a bull in a china shop

_____

5. works like a charm

_____

Name _____

Metaphors

A **metaphor** makes a direct comparison between two unlike things. A noun must be used in the comparison. The words **like** and **as** are not used.

Examples:
   Correct: The exuberant puppy was a **bundle of energy**.
   Incorrect: The dog is **happy**. (**Happy** is an adjective.)

Directions: Circle the two objects being compared.

1. The old truck was a heap of rusty metal.

2. The moon was a silver dollar in the sky.

3. Their vacation was a nightmare.

4. That wasp is a flying menace.

5. The prairie was a carpet of green.

6. The flowers were jewels on stems.

7. This winter, our pond is glass.

8. The clouds were marshmallows.

Directions: Complete the metaphor in each sentence.

9. The ruby was _____ .

10. The hospital is _____ .

11. The car was _____ .

12. This morning when I awoke, I was _____ .

13. When my brother is grumpy, he is _____ .

14. Her fingers on the piano keys were _____ .

Writing: Similes and Metaphors

Using **similes** and **metaphors** to describe things makes writing interesting. Similes are comparisons that use **like** or **as**.

Examples: She looked like a frightened mouse.
She looked as frightened as a mouse.

Metaphors are direct comparisons that do not use **like** or **as**.

Example: She was a frightened mouse.

Directions: Rewrite each sentence two different ways to make it more interesting. In the first sentence (a), add at least one adjective and one adverb. In the second sentence (b), compare something in the sentence to something else, using a simile or metaphor.

Example: The baby cried.
a. The sick baby cried softly all night.
b. The baby cried louder and louder, like a storm gaining strength.

1. The stranger arrived.

   a. _____

   b. _____

2. The dog barked.

   a. _____

   b. _____

3. The children danced.

   a. _____

   b. _____

4. The moon rose.

   a. _____

   b. _____

Writing: Similes and Metaphors in Poetry

Many poems use similes and metaphors to create a more interesting description of what the poem is about.

Directions: Read the following poems and underline any similes or metaphors you see.

Flint

An emerald is as green as grass,
    A ruby red as blood;
A sapphire shines as blue as heaven;
    A flint lies in the mud.

A diamond is a brilliant stone,
    To catch the world's desire;
An opal holds a fiery spark;
    But a flint holds fire.

—Christina Rossetti

The Night Is a Big Black Cat

The night is a big black cat
    The moon is her topaz eye,
The stars are the mice she hunts at night,
    In the field of the sultry sky.

—G. Orr Clark

Directions: Now, write your own poem, using at least one simile and one metaphor.

_____

_____

_____

_____

_____

_____

_____

_____

_____

_____

Writing: Rhyming Words

Words that share the same vowel sound in their last syllables are **rhyming words**. Rhyming words can have the same number of syllables, like **spike** and **hike**, or different numbers of syllables, like **tent** and **excellent** or **nation** and **conversation**.

Directions: Write words that rhyme with the words below and have the number of syllables shown. The first one has been done for you.

1. table _____*unable*_____ (3)

2. green _____ (3)

3. instead _____ (1)

4. store _____ (2)

5. remember _____ (3)

6. concentration _____ (4)

7. stars _____ (2)

8. giraffe _____ (1)

9. neighbor _____ (2)

10. berry _____ (4)

11. vein _____ (3)

12. bath _____ (1)

13. celebration _____ (4)

14. master _____ (2)

15. baby _____ (2)

They share the same vowel sound in their last syllables.

spike
hike
like
Mike

Writing: Poetry

Directions: For the first group of poems below, both lines should rhyme. The first line is given. Complete each poem, using one of the given rhyming words, or use one of your own. Make sure to add the correct punctuation.

Example: mile   Dylan James has a certain style.
             pile
             dial   <u>To get his way, he'd walk a mile.</u>

ape   Mindy Lou got a very bad scrape!
grape
cape   _____

hide   Sometimes you have to swallow your pride.
fried
cried   _____

Directions: Complete these poems, using one of the given words, or use one of your own. Each poem should have four lines. The second and fourth lines should rhyme.

Example: cape   Kenny skidded on his bike.
             tape   And got himself all **scraped**.
             grape   Now his bike has a flat tire,
                     And his whole leg is **taped**.

I   I put some water in a bucket
cry   And then threw in some **dye**.
my   _____

           _____

file   Kelly got her hair cut,
dial   But I don't like the **style**.
Nile   _____

           _____

ride   When Billy Joe didn't win the race,
hide   It really hurt his **pride**.
cried   _____

           _____

Haiku

Haiku is a form of unrhymed Japanese poetry. Haiku have three lines. The first line has five syllables, the second line has seven syllables, and the third line has five syllables.

Example:

The Fall

Leaves fall from the trees.
Do they want to leave their home?
They float on the breeze.

Directions: Write a haiku about nature. Write the title on the first line. Then, illustrate your haiku.

Nature _____

_____

_____

_____

Lantern

Lantern is another type of five-line Japanese poetry. It takes the shape of a Japanese lantern. Each line must contain the following number of syllables.

Line 1:   1 syllable
Line 2:   2 syllables
Line 3:   3 syllables
Line 4:   4 syllables
Line 5:   1 syllable

Example: Cats—
                    Stealthy
                wild creatures
                want to be your
                    pet.

Directions: Write and illustrate your own lantern.

_____

_____

_____

_____

_____

Alliterative Poetry

Alliteration is the repetition of a consonant sound in a group of words.

Example: Barney Bear bounced a ball.

Alliterative story poems can be fun to read and write. Any of several rhyming patterns can be used. Possibilities include:
   Every two lines rhyme.
   Every other line rhymes.
   The first line rhymes with the last line, and the two middle lines rhyme with each other.
   All four lines rhyme.

Example:

Thomas Tuttle tries to dine,
On turkey, tea, and treats so fine.
Thomas eats tomatoes and tortellini,
He devours tuna and tettrazini.

When tempting tidbits fill the table,
Thomas tastes as much as he is able,
He stuffs himself from top to toes,
Where he puts it, goodness knows!

Directions: Write an alliterative story poem using any rhyming pattern listed above. Your poem should be at least four lines long.

_____

_____

_____

_____

_____

_____

_____

Name _____

How to Write a Book Report

Writing a book report should not be a chore. Instead, consider it an opportunity to recommend a book you have enjoyed. Simply writing, "I really liked this book. You will, too!" is not enough. You need to explain what makes the book worth reading.

Like other essays, book reports have three parts. An essay is a short report that presents the personal views of the writer. The three parts of an essay (and a book report) are introduction, body, and conclusion.

The **introduction** to a book report should be a full paragraph that will capture the interest of your readers. The **body** paragraphs contain the main substance of your report. Include a brief overview of the plot of your book, along with supporting details that make it interesting. In the **conclusion**, summarize the central ideas of your report. Sum up why you would or would not recommend it to others.

Directions: Answer these questions about writing book reports.

1. Which of these introductory sentences is more interesting?

   ☐ Brian, a thirteen-year-old boy, must survive in the Canadian wilderness after his plane crashes.

   ☐ *Hatchet* is an interesting book about survival and the wilderness.

2. In a report on a fiction book about a teenage survivor of a plane crash, where would these sentences go?

   "Brian is flying in a plane to visit his father when the plane's pilot dies unexpectedly of a heart attack."

   ☐ introduction

   ☐ conclusion

3. In the same report, where would these sentences go?

   "Author Gary Paulsen has written an exciting adventure story about a boy's patience and courage as he survives alone for two months in the wilderness. I strongly recommend the book to people of all ages."

   ☐ body

   ☐ conclusion

Book Report: A Book I Devoured

Directions: Follow the writing prompts to write a short book report on a book you truly enjoyed.

Recently, I read a book I could not put down.

Its title is _____

One reason I "devoured" this book was _____

_____

_____

If I could be one of the characters, I'd be _____ because _____

_____

_____

_____

My favorite part of the story was when _____

_____

_____

_____

_____

_____

_____

_____

Book Report: Comparing Two Books

Directions: Follow the writing prompts to write a short book report comparing two books on the same subject.

Two books I recently read on the same subject

are _____

by _____

and _____

by _____

I liked _____ better because _____

_____

_____

_____

The best part of this book was when _____

_____

_____

_____

_____

_____

_____

Even though I did not like it as well, one good thing I can say about the other book is

_____

_____

_____

Reference Sources: Languages, Social Studies

Reference sources are books and other materials that provide facts and information. Dictionaries, encyclopedias, and nonfiction books are reference books. Magazine and newspaper articles, the Internet, and computer CDs are also reference sources.

There are many other kinds of reference sources on specific topics. Some of these are listed below by the topics covered.

Language:
1. *The American Heritage Dictionary*
2. *Dictionary of American Idioms* by Adam Makkai
3. *Math Dictionary for Kids* by Theresa Fitzgerald
4. *Oxford Dictionary of Foreign Words and Phrases* by Andrew Delahunty
5. *Scholastic Children's Thesaurus*

Social Studies:
1. *Book of Black Heroes from A to Z* by Wade Hudson and Valerie Wilson Wesley
2. *If You Lived When Women Won Their Rights* by Anne Kamma
3. *Understanding Myself: A Kid's Guide to Intense Emotions and Strong Feelings* by Mary C. Lamia
4. *Merriam Webster's Geographical Dictionary*

Directions: Answer the questions.

1. Which book would be the best source for finding the meaning of the Spanish term, *que pasa*?

_____

2. Which book would be the best source of information on Martin Luther King, Jr.?

_____

3. Where would you find information on the average yearly rainfall in the Amazon?

_____

4. Which book would have information on women getting the right to vote?

_____

5. Where would you look for a list of terms that mean the same as **incredible**?

_____

Reference Sources:
General, Science, and Technology

These reference sources are listed by the topics covered.

General:
1. *How Things Work Encyclopedia*
2. *Children's Encyclopedia of American History*
3. *World Book Encyclopedia Kids* (online subscription)
4. *National Geographic Student World Atlas*
5. United States Census Bureau website (www.census.gov)

Science and Technology:
1. *A Field Guide to Rocks and Minerals* by Frederick H. Pough
2. *Encyclopedia of Animals*
3. *National Wildlife Federation Field Guide to Trees of North America*
4. *The Universe (Discovery Kids)*
5. *The Complete Human Body* (book and DVD-ROM) by Dr. Alice Roberts

Directions: Answer the questions.

1. Which reference source would you check to find a map of Poland?

    _____

2. Which source would you consult to find the most recent statistics on the number of single parents in the United States?

    _____

3. Where would you find the most complete information on the Milky Way and other galaxies?

    _____

4. Where would you find the most complete information about a rock crystal called quartz?

    _____

5. Where would you find the most complete information on the Boston Tea Party?

    _____

Using the Library Catalog

Directions: Read about library catalogs. Use this information to answer the questions on the next page.

A **library catalog** is a digital listing of all the books, DVDs, CDs, etc. in the library's collection. Most libraries offer many search options. The most common ways to search are by title, author, subject, or keyword. If you don't find the book you are looking for at first, you may find it by changing your search. For example, if you can't find a book by title, try doing a keyword search using only one or two main words from the title.

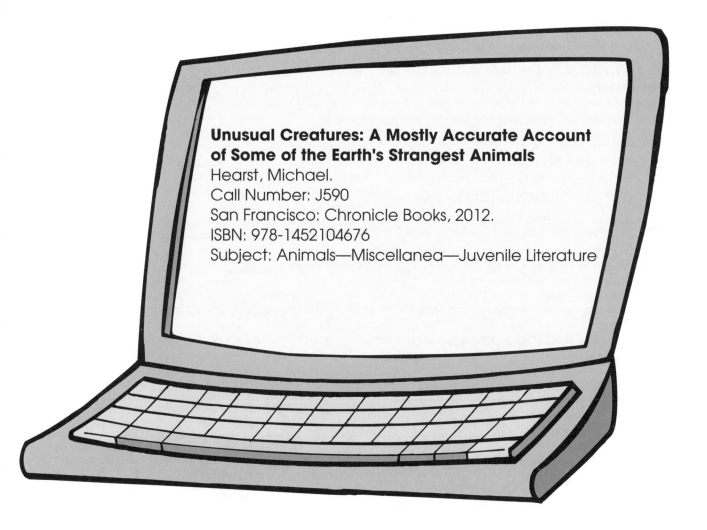

Unusual Creatures: A Mostly Accurate Account of Some of the Earth's Strangest Animals
Hearst, Michael.
Call Number: J590
San Francisco: Chronicle Books, 2012.
ISBN: 978-1452104676
Subject: Animals—Miscellanea—Juvenile Literature

Using the Library Catalog

The **call number** for a book is printed on its spine and also appears in the library catalog. Nonfiction books are shelved in order by call number.

Directions: Use what you learned about library catalogs to answer these questions.

1. What should you type into a library's computerized catalog for a listing of all the books the library has on birds?   _____

2. What should you type into the library's catalog for a list of all the books by Louisa May Alcott?   _____

3. What should you type into the library's catalog to see if the library owns a book called *Birds of North America*?   _____

4. According to the catalog entry shown on the previous page, what company published the book *Unusual Creatures*?   _____

5. Under what subject is *Unusual Creatures* listed?   _____

6. What is the call number for *Unusual Creatures*?   _____

7. What are three ways to find a book in the library? _____

_____

8. If you don't find the book you were looking for after your first catalog search, what else can you try?

_____

_____

9. Besides the call number, title, and author, what are three other types of information given for a book in a library catalog?

_____

_____

_____

Research

Directions: Read about doing research. Then, answer the questions.

Step 1: Look in a general online encyclopedia, such as *Encyclopedia Britannica Kids* or *Fact Monster* (which uses the *Columbia Encyclopedia*), for background information on your topic. Check for a bibliography at the end of the article for clues to other sources. A **bibliography** lists all the books and magazines used to write the article.

Step 2: Use a special encyclopedia for more specific information or for definitions of special terms. *How Things Work Encyclopedia*, *Children's Encyclopedia of American History*, and *Human Body: A Visual Encyclopedia* are examples of special encyclopedias.

Step 3: Look for a general book on your topic using the subject headings in the library catalog. Be sure to note the copyright date (date published) on all books you select. For current topics, such as medical research or computers, you will want to use only the most recently published and up-to-date sources. You will be most likely to find these using online resources.

Step 4: When using the Internet to research a topic, be sure to use only trustworthy, reliable sites. Choose sites that are run by companies, schools, or organizations you've heard of, such as NASA, the Smithsonian Institution, National Geographic Kids, Time Magazine, PBS, or the National Gallery of Art. If you're not sure whether a site is reliable, ask a parent or a teacher.

1. Name two general encyclopedias. _____

_____

2. Name three special encyclopedias. _____

_____

_____

3. How can you tell whether a website contains trustworthy, reliable information?

_____

Name _____

Research

Directions: Read the following questions. Use the Internet or library resources to answer them.

1. Choose two figures from history. Research them on www.biography.com. Write two facts you found about each person.

_____

_____

_____

_____

2. Use a resource book or online search to find out during what period the dinosaur Diplodocus lived.

_____

3. What were the last three winners of the Newbery Award for best children's books?

_____

4. Name three types of mollusks. List the source of your information.

_____

5. Visit the site www.libraryspot.com. Write three questions that a classmate could answer by using this site.

_____

_____

_____

6. Use a library catalog to search for books about ancient Egypt. List the titles and call numbers of three books you find.

_____

_____

Research

Directions: Read the following questions. Use the Internet or library resources to answer them.

1. Use a print or online children's almanac to find two facts about the weather or weather-related events.

_____

_____

_____

2. What is the world's tallest building? How tall is it?

_____

3. List two sources you could use to find current information about global warming.

_____

_____

4. Use a print or online atlas to find out what African countries and what body of water border Namibia.

_____

5. Use an online encyclopedia to research the Chinese New Year. Briefly describe what it is below.

_____

_____

_____

6. How are hurricanes named? What source did you use to find the answer?

_____

_____

Fiction, Nonfiction, and Biographies

Fiction books are stories that are not based on facts or real events. They are based on the imagination of the author.

Examples: picture book stories and novels

Nonfiction books are about facts or events that actually occurred.

Examples: reference books and history books

Biographies are written about a person's life. They are based on true events. Biographies have been written about Presidents and First Ladies, as well as other people.

Directions: Use your library to answer the following questions.

1. What are the titles and authors of three fiction books? _____

_____

_____

2. What are the titles and authors of three nonfiction books? _____

_____

_____

3. What are the call numbers of the three nonfiction books you listed? _____

_____

Directions: Use the library catalog to locate two biographies of each of the people listed. Write the titles, authors, and call numbers.

4. Abraham Lincoln _____

5. George Washington Carver _____

6. John F. Kennedy _____

7. Princess Diana _____

8. Pocahontas _____

Book Search: Fiction

 Have you ever been on a scavenger hunt? Usually, when you go on a scavenger hunt, you need to find unusual items on a list. This scavenger hunt will take place at your library. Instead of finding unusual items, you will need to find books.

Directions: Find these books at your library. They will be in alphabetical order by the author's last name in the picture book section of the children's department. Then, answer the questions.

Author: Margaret Wise Brown   **Title:** *Goodnight Moon*

1. Where is the cow jumping over the moon? _____

2. What is the old lady whispering? _____

3. How many kittens are in the story? _____

Author: Audrey Wood   **Title:** *Napping House*

4. In the beginning, what is everyone in the house doing? _____

5. What kind of flea is in this story? _____

6. What breaks at the end of the story? _____

Author: Mo Willems   **Title:** *Knuffle Bunny: A Cautionary Tale*

7. Who is Knuffle Bunny?

_____

8. How does Trixie explain her problem to her father?

_____

_____

9. How does the story end?

_____

_____

Book Search: Nonfiction

Directions: Look in your library catalog to find the types of nonfiction books listed. Then, go to the shelf in the nonfiction section, and locate the books. Write the information requested for each book.

A book about gorillas

    Title: _____

    Author: _____

    Call number: _____

    First sentence in book: _____

A book about the solar system

    Title: _____

    Author: _____

    Call number: _____

    Last sentence in book: _____

A book about baseball

    Title: _____

    Author: _____

    Call number: _____

    Color of book's cover: _____

A book about flowers

    Title: _____

    Author: _____

    Call number: _____

    Name of a flower pictured in book: _____

Book Search: Biographies

Biographies may be located in the 920 section in your library or may be filed by call number according to subject.

Directions: Use the library catalog and the actual books to answer these questions.

1. How many books can you find about Elizabeth Blackwell? _____

2. What is the title of one of the books? _____

3. How many books can you find about Kareem Abdul-Jabar? _____

4. What are the titles, authors, and call numbers of three books about George Washington?

_____

_____

_____

5. What are the titles, authors, and call numbers of three books about Martin Luther King, Jr.?

_____

_____

_____

6. What are the titles, authors, and call numbers of three books about Eleanor Roosevelt?

_____

_____

_____

7. What are the titles, authors, and call numbers of three books about Marie Curie?

_____

_____

_____

Reports: Choosing a Topic

Directions: Read about how to write a report. Then, answer the questions.

A report is a written paper based on the writer's research. It is logically organized and, if it is a good report, presents information in an interesting way. Reports can focus on many different topics. A social studies report may provide information about a city or state. A science report may explain why the oceans are polluted.

If possible, choose a topic you're interested in. Sometimes a teacher assigns a general topic to the whole class, such as the solar system. This is a very broad topic, so you must first narrow it to a smaller topic about which you can write an interesting four- or five-page report. For example, your report could be on "The Sun, the Center of the Solar System" or "Jupiter, the Jumbo Planet."

A narrower topic gives your paper a better focus. Be careful not to make your topic too narrow, because then you may not be able to find much information about it for your report.

The inverted pyramid on the right shows how to narrow your topic from the general, at the top of the pyramid, to the specific, at the bottom.

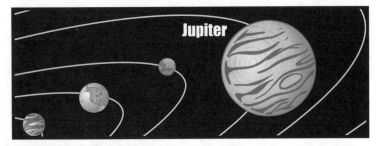

The solar system

Planets in the solar system

Jupiter, the jumbo planet

Directions: Select a topic for a paper you will write. You may choose one of these topics or select one of your own. Then, answer the questions.

American wars   Games   Presidents   States
Famous American women   Solar system   Sports heroes   Ecology

1. What is a report? _____

_____

2. Which general topic did you choose? _____

3. What specific topic will you write about? _____

_____

Reports: Doing Research

Directions: Review the information on pages 333–335 about doing library research. Then, read about how to do research for a report, and answer the questions.

Before starting your report, locate the most likely places to find relevant information for your research. Ask the librarian for help if necessary. A good report will be based on at least three or four sources, so it's important to find references that provide varied information.

Is the topic a standard one, such as a report on the skeletal system? A children's encyclopedia of the human body is a good place to begin your research. You may also want to look online for some children's websites about the body and how it works.

Does your report require current statistics and/or facts? Specific websites will probably be your best source for information. For example, if you want to know the current population of various endangered animals, you could visit the World Wildlife Fund site. Be sure to use sites that are credible and reliable. If you are not sure whether a site is reliable, ask a parent or teacher.

For current magazine articles, see if your school has a membership to the *Reader's Guide to Periodical Literature*, which lists the names and page numbers of magazine articles related to a variety of topics. If you need geographical information about a country, check an atlas such as the *National Geographic Student World Atlas*.

1. How many reference sources should you consult before writing your report? _____

2. What are two references that provide statistics and facts? _____

_____

3. Where will you find a listing of magazine articles? _____

_____

4. Where should you look for geographical information? _____

_____

5. If you're stumped or don't know where to begin, who can help? _____

_____

Reports: Taking Notes

Directions: Read about taking notes for your report. Use the "index card" below to write a sample note from one of your reference sources.

When gathering information for a report, it is necessary to take notes. You'll need to take notes when you read encyclopedia entries, books, and magazine or news articles related to your topic.

Before you begin gathering information for a report, organize your thoughts around the who, what, when, where, why, and how questions of your topic. This organized approach will help direct you to the references that best answer these questions. It will also help you select and write in your notes only useful information.

There are different ways of taking notes. Some people use notebook paper. If you write on notebook paper, put a heading on each page. Write only notes related to each heading on specific pages. Otherwise, your notes will be disorganized, and it will be difficult to begin writing your paper.

Many people prefer to put their notes on index cards. Index cards can be easily sorted and organized when you begin writing your report and are helpful when preparing an outline. If you use index cards for your notes, put one fact on each card.

Take several notes from each reference source you use. Having too many notes is better than not having enough information when you start to write your report.

_____

_____

_____

_____

_____

_____

_____

_____

_____

_____

Encyclopedia Skills: Taking Notes

A **biography** is a written report of a person's life. It is based on facts and actual events. To prepare to write a biographical essay, you could look up information about the person in a biographical or online encyclopedia.

Directions: Select one of the people listed below. Read about that person in an encyclopedia. Take notes to prepare for writing a biographical essay. Then, use your notes to answer the questions.

Babe Ruth

Mikhail Baryshnikov

Jane Goodall

Jesse Owens

J.K. Rowling

Ben Carson

Steve Jobs

Woodrow Wilson

Charles Darwin

Marie Curie

My Notes:

1. Where and when was he or she born? _____

2. If deceased, when did the person die? _____

3. When and why did he or she first become famous? _____

_____

_____

4. What are some important points about this person's career?

_____

_____

_____

_____

_____

_____

_____

Reports: Making an Outline

An outline will help you organize your ideas before you begin writing your report.

Title

I. First Main Idea

   A. A supporting idea or fact

   B. Another supporting idea or fact

      1. An example or related fact

      2. An example or related fact

II. Second Main Idea

   A. A supporting idea or fact

   B. Another supporting idea or fact

III. Third Main Idea

   A. A supporting idea or fact

   B. Another supporting idea or fact

Directions: Use information from your notes to write an outline for your report. Follow the above format, but expand your outline to include as many main ideas, facts, and examples as necessary.

_____

_____

_____

_____

_____

_____

_____

_____

_____

Reports: Writing the Paper

Directions: Read more about writing a report. Then, write your report.

Before you begin, be certain you clearly understand what is expected. How long should your report be? Must it be typed? Can it be written in pen? Should it be double-spaced?

Begin the first draft of your report with a general introduction of your topic. In the introduction, briefly mention the main points you will write about. One paragraph is usually enough to introduce your paper.

Next, comes the body of your report. Start a new paragraph for each main point. Include information that supports that point. If you are writing a long report, you may need to write a new paragraph for each supporting idea and/or each example. Follow your outline to be certain you cover all points. Depending on the number of words required to cover your topic, the body of the report will be anywhere from three or four paragraphs to several pages long.

In one or two concluding paragraphs, briefly summarize the main points you wrote about in the body of the report, and state any conclusions you have drawn as a result of your research.

Once you finish the first draft, you will need to edit and rewrite your report to make it read smoothly and correct errors. You may need to rewrite your report more than once to make it the best it can be.

If possible, put the report aside for a day or two before you rewrite it so you can look at it with fresh eyes and a clear mind. Professional writers often write several drafts, so don't be discouraged about rewrites! Rewriting and editing are the keys to good writing—keys that every writer, no matter how old or experienced, relies on.

Directions: Circle the words in the puzzle related to writing a report.

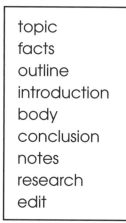

```
K  K  N  K  T  O  P  I  C  D  T  B
L  D  O  B  T  T  O  D  P  T  D  O
I  N  T  R  O  D  U  C  T  I  O  N
E  N  E  R  G  D  E  E  O  O  O  N
D  W  S  R  G  E  Y  C  P  C  X  R
S  A  F  E  A  T  T  E  I  E  Y  O
R  W  A  Q  U  B  W  P  C  D  G  F
L  I  C  O  N  C  L  U  S  I  O  N
O  U  T  L  I  N  E  U  T  T  E  D
R  E  S  E  A  R  C  H  R  E  S  E
```

topic
facts
outline
introduction
body
conclusion
notes
research
edit

Comprehensive Curriculum - **Grade 5**

Review

1. Why should you narrow your topic when writing a report?

   ☐ So you can include specific, relevant information

   ☐ So you can write a short paper

   ☐ So you can use only one reference book

2. Which of the following is not a reference book?

   ☐ *The American Heritage Children's Thesaurus*

   ☐ *National Geographic Student World Atlas*

   ☐ *Flowers for Cosmo*

   ☐ *How Things Work Encyclopedia*

3. Writing an outline for your report will help you

   ☐ narrow your topic.

   ☐ gather many notes.

   ☐ get organized and follow a plan.

   ☐ broaden your topic.

4. Which of the following is not a part of a finished report?

   ☐ Introduction

   ☐ Conclusion

   ☐ Body

   ☐ Outline

5. When taking notes, index cards will help you

   ☐ check spelling, grammar, and punctuation.

   ☐ organize your writing later.

   ☐ find things quickly on the shelves.

   ☐ transfer facts to your notebook.

Editing

To **edit** means to revise and correct written work. Learning how to edit your work will help you become a better writer. First you should write a rough draft of your paper, and then edit it to make it better. Remember these things when writing your rough draft:

▶ **Do not overcrowd your page.** Leave space between every line and at the sides of your pages to make notes and changes.

▶ **Write so you can read it.** Don't be sloppy just because you're only writing a rough draft.

▶ **Number your pages.** This will help you keep everything in order.

▶ **Write on only one side of the page.** This gives you plenty of space if you want to make changes or add information between paragraphs.

▶ **Use the same size notebook paper for all drafts.** If all pages are the same size, you're less likely to lose any.

Before turning in your report or paper, ask yourself these questions:

▶ **Have I followed my outline?**

▶ **Have I told who, what, when, where, why, and how?**

▶ **Have I provided too much information?** (Good writers are concise. Don't repeat yourself after you have made a point.)

▶ **Do I still have unanswered questions?** (If you have questions, you can bet your readers will also. Add the missing information.)

It is always a good idea to let a day or so pass before rereading your paper and making final corrections. That way you will see what you actually wrote, instead of what you **think** you wrote.

When you edit your work, look for:

▶ **Correct grammar.**

▶ **Correct spelling.** Use the dictionary if you are not 100 percent sure.

▶ **Correct punctuation.**

▶ **Complete sentences.** Each should contain a complete thought.

Directions: Answer these questions about editing by writing **T** for true or **F** for false.

___ 1. When you are editing, you should look for correct grammar and spelling.

___ 2. Editors do not look for complete sentences.

___ 3. Editors do not have to read each word of a story.

___ 4. It is best to use both sides of a sheet of paper when writing the rough draft of your report.

___ 5. It does not matter how neat your first draft is.

___ 6. Editors make sure that sentences are punctuated correctly.

Name _____

Editing

Editors and proofreaders use certain marks to note the changes that need to be made. In addition to circling spelling errors and fixing capitalization mistakes, editors and proofreaders also use the following marks to indicate other mistakes that need to be corrected.

~~the~~	Delete.	∧	Insert a comma.	is ∧	Insert a word.
a͡ nt	Remove the space.	⌄	Insert an apostrophe.	⊙	Insert a period.
In#this	Insert a space.	⌄⌄	Insert quotation marks.	sara̲	Capitalize.

Directions: Use editing marks to correct the errors in these sentences. Then, write the sentences correctly on the lines.

1. Mr. Ramsey was a man who liked to do nothing

_____

2. Lili a young hawaiian girl, liked to swim in the sea.

_____

3. Youngsters who play baseballalways have a favorite player.

_____

4. Too many people said, That movie was terrible."

_____

5. I didn't wantto go to the movie with jaden

_____

6. Prince charles has two adult sons

_____

7. The little boy's name was albert leonard longfellow

_____

Editing

Directions: Use editing marks to show the changes that need to be made in the following sentences.

1. billy bob branstool was was the biggest bully at our school

2. mr. Ling told my mother that i was a good student

3. I heard your mom say, "give your mother a kiss.

4. david and justin liked reading about dinosaurs especially tyrannosaurus rex.

5. milton said to to mabel "maybe we can play tomorrow."

6. ana and Liam knew the answers to the questions but they would not raise hands

7. too many people were going to see the movie so we decided to go get pizza instead

8. tillie's aunt teresa was coming to visit for the month of may

9. we lived in a small town called sophia, north carolina, for 20 days before we decided to move away.

10. we saw the mother fox bringing food to her cubs in the den

11. i was reading the book called, haunting at midnight.

12. kevin and i decided that we would be detective bob and detective joe.

13. there were thirteen questions on the test. kevin missed all but the first one

14. thirty of us were going on a fieldtrip when suddenly the teachertold the bus driver to turn around.

Editing

⁀not⁀is⁀	Flip the words around; transpose.
wan⌢l⌢ut	Flip letters around; transpose.
¶That was when Peter began talking.	Indent the paragraph or start a new paragraph.
with you.⌐The movie we went to see was good.	Move text down to line below.
There were no people there. ⌐ Jason thought we should go.	Move text up to line above.

Directions: Use editing marks to edit this story.

The Fallen Log

There was once a log on the floor of a very damp and eerie forest two men came upon the log and sat down for a rest. these two men, leroy and larry, did not know that someone could hear every word they said. "I'm so tired, moaned larry, as he began unlacing his heavy hikingboots. "and my feet hurt, too."

"Quit complaining" friend his said. We've got miles to walk before we'll find the cave with the hidden treasure. besides, if you think you're tired at look feet my. with that he kicked off his tennis shoe and discovered a very red big toe. "i think i won't be able to go any farther.

"Sh-h-h, already!" the two men heard a voice. "enough about feet, enough!" Larry and Leroy began loking around them. theycouldn't see anyone, though. "I'm in hree the voice said hoarsely.

Editing

Directions: Use editing marks to edit the continuing story of Larry and Leroy.

Larry and Leroy

larry and leroy jumped up from the log as soon as they realized that they were sitting on something that had a voice. "Hey, that was fast, said the voice. "How did you figure out where i was?"

By this time larry and leroy felt a little silly. Theycertainly didn't want to talk to a log. they looked at each other and then back at the log again. together they turned around and started walking down the path that had brought them to this point in the forest. "Hey were are you going?" the voice called.

"Well, i-i-i don't know," Larry replied, wondering if he sould be answering a log. "Who are you?"

"I'm a tiny elf who has been lostin this tree foryears," said the voice.

"Sure you are," replied larr. with that he and lroy began running for their lives.

Name _____

Editing

Directions: Draw a line from the editing mark on the left to its meaning on the right.

copmlain

Close up a word.

The two boys came to class.
The girls, though,

Insert an apostrophe.

¶ This is the best pie ever.

Insert a comma.

this

Delete a word.

copy editor

We went zoo to the.

Transpose words.

There were two of us in the house.

Transpose letters.

Insert a space.

Once upon a time there were

Capitalize.

leonardo da vinci

Move text down to line below.

Thomas was the best.

Change letter to lower case.

The two girls came to class. The two
boys never came back until the
principal left.

Start a new paragraph.

Now, I will end the story

Move text up to line above.

was
My mother the best lady I know

Insert a period.

This is my mothers hat.

Insert a word.

Review

Directions: Use editing marks to edit the story. Also watch for and change:
Important details that may have been left out.
Places where the wording could be livelier.
Information that is not related to the story.

My friend Annie and I decided to go windsurfing one day. We gathered up our equipment—our windsuring boards and sails—and headed down to the lake. The air was coolthat day so annie and I didn't wear our bathing suits. we were just in cut-off shorts and t-shirts.

Ittook us a few minutes to get our windsails puttogether. Thiswas the first time Annie and I had ever did this alone. Usually ourbig brothers helped us. They had to be in school, though, and and annie and I don't so we decidedto try the sport alone.

Annie's smile was ok. But I was glad the sun was shining brighty.It made it feel like it was warming outside than it really was. "Are you sure we should do this?" saic annie, just as I was pulling my windsurf board down to the water. "It will be fine, I assured her. I had gum in my mouth.

I put my toe into the lake.

"Wow is it cold!" I yelled back to Annie. She pulled her windsurf board down beside mine. Hers was orange, blue and yellow. Mine was just purple and green. I finally got inot the water with my board Annie was right beside me. We got onto our boards and finally, both of us were standing up. But our windsails wouldn't move. Then Annie and I realized there was no wind that day!

Proofreading

Proofreading, or "proofing," means to carefully look over what has been written, checking for spelling, grammar, punctuation, and other errors. All good writers carefully proofread and correct their own work before turning it into an editor—or a teacher.

Here are three common proofreading marks:

Correct spelling   dog
                           ~~dot~~

Replace with lower case letter   A̸

Replace with capital letter   a̲̲

Directions: Carefully read the following paragraphs. Use proofreading marks to mark errors in the second paragraph. Correct all errors. The first sentence has been done for you.

         alarm
    A six-~~alurm~~ fire at 2121 w̲indsor Terrace on the northeast

side awoke apartment /Residents at 3 A.M. yesterday morning.

Elven people were in the biulding. No one was hurt in the

blase, which caused $200,000 of property damage.

    Proporty manager Jim Polaski credits a perfectly Functioning smoke alurm

system for waking residents so they could get out safely. A springkler system

were also in plase. "There was No panick," Polaski said proudly. "Everone was

calm and Orderly."

Proofreading

Directions: Proofread the news article. Mark and correct the 20 errors in capitalization and spelling.

Be Wise When Buying a Car

Each year, about five percent of the U.S. popalation buys a new car, acording to J.D. Link and Associates, a New York-based auto industry reseerch company.

"A new car is the second most expenseve purchase most people Ever make," says Link. "it's amazing how litle reseerch people do before they enter the car showroom."

Link says reseerch is the most impotant Thing a new car buyer can do to pertect himself or herself. That way, he or she wil get the Best car at the best price.

"the salespeople are not trying to get You the best deal," says Link. "they're trying to get themselves the best deal. Bee smart! Read up on new cars online and in magazines like *Car and Driver* and *motortrend* before you talk to a saleperson!"

NEW MODELS

Editing: Check Your Proofreading Skills

Directions: Read about the things you should remember when you are revising your writing. Then, follow the instructions to revise the paper below.

After you have finished writing your rough draft, you should reread it later to determine what changes you need to make to ensure it's the best possible paper you are capable of writing.

Ask yourself the following questions:
Does my paper stick to the topic?
Have I left out any important details?
Can I make the writing more lively?
Have I made errors in spelling, punctuation, or capitalization?
Is there any information that should be left out?

Directions: Revise the following story by making changes to correct spelling, punctuation, and capitalization; add details; and cross out words or sentences that do not stick to the topic.

Hunting for Treasure

No one really believes me when I tell them that I'm a treasure hunter. But really i am. It isn't just any treasure that I like to hunt, though. I like treasures related to coins. Usually when I go treasure huting I go alone. I always wear my blue coat.

One day my good friend Jesse wanted to come with me. Why would you want to do that?" I said. "Because I like coins, too," he replied. What Jesse did not know was that the Coins that I dig to find are not the coins that just anyone collects. The coins i like are special. They are coins that have been buried in dirt for years!

Ancient Egypt

Have you ever wished you could visit Egypt for a first-hand look at the pyramids and ancient mummies? For most people, learning about Egypt is the closest they will come to visiting these ancient sites.

Directions: Test your knowledge about Egypt by writing as many of the answers as you can.

1. Write a paragraph describing what you already know about Egypt.

_____

_____

_____

_____

_____

_____

2. Name at least two famous Egyptian kings or queens. _____

_____

3. What was the purpose of a pyramid? _____

_____

_____

_____

4. What was the purpose of mummification? _____

_____

_____

_____

5. What major river runs through Egypt? _____

Name _____

Taking Notes: Egyptian Mummies

Taking notes is the process of writing important points to remember, such as taking notes on material prepared by your teacher, what is discussed in class, or an article you read. Taking notes is useful when preparing for a test or when writing a report.
When taking notes, follow these steps:

1. Read the article carefully.
2. Select one or two important points from each paragraph.
3. Write your notes in your own words.
4. Reread your notes to be sure you understand what you have written.
5. Abbreviate words to save time.

Directions: Read about Egyptian mummies. Select one or two important points from each paragraph. Write your notes in your own words.

After the Egyptians discovered that bodies buried in the hot, dry sand of the desert became mummified, they began searching for ways to improve the mummification process. The use of natron became a vital part of embalming.

Natron is a type of white powdery salt found in oases throughout Egypt. An oasis is a place in the desert where underground water rises to the surface. This water contains many types of salts, including table salt. It also contained natron. As the water evaporated in the hot sun of the desert, the salts were left behind. Natron was then collected for use in the mummification process.

The body was dried in natron for up to 40 days. The natron caused the body to shrink and the skin to become leathery. For thousands of years, natron was a vital ingredient in preserving the bodies of kings, queens, and other wealthy Egyptian citizens.

Sample notes:

Paragraph 1 _Bodies buried in hot dry sand became mummified._
Natron is vital for embalming.

Paragraph 2 _____
_____

Paragraph 3 _____
_____

Outlining

Outlining is a way to organize information before you write an essay or informational paragraph. Outlining helps you understand the information you read.

This sample form will help you get started. When outlining, you can add more main points, more smaller points, and/or more examples.

Title
I. First Main Idea
   A. A smaller idea
      1. An example
      2. An example
   B. Another smaller idea
II. Second Main Idea
   A. A smaller idea
   B. Another smaller idea
      1. An example
      2. An example
III. Third Main Idea
   A. A smaller idea
   B. A smaller idea

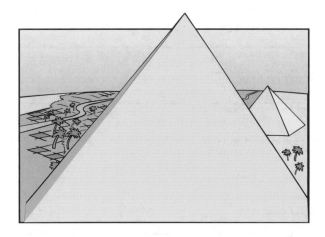

Directions: Read about building pyramids. Then, complete the outline on the next page.

The process of building pyramids began as a way to honor a king or queen. Since the Egyptians believed in an afterlife, they thought it only fitting for their kings and queens to have elaborate burial tombs filled with treasures to enjoy in the afterlife. Thus, the idea of the pyramid was born.

At first, pyramids were not built as they are known today. In the early stages of the Egyptian dynasty, kings were entombed in a *mastaba*. Mastabas were tombs made of mud-dried bricks. They formed a rectangular tomb with angled sides and a flat roof.

Later, as the Egyptian kingdom became more powerful, kings felt they needed grander tombs. The step pyramid was developed. These pyramids were made of stone, rather than mud, and were much taller. A large mastaba was built on the ground. Then, four more mastabas (each smaller than the previous) were stacked on top.

Finally, the pyramids took the shape that is familiar today. They were constructed with a flat bottom and four slanting sides that ascended to a final point. One of the tallest is over 400 feet high. These pyramids were also built of stone and were finished with an exterior of white limestone.

Outlining: Egyptian Pyramids

Directions: Complete the outline. Then, answer the question.

_____
(title)

I. Mastabas
   A. _____

   B. _____

   C. _____

II. Step pyramids
   A. _____

   B. _____

   C. _____

III. Pyramids
   A. _____

   B. _____

   C. _____

What do you find is the most interesting aspect about the pyramids of ancient Egypt? Why?

_____

_____

_____

_____

_____

_____

_____

Summarizing

A **summary** includes the main points from an article, book, or speech.

Example:

Tomb robbing was an important business in ancient Egypt. Often, entire families participated in the plunder of tombs. These robbers may have been laborers, officials, tomb architects, or guards, but they all probably had one thing in common. They were involved in the building or designing of the tomb, or they wouldn't have had the knowledge necessary to successfully rob the burial sites. Not only did tomb robbing ensure a rich life for the robbers, but it also enabled them to be buried with many riches themselves.

Summary:

Tomb robbing occurred in ancient Egypt. The robbers stole riches to use in their present lives or in their burials. Tomb robbers usually had some part in the building or design of the tomb. This allowed them to find the burial rooms where the treasures were stored.

Directions: Read about life in ancient Egypt. Then, write a three- to five-sentence summary.

Egyptologists have learned much from the pyramids and mummies of ancient Egypt from the items left by grave robbers.

Women of ancient Egypt wore makeup to enhance their features. Dark colored minerals called *kohl* were used as eyeliner and eye shadow. Men also wore eyeliner. Women used another mineral called *ocher* on their cheeks and lips to redden them. Henna, a plant which produces an orange dye, tinted the fingernails, the palms of their hands, and the soles of their feet.

Perfume was also important in ancient Egypt. Small cones made of wax were worn on top of the head. These cones contained perfume oils. The sun slowly melted the wax, and the perfume would scent the hair, head, and shoulders.

_____

_____

_____

_____

Name _____

Summarizing: King Tut

Directions: Read about King Tut. Then, write a five- to seven-sentence summary.

King Tutankhamen (TO-TAN-KO-MEN) became king of Egypt when he was only nine years old. Known today as "King Tut," he died in 1355 B.C. when he was 18. Because King Tut died so young, not much is known about what he did while he was king.

After his death, Tut's body was mummified and buried in a pyramid in the Valley of the Kings in Egypt. Many other kings of ancient Egypt were buried there also.

In 1922, King Tut became famous when an Englishman named Howard Carter discovered and explored his tomb. The king's mummy, wearing a gold mask decorated with precious stones, was found intact. Amazingly, all King Tut's riches were still in his tomb. His was the only one in the Valley of the Kings that had not been discovered and robbed.

The king's tomb contained four rooms. One contained his mummy. The other rooms were filled with beautiful furniture, including King Tut's throne. Also found in Tut's tomb were more than 3,000 objects, like clothes, jewelry, wine, food—and a trumpet that could still be played. Obviously, King Tut planned to live royally in the next world!

_____

_____

_____

_____

_____

_____

_____

_____

_____

Name _____

Place Value

The place value of a digit or numeral is shown by where it is in the number. In the number 1,234, 1 has the place value of thousands, 2 is hundreds, 3 is tens, and 4 is ones.

Example: 1,250,000,000

Read: One billion, two hundred fifty million

Write: 1,250,000,000

Billions			**Millions**			**Thousands**			**Ones**		
h	t	o	h	t	o	h	t	o	h	t	o
		1,		2	5	0,	0	0	0,	0	0	0

Directions: Read the words. Then, write the numbers.

twenty million, three hundred four thousand _____

five thousand, four hundred twenty-three _____

one hundred fifty billion, eight million,
one thousand, five hundred _____

sixty billion, seven hundred million,
one hundred thousand, three hundred twelve _____

four hundred million, fifteen thousand,
seven hundred one _____

six hundred ninety-nine million, four thousand,
nine hundred forty-two _____

Here's a game to play with a partner.

Write a 10-digit number using each digit, 0 to 9, only once. Do not show the number to your partner. Give clues like: "There is a five in the hundreds place." The clues can be given in any order. See if your partner can write the same number you have written.

Name _____

Place Value

Directions: Draw a line to connect each number to its correct written form.

1. 791,000

2. 350,000

3. 17,500,000

4. 3,500,000

5. 70,910

6. 35,500,000

7. 17,000,500,000

Three hundred fifty thousand

Seventeen million, five hundred thousand

Seven hundred ninety-one thousand

Seventy thousand, nine hundred ten

Three million, five hundred thousand

Seventeen billion, five hundred thousand

Thirty-five million, five hundred thousand

Directions: Look carefully at this number: 2,071,463,548. Write the numeral for each of the following places.

8. _____ ten thousands

9. _____ millions

10. _____ hundreds

11. _____ billions

12. _____ hundred thousands

13. _____ ten millions

14. _____ one thousands

15. _____ hundred millions

Comprehensive Curriculum - **Grade 5**

Name _____

Addition

Addition is putting together two or more numbers to find the sum.

Directions: Add. Fill the backpacks with the right answers.

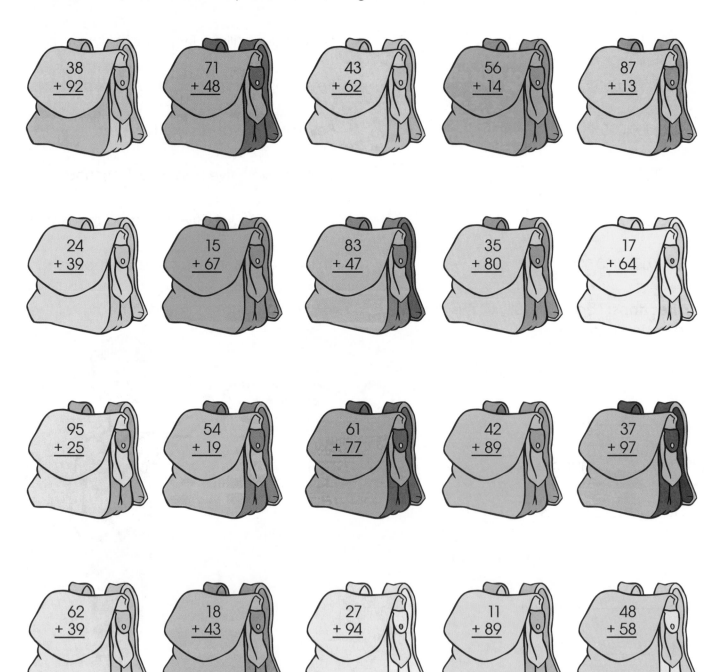

$$\begin{array}{r} 38 \\ + 92 \\ \hline \end{array}$$
$$\begin{array}{r} 71 \\ + 48 \\ \hline \end{array}$$
$$\begin{array}{r} 43 \\ + 62 \\ \hline \end{array}$$
$$\begin{array}{r} 56 \\ + 14 \\ \hline \end{array}$$
$$\begin{array}{r} 87 \\ + 13 \\ \hline \end{array}$$

$$\begin{array}{r} 24 \\ + 39 \\ \hline \end{array}$$
$$\begin{array}{r} 15 \\ + 67 \\ \hline \end{array}$$
$$\begin{array}{r} 83 \\ + 47 \\ \hline \end{array}$$
$$\begin{array}{r} 35 \\ + 80 \\ \hline \end{array}$$
$$\begin{array}{r} 17 \\ + 64 \\ \hline \end{array}$$

$$\begin{array}{r} 95 \\ + 25 \\ \hline \end{array}$$
$$\begin{array}{r} 54 \\ + 19 \\ \hline \end{array}$$
$$\begin{array}{r} 61 \\ + 77 \\ \hline \end{array}$$
$$\begin{array}{r} 42 \\ + 89 \\ \hline \end{array}$$
$$\begin{array}{r} 37 \\ + 97 \\ \hline \end{array}$$

$$\begin{array}{r} 62 \\ + 39 \\ \hline \end{array}$$
$$\begin{array}{r} 18 \\ + 43 \\ \hline \end{array}$$
$$\begin{array}{r} 27 \\ + 94 \\ \hline \end{array}$$
$$\begin{array}{r} 11 \\ + 89 \\ \hline \end{array}$$
$$\begin{array}{r} 48 \\ + 58 \\ \hline \end{array}$$

Addition

Teachers of an Earth science class planned to take 50 students on an overnight hiking and camping experience. After planning the menu, they went to the grocery store for supplies.

Breakfast	**Lunch**	**Dinner**	**Snacks**
bacon	sandwiches	pasta	graham crackers
eggs	apples	sauce	marshmallows
fruit	pretzels	garlic bread	chocolate bars
cereal	juice	salad	
juice	granola bars		
$34.50	$ 52.15	$ 47.25	$ 23.40

Directions: Answer the questions. Write the total amount spent on food for the trip.

What information do you need to answer the question? _____

_____

What is the total? _____

Directions: Add.

462 + 574	918 + 359	527 + 582	386 + 745	295 + 764
397 + 448	524 + 725	906 + 337	750 + 643	891 + 419
1,568 + 2,341	3,214 + 2,896	5,147 + 4,285	7,259 + 2,451	9,317 + 3,583

Name _____

Addition

Directions: Add.

1. Tourists travel to national parks to see the many animals that live there. Park rangers estimate 384 buffalo, 282 grizzly bears, and 426 deer are in the park. What is the total number of buffalo, bears, and deer estimated to be in the park?

_____

2. Last August, 2,248 visitors drove motor homes into the campgrounds for overnight camping. 647 set up campsites with tents. How many campsites were there altogether in August?

_____

3. During a three-week camping trip, Carlos and his family hiked 42 miles, took a 126-mile canoeing trip, and drove their car 853 miles. How many miles did they travel in all?

_____

4. Old Faithful is a geyser that spouts water high into the air. 10,000 gallons of water burst into the air regularly. Two other geysers spout 2,400 gallons of water during each eruption. What is the amount of water thrust into the air during one cycle?

_____

5. Yellowstone National Park covers approximately 2,221,772 acres of land. Close by, the Grand Tetons cover approximately 310,350 acres. How many acres of land are there in these two parks?

_____

6. Hiking trails cover 486 miles, motor routes around the north rim total 376 miles, and another 322 miles of road allow visitors to follow a loop around the southern part of the park. How many miles of trails and roadways are there?

_____

Addition

Bob the butcher is popular with the dogs in town. He was making a delivery this morning when he noticed he was being followed by two dogs. Bob tried to climb a ladder to escape from the dogs. Solve the following addition problems, and shade in the answers on the ladder. If all the numbers are shaded when the problems have been solved, Bob made it up the ladder. Some answers may not be on the ladder.

1. 986,145 621,332 + 200,008	2. 1,873,402 925,666 + 4,689	3. 506,328 886,510 + 342,225
4. 43,015 2,811,604 + 987,053	5. 18,443 300,604 + 999,999	6. 8,075 14,608 + 33,914
7. 9,162 7,804 + 755,122	8. 88,714 213,653 + 5,441,298	9. 3,244,662 1,986,114 + 521,387
10. 4,581 22,983 + 5,618,775	11. 818,623 926 + 3,260,004	12. 80,436 9,159 + 3,028,761

Ladder:
- 1,319,046
- 2,803,757
- 5,743,665
- 3,118,356
- 56,597
- 4,079,553
- 1,807,485
- 2,943,230
- 18,344,666
- 1,735,063
- 5,752,163
- 896,316
- 3,841,672
- 5,646,339

Does Bob make it? _____

Subtraction

Subtraction is taking away one number from another to find the difference between the two numbers.

Directions: Subtract.

76	93	68	49	88	54
− 23	− 14	− 25	− 17	− 39	− 25

Brent saved $75.00 of the money he earned delivering the local newspaper in his neighborhood. He wanted to buy a new bicycle that cost $139.00. How much more would he need to save in order to buy the bike?

_____

38	74	67	92	43	85
− 29	− 25	− 49	− 35	− 26	− 37

When Brent finally went to buy the bicycle, he saw a light and basket for the bike. He decided to buy them both. The light was $5.95, and the basket was $10.50. He gave the clerk a 20-dollar bill that his grandmother had given him for his birthday. How much change did he get back?

_____

Subtraction

When working with larger numbers, it is important to keep the numbers lined up according to place value.

Directions: Subtract.

$$
\begin{array}{r} 398 \\ -\ 149 \\ \hline \end{array}
\qquad
\begin{array}{r} 543 \\ -\ 287 \\ \hline \end{array}
\qquad
\begin{array}{r} 491 \\ -\ 311 \\ \hline \end{array}
$$

$$
\begin{array}{r} 786 \\ -\ 597 \\ \hline \end{array}
\qquad
\begin{array}{r} 1,825 \\ -\ 495 \\ \hline \end{array}
\qquad
\begin{array}{r} 4,172 \\ -\ 2,785 \\ \hline \end{array}
$$

$$
\begin{array}{r} 8,391 \\ -\ 5,492 \\ \hline \end{array}
\qquad
\begin{array}{r} 63,852 \\ -\ 34,765 \\ \hline \end{array}
\qquad
\begin{array}{r} 24,107 \\ -19,350 \\ \hline \end{array}
\qquad
\begin{array}{r} 52,900 \\ -\ 43,081 \\ \hline \end{array}
$$

Eagle Peak is the highest mountain peak at Yellowstone National Park. It is 11,353 feet high. The next highest point at the park is Mount Washburn. It is 10,243 feet tall. How much higher is Eagle Peak?

_____

The highest mountain peak in North America is Mount McKinley, which stretches 20,320 feet toward the sky. Two other mountain ranges in North America have peaks at 10,302 feet and 8,194 feet. What is the greatest difference between the peaks?

_____

Name _____

Checking Subtraction

You can check your subtraction by using addition.

Example: 34,436   Check: → 22,172
                 − 12,264   + 12,264
                 22,172   34,436

Directions: Subtract. Then, check your answers by adding.

15,326 − 11,532	Check:	28,615 − 25,329	Check:
96,521 − 47,378	Check:	46,496 − 35,877	Check:
77,911 − 63,783	Check:	156,901 −112,732	Check:
395,638 −187,569	Check:	67,002 − 53,195	Check:
16,075 −15,896	Check:	39,678 −19,769	Check:
84,654 − 49,997	Check:	12,335 −10,697	Check:

During the summer, 158,941 people visited Yellowstone National Park. During the fall, there were 52,397 visitors. How many more visitors went to the park during the summer than the fall?

_____

Addition and Subtraction

Directions: Check the answers. Write **T** if the answer is true and **F** if it is false.

Example: 48,973   Check: 35,856
      − 35,856   **F**   +13,118
        13,118   48,974

18,264   Check: 458,342   Check:
+ 17,893   − 297,652
36,157   _____   160,680   _____

39,854   Check: 631,928   Check:
+ 52,713   − 457,615
92,577   _____   174,313   _____

14,389   Check: 554,974   Check:
+ 93,587   − 376,585
107,976   _____   178,389   _____

87,321   Check: 109,568   Check:
− 62,348   + 97,373
24,973   _____   206,941   _____

Directions: Read the story problem. Write the equation, and check the answer.

A camper hikes 53,741 feet out into the wilderness. On his return trip, he takes a shortcut, walking 36,752 feet back to his cabin. The shortcut saves him 16,998 feet of hiking. True or false?

Name _____

Addition and Subtraction

Directions: Add or subtract to find the answers.

Eastland School hosted a field day. Students could sign up for a variety of events. 175 students signed up for individual races. Twenty two-person teams competed in the mile relay, and 36 kids took part in the high jump. How many students participated in the activities?

_____

Westmore School brought 42 students and 7 adults to the field day event. Northern School brought 84 students and 15 adults. There was a total of 300 students and 45 adults at the event. How many were from other schools?

_____

The Booster Club sponsored a concession stand during the day. Last year, they made $1,000 at the same event. This year they hoped to earn at least $1,250. They actually raised $1,842. How much more did they make than they had anticipated?

_____

Each school was awarded a trophy for participating in the field day's activities. The Booster Club planned to purchase three plaques as awards, but they only wanted to spend $150. The first-place trophy they selected was $68. The second-place award was $59. How much would they be able to spend on the third-place award if they stay within their budgeted amount?

_____

The Booster Club decided to spend $1,000 to purchase several items for the school with the money they had earned. Study the list of items suggested, and decide which combination of items they could purchase.

A. Swing set $425 _____

B. Sliding board $263 _____

C. Scoreboard $515 _____

D. Team uniforms $180 _____

Rounding

Rounding a number means to express it to the nearest ten, hundred, thousand, and so on. When rounding a number to the nearest ten, if the number has five or more ones, round up. Round down if the number has four or fewer ones.

Examples:

Round to the nearest ten:	84 ⟶	<u>80</u>	86 ⟶	<u>90</u>	
Round to the nearest hundred:	187 ⟶	<u>200</u>	120 ⟶	<u>100</u>	
Round to the nearest thousand:	981 ⟶	<u>1,000</u>	5,480 ⟶	<u>5,000</u>	

Directions: Round these numbers to the nearest ten.

87 ⟶ _____   53 ⟶ _____   48 ⟶ _____   32 ⟶ _____   76 ⟶ _____

Directions: Round these numbers to the nearest hundred.

168 ⟶ _____   243 ⟶ _____   591 ⟶ _____   743 ⟶ _____   493 ⟶ _____

Directions: Round these numbers to the nearest thousand.

895 ⟶ _____   3,492 ⟶ _____   7,521 ⟶ _____   14,904 ⟶ _____   62,387 ⟶ _____

City Populations	
City	Population
Cleveland	390,113
Seattle	652,405
Omaha	434,353
Kansas City	467,007
Atlanta	447,841
Austin	885,400

Directions: Use the city population chart to answer the questions.

Which city has a population of about 500,000?

_____

Which city has a population of about 900,000?

_____

How many cities have a population of about 400,000? _____

Which ones? _____

_____

Estimating

To **estimate** means to give an approximate rather than an exact answer. Rounding each number first makes it easy to estimate an answer.

Example:

$$\begin{array}{r} 93 \\ + 48 \\ \hline \end{array} \longrightarrow \begin{array}{r} 90 \\ + 50 \\ \hline 140 \end{array} \qquad \begin{array}{r} 321 \\ + 597 \\ \hline \end{array} \longrightarrow \begin{array}{r} 300 \\ + 600 \\ \hline 900 \end{array} \qquad \begin{array}{r} 1{,}859 \\ - 997 \\ \hline \end{array} \longrightarrow \begin{array}{r} 2{,}000 \\ - 1{,}000 \\ \hline 1{,}000 \end{array}$$

Directions: Estimate the sums and differences by rounding the numbers first.

$\begin{array}{r} 68 \\ + 34 \\ \hline \end{array} \longrightarrow$	$\begin{array}{r} 12 \\ + 98 \\ \hline \end{array} \longrightarrow$	$\begin{array}{r} 89 \\ + 23 \\ \hline \end{array} \longrightarrow$
$\begin{array}{r} 638 \\ - 395 \\ \hline \end{array} \longrightarrow$	$\begin{array}{r} 281 \\ - 69 \\ \hline \end{array} \longrightarrow$	$\begin{array}{r} 271 \\ - 126 \\ \hline \end{array} \longrightarrow$
$\begin{array}{r} 1{,}532 \\ - 998 \\ \hline \end{array} \longrightarrow$	$\begin{array}{r} 8{,}312 \\ - 4{,}789 \\ \hline \end{array} \longrightarrow$	$\begin{array}{r} 6{,}341 \\ + 9{,}286 \\ \hline \end{array} \longrightarrow$

Alejandra has $50 to purchase tennis shoes, a tennis racquet, and tennis balls. Does she have enough money?

_____

$23.00

$16.00

$3.00

Rounding and Estimating

Rounding numbers and estimating answers is an easy way of finding the approximate answer without writing out the problem or using a calculator.

Directions: Circle the correct answer.

Round to the nearest **ten**:

73 ⟶ 70
       80

48 ⟶ 40
       50

65 ⟶ 60
       70

85 ⟶ 80
       90

92 ⟶ 90
       100

37 ⟶ 30
       40

Round to the nearest **hundred**:

139 ⟶ 100
        200

782 ⟶ 700
        800

390 ⟶ 300
        400

640 ⟶ 600
        700

525 ⟶ 500
        600

457 ⟶ 400
        500

Round to the nearest **thousand**:

1,375 ⟶ 1,000
          2,000

21,800 ⟶ 21,000
           22,000

36,240 ⟶ 36,000
           37,000

Sam wanted to buy a new computer. He knew he had about $1,200 to spend. Which of the following ones could he afford to buy?

 $1,165

 $1,279

 $1,249

If Sam spent $39 on software for his new computer, $265 for a printer, and $38 for a cordless mouse, about how much money did he need?

_____

Name _____

Prime Numbers

Example: 3 is a prime number because 3 ÷ 1 = 3 and 3 ÷ 3 = 1. Any other divisor will result in a mixed number or fraction.

> A prime number is a positive whole number that can be divided evenly only by itself or one.

A **prime number** is any number greater than 1 that can only be divided by itself and the number 1.

A **composite number** is not a prime number. That is, it can be divided evenly by numbers other than itself and 1.

Directions: Write the first 15 prime numbers. Test them by dividing by 2 and by 3.

Prime Numbers:

_____   _____   _____   _____   _____

_____   _____   _____   _____   _____

_____   _____   _____   _____   _____

How many prime numbers are there between 0 and 100? _____

Prime Numbers

Directions: Circle the prime numbers.

71	3	82	20	43	69
128	97	23	111	75	51
13	44	137	68	171	83
61	21	77	101	34	16
2	39	92	17	52	29
19	156	63	99	27	147
121	25	88	12	87	55
57	7	139	91	9	37
67	183	5	59	11	95

Multiples

A **multiple** is the product of a specific number and any other number. When you multiply two numbers, the answer is called the **product**.

Example:

The multiples of 2 are 2 (2 x 1), 4 (2 x 2), 6, 8, 10, 12, and so on.

The **least common multiple** (LCM) of two or more numbers is the smallest number other than 0 that is a multiple of each number.

Example:

Multiples of 3 are 3, **6**, 9, **12**, 15, **18**, 21, **24**, etc.
Multiples of 6 are **6**, **12**, **18**, **24**, 30, 36, 42, etc.
Multiples that 3 and 6 have in common are 6, 12, 18, 24.
The LCM of 3 and 6 is 6.

Directions: Write the first nine multiples of 3, 4, and 6. Write the LCM.

3: _____ , _____ , _____ , _____ , _____ , _____ , _____ , _____ , _____

4: _____ , _____ , _____ , _____ , _____ , _____ , _____ , _____ , _____

6: _____ , _____ , _____ , _____ , _____ , _____ , _____ , _____ , _____

LCM = _____

Directions: Write the first nine multiples of 2 and 5. Write the LCM.

2: _____ , _____ , _____ , _____ , _____ , _____ , _____ , _____ , _____

5: _____ , _____ , _____ , _____ , _____ , _____ , _____ , _____ , _____

LCM = _____

Directions: Find the LCM for each pair of numbers.

7 and 3 _____   4 and 6 _____   6 and 9 _____

5 and 15 _____   5 and 4 _____   3 and 18 _____

Directions: Fill in the missing numbers.

30 has multiples of 5 and _____ , of 2 and _____ , of 3 and _____ .

Factors

Factors are the numbers multiplied together to give a product. The **greatest common factor** (GCF) is the largest number for a set of numbers that divides evenly into each number in the set.

Example:

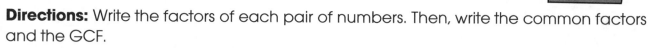

The factors of 12 are 3 x 4, 2 x 6, and 1 x 12.

We can write the factors like this: 3, 4, 2, 6, 12, 1.

The factors of 8 are 2, 4, 8, 1.

The common factors of 12 and 8 are 2 and 4 and 1.

The GCF of 12 and 8 is 4.

Directions: Write the factors of each pair of numbers. Then, write the common factors and the GCF.

1. 12: _____ , _____ , _____ , _____ , _____ , _____

    15: _____ , _____ , _____ , _____

    The common factors of 12 and 15 are _____ , _____ .

    The GCF is _____ .

2. 20: _____ , _____ , _____ , _____ , _____ , _____

    10: _____ , _____ , _____ , _____

    The common factors of 10 and 20 are _____ , _____ , _____ , _____ .

    The GCF is _____ .

3. 32: _____ , _____ , _____ , _____ , _____ , _____

    24: _____ , _____ , _____ , _____ , _____ , _____ , _____ , _____

    The common factors of 24 and 32 are _____ , _____ , _____ , _____ .

    The GCF is _____ .

Directions: Write the GCF for the following pairs of numbers.

28 and 20 _____   42 and 12 _____

36 and 12 _____   20 and 5 _____

Comprehensive Curriculum - **Grade 5**

Factor Trees

A **factor tree** shows the prime factors of a number. The factors for a prime number, such as 7, are only itself and 1.

Example:

30
6 x 5
3   2   5

30 = 3 x 2 x 5.

3, 2, and 5 are prime numbers.

Directions: Fill in the numbers in the factor tree.

Factor Trees

Directions: Fill in the numbers in the factor trees. The first one has been done for you.

Tree 1:

13,720

140 X 98

10 X 14 X 7

5 X 2 X 7 X 1

Tree 2:

[ ]

[ ] X [ ]

[ ] X [ ] X [ ]

1 X 2 X 2 X 3

Tree 3:

[ ]

[ ] X [ ]

[ ] X [ ] X [ ]

3 X 5 X 1 X 3

Comprehensive Curriculum - **Grade 5**

Name

Name _____

Greatest Common Factor

Directions: Write the greatest common factor for each set of numbers.

10 and 35 _____

2 and 10 _____

42 and 63 _____

16 and 40 _____

25 and 55 _____

12 and 20 _____

14 and 28 _____

8 and 20 _____

6 and 27 _____

15 and 35 _____

18 and 48 _____

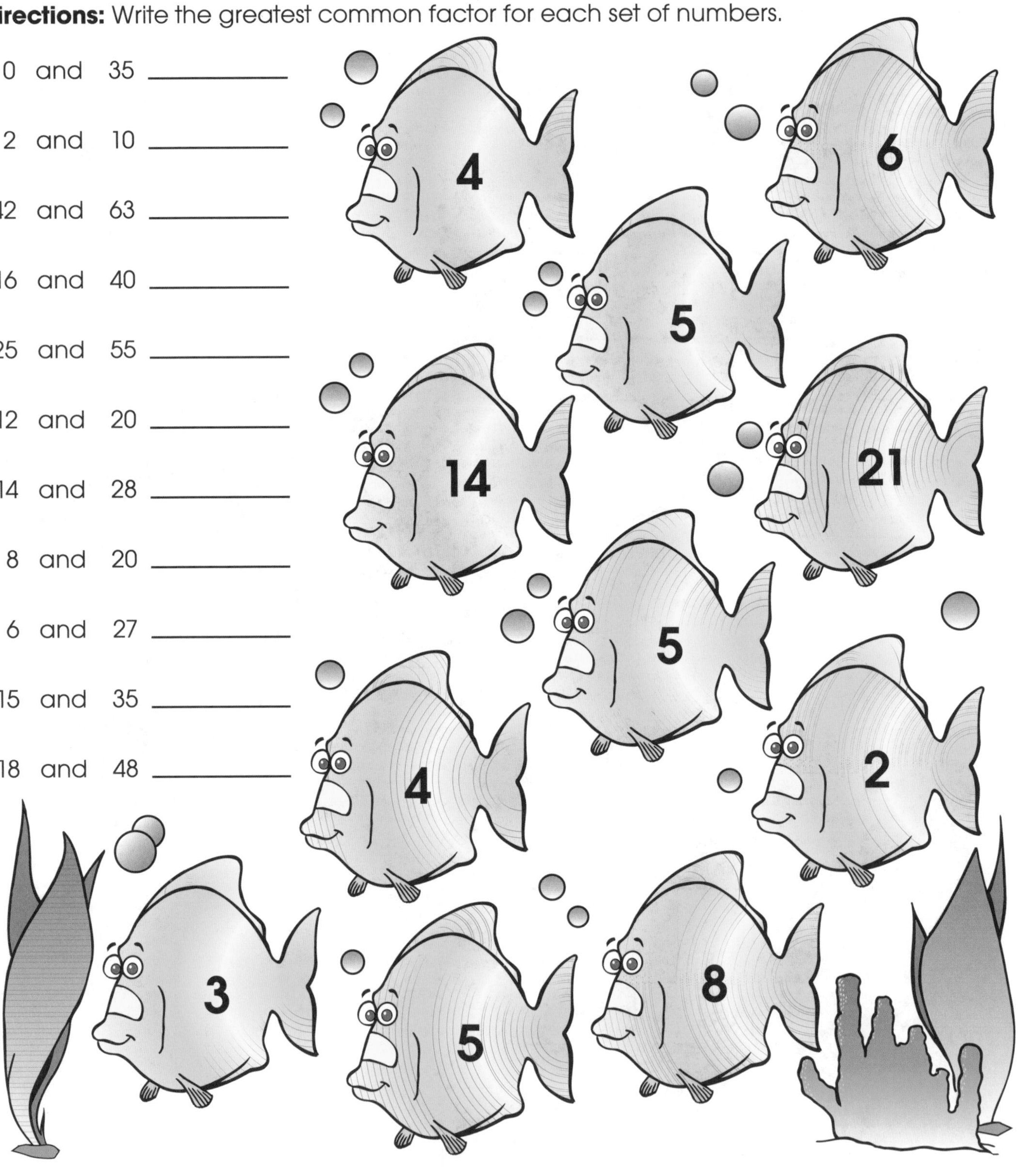

Least Common Multiple

Directions: Write the least common multiple for each pair of numbers.

12 and 7 _____

2 and 4 _____

22 and 4 _____

6 and 10 _____

3 and 7 _____

6 and 8 _____

5 and 10 _____

8 and 12 _____

9 and 15 _____

7 and 5 _____

3 and 8 _____

9 and 4 _____

Name _____

Multiplication

Multiplication is a process of quick addition of a number a certain number of times.

Example: 3 x 15 = 45   is the same as adding   15 + 15 + 15 = 45
15 three times.

Directions: Multiply.

32	48	26	19	63
x 3	x 7	x 5	x 6	x 2

251	523	915	431	275
x 4	x 8	x 3	x 7	x 3

412	643	526	742
x 21	x 17	x 22	x 35

256	874	372	951
x 74	x 15	x 45	x 34

Kerry is on the cross country team. She runs 3 miles every day except on her birthday. How many miles does she run each year?

_____

Multiplication

Be certain to keep the proper place value when multiplying by tens and hundreds.

Examples:

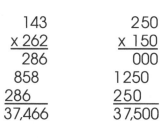

```
   143            250
 x 262          x 150
   286            000
   858           1250
   286            250
 37,466         37,500
```

Directions: Multiply.

```
   701            621            348            597
 x 308          x 538          x 200          x 424
```

```
   537            416            682            180
 x 189          x 727          x 472          x 340
```

```
   878            267            893            907
 x 638          x 196          x 214          x 428
```

An airplane flies 720 trips a year between the cities of Chicago and Columbus. Each trip is 375 miles. How many miles does the airplane fly each year?

_____

Name _____

Division

Division is the reverse of multiplication. It is the process of dividing a number into equal groups of smaller numbers.

Directions: Divide.

Greg had 936 marbles to share with his two brothers. If the boys divided them evenly, how many will each one get? _____

The marbles Greg kept were four different colors: blue, green, red, and orange. He had the same number of each color. He divided them into two groups. One group had only orange marbles. The rest of the marbles were in the other group. How many marbles did he have in each group?   orange _____ others _____

The **dividend** is the number to be divided by another number. In the problem $28 \div 7 = 4$, 28 is the dividend.

The **divisor** is the number by which another number is divided. In the problem $28 \div 7 = 4$, 7 is the divisor.

The **quotient** is the answer in a division problem. In the problem $28 \div 7 = 4$, 4 is the quotient.

The **remainder** is the number left over in the quotient of a division problem. In the problem $29 \div 7 = 4\ r1$, 1 is the remainder.

Directions: Write the answers.

In the problem $25 \div 8 = 3\ r1$ . . .

What is the divisor? _____   What is the remainder? _____

What is the quotient? _____   What is the dividend? _____

Directions: Divide.

$9\overline{)2,025}$ $6\overline{)2,508}$ $3\overline{)225}$ $5\overline{)400}$ $2\overline{)1,156}$

Division

The remainder in a division problem must always be less than the divisor.

Example:

$$
\begin{array}{r}
244\ r\ 23 \\
26\overline{)6{,}367} \\
\underline{52} \\
116 \\
\underline{104} \\
127 \\
\underline{104} \\
23
\end{array}
$$

Directions: Divide.

53)1,220   37)1,528   83)6,270   26)3,618

14)389   29)2,645   60)8,010   57)5,406

35)2,546   43)492   83)4,608   19)185

The Oregon Trail is 2,197 miles long. How long would it take a
covered wagon traveling 20 miles a day to complete the trip?

_____

Name _____

Checking Division

Answers in division problems can be checked by multiplying.

Example:

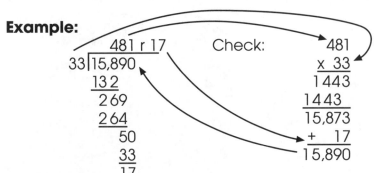

$$
\begin{array}{r}
481 \text{ r } 17 \\
33\overline{)15,890} \\
13\,2 \\
2\,69 \\
2\,64 \\
50 \\
33 \\
\hline
17
\end{array}
$$

Check:

$$
\begin{array}{r}
481 \\
\times\ 33 \\
\hline
1443 \\
1443 \\
\hline
15,873 \\
+\ \ 17 \\
\hline
15,890
\end{array}
$$

Add the
remainder

Directions: Divide and check your answers.

$61\overline{)2,736}$ Check:	$73\overline{)86,143}$ Check:
$59\overline{)9,390}$ Check:	$43\overline{)77,141}$ Check:
$33\overline{)82,050}$ Check:	$93\overline{)84,039}$ Check:

Denny has a baseball card collection. He has 13,789 cards. He wants to put the cards in a scrapbook that holds 15 cards on a page. How many pages does Denny need in his scrapbook? _____

Multiplication and Division

Directions: Multiply or divide to find the answers.

Brianne's summer job is mowing lawns for three of her neighbors. Each lawn takes about 1 hour to mow and needs to be done once every week. At the end of the summer, she will have earned a total of $630. She collected the same amount of money from each job. How much did each neighbor pay for her summer lawn service?

_____

If the mowing season lasts for 14 weeks, how much will Brianne earn for each job each week? _____

If she had worked for two more weeks, how much would she have earned? _____

Brianne agreed to shovel snow from the driveways and sidewalks for the same three neighbors. They agreed to pay her the same rate. However, it only snowed seven times that winter. How much did she earn shoveling snow? _____

What was her total income for both jobs? _____

Directions: Multiply or divide.

$$12\overline{)7{,}476} \qquad 23\overline{)21{,}620} \qquad 40\overline{)32{,}600}$$

$$32 \times 45 = \text{_____} \qquad 28 \times 15 = \text{_____} \qquad 73 \times 14 = \text{_____} \qquad 92 \times 30 = \text{_____}$$

Adding and Subtracting Like Fractions

A **fraction** is a number that names part of a whole. Examples of fractions are $\frac{1}{2}$ and $\frac{1}{3}$. **Like fractions** have the same **denominator**, or bottom number. Examples of like fractions are $\frac{1}{4}$ and $\frac{3}{4}$.

To add or subtract fractions, the denominators must be the same. Add or subtract only the **numerators**, the numbers above the line in fractions.

Example:

numerators
denominators
$\frac{5}{8} - \frac{1}{8} = \frac{4}{8}$

$\frac{5}{8}$ $\frac{1}{8}$ $\frac{4}{8}$

Directions: Add or subtract these fractions.

$\frac{6}{12} - \frac{3}{12} =$	$\frac{4}{9} + \frac{1}{9} =$	$\frac{1}{3} + \frac{1}{3} =$	$\frac{5}{11} + \frac{4}{11} =$
$\frac{3}{5} - \frac{1}{5} =$	$\frac{5}{6} - \frac{2}{6} =$	$\frac{3}{4} - \frac{2}{4} =$	$\frac{5}{10} + \frac{3}{10} =$
$\frac{3}{8} + \frac{2}{8} =$	$\frac{1}{7} + \frac{4}{7} =$	$\frac{2}{20} + \frac{15}{20} =$	$\frac{11}{15} - \frac{9}{15} =$

Directions: Color the part of each pizza that equals the given fraction.

$$\frac{2}{4} \qquad + \qquad \frac{1}{4} \qquad =$$

  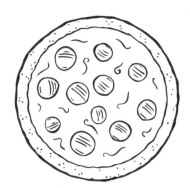

Adding and Subtracting Unlike Fractions

Unlike fractions have different denominators. Examples of unlike fractions are $\frac{1}{4}$ and $\frac{2}{5}$. To add or subtract fractions, the denominators must be the same.

Example:

Step 1: Make the denominators the same by finding the least common denominator. The LCD of a pair of fractions is the same as the least common multiple (LCM) of their denominators.

$$\frac{1}{3} + \frac{1}{4} =$$

Multiples of 3 are 3, 6, 9, **12**, 15.
Multiples of 4 are 4, 8, **12**, 16.
LCM (and LCD) = 12

Step 2: Multiply by a number that will give the LCD. The numerator and denominator must be multiplied by the same number.

A. $\frac{1}{3} \times \frac{4}{4} = \frac{4}{12}$ **B.** $\frac{1}{4} \times \frac{3}{3} = \frac{3}{12}$

Step 3: Add the fractions. $\frac{1}{3} + \frac{1}{4} = \frac{4}{12} + \frac{3}{12} = \frac{7}{12}$

Directions: Follow the above steps to add or subtract unlike fractions. Write the LCM.

$\frac{2}{4} + \frac{3}{8} =$ LCM = _____	$\frac{3}{6} + \frac{1}{3} =$ LCM = _____	$\frac{4}{5} - \frac{1}{4} =$ LCM = _____
$\frac{2}{3} + \frac{2}{9} =$ LCM = _____	$\frac{4}{7} - \frac{2}{14} =$ LCM = _____	$\frac{7}{12} - \frac{2}{4} =$ LCM = _____

The basketball team ordered two pizzas. They left $\frac{1}{3}$ of one and $\frac{1}{4}$ of the other. How much pizza was left?

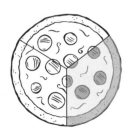 

_____

Reducing Fractions

A fraction is in lowest terms when the GCF of both the numerator and denominator is 1. These fractions are in lowest possible terms: $\frac{2}{3}$, $\frac{5}{8}$, and $\frac{99}{100}$.

Example: Write $\frac{4}{8}$ in lowest terms.

Step 1: Write the factors of 4 and 8.

Factors of 4 are **4**, 2, 1.

Factors of 8 are 1, 8, 2, **4**.

Step 2: Find the GCF: 4.

Step 3: Divide both the numerator and denominator by 4.

Directions: Write each fraction in lowest terms.

$\frac{6}{8}$ = _____ lowest terms $\frac{9}{12}$ = _____ lowest terms

factors of 6: 6, 1, 2, 3   factors of 9: _____ , _____ , _____   _____ GCF

factors of 8: 8, 1, 2, 4   factors of 12: _____ , _____ , _____ , _____ , _____ , _____   _____ GCF

$\frac{2}{6}$ =	$\frac{10}{15}$ =	$\frac{8}{32}$ =	$\frac{4}{10}$ =
$\frac{12}{18}$ =	$\frac{6}{8}$ =	$\frac{4}{6}$ =	$\frac{3}{9}$ =

Directions: Color the pizzas to show that $\frac{4}{6}$ in lowest terms is $\frac{2}{3}$.

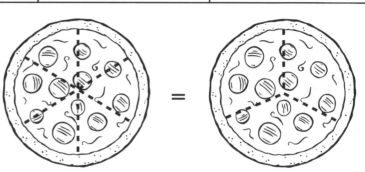

Improper Fractions

An **improper fraction** has a numerator that is greater than its denominator. An example of an improper fraction is $\frac{7}{6}$. An improper fraction should be reduced to its lowest terms.

Example: $\frac{5}{4}$ is an improper fraction because its numerator is greater than its denominator.

Step 1: Divide the numerator by the denominator: $5 \div 4 = 1, r1$

Step 2: Write the remainder as a fraction: $\frac{1}{4}$

$\frac{5}{4} = 1\frac{1}{4}$ $1\frac{1}{4}$ is a mixed number—a whole number and a fraction.

Directions: Follow the steps above to change the improper fractions to mixed numbers.

$\frac{9}{8} =$	$\frac{11}{5} =$	$\frac{5}{3} =$	$\frac{7}{6} =$	$\frac{8}{7} =$	$\frac{4}{3} =$
$\frac{21}{5} =$	$\frac{9}{4} =$	$\frac{3}{2} =$	$\frac{9}{6} =$	$\frac{25}{4} =$	$\frac{8}{3} =$

Sara had 29 duplicate stamps in her stamp collection. She decided to give them to four of her friends. If she gave each of them the same number of stamps, how many duplicates will she have left? _____

Name the improper fraction in this problem. _____

What step must you do next to solve the problem? _____

_____

Write your answer as a mixed number. _____

How many stamps could she give each of her friends? _____

Name _____

Mixed Numbers

A **mixed number** is a whole number and a fraction together. An example of a mixed number is $2\frac{3}{4}$. A mixed number can be changed to an improper fraction.

Example: $2\frac{3}{4}$

Step 1: Multiply the denominator by the whole number: $4 \times 2 = 8$

Step 2: Add the numerator: $8 + 3 = 11$

Step 3: Write the sum over the denominator: $\frac{11}{4}$

Directions: Follow the steps above to change the mixed numbers to improper fractions.

$3\frac{2}{3}$ =	$6\frac{1}{5}$ =	$4\frac{7}{8}$ =	$2\frac{1}{2}$ =
$1\frac{4}{5}$ =	$5\frac{3}{4}$ =	$7\frac{1}{8}$ =	$9\frac{1}{9}$ =
$8\frac{1}{2}$ =	$7\frac{1}{6}$ =	$5\frac{3}{5}$ =	$9\frac{3}{8}$ =
$12\frac{1}{5}$ =	$25\frac{1}{2}$ =	$10\frac{2}{3}$ =	$14\frac{3}{8}$ =

Adding Mixed Numbers

To add mixed numbers, first find the least common denominator.

Always reduce the answer to lowest terms.

Example:

$$5 \frac{1}{4} \longrightarrow 5 \frac{3}{12}$$

$$+ 6 \frac{1}{3} \longrightarrow + 6 \frac{4}{12}$$

$$11 \frac{7}{12}$$

Directions: Add. Reduce the answers to lowest terms.

$$8 \frac{1}{2}$$
$$+ 7 \frac{1}{4}$$

$$5 \frac{1}{4}$$
$$+ 2 \frac{3}{8}$$

$$9 \frac{3}{10}$$
$$+ 7 \frac{1}{5}$$

$$8 \frac{1}{5}$$
$$+ 6 \frac{7}{10}$$

$$4 \frac{4}{5}$$
$$+ 3 \frac{3}{10}$$

$$3 \frac{1}{2}$$
$$+ 7 \frac{1}{4}$$

$$4 \frac{1}{2}$$
$$+ 1 \frac{1}{3}$$

$$6 \frac{1}{12}$$
$$+ 3 \frac{3}{4}$$

$$5 \frac{1}{3}$$
$$+ 2 \frac{3}{9}$$

$$6 \frac{1}{3}$$
$$+ 2 \frac{2}{5}$$

$$2 \frac{2}{7}$$
$$+ 4 \frac{1}{14}$$

$$3 \frac{1}{2}$$
$$+ 3 \frac{1}{4}$$

The boys picked $3 \frac{1}{2}$ baskets of apples. The girls picked $5 \frac{1}{2}$ baskets. How many baskets of apples did the boys and girls pick in all?

_____

Subtracting Mixed Numbers

To subtract mixed numbers, first find the least common denominator. Reduce the answer to its lowest terms.

Directions: Subtract. Reduce to lowest terms.

Example:

$$6 \frac{5}{8} \rightarrow 6 \frac{10}{16}$$
$$- 3 \frac{4}{16} \rightarrow - 3 \frac{4}{16}$$
$$\overline{\qquad \qquad \qquad 3 \frac{6}{16} = 3 \frac{3}{8}}$$

$$2 \frac{3}{7}$$
$$- 1 \frac{1}{14}$$

$$7 \frac{2}{3}$$
$$- 5 \frac{1}{8}$$

$$6 \frac{3}{4}$$
$$- 2 \frac{3}{12}$$

$$9 \frac{5}{12}$$
$$- 5 \frac{9}{24}$$

$$5 \frac{1}{2}$$
$$- 3 \frac{1}{3}$$

$$7 \frac{3}{8}$$
$$- 5 \frac{1}{6}$$

$$8 \frac{3}{8}$$
$$- 6 \frac{5}{12}$$

$$11 \frac{5}{6}$$
$$- 7 \frac{1}{12}$$

$$9 \frac{3}{5}$$
$$- 7 \frac{1}{15}$$

$$4 \frac{4}{5}$$
$$- 2 \frac{1}{4}$$

$$9 \frac{2}{3}$$
$$- 4 \frac{1}{6}$$

$$14 \frac{3}{8}$$
$$- 9 \frac{3}{16}$$

The Rodriguez Farm has $9\frac{1}{2}$ acres of corn. The Johnson Farm has $7\frac{1}{3}$ acres of corn. How many more acres of corn does the Rodriguez Farm have? _____

Comparing Fractions

Directions: Use the symbol **>** (greater than), **<** (less than), or **=** (equal to) to show the relationship between each pair of fractions.

$\frac{1}{2}$ _____ $\frac{1}{3}$ $\frac{2}{5}$ _____ $\frac{3}{7}$ $\frac{3}{8}$ _____ $\frac{2}{4}$

$\frac{3}{4}$ _____ $\frac{6}{8}$ $\frac{2}{3}$ _____ $\frac{4}{5}$ $\frac{3}{9}$ _____ $\frac{1}{3}$

$\frac{3}{12}$ _____ $\frac{1}{4}$ $\frac{2}{14}$ _____ $\frac{1}{7}$ $\frac{5}{15}$ _____ $\frac{2}{3}$

If Kelly gave $\frac{1}{3}$ of a pizza to Holly and $\frac{1}{5}$ to Zoe, how much did she have left?

_____

Holly decided to share $\frac{1}{2}$ of her share of the pizza with Lila. How much did each of them actually get?

_____

Name _____

Ordering Fractions

When putting fractions in order from smallest to largest or largest to smallest, it helps to find a common denominator first.

Example:

$\frac{1}{3}$, $\frac{1}{2}$ changed to $\frac{2}{6}$, $\frac{3}{6}$

Directions: Put the following fractions in order from least to largest value.

				Least			Largest
$\frac{1}{2}$	$\frac{2}{7}$	$\frac{4}{5}$	$\frac{1}{3}$	_____	_____	_____	_____
$\frac{3}{12}$	$\frac{3}{6}$	$\frac{1}{3}$	$\frac{3}{4}$	_____	_____	_____	_____
$\frac{2}{5}$	$\frac{4}{15}$	$\frac{3}{5}$	$\frac{5}{15}$	_____	_____	_____	_____
$3\frac{4}{5}$	$3\frac{2}{5}$	$\frac{9}{5}$	$3\frac{1}{5}$	_____	_____	_____	_____
$9\frac{1}{3}$	$9\frac{2}{3}$	$9\frac{9}{12}$	$8\frac{2}{3}$	_____	_____	_____	_____
$5\frac{8}{12}$	$5\frac{5}{12}$	$5\frac{4}{24}$	$5\frac{3}{6}$	_____	_____	_____	_____
$4\frac{3}{5}$	$5\frac{7}{15}$	$6\frac{2}{5}$	$5\frac{1}{5}$	_____	_____	_____	_____

Four dogs were selected as finalists at a dog show. They were judged in four separate categories. One received a perfect score in each area. The dog with a score closest to four is the winner. Their scores are listed below. Which dog won the contest? _____

Dog A $3\frac{4}{5}$ Dog B $3\frac{2}{3}$ Dog C $3\frac{5}{15}$ Dog D $3\frac{9}{12}$

Multiplying Fractions

To multiply fractions, follow these steps:

$\frac{1}{2}$ x $\frac{3}{4}$ =   **Step 1:** Multiply the numerators.   1 x 3 = $\frac{3}{8}$
                   Step 2: Multiply the denominators.   2 x 4 = 8

When multiplying a fraction by a whole number, first change the whole number to a fraction.

Example:

$\frac{1}{2}$ x 8 = $\frac{1}{2}$ x $\frac{8}{1}$ = $\frac{8}{2}$ = 4 reduced to lowest terms

Directions: Multiply. Reduce your answers to lowest terms.

$\frac{3}{4}$ x $\frac{1}{6}$ =	$\frac{1}{2}$ x $\frac{5}{8}$ =	$\frac{2}{3}$ x $\frac{1}{6}$ =	$\frac{2}{3}$ x $\frac{1}{2}$ =
$\frac{5}{6}$ x 4 =	$\frac{3}{8}$ x $\frac{1}{16}$ =	$\frac{1}{5}$ x 5 =	$\frac{7}{8}$ x $\frac{3}{4}$ =
$\frac{7}{11}$ x $\frac{1}{3}$ =	$\frac{2}{9}$ x $\frac{9}{4}$ =	$\frac{1}{3}$ x $\frac{1}{3}$ x $\frac{1}{3}$ =	$\frac{1}{8}$ x $\frac{1}{4}$ x $\frac{1}{2}$ =

Amina has 10 pets. Two-fifths of the pets are cats, one-half are fish, and one-tenth are dogs. How many of each pet does she have?

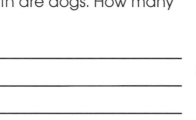

_____

_____

_____

Multiplying Mixed Numbers

Multiply mixed numbers by first changing them to improper fractions. Always reduce your answers to lowest terms.

Example:

$$2\frac{1}{3} \times 1\frac{1}{8} = \frac{7}{3} \times \frac{9}{8} = \frac{63}{24} = 2\frac{15}{24} = 2\frac{5}{8}$$

Directions: Multiply. Reduce to lowest terms.

$4\frac{1}{4} \times 2\frac{1}{5} =$	$1\frac{1}{3} \times 3\frac{1}{4} =$	$1\frac{1}{9} \times 3\frac{3}{5} =$
$1\frac{6}{7} \times 4\frac{1}{2} =$	$2\frac{3}{4} \times 2\frac{3}{5} =$	$4\frac{2}{3} \times 3\frac{1}{7} =$
$6\frac{2}{5} \times 2\frac{1}{8} =$	$3\frac{1}{7} \times 4\frac{5}{8} =$	$7\frac{3}{8} \times 2\frac{1}{9} =$

Sunnyside Farm has two barns with 25 stalls in each barn. Cows use $\frac{3}{5}$ of the stalls, and horses use the rest.

How many stalls are for cows? _____

How many are for horses? _____

(Hint: First, find how many total stalls are in the two barns.)

Dividing Fractions

To divide fractions, follow these steps:

$$\frac{3}{4} \div \frac{1}{4} =$$

Step 1: Invert the divisor. That means to turn it upside down.

$$\frac{3}{4} \div \frac{4}{1}$$

Step 2: Multiply the two fractions:

$$\frac{3}{4} \times \frac{4}{1} = \frac{12}{4}$$

Step 3: Reduce the fraction to lowest terms by dividing the denominator into the numerator.

$$12 \div 4 = 3$$

$$\frac{3}{4} \div \frac{1}{4} = 3$$

Directions: Follow the above steps to divide fractions.

$\frac{1}{4} \div \frac{1}{5} =$	$\frac{1}{3} \div \frac{1}{12} =$	$\frac{3}{4} \div \frac{1}{3} =$
$\frac{5}{12} \div \frac{1}{3} =$	$\frac{3}{4} \div \frac{1}{6} =$	$\frac{2}{9} \div \frac{2}{3} =$
$\frac{3}{7} \div \frac{1}{4} =$	$\frac{2}{3} \div \frac{4}{6} =$	$\frac{1}{8} \div \frac{2}{3} =$
$\frac{4}{5} \div \frac{1}{3} =$	$\frac{4}{8} \div \frac{1}{2} =$	$\frac{5}{12} \div \frac{6}{8} =$

Dividing Whole Numbers by Fractions

Follow these steps to divide a whole number by a fraction:

$$8 \div \frac{1}{4} =$$

Step 1: Write the whole number as a fraction:

$$\frac{8}{1} \div \frac{1}{4} =$$

Step 2: Invert the divisor.

$$\frac{8}{1} \div \frac{4}{1} =$$

Step 3: Multiply the two fractions:

$$\frac{8}{1} \times \frac{4}{1} = \frac{32}{1}$$

Step 4: Reduce the fraction to lowest terms by dividing the denominator into the numerator: $32 \div 1 = 32$

Directions: Follow the above steps to divide a whole number by a fraction.

$6 \div \frac{1}{3} =$	$4 \div \frac{1}{2} =$	$21 \div \frac{1}{3} =$
$8 \div \frac{1}{2} =$	$3 \div \frac{1}{6} =$	$15 \div \frac{1}{7} =$
$9 \div \frac{1}{5} =$	$4 \div \frac{1}{9} =$	$12 \div \frac{1}{6} =$

Three-fourths of a bag of popcorn fits into one bowl.
How many bowls do you need if you have six bags of popcorn? _____

Decimals

A **decimal** is a number with one or more places to the right of a decimal point.

Examples: 6.5 and 2.25

Fractions with denominators of 10 or 100 can be written as decimals.

Examples:

$$\frac{7}{10} = 0.7 \qquad \frac{0}{\text{ones}} . \frac{7}{\text{tenths}} \frac{0}{\text{hundredths}}$$

$$1\frac{52}{100} = 1.52 \qquad \frac{1}{\text{ones}} . \frac{5}{\text{tenths}} \frac{2}{\text{hundredths}}$$

Directions: Write the fractions as decimals.

$$\frac{1}{2} = \frac{}{10} = 0.\underline{\hspace{1cm}}$$

$$\frac{2}{5} = \frac{}{10} = 0.\underline{\hspace{1cm}}$$

$$\frac{1}{5} = \frac{}{10} = 0.\underline{\hspace{1cm}}$$

$$\frac{3}{5} = \frac{}{10} = 0.\underline{\hspace{1cm}}$$

$\frac{1}{2}$	$\frac{1}{4}$	$\frac{1}{5}$	1/10
			1/10
	$\frac{1}{4}$	$\frac{1}{5}$	1/10
			1/10
		$\frac{1}{5}$	1/10
$\frac{1}{2}$	$\frac{1}{4}$		1/10
		$\frac{1}{5}$	1/10
			1/10
	$\frac{1}{4}$	$\frac{1}{5}$	1/10
			1/10

$\frac{63}{100}$ =	$2\frac{8}{10}$ =	$38\frac{4}{100}$ =	$6\frac{13}{100}$ =
$\frac{1}{4}$ =	$\frac{2}{5}$ =	$\frac{1}{50}$ =	$\frac{100}{200}$ =
$5\frac{2}{100}$ =	$\frac{4}{25}$ =	$15\frac{3}{5}$ =	$\frac{3}{100}$ =

Name _____

Decimals and Fractions

Directions: Write the letter of the fraction that is equal to the decimal.

0.25 = _____

0.5 = _____

0.7 = _____

0.8 = _____

0.37 = _____

0.2 = _____

0.65 = _____

0.75 = _____

0.6 = _____

0.12 = _____

0.33 = _____

0.95 = _____

0.24 = _____

0.3 = _____

0.4 = _____

A. $\dfrac{33}{100}$

B. $\dfrac{3}{4}$

C. $\dfrac{13}{20}$

D. $\dfrac{3}{5}$

E. $\dfrac{3}{25}$

F. $\dfrac{19}{20}$

G. $\dfrac{1}{4}$

H. $\dfrac{2}{5}$

I. $\dfrac{3}{10}$

J. $\dfrac{37}{100}$

K. $\dfrac{1}{5}$

L. $\dfrac{1}{2}$

M. $\dfrac{6}{25}$

N. $\dfrac{4}{5}$

O. $\dfrac{7}{10}$

Adding and Subtracting Decimals

Add and subtract with decimals the same way you do with whole numbers. Keep the decimal points lined up so that you work with hundreths, then tenths, then ones, and so on.

Directions: Add or subtract. Remember to keep the decimal point in the proper place.

$$
\begin{array}{r} 0.5 \\ + 0.8 \\ \hline \end{array}
\qquad
\begin{array}{r} 0.35 \\ + 0.25 \\ \hline \end{array}
\qquad
\begin{array}{r} 47.5 \\ - 32.7 \\ \hline \end{array}
\qquad
\begin{array}{r} 85.7 \\ - 9.8 \\ \hline \end{array}
$$

$$
\begin{array}{r} 13.90 \\ + 4.23 \\ \hline \end{array}
\qquad
\begin{array}{r} 9.53 \\ - 8.16 \\ \hline \end{array}
\qquad
\begin{array}{r} 72.8 \\ - 63.9 \\ \hline \end{array}
\qquad
\begin{array}{r} 6.43 \\ + 4.58 \\ \hline \end{array}
$$

$$
\begin{array}{r} 638.07 \\ - 19.34 \\ \hline \end{array}
\qquad
\begin{array}{r} 811.060 \\ + 78.430 \\ \hline \end{array}
\qquad
\begin{array}{r} 521.09 \\ - 148.75 \\ \hline \end{array}
$$

$$
\begin{array}{r} 916.635 \\ + 172.136 \\ \hline \end{array}
\qquad
\begin{array}{r} 287.768 \\ - 63.951 \\ \hline \end{array}
\qquad
\begin{array}{r} 467.05 \\ - 398.19 \\ \hline \end{array}
$$

Sean ran a 1-mile race in 5.58 minutes. Carlos ran it in 6.38 minutes. How much less time did Sean need?

_____

Multiplying Decimals

Multiply with decimals the same way you do with whole numbers. The decimal point moves in multiplication. Count the number of decimal places in the problem, and use the same number of decimal places in your answer.

Example:

$$\begin{array}{r} 3.5 \\ \times\ 1.5 \\ \hline 175 \\ 35 \\ \hline 5.25 \end{array}$$

Directions: Multiply.

$$\begin{array}{r} 2.5 \\ \times\ .9 \\ \hline \end{array} \qquad \begin{array}{r} 67.4 \\ \times\ 2.3 \\ \hline \end{array} \qquad \begin{array}{r} 83.7 \\ \times\ 9.8 \\ \hline \end{array} \qquad \begin{array}{r} 13.35 \\ \times\ 3.06 \\ \hline \end{array}$$

$$\begin{array}{r} 9.06 \\ \times\ 2.38 \\ \hline \end{array} \qquad \begin{array}{r} 28.97 \\ \times\ 5.16 \\ \hline \end{array} \qquad \begin{array}{r} 33.41 \\ \times\ .93 \\ \hline \end{array} \qquad \begin{array}{r} 28.7 \\ \times\ 11.9 \\ \hline \end{array}$$

The jet flies 1.5 times faster than the plane with a propeller. The propeller plane flies 165.7 miles per hour. How fast does the jet fly?

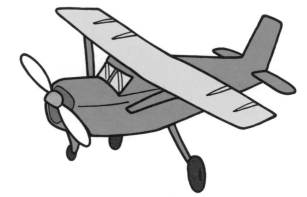

_____

Dividing with Decimals

When the dividend has a decimal, place the decimal point for the answer directly above the decimal point in the dividend. The first one has been done for you.

$$
\begin{array}{r}
12.5 \\
3\,\overline{)37.5} \\
-3 \\
\hline
07 \\
-6 \\
\hline
15 \\
-15 \\
\hline
0
\end{array}
$$

$4\,\overline{)34.4}$ $\qquad$ $2\,\overline{)31.6}$ $\qquad$ $3\,\overline{)131.4}$

$5\,\overline{)187.5}$ $\qquad$ $7\,\overline{)181.3}$ $\qquad$ $6\,\overline{)340.8}$ $\qquad$ $9\,\overline{)294.3}$

$3\,\overline{)135.6}$ $\qquad$ $5\,\overline{)264.5}$ $\qquad$ $2\,\overline{)134.6}$ $\qquad$ $8\,\overline{)754.4}$

$5\,\overline{)35.25}$ $\qquad$ $7\,\overline{)79.45}$ $\qquad$ $9\,\overline{)28.71}$ $\qquad$ $36\,\overline{)199.44}$

Name _____

Dividing Decimals by Decimals

When the divisor has a decimal point, you must eliminate it before dividing. You can do this by moving the decimal point to the right to create a whole number. You must also move the decimal point the same number of spaces to the right in the dividend.

Sometimes you need to add zeros to do this.

Example:

$0.25\overline{)85.50}$ changes to

$$
\begin{array}{r}
342 \\
25\overline{)8550} \\
-\underline{75} \\
105 \\
-\underline{100} \\
50 \\
\underline{50} \\
0
\end{array}
$$

Directions: Divide.

$0.3\overline{)27.9}$ $0.6\overline{)42.6}$ $0.9\overline{)81.9}$ $0.7\overline{)83.3}$

$0.4\overline{)23.2}$ $0.7\overline{)56.7}$ $1.2\overline{)10.8}$ $2.2\overline{)138.6}$

$12.6\overline{)5,670}$ $4.7\overline{)564}$ $8.6\overline{)842.8}$ $3.7\overline{)2,009.1}$

$5.9\overline{)1,917.5}$ $4.3\overline{)1,376}$ $2.9\overline{)922.2}$ $2.7\overline{)5613.3}$

Geometry

Geometry is the branch of mathematics that has to do with points, lines, and shapes.

Directions: Write the word from the box that fits each description. Use the glossary on pages 446-455 if you need help.

triangle	square	cube	angle
line	ray	segment	rectangle

a collection of points on a straight path that goes on and on in opposite directions _____

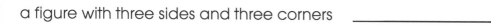

a figure with three sides and three corners _____

a figure with four equal sides and four corners _____

part of a line that has one end point and goes on and on in one direction _____

part of a line having two end points _____

a space figure with six square faces _____

two rays with a common end point _____

a figure with four corners and four sides _____

Comprehensive Curriculum - **Grade 5**

Geometry

Review the definitions on the previous page before completing the problems below.

Directions: Identify the labeled section of each of the following diagrams.

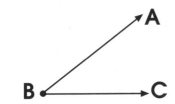

AB = _____

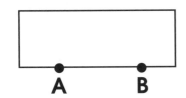

ABC = _____

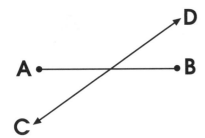

AB = _____

CD = _____

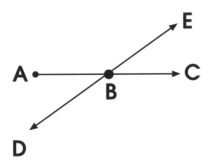

AC = _____

AB = _____

EBC = _____

BC = _____

Similar, Congruent, and Symmetrical Figures

Similar figures have the same shape but have varying sizes.

Figures that are **congruent** have identical shapes but different orientations. That means they face in different directions.

Symmetrical figures can be divided equally into two identical parts.

Directions: Cross out the shape that does not belong in each group. Label the two remaining shapes as similiar, congruent, or symmetrical.

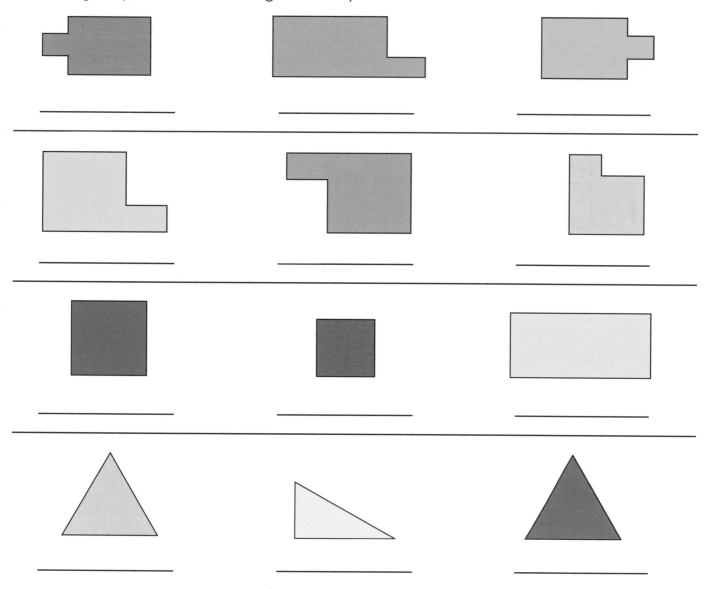

Comprehensive Curriculum - **Grade 5**

Perimeter and Area

The **perimeter (P)** of a figure is the distance around it. To find the perimeter, add the lengths of the sides.

The **area (A)** of a figure is the number of units in a figure. Find the area by multiplying the length of a figure by its width.

Example:

P = 16 units
A = 16 units

Directions: Find the perimeter and area of each figure.

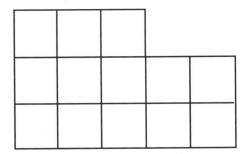

P = _____

A = _____

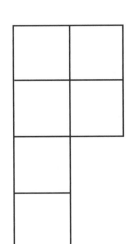

P = _____

A = _____

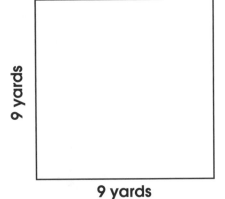

9 yards

P = _____

A = _____

2 miles

45 miles

P = _____

A = _____

Volume

The formula for finding the volume of a box is length times width times height **(L x W x H)**. The answer is given in cubic units.

Directions: Solve the problems.

Example:

Height 8 ft.
Length 8 ft.
Width   8 ft. **L** x **W** x **H** = **volume**
8' x 8' x 8' = 512 cubic ft. or 512 ft.³

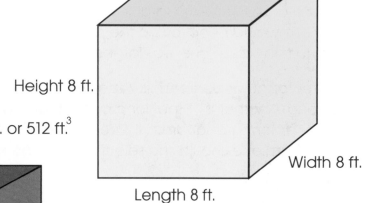

Height 8 ft.
Width 8 ft.
Length 8 ft.

4 ft.
12 ft.
6 ft.

V = _____

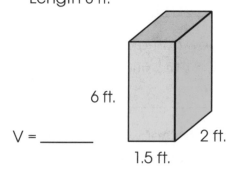

6 ft.
2 ft.
1.5 ft.

V = _____

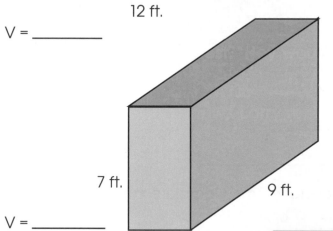

7 ft.
9 ft.
3 ft.

V = _____

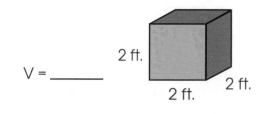

2 ft.
2 ft.
2 ft.

V = _____

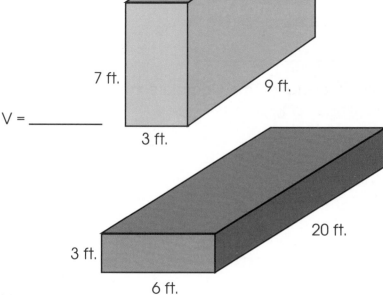

3 ft.
6 ft.
20 ft.

V = _____

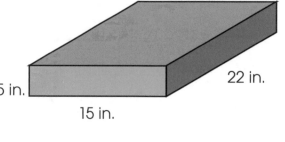

5 in.
15 in.
22 in.

V = _____

Perimeter and Area

Directions: Use the formulas for finding perimeter and area to solve these problems.

Julie's family moved to a new house. Her parents said she could have the largest bedroom. Julie knew she would need to find the area of each room to find which one was largest.

One rectangular bedroom is 7 feet wide and 12 feet long. Another is 11 feet long and 9 feet wide. The third bedroom is a square. It is 9 feet wide and 9 feet long. Which one should she select to have the largest room?

_____

The new home also has a swimming pool in the backyard. It is 32 feet long and 18 feet wide. What is the perimeter of the pool?

_____

Julie's mother wants to plant flowers on each side of the new house. She will need three plants for every foot of space. The house is 75 feet across the front and back and 37.5 feet along each side. Find the perimeter of the house.

_____

How many plants should she buy? _____

The family decided to buy new carpeting for several rooms. Complete the necessary information to determine how much carpeting to buy.

Den: 12 ft. x 14 ft. = _____ sq. ft.

Master bedroom: 20 ft. x _____ = 360 sq. ft.

Family room: _____ x 25 ft. = 375 sq. ft.

Total square feet of carpeting: _____

Perimeter, Area, and Volume

Directions: Find the perimeter and area.

1. Length = 8 ft.

   Width = 11 ft.

   P = _____ A = _____

2. Length = 12 ft.

   Width = 10 ft.

   P = _____ A = _____

3. Length = 121 ft.

   Width = 16 ft.

   P = _____ A = _____

4. Length = 72 in.

   Width = 5 ft.

   P = _____ A = _____

Directions: Find the perimeter, area, and volume.

5. Length = 7 ft.

    Width = 12 ft.

    Height = 10 ft.

    P = _____

    A = _____

    V = _____

6. Length = 48 in.

    Width = 7 ft.

    Height = 12 in.

    P = _____

    A = _____

    V = _____

7. Length = 12 in.

    Width = 15 in.

    Height = 20 in.

    P = _____

    A = _____

    V = _____

8. Length = 22 ft.

    Width = 40 ft.

    Height = 10 ft.

    P = _____

    A = _____

    V = _____

Circumference

Circumference is the distance around a circle. The **diameter** is a line segment that passes through the center of a circle and has both end points on the circle.

To find the circumference of any circle, multiply 3.14 times the diameter. The number 3.14 represents **pi** (pronounced *pie*) and is often represented by this Greek symbol, π.

The formula for circumference is C = π x d

> C = circumference
>
> d = diameter
>
> π = 3.14

Example:

Circle A
d = 2 in.
C = 3.14 x 2 in.
C = 6.28 in.

Directions: Find the circumference of each circle.

4 in.

C = _____

6 in.

C = _____

d = 10 in.

C = _____

d = 14 in.

C = _____

d = 3 yd.

C = _____

d = 4 ft.

C = _____

d = 8 ft.

C = _____

d = 12 ft.

C = _____

Circumference

The **radius** of a circle is the distance from the center of the circle to its outside edge. The diameter equals two times the radius.

Find the circumference by multiplying π (3.14) times the diameter or by multiplying π (3.14) times 2r (2 times the radius).

C = π x d or C = π x 2r

Directions: Write the missing radius, diameter, or circumference.

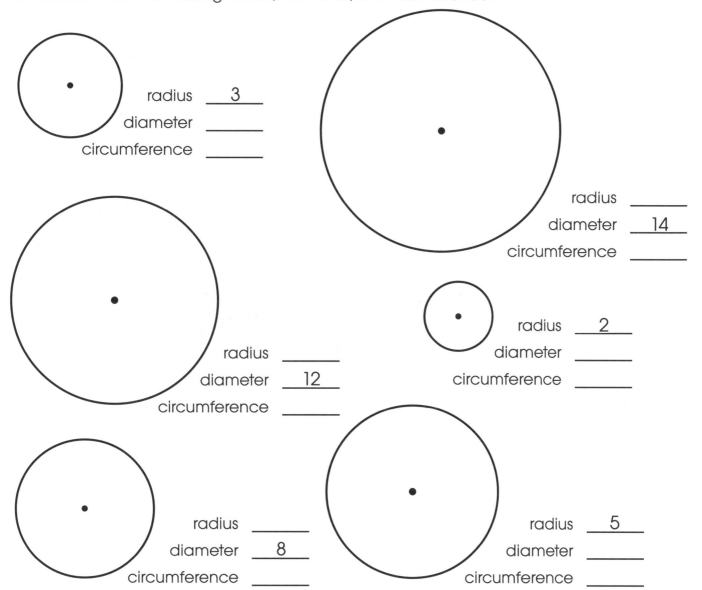

radius ___3___
diameter _____
circumference _____

radius _____
diameter ___14___
circumference _____

radius _____
diameter ___12___
circumference _____

radius ___2___
diameter _____
circumference _____

radius _____
diameter ___8___
circumference _____

radius ___5___
diameter _____
circumference _____

Name _____

Diameter, Radius, and Circumference

C = π x d or C = π x 2r

Directions: Write the missing radius, diameter, or circumference.

Katie was asked to draw a circle on the playground for a game during recess. If the radius of the circle needed to be 14 inches, how long is the diameter? _____

What is the circumference? _____

A friend told her that more kids could play the game if they enlarged the circle. She had a friend help her. They made the diameter of the circle 45 inches long.

What is the radius? _____

What is the circumference? _____

Jamie was creating an art project. He wanted part of it to be a sphere. He measured 24 inches for the diameter.

What would the radius of the sphere be? _____

Find the circumference. _____

Unfortunately, Jamie discovered that he didn't have enough material to create a sphere that large, so he cut the dimensions in half. What are the new dimensions for his sphere?

Radius _____

Diameter _____

Circumference _____

Triangle Angles

A **triangle** is a figure with three corners and three sides. Every triangle contains three angles. The sum of the angles is always 180°, regardless of the size or shape of the triangle.

If you know two of the angles, you can add them together, and then subtract the total from 180 to find the number of degrees in the third angle.

Directions: Find the number of degrees in the third angle of each triangle.

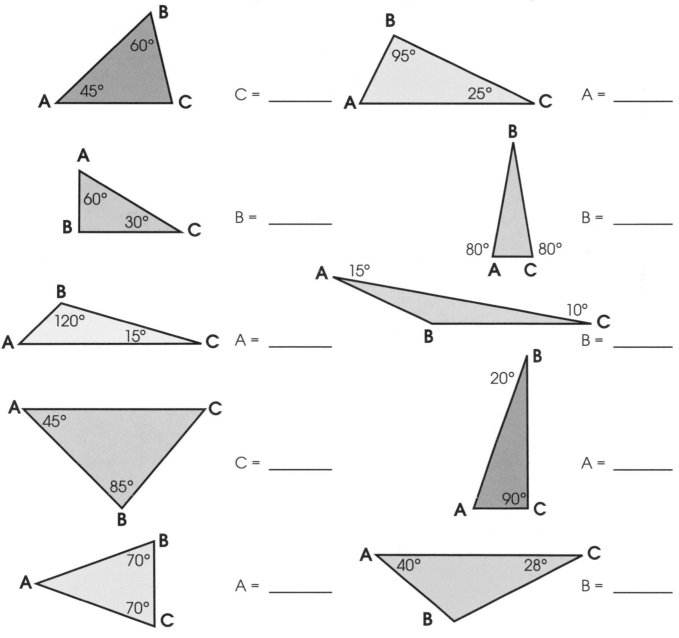

C = _____

A = _____

B = _____

B = _____

A = _____

B = _____

C = _____

A = _____

A = _____

B = _____

Name _____

Area of a Triangle

The area of a triangle is found by multiplying $\frac{1}{2}$ times the base times the height.
$A = \frac{1}{2} \times b \times h$

Example:

$\overline{CD}$ is the height.   4 in.

$\overline{AB}$ is the base.   8 in.

Area $= \frac{1}{2} \times 4 \times 8 = \frac{32}{2} = 16$ sq. in.

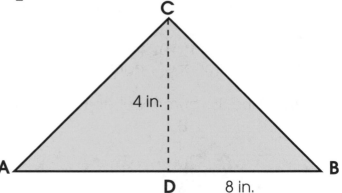

Directions: Find the area of each triangle.

4 in.

2 in.

A = _____

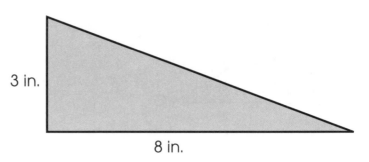

3 in.

8 in.

A = _____

9 in.

4 in.

A = _____

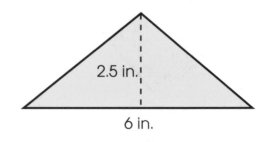

2.5 in.

6 in.

A = _____

Space Figures

Space figures are figures whose points are in more than one plane. Cubes and cylinders are space figures.

 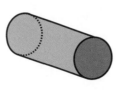 sphere

rectangular prism **cone** **cube** **cylinder** **sphere** **pyramid**

A **prism** has two identical, parallel bases.

All of the faces on a **rectangular prism** are rectangles.

A **cube** is a prism with six identical, square faces.

A **pyramid** is a space figure whose base is a polygon and whose faces are triangles with a common vertex—the point where two rays meet.

A **cylinder** has a curved surface and two parallel bases that are identical circles.

A **cone** has one circular, flat face and one vertex.

A **sphere** has no flat surface. All points are an equal distance from the center.

Directions: Circle the name of the figure you see in each of these familiar objects

cone	sphere	cylinder
cone	sphere	cylinder
cube	rectangular prism	pyramid
cone	pyramid	cylinder

Name _____

Length

Inches, **feet**, **yards**, and **miles** are used to measure length in the United States.

12 inches = 1 foot (ft.)

3 feet = 1 yard (yd.)

36 inches = 1 yard

1,760 yards = 1 mile (mi.)

Directions: Circle the best unit to measure each object. The first one has been done for you.

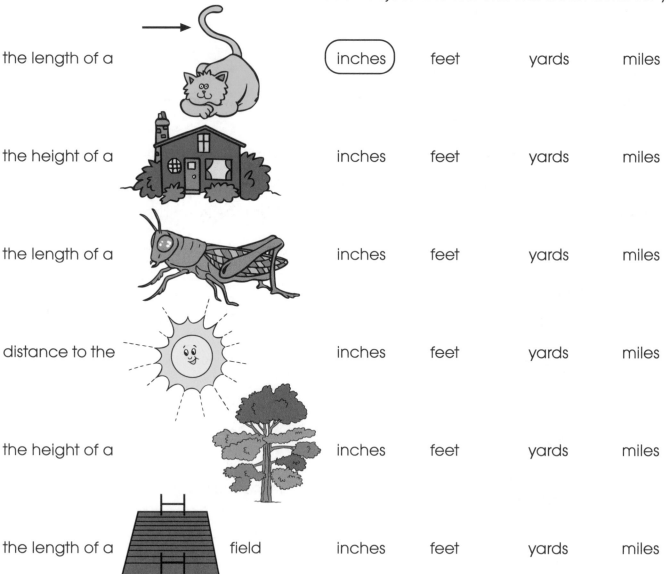

	inches	feet	yards	miles
the length of a	(inches)	feet	yards	miles
the height of a	inches	feet	yards	miles
the length of a	inches	feet	yards	miles
distance to the	inches	feet	yards	miles
the height of a	inches	feet	yards	miles
the length of a field	inches	feet	yards	miles

Length

Directions: Use a ruler to find the shortest paths. Round your measurement to the nearest quarter inch. Then, convert to yards using the scale.

Scale: 1 inch = 100 yards

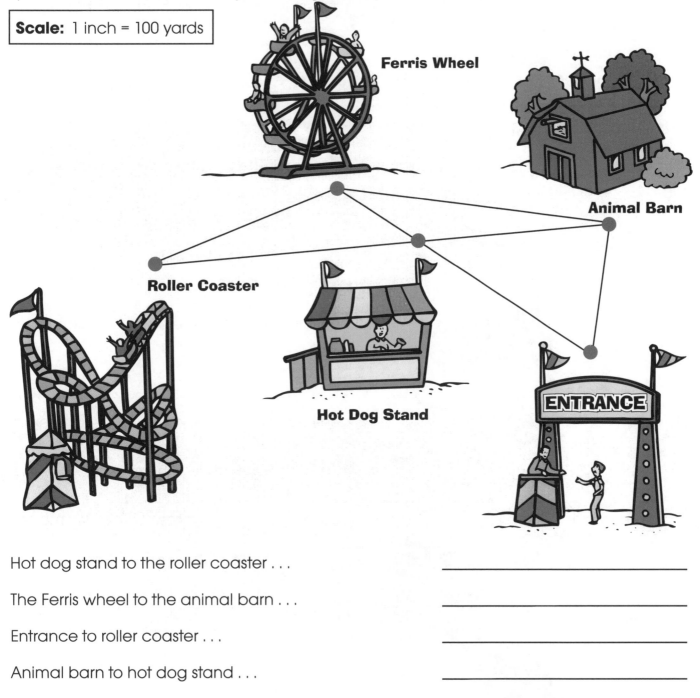

Hot dog stand to the roller coaster . . .   _____

The Ferris wheel to the animal barn . . .   _____

Entrance to roller coaster . . .   _____

Animal barn to hot dog stand . . .   _____

Ferris wheel to roller coaster to entrance . . .   _____

Name _____

Length: Metric

Millimeters, **centimeters**, **meters**, and **kilometers** are used to measure length in the metric system.

1 meter = 39.37 inches

1 kilometer = about $\frac{5}{8}$ mile

10 millimeters = 1 centimeter (cm)

100 centimeters = 1 meter (m)

1,000 meters = 1 kilometer (km)

Directions: Circle the best unit to measure each object. The first one has been done for you.

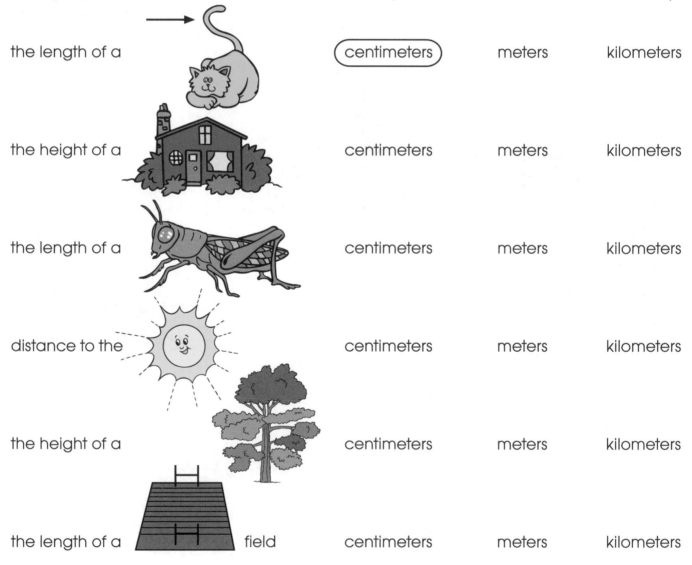

the length of a	(centimeters)	meters	kilometers
the height of a	centimeters	meters	kilometers
the length of a	centimeters	meters	kilometers
distance to the	centimeters	meters	kilometers
the height of a	centimeters	meters	kilometers
the length of a _____ field	centimeters	meters	kilometers

Weight

Ounces, **pounds**, and **tons** are used to measure weight in the United States.

16 ounces = 1 pound (lb.)
2,000 pounds = 1 ton (tn.)

Directions: Circle the most reasonable estimate for the weight of each object. The first one has been done for you.

10 ounces	(10 pounds)	10 tons
6 ounces	6 pounds	6 tons
2 ounces	2 pounds	2 tons
3 ounces	3 pounds	3 tons
1,800 ounces	1,800 pounds	1,800 tons
20 ounces	20 pounds	20 tons
1 ounce	1 pound	1 ton

Weight: Metric

Grams and **kilograms** are units of weight in the metric system. A paper clip weighs about 1 gram. A kitten weighs about 1 kilogram.

1 kilogram (kg) = about 2.2 pounds

1,000 grams (g) = 1 kilogram

Directions: Circle the best unit to weigh each object.

kilogram
gram

kilogram
gram

kilogram
gram

kilogram
gram

kilogram
gram

kilogram
gram

kilogram
gram

kilogram
gram

kilogram
gram

kilogram
gram

Capacity

The **fluid ounce**, **cup**, **pint**, **quart**, and **gallon** are used to measure capacity in the United States.

1 cup

1 pint

1 quart

1 half gallon

1 gallon

> **8 fluid ounces (fl. oz.) = 1 cup (c.)**
> **2 cups = 1 pint (pt.)**
> **2 pints = 1 quart (qt.)**
> **2 quarts = 1 half gallon ($\frac{1}{2}$ gal.)**
> **4 quarts = 1 gallon (gal.)**

Directions: Convert the units of capacity.

13 gal. = _____ qt.   10 pt. = _____ c.   12 c. = _____ pt.

4 gal. = _____ qt.   16 qt. = _____ gal.   5 c. = _____ pt.

36 pt. = _____ gal.   12 qt. = _____ pt.   6 gal. = _____ pt.

16 c. = _____ qt.   32 oz. = _____ c.   16 oz. = _____ pt.

Capacity: Metric

Milliliters and liters are units of capacity in the metric system. A can of soda contains about 350 milliliters of liquid. A large plastic bottle contains 1 liter of liquid. A liter is about a quart.

1,000 milliliters (mL) = 1 liter (L)

Directions: Circle the best unit to measure each liquid.

milliliters
liters

milliliters
liters

milliliters
liters

milliliters
liters

milliliters
liters

milliliters
liters

milliliters
liters

milliliters
liters

milliliters
liters

milliliters
liters

Comparing Measurements

Directions: Use the symbols greater than (>), less than (<), or equal to (=) to complete each statement.

10 inches   _____   10 centimeters

40 feet   _____   120 yards

25 grams   _____   25 kilograms

16 quarts   _____   4 gallons

2 liters   _____   2 milliliters

16 yards   _____   6 meters

3 miles   _____   3 kilometers

20 centimeters _____ 20 meters

85 kilograms   _____   8 grams

2 liters   _____   1 gallon

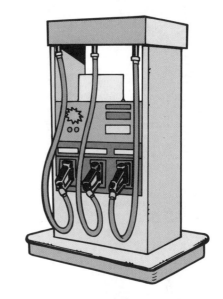

Name _____

Temperature: Fahrenheit

Degrees Fahrenheit (°F) is a unit for measuring temperature.

Directions: Write the temperature in degrees Fahrenheit (°F).

Example:

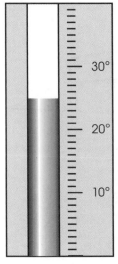
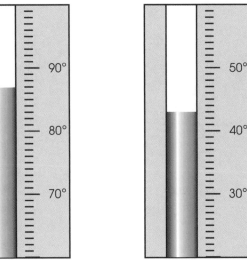
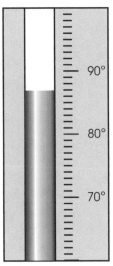

25°F   _____   _____   _____

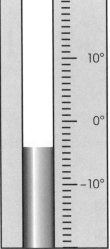
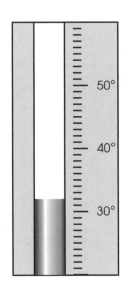

_____   _____   _____   _____

Temperature: Celsius

Degrees Celsius (°C) is a unit for measuring temperature in the metric system. Zero °C is equivalent to 32°F.

Directions: Write the temperature in degrees Celsius (°C).

Example:

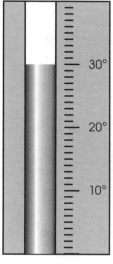 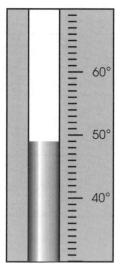 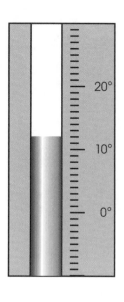 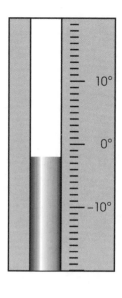

$30°C$

_____ _____ _____

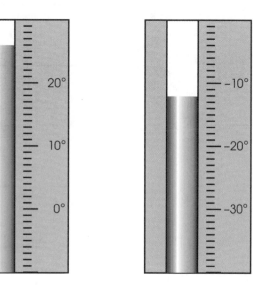 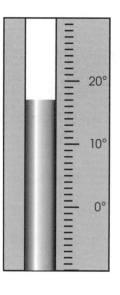

_____ _____ _____ _____

Review

Directions: Write the best unit to measure each item: inch, foot, yard, mile, ounce, pound, ton, fluid ounce, cup, pint, quart, or gallon.

distance from New York to Chicago _____

weight of a goldfish _____

height of a building _____

water in a large fish tank _____

glass of milk _____

weight of a whale _____

length of a pencil _____

distance from first base to second base _____

distance traveled by a space shuttle _____

length of a soccer field _____

amount of paint needed to cover a house _____

material needed to make a dress _____

Ratio

A **ratio** is a comparison of two quantities.

Ratios can be written three ways: 2 to 3 or 2 : 3 or $\frac{2}{3}$. Each ratio is read: two to three.

Example:

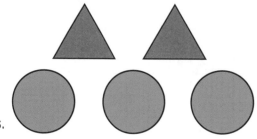

The ratio of triangles to circles is 2 to 3.

The ratio of circles to triangles is 3 to 2.

Directions: Write the ratio that compares these items.

ratio of tulips to cacti _____

ratio of cubes to triangles _____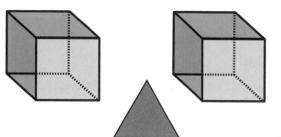

ratio of pens to pencils _____

Name _____

Percent

Percent is a ratio meaning "per hundred." It is written with a % sign. 20% means 20 percent or 20 per hundred.

Example:

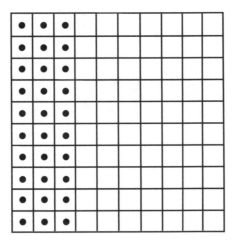

ratio = $\dfrac{30}{100}$

percent = 30%

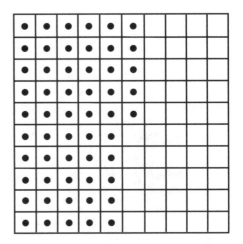

ratio = _____

percent = _____

Directions: Write the percent for each ratio.

Book Sale

$\dfrac{7}{100} =$	$\dfrac{38}{100} =$
$\dfrac{63}{100} =$	$\dfrac{3}{100} =$
$\dfrac{40}{100} =$	$\dfrac{1}{5} =$

The school received 100 books for the Book Fair. It sold 43 books.

What is the ratio of books sold to books received? _____

What percentage of books sold? _____

Probability

Probability is the ratio of favorable outcomes to possible outcomes of an experiment.

Vehicle	Number Sold
4 door	26
2 door	18
Sport	7
Van	12
Wagon	7
Compact	5
Total	75

Example:

This table records vehicle sales for 1 month. What is the probability of a person buying a van?

number of vans sold = 12   total number of cars = 75

The probability that a person will choose a van is 12 in 75 or $\frac{12}{75}$.

Directions: Look at the chart of flowers sold in a month. What is the probability that a person will buy each type of flower?

Roses   _____

Tulips   _____

Violets   _____

Orchids   _____

Flowers	Number Sold
Roses	48
Tulips	10
Violets	11
Orchids	7
Total	76

How would probability help a flower store owner keep the correct quantity of each flower in the store?

_____

_____

_____

Using Calculators to Find Percent

A **calculator** is a machine that rapidly does addition, subtraction, multiplication, division, and other mathematical functions.

Example:

Carlos got 7 hits in 20 "at bats."

$$\frac{7}{20} = \frac{35}{100} = 35\%$$

To use a calculator:

Step 1: Press 7.

Step 2: Press the ÷ symbol.

Step 3: Press 20.

Step 4: Press the = symbol.

Step 5: 0.35 appears.
0.35 = 35%.

Directions: Use a calculator to find the percent of hits to the number of "at bats" for each baseball player. Round your answer to two digits. For example, if your calculator displays the answer 0.753, round it to 0.75 or 75%.

Player	Hits	At Bats	Percent
Carlos	7	20	35%
Troy	3	12	_____
Sasha	4	14	_____
Dan	8	18	_____
Jaye	5	16	_____
Keesha	9	17	_____
Martin	11	16	_____
Robi	6	21	_____
Devan	4	15	_____

Who is most likely to get a hit? _____

Finding Percents

Find percent by dividing the number you have by the number possible.

Example:

15 out of 20 possible:

$$\begin{array}{r} 0.75 \\ 20\,\overline{)15.00} \\ -\underline{140} \\ 100 \\ \underline{100} \end{array} = 75\%$$

Annie has been keeping track of the scores she earned on each spelling test during the grading period.

Directions: Find out each percentage grade she earned. The first one has been done for you.

Week	Number Correct		Total Number of Words	Score in Percent
1	14	(out of)	20	70%
2	16		20	_____
3	18		20	_____
4	12		15	_____
5	16		16	_____
6	17		18	_____
Review Test	51		60	_____

If Carmen scored 5% higher than Annie on the review test, how many words did she get right?   _____

Carrie scored 10% lower than Carmen on the review test. How many words did she spell correctly?   _____

Of the 24 students in Annie's class, 25% had the same score as Annie. Only 10% had a higher score. What percent had a lower score?   _____

Is that answer possible? _____

Why? _____

Locating Points on a Grid

To locate points on a grid, read the first coordinate, and follow it to the second coordinate.

Example: C, 3

Directions: Maya is new in town. Help her learn the way around her new neighborhood. Place the following locations on the grid below.

Grocery	C, 10
Home	B, 2
School	A, 12
Playground	B, 13
Library	D, 6
Bank	G, 1
Post Office	E, 7
Ice-Cream Shop	D, 3

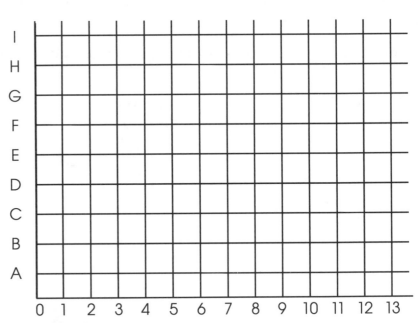

Is her home closer to the bank or the grocery store? _____

Does she pass the playground on her way to school? _____

If she needs to stop at the library after school, will she
be closer to home or farther away? _____

Graphs

A **graph** is a drawing that shows information about changes in numbers.

Directions: Use the graph to answer the questions.

Line Graph

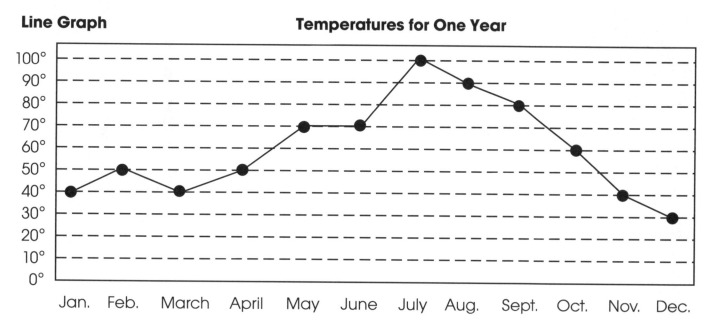

Temperatures for One Year

Which month was the coldest?   _____

Which month was the warmest?   _____

Which three months were 40 degrees?   _____

How much warmer was it in May than October?   _____

Bar Graph

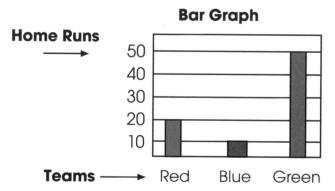

Home Runs →

	50			
	40			
	30			
	20			
	10			

Teams ⟶   Red   Blue   Green

How many home runs did the Green team hit? _____

How many more home runs did the Green team
hit than the Red team and Blue team combined? _____

Name _____

Graphs

Directions: Read each graph, and follow the directions.

List the names of the students from the shortest to the tallest.

1. _____   4. _____

2. _____   5. _____

3. _____   6. _____

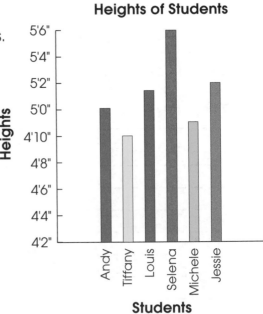

Heights of Students

List how many lunches the students bought each day, from the day the most were bought to the least.

1. _____   4. _____

2. _____   5. _____

3. _____

Lunches Bought

List the months in the order of the most number of outside recesses to the least number.

1. _____   6. _____

2. _____   7. _____

3. _____   8. _____

4. _____   9. _____

5. _____   10. _____

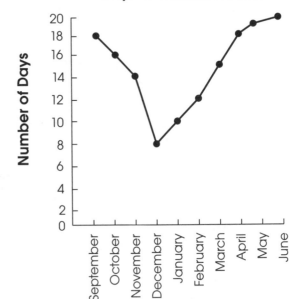

Days of Outside Recess

Graphs

Directions: Complete the graph using the information in the table.

Student	Books read in February
Piper	20
Joe	8
Peter	12
Suki	16
Logan	15
Lexi	8

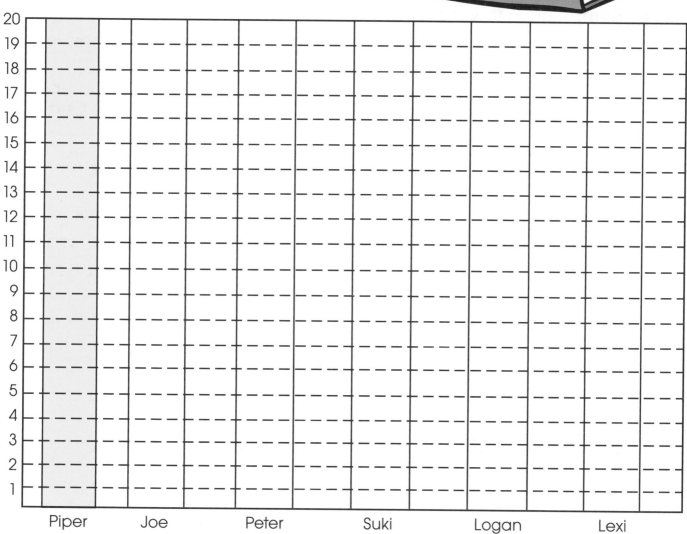

GLOSSARY

Abstract Noun: A noun that names something that cannot be touched or seen, such as an idea, a thought, or a feeling.

Addition: The process of putting together two or more numbers to find the sum.

Adjective: A word that describes a noun or pronoun, telling which one, what kind, or how many.

Adverb: A word that describes a verb, adjective, or other adverb, telling how, when, where, how often, or in what manner.

Alliteration: The repetition of a certain consonant sound in a group of words.

Analogy: A way of comparing items to show how they are related.

Angle: The shape formed by two rays with the same end point.

Antecedent: A noun to which a pronoun refers.

Antonym: A word with the opposite meaning of another word. Example: hot and cold.

Appositive: A word or words that gives the reader more information about a previous noun or pronoun. Example: My teacher, *Ms. Wright*, gave us a test.

Area: The number of square units in a figure.

Author's Purpose: The reason why an author writes, such as to inform, to entertain, or to persuade.

Bibliography: A list of all books and magazines used to write an article.

Biography: A book written about the life of a person by another person.

Body: The middle paragraphs of a report that contain the main substance of the information, examples, and supporting details.

Calculator: A machine that rapidly does addition, subtraction, multiplication, division, and other mathematical functions.

Cause: An event or reason that has an effect on something else.

Celsius: A measurement of temperature in the metric system using units called *degrees Celsius*.

Centimeter (cm): A metric measurement of length equal to $\frac{1}{100}$ of a meter. There are 2.54 centimeters in an inch.

Circumference: The distance around a circle.

Classifying: Putting items into categories based on similar characteristics.

Clause: A group of words with a subject and a verb.

Comma: A punctuation mark that tells a reader where to pause when reading a sentence.

Command: A sentence that orders someone to do something. It ends with a period (.) or exclamation mark (!).

Common Noun: A noun that names a nonspecific person, place, or thing.

Comparative: A form of adjective or adverb used to compare things. Examples: Adjective—*quick, quicker*; adverb—*quickly, more quickly*

Compound Predicate: A predicate with two or more verbs joined by a conjunction.

Compound Subject: A subject with two or more nouns or pronouns joined by a conjunction.

Comprehension: Understanding what is seen, heard, or read.

Conclusion: The final one or two paragraphs of a report that sum up the main ideas and restate any conclusions the writer has drawn as a result of research.

Concrete Noun: A noun that names something that can be touched or seen.

Cone: A space figure having one circular surface, one flat face, and one vertex.

Congruent Figures: Figures having identical shapes but different orientations, that is, facing in different directions.

Conjunction: A word used to join words or groups of words in a sentence or to combine sentences. Examples: *and, or, but*, and *because*

Consonants: Letters in the alphabet that are not vowels.

Context: The rest of the words in a sentence or the sentences before or after a word that help show its meaning.

Context Clue: A way to determine the meaning of new words by relating them to other words in the sentence.

Cube: A space figure with six square faces.

Cup (c.): A measurement of capacity equal to 8 fluid ounces.

Cylinder: A space figure with a curved surface and two parallel bases that are identical circles.

Decimal: A number with one or more places to the right of a decimal point, such as 6.5 or 2.25.

Demonstrative Adjective: An adjective that identifies a particular person, place or thing. Examples: *this, these, that,* and *those*

Denominator: The number below the fraction bar in a fraction.

Descriptive Sentence: A sentence that gives readers a vivid image and helps them imagine a scene clearly.

Diameter: A line segment that passes through the center of a circle and has both end points on the circle.

Dictionary: A reference book that lists words in alphabetical order and gives their definitions, pronunciation, and parts of speech. Some dictionaries provide illustrations and further information about words.

Digraph: Two letters pronounced as one sound. Examples: *sh—shell, ch—chew, th—thin*

Direct Address: A noun or pronoun that names or refers to the person addressed. Example: *John,* are you ready yet?

Direct Object: A word that follows a verb and completes its meaning. Example: I called *Mary.*

Dividend: The number that is divided by another number (the divisor) in a division problem. In the problem 28 ÷ 7 = 4, 28 is the dividend.

Division: The process of dividing a number into equal groups of smaller numbers.

Divisor: The number by which another number (the dividend) is divided in a division problem. In the problem 28 ÷ 7 = 4, 7 is the divisor.

Editing: Revising and correcting written work.

Effect: An event that results from a cause.

Encyclopedia: A set of reference books or an online resource that provides information about different subjects in alphabetical order.

Estimate: To give an approximate rather than an exact answer.

Exclamation: A sentence that shows strong feeling or excitement. It ends with an exclamation mark (!).

Fact: Information that can be proven true.

Factors: The numbers multiplied together to give a product.

Fahrenheit: A measurement of temperature using units called degrees Fahrenheit.

Fiction: Books that are not based on facts or real events.

Fluid Ounce (fl. oz.): A measure of capacity equal to $\frac{1}{8}$ of a cup.

Following Directions: Doing what the directions say to do, step by step, in the correct order.

Foot (ft.): A measurement of length equal to 12 inches.

Fraction: A number that names part of a whole. It is usually shown as one number (the part) above a second number (the whole), with a horizontal line between. Examples: $\frac{1}{2}$ and $\frac{1}{4}$

Fragment: A sentence that does not contain both a subject and a predicate.

Future-Tense Verb: A verb that tells about something that will happen in the future.

Gallon (gal.): A measurement of capacity equal to 4 quarts.

Geometry: The branch of mathematics that has to do with points, lines, and shapes.

Gram (g): A metric measurement of weight. 1,000 grams = 1 kilogram.

Graph: A drawing that shows information about changes in numbers.

Greatest Common Factor (GCF): The largest number that is a factor of every number in a given set of numbers. Example: The greatest common factor of 9, 15, and 27 is 3 (3 x 3 = 9, 3 x 5 = 15, and 3 x 9 = 27), while the GCF of 9, 15, and 25 is 1.

Guide Words: Words that appear at the top of a dictionary page to indicate the first and last words, alphabetically, found on that page.

Haiku: A three-line, unrhymed Japanese verse with five, seven, and five syllables.

Helping Verb: A verb used to support another verb. Examples: *is* helping; *are* working

Homographs: Words that have the same spelling but different meanings and pronunciations.

Homophones: Words that are pronounced the same but are spelled differently and have different meanings.

Idiom: A figure of speech that has a meaning different from the literal one.

Improper Fraction: A fraction in which the numerator is greater than its denominator.

Inch: A measurement of length. 12 inches = 1 foot.

Indefinite Adjective: An adjective that does not identify a particular person, place, or thing, but rather a group or number.

Indefinite Pronoun: A pronoun that ends with *body*, *one*, or *thing*. Examples: *all*, *any*, *both*, and *many*

Index: The section in the back of an encyclopedia or nonfiction book that indicates the page number and/or volume where information on a specific topic can be found.

Indirect Object: Words that come between the verb and the direct object. Indirect objects tell to whom or for whom something is done. Example: She cooked *me* a great dinner.

Interrogative Adjective: An adjective that is used when asking a question. *What* and *which* are interrogative adjectives.

Interrogative Pronoun: A pronoun that is used when asking a question, such as *who*, *what* and *which*.

Intransitive Verb: A verb that can stand alone in the predicate because its meaning is complete.

Introduction: A paragraph at the beginning of a report that states the main parts to be covered in the report.

Inverted Pyramid: A style of newswriting that places the most important facts at the beginning of the article.

Irregular Verb: A verb that changes completely in the past tense. Example: *eat—ate*.

Kilogram (kg): A metric measurement of weight equal to 1,000 grams. 1 kilogram = about 2.2 pounds

Kilometer (km): A metric measure of distance equal to 1,000 meters or about $\frac{5}{8}$ mile.

Lantern: A five-line Japanese verse in the shape of a lantern. Each line must contain a specific number of syllables.

Least Common Denominator (LCD): The least common multiple of the denominators in a given set of fractions.

Least Common Multiple (LCM): The smallest number other than 0 that is a multiple of each number in a given set of more numbers. Example: The least common multiple of 3, 5, and 6 is 30 (3 x 10, 5 x 6, 6 x 5).

Library Catalog: A listing on separate index cards or in a computer file of all the books, DVDs, CDs, etc., in a library collection. Materials are listed by title, by author, and by subject.

Like Fractions: Fractions with the same denominator, or bottom number.

Line: A collection of points on a straight path that goes on and on in opposite directions.

Linking Verb: A verb that links a noun or adjective in the predicate to the subject.

Liter (L): A metric measurement of capacity equal to about 1 quart.

Main Idea: The most important idea, or main point, in a sentence, paragraph, or story.

Metaphor: A direct comparison between two unlike things that doesn't use the words *like* or *as*. Example: *She was a frightened mouse.*

Meter (m): A metric measurement of length equal to 39.37 inches.

Mile (mi.): A measurement of distance equal to 1,760 yards.

Milliliter (mL): A metric measurement of capacity. 1,000 milliliters = 1 liter.

Millimeter (mm): A metric measurement of length equal to $\frac{1}{1000}$ of a meter. 10 millimeters = 1 centimeter.

Mixed Number: A number written as a whole number and a fraction.

Multiple: The product of a specific number and any other number. Example: The multiples of 2 are 2 (2 x 1), 4 (2 x 2), 6, 8, 10, 12, and so on.

Multiplication: The process of quickly adding a number a certain number of times.

Narrative: A spoken or written account of an actual event.

Newswriting: A style of writing used by newspaper reporters and other journalists who write for periodicals.

Nonfiction: Books based on facts or events that actually occurred.

Noun: A word that names a person, place, or thing.

Numerator: The number above the fraction bar in a fraction.

Object of a Preposition: A noun or pronoun that follows a preposition and completes its meaning.

Opinion: Information that tells what someone thinks or believes about something or someone.

Ounce (oz.): A measurement of weight. 16 ounces = 1 pound.

Outlining: A way to organize information in preparation for writing a paper or a report.

Paragraph: A group of related sentences about a topic.

Past-Tense Verb: A verb that tells what already happened.

Percent: A ratio that means "per hundred."

Perimeter: The distance around an object found by adding the lengths of the sides.

Periodicals: Newspapers, magazines, and newsletters that are published regularly.

Personal Narrative: Tells about a person's own experiences.

Personification: A figure of speech in which an object or animal is given human qualities. Example: *The wind sighed and moaned.*

Pi (π): A symbol representing a number equal to approximately 3.14.

Pint (pt.): A measurement of capacity equal to 2 cups.

Place Value: The value of a digit as representing ones, tens, hundreds, and so on, according to its position, or place, in a number.

Point of View: The attitude someone has about a particular topic as a result of his or her personal experience or knowledge.

Possessive Adjective: An adjective that shows ownership. Examples: *our, your, her, his, its, my,* and *their*

Possessive Pronoun: A pronoun that shows ownership. Examples: *his, theirs,* and *its*

Pound (lb.): A measurement of weight equal to 16 ounces.

Predicate: The part of the sentence that tells what the subject does, did, or is doing.

Prefix: A syllable added to the beginning of a word that changes the word's meaning.

Preposition: A word that comes before a noun or pronoun and shows the relationship of that noun or pronoun to other words in the sentence.

Prepositional Phrase: Includes a preposition and the object(s) of the preposition.

Present-Tense Verb: A verb that tells what is happening now.

Prime Number: A positive whole number that can be divided evenly only by itself or one.

Prior Knowledge: What one already knows.

Prism: A space figure with two identical, parallel bases.

Probability: The ratio of favorable outcomes to possible outcomes of an experiment.

Product: The quantity that results from multiplying two or more numbers.

Pronoun: A word used in place of a noun. Examples: *Wanda—her; Brian—him*

Proofreading: Carefully checking over what has been written for spelling, grammar, punctuation, and other errors.

Proper Noun: A noun that names a specific person, place, or thing.

Pyramid: A space figure whose base is a polygon and whose faces are triangles with a common vertex—the point where two rays meet.

Quart (qt.): A measurement of capacity equal to 4 cups or 2 pints.

Question: A sentence that asks something. It ends with a question mark (?).

Quotation Marks: Punctuation marks used to identify a person's exact words used in a sentence.

Quotient: The answer found by dividing one number by another number.

Radius: A line segment with one end point on the circle and the other end point at the center.

Ratio: A comparison of two quantities.

Ray: A part of a line with one end point that goes on and on in one direction.

Recalling Details: Being able to pick out and remember the who, what, when, where, why, and how of what has been read.

Rectangle: A figure with four equal angles and four sides, with the sides opposite each other of equal length.

Rectangular Prism: A space figure with six sides, or faces, all of which are rectangles.

Reference Sources: Nonfiction books and other materials that provide facts and information.

Relative Pronoun: A pronoun that refers to the nouns which come before it. Examples: *who, whom, which,* and *that*

Remainder: The number left over in the quotient of a division problem.

Report Writing: Researching and collecting information about a particular topic and writing about it.

Request: A sentence that asks someone to do something. It ends with a period (.) or question mark (?).

Rhyming Words: Words that share the same vowel sound in their last syllables. Example: *cane* and *explain*

Root Word: The common stem that gives related words their basic meanings. Example: The root word of *arrangement* is *arrange*.

Rounding: Expressing a number to the nearest ten, hundred, thousand, and so on. Examples: round 18 up to 20; round 113 down to 100.

Run-on Sentence: Two or more sentences that are joined together without correct punctuation.

Segment: A part of a line having two end points.

Sentence: A group of words that expresses a complete thought.

Sequencing: Placing events or objects in the correct order.

Similar Figures: Figures having the same shape but different sizes.

Simile: A comparison using the words like or as. Example: *She looked as frightened as a mouse.*

Skimming: To read quickly, looking for headings and key words, in order to identify the overall idea of the material's content or to find a particular fact.

Space Figures: Figures whose points are in more than one plane.

Sphere: A space figure with no flat surface. All points are an equal distance from the center.

Square: A figure with four equal sides and four equal angles.

Statement: A sentence that tells something. It ends with a period (.).

Subject: The part of a sentence that tells whom or what the sentence is about.

Subtraction: The process of taking away one number from another. It is used to find the difference between two numbers.

Suffix: A syllable at the end of a word that changes its meaning.

Summarizing: Writing a short report containing only the main points found in an article, book, or speech.

Summary: A short description of what a selection or book is about.

Superlative: A form of adjectives or adverbs that compare by pointing out the most extreme case. Examples: *tallest, softest, most important*

Supporting Sentences: The sentences in a paragraph that follow the topic sentence and provide details about the topic.

Syllable: A word part with only one vowel sound.

Symmetrical Figure: A figure that can be divided equally into two identical parts.

Synonym: A word that means the same or nearly the same as another word. Example: *jump* and *hop.*

Taking Notes: The process of writing important information from a story, article, or lecture that can be used later when writing a report or taking a test.

Tall Tale: A fictional story with exaggerated details.

Thesaurus: A type of reference book that lists words in alphabetical order followed by their synonyms and antonyms. Some types of thesauri also list idioms, related words, examples, and other information.

Ton (tn.): A measurement of weight equal to 2,000 pounds.

Topic Sentence: The sentence that tells the main idea of a paragraph.

Transitive Verb: A verb that needs a direct object to complete its meaning.

Triangle: A figure with three sides and three angles.

Unlike Fractions: Fractions with different denominators, or bottom numbers.

Venn Diagram: A diagram used to chart information comparing two things, showing their similarities and differences.

Verb: The action word in a sentence that tells what the subject does or that it exists.

Volume: The number of cubic units inside a space figure.

Vowels: The letters *a, e, i, o, u,* and sometimes *y.*

Word Family: A group of words based on the same word. Example: *play—playful, playground, playing*

Yard (yd.): A measurement of distance equal to 3 feet.

Spelling: Digraphs

A **digraph** is two consonants pronounced as one sound.

Examples: sh as in **shell**, **ch** as in **chew**, **th** as in **thin**

Directions: Write **sh**, **ch**, or **th** to complete each word below.

1. __th__ reaten
2. __ch__ ill
3. __sh__ ock
4. __sh__ iver
5. __th__ aw
6. __ch__ allenge
7. peri __sh__
8. __sh__ ield
9. __ch__ art
10. __th__ rive

Directions: Complete these sentences with a word, or form of the word, from the list above.

1. A trip to the South Pole would really be a (**ch**) __challenge__ .
2. The ice there never (**th**) __thaws__ because the temperature averages –50℃.
3. How can any living thing (**th**) __thrive__ or even live when it's so cold?
4. With 6 months of total darkness and those icy temperatures, any plants would soon (**sh**) __perish__ .
5. Even the thought of that numbing cold makes me (**sh**) __shiver__ .
6. The cold and darkness (**th**) __threaten__ the lives of explorers.
7. The explorers take along maps and (**ch**) __charts__ to help them find their way.
8. Special clothing helps protect and (**sh**) __shield__ them from the cold.
9. Still, the weather must be a (**sh**) __shock__ at first.
10. Did someone leave a door open? Suddenly, I feel a (**ch**) __chill__ .

Page 6

Spelling: Listening for Sounds

Not every word spelled with **ow** is pronounced **ou** as in **powder** and **however**. In the same way, not every word spelled with **ou** is pronounced **ou** as in **amount** and **announce**. The letters **ou** can be pronounced a number of ways.

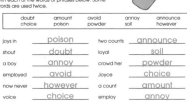

Directions: Write the word from the box that rhymes with each of the words or phrases below. Some words are used twice.

| doubt | amount | avoid | annoy | announce |
| choice | poison | powder | soil | however |

joys in __poison__
shout __doubt__
a boy __annoy__
employed __avoid__
now never __however__
voice __choice__
a bounce __announce__
enjoyed __avoid__

two counts __announce__
loyal __soil__
crowd her __powder__
Joyce __choice__
a count __amount__
employ __annoy__
louder __powder__
trout __doubt__

Page 7

Spelling: The *J* and *Ch* Sounds

The **j** sound can be spelled with a **j** as in **jump**, with a **g** before **e** or **i** as in **agent** and **giant**, or with **ge** at the end of a word as in **page**.

The **ch** sound is often spelled with the letters **ch** but can also be spelled with a **t** before **u**, as in **nature**.

Directions: Use words from the box to complete the exercises below.

| statue | imagination | jealous | future | arrangements |
| furniture | stranger | project | justice | capture |

1. Say each word, and then write it in the correct row, depending on whether it has the **j** or **ch** sound.

j __imagination__ __jealous__ __arrangements__
__stranger__ __project__ __justice__
ch __statue__ __future__ __furniture__ __capture__

2. Write a word from the box that belongs to the same word family as each word below.

imagine __imagination__ arranging __arrangements__
strangely __stranger__ furnish __furniture__
just __justice__ jealousy __jealous__

Directions: Complete each sentence with a word containing the given sound.

1. What is your group's (**j**) __project__ this week?
2. There is a (**ch**) __statue__ of George Washington in front of our school.
3. She used her (**j**) __imagination__ to solve the problem.
4. My sister keeps rearranging the (**ch**) __furniture__ in our room.

Page 8

Spelling: Words with Silent Letters

Some letters in words are not pronounced, such as the **s** in **island**, the **t** in **listen**, the **k** in **knee**, the **h** in **hour**, and the **w** in **write**.

Directions: Use words from the box to complete the exercises below.

| wrinkled | honest | aisle | knife | wrist |
| rhyme | exhaust | glisten | knowledge | wrestle |

1. Write each word beside its silent letter. Two words have two silent letters—write them twice.

s __aisle__
t __glisten__ __wrestle__
h __honest__ __rhyme__ __exhaust__
w __wrinkled__ __wrist__ __wrestle__ __knowledge__
k __knife__ __knowledge__

2. Write in the missing letter or letters for each word.

w res __t__ le   ex __h__ aust   __k__ nife   glis __t__ en   ai __s__ le
__k__ nowledge   __w__ rinkle   r __h__ yme   __h__ onest   __w__ rist

Directions: Complete each sentence with a word that has the given silent letter. Use each word only once.

1. He always tells the truth. He's very (**h**) __honest__ .
2. I like (**s**) __aisle__ seats in airplanes.
3. I need a sharper (**k**) __knife__ to cut this bread.
4. I think a long hike might (**h**) __exhaust__ me.
5. Did you sleep in that shirt? It is so (**w**) __wrinkled__ .
6. The snow seemed to (**t**) __glisten__ in the sunlight.
7. To play tennis, you need a strong (**w**) __wrist__ .

Page 9

Spelling: Syllables

A **syllable** is a part of a word with only one vowel sound. Some words have only one syllable, like **cat**, **leaf**, and **ship**. Some words have two or more syllables. **Be-lief** and **trac-tor** have two syllables, **to-geth-er** and **ex-cel-lent** have three syllables, and **con-ver-sa-tion** has four syllables. Some words can have six or more syllables! The word **ex-tra-ter-res-tri-al**, for example, has six syllables.

Directions: Follow the instructions below.

1. Count the syllables in each word below, and write the number of syllables on the line.

a. badger __2__
b. location __3__
c. award __2__
d. national __3__
e. necessary __4__
f. grease __1__
g. relationship __4__
h. communication __5__
i. government __3__
j. Braille __1__

2. Write four words with four syllables each in the blanks. Answers will vary. Possible answers:

a. __calculator__   c. __centimeter__
b. __testimony__   d. __geography__

3. Write one word with five syllables and one with six syllables. If you need help, use a dictionary. Answers will vary. Possible answers:

Five syllables: __refrigerator__
Six syllables: __responsibility__

Page 10

Writing: Sounding Out Syllables

Directions: Use words from the box to complete the exercises below.

| decision | division | pressure | addition | ancient |
| subtraction | confusion | multiplication | social | correction |

1. Write each word in the row showing the correct number of syllables.

Two: __pressure__ __ancient__ __social__
Three: __decision__ __division__ __addition__
__subtraction__ __confusion__ __correction__
Five: __multiplication__

2. Write in the missing syllables for each word.

__so__ cial   sub __trac__ tion   mul __ti__ pli __ca__ tion   pres __sure__
di __vi__ sion   an __cient__   deci __sion__   ad __di__ tion
__con__ fusion   cor __rec__ tion

Order of answers may vary.

3. Beside each word below, write a word with the same number of syllables. Use each word from the box only once.

daily __pressure__   challenging __subtraction__
syllable __decision__   election __confusion__
decreasing __division__   threaten __social__
advantage __addition__   shivering __correction__
title __ancient__   experimenting __multiplication__

Page 11

Writing: Word Families

A **word family** is a group of words based on the same word. For example, **playful**, **playground**, and **playing** are all based on the word **play**.

Directions: Use words from the box to complete the exercises below.

decision	division	pressure	addition	create
subtraction	confusion	multiplication	social	correction

1. Write the word that belongs to the same word family as each word below.

correctly	correction	confused	confusion
divide	division	subtracting	subtraction
pressing	pressure	society	social
multiply	multiplication	decide	decision
added	addition	creativity	create

2. Complete each sentence by writing the correct form of the given word.

Example: Have you (decide) _decided_ what to do? Did you make a (decide) _decision_ yet?

I am (add) _adding_ the numbers right now. Would you check my (add) _addition_ ?

This problem has me (confuse) _confused_ . Can you clear up my (confuse) _confusion_ ?

This is a (press) _pressing_ problem. We feel (press) _pressure_ to solve it right away.

Is he (divide) _dividing_ by the right number? Will you help him with his (divide) _division_ ?

Try to answer (correct) _correctly_ . Then, you won't have to make any (correct) _corrections_ on your paper later on.

Page 12

Writing: Word Families

Directions: Write the word that belongs to the same word family as each word below.

doubt	amount	avoid	annoy	announce
choice	poison	powder	soil	however

avoidance	avoid	annoyance	annoy
doubtful	doubt	soiled	soil
announcement	announce	poisonous	poison
choose	choice	amounted	amount
powdery	powder	whenever	however

Directions: Complete each sentence by writing the correct form of the given word.

Example: Are you (doubt) _doubting_ my word? You never (doubt) _doubted_ it before.

1. The teacher is (announce) _announcing_ the next test. Did you hear what he (announce) _announced_ ?

2. This stream was (poison) _poisoned_ by a chemical from a factory nearby.

3. Is the chemical (poison) _poisoning_ any other water supply? How many (poison) _poisons_ does the factory produce?

4. My cat always (annoy) _annoys_ our dog.

5. Last night, Carrie (annoy) _annoyed_ Lucas for hours.

6. I think Carrie is (avoid) _avoiding_ me. Yesterday, she (avoid) _avoided_ walking home with me.

Page 13

Spelling: Double Consonants

When adding endings such as **ing** and **ed** to verbs, use the following rule: Double the final consonant of verbs that have short vowel sounds and end with only one consonant. For example, **rip** becomes **ripped**, and **beg** becomes **begging**. However, do not double the final consonant in words that end in double consonants. For example, **rock** ends with two consonants, **ck**. So even though it has a short vowel sound, **rock** becomes **rocked**.

Directions: Add **ed** to the verbs below. Remember, when a verb ends with **e**, drop the **e** before adding an ending (**taste**, **tasting**). The first one has been done for you.

top	topped	rip	ripped
pet	petted	punch	punched
sob	sobbed	rinse	rinsed
brag	bragged	stock	stocked
scrub	scrubbed	lack	lacked
flip	flipped	dent	dented

Directions: Add **ing** to the verbs below. The first one has been done for you.

flap	flapping	snack	snacking
scrub	scrubbing	flip	flipping
stock	stocking	rinse	rinsing
dent	denting	brag	bragging
pet	petting	lack	lacking
sob	sobbing	punch	punching

Page 14

Writing: Verb Forms

Directions: In the following story, some of the verbs are missing. Write the proper form of the verbs shown, adding **ed** or **ing** when necessary.

Yesterday, I was (brag) _bragging_ to my brother about how much I (help) _helped_ our mother around the house. I had (scrub) _scrubbed_ the kitchen floor, (wipe) _wiped_ off all the counters, and (rinse) _rinsed_ out the sink. I was (pour) _pouring_ the dirty water out of the bucket when our mother came in. She looked around the kitchen and (smile) _smiled_ , "Who did all this work?" she (ask) _asked_ .

I was (get) _getting_ ready to tell her what I had done when my brother (interrupt) _interrupted_ me. "We both did! We've been (work) _working_ very hard!" he said. "He's not (tell) _telling_ the truth!" I said to Mom. "I did everything!" My brother (glare) _glared_ at me.

"Is that true?" asked Mom. My brother (look) _looked_ at the floor and (nod) _nodded_ . He was (think) _thinking_ about all the trouble he would get into. Instead, Mom smiled again. "Well, that's okay," she said. "The rest of the house needs to be (clean) _cleaned_ , too. You can get (start) _started_ right away!"

Page 15

Spelling: Math Plurals

To make most nouns plural, add **s**. When a noun ends with **s**, **ss**, **sh**, **ch**, or **x**, add **es**: bus—**buses**, cross—**crosses**, brush—**brushes**, church—**churches**, box—**boxes**. When a noun ends with a consonant and **y**, change the **y** to **i** and add **es**: berry—**berries**. For some words, instead of adding **s** or **es**, the spelling of the word changes: man—**men**, mouse—**mice**.

Directions: Write the correct plural or singular form of the words in these math problems. Write whether the problem requires addition (**A**), subtraction (**S**), multiplication (**M**), or division (**D**). The first one has been done for you.

1. 3 (box) _boxes_ – 2 (box) _boxes_ = _1 box_ S
2. 2 (supply) _supplies_ + 5 (supply) _supplies_ = _7 supplies_ A
3. 4 (copy) _copies_ x 2 (copy) _copies_ = _8 copies_ M
4. 6 (class) _classes_ ÷ 2 (class) _classes_ = _3 classes_ D
5. 5 (factory) _factories_ – 3 (factory) _factories_ = _2 factories_ S
6. 3 (daisy) _daisies_ x 3 (daisy) _daisies_ = _9 daisies_ M
7. 8 (sandwich) _sandwiches_ – 4 (sandwich) _sandwiches_ = _2 sandwiches_ A
8. 3 (child) _children_ – 1 (child) _child_ = _2 children_ S
9. 10 (brush) _brushes_ + 5 (brush) _brushes_ = _2 brushes_ D
10. 4 (goose) _geese_ + 1 (goose) _goose_ = _5 geese_ A
11. 3 (mouse) _mice_ + 1 (mouse) _mouse_ = _4 mice_ A

Page 16

Spelling: More Plurals

Remember, in some words, an **f** changes to a **v** to make the plural form.

Examples: life — lives   wife — wives   knife — knives   leaf — leaves

Directions: Complete these sentences by writing the correct plural form of the given word. Also, circle the spelling errors, and write the words correctly on the lines to the right.

1. The (leaf) _leaves_ are dry and (rinkled). — wrinkled
2. The (knife) _knives_ (glisened) in the sun. — glistened
3. I think the (child) _children_ in this school are (honist). — honest
4. The (supply) _supplies_ were stacked in the (isle). — aisle
5. (mouse) _Mice_ (rimes) with **twice**. — rhymes
6. Some people feel (exausted) all their (life) _lives_ . — exhausted
7. The (class) _classes_ were trying to gain more (knowlege) about Olympic athletes. — knowledge
8. The kittens were (wresling) in the (bush) _bushes_ . — wrestling
9. Jamie nearly broke his (rist) trying to carry all those (box) _boxes_ . — wrist
10. Some kings had several (wife) _wives_ who (new) about each other. — knew
11. (Daisy) _Daisies_ are (knot) expensive. — not
12. (Rite) your name on both (copy) _copies_ . — Write
13. We watched the (monkey) _monkeys_ play on the swings for (ours). — hours
14. Do you like (strawberry) _strawberries_ (hole) or sliced? — whole

Page 17

Comprehensive Curriculum - Grade 5

Spelling: Finding Mistakes

Directions: Circle the four spelling mistakes in each paragraph. Then, write the words correctly on the lines below.

Last nite our family went to a nice restaurant. As we were looking at the menus, a waiter walked in from the kichen carrying a large tray of food. As he walked by us, he triped and the tray went flying! The food flew all over our table and all over us, too!

night	looking
kitchen	tripped

Last week, while my dad was washing the car, our dog Jack dicided to help. He stuck his nose in the pale of soapy water, and tipped over and soaked him! As he shook himself off, the water from his fur went all over the car. "Look!" Dad laffed "Jack is doing his part!"

decided	pail
tipped	laughed

For our next feild trip, my class is going to the zoo. We have been studying about animals in sceince class. I'm very eksited to see the elephants, but my freind Tasha really wants to see the monkeys. She has been to the zoo before, and she says the monkeys are the most fun to watch.

field	science
excited	friend

It seems the rain will never stop! It has been raining for seven days now, and the sky is always dark and clowdy. Everyone at school is in a bad mood, because we have to stay inside during recess. Will we ever see the son again?

raining	cloudy
recess	sun

Page 18

Spelling: Finding Mistakes

Directions: Circle the four spelling mistakes in each paragraph. Then, write the misspelled words correctly on the lines below.

According to the newspaper, a man came into the store and stood near a clerk. The clerk was stocking the shelves with watches. Then, the man suddenly grabed several watches and raced out of the store. The clerk shouted, "Stop him! He's robing us!" The police searched for the man, but they still lak a suspect.

stocking	grabbed
robbing	lack

Tony always braged about the tricks he could do with his skateboard. One day, he tried to skate up a ramp and jump over three bikes. Well, he landed on the last bike and dented it. The last I saw Tony, he was runing down the street. The owner of the bike was chasing him.

bragged	dented
running	chasing

One day, I was peting my dog when I felt something sticky in his fur. It was time for a bath! I put him in a tub of water and scrubed as best I could. Then, I rinced the soap out of his fur. He jumped out of the tub, soaking wet, and rolled in some dirt. I sighed and draged him back into the tub. This dog makes me tired sometimes!

petting	scrubbed
rinsed	dragged

Last night, my little sister started braging about how fast she could wash the dishes. I told her to prove it. (It was my turn to do the dishes.) She started fliping the dishes around in the sink, washing them as fast as she could. I noticed she was rinseing only about half of them. Finally, it happened. She droped a cup on the floor. Dad made me finish the dishes, but at least she did some of them.

bragging	flipping
rinsing	dropped

Page 19

Spelling: Finding Mistakes

Directions: Circle the spelling mistakes in each paragraph. Write the words correctly on the lines below.

Some poisons that kill insects can also threten people. Often these powders and sprays are used on corn, beans, and other plants we eat. Unless these plants are well scrubed, we may eat a small amount of the poison.

poisons	threaten	powders	scrubbed

Sometimes the poison is put into the soyl and moves into the plant through its roots. Then, it stays in the plant in spyte of all our rinseing. All we can do is avoyd eating food that has been grown this way. Howevr, that also means we have to expect more insects in our food. It's a hard choise. Some people dout that a little bit of poison will hurt them, while others have made a dicision to grow their own food.

soil	spite	rinsing	avoid
However	It's	choice	doubt
	poison	decision	

Yesterday, the teacher anounced a new projict. She chalenged us to think of a new arrangment for the furnichure in the room. We voated to put the chairs in groups. Then, Brian said it would be easier to cheit that way. I was annoyd. I told him we had more pryde than that!

announced	project	challenged
arrangement	furniture	voted
cheat	annoyed	pride

Page 20

Spelling: Proofreading Practice

Directions: Circle the six spelling and pronoun mistakes in each paragraph. Write the words correctly on the lines below.

Jenna always braged about being ready to meet any chalenge or reach any goel. When it was time for our class to elekt it's new officers, Jenna said we should voat for her to be president.

bragged	challenge	goal
elect	its	vote

Simon wanted to be our president, too. He tried to coaks everyone to vote for his. He even lowned kids money to get their votes! Well, Jenna may have too much pryde in herself, but I like her in spit of that. At least she didn't try to buy our votes!

our	coax	him
loaned	pride	spite

Its true that Jenna tried other ways to get us to vote for hen. She scrubed the chalkboards even though it was my dayly job for that week. One day, I saw her rinseing out the paintbrushes when it was Peter's turn to do it. Then, she made sure we knew about her good deeds so we would prayse her.

It's	her	scrubbed
daily	rinsing	praise

We held the election, but I was shalked when the teacher releesed the results. Simon won! I wondered if he cheeted somehow. I feel like our class was robed. Now, Simon is the one who's braging about how great he is. I wish he knew the titel of president doesn't mean anything if no one wants to be around you!

shocked	released	cheated
robbed	bragging	title

Page 21

Adding Suffixes

A **suffix** is a syllable at the end of a word that changes its meaning. The suffixes **ant** and **ent** mean "a person or thing that does something."

Examples:
A person who occupies a place is an **occupant**.
A person who obeys is **obedient**.

A **root word** is the common stem that gives related words their basic meanings.

When a word ends in silent **e**, keep the **e** before adding a suffix beginning with a consonant. Drop the **e** before adding a suffix beginning with a vowel.

Examples:
announce + ment = **announcement**
announce + ing = **announcing**

Announce is the root word in this example.

Directions: Combine each root word and suffix to make a new word. The first one has been done for you.

Root word	Suffix	New word
observe	ant	observant
contest	ant	contestant
please	ant	pleasant
preside	ent	president
differ	ent	different

Directions: Use the meanings in parentheses to complete the sentences with one of the above new words. The first one has been done for you.

1. To be a good scientist, you must be very **observant**. (pay careful attention)
2. Her perfume had a strong but very **pleasant** smell. (nice)
3. Because the bridge was out, we had to find a **different** route home. (not the same)
4. The game show **contestant** jumped up and down when she won the grand prize. (person who competes)
5. Next week, we will elect a new student council **president**. (highest office)

Page 22

Adding Suffixes

The suffix **less** means "without"; **ative** means "having the nature of" or "relating to"; **ive** means "having" or "tending to be."

Examples:
Faultless means "without fault or blame."
Formative means "something that can be formed or molded."
Corrective means "something that fixes a problem."

Directions: Combine each root word and suffix to form a new word. The first one has been done for you.

Root word	Suffix	New word
sleep	less	sleepless
imagine	ative	imaginative
talk	ative	talkative
impress	ive	impressive
attract	ive	attractive

Directions: Use the meanings in parentheses to complete the sentences with one of the above new words.

1. The night before his birthday, Michael spent a **sleepless** night. (wide awake)
2. Our history teacher is a rather **talkative** man who likes to tell jokes and stories. (fond of speaking)
3. That book has such an **imaginative** plot! (showing creativity)
4. Monica thought the dress in the store window was very **attractive**. (pleasing)
5. The high school basketball team was **impressive** in its Friday night game, beating its rivals by 30 points. (making an impact on the mind or emotions)

Page 23

Adding Prefixes

A **prefix** is a syllable at the beginning of a word that changes its meaning. The prefixes **il, im, in,** and **ir** all mean "not."

Examples:
Illogical means "not logical or practical."
Impossible means "not possible."
Invisible means "not visible."
Irrelevant means "not relevant or practical."

Directions: Divide each word into its prefix and root word. The first one has been done for you.

	Prefix	Root Word
illogical	il	logical
impatient	im	patient
immature	im	mature
incomplete	in	complete
insincere	in	sincere
irresponsible	ir	responsible
irregular	ir	regular

Directions: Use the meanings in parentheses to complete the sentences with one of the above words.

1. I had to turn in my assignment __incomplete__ because I was sick last night. (not finished)
2. It was __illogical__ for Jimmy to give me his keys because he can't get into his house without them. (not practical)
3. Yoko and Joel were __irresponsible__ to leave their bikes out in the rain. (not doing the right thing)
4. I sometimes get __impatient__ waiting for my ride to school. (restless)
5. The boys sounded __insincere__ when they said they were sorry. (not honest)
6. These towels didn't cost much because they are __irregular__. (not straight or even)

Page 24

Adding Prefixes

The prefix **pre** means "before." The prefix **re** means "again."

Examples:
Preview means "to see in advance."
Redo means "to do again."

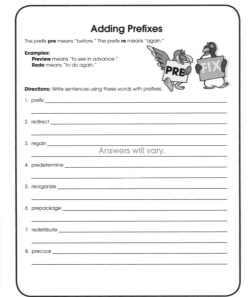

Directions: Write sentences using these words with prefixes.

1. prefix _____

2. redirect _____

3. regain _____
   Answers will vary.

4. predetermine _____

5. reorganize _____

6. prepackage _____

7. redistribute _____

8. precook _____

Page 25

Synonyms

A **synonym** is a word with the same or similar meaning as another word.

Examples: bucket — pail   happy — cheerful   dirty — messy

Directions: Match the words on the left with their synonyms on the right. The first one has been done for you.

tired
start
get
fire
dull
big
noisy
crowded
sofa
drink
sign
stop

beverage
notice
boring
busy
sleepy
couch
receive
begin
loud
halt
large
flames

Noisy!

Directions: Rewrite the sentences below using synonyms for the bold words.
Answers will vary. Possible answers:

1. Because the road was **rough**, we had a **hard** time riding our bikes on it.
Because the road was bumpy, we had a difficult time riding bikes on it.

2. After the accident, the driver appeared to be **hurt**, so someone **ran** to call an ambulance.
After the accident, the driver appeared to be injured, so someone sprinted to call an ambulance.

3. Yesterday, everyone stayed after school to pick up litter, and now the school yard is **nice** and **clean**.
Yesterday, everyone stayed after school to pick up litter, and now the school yard is lovely and tidy.

Page 26

Synonyms

Directions: Circle a word or a phrase in each sentence that is a synonym for a word in the box. Write the synonym on the line.

challenged	shocked	thaw	chart	frighten
perish	chill	shivering	thrive	shield

Example: The writing was in an old code.   __ancient__

1. A fish out of water will quickly die.   __perish__
2. The ice carving is beginning to melt.   __thaw__
3. I was amazed when I saw how he looked.   __shocked__
4. The puppy was trembling with excitement.   __shivering__
5. Ferns need moisture to grow well.   __thrive__
6. Are you trying to scare me?   __frighten__
7. Let the salad get cold in the refrigerator.   __chill__
8. She tried to protect him from the truth.   __shield__
9. He made a list of different kinds of birds.   __chart__
10. They dared us to enter the contest.   __challenged__

Directions: Write your own sentences using five words from the box. If you're not sure what a word means, look it up in a dictionary.

Sentences will vary.

Page 27

Finding Synonyms

Directions: Circle a word, or group of words, in each sentence that is a synonym for a word in the box. Write the synonym on the line.

statue	imagination	jealous	future	arrangements
furniture	stranger	project	justice	capture

Example: She will lend me her book.   __loan__

1. He tried to catch the butterfly.   __capture__
2. No one knows what will happen in the time to come.   __future__
3. They are loading the chairs, tables, and beds into the moving van.   __furniture__
4. We almost finished our team assignment.   __project__
5. They made plans to have a class party.   __arrangements__
6. Penny made a model of a horse.   __statue__
7. The accused man asked the judge for fairness.   __justice__

Directions: Write your own sentences for these words: **stranger, imagination, jealous.** Then, choose one other word from the box, and use it in a sentence. Make each sentence at least 10 words long. The sentences should show that you know what the word means.

1. _____   *Sentences will vary.*
2. _____
3. _____
4. _____

Page 28

Synonyms

Synonyms are words that mean the same or nearly the same.

Examples:
small and **little**
big and **large**
bright and **shiny**
unhappy and **sad**

little

small

Directions: Write a synonym for each word. Then, use it in a sentence. Use a dictionary if you are unsure of the meaning of a word.

1. cup _____   *Answers will vary.*
2. book _____
3. looking glass _____
4. hop _____
5. discover _____
6. plan _____
7. lamp _____
8. friend _____
9. discuss _____
10. rotate _____

Page 29

Comprehensive Curriculum - **Grade 5**

Antonyms

An **antonym** is a word with the opposite meaning of another word.

Examples: hot — cold
up — down
start — stop

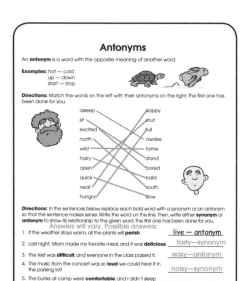

Directions: Match the words on the left with their antonyms on the right. The first one has been done for you.

asleep — slow
sit — sloppy
excited — shut
north — full
wild — awake
hairy — tame
open — stand
quick — bored
neat — bald
hungry — south

Directions: In the sentences below, replace each bold word with a synonym or an antonym so that the sentence makes sense. Write the word on the line. Then, write either **synonym** or **antonym** to show its relationship to the given word. The first one has been done for you.

Answers will vary. Possible answers:
1. If the weather stays warm, all the plants will **perish**. _live — antonym_
2. Last night, Mom made my favorite meal, and it was **delicious**. _tasty—synonym_
3. The test was **difficult**, and everyone in the class passed it. _easy—antonym_
4. The music from the concert was so **loud** we could hear it in the parking lot! _noisy—synonym_
5. The bunks at camp were **comfortable**, and I didn't sleep very well. _uncomfortable—antonym_

Page 30

Finding Antonyms

Directions: Write a word that is an antonym for each bold word in the sentences below.
Answers will vary. Possible answers:
1. Jared made his way **quickly** through the crowd. _slowly_
2. My friends and I arrived **late** to the party. _early_
3. My sister loves to watch airplanes **take off**. _land_
4. The teacher seems especially **cheerful** this morning. _depressed_
5. When are you going to **begin** your project? _finish_

Directions: Write antonyms for the following words on the lines. Then, write a short paragraph using all the words you wrote. Answers will vary. Possible answers:

dirty _clean_   whisper _yell_
old _young_   carefully _carelessly_
down _up_   night _day_
sit _stand_   happy _sad_

Paragraphs will vary.

Page 31

Antonyms

Antonyms are words that mean the opposite.

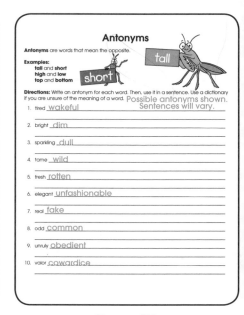

Examples:
tall and **short**
high and **low**
top and **bottom**

Directions: Write an antonym for each word. Then, use it in a sentence. Use a dictionary if you are unsure of the meaning of a word. Possible antonyms shown. Sentences will vary.

1. tired _wakeful_
2. bright _dim_
3. sparkling _dull_
4. tame _wild_
5. fresh _rotten_
6. elegant _unfashionable_
7. real _fake_
8. odd _common_
9. unruly _obedient_
10. valor _cowardice_

Page 32

Homophones

Homophones are words that sound alike but have different spellings and meanings. The words **no** and **know** are homophones. They sound alike, but their spellings and meanings are very different.

Directions: Use words from the box to complete the exercises below.

| hour | wring | knot | whole | knew |
| wrap | knight | piece | write | |

1. Write each word beside its homophone.
peace _piece_   new _knew_   ring _wring_
hole _whole_   rap _wrap_   night _knight_
not _knot_   right _write_   our _hour_
2. Write three words that have a silent **k**. _knot knew knight_
3. Write one word that has a silent **h**. _hour_

Directions: Circle the misused homophones in each sentence. Then, rewrite the sentences, using the correct homophones.
1. By the time knight fell, I new she was knot coming.
   By the time night fell, I knew she was not coming.
2. I would never have any piece until I new the hole story.
   I would never have any peace until I knew the whole story.
3. He spent an our fighting down what had happened.
   He spent an hour writing down what had happened.
4. I could see write through the whole in the night's armor.
   I could see right through the hole in the knight's armor.

Page 33

Homophones

Homophones are words that are pronounced the same but are spelled differently and have different meanings.

Example: to, two, too

Directions: Use these homophones in sentences of your own.
1. forth _Sentences will vary._
2. fourth
3. shown
4. shone
5. they're
6. their
7. there
8. not
9. knot

Page 34

Homophones

Directions: Complete the story below by writing the correct homophones for the words in parentheses.

Last Saturday, I went to (meat) _meet_ my friend, Andrea, at the mall.

When I got there, I noticed she looked a little (pail) _pale_.

"What's wrong?" I asked her.

She (side) _sighed_. "I'm (knot) _not_ feeling so (grate) _great_," she said. "I don't (no) _know_ what's wrong with me."

"Maybe you (knead) _need_ to drink some water or some juice," I said.

"Let's go to the drugstore. It's this (weigh) _way_."

As we were walking, we passed a (flour) _flower_ shop, and I bought (sum) _some_ roses for my mother. Then, we found the drugstore, and Andrea bought some juice. An (our) _hour_ later, she felt much better.

That (knight) _night_, I gave the roses to my mother. "You shouldn't (waist) _waste_ your money on (presence) _presents_ for me!" she said, but she was smiling. I (new) _knew_ she was pleased.

"That's okay, Mom, I wanted to buy them for you," I said. "But now I'm broke. How about a (lone) _loan_?"

Page 35

Homographs

Homographs are words that have the same spelling but different meanings and pronunciations.

pres´ent	n.	a gift
pre sent´	v.	to introduce or offer to view
rec´ord	n.	written or official evidence
re cord´	v.	to keep an account of
wind	n.	air in motion
wind	v.	to tighten the spring by turning a key
wound	n.	an injury in which the skin is broken
wound	v.	past tense of **wind**

Directions: Write the definition for the bold word in each sentence.

1. I would like to **present** our new student council president, Olivia Hall.
   to introduce
2. The store made a **record** of all my payments.
   written or official evidence
3. **Wind** the music box to hear the song.
   to tighten the spring by turning a key
4. His **wound** was healing quickly.
   an injury in which the skin is broken
5. The **wind** knocked over my bicycle.
   air in motion
6. I bought her a birthday **present** with my allowance.
   a gift

Page 36

Similes

A **simile** uses the words **like** or **as** to compare two things.

Examples:
The snow glittered **like** diamonds.
He was **as** slow **as** a turtle.

Directions: Circle the two objects being compared in each sentence.

1. The kittens were like gymnasts performing tricks.
2. My old computer is as slow as molasses.
3. When the lights went out in the basement it was as dark as night.
4. The sun was like a fire, heating up the earth.
5. The young girl was as graceful as a ballerina.
6. The puppy cried like a baby all night.
7. He flies that airplane like a daredevil.
8. The girl was as pretty as a picture.
9. The snow on the mountaintops was like whipped cream.
10. The tiger's eyes were like emeralds.

Directions: Complete the simile in each sentence.

Answers will vary.

11. My cat is as _____ as _____.
12. He was as _____ as _____.
13. Melissa's eyes shone like _____.
14. The paints were like _____.
15. The opera singer's voice was as _____ as _____.
16. My friend is as _____ as _____.

Page 37

Metaphors

A **metaphor** is a direct comparison between two things. The words **like** or **as** are not used in a metaphor.

Example: The sun is a **yellow ball** in the sky.

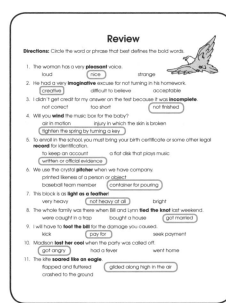

Directions: Underline the metaphor in each sentence. Write the two objects being compared on the line.

1. As it bounded toward me, the dog was a quivering furball of excitement.
   dog/furball of excitement
2. The snow on was mashed potatoes.
   snow/mashed potatoes
3. Diego is a mountain goat when it comes to rock climbing.
   Diego/mountain goat
4. The light is a beacon shining into the dark basement.
   light/beacon
5. The famished child was a wolf, eating for the first time in days.
   famished child/a wolf
6. The man's arm was a tireless lever as he fought to win the wrestling contest.
   arm/tireless lever
7. The flowers were colorful polkadots against the green of the yard.
   flowers/colorful polkadots

Page 38

Idioms

An **idiom** is a phrase that says one thing but actually means something quite different.

Example: A **horse of a different color** means something quite unusual.

Directions: Write the letter of the correct meaning for each bold phrase. The first one has been done for you.

a. refusal to see or listen
b. misbehaving, acting in a wild way
c. made a thoughtless remark
d. lost an opportunity
e. got angry
f. pay for
g. unknowing
h. feeling very sad
i. get married
j. excited and happy

f 1. My parents will **foot the bill** for my birthday party.
i 2. Antonio and Lisa will finally **tie the knot** in June.
h 3. Sam was **down in the dumps** after he wrecked his bicycle.
c 4. Sarah **put her foot in her mouth** when she was talking to our teacher.
d 5. I really **missed the boat** when I turned down the chance to work after school.
a 6. I got the **brush-off** from Malia when I tried to ask her where she was last night.
g 7. Mickey is **in the dark** about our plans to throw a surprise birthday party for him.
b 8. The children were **bouncing off the walls** when the baby-sitter tried to put them to bed.
j 9. The students were **flying high** on the last day of school.
e 10. My sister **lost her cool** when she discovered I had spilled chocolate milk on her new sweater.

Page 39

Idioms

An **idiom** is a figure of speech that has a meaning different from the literal one.

Example:
Dad is **in the doghouse** because he was late for dinner.

Meaning: Dad is in trouble because he was late for dinner.

Directions: Write the meanings of the idioms in bold.

Answers will vary.

1. He was a **bundle of nerves** waiting for his test scores.
   very nervous
2. It was **raining cats and dogs**.
   raining very hard
3. My friend and I decided to **bury the hatchet** after our argument.
   make peace
4. He gave me the **cold shoulder** when I spoke to him.
   ignored
5. My mom **blew up** when she saw my poor report card.
   got angry
6. I was **on pins and needles** before my skating performance.
   anxious; nervous
7. When the student didn't answer, the teacher asked, "**Did the cat get your tongue?**"
   Why aren't you speaking?
8. The city **rolled out the red carpet** for the returning Olympic champion.
   welcomed
9. They hired a clown for the young boy's birthday party to help **break the ice**.
   put everyone at ease

Page 40

Review

Directions: Circle the word or phrase that best defines the bold words.

1. The woman has a very **pleasant** voice.
   loud   *nice*   strange
2. He had a very **imaginative** excuse for not turning in his homework.
   creative   difficult to believe   acceptable
3. I didn't get credit for my answer on the test because it was **incomplete**.
   not correct   too short   *not finished*
4. Will you **wind** the music box for the baby?
   air in motion   injury in which the skin is broken
   tighten the spring by turning a key
5. To enroll in the school, you must bring your birth certificate or some other legal **record** for identification.
   to keep an account   a flat disk that plays music
   written or official evidence
6. We use the crystal **pitcher** when we have company.
   printed likeness of a person or object
   baseball team member   *container for pouring*
7. This block is as **light as a feather**!
   very heavy   *not heavy at all*   bright
8. The whole family was there when Bill and Lynn **tied the knot** last weekend.
   were caught in a trap   bought a house   *got married*
9. I will have to **foot the bill** for the damage you caused.
   kick   *pay for*   seek payment
10. Madison **lost her cool** when the party was called off.
    got angry   had a fever   went home
11. The kite **soared like an eagle**.
    flapped and fluttered   *glided along high in the air*
    crashed to the ground

Page 41

Comprehensive Curriculum - **Grade 5**

ANSWER KEY

Review
Answers will vary. Possible answers:

Directions: Write a synonym for each word.
1. amusing __entertaining__
2. prison __jail__
3. terrifying __frightening__
4. flee __escape__

Directions: Write an antonym for each word.
5. insult __compliment__
6. famine __abundance__
7. discourage __encourage__
8. generous __stingy__

Directions: Write a homophone pair.
9. _____ **Answers will vary.**

Directions: Write a sentence containing a simile.
10. _____

Directions: Write a sentence containing a metaphor.
11. _____

Directions: Write the letter of the correct meaning for the idiom in each sentence.

a. made a thoughtless remark
b. lost an opportunity
c. pay for
d. feeling very sad
e. excited and happy

__c__ 12. My uncle promised to foot the bill for a new computer if I got terrific grades this year.
__d__ 13. Takeo was down in the dumps when his team lost the game.
__e__ 14. The opposing team was flying high after the win.
__a__ 15. Jonah put his foot in his mouth when he told his mother what he really thought of her new hairdo.
__b__ 16. Sean really missed the boat when he turned down the chance to travel to England.

Page 42

Using a Dictionary
Directions: Read about dictionaries. Then, answer the questions.

Dictionaries are books that give definitions of words. Dictionaries list words in alphabetical order. **Guide words** at the top of each page show the first and last words listed on the page. All other words on the page are listed in alphabetical order between the guide words. This helps you locate the word you want quickly and easily.

In addition to definitions, dictionaries also show the following: how to pronounce, or say, each word; the individual syllables found in each word; the part of speech for each word; and the plural form or verb forms if the base word changes.

Some dictionaries provide considerably more information. For example, The Tormont Webster's Illustrated Encyclopedic Dictionary includes many color illustrations of terms, a pronunciation key on every other page and two pages of introductory information on how to use the dictionary effectively.

Other highlights of the Tormont Webster are **historical labels** that tell the history of words no longer in common use; **geographic labels** that tell in what part of the world uncommon words are used; **stylistic labels** that tell whether a word is formal, informal, humorous or a slang term; and **field labels** that tell what field of knowledge—such as medicine—the word is used in.

1. Where are guide words found? __at the top of each page__
2. What is the purpose of guide words? __They show the first and last words listed on the page.__
3. Which label tells if a word is a slang term? __stylistic__
4. Which label tells the history of a word? __historical__
5. Which type of information is not provided for each word in the dictionary?
☐ definition
☐ part of speech
☒ picture

Page 43

Using a Dictionary
Directions: Use the dictionary entry below to answer the questions.

ad·he·sive (ad-he′-siv) adj. 1. Tending to adhere; sticky. 2. Gummed so as to adhere. n. 3. An adhesive substance such as paste or glue. **ad·he·sive·ly** adv. **ad·he·sive·ness** n.

1. Based on the first definition of **adhesive**, what do you think **adhere** means? __to stick to something__
2. Which definition of **adhesive** is used in this sentence? The tape was so adhesive that we couldn't peel it loose. __tending to adhere; sticky__
3. Which part of speech is **adhesive** used as in this sentence? We put a strong adhesive on the package to keep it sealed. __noun__
4. How many syllables does **adhesive** have? __three__
5. Is **adhesive** used as a noun or an adjective in this sentence? The adhesive we chose to use was not very gummy. __noun__
6. **Adhesive** and variations of the word can be used as what parts of speech? __adjective, noun, or adverb__

Directions: Write sentences using these words.
7. adhesiveness __Answers will vary.__
8. adhesively _____
9. adhere _____

Page 44

Using a Dictionary
Guide words are the words that appear at the top of dictionary pages. They show the first and last words on each page.

Directions: Read the guide words on each dictionary page below. Then, look around for objects whose names come between the guide words. Write the names of the objects, and then number them in alphabetical order.

Answers will vary.

babble	buzz	magic	myself
cabin	cycle	pea	puzzle
dairy	dwarf	scar	sword
feast	future	tack	truth

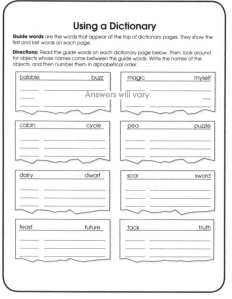

Page 45

Using a Dictionary: Guide Words
Directions: Use the guide words and page numbers shown on the top of the dictionary pages below. Write the page number where each word would be found.

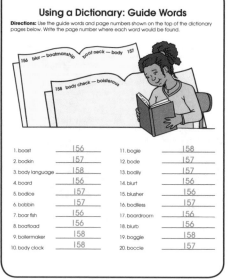

156 blur – boatmanship boat neck – body 157
158 body check – boisterous

1. boast __156__
2. bodkin __157__
3. body language __158__
4. board __156__
5. bodice __157__
6. bobbin __157__
7. boar fish __156__
8. boatload __156__
9. boilermaker __158__
10. body clock __158__
11. bogie __158__
12. bode __157__
13. bodily __157__
14. blurt __156__
15. blusher __156__
16. bodiless __157__
17. boardroom __156__
18. blurb __156__
19. boggle __158__
20. boccie __157__

Page 46

Using a Dictionary: Multiple Meanings
If a word has more than one meaning, you will find that information in a dictionary.

Directions: Use the dictionary entry below to answer the questions about the word **record**.

re·cord v. (rĭ kôrd′) **1.** a) to put in writing, print, etc. for future use; draw up an account of (to record the day's events); b) to make a permanent or official note of (to record a vote) **2.** a) to indicate automatically or permanently, as on a graph or chart (a seismograph records earthquakes); b) to show, as on a dial (a thermometer records temperatures) **3.** to remain as evidence of (metal tools record a superior civilization) **4.** a) to register (sound or visual images) in some permanent form, such as digitally or on a phonograph disc, magnetic tape, etc. for reproduction on a playback device; b) to register the performance of (a musician, actor, composition, etc.) in this way. (for n. & adj. rek′ erd) **5.** an account of facts or events preserved, esp. in writing **6.** information or knowledge about a person's achievements or performances **7.** standing with respect to contests won, lost, and tied **8.** the best performance of its kind to date **9.** something, as in a disk, on which sound or images have been recorded **10.** adj. surpassing all others.

1. How many and which parts of speech are listed for all definitions of **record**? __10; verb, noun, adjective__
2. Including all the subheadings, how many definitions are listed? __13__
3. Which definition uses the example of a thermometer recording a temperature? __2b__
4. Which definition describes a record you might play to listen to music? __9__
5. Is **record** used as a noun or a verb in this sentence? She held the all-time record for most wins. __noun__
6. Is **record** used as a noun or a verb in this sentence? I will record our conversation. __verb__

Page 47

Multiple Meanings

Directions: Circle the correct definition of the bold word in each sentence. The first one has been done for you.

1. Try to **flag** down a car to get us some help!
   - (to signal to stop)
   - cloth used as symbol

2. We listened to the **band** play the National Anthem.
   - (group of musicians)
   - a binding or tie

3. He was the **sole** survivor of the plane crash.
   - bottom of the foot
   - (one and only)

4. I am going to **pound** the nail with this hammer.
   - (to hit hard)
   - a unit of weight

5. He lived on what little **game** he could find in the woods.
   - (animals for hunting)
   - form of entertainment

6. We are going to **book** the midnight flight from Miami.
   - (to reserve in advance)
   - a written work

7. The **pitcher** looked toward first base before throwing the ball.
   - (baseball team member)
   - container for pouring

8. My grandfather and I played a **game** of checkers last night.
   - animals for hunting
   - (form of entertainment)

9. They raise the **flag** over City Hall every morning.
   - to signal to stop
   - (cloth used as symbol)

Page 48

Using a Dictionary: Choosing the Correct Word

Directions: Use a dictionary to look up the words in parentheses. Then, write the correct word in the blanks.

1. gallery — Our class visited an art (galley/gallery) last week to learn about paintings and sculptures.
2. scrutinize — He didn't (scrutinize/scruple) his essay very carefully before handing it in.
3. pliable — She squeezed the clay in her hands until it became (plentiful/pliable).
4. laudable — The quarterback's (laudable/laughable) performance helped his team win the game.
5. astronomy — The science that deals with the universe beyond Earth's atmosphere is known as (astronomy/astrology).
6. grateful — My mother was (grateful/graphic) that I helped her with the dishes.
7. tangible — The police did not have any (tantamount/tangible) evidence that the man was guilty.
8. unfortunate — It was very (unfortunate/unfamiliar) that she broke her arm right before the big game.
9. trowel — The gardener was using a (trough/trowel) to dig up the flowers.
10. apparel — That company manufactures men's and women's (appendage/apparel).
11. decompose — After vegetable scraps (decompose/decongest), you can put them on your garden as fertilizer.
12. nocturnal — Most bats are (nocturnal/noble) and sleep during the day.
13. venetian — We bought some (venerable/venetian) blinds for our windows instead of curtains.
14. exasperated — The noisy class (exasperated/exaggerated) the teacher.
15. parole — The prisoner was released on (parody/parole).

Page 49

Learning New Words

Directions: Write a word from the box to complete each sentence. Use a dictionary to look up words you are unsure of.

bouquet	unconscious	inspire	disability
inherit	hovering	assault	enclosure
commotion	criticize		

1. He was knocked **unconscious** by the blow to his head.
2. Megan never let her **disability** stand in the way of accomplishing what she wanted.
3. The teacher burst into the noisy room and demanded to know what all the **commotion** was about.
4. He offered her a **bouquet** of flowers as a truce after their argument.
5. The zoo was in the process of building a new **enclosure** for the elephants.
6. The mother was **hovering** over her sick child.
7. The movie was meant to **inspire** people to do good deeds.
8. My friend will eventually **inherit** a fortune from his grandmother.
9. Not many people enjoy having someone **criticize** their work.
10. The female leopard led the **assault** on the herd of zebras.

Page 50

Learning New Words

Directions: Use a dictionary. Define the following words. Then, use each word in a sentence. *Sentences will vary.*

1. mechanical **pertaining to or involving machines**
2. cashmere **fine, soft wool made from the fleece of Kashmir goats**
3. deplorable **lamentable; wretched; regrettable**
4. illusion **something that appears different from what it is**
5. rivalry **competition**
6. traction **the force that causes something in motion to stick to the surface it is moving on**
7. whittle **to carve an object from wood with a knife**
8. pageant **a show or exhibition**
9. nectarine **a smooth-skinned stone fruit, similar to a peach**
10. javelin **a lightweight spear**

Page 51

Using a Thesaurus

A **thesaurus** is a type of reference book that lists words in alphabetical order followed by their synonyms and antonyms. **Synonyms** are words that mean the same. **Antonyms** are words that mean the opposite.

A thesaurus is an excellent tool for finding just the right word. It is also a valuable resource for finding a variety of synonyms and/or antonyms to make your writing livelier.

Each main entry in a thesaurus consists of a word followed by the word's part of speech, its definition, an example, a list of related words, and other information. You can also find several thesauruses online.

Here is a typical entry in a thesaurus, with an explanation of terms below:

SLOW
ADJ **SYN** deliberate, dilatory, laggard, leisurely, unhasty, unhurried **REL** lateness, limited, measured, slowish, steady, unhurrying, slowfooted, plodding, pokey, straggling, snail-like **IDIOM** as slow as molasses in January; as slow as a turtle **CON** blitz, quick, rapid, swift **ANT** fast

- **ADJ** means "adjective"
- **CON** means "contrasted words"
- **SYN** means "synonym"
- **ANT** means "antonym"
- **REL** means "related words"
- **idiom** means "a common phrase that is not literal"

Directions: Use the thesaurus entry to answer the questions.

1. What is the antonym listed for **slow**? **fast**
2. How many contrasting words are listed for **slow**? **4**
3. How many synonyms are listed for **slow**? **6**
4. What is **slow** compared to in the two idioms listed? **molasses; a turtle**
5. What is the last related word listed for **slow**? **snail-like**

Page 52

Using a Thesaurus to Find Synonyms

A thesaurus can help you find synonyms.
Example:
FIND: VERB **SYN** locate, discover, detect, uncover, see, etc.

Directions: Use a thesaurus. Replace each word in bold with a synonym. *Answers will vary. Possible answers:*

1. My father does not like our **artificial** Christmas tree.
   fake
2. The **fabulous** home sat on a large hill overlooking a wooded ravine.
   wonderful
3. My dog is allowed to be **loose** if someone is home.
   free
4. A **peaceful** rally was held to bring attention to the needs of the homeless.
   nonviolent
5. The artist completed his **sketch** of the girl.
   drawing
6. The **timid** boy could not bring himself to speak to the man at the counter.
   shy
7. My family is cutting down the **timber** at the back of our property.
   trees
8. Her necklace was very **attractive**.
   appealing
9. The girl looked hopelessly at her **clothes** and moaned that she had nothing to wear.
   garments
10. The team's **feat** of winning 20 games in a row was amazing.
    accomplishment

Page 53

Comprehensive Curriculum - **Grade 5**

Page 54

Answers will vary. Possible answers:
Using a Thesaurus

Directions: Use a thesaurus to list as many synonyms as possible for the following words.

1. calm __placid, serene, tranquil, peaceful__
2. hunt __chase, stalk, pursue__
3. quilt __bed cover, blanket, coverlet, comforter__
4. tender __gentle, kind, affectionate__
5. vacate __abandon, evacuate, leave, quit__

Directions: Use a thesaurus to list as many related words as possible for the following words.

6. value __importance, goodness, measurement__
7. difference __unconformity, deviation, change, inequality__
8. enable __empower, allow, permit__

Directions: Use a thesaurus to list one idiom for each of the following words.

9. beauty __Beauty is only skin deep.__
10. cake __You can't have your cake and eat it too.__

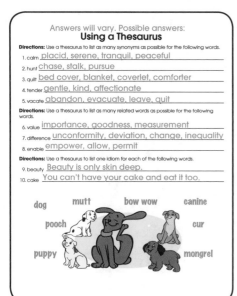

Page 54

Page 55

Using a Thesaurus to Find Antonyms

Antonyms are words that mean the opposite. Antonyms can be found in some thesauruses. They are identified by the abbreviation **ANT**.

Examples:

FOUND:
VERB **ANT** misplaced, gone, lost, missing, mislaid, etc.

RIDDLE:
NOUN **ANT** key, solution, answer, etc.

ANCIENT:
ADJECTIVE **ANT** new, recent, current, etc.

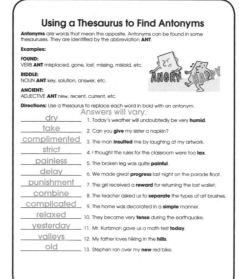

Directions: Use a thesaurus to replace each word in bold with an antonym.
Answers will vary.

dry _____ 1. Today's weather will undoubtedly be very **humid**.
take _____ 2. Can you **give** my sister a napkin?
complimented __ 3. The man **insulted** me by laughing at my artwork.
strict _____ 4. I thought the rules for the classroom were too **lax**.
painless _____ 5. The broken leg was quite **painful**.
delay _____ 6. We made great **progress** last night on the parade float.
punishment ____ 7. The girl received a **reward** for returning the lost wallet.
combine _____ 8. The teacher asked us to **separate** the types of art brushes.
complicated ___ 9. The home was decorated in a **simple** manner.
relaxed _____ 10. They became very **tense** during the earthquake.
yesterday _____ 11. Mr. Kurtzman gave us a math test **today**.
valleys _____ 12. My father loves hiking in the **hills**.
old _____ 13. Stephen ran over my **new** red bike.

Page 55

Page 56

Comprehension: Word Origins

Did you ever wonder why we call our midday meal "lunch"? Or where the name "Abraham" came from? Or why one of our lovely eastern states is called "Vermont"?

These and other words have a history. The study of where words came from and how they began is called **etymology** (ett-a-mol-o-gee).

The word **lunch** comes from the Spanish word **lonja** which means "a slice of ham." Long ago, Spanish people ate a slice of ham for their midday meal. Eventually, what they ate became the word for the meal itself. Still later, it came to be pronounced "lunch" in English.

Abraham also has an interesting history. Originally, it came from the Hebrew word **avaraham**. Abraham means "father of many."

City and state names are often based on the names of Native American tribes or describe the geography of the area. **Vermont** is actually made from two French words. **Vert** is French for "green." **Mont** is French for "mountain."

Directions: Answer these questions about word origins.

1. What is the study of the history and origin of words? ___etymology___
2. From which language did the word **lunch** come? ___Spanish___
3. What is the French word for "green"? ___vert___
4. **Vermont** comes from two words of what language?
   ☐ Spanish ☐ English ☒ French
5. Which is not correct about the origin of names of cities and states?
   ☐ They describe geography.
   ☐ They name Native American tribes.
   ☒ They are mostly French in origin.

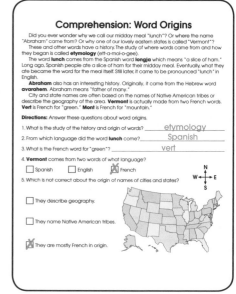

Page 56

Page 57

Comprehension and Context

Comprehension is understanding what is seen, heard, or read.

Context is the rest of the words in a sentence or the sentences before or after a word. Context can help with comprehension.

Context clues help you figure out the meaning of a word by relating it to other words in the sentence.

Directions: Use the context clues in the sentences to find the meanings of the bold words.

1. Ana was a **wizard** at games. She mastered them in no time and seldom lost.
   ☐ evil magician ☒ gifted person ☐ average player

2. The holiday was so special that she was sure she'd never forget it. The memory would be **imprinted** forever on her mind.
   ☐ found ☐ weighed ☒ fixed

3. "John will believe anything anyone tells him," his teacher said. "He's a very **impressionable** young man."
   ☒ easily influenced ☐ unhappy ☐ unintelligent

4. "Do you really think it's **prudent** to spend all your money on clothes?" his mother asked crossly.
   ☐ foolish ☒ wise ☐ funny

5. "Your plan has **merit**," Elizabeth's father said. "Let me give it some thought."
   ☒ value ☐ awards ☐ kindness

6. Isaiah was very **gregarious** and loved being around people.
   ☐ shy ☒ outgoing ☐ unfriendly

Page 57

Page 58

Classifying

Classifying means putting items into categories based on similar characteristics.

Example: Tag, hide-and-seek, and tic-tac-toe could be classified as games.

Directions: ... of your ow ... Answers will vary. Possible answers: ...ord

1. wren	robin	fea**her**
sparrow	eagle	**bluebird**
2. sofa	stool	chair
ca**r**et	bench	**armchair**
3. lettuce	s**p**d	corn
broccoli	spinach	**carrots**
4. pencil	chalk	crayon
pen	dra**w**ing	**marker**
5. perch	shark	pen**g**uin
bass	tuna	**salmon**
6. rapid	quick	un**h**ed
swift	speedy	**fast**
7. lemon	a**p**e	melon
lime	grapefruit	**blueberry**

Directions: Write a category name above each group of words. Then, write a word of your own that belongs in each group. Answers will vary.

Weather
blizzard
hurricane
thunder
__tornado__

Parts of a Leg
ankle
shin
thigh
__knee__

Parts of a Car
engine
horn
steering wheel
__headlights__

Sports
hockey
ice skating
bobsledding
__soccer__

Page 58

Page 59

Classifying

Directions: Writ **Answers will vary. Possible answers:**

1. whales	humpback	blue	killer
2. songs	Happy Birthday	Blue Suede Shoes	We Will Rock You
3. sports stars	LeBron James	Serena Williams	Michael Jordan
4. fruit	lemon	apple	kiwi
5. schools	elementary	university	high school
6. teachers	Mr. Samberg	Ms. Wong	Mrs. Campbell
7. tools	hammer	saw	wrench
8. friends	Cameron	Aisha	Sam
9. books	Alice in Wonderland	The Golden Compass	Wonder
10. mammals	bat	polar bear	fox
11. fish	guppy	tuna	minnow
12. snacks	pretzels	granola bars	apple slices
13. cars	race car	station wagon	convertible
14. hobbies	dancing	collecting rocks	drawing
15. vegetables	radishes	cucumbers	asparagus
16. insects	ladybugs	crickets	cockroaches

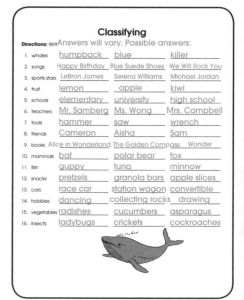

Page 59

Classifying: Regional Forecast

Directions: Read the forecast. Then, write words in the correct categories.

The very warm, early spring weather will continue to spread along the East Coast today. With some sunshine, afternoon temperatures will climb to 90 degrees in many places. Columbia, South Carolina, and neighboring areas could reach 100 degrees. Showers are expected from Washington, D.C., to New York City. Severe thunderstorms are likely in Virginia and North Carolina. Central South Carolina will be under a tornado watch during the afternoon.

Cities
Columbia
Washington, D.C.
New York City

States
South Carolina
Virginia
North Carolina

Weather Conditions
showers
severe thunderstorms
tornado watch
warm, sunny weather

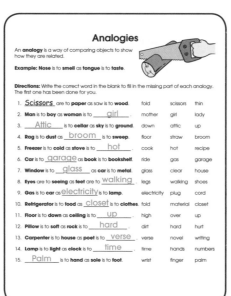

Page 60

Analogies

An **analogy** is a way of comparing objects to show how they are related.

Example: Nose is to **smell** as **tongue** is to **taste**.

Directions: Write the correct word in the blank to fill in the missing part of each analogy. The first one has been done for you.

1. __Scissors__ are to **paper** as **saw** is to **wood.**   fold   scissors   thin
2. **Man** is to **boy** as **woman** is to __girl__.   mother   girl   lady
3. __Attic__ is to **cellar** as **sky** is to **ground.**   down   attic   up
4. **Rag** is to **dust** as __broom__ is to **sweep.**   floor   straw   broom
5. **Freezer** is to **cold** as **stove** is to __hot__.   cook   hot   recipe
6. **Car** is to __garage__ as **book** is to **bookshelf.**   ride   gas   garage
7. **Window** is to __glass__ as **car** is to **metal.**   glass   clear   house
8. **Eyes** are to **seeing** as **feet** are to __walking__.   legs   walking   shoes
9. **Gas** is to **car** as __electricity__ is to **lamp.**   electricity   plug   cord
10. **Refrigerator** is to **food** as __closet__ is to **clothes.**   fold   material   closet
11. **Floor** is to **down** as **ceiling** is to __up__.   high   over   up
12. **Pillow** is to **soft** as **rock** is to __hard__.   dirt   hard   hurt
13. **Carpenter** is to **house** as **poet** is to __verse__.   verse   novel   writing
14. **Lamp** is to **light** as **clock** is to __time__.   time   hands   numbers
15. __Palm__ is to **hand** as **sole** is to **foot.**   wrist   finger   palm

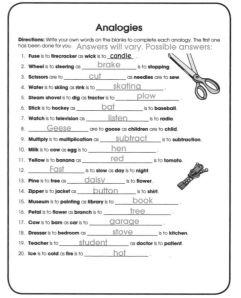

Page 61

Analogies

Directions: Write your own words on the blanks to complete each analogy. The first one has been done for you.   Answers will vary. Possible answers:

1. **Fuse** is to **firecracker** as **wick** is to __candle__.
2. **Wheel** is to **steering** as __brake__ is to **stopping.**
3. **Scissors** are to __cut__ as **needles** are to **sew.**
4. **Water** is to **skiing** as **rink** is to __skating__.
5. **Steam shovel** is to **dig** as **tractor** is to __plow__.
6. **Stick** is to **hockey** as __bat__ is to **baseball.**
7. **Watch** is to **television** as __listen__ is to **radio.**
8. __Geese__ are to **goose** as **children** are to **child.**
9. **Multiply** is to **multiplication** as __subtract__ is to **subtraction.**
10. **Milk** is to **cow** as **egg** is to __hen__.
11. **Yellow** is to **banana** as __red__ is to **tomato.**
12. __Fast__ is to **slow** as **day** is to **night.**
13. **Pine** is to **tree** as __daisy__ is to **flower.**
14. **Zipper** is to **jacket** as __button__ is to **shirt.**
15. **Museum** is to **painting** as **library** is to __book__.
16. **Petal** is to **flower** as **branch** is to __tree__.
17. **Cow** is to **barn** as **car** is to __garage__.
18. **Dresser** is to **bedroom** as __stove__ is to **kitchen.**
19. **Teacher** is to __student__ as **doctor** is to **patient.**
20. **Ice** is to **cold** as **fire** is to __hot__.

Page 62

Synonym and Antonym Analogies

Analogies are a way of comparing items to show how they are related. Analogies can show different types of relationships. Two relationships analogies might show are synonyms or antonyms.

Examples:
Antonyms: hot is to **cold** as **happy** is to **sad**
Synonyms: happy is to **glad** as **run** is to **jog**

You can write an analogy this way:
slow : fast :: up : down
You read it this way:
Slow is to **fast** as **up** is to **down.**

Directions: Write **S** for synonym or **A** for antonym in the blanks in front of each analogy. Then, complete the analogies by choosing a word from the box.

life	run	comforter	fail	photograph
above	feline	play	drape	different

__S__ 1. dog : canine :: cat : __feline__
__S__ 2. coat : parka :: curtain : __drape__
__A__ 3. asleep : awake :: work : __play__
__A__ 4. ground : sky :: below : __above__
__A__ 5. freeze : thaw :: stroll : __run__
__S__ 6. dangerous : treacherous :: picture : __photograph__
__S__ 7. ancient : old :: bedspread : __comforter__
__A__ 8. win : lose :: succeed : __fail__
__S__ 9. manmade : artificial :: unique : __different__
__A__ 10. wealthy : poor :: death : __life__

Page 63

Part/Whole and Cause/Effect Analogies

Other types of analogies are part to whole and cause and effect.

Example:
Part to whole: fingers : hand :: toes : foot
Cause and effect: rain : flood :: matches : fire

Directions: Write **P** for part to whole or **C** for cause and effect in the blanks in front of each analogy. Then, complete the analogies by choosing a word from the box.

tree	bike	punishment	stomachache
beach	laugh	fingers	hawk
pencil	blizzard		

__P__ 1. hair : head :: fingernails : __fingers__
__C__ 2. germ : virus :: misbehavior : __punishment__
__C__ 3. fall : injury :: overeating : __stomachache__
__P__ 4. keyboard : computer :: wheels : __bike__
__P__ 5. tongue : shoe :: sand : __beach__
__C__ 6. practice : win :: joke : __laugh__
__C__ 7. read : learn :: snow : __blizzard__
__P__ 8. pouch : kangaroo :: beak : __hawk__
__P__ 9. leaf : plant :: bark : __tree__
__P__ 10. ink : pen :: lead : __pencil__

Page 64

Facts and Opinions

A **fact** is information that can be proved.

Example: Hawaii is a state.

An **opinion** is a belief. It tells what someone thinks. It cannot be proved.

Example: Hawaii is the prettiest state.

Directions: Write **F** (fact) or **O** (opinion) on the line by each sentence. The first one has been done for you.

__F__ 1. Hawaii is the only island state.
__O__ 2. The best fishing is in Michigan.
__O__ 3. It is easy to find a job in Wyoming.
__F__ 4. Trenton is the capital of New Jersey.
__F__ 5. Kentucky is nicknamed the Bluegrass State.
__O__ 6. The friendliest people in the United States live in Georgia.
__O__ 7. The cleanest beaches are in California.
__O__ 8. Summers are most beautiful in Arizona.
__F__ 9. Only one percent of North Dakota's forest or woodland.
__F__ 10. New Mexico produces almost half of the nation's uranium.
__F__ 11. The first shots of the Civil War were fired in South Carolina on April 12, 1861.
__F__ 12. The varied geographical features of Washington include mountains, deserts, a rainforest, and a volcano.
__F__ 13. In 1959, Alaska and Hawaii became the 49th and 50th states admitted to the Union.
__F__ 14. Wyandotte Cave, one of the largest caves in the United States, is in Indiana.

Directions: Write one fact and one opinion about your own state.
Fact: __Answers will vary.__

Opinion: _____

Page 65

Comprehensive Curriculum - **Grade 5**

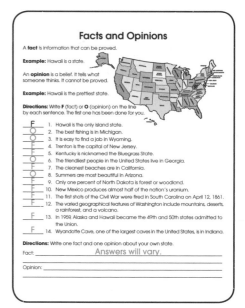

ANSWER KEY

Facts and Opinions

A **fact** is a statement based on truth. It can be proven. **Opinions** are the beliefs of an individual that may or may not be true.

Examples:
Fact: Alaska is a state.
Opinion: Alaska is the most magnificent state.

Directions: Write **F** if the statement is a fact. Write **O** if the statement is an opinion.

1. O The Grand Canyon is the most scenic site in the United States.
2. F Dinosaurs roamed Earth millions of years ago.
3. F Scientists have discovered how to clone sheep.
4. O All people should attend this fair.
5. O Purebreds are the best dogs to own because they are intelligent.
6. O Nobody likes being bald.
7. O Students should be required to get straight A's to participate in extracurricular activities.
8. F Reading is an important skill that is vital in many careers.
9. O Snakes do not make good pets.
10. F Many books have been written about animals.
11. F Thomas Edison invented the lightbulb.
12. O Most people like to read science fiction.
13. F Insects have three body parts.

Page 66

Facts and Opinions

Directions: Read the articles about cats. List the facts and opinions.

Cats make the best pets. Domestic or house cats were originally produced by crossbreeding several varieties of wild cats. They were used in ancient Egypt to catch rats and mice, which were overrunning bins of stored grain. Today, they are still the most useful domestic animal.

Facts: Domestic or house cats were originally produced by crossbreeding several varieties of wild cats. They were used in ancient Egypt to catch rats and mice,
Opinions: which were overrunning bins of stored grain. Cats make the best pets. Today, they are still the most useful domestic animal.

It is bad luck for a black cat to cross your path. This is one of the many legends about cats. In ancient Egypt, for example, cats were considered sacred and often were buried with their masters. During the Middle Ages, cats often were killed for taking part in what people thought were evil deeds. Certainly, cats sometimes do bring misfortune.

Facts: This is one of the many legends about cats. In ancient Egypt, for example, cats were considered sacred and often were buried with their masters. During the Middle Ages, cats often were killed for
Opinions: taking part in what people thought were evil deeds. It is bad luck for a black cat to cross your path. Certainly, cats sometimes do bring misfortune.

Page 67

Facts and Opinions

Directions: Write nine statements that are facts and nine statements that are opinions.

FACTS

Answers will vary.
1.
2.
3.
4.
5.
6.
7.
8.
9.

OPINIONS
1.
2.
3.
4.
5.
6.
7.
8.
9.

Page 68

Cause and Effect

A **cause** is an event or reason that has an effect on something else.

Example:
The heavy rains produced flooding in Chicago.
Heavy rains were the **cause** of the flooding in Chicago.

An **effect** is an event that results from a cause.

Example:
Flooding in Chicago was due to the heavy rains.
Flooding was the **effect** caused by the heavy rains.

Directions: Read the paragraphs. Complete the charts by writing the missing cause (reason) or effect (result).

Club-footed toads are small toads that live in the rainforests of Central and South America. Because they give off a poisonous substance on their skins, other animals cannot eat them.

Cause:
They give off a poisonous substance.
Effect: Other animals cannot eat them.

Civets (siv its) are weasel-like animals. The best known of the civets is the mongoose, which eats rats and snakes. For this reason, it is welcome around homes in its native India.

Cause: The mongoose eats rats and snakes.
Effect: It is welcome around homes in its native India.

Bluebirds can be found in most areas of the United States. Like other members of the thrush family of birds, young bluebirds have speckled breasts. This makes them difficult to see and helps them hide from their enemies. The Pilgrims called them "blue robins" because they are much like the English robin. They are the same size and have the same red breast and friendly song as the English robin.

Cause: Young bluebirds have speckled breasts. Bluebirds are much like the English robin.
Effect: This makes them difficult to see and helps them hide from their enemies. The Pilgrims called them "blue robins."

Page 69

Review

Directions: Write the answers.

1. Define classifying.
Answers will vary. Possible answers:
2. Add words to these classifications.

meat:	music groups:
hamburger	the Backstreet Boys
steak	the Beatles
sirloin tip	One Direction
pork chops	Justin Bieber
chicken	Taylor Swift

breakfast drinks:	colors:
orange juice	blue
cranberry juice	fuschia
grapefruit juice	melon
coffee	light green
tea	rose
milk	black

3. What is an analogy? a way of comparing objects to show how they relate
4. Give an example of an analogy. Answers will vary.
5. Write two sentences that are facts. Answers will vary.
6. Write two sentences that are opinions. Answers will vary.
7. Write an example of cause and effect. Underline the cause. Circle the effect. Answers will vary.

Page 70

Review

Directions: Write three statements about yourself that are facts.
1. Answers will vary.
2.
3.

Directions: Write three statements about yourself that are opinions.
4. Answers will vary.
5.
6.

Directions: Write a category name for each set of words.
7. Arizona, Wisconsin, Texas — states
8. mouse, rat, squirrel — rodents
9. saddle, reins, halter — horse equipment

Directions: Finish the analogies with words from the box. Not all words will be used.
10. look : see :: kind : nice
11. bald : hairy :: difficult : easy
12. insomnia : nightmares :: crumbs : pretzels
13. engine : car :: heart : human

friend, nice, ants, pretzels, human, hard, easy, alone

Page 71

Main Idea

The **main idea** is the most important idea, or main point, in a sentence, paragraph, or story.

Directions: Read the paragraphs below. For each paragraph, underline the sentence that tells the main idea.

Sometimes, people think they have to choose between exercise and fun. For many people, it is more fun to watch television than to run 5 miles. Yet, if you don't exercise, your body gets soft and out of shape. You move more slowly. You may even think more slowly. But why do something that isn't fun? Well, there are many ways to exercise and have fun.

One family solved the exercise problem by using their TV. They hooked up the television to an electric generator. The generator was operated by an exercise bike. Anyone who wanted to watch TV had to ride the bike. The room with their television in it must have been quite a sight!

Think of the times when you are just hanging out with your friends. You go outside and jump rope, play ball, run races, and so on. Soon, you are all laughing and having a good time. _Many group activities can provide you with exercise and be fun, too._

Maybe there aren't enough kids around after school for group games. Perhaps you are by yourself. Then what? _You can get plenty of exercise just by walking, biking, or even dancing._ In the morning, walk the long way to the bus. Ride your bike to and from school. Practice the newest dance by yourself. Before you know it, you will be the fittest dancer of all your friends!

Directions: Write other ideas you have for combining fun and exercise below.

Answers will vary.

Page 72

Reading Skills: Skimming

Skimming an article means to read quickly, looking for headings and key words to give an overall idea of the content of an article or to find a particular fact. When skimming for answers, read the questions first. Then, look for specific words that will help locate the answers.

Directions: Skim the paragraph to answer this question.

1. What "marvel" is the paragraph about? the Grand Canyon

In America, there is so much magnificent scenery. Perhaps the most stunning sight of all is the Grand Canyon. This canyon is in northern Arizona. It is the deepest, widest canyon on Earth. The Grand Canyon is 217 miles long, 4 to 18 miles wide and, in some places, more than a mile deep. The rocks at the bottom of the steep walls are at least 500 million years old. Most of the rocks are sandstone, limestone, and shale. By studying these rocks, scientists know that this part of the world was once under the sea.

Directions: Skim the paragraph again to find the answers to these questions.

1. How deep are the lowest points in the Grand Canyon?
   more than a mile deep

2. How old are the rocks at the bottom of the Grand Canyon?
   at least 500 million years old

3. What kinds of rocks would you find in the Grand Canyon?
   sandstone, limestone, and shale

4. What do these rocks tell us?
   This part of the world was once under the sea.

Page 73

Reading Skills: Maps

Directions: Use this map to answer the questions.

1. What state borders Louisiana to the north?
   Arkansas

2. What is the state capital of Louisiana?
   Baton Rouge

3. What cities are located near Lake Pontchartrain?
   New Orleans and Baton Rouge

4. In which direction would you be traveling if you drove from Monroe to Alexandria?
   southwest

5. About how far is it from Alexandria to Lake Charles?
   about 125 miles

6. Besides Arkansas, name one other state that borders Louisiana.
   Mississippi or Texas

Page 74

Reading Skills: Maps

Directions: Use this map of Columbus, Ohio, to answer the questions.

1. Does Highway 104 run east and west or north and south?
   east and west

2. What is the name of the freeway numbered 315?
   Olentangy Freeway

3. Which is farther south, Bexley or Whitehall?
   Whitehall

4. What two freeways join near the Port Columbus International Airport?
   270 and 670

5. Which two suburbs are farther apart, Dublin and Upper Arlington, or Dublin and Worthington?
   They are about the same distance apart.

6. In which direction would you be traveling if you drove from Grove City to Worthington?
   north

Page 75

Sequencing: Maps

Directions: Read the information about planning a map.

Maps have certain features that help you to read them. A **compass rose** points out directions. Color is often used so you can easily see where one area (such as a county, state, or country) stops and the next starts.

To be accurate, a map must be drawn to scale. The **scale** of a map shows how much area is represented by a given measurement. The scale can be small: 1 inch = 1 mile; or large: 1 inch = 1,000 miles.

Symbols are another map tool. An airplane may represent an airport. Sometimes, a symbol does not look like what it represents. Cities are often represented by dots. A map **legend** tells what each symbol means.

One of the best ways to learn about maps is to make one of your own. You may be surprised at how much you learn about your neighborhood, too. You will need a large piece of paper, a ruler, a pencil, and colored pencils.

You will need to choose the area you want to map out. It is important to decide on the scale for your map. It could be small: 1 inch = 3 feet, if you are mapping out your own backyard. Be sure to include symbols, like a picnic table to represent a park or a flag to represent a school. Don't forget to include the symbols and other important information in your legend.

Directions: Number in order the steps to making your own map.

3 Figure out the scale that will work best for your map.

1 Obtain a large piece of paper, ruler, pencil, and colored pencils.

5 Make a legend explaining the symbols you used.

6 Draw your map!

4 Draw symbols to represent features of the area you are mapping.

2 Decide on the area you want to map out.

Page 76

Following Directions

Directions: Read and follow the directions.

1. Draw a vertical line from the top mid-point of the square to the bottom mid-point of the square.
2. Draw a diagonal line from top left to bottom right of the square.
3. In each of the two triangles, draw a heart.
4. Draw a picture of a cat's face below the square.
5. Draw a horizontal line from the left mid-point to the right mid-point of the square.
6. Draw two intersecting lines in each of the two smaller squares so they are equally divided into four quadrants.
7. Draw a triangle-shaped roof on the square.
8. Draw a circle next to each heart.
9. Write your name in the roof section of your drawing.

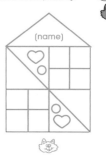

Page 78

Comprehensive Curriculum - **Grade 5**

Following Directions: Continents

Directions: Read the facts about the seven continents, and follow the directions.

1. Asia is the largest continent. It has the largest land mass and the largest population. Draw a star on Asia.
2. Africa is the second largest continent. Write a **2** on Africa.
3. Australia is the smallest continent in area: 3 million square miles, compared to 17 million square miles for Asia. Write **3,000,000** on Australia.
4. Australia is not a very crowded continent, but it does not rank lowest in population. That honor goes to Antarctica, which has no permanent population at all! This ice-covered continent is too cold for life. Write **zero** on Antarctica.
5. Australia and Antarctica are the only continents entirely separated by water. Draw circles around Australia and Antarctica.
6. North America and South America are joined together by a narrow strip of land. It is called Central America. Write an **N** on North America, an **S** on South America, and a **C** on Central America.
7. Asia and Europe are joined together over such a great distance that they are sometimes called one continent. The name given to it is Eurasia. Draw lines under the names of the two continents in Eurasia.

Page 79

Reading a Recipe

Directions: Read the recipe. Then, answer the questions.

Black Bean and Cheese Tacos

1 15-ounce can of black beans
½ c. mild salsa
½ tsp. salt
¼ tsp. garlic powder
1 head of lettuce
8 taco shells
1 cup shredded cheddar cheese

Drain the beans, and then combine them with ¼ cup of the salsa in a medium bowl. Microwave for 1 to 2 minutes. Stir in the salt and garlic powder. Next, wash the lettuce, and tear or cut it into small pieces. Place two taco shells on each plate. Divide the bean mixture among the taco shells. Top with lettuce, cheddar, and remaining salsa.

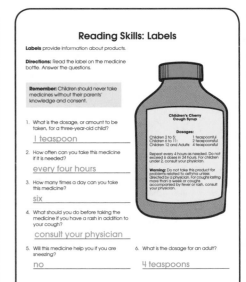

1. What do these abbreviations stand for?

   tsp. __teaspoon__

   c. __cup__

2. Number the steps in the correct order.

   __4__ Wash the lettuce.

   __5__ Place two taco shells on each plate.

   __3__ Microwave the beans and salsa.

   __1__ Drain the beans.

   __2__ Combine the beans with a quarter cup of the salsa.

3. Why is it important to follow the correct sequence when cooking?

   __to be certain the dish turns out correctly__

Page 80

Reading Skills: Labels

Labels provide information about products.

Directions: Read the label on the medicine bottle. Answer the questions.

Remember: Children should never take medicines without their parents' knowledge and consent.

Children's Cherry Cough Syrup

Dosages:
Children 2 to 5: 1 teaspoonful
Children 6 to 11: 2 teaspoonful
Children 12 and Adults: 4 teaspoonful

Repeat every 4 hours as needed. Do not exceed 6 doses in 24 hours. For children under 2, consult your physician.

Warning: Do not take this product for problems related to asthma unless directed by a physician. For coughs lasting more than a week or coughs accompanied by fever or rash, consult your physician.

1. What is the dosage, or amount to be taken, for a three-year-old child?

   __1 teaspoon__

2. How often can you take this medicine if it is needed?

   __every four hours__

3. How many times a day can you take this medicine?

   __six__

4. What should you do before taking the medicine if you have a rash in addition to your cough?

   __consult your physician__

5. Will this medicine help you if you are sneezing?

   __no__

6. What is the dosage for an adult?

   __4 teaspoons__

Page 81

Reading Skills: News Stories

Directions: Write the answers.

__Answers will vary.__

1. What is the name of your daily local newspaper?

2. List the sections included in your local newspaper. If you do not get a newspaper at home, you can visit your local newspaper's Web site or look for a copy at a library.

3. Do you read news stories (in newspapers, magazines, or online) on a regular basis? If so, where? If not, how do you learn about current events? _____

4. Ask a parent where he or she reads the news. Is it a newspaper, an online news site, or a variety of sources? _____

5. Find the editorial section of your newspaper. An editorial is the opinion of one person. Write the main idea of one editorial. _____

6. If you could work as a news reporter, what sorts of stories would you like to report on?

7. Go online, and search for a news source intended for kids. (Some options are www.timeforkids.com, www.dogonews.com, and www.magazines.scholastic.com.) Write down two headlines that interest you.

Page 82

Reading Skills: A Newspaper Index

An **index** is a listing in a book, magazine, or newspaper that tells where to find items or information.

Newspapers provide many kinds of information. You can read about national events, local news, the weather, and sports. You will also find opinions, feature stories, advice columns, comics, entertainment, recipes, advertisements, and more. A guide that tells you where to find different types of information in a newspaper is called a **newspaper index**. An index of the newspaper usually appears on the front page. In an online version of a newspaper, the index appears on the paper's home page. There are usually drop-down menus that allow you to chose more specific topics within a section.

Directions: Use the newspaper index to answer the questions.

Business.........................8	Local News.................5–7
Classified Ads.........18–19	National News.............1–4
Comics..........................20	Television........................17
Editorials..........................9	Sports.......................11–13
Entertainment..........14–16	Weather...........................10

1. Where would you look for results of last night's basketball games?
   Section: __Sports__ Page(s) __11-13__
2. Where would you find your favorite cartoon strip?
   Section: __Comics__ Page(s) __20__
3. Where would you find opinions of upcoming elections?
   Section: __Editorials__ Page(s) __9__
4. Where would you look to locate a used bicycle to buy?
   Section: __Classified Ads__ Page(s) __18-19__
5. Where would you find out if you need to wear your raincoat tomorrow?
   Section: __Weather__ Page(s) __10__
6. Which would be first, a story about the president's trip to Europe or a review of the newest movie?
   __story about the president's trip to Europe__

Page 83

Reading Skills: Classified Ads

A **classified ad** is an advertisement found in a newspaper, online, or in a magazine offering a product or service for sale or rent.

Example: For Sale: Used 26" 30-speed bike. $100. Call 555-5555.

Directions: Read these advertisements. Answer the questions.

Pet Sitter
Going on Vacation? Away for the Weekend?
...
Call Riley Trent
Phone: 999-8250

1.
Yard Work
Breaking Your Back?
Give Mike and Jane a crack! Mowing, raking, trash hauled. References provided.
Call 555-9581 or email yrdwrk@linknet.com.

2.
Pet Sitter:
Going on vacation? Away for the weekend? I am 14 years old and have experience caring for dogs and cats. Your home or mine. Excellent references.
Call Riley Trent.
Phone: 999-8250

3.
Singing Lessons for All Ages!
Be popular at parties! Fulfill your dreams! 20 years coaching experience. Madame Rinaud - Coach to the Stars.
Call 555-5331 or email songbird@global.com.

1. What is promised in the third ad? __popularity and fulfillment of dreams__
2. Is it fact or opinion? __opinion__
3. What fact is offered in the third ad? __20 years coaching experience__
4. Give an example of a slogan, or easy-to-remember phrase, that appears in one of the ads. __Yard work breaking your back? Give Mike and Jane a crack!__
5. Which ad gives the most facts? __2__
6. Which ad is based mostly on opinion? __3__

Page 84

Reading Skills: Classified Ads

Directions: Write a classified ad for these topics. Include information about the item, a phone number or email address, and an eye-catching title.

1. An ad to wash cars
Answers will vary.

2. An ad for free puppies

3. An ad for something you would like to sell

4. An ad to sell your house

Page 85

Reading Skills: Schedules

A **schedule** lists events or programs by time, date, and place or channel.
Example:

Packer Preseason Games		
August 14	7 P.M.	NY Jets at Green Bay
August 28	7 P.M.	Denver Broncos at Madison
August 28	3 P.M.	Saints at New Orleans
September 2	Noon	Miami Dolphins at Green Bay

Directions: Use this television schedule to answer the questions.

Evening
6:00 ANM Let's Talk! Guest: Animal expert Jim Porter
      CAR Cartoons
      NTV News
      WMU News
7:00 FRM Farm Report
      COM Movie. A Laugh a Minute (1955) James
           Rayburn. Comedy about a boy who wants to join the circus.
      GMS Spin for Dollars!
      CKG Cooking with Cathy. Tonight: Chicken with mushrooms
7:30 COM Double Trouble (comedy). The twins disrupt the high school dance.
      WST Wall Street Today: Stock Market Report
8:00 STS NBA Basketball. Teams to be announced.
      WMU News Special. "Saving Our Waterways: Pollution in the Mississippi."
      THT Movie. At Day's End (2009). Michael Collier, Julie Romer. Drama set
           in World War II.

1. What two stations have the news at 6:00? NTV and WMU
2. What time would you turn on the television to watch a funny movie? 7:00 P.M.
   What channel? COM
3. What could you watch if you are a sports fan? NBA basketball
   What time and channel is it on? 8:00 P.M./STS
4. Which show title sounds like it could be a game show? Spin for Dollars!
5. What show might you want to watch if you are interested in the environment?
   "Saving Our Waterways: Pollution in the Mississippi"
   What time and channel is it on? 8:00 P.M./WMU

Page 86

Review

Directions: Write the answers.

1. What is the purpose of a classified ad? to sell an item or service

2. Skim a paper or digital version of your local newspaper. List at least six categories of classified ads.
   Answers will vary.

3. What sections are included in the index of your local newspaper?
   Answers will vary.

4. What four pieces of information should a television program schedule contain?
   channels   time of programs
   program names   day/date

5. What information is present on a medicine bottle?
   type of medicine/name   directions
   dosage   warnings

6. Why is it important for medicine labels to include warnings?
   so people know when to consult a physician

Page 87

Using Prior Knowledge: Books

Directions: Before reading about books in the following section, answer these questions.

1. What books have you read recently?
   Answers will vary.

2. Write a summary of one of the books you listed above.
   Answers will vary.

3. Define the following types of books and, if possible, give an example of each.
   Examples will vary.
   biography: the story of a person's life, told by someone else

   fiction: a made-up story

   mystery: a story in which something puzzling occurs

   nonfiction: a factual piece of writing

Page 88

Context Clues: Remember Who You Are

Directions: Read each paragraph. Then, use context clues to figure out the meanings of the bold words.

During the 1940s, Esther Hautzig lived in the town of Vilna, which was then part of Poland. Shortly after the **outbreak** of World War II, she and her family were **deported** to Siberia by Russian communists who hated Jews. She told what happened to her and other Polish Jews in a book. The book is called *Remember Who You Are: Stories About Being Jewish*.

1. Choose the correct definition of **deported**.
   ☒ sent away   ☐ asked to go   ☐ invited to visit

2. Choose the correct definition of **outbreak**.
   ☒ a sudden occurrence   ☐ to leave suddenly

Remember Who You Are: Stories About Being Jewish is a nonfiction book that tells true stories. An interesting **fiction** book is *Wonder* by R.J. Palacio. It tells the story of a boy named August Pullman who was born with a facial difference. He begins fifth grade at a new school, and all he wants is to fit in. However, his classmates have a hard time showing **empathy** and getting past what he looks like on the outside.

3. Choose the correct definition of **fiction**.
   ☐ stories that are true   ☒ stories that are not true

4. Choose the correct definition of **empathy**.
   ☐ interesting   ☒ understanding   ☐ rejection

Page 89

Comprehension: Books and More Books!

Variety is said to be the spice of life. Where books are concerned, variety is the key to reading pleasure. There is a type of book that appeals to every reader.

Each year, hundreds of new books are published for children. A popular series for girls between the ages of 8 and 12 is *Dear America*. Each book focuses on a different time period or event in American history. The stories are told through the fictional diary entries of a girl living in that period.

If you like legends, an interesting book is *Dream Wolf* by Paul Goble. *Dream Wolf* is a retelling of an old Native American legend. Legends are stories passed down from one generation to another that may or may not be true. Some of them are scary! *The Legend of Sleepy Hollow*, for example, is about a headless horseman. Other legends are about a person's brave or amazing deeds. For example, there are many legends about Robin Hood, who stole from the rich and gave to the poor.

Many children like to read nonfiction books, which are about things that really exist or really happened. Those interested in information about Native Americans might like to read these books: *North American Indian* by David S. Murdoch, *Native American History for Kids* by Karen Bush Gibson, and *If You Lived with the Indians of the Northwest Coast* by Anne Kamma.

Directions: Answer these questions about different types of books.

1. What is the name of a book series that takes place in different periods of American history? *Dear America*

2. What legend is about a headless horseman? *The Legend of Sleepy Hollow*

3. Which of the following is not correct about legends?
   ☐ Legends are passed down through the generations.
   ☒ All legends are scary.
   ☐ Some legends are about people who did brave things.

Page 90

Comprehensive Curriculum - **Grade 5**

Comprehension: Shel Silverstein

Who is your favorite author? For many young people, the answer is Shel Silverstein. Shel's first book was published in the 1960s, and since then, his children's books have sold more than 20 million copies!

Shel Silverstein was born in Chicago, Illinois, in 1932. Although he was best known for writing children's poetry, Shel was creative in many ways. He was a talented singer, songwriter, composer, and illustrator. In fact, Shel illustrated all of his children's books himself. That is one reason the pictures seem to accompany the poetry so perfectly.

Shel's *Where the Sidewalk Ends*, first published in 1984, is one of the most beloved children's books of all time. What makes Shel's poetry so timeless and popular? His poems are often hilarious, with exaggerated situations, funny characters, and clever language. Shel's poems often rhyme and have a good rhythm, making them easy and interesting to read.

Shel Silverstein died in 1999 at his home in Key West, Florida. However, his quirky humor and incredible imagination will live on in his work, bringing joy to young readers for many generations to come.

Directions: Answer these questions about Shel Silverstein.

1. What is Shel Silverstein best known for? writing children's poetry

2. Who illustrated Shel Silverstein's books? he did

3. In what year was *Where the Sidewalk Ends* published? 1984

4. Which two words best describe Shel Silverstein's writing?
☒ hilarious ☒ rhythmic ☐ serious

5. Where was Shel Silverstein born?
☐ London, England
☐ Key West, Florida
☒ Chicago, Illinois

Page 91

Fact or Opinion?

Directions: Read the paragraphs below. Then, in the corresponding numbered blanks, write whether each numbered sentence is a fact or an opinion.

Have you ever seen the show Reading Rainbow? **(1)** It's a show about books, and its host is LeVar Burton. **(2)** Reading Rainbow was broadcast for more than 20 years on PBS stations across the country.

Some books that have been featured on the show are I Can Be an Oceanographer by Paul Sipiera, Soccer Sam by Jean Marzollo, Redbird by Patrick Fort, and Miss Nelson Has a Field Day by Harry Allard. **(3)** Miss Nelson Has a Field Day sounds like the most interesting book of all!

(4) On Reading Rainbow, children give informal book reports about books they have read. **(5)** All the children are adorable! In about 1 minute, each child describes his or her book. **(6)** While the child is talking, pictures of some of the pages from the book are shown. **(7)** Seeing the pictures will make you want to read the book. A few books are described on each show. **(8)** Other activities include trips with LeVar to places the books tell about. **(9)** Every child should make time to watch Reading Rainbow! **(10)** It's a fabulous show!

1. fact
2. fact
3. opinion
4. fact
5. opinion
6. fact
7. opinion
8. fact
9. opinion
10. opinion

Page 92

Context Clues: Kids' Books Are Big Business

Between 1978 and 1988, the number of children's books published in the United States doubled. The publishing industry, which prints, promotes, and sells books, does not usually move this fast. Why? Because if publishers print too many books that don't sell, they lose money. They like to wait, if they can, to see what the demand is for certain types of books. Then, they accept manuscripts from writers who have written the types of books the public seems to want. More than 4,600 children's books were published in 1988, because publishers thought they could sell that many titles. Many copies of each title were printed and sold to bookstores and libraries. The publishers made good profits and, since then, the number of children's books published each year has continued to grow. Today, more than 30,000 children's books are published each year!

Some people are worried that old-fashioned books will soon be a thing of the past. More and more information is available for free on the Internet. In addition, many people choose to read their books in digital form, on a tablet or computer screen. There is something special about reading an actual book with paper pages. Humans may have entered the digital age, but I'm sure that old-fashioned books are here to stay!

Directions: Answer these questions about how interest in writing, reading, and selling children's books has grown.

1. Use context clues to choose the correct definition of **industry**.
☐ booksellers ☐ writers ☒ entire business

2. If 4,600 books were sold in 1988, how many books were sold in 1978? 2,300

3. The number of children's books published in the United States doubled between 1978 and 1988. (Fact) Opinion

4. More and more information is available for free on the Internet. (Fact) Opinion

5. Many people choose to read their books in digital form, on a tablet or computer screen. (Fact) Opinion

6. There is something special about reading an actual book with paper pages. Fact (Opinion)

Page 93

Review

Directions: Follow the instructions below.

1. Write a summary of the selection "Shel Silverstein" (page 91).
Answers will vary.

2. What skills must a writer have in order to produce a book?
Answers will vary.

3. Define the following words from this section.
appeal: is attractive to
legend: a story passed down from generation to generation
deed: an act
generation: a group of people born and living at the same time
profit: money made or gained
distribute: to give, deliver, or divide something
suspense: a feeling of excitement, related to curiosity about what will happen
manuscript: a piece of writing before it has been printed/published

4. Interview the members of your family. Ask each person his or her favorite book title and the reason he or she enjoyed it. Then, summarize your findings in a paragraph.
Answers will vary.

Page 94

Using Prior Knowledge: Music

Using **prior knowledge** means being able to use what one already knows to find an answer or get information.

Directions: Before reading about music in the following section, answer these questions.

1. In your opinion, why is music important to people?
Answers will vary.

2. Name as many styles of music as you can.

3. What is your favorite type of music? Why?

4. If you could choose a musical instrument to play, what would it be? Why?

5. Name a famous musician, and describe what you know about him or her.

Page 96

Main Idea: Where Did Songs Come From?

Historians say the earliest music was probably connected to religion. Long ago, people believed the world was controlled by a variety of gods. Singing was among the first things humans did to show respect to the gods.

Singing is still an important part of most religions. Buddhists (bood-ists), Christians, Muslims, and Jews all use chants and/or songs in their religious ceremonies. If you have ever sung a song—religious or otherwise—you know that singing is fun. The feeling of joy that comes from singing must have also made ancient people feel happy.

Another time people sang was when they worked. Egyptian slaves sang as they carried the heavy stones to build the pyramids. Soldiers sang as they marched into battle. Farmers sang one song as they planted and another when they harvested. Singing made the work less burdensome. People used the tunes to pace themselves. Sometimes, they followed instructions through songs. For example, "Yo-oh, heave ho!/Yo-oh, heave ho!" was sung when sailors pulled on a ship's ropes to lift the sails. **Heave** means "to lift," and that is what they did as they sang the song. The song helped sailors work together and pull at the same time. This made the task easier.

Directions: Answer these questions about music.

1. Circle the main idea:

Singing is fun, and that is why early people liked it so much.

Singing began as a way to show respect to the gods and is still an important part of most religious ceremonies.

(Traditionally, singing has been important as a part of religious ceremonies and as inspiration for workers.)

2. Besides religious ceremonies, what other activity fostered singing? People often sang as they worked.

3. When did farmers sing two different songs? when they planted and when they harvested

4. How did singing "Yo-oh, heave ho!" help sailors work?
It helped them work together and pull at the same time.

Page 97

Comprehension: Facts About Folk Music

Folk music literally means music "of the folk," and it belongs to everyone. The names of the musicians who composed most folk music have long been forgotten. Even so, folk music has remained popular because it tells about the lives of people. Usually, the tune is simple, and even though folk songs often have many verses, the words are easy to remember. Do you know the words to "She'll Be Comin' 'Round the Mountain"?

Although no one ever says who "she" is, the verses tell you that she will be "riding six white horses" and that "we'll go out to greet her." The song also describes what will be eaten when she comes (chicken and dumplings) and what those singing will be wearing (red pajamas).

"Clementine" is a song that came out of the California gold rush in the mid-1800s. It tells the story of a woman who was "lost and gone forever" when she was killed. ("In a cavern, in a canyon, excavating for a mine/Met a miner '49er and his daughter, Clementine.")

Another famous folk song is "Swing Low, Sweet Chariot." This song was sung by slaves in the United States and today is sung by people of all races. The words "Swing low, sweet chariot, coming for to carry me home . . ." describe the soul being united with God after death. Like other folk songs that sprang from slaves, "Swing Low, Sweet Chariot" is simple, moving, and powerful.

Directions: Answer these questions about folk music.

1. What is the purpose of folk music? It tells about the lives of people.
   _____

2. What food is sung about in "She'll Be Comin' 'Round the Mountain"?
   chicken and dumplings

3. Should Clementine live?
   ☐ Florida   ☐ Mississippi   ☒ California

4. Where in the United States do you think "Swing Low, Sweet Chariot" was first sung?
   ☐ the North   ☐ the West   ☒ the South

Page 98

Recalling Details: Woodwinds

There are four kinds of woodwind instruments in modern bands. They are flutes, oboes, clarinets, and bassoons. They are called "woodwind" instruments for two sensible reasons. In the beginning, they were all made of wood. Also, the musician's breath, or "wind," was required to play them.

Although they are all woodwinds, these instruments look different and are played differently. To play an oboe, the musician blows through a mouthpiece on the front of the instrument. The mouthpiece, called a reed, is made of two flat pieces of wood called cane. Clarinet players also blow into a reed mouthpiece. The clarinet has only one reed in its mouthpiece.

To play the flute, the musician blows across a hole near one end of the instrument. The way the breath is aimed helps to make the flute's different sounds. The bassoon is the largest woodwind instrument. Bassoon players blow through a mouthpiece that goes through a short metal pipe before it goes into the body of the bassoon. It makes a very different sound from the clarinet or the oboe.

Woodwind instruments also have keys—but not the kind of keys that open locks. These keys are more like levers that the musician pushes up and down. The levers cover holes. When the musician pushes down on a lever, it closes that hole. When he or she lifts his or her finger, it opens the hole. Different sounds are produced by controlling the amount of breath, or "wind," that goes through the holes.

Directions: Answer these questions about woodwind instruments.

1. What instruments are in the woodwind section? flutes, oboes, clarinets, and bassoons

2. Why are some instruments called woodwinds? At first, they were all made of wood, and the musician's breath, or "wind," was needed to play them.

3. How is a flute different from the other woodwinds? The way breath is aimed makes different sounds.

4. What happens when a musician pushes down on a woodwind key? Different sounds are made by controlling the amount of breath that goes through the holes.

5. How would a woodwind musician open the holes on his/her instrument? by lifting a finger on a key

Page 99

Comprehension: Harp Happenings

If you have ever heard a harpist play, you know what a lovely sound a harp makes. Music experts say the harp is among the oldest of instruments. It probably was invented several thousand years ago in or near Egypt.

The first harps are believed to have been made by stretching a string tightly between an empty tortoise shell and a curved pole. The empty shell magnified the sound the string made when it was plucked. More strings were added later so that more sounds could be made. Over the centuries, the shape of the harp gradually was changed into that of the large, graceful instruments we recognize today.

Here is how a harpist plays a harp. First, he or she leans the harp against his or her right shoulder. Then, the harpist puts his or her hands on either side of the harp and plucks its strings with both hands.

A harp has seven pedals on the bottom back. The audience usually cannot see these pedals. Most people are surprised to learn about them. The pedals are connected to the strings. Stepping on a particular pedal causes certain strings to tighten. The tightening and loosening of the strings makes different sounds; so does the way the strings are plucked with the hands.

At first glance, harps look like simple instruments. Actually, they are rather complicated and difficult to keep in tune. A harpist often spends as long as half an hour before a performance tuning his or her harp's strings so it produces the correct sounds.

Directions: Answer these questions about harps.

1. When were harps invented? Several thousand years ago

2. Where were harps invented? Egypt

3. What is a person called who plays the harp? harpist

4. The harpist leans the harp against his or her
   ☒ right shoulder.   ☐ left shoulder.   ☐ left knee.

5. How many pedals does a harp have?
   ☐ five   ☐ six   ☒ seven

6. Harps are easy to play.
   ☐ yes   ☒ no

Page 100

Comprehension: Brass Shows Class

If you like band music, you probably love the music made by brass instruments. Bright, loud, moving, and magnificent—all these words describe the sounds made by brass.

Some of the earliest instruments were horns. Made from hollowed-out animal horns, these primitive instruments could not possibly have made the rich sounds of modern horns that are made of brass.

Most modern brass bands have three instruments—tubas, trombones, and trumpets. Combined, these instruments can produce stirring marches, as well as haunting melodies.

The most famous composer for brass instruments was John Philip Sousa. Born in Washington, D.C., in 1854, Sousa was a military band conductor and composer. He died in 1932, but his music is still popular today. One of Sousa's most famous tunes for military bands is "Stars and Stripes Forever."

Besides composing band music, Sousa also invented a practical band instrument—the sousaphone. The sousaphone is a huge tuba that makes very low noises. Because of the way it curls around the body, a sousaphone is easier to carry than a tuba, especially when the musician must march. This is exactly why John Philip Sousa invented it!

Directions: Answer these questions about brass instruments.

1. Who invented the sousaphone? John Philip Sousa

2. What were the first horns made from? hollowed-out animal horns

3. Where was John Philip Sousa born? Washington, D.C.

4. When did John Philip Sousa die? 1932

5. Why did Sousa invent the sousaphone? Because it was easier to hold when marching.

6. What types of instruments make up a modern brass band? tubas, trombones, and trumpets

Page 101

Comprehension: Violins

If you know anything about violin music, chances are you have heard the word **Stradivarius** (Strad-uh-vary-us). Stradivarius is the name for the world's most magnificent violins. They are named after their creator, Antonio Stradivari.

Stradivari was born in northern Italy and lived from 1644 to 1737. Cremona, the town he lived in, was a place where violins were manufactured. Stradivari was very young when he learned to play the violin. He grew to love the instrument so much that he began to make them himself.

Violins were new instruments during Stradivari's time. People made them in different sizes and shapes and of different types of wood. Stradivari is said to have been very particular about the wood he selected for his violins. He took long walks alone in the forest to find just the right tree. He is also said to have used a secret and special type of varnish to put on the wood. Whatever the reasons, his violins are the best in the world.

Stradivari put such care and love into his violins that they are still used today. Many of them are in museums. But some wealthy musicians, who can afford the thousands and thousands of dollars they cost, own Stradivarius violins.

Stradivari passed his methods on to his sons. But the secrets of making Stradivarius violins seem to have died out with the family. Their rarity, as well as their mellow sound, make Stradivarius violins among the most prized instruments in the world.

Directions: Answer these questions about Stradivarius violins.

1. Where did Stradivari live? northern Italy

2. Why did he begin making violins? He loved the instrument.

3. Why are Stradivarius violins special? Stradivari chose the wood carefully, used a special varnish, and made the violins with love and care.

4. Where can Stradivarius violins be found today? Most are in museums, but some are owned by wealthy musicians.

5. How did Stradivari select the wood for his violins? He took long walks alone in the forest to find just the right tree.

6. Who else knew Stradivari's secrets for making such superior violins? his sons

Page 102

Review

Directions: Complete the following exercises.

1. Write a four-sentence summary of the selection "Where Did Songs Come From?" (page 97).
   Answers will vary.
   _____

2. Describe the main difference between a clarinet and an oboe.
   The oboe has two reeds in its mouthpiece, while the clarinet has only one.

3. How do the keys of woodwind instruments work?
   The keys are like levers that, when pressed, cover the holes. This changes the sound.

4. Write a summary of the history of the harp.
   Answers will vary.
   _____

5. Define the following words from the selection "Facts About Folk Music" (page 98).
   verses: stanza of a poem or a song
   excavating: making a hole or channel by digging
   chariot: two-wheeled vehicle drawn by a horse
   composed: created in music or writing

Page 103

Using Prior Knowledge: Art

Directions: Before reading about art in the following section, answer these questions.

1. Write a short paragraph about a famous artist of your choice.

   Answers will vary.

2. Many artists paint realistic scenes. Other artists paint imaginary scenes. Which do you prefer? Why?

3. Although we often think of art as painting and drawing, art also includes sculpture, fabric weavings, and metalwork. Are you talented at a particular type of art? If so, what type? If not, what would you like to learn?

4. Why are art museums important to society?

5. Why do you think some artwork is worth so much money? Would you pay several thousand dollars for a piece of artwork? Why or why not?

Page 104

Main Idea: Creating Art

No one knows exactly when the first human created the first painting. Crude drawings and paintings on the walls of caves show that humans have probably always expressed themselves through art. These early cave pictures show animals being hunted, people dancing, and other events of daily life. The simplicity of the paintings reflect the simple lifestyles of these primitive people.

The subjects of early paintings also help to make another important point. Art is not created out of nothing. The subjects an artist chooses to paint reflect the history, politics, and culture of the time and place in which he or she lives. An artist born and raised in New York City, for example, is not likely to paint scenes of the Rocky Mountains. An artist living in the Rockies is not likely to paint pictures of city life.

Of course, not all paintings are realistic. Many artists choose to paint pictures that show their own "inner vision" as opposed to what they see with their eyes. Many religious paintings of earlier centuries look realistic but contain figures of angels. These paintings combine the artist's inner vision of angels with other things, such as church buildings, that can be seen.

Directions: Answer these questions about creating art.

1. Circle the main idea:

   Art was important to primitive people because it showed hunting and dancing scenes, and it is still important today.

   (Through the ages, artists have created paintings that reflect the culture, history, and politics of the times, as well as their own inner visions.)

2. Why is an artist living in the Rocky Mountains less likely to paint city scenes?

   Artists tend to paint things that are a part of the time and place where they live.

3. In addition to what the artists see with their eyes, what do some paintings also show?

   Some paintings show an artist's inner vision.

Page 105

Comprehension: Leonardo da Vinci

Many people believe that Leonardo da Vinci, an Italian artist and inventor who lived from 1452 to 1519, was the most brilliant person ever born. He was certainly a man ahead of his time! Records show that da Vinci loved the world and was curious about everything in it.

To learn about the human body, he dissected corpses to find out what was inside. In the 15th and 16th centuries, dissecting the dead was against the laws of the Catholic Church. Leonardo was a brave man!

He was also an inventor. Leonardo invented a parachute and designed a type of helicopter—five centuries before airplanes were invented! Another of da Vinci's major talents was painting. You have probably seen a print, or copy, of one of his most famous paintings. It is called The Last Supper, and it shows Jesus eating his final meal with his disciples. It took da Vinci three years to paint The Last Supper. The man who hired da Vinci to do the painting was upset. He went to da Vinci to ask why it was taking so long. The problem, said da Vinci, was that in the painting, Jesus has just told the disciples that one of them would betray him. He wanted to get their expressions exactly right as each one cried out, "Lord, am I the one?"

Another famous painting by da Vinci is called the Mona Lisa. Have you seen a print of this painting? Maybe you have been lucky enough to see the original hanging in a Paris art museum called the Louvre (loov). If so, you know that Mona Lisa has a wistful expression on her face. The painting is of a real woman, the wife of an Italian merchant. Art historians believe she looks wistful because one of her children had recently died.

Directions: Answer these questions about Leonardo da Vinci.

1. How old was da Vinci when he died? 67

2. Name two of da Vinci's inventions. the parachute and the helicopter

3. Name two famous paintings by da Vinci. The Last Supper and Mona Lisa

4. In which Paris museum does Mona Lisa hang? ☐ Lourre ☐ Loure ☒ Louvre

Page 106

Context Clues: Leonardo da Vinci

Directions: Read the sentences below. Use context clues to figure out the meaning of the bold words.

1. Some people are **perplexed** when they look at The Last Supper, but others understand it immediately.
   ☐ unhappy   ☐ happy   ☒ puzzled

2. Because his model felt **melancholy** about the death of her child, da Vinci had music played to lift her spirits as he painted the Mona Lisa.
   ☒ sad   ☐ unfriendly   ☐ hostile

3. Because da Vinci's work is so famous, many people **erroneously** assume that he left behind many paintings. In fact, he left only 20.
   ☐ rightly   ☐ correctly   ☒ wrongly

4. Leonardo da Vinci was not like most other people. He didn't care what others thought of him—he led an interesting and **unconventional** life.
   ☐ dull   ☐ not ordinary   ☐ ordinary

5. The **composition** of The Last Supper is superb. All the parts of the painting seem to fit together beautifully.
   ☐ the picture frame   ☒ parts of the picture

6. Leonardo's **genius** set him apart from people with ordinary minds. He never married, he had few friends, and he spent much of his time alone.
   ☒ great mental abilities   ☐ great physical abilities
   ☐ improper way to do things   ☐ proper way to do things

7. Because he was a loner, da Vinci worried no one would come to his funeral when he died. In his will, he set aside 70 cents each to hire 60 **mourners** to accompany his body to his grave.
   ☐ friends   ☒ people who grieve   ☐ people who smile

Page 107

Comprehension: Michelangelo

Another famous painter of the late 14th and early 15th centuries was Michelangelo Buonarroti. Michelangelo, who lived from 1475 to 1564, was also an Italian. Like da Vinci, his genius was apparent at a young age. When he was 13, the ruler of his hometown of Florence, Lorenzo Medici (muh-dee-chee), befriended Michelangelo and asked him to live in the palace. There, Michelangelo studied sculpture and met many artists.

By the time he was 18, Michelangelo was a respected sculptor. He created one of his most famous religious sculptures, the Pieta (pee-ay-tah), when he was only 21. Then, the Medici family abruptly fell from power and Michelangelo had to leave Florence.

Still, his work was well known, and he was able to make a living. In 1503, Pope Julius II called Michelangelo to Rome. He wanted Michelangelo to paint the tomb where he would someday be buried. Michelangelo preferred sculpting to painting, but no one turned down the pope! Before Michelangelo finished his painting, however, the pope ordered Michelangelo to begin painting the ceiling of the Sistine Chapel inside the Vatican. (The Vatican is the palace and surrounding area where the pope lives in Rome.)

Michelangelo was very angry! He did not like to paint. He wanted to create sculptures. But no one turns down the pope. After much complaining, Michelangelo began work on what would be his most famous project.

Directions: Answer these questions about Michelangelo.

1. How old was Michelangelo when he died? 89

2. What was the first project Pope Julius II asked Michelangelo to paint?
   He wanted Michelangelo to paint the tomb where he would someday be buried.

3. What is the Vatican? the palace and surrounding area where the pope lives in Rome

4. What was the second project the pope asked Michelangelo to do?
   ☐ paint his tomb's ceiling   ☒ paint the Sistine Chapel's ceiling

Page 108

Comprehension: Rembrandt

Most art critics agree that Rembrandt (Rem-brant) was one of the greatest painters of all time. This Dutch artist, who lived from 1606 to 1669, painted some of the world's finest portraits.

Rembrandt, whose full name was Rembrandt van Rijn, was born in Holland to a wealthy family. He was sent to a fine university, but he did not like his studies. He only wanted to paint. He sketched the faces of people around him. During his lifetime, Rembrandt painted 11 portraits of his father and nearly as many of his mother. From the beginning, the faces of old people fascinated him.

When he was 25, Rembrandt went to paint in Amsterdam, a large city in Holland where he lived for the rest of his life. There, he married a wealthy woman named Saskia, whom he loved deeply. She died from a disease called tuberculosis (ta-bur-ku-lo-sis) after only eight years, leaving behind a young son named Titus (Ty-tuss).

Rembrandt was heartbroken over his wife's death. He began to spend all his time painting. But instead of painting what his customers wanted, he painted exactly the way he wanted. Unsold pictures filled his house. They were wonderful paintings, but they were not the type of portraits people wanted. Rembrandt could not pay his debts. He and his son were thrown into the streets. The creditors took his home, his possessions, and his paintings. One of the finest painters on Earth was treated like a criminal.

Directions: Answer these questions about Rembrandt.

1. How old was Rembrandt when he died? 63

2. In what city did he spend most of his life? Amsterdam

3. How many children did Rembrandt have? one

4. Rembrandt's wife was named
   ☐ Sasha.   ☒ Saskia.   ☐ Saksia.

5. These filled his house after his wife's death.
   ☐ friends   ☐ customers   ☒ unsold paintings

Page 109

Review

Directions: Follow the instructions below.

1. Write a one-sentence main idea for the selection "Leonardo da Vinci" (page 106).

Leonardo da Vinci was a brilliant Italian artist and inventor who is known as a man ahead of his time.

2. Write a summary of the selection "Leonardo da Vinci" (page 106).

Answers will vary.

3. Complete the sequence of events from the selection "Michelangelo" (page 108). Possible answers:

1) Michelangelo was born in 1475 in Italy.
2) At 13, Michelangelo moved into Medici's palace to study sculpture.
3) Michelangelo created the Pieta when he was 21.
4) Michelangelo had to leave Florence when the Medicis fell from power.
5) Pope Julius II asked Michelangelo to paint his tomb in 1503.
6) The pope asked Michelangelo to paint the ceiling of the Sistine Chapel.
7) Michelangelo did not want to do the painting, but it turned out to be his most famous work.

4. Define the following words from this section. Possible answers:

crude: simple, basic, primitive

dissect: to cut open in order to examine

disciples: people who help spread the teachings of a famous person

merchant: a storekeeper

wistful: feeling a yearning or sadness for something one wants

Page 110

Using Prior Knowledge: Big Cats

Directions: Before reading about big cats in the following section, answer these questions.

1. Name at least four big wild cats.

Answers will vary.

2. Compare and contrast a house cat with a wild cat.

3. What impact might the expansion of human population and housing have on big cats?

4. Do you have a cat? What are the special qualities of this pet? Write about your cat's name and its personality traits. If you don't have a cat, write about a cat you would like to have.

Page 111

Comprehension: Jaguars

The jaguar is a large cat, standing up to 2 feet tall at the shoulder. Its body can reach 73 inches long, and the tail can be another 30 inches long. The jaguar is characterized by its yellowish-red coat covered with black spots. The spots themselves are made up of a central spot surrounded by a circle of spots.

Jaguars are not known to attack humans, but some ranchers claim that jaguars attack their cattle. This claim has given jaguars a bad reputation.

The jaguar can be found in southern North America, but is most populous in Central and South America. Jaguars are capable climbers and swimmers, and they eat a wide range of animals.

Female jaguars have between one and four cubs after a gestation of 93 to 105 days. Cubs stay with the mother for two years. Jaguars are known to have a life expectancy of at least 22 years.

Directions: Use context clues for these definitions. Possible answers:

1. populous: having greatest population
2. reputation: the opinion of others about a person or thing
3. gestation: pregnancy

Directions: Answer these questions about jaguars.

4. Describe the spots on a jaguar's coat.

The spots are made up of a central spot surrounded by a circle of spots.

5. Why would it be to a jaguar's advantage to have spots on its coat?

Possible answer: The spots may help camouflage the jaguar.

Page 112

Comprehension: Leopards

The leopard is a talented nocturnal hunter and can see very well in the dark. Because of its excellent climbing ability, the leopard is able to stalk and kill monkeys and baboons. Leopards are also known to consume mice, porcupines, and fruit.

Although the true leopard is characterized by a light beige coat with black spots, some leopards can be entirely black. These leopards are called black panthers. Many people refer to other cat species as leopards. Cheetahs are sometimes referred to as hunting leopards. The clouded leopard lives in southeastern Asia and has a grayish spotted coat. The snow leopard, which has a white coat, lives in Central Asia. A leopard's spots help to camouflage (cam-o-flaj) it as it hunts.

True leopards can grow to over 6 feet long, not including their 3-foot-long tail. Leopards can be found in Africa and Asia.

Directions: Use context clues for these definitions. Possible answers:

1. consume: eat
2. ability: skill
3. nocturnal: active at night

Directions: Answer these questions about leopards.

4. List three differences between the leopard and the jaguar.

Answers will vary.

5. What makes a leopard able to hunt monkeys and baboons?

It is an excellent climber.

Page 113

Comprehension: Lynxes

Lynxes are strange-looking cats with very long legs and large paws. Their bodies are a mere 51 inches in length, and they have short little tails. Most lynxes have a clump of hair that extends past the tip of their ears.

Lynxes are known to chase down their prey and also to leap on them from a perch above the ground. They eat small mammals and birds, as well as an occasional deer.

There are four types of lynxes. Bobcats can be found in all areas of the United States except the Midwest. The Spanish lynx is an endangered species. The Eurasian lynx, also known as the northern lynx, and the Canadian lynx are two other kinds of lynxes.

Directions: Use context clues for these definitions. Possible answers:

1. prey: animals hunted by other animals
2. perch: a high-up resting place

Directions: Answer these questions about lynxes.

3. What are the four types of lynxes? bobcats, Spanish lynxes, Eurasian lynxes, Canadian lynxes

4. Use the following words in a sentence of your own.

mammal Answers will vary.

endangered

5. Do you believe it is important to classify animals as "endangered" to protect a species that is low in population? Explain your answer.

Answers will vary.

Page 114

Comprehension: Pumas

The puma is a cat most recognized by the more popular names of "cougar" or "mountain lion." Just like other large cats, the puma is a carnivore. It feeds on deer, elk, and other mammals. It can be found in both North and South America.

Pumas have small heads with a single black spot above each eye. The coat color ranges from bluish-gray (North America) to reddish-brown (South America). The underside of the body, as well as the throat and muzzle, are white. The puma's body can be almost 6 feet long, not including the tail.

Female pumas give birth to two to four young. When first born, pumas have brown spots on their backs, and their tails are lined with dark brown rings.

As with the jaguar, pumas are blamed for killing cattle. Because of this, pumas are either nonexistent in some areas or are endangered.

Directions: Answer these questions about pumas.

1. What is a muzzle? the nose and mouth of an animal

2. As the population increases in North America, predict what might happen to pumas.

Answers will vary.

3. What are two other popular names for the puma? cougar and mountain lion

4. What other cat besides the puma is blamed for killing cattle? the jaguar

5. Reviewing the sizes of cats discussed so far, write their names in order, from smallest to largest.

1) lynx
2) puma
3) jaguar
4) leopard

Page 115

ANSWER KEY

Comprehension: Tigers

Tigers live on the continent of Asia. The tiger is the largest cat, often weighing over 500 pounds. Its body can grow to be 9 feet long and the tail can be up to 36 inches in length.

There are three types of tigers. The Siberian tiger is very rare and has a yellow coat with dark stripes. The Bengal tiger can be found in southeastern Asia and central India. Its coat is more orange, and its stripes are darker. There is a tiger that lives on the island of Sumatra as well. It is smaller and darker in color than the Bengal tiger.

Tigers lead solitary lives. They meet with other tigers only to mate and share food or water. Tigers feed primarily on deer and cattle but are also known to eat fish and frogs. If necessary, tigers will also eat dead animals.

Female tigers bear one to six cubs at a time. The cubs stay with their mother for almost two years before going out on their own.

Because tiger parts are in high demand for use in Chinese medicine and recipes, tigers have been hunted almost to extinction. All tigers are currently listed as endangered.

Directions: Use context clues for these definitions. **Possible answers:**

1. rare: not common

2. solitary: alone; not part of a group

3. extinction: when a species has completely died out

Directions: Answer these questions about tigers.

4. Why have tigers been hunted almost to extinction?
Tiger parts are in high demand for use in Chinese medicine and recipes.

5. Name the three types of tigers.
Siberian, Bengal, Sumatran

Page 116

Comprehension: Lions

The lion, often referred to as the king of beasts, once commanded a large territory. Today, lions' territory is very limited. Lions are savanna-dwelling animals, which has made them easy targets for hunters. The increasing population of humans and their livestock has also contributed to the lion's decreased population.

Lions are heavy cats. Males weigh over 500 pounds and can grow to be over 8 feet in length, with a tail over 36 inches long. Males are characterized by a long, full mane that covers the neck and most of the head and shoulders. Females do not have a mane and are slightly smaller in size. Both males and females have beige coats, hooked claws, and powerful jaws. Their roars can be heard up to 5 miles away!

Lions tend to hunt in the evening and spend the day sleeping. They prefer hunting zebra or giraffe but will eat almost anything. A lion is capable of eating over 75 pounds of meat at a single kill and then going a week without eating again. Generally, female lions do the hunting, and the males come to share the kill.

Lions live in groups called prides. Each pride has between four and 37 lions. Females bear one to four cubs approximately every two years.

Directions: Answer these questions about lions.

1. What are the differences between male and female lions? Females are smaller and do not have a mane.

2. Why would living on a savanna make the lion an "easy target"? Savannas are flat grasslands, so lions don't have many places to hide.

Directions: Use context clues for these definitions. **Possible answers:**

3. pride: a group of lions

4. territory: a particular geographic area

5. savanna: a flat grassland

6. capable: able to do something

Page 117

Review

Directions: Follow the instructions below.

1. Choose any two big cats from this section, and compare them.
Answers will vary.

2. Why are each of these big cats endangered or decreasing in number?

3. What can be done to get these big cats off the endangered list?

4. Now that you have read about big cats, compare and contrast them with a house cat. What do you know now that you didn't know before reading this section?

Page 118

Using Prior Knowledge: Farm Animals

Directions: Before reading about farm animals in the following section, answer these questions.

1. List at least nine types of farm animals by mother and baby names.
Example: sow—piglet
Answers will vary.

2. If you owned a large ranch, what type of livestock would you enjoy keeping? Why?

3. Some animals routinely give birth to twins, triplets, or larger litters. Which animals give birth to more than one baby at a time?

4. Would you enjoy living on a farm? Why or why not?

5. What is the importance of raising livestock today?

Page 119

Comprehension: All About Sheep

Did you ever wonder what really happened to the tails of Little Bo-Peep's sheep? Here's the real story.

When sheep are born, they are called lambs. Lambs are born with long tails. A few days after lambs are born, the shepherd cuts off their tails. Because they get dirty, the lambs' long tails can pick up lots of germs. Cutting them off helps to prevent disease. The procedure is called "docking." This is probably what happened to Bo-Peep's sheep! Another shepherd must have cut their tails off without telling her.

Little lambs are cute. A lamb grows inside its mother for 150 days before it is born. This is called the "gestation period." Some types of sheep, such as hill sheep, give birth to one lamb at a time. Other types of sheep, such as lowland sheep, give birth to two or three lambs at a time.

After it is born, it takes a lamb three or four days to recognize its mother. Once it does, it stays close to her until it is about 3 weeks old. After that, the lamb becomes friendly toward other sheep.

Young lambs then form play groups. They chase each other in circles. They butt into each other. Like children, they pretend to fight. When play gets too rough, the lambs run back to their mothers for protection.

Lambs follow their mothers as they graze on grass. Usually, sheep move in single file behind an older female sheep. Female sheep are called ewes. The ewes teach their lambs how to keep themselves clean. This is called "grooming." Sheep groom only their faces. Here is how they do it: They lick one of their front legs, and then they rub their faces against the spot they have licked.

Directions: Follow the instructions below.

1. Define the word **docking**. cutting off a lamb's tail to prevent disease

2. Name a type of sheep that gives birth to one lamb at a time. hill sheep

3. Name a type of sheep that gives birth to two or three lambs at a time.
lowland sheep

4. Female sheep are called
☐ grazers. ☒ ewes. ☐ dockers.

5. Lambs begin playing in groups when they are
☐ 2 weeks old. ☒ 3 weeks old. ☐ 4 weeks old.

Page 120

Comprehension: Pigs Are Particular

Have you ever wondered why pigs wallow in the mud? It's not because they are dirty animals. Pigs have no sweat glands. They can't sweat, so they roll in the mud to cool themselves. When people who are hot say, "I'm sweating like a pig!" that's not really true. Humans can sweat, but pigs cannot.

Actually, pigs are particular about their pens. They are very clean animals. They prefer to sleep in clean, dry places. They move their bowels and empty their bladders in another area. They do not want to get their homes dirty.

Another misconception about pigs is that they are smooth. Only cartoon pigs are pink, smooth, and shiny-looking. The skin of real pigs is covered with bristles—small, stiff hairs. Their bristles protect their tender skin.

Female pigs are called sows. Sows have babies twice a year and give birth to 10 to 14 piglets at a time. The babies have a gestation period of 16 weeks before they are born.

All the piglets together are called a litter. Newborn piglets are on their tiny feet within a few minutes after birth. Can you guess why? They are hungrily looking for their mother's teats so they can get milk. As they nurse, piglets snuggle in close to their mother's belly to keep warm.

Directions: Answer these questions about pigs.

1. Why do pigs wallow in mud? to keep cool since they cannot sweat

2. How long is the gestation period for pigs? 16 weeks

3. What is one misconception about pigs? They are smooth. Pigs actually have bristles.

4. Tell two reasons pigs are on their feet soon after they are born.
a.) They want to nurse. b.) They want to snuggle and get warm.

5. A female pig is called a
☐ bristle. ☐ piglet. ☒ sow.

6. Together, the newborn piglets are called a
☐ group. ☐ family. ☒ litter.

Page 121

Context Clues: No Kidding About Goats

Goats are independent creatures. Unlike sheep, which move easily in herds, goats cannot be driven along by a goatherd. They must be moved one or two at a time. Moving a big herd of goats can take a long time, so goatherds must be patient people.

Both male and female goats can have horns, but some goats don't have them at all. Male goats have longer and bushier beards than females. Males goats also have thicker and shaggier coats than females. During breeding season, when goats mate, male goats have a very strong smell.

Goats are kept in paddocks with high fences. The fences are high because goats are good jumpers. They like to nibble on hedges and on the tips of young trees. They can cause a lot of damage this way! That is why many farmers keep their goats in a paddock.

Baby goats are called "kids," and two or three at a time are born to the mother goat. Farmers usually begin to bottle-feed kids when they are a few days old. They milk the mother goat and keep the milk. Goat's milk is much easier to digest than cow's milk, and many people think it tastes delicious.

Directions: Answer these questions about goats.

1. Use context clues to choose the correct definition of **goatherd**.

   [x] person who herds goats   [ ] goats in a herd   [ ] person who has heard of goats

2. Use context clues to choose the correct definition of **paddock**.

   [ ] pad   [ ] fence   [x] pen

3. Use context clues to choose the correct definition of **nibble**.

   [x] take small bites   [ ] take small drinks   [ ] take little sniffs

4. Use context clues to choose the correct definition of **delicious**.

   [ ] delicate   [x] tasty   [ ] terrible

Page 122

Comprehension: Cows Are Complicated

Would you believe cows have four stomachs? It sounds incredible, but it's true.

Here are the "hows" and "whys" of a cow's digestive system. First, it's important to know that cows do not have front teeth. They eat grass by wrapping their tongues around it and pulling it from the ground. They do have back teeth, but still they cannot properly chew the grass.

Cows swallow grass without chewing it. When it's swallowed, the grass goes into the cow's first stomach, called a **rumen** (roo-mun). There, it is broken up by the digestive juices and forms into a ball of grass. This ball is called cud. The cow is able to bring the cud back up into its mouth. Then, the cow chews the cud into a pulp with its back teeth and re-swallows it.

After it is swallowed the second time, the cud goes into the cow's second stomach. This second stomach is called the **reticulum** (re-tick-u-lum). The reticulum filters the food to sort out any small stones or other non-food matter. Then, it passes the food onto the cow's third stomach. The third stomach is called the **omasum** (oh-mass-um).

From there, any food that is still undigested is sent back to the first stomach so the cow can bring it back up into her mouth and chew it some more. The rest goes into the cow's fourth stomach. The fourth stomach is called the **abomasum** (ab-oh-ma-sum). Digesting food that can be turned into milk is a full-time job for cows!

Directions: Answer these questions about cows.

1. List in order the names of a cow's four stomachs.

   a) _rumen_   b) _reticulum_   c) _omasum_   d) _abomasum_

2. What is the name of the ball of grass a cow chews on? _the cud_

3. A cow has no

   [x] front teeth.   [ ] back teeth.   [ ] fourth stomach.

4. Which stomach acts as a filter for digestion?

   [x] reticulum   [ ] rumen   [ ] abomasum

Page 123

Context Clues: Dairy Cows

Some cows are raised for their beef. Other cows, called dairy cows, are raised for their milk. A dairy cow cannot produce any milk until after its first calf is born. Cows are not mature enough to give birth until they are 2 years old. A cow's gestation period is 40 weeks long, and she usually gives birth to one calf. Then, she produces a lot of milk to feed it. When the calf is 2 days old, the dairy farmer takes the calf away from its mother. After that, the cow is milked twice a day.

The dairy cow's milk comes from the large, smooth udder beneath her body. The udder has four openings called teats. To milk the cow, the farmer grasps a teat and squeezes it with his thumb and forefinger. Then, he gently but firmly pulls his hand down the teat to squeeze the milk out. Milking machines that are hooked to the cow's teats duplicate this action and can milk many cows quickly.

A dairy cow's milk production is not at the same level all the time. When the cow is pregnant, milk production gradually decreases. For two months before her calf is born, a cow is said to be "dry" and is not milked. This happens because, like humans, much of the cow's food is actually being used to nourish the unborn calf.

Farmers give the cow extra food at this time to make sure the mother and unborn calf are well nourished. Again, like humans, well-nourished mothers are more likely to produce healthy babies.

Directions: Answer these questions about dairy cows.

1. Use context clues to choose the correct definition of **grasp**.

   [ ] pull firmly   [x] hold firmly   [ ] hold gently

2. Use context clues to choose the correct definition of **duplicate**.

   [ ] correct   [ ] make   [x] copy

3. Use context clues to choose the correct definition of **decrease**.

   [ ] become more   [x] become less   [ ] become quicker

4. Use context clues to choose the correct definition of **nourish**.

   [ ] to be happy   [ ] to be friendly   [x] to feed

Page 124

Comprehension: Chickens

Have you ever heard the expression "pecking order"? In the pecking order of a school, the principal is at the top of the order. Next comes the assistant principal, then the teachers and students.

In the pecking order of chickens, the most aggressive chicken is the leader. The leader is the hen that uses her beak most often to peck the chickens she bosses. These chickens, in turn, boss other chickens by pecking them, and so on. Chickens can peck all others who are "below" them in the pecking order. They never peck "above" themselves by pecking their bosses.

Directions: Answer these questions about chickens.

1. Put this pecking order of four chickens in order.

   _2_ This chicken pecks numbers 3 and 4 but never 1.

   _1_ No one pecks this chicken. She's the top boss.

   _4_ This chicken can't peck anyone.

   _3_ This chicken pecks chicken number 4.

2. Use context clues to figure out the definition of **aggressive**. _Possible answer:_ _pushy; bossy; ready to fight_

3. Who is at the top of the pecking order in a school? _the principal_

Page 125

Review

Directions: Follow the instructions for each section.

1. Write a summary of the selection "All About Sheep" (page 120).
   Answers will vary.

2. What is the purpose of a pig's bristles?
   to protect the pig's skin

3. Write a summary of the selection "No Kidding About Goats" (page 122).
   Answers will vary.

4. What is the purpose of a cow's four stomachs?
   to digest food that can be turned into milk

5. How do chickens establish leaders and followers?
   Chickens peck each other to determine
   dominance. Chickens will only peck another
   chicken who is "below" them in the pecking order.

6. What is cud?
   the ball of grass formed by the rumen

Page 126

Using Prior Knowledge: Stamp Collecting

Directions: Before reading about stamp collecting in the following section, answer these questions.

1. Why do you think people collect stamps?
   Answers will vary.

2. What hobby do you most enjoy? Why?

3. Name at least six famous people who have been pictured on a stamp.

4. Why do you think the postal service issues many different stamps each year? Why not just issue one stamp?

5. Most stamps today are self-stick stamps. What are the benefits of these stamps? Do you think these create any drawbacks for collectors?

Page 127

Fact or Opinion?

Directions: Read the paragraphs below. Then, in the corresponding numbered blanks, write whether each numbered sentence is a fact or an opinion.

(1) An important rule for stamp collectors to follow is never to handle stamps with their fingers. (2) Instead, to keep the stamps clean, collectors use stamp tongs to pick up stamps. (3) Stamps are stored by being placed on mounts. (4) Stamp mounts are plastic holders that fit around the stamp and keep it clean. (5) The backs of the mounts are sticky, so they can be stuck onto a stamp album page. (6) What a great idea!
(7) The stamps are mounted in stamp albums that have either white or black pages. (8) Some people prefer black pages, claiming that the stamps "show" better. (9) Some people prefer white pages, claiming that they give the album a cleaner look. (10) I think this foolish bickering over page colors is ridiculous!

1. fact
2. fact
3. fact
4. fact
5. fact
6. opinion
7. fact
8. opinion
9. fact
10. opinion

Page 128

Comprehension: More Stamp Collecting

Many people collect stamps in blocks of four. Each stamp in the block is stuck to the other stamps along the edges. Collectors do not tear the stamps apart from one another. They buy blocks of stamps bearing new designs directly from the post office. Then, they mount the blocks of stamps and place them in their albums.

Collectors also get their stamps off envelopes. This is a bit tricky, because the stamps are glued on. Usually, collectors soak the stamps in warm water to loosen the glue. Then, they gently pull the stamps from the paper and let them dry before mounting them.

Some beginners start their collections by buying a packet of mixed stamps. The packets, or bags, contain a variety of different stamps. Beginners buy these packets from companies that supply stamps to philatelists (fuh-lay-tell-ists). Philately (fuh-lay-tell-lee) is the collection and study of postage stamps. Philatelists are the people who collect and study them.

Packets of stamps usually contain stamps from many different countries. Often, they contain duplicates of some of the stamps. Suppliers usually don't sort the stamps that go into the packets for beginners. They leave that for beginning philatelists to enjoy!

Directions: Answer these questions about stamp collecting.

1. Name three places some people get stamps. from the post office, from envelopes, by buying a packet of mixed stamps

2. What is the word that describes the collection and study of stamps? philately

3. What are people called who collect and study stamps? philatelists

4. The bag that a mixture of stamps comes in is called a
☐ postal bag.   ☒ packet.   ☐ philatelist.

5. Do stamp mixtures usually include only U.S. stamps?
☐ Yes   ☒ No

Page 129

Recalling Details: Philately Abbreviations

Like other hobbies, philately has its own jargon and symbols. Collectors and dealers know what they mean, but outsiders would be puzzled if they saw the following abbreviations without their definitions. Read them carefully, and then refer to them when answering the questions below.

Avg. — average condition
blk. — block of four stamps
C — cancelled (used) stamp
OG — original gum
   (glue on back of stamp)
G — good condition
M — mint (excellent and unused) condition
s — single stamp
U — used stamp
VF — very fine condition
Wmk — watermark (can occur when water is used to remove stamp from envelope)

Directions: Answer these questions about the abbreviations used by stamp dealers and collectors.

1. If a philatelist wrote the following description, what would he or she mean?
I have a blk. in VF. I have a block of four stamps in very fine condition.

2. What does this mean? **s with OG, condition M** a single stamp with original gum in mint condition

3. What other abbreviation would most likely be used do describe a used (U) stamp? C

4. What does this mean? **s in Avg. with Wmk** a single stamp in average condition with a watermark

5. Which is more valuable, a rare stamp in **M** or **VF** condition? M

6. Would you rather own a single U stamp or a blk. in M? blk. in M

Page 130

Comprehension: Faces on Stamps

Most faces that appear on postage stamps are of famous people who are no longer alive. In fact, since 2011, the U.S. Postal Service had a rule that no living people could be featured on stamps. Until 2011, a person had to be deceased for five years before appearing on a stamp. The Postal Service changed the rule in 2011. The actors from the Harry Potter movies were among the first to be honored on a series of stamps.

Many U.S. presidents' faces have been on postage stamps, as have pictures of the faces of other important people in U.S. history. Some people's faces have been on many different stamps. Through the years, George Washington and Benjamin Franklin have been on dozens of different types of stamps!

Other people whose pictures have been on stamps include John Quincy Adams, the sixth president of the United States; Jane Addams, a U.S. social worker and writer; Louisa May Alcott, author of *Little Women* and many other books; Clara Barton, nurse and founder of the American Red Cross; Alexander Graham Bell, inventor of the telephone; and poet, Emily Dickinson. These are only a few of the hundreds of famous Americans whose faces have appeared on U.S. postage stamps.

Directions: Answer these questions about some of the people whose faces have appeared on U.S. stamps.

1. Name six occupations of people whose faces have appeared on postage stamps.
Possible answers: actor, president, writer, inventor, nurse, and poet

2. What two people's pictures have appeared on more stamps than on any others?
George Washington and Benjamin Franklin

3. What living person do you think should appear on a stamp? Why does he or she deserve this honor? Answers will vary.

4. Which person featured on a postage stamp was a social worker?
☐ Clara Barton   ☐ Louisa May Alcott   ☒ Jane Addams

5. Which person featured on a postage stamp was an inventor?
☐ Emily Dickinson   ☒ Alexander Graham Bell   ☐ John Quincy Adams

Page 131

Comprehension: Valuable Stamps

Most people collect stamps as a hobby. They spend small sums of money to get the stamps they want, or they trade stamps with other collectors. They rarely make what could be considered "big money" from their philately hobby.

A few collectors are in the business of philately as opposed to the hobby. To the people who can afford it, some stamps are very valuable. For example, a U.S. airmail stamp with a face value of 24 cents when it was issued in 1918 is now worth more than $35,000 if a certain design appears on the stamp. Another stamp, the British Guiana, an ugly stamp that cost only a penny when it was issued, later sold for $280,000!

The *Graf Zeppelin* is another example of an ugly stamp that became valuable. *Graf Zeppelin* is the name of a type of airship, similar to what we now call a blimp, invented around the turn of the century. Stamps were issued to mark the first roundtrip flight the *Zeppelin* made between two continents. A set of three of these stamps cost $4.55 when they were issued. The stamps were ugly, and few of them sold. The Postal Service destroyed the rest. Now, because they are rare, each set of the *Graf Zeppelin* stamps is worth hundreds of dollars.

Directions: Answer these questions about valuable stamps.

1. What is the most valuable stamp described? the British Guiana

2. For how much did this stamp originally sell? a penny

3. What did a collector later pay for it? $280,000

4. The *Graf Zeppelin* stamps originally sold for $4.55 for a set of
☐ four.   ☐ six.   ☒ three.

5. Which stamp did the Postal Service destroy because it didn't sell?
☐ British Guiana   ☒ Graf Zeppelin   ☐ British Zeppelin

Page 132

Fact or Opinion?

Directions: Read the paragraphs below. Then, in the corresponding numbered blanks, write whether each numbered sentence is a fact or an opinion.

(1) Nearly every valuable stamp on Earth has been counterfeited (coun-ter-fit-tid) at one time or another. (2) A counterfeit is a fake that looks nearly identical to the original. (3) It takes a lot of nerve to try to pass off counterfeits as the real thing. (4) Counterfeiting is big business, especially with stamps from overseas. (5) Because a collector often has no original for comparison, he or she can be easily fooled by a good counterfeit!
(6) One way people can make sure a stamp is real is to have it checked by a company that authenticates (aw-then-ti-kates) stamps. (7) To authenticate means to prove the stamp is real. (8) Of course, there is a fee for this service. (9) But I think paying a reasonable fee is worth what collectors get in return. (10) Those counterfeiters should be locked up forever!

1. fact
2. fact
3. opinion
4. fact
5. opinion
6. fact
7. fact
8. fact
9. opinion
10. opinion

Page 133

Comprehension: Stamp Value

It's nearly impossible to predict which stamps will rise in value. Why? Because the value is based on the law of supply and demand. How much does someone or a group of "someones" want a particular stamp? If many people want a stamp, the value will increase, especially if few of the stamps exist.

However, collectors are also always on the lookout for things that can lower the value of a stamp. Are the stamp's perforations (per-four-ay-shuns) torn along the edges? (Perforations are ragged edges where stamps tear apart.) Is there a watermark on the stamp? Has the gum worn off the back? All these things can make a stamp less valuable.

Directions: Answer these questions about determining the value of stamps.

1. Name three things that can lower the value of a stamp.
   perforations that are torn along the edges, a watermark, gum worn off the back

2. Collecting stamps is a fascinating hobby.   Fact   (Opinion)

3. What is one thing the value of stamps is based upon? the law of supply and demand

4. What will happen if many people want a rare stamp? the value will increase

5. Explain how to spot a stamp that will become valuable. Answers will vary.

Page 134

Review

Directions: Follow the instructions below.

1. Define the following words from this section. Possible answers:
   mount: to display
   bickering: arguing
   philately: the collection and study of postage stamps
   counterfeit: fake
   authenticate: to prove to be real or authentic
   perforations: ragged edges where stamps tear apart

2. Choose two of the words above, and use each in a sentence.
   a) Answers will vary.
   b)

3. Write a one-sentence main idea for the selection "Stamp Value" (page 134).
   Answers will vary.

4. Write a summary of the selection "Faces on Stamps" (page 131).
   Answers will vary.

5. Write a summary of the selection "More Stamp Collecting" (page 129).
   Answers will vary.

Page 135

Using Prior Knowledge: Cooking

Directions: Before reading about cooking in the following section, answer these questions.

1. What is your favorite recipe? Why?
   Answers will vary.

2. What do you most like to cook? Why?

3. Have you tried food from cultures other than your own? If so, which type of food do you like most? Why?

4. Why is it important to follow the correct sequence when preparing a recipe?

5. What safety precautions must be followed when working in a kitchen?

Page 136

Following Directions: Chunky Tomato and Green Onion Sauce

Following directions means to do what the directions say to do, step by step, in the correct order.

Directions: Read the recipe for chunky tomato and green onion sauce. Answer the questions below.

Ingredients:
- 2 tablespoons corn oil
- 2 cloves of garlic, finely chopped
- 1½ pounds plum tomatoes, cored, peeled, seeded, then coarsely chopped
- 3 green onions, cut in half lengthwise, then thinly sliced
- salt
- freshly ground pepper

Heat oil in a heavy skillet over medium heat. Add garlic, and cook until yellow, about 1 minute. Stir in tomatoes. Season with salt and pepper. Cook until thickened, about 10 minutes. Stir in green onions and serve.

1. What is the last thing the cook does to prepare the tomatoes before cooking them?
   coarsely chop them

2. What kind of oil does the cook heat in the heavy skillet? corn oil

3. How long should the garlic be cooked? about a minute

4. What does the cook do to the tomatoes right before removing the seeds?
   peel them

5. Is the sauce served hot or cold? hot

Page 137

Comprehension: Cooking with Care

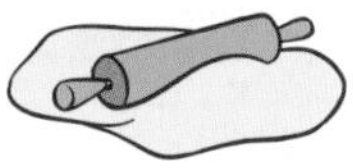

People are so busy these days that many have no time to cook. This creates a problem, because most families love home cooking! The food tastes good and warm, and a family meal brings everyone together. In some families, meals are often the only times everyone sees one another at the same time.

Another reason people enjoy home cooking is that it is often more nutritious than prepared foods. Restaurant meals and prepared foods are often much higher in fat, salt, and preservatives. At home, people tend to make more wholesome foods. You know what every ingredient is in a meal when you cook from home!

There's also something about the smell of good cooking that appeals to people of all ages. It makes most of us feel secure and loved—even if we are the ones doing the cooking! Next time you smell muffins baking, stop for a moment and pay attention to your mood. Chances are, the good smell is making you feel happy.

Real estate agents know that good cooking smells are important. They sometimes advise people whose homes are for sale to bake cookies or bread if prospective buyers are coming to see the house. The good smells make the place "feel like home." These pleasant smells help convince potential buyers that the house would make a good home for their family, too!

Directions: Answer these questions about good cooking.

1. Why do fewer people cook nowadays? People are very busy.

2. Why are family meals important? Meals are often the only times everyone sees one another at the same time.

3. Why are home-cooked meals usually more nutritious than prepared foods?
   They are lower in fat, salt, and preservatives. People also tend to make more wholesome foods at home.

4. Real estate agents often advise home sellers holding open houses to
   ☐ clean the garage.   ☒ bake cookies or bread.

5. The smell of baking at open houses may encourage buyers to
   ☐ bake cookies.   ☒ buy the house.   ☐ bake bread.

Page 138

Sequencing: Pumpkin-Nut Muffins

2¼ cups flour	1 cup canned pumpkin
2 teaspoons pumpkin pie spice	½ cup buttermilk
1½ teaspoons baking soda	½ cup canola oil
1 teaspoon ground ginger	¼ cup maple syrup
¼ teaspoon salt	1 teaspoon vanilla extract
½ cup chopped pecans	2 large eggs
1 cup packed brown sugar	

Before you begin, preheat the oven to 400°. Combine the flour, pumpkin pie spice, baking soda, ginger, and salt in a medium bowl. Stir the dry ingredients with a whisk. Stir in the nuts. Next, make a well in the center of the mixture. In a separate bowl, combine the brown sugar, canned pumpkin, buttermilk, canola oil, maple syrup, vanilla extract, and eggs. Stir well with a whisk. Now, add the sugar mixture to the flour mixture, and stir just until moist.

Scoop the batter into 18 muffin cups coated with cooking spray. Bake at 400° for about 15 minutes, or until a wooden pick inserted in the center of a muffin comes out clean. Cool the muffins on a wire rack. Eat and enjoy!

Directions: Number in correct order the steps for making pumpkin-nut muffins.

2 Combine the dry ingredients.
3 Stir in the nuts.
5 Whisk together the wet ingredients.
7 Cool the muffins on a wire rack.
1 Preheat the oven to 400°.
6 Add the sugar mixture to the flour mixture.
8 Eat and enjoy!
4 Make a well in the center of the mixture.

Page 139

Comprehensive Curriculum - **Grade 5**

ANSWER KEY

Comprehension: Eating High-Fiber Foods

Have you heard your parents or other adults talk about "high-fiber" diets? Foods that are high in fiber, like oats and other grains, are believed to be very healthy. Here's why: The fiber adds bulk to the food the body digests and helps keep the large intestines working properly. Corn, oatmeal, apples, celery, nuts, and other chewy foods also contain fiber that helps the body's systems for digesting and eliminating food keep working properly.

Researchers at the University of Minnesota have found another good reason to eat high-fiber food, especially at breakfast. Because fiber is bulky, it absorbs a lot of liquid in the stomach. As it absorbs the liquid, it swells. This fools the stomach into thinking it's full. As a result, when lunchtime comes, those who have eaten a high-fiber breakfast are not as hungry. They eat less food at lunch. Without much effort on their parts, dieters eating a high-fiber breakfast can lose weight.

The university researchers say a person could lose 10 pounds in a year just by eating a high-fiber breakfast! This is good news to people who are only slightly overweight and want an easy method for losing that extra 10 pounds.

Directions: Answer these questions about eating high-fiber foods.

1. Why is fiber healthy? Fiber adds bulk to the food the body digests and helps keep the large intestines working properly.

2. How does fiber fool the stomach? Fiber absorbs liquid in the stomach and swells. This fools the stomach into thinking it's full.

3. Name four examples of healthy, fiber-rich foods. Possible answers: corn, oatmeal, apples, celery

4. How many pounds could a dieter eating a high-fiber breakfast lose in a year?
☐ 20 pounds ☐ 30 pounds ☒ 10 pounds

5. The university that did the research is in which state?
☐ Michigan ☒ Minnesota ☐ Montana

Page 140

Main Idea: New Corn

I will clothe myself in spring clothing
And visit the slopes of the eastern hill.
By the mountain stream, a mist hovers,
Hovers a moment and then scatters.
Then comes a wind blowing from the south
That brushes the fields of new corn.

Directions: Answer these questions about this ancient poem, which is translated from Chinese.

1. Circle the main idea:

[The poet will dress comfortably and go to where the corn grows so he or she can enjoy the beauty of nature.]

The poet will dress comfortably and visit the slopes of the eastern hill, where he or she will plant corn.

2. From which direction does the wind blow? the south

3. Where does the mist hover? by the mountain stream

4. What do you think the poet means by "spring clothing"? _____
Answers will vary.

Page 141

Comprehension: The French Eat Differently

Many people believe that French people are very different from Americans. This is certainly true where eating habits are concerned! Obesity rates are about three times higher in America than they are in France. And yet, the French are known for their rich cheeses and delicious pastries. So how do the French manage to stay fit and healthy? There are several differences between the eating habits of Americans and the French.

One difference has to do with quality versus quantity. In America, portion sizes are known for being very large. In France, portions are much smaller, which means the French consume fewer calories. Also, when the foods are high quality, a small amount can be very satisfying.

In general, the French also really savor and enjoy their food. Americans are often in a hurry and rush through meals. Eating quickly or mindlessly can lead to overeating. The French take their time with meals. They eat more slowly, which gives the body a chance to recognize when it is full.

Finally, the French tend to cook at home more often than Americans do. In the United States, eating out is a popular pastime. The problem is that restaurant foods and processed foods are higher in fat and calories. Eating at home, like the French tend to do, results in healthier meals.

French meals are high in quality and flavor, and the French leave a meal feeling satisfied. Their eating habits keep them fit and healthy. Eating like the French could make America healthier, too!

Directions: Answer these questions about the eating habits of French and American people.

1. Why is it surprising that the French tend to be healthy and have low rates of obesity? The French are known for their rich cheeses and delicious pastries.

2. Are Americans or the French more likely to rush through meals? Americans

3. Why is eating at home generally a better idea than eating out or eating processed foods? Restaurant foods and processed foods are usually higher in fat and calories.

4. What is the difference between portion sizes in France and America? In America, portion sizes tend to be large, while in France, portions are much smaller.

5. What is a benefit of eating slowly? The body has a chance to recognize when it is full.

Page 142

Comprehension: Chinese Cabbage

Many Americans enjoy Chinese food. It's a popular take-out meal in cities across the United States. Because it tastes so good, many people are curious about the ingredients in Chinese food. Siu choy and choy sum are two types of Chinese cabbage that many people enjoy eating. Siu choy grows to be 2 to 3 feet! Of course, it is chopped into small pieces before it is cooked and served. Its leaves are light green and soft. It is not crunchy like American cabbage. Siu choy is used in soups and stews. Sometimes, it is pickled with vinegar and other ingredients and served as a side dish to other courses.

Choy sum looks and tastes different than siu choy. Choy sum grows to be only 8 to 10 inches. It is a flowering cabbage that grows small yellow flowers, which are edible. Its leaves are long and bright green. After its leaves are boiled for four minutes, choy sum is often served as a salad. Oil and oyster sauce are mixed together and poured over choy sum as a salad dressing.

Directions: Answer these questions about Chinese cabbage.

1. Which Chinese cabbage grows small yellow flowers? choy sum

2. Which Chinese cabbage is served as a salad? choy sum

3. Is siu choy crunchy? no

4. What ingredients are in the salad dressing used on choy sum? oil and oyster sauce

5. To what size does siu choy grow? 2 to 3 feet

6. Name two main dishes in which siu choy is used. soups and stews

Page 143

Review

Here's a recipe for a special mashed potato treat that serves two people. The recipe is fast and easy to follow, and the results are delicious!

Begin by peeling two large potatoes and cooking them in a pot of boiling water. When a fork or knife inserted into them pulls out easily, you will know they are done. Then, take them from the pot, and drain them well. Place them in a large mixing bowl, and add 2 tablespoons of milk and 2 tablespoons of butter. Mash with a potato masher until the lumps are gone.

In a skillet, melt a tablespoon of butter, and add one bunch of chopped green onions. Cook them about 1 minute. Add them to the potatoes, and mix gently. Season with salt and pepper. Serve and eat!

Directions: Answer these questions about how to make mashed potatoes with green onions.

1. Circle the main idea:

[This recipe is fast and easy, and the potatoes are delicious.]

This recipe has only four ingredients (plus salt and pepper).

2. Name the main ingredients in this recipe (not including salt and pepper).
potatoes, milk, butter, and green onions

3. How many people does this recipe serve? two

4. Number in order the steps for making mashed potatoes with green onions.
4 Cook the chopped green onions for 1 minute.
1 Peel two potatoes.
6 Season with salt and pepper and serve.
3 Put the cooked potatoes in a bowl with milk and butter, then mash.
5 Add the onions to the mashed potatoes.
2 Boil the potatoes until they are done.

Page 144

Using Prior Knowledge: Greek and Roman Mythology

Directions: Before reading about Greek and Roman mythology in the following section, answer these questions.

1. Hercules is a man from Greek and Roman mythology. Write a short paragraph describing what you know about Hercules.
Answers will vary.

2. Can you think of anything today that derived its name from a Greek or Roman myth?

3. Compare and contrast what you know of Greek and Roman beliefs about mythology with your beliefs.

4. Many constellations are named after gods, goddesses, and mythical creatures. Name at least six.

Page 145

Comprehension: Roman Legends

Long ago, people did not know as much about science and astronomy as they do today. When they did not understand something, they thought the gods were responsible. The ancient Romans believed there were many gods and that each god or goddess (a female god) was responsible for certain things.

For example, the Romans believed Ceres (Sir-eez) was the goddess who made flowers, plants, trees, and other things grow. She was a lot like what people today refer to as Mother Nature. Ceres was also responsible for the good weather that made crops grow. You can see why Ceres was such an important goddess to the ancient Romans.

Apollo was the god of the sun. People believed he used his chariot to pull the sun up each day and take it down at night. Apollo was extremely good-looking. His home was a golden palace near the sun surrounded by fluffy white clouds. Apollo had to work every single day, but he lived a wonderful life.

Jupiter was the most important god of all. He was the god who ruled all of the other gods, as well as the people. Jupiter was also called Jove. Maybe you have heard someone use the exclamation, "By Jove!" That person is talking about Jupiter! The word **father** is derived from the name of Jupiter. Although he did not really exist, Jupiter influenced our language.

Directions: Answer these questions about Roman legends.

1. What imaginary figure is Ceres compared to today? _Mother Nature_

2. Where did Apollo live? _a golden palace near the sun_

3. The word **father** is derived from the name of this god:
☐ Ceres ☐ Apollo ☒ Jupiter

4. Which is not true of Apollo?
☐ He had to work every day.
☒ He lived in a mountain cave.
☐ He was very handsome.

Page 146

Comprehension: Apollo and Phaethon

Apollo, the sun god, had a son named Phaethon (Fay-a-thun). Like most boys, Phaethon was proud of his father. He liked to brag to his friends about Apollo's father. But no one believed that the great Apollo was his father.

Phaethon thought of a way to prove to his friends that he was telling the truth. He went to Apollo and asked if he could drive the chariot of the sun. If his friends saw him making the sun rise and set, they would be awestruck!

Apollo did not want to let Phaethon drive the chariot. He was afraid Phaethon was not strong enough to control the horses. But Phaethon begged until Apollo gave in. "Stay on the path," Apollo said. "If you dip too low, the sun will catch Earth on fire. If you go too high, people will freeze."

Unfortunately, Apollo's worst fears came true. Phaethon could not control the horses. He let them pull the chariot of the sun too close to Earth. To keep Earth from burning, Jupiter, father of the gods, sent a thunderbolt that hit Phaethon and knocked him from the driver's seat. When Phaethon let go of the reins, the horses pulled the chariot back up onto the proper path. Phaethon was killed as he fell to Earth. His body fell and became a shooting star.

Directions: Answer these questions about the Roman legend of Apollo and his son.

1. Who did not believe Apollo was Phaethon's father? _No one believed that Apollo was his father._

2. What did Phaethon do to prove Apollo was his father? _He asked if he could drive the chariot of the sun._

3. Why did Jupiter send a lightning bolt? _to knock Phaethon from the driver's seat and keep Earth from burning_

4. Which was not a warning from Apollo to Phaethon?
☐ Don't go too close to Earth. It will burn up.
☒ Don't pet the horses. They will run wild.
☐ Don't go too far from Earth. It will freeze.

Page 147

Context Clues: Mighty Hercules

Some people lift weights to build their strength. But Hercules (Her-cu-lees) had a different idea. He carried a calf on his shoulders every day. As the calf grew, it got heavier, and Hercules got stronger. Eventually, Hercules could carry a full-grown bull!

Hercules used his enormous strength to do many kind things. He became famous. Even the king had heard of Hercules! He called for Hercules to kill a lion that had killed many people in his kingdom. Hercules tracked the lion to its den and strangled it. Then, Hercules made clothes for himself from the lion's skin. This kind of apparel was unusual, and soon Hercules was recognized everywhere he went. Hercules was big, and his clothes made it easy to pick him out in a crowd!

The king asked Hercules to stay in his kingdom and help protect the people who lived there. Hercules performed many feats of strength and bravery. He caught a golden deer for the king. The deer had outrun everyone else. Then, Hercules killed a giant, a dragon, and other dangerous creatures. Hercules became a hero and was known throughout the kingdom.

Directions: Answer these questions about Hercules.

1. Use context clues to choose the correct definition of **enormous**.
☒ huge ☐ tiny ☐ smart

2. Use context clues to choose the correct definition of **strangle**.
☐ beat ☒ choke ☐ tickle

3. Use context clues to choose the correct definition of **den**.
☐ pond ☐ hutch ☒ home

4. Use context clues to choose the correct definition of **apparel**.
☐ appearance ☒ clothing ☐ personality

5. Use context clues to choose the correct definition of **feat**.
☐ trick ☐ treat ☒ act

Page 148

Comprehension: Ceres and Venus

Remember Ceres? She was like Mother Nature to the ancient Romans.

Ceres made the flowers, plants, and trees grow. She made crops come up and rain fall. Ceres was a very important goddess. The ancient Romans depended on her for many things.

Although the gods and goddesses were important, they had faults like ordinary people. They argued with one another. Sometimes they got mad and lost their tempers. This is what happened to Ceres and another goddess named Venus (Veen-us). Venus, who was the goddess of love and beauty, got mad at Ceres. She decided to hurt Ceres by causing Pluto, gloomy god of the underworld, to fall in love with Cere's daughter, Proserpine (Pro-sur-pin-ay).

To accomplish this, Venus sent her son Cupid to shoot Pluto with his bow and arrow. Venus told Cupid that the man shot by this arrow would fall in love with the first woman he saw. Venus instructed Cupid to make sure that woman was Ceres's daughter. Cupid waited with his bow and arrow until Pluto drove by Ceres's garden in his chariot. In the garden was Proserpine. Just as Pluto's chariot got near her, Cupid shot his arrow.

Ping! The arrow hit Pluto. It did not hurt, but it did its job well. Pluto fell instantly in love with poor Proserpine, who was quietly planting flowers. Pluto was not a gentleman. He did not even introduce himself! Pluto swooped down and carried Proserpine off in his chariot before he could call for help.

Directions: Answer these questions about Ceres and Venus.

1. With whom was Venus angry? _Ceres_

2. How did Venus decide to get even? _She decided to hurt Ceres by causing Pluto to fall in love with Ceres's daughter, Proserpine._

3. Ceres's daughter's name was
☐ Persperpine. ☐ Prosperline. ☒ Proserpine.

4. Venus's son's name was
☐ Apollo. ☒ Cupid. ☐ Persperpine.

Page 149

Comprehension: Proserpine and Pluto

Proserpine was terrified in Pluto's palace in the underworld. She missed her mother, Ceres, and would not stop crying.

When Ceres discovered her daughter was missing, she searched the whole Earth looking for her. Of course, she did not find her. Ceres was so unhappy about Proserpine's disappearance that she refused to do her job, which was to make things grow. When Ceres did not work, rain could not fall and crops could not grow. Finally, Ceres went to Jupiter for help.

Jupiter was powerful, but so was Pluto. Jupiter told Ceres he could get Proserpine back from Pluto if she had not eaten any of Pluto's food. As it turned out, Proserpine had eaten something. She had swallowed six seeds from a piece of fruit. Because he felt sorry for the people on Earth who were suffering, Pluto told Jupiter that Proserpine could return temporarily to Ceres so she would cheer up and make crops grow again. But Pluto later came back for Proserpine and forced her to spend six months each year with him in the underworld—one month for each seed she had eaten. Every time she returned to the underworld, Ceres mourned and refused to do her job. This is how the Romans explained the seasons—when Proserpine is on Earth with Ceres, it is spring and summer; when Proserpine goes to the underworld, it is fall and winter.

Directions: Answer these questions about Proserpine and Pluto.

1. What happened to Ceres when Pluto took her daughter? _Ceres was so unhappy that she refused to do her job, which was to make things grow._

2. Whom did Ceres ask for help to get her daughter back? _Jupiter_

3. Why did Proserpine have to return to Pluto's underworld? _because she had swallowed six seeds from a piece of Pluto's fruit_

4. How long did Proserpine have to stay in the underworld each time she returned? _six months each year_

Page 150

Comprehension: Orpheus Saves the Day

Orpheus (Or-fee-us) was a talented Greek musician. Once, by playing beautiful music on his lyre (ly-er), he caused a ship that was stuck in the sand to move into the water. (A lyre is a stringed instrument that looks like a small harp and fits in the musician's lap.) The music was so wonderful it was to sail upon the sea. The ship must have thought the song was wonderful, too, because it slipped into the water and sailed away!

There was a reason the ship understood Orpheus's song. Inside the ship was a piece of wood that a goddess had given to the captain of the ship. The captain's name was Jason. Once, Jason had helped an old woman across a deep river. He later learned that the old woman was a goddess. To thank him, the goddess gave Jason a piece of wood that could talk. She told him to use the wood when he built a new ship. If he ever got stuck while building the ship and did not know what to do, the goddess told Jason to ask the wood.

Several times, Jason and his crew got instructions from the wood. Finally, the ship was finished. It was beautiful and very large. Because it was so big, Jason and his men were unable to move it into the water. They called on Hercules for help, and even he could not make it budge. That's when Orpheus saved the day with his lyre.

Directions: Answer these questions about Orpheus's amazing talent.

1. Who owned the ship that was stuck? _Jason_

2. Where was the ship stuck? _in the sand_

3. Why did the ship get stuck? _because it was so big_

4. A lyre looks like what other instrument?
☐ harmonica ☐ guitar ☒ harp

5. Who did Jason first ask for help to move the ship?
☐ Orpheus ☒ Hercules ☐ Jupiter

Page 151

Comprehensive Curriculum - **Grade 5**

Review

Directions: Follow the instructions below.

1. Define the following words from this section.

astronomy: the study of the stars, planets, and space

reins: straps used to guide or control a horse

lyre: a stringed instrument that looks like a small harp

centaur: a creature from mythology that is part human and part horse

minotaur: a creature from mythology that is part human and part bull

myth: a story from an ancient culture that explains a belief or something found in nature

2. Choose two words from above, and use each in a sentence.

a) Answers will vary.

b)

3. Write a summary of the selection "Mighty Hercules" (page 148).

Answers will vary.

4. Complete the sequence of events from the selection "Proserpine and Pluto" (page 150).
Possible answers:
a) Pluto fell in love with Proserpine and kidnapped her in his chariot.
b) Ceres was so unhappy about that she refused to do her job and make things grow.
c) Pluto told Jupiter that Proserpine could return temporarily to Ceres so she would cheer up and make crops grow again.
d) Pluto later came back for Proserpine and forced her to spend six months each year with him.
e) Every time she returned to the underworld, Ceres mourned and refused to do her job.

Page 152

Using Prior Knowledge: Famous Ships

Directions: Before reading about famous ships in the following section, answer these questions.

1. Look up the following terms in a dictionary, and write their definitions.

vessel: _____ Answers will vary. _____

bow: _____

stern: _____

poop deck: _____

hull: _____

caravel: _____

mast: _____

frigate: _____

lateen: _____

spar: _____

fore: _____

aft: _____

2. Have you ever been on a large ship? If so, describe the experience. If not, on what kind of ship or boat would you like to ride? Why?

_____

3. Name at least one famous ship, and write what you know about it.

_____

Page 153

Comprehension: The *Constitution*

The Constitution, or "Old Ironsides," was built by the United States Navy in 1798. Its success in battle made it one of the most famous vessels in the United States.
The Constitution's naval career began with the war with Tripoli from 1803 to 1804. Later, it was also used in the War of 1812. During this war, it was commanded by Isaac Hull. The Constitution won a 30-minute battle with the British ship, Guerriere, in August of 1812. The Guerriere was nearly demolished. Later that same year, the Constitution was used to capture a British frigate near Brazil.
The Constitution was taken out of service in 1829 and was rebuilt many times over the years. Today, it is on display at the Boston Navy Yard.

Directions: Answer these questions about the Constitution.

1. What is the main idea of the selection? Possible answer: The Navy ship the *Constitution* has a long and colorful history.

2. Which ship was almost demolished by the Constitution? the *Guerriere*

3. In which two wars was the Constitution used? the war with Tripoli and the War of 1812

4. Where is the Constitution now on display? the Boston Navy Yard

5. Complete the following time line with dates and events described above.
Possible answers:

the Constitution was built	War with Tripoli	War of 1812/ Battle w/ Guerriere	taken out of service	on display at Boston Navy Yard
1798	1803-1804	1812	1829	present day

Page 154

Comprehension: The *Santa Maria*, *Niña*, and *Pinta*

When Christopher Columbus decided to attempt a voyage across the ocean, the ships he depended upon to take him there were called "caravels." A caravel is a small sailing ship built by Spain and Portugal in the 15th and 16th centuries. The caravels Columbus used to sail to the New World were named the Santa Maria, Niña, and Pinta.
The ships were not very large. It is believed the Santa Maria was only 75 to 90 feet long, and the Niña and Pinta were only about 70 feet long. Caravels typically had three to four masts with sails attached. The foremast carried a square sail, while the others were more triangular in shape. These triangular-shaped sails were called "lateen sails."
These three small ships were quite seaworthy and proved excellent ships for Columbus. They carried him safely to the other side of the world!

Directions: Answer these questions about the Santa Maria, Niña, and Pinta.

1. What is a lateen sail? a triangular-shaped sail

2. What is the main idea of the selection? Possible answer: Christopher Columbus voyaged to the New World with three reliable ships called caravels.

3. What is a caravel? a small sailing ship built by Spain and Portugal in the 15th and 16th centuries

4. Where did Columbus sail in his caravels? across the ocean to the New World

5. Do some research, and compare a 15th-century caravel with a ship built in the 20th century.

Answers will vary.

Page 155

Comprehension: The *Lusitania*

The Lusitania was a British passenger steamship. It became famous when it was torpedoed and sunk by the Germans during World War I. On May 7, 1915, the Lusitania was traveling off the coast of Ireland when a German submarine fired on it without warning. The ship stood no chance of surviving the attack and sunk in an astonishing 20 minutes. Of the 1,198 people who perished, 128 were American citizens. At the time the ship was torpedoed, the United States was not yet involved in the war. Public opinion over the attack put pressure on President Woodrow Wilson to declare war on Germany. The Germans proclaimed that the Lusitania was carrying weapons for the allies.
This claim was later proven to be true. President Wilson demanded that the German government apologize for the sinking and make amends. Germany did not accept responsibility but did promise to avoid sinking any more passenger ships without first giving a warning.

Directions: Answer these questions about the Lusitania. Possible answers:

1. What does **proclaimed** mean? stated publicly

2. What does **perished** mean? died

3. What does **amends** mean? to correct a mistake

4. What does **allies** mean? countries that were on the same side in the war

5. If the Lusitania was carrying arms, do you think the Germans had a right to sink it? Why or why not?

Answers will vary.

Page 156

Comprehension: The *Titanic*

The British passenger ship, Titanic, debuted in the spring of 1912. It was billed as an unsinkable ship due to its construction. It had 16 watertight compartments that would hold the ship afloat even in the event that four of the compartments were damaged.
But on the evening of April 14, 1912, during Titanic's first voyage, its design proved unworthy. Just before midnight, Titanic struck an iceberg, which punctured 5 of the 16 compartments. The ship sunk in a little under 3 hours. Approximately 1,513 of the over 2,220 people onboard died. Most of these people died because there weren't enough lifeboats to accommodate everyone onboard. These people were left floating in the water. Many died from exposure, since the Atlantic Ocean was near freezing in temperature. It was one of the worst ocean disasters in history.
Because of the investigations that followed the Titanic disaster, the passenger ship industry instituted many reforms. It is now required that there is ample lifeboat space for all passengers and crew. An international ice patrol and full-time radio coverage were also instituted to prevent such disasters in the future.

Directions: Answer these questions about the Titanic.

1. How did most of the 1,513 people onboard the Titanic die? there weren't enough lifeboats

2. Why did this "unsinkable" ship sink? It hit an iceberg that punctured about a third of its compartments.

3. What changes have been made in ship safety as a result of the Titanic tragedy? There must be lifeboats for all passengers and crew. Today, there is an international ice patrol and full-time radio coverage.

4. There have been many attempts to rescue artifacts from the Titanic. But many families of the dead wish the site to be left alone, as it is the final resting place of their relatives. They feel burial sites should not be disrupted. Do you agree or disagree? Why?

Answers will vary.

Page 157

Venn Diagram: *Lusitania* and *Titanic*

A **Venn diagram** is used to chart information that shows similarities and differences between two things.

Example:

Dogs	Both	Cats
bark	good pets	one size
dependent	can live inside or outside	kill mice
large and small breeds	have fur	can use litterbox
protect the home	four legs	independent

Directions: Complete the Venn diagram for the *Lusitania* and the *Titanic*.

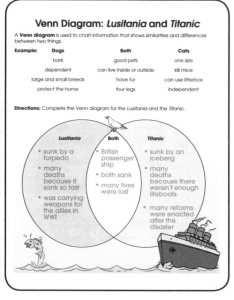

Lusitania
- sunk by a torpedo
- many deaths because it sank so fast
- was carrying weapons for the allies in WWI

Both
- British passenger ship
- both sank
- many lives were lost

Titanic
- sunk by an iceberg
- many deaths because there weren't enough lifeboats
- many reforms were enacted after the disaster

Page 158

Comprehension: The *Monitor* and the *Virginia*

During the Civil War, it became customary to cover wooden warships with iron. This increased their durability and made them more difficult to sink. Two such ships were built using iron. They were the *Monitor* and the *Virginia*.

Most people are more familiar with the name the *Merrimack*. The *Merrimack* was a U.S. steam frigate that had been burnt and sunk by Union forces when the Confederates were forced to abandon their navy yard. The Confederate Navy raised the hull of the *Merrimack* and rebuilt her as the ironclad *Virginia*.

Both the *Monitor* and the *Virginia* engaged in battle on March 9, 1862. After several hours of battle, the bulky *Virginia* had no choice but to withdraw in order to avoid the lowering tides. This battle, called Hampton Roads, was considered to be a tie between the two ships.

Although both ships survived the battle, they were later destroyed. Two months later, the *Virginia* was sunk by her crew to avoid capture. The *Monitor* sunk on December 31, 1862, during a storm off the coast of North Carolina.

Directions: Use context clues for these definitions. Possible answers:

1. customary: common
2. durability: strength; ability to last
3. ironclad: covered in iron

Directions: Answer these questions about the *Monitor* and the *Virginia*.

4. Who won the battle between the *Virginia* and the *Monitor*? It was a tie.

5. Why would lowering tides present danger to a ship? Possible answer: The ship could run aground.

6. Describe how each ship was finally destroyed. The *Virginia* was sunk by her crew to avoid capture. The *Monitor* sank during a storm off the coast of North Carolina.

Page 159

Review

1. Use the Venn diagram you completed comparing the *Lusitania* and the *Titanic* (page 158) to write a two-paragraph compare/contrast essay about the two ships. Describe their similarities in the first paragraph and their differences in the second.

Answers will vary.

2. Describe the differences in the structure of the following ships: Santa Maria, Monitor, and Titanic.

The *Santa Maria* was a relatively small sailing ship. The *Monitor* was an ironclad warship. The *Titanic* was a luxury passenger ship with 16 airtight compartments to make it "unsinkable."

3. Why did people think the Titanic was unsinkable? After the ship actually did sink, how do you think this affected the way people thought about new technology?

Answers will vary.

Page 160

Reading Comprehension: Railroads

Directions: Read the information about railroads. Then, answer the questions.

As early as the 1550s, a rough form of railroad was already being used in parts of Europe. Miners in England and other areas of western Europe used horse- or mule-drawn wagons on wooden tracks to pull loads out of mines. With these tracks, the horses could pull twice as much weight as they could without them. No one could have known then that one day this simple idea would change the world.

There were many developments along the way that helped make railroads a practical and valuable form of transportation. Two of the most important were the iron track and the "flanged" wheel, which has a rim around it to hold it onto the track. The most important invention was the steam engine by James Watt in 1765.

The first railroads in the United States were built during the late 1820s and caused a lot of excitement. They were faster than other forms of travel, and they could provide service year-round, unlike boats and stagecoaches. Trains were soon the main means of travel in the U.S.

Railroads played a major part in the Industrial Revolution—the years of change when machines were first used to do work that had been done by hand for many centuries. Trains provided cheaper rates and quicker service for transporting goods. Because manufacturers could ship their goods over long distances, they could sell their products all over the nation instead of only in the surrounding cities and towns. This meant greater profits for the companies. Trains also brought people into the cities to work in factories.

1. What was the source of power for the earliest railroads? horses or mules

2. What were three important developments that made railroads a practical means of transportation? the iron track, the "flanged" wheel, and the steam engine

3. What is meant by the Industrial Revolution? the years or change from human-made to machine-made products

4. What were two ways that railroads changed life in America? They provided more reliable and faster transportation for people and products.

Page 161

Main Idea: Locomotives

Directions: Read the information about locomotives. Then, answer the questions.

In the 1800s, the steam locomotive was considered by many to be a symbol of the new Industrial Age. It was, indeed, one of the most important inventions of the time. Over the years, there have been many changes to the locomotive. One of the most important has been its source of power. During its history, the locomotive has gone from steam to electric to diesel power.

The first railroads used horses or mules for power, but the development of the steam locomotive made railroads a practical means of transportation. The first steam locomotive was built in 1804 in Great Britain by Richard Trevithick. It could haul 50,000 pounds, but it was not very successful because it was so heavy it caused the tracks to fall apart. However, it encouraged other engineers to try to build steam locomotives. Two of the most important men to accept the challenge were George Stephenson and his son, Robert. Robert once won a contest to build the best locomotive. The *Rocket*, as he called it, had a top speed of 29 miles per hour.

In America, developments in steam engines were close behind those of the British. In 1830, Peter Cooper's tiny locomotive, called Tom Thumb, lost a famous race against a horse-drawn coach. In spite of the loss, it still convinced railroad officials that steam power was more practical than horsepower.

Just before the turn of the century, the electric locomotive was widely used. At its peak in the 1940s, U.S. railroads had 2,400 miles of electric routes.

The diesel locomotive was invented in the 1890s by Rudolf Diesel, a German engineer. The power of this locomotive was supplied by a diesel fuel engine. The diesel locomotive is still used today. It costs about twice as much as a steam locomotive to build, but it is much cheaper to operate.

1. What is the main idea of this selection?
___ The steam locomotive was considered a symbol of the Industrial Age.
_X_ Over the years, there have been many changes to the locomotive.

2. Who built the first steam locomotive in 1804? Richard Trevithick

3. How fast could the *Rocket* travel? 29 miles per hour

4. Who built the locomotive called Tom Thumb? Peter Cooper

5. Tom Thumb was in a race against a horse-drawn coach. Which won? the horse-drawn coach

6. What kind of fuel does a diesel engine use? diesel fuel

Page 162

Review

Directions: Define these words as used in the selections "Railroads" and "Locomotives."

1. flanged wheel a wheel that has a rim around it to hold it to the track

2. transportation a way to move people and products from one place to another

3. profit money earned

4. locomotive a vehicle that pulls a train

5. diesel a type of fuel

6. engineer a person who drives a train

Directions: Use information from the selection "Locomotives" to create a time line of the invention of locomotives.

7.

1804	early 1800s	1830	1890
first steam locomotive built in Great Britain by Richard Trevithick	George and Robert Stephenson build the *Rocket*	Tom Thumb built by Peter Cooper	diesel locomotive invented by Rudolf Diesel

Directions: Write your answer in a complete sentence.

8. The world is going through another "revolution" in industry today. What new technology is leading this change, and how might it affect workers in the future?

Answers will vary.

Page 163

Reading Comprehension: Railroad Pioneer

Directions: Read the information about railroad pioneers. Then, answer the questions by circling **Yes** or **No**.

George Stephenson was born in Wylam, England, in 1781. His family was extremely poor. When he was young, he didn't go to school but worked in the coal mines. In his spare time, he taught himself to read and write. After a series of explosions in the coal pits, Stephenson built a miner's safety lamp. This helped bring him to the attention of the owners of the coal mines. They put him in charge of all the machinery.

In 1812, Stephenson became an engine builder for the mines. The owners were interested in locomotives because the cost of horse feed was so high. They wanted Stephenson to build a locomotive to pull the coal cars from the mines. His first locomotive, the Blucher, was put on the rails in 1814.

Stephenson was a good engineer, and he was fortunate to work for a rich employer. Between 1814 and 1826, Stephenson was the only man in Great Britain building locomotives. When the Stockholm and Darlington Railway, the first public railroad system, was planned, Stephenson was named company engineer. He convinced the owners to use steam power instead of horses. He built the first locomotive on the line. The Locomotion, as it was called, was the best locomotive that had been built anywhere in the world up to that time. Over the years, Stephenson was responsible for many other important developments in locomotive design, such as improved cast-iron rails and wheels, and the first steel springs strong enough to carry several tons.

Stephenson was convinced that the future of railroads lay in steam power. His great vision of what the railroad system could become was a driving force in the early years of its development.

1. George Stephenson was an excellent student in school. Yes **No**
2. Stephenson's first invention was a miner's safety lamp. **Yes** No
3. Between 1814 and 1826, Stephenson was one of many engineers building locomotives in Great Britain. Yes **No**
4. The Stockholm and Darlington Railway was the first public railroad system. **Yes** No
5. The first locomotive on the Stockholm and Darlington line was the Locomotion, built by Stephenson. **Yes** No
6. Stephenson's ideas did not influence the development of the railroad system. Yes **No**

Page 164

Tall Tales

A **tall tale** is a fictional story with exaggerated details and a "super" hero. The main character in a tall tale is much larger, stronger, smarter, or better than a real person. Tall tales may be unbelievable, but they are fun to hear.

America had nearly 200,000 miles of railroad track by 1900. Because of the rapid growth and the excitement over the railroads, many colorful tall tales about railroad heroes and their adventures were told.

Directions: Read the story about John Henry. Then, answer the questions.

A Steel-Driving Man

On the night John Henry was born, forked lightning split the air and the earth shook. He weighed 44 pounds at birth, and the first thing he did was reach for a hammer hanging on the wall. "He's going to be a steel-driving man," his father told his mother.

Every time his hammer hit a spike, the sky lit up with the sparks. "I dreamed that the railroad was going to be the end of me, and I'd die with a hammer in my hand," he said. When John Henry grew up, he did work for the railroad. He was the fastest, most powerful steel-driving man in the world.

In about 1870, the steam drill was invented. One day, the company at the far end of a tunnel tried it out. John Henry's company, working at the other end, continued to use men to do the drilling. There was much bragging from both companies as to which was faster. Finally, they decided to have a contest. John Henry was matched against the best man with a steam drill.

John Henry swung a 20-pound hammer in each hand. The sparks flew so fast and hot that they burned his face. At the end of the day, the judges said John Henry had beaten the steam drill by 4 feet!

That night, John Henry said, "I was a steel-driving man." Then, he laid down and closed his eyes forever.

1. How much was John Henry said to have weighed at birth? **44 pounds**
2. Why did his father think he would be a steel-driving man? **He reached for a hammer**
3. What invention was John Henry in a contest against? **the steam drill** first.
4. Why was the contest held? **to see who was faster**
5. What tools did John Henry use in the contest? **two 20-pound hammers**
6. Who won the contest? **John Henry**
7. What happened to John Henry after the contest? **He died.**

Page 165

Tall Tales

Directions! Write a tall tale about yourself. Be sure to make it a fantastic and incredible story!

Stories will vary.

Directions: Reread your tall tale. Does it make sense? Check and correct spelling and grammar mistakes. Does your story fit the category of tall tale?

Page 166

Context Clues: Passenger Cars

Directions: Read the information about passenger cars. Use context clues to determine the meaning of words in bold. Check the correct answers.

Early railroad passenger cars were little more than stagecoaches fitted with special wheels to help them stay on the tracks. They didn't hold many passengers, and because they were made out of wood, they were fire **hazards**. They also did not hold up very well if the train came off the track or had a **collision** with another train.

In the United States, it wasn't long before passenger cars were lengthened to hold more people. Late in the 1830s, Americans were riding in **elongated** cars with double seats on either side of a center aisle. By the early 1900s, most cars were made of metal instead of wood.

Sleeping and dining cars were introduced in the United States by the early 1860s. Over the next 25 years, other improvements were made, including electric lighting, steam heat, and covered **vestibules** that allowed passengers to walk between cars. All of these **luxuries** helped make railroad travel much more comfortable.

1. Based on the other words in the sentence, what is the correct definition of **hazards**?
   ___ engines   **X** risks   ___ stations
2. Based on the other words in the sentence, what is the correct definition of **collision**?
   X crash   ___ race   ___ track
3. Based on the other words in the sentence, what is the correct definition of **elongated**?
   ___ wooden   ___ new   **X** lengthened
4. Based on the other words in the sentence, what is the correct definition of **vestibules**?
   X passageways   ___ cars   ___ depots
5. Based on the other words in the sentence, what is the correct definition of **luxuries**?
   ___ additions   **X** things offering the greatest comfort   ___ inventions

Page 167

Reading Skills: Railroads

Directions: Read the information about railroads. Then, answer the questions.

When railroads became the major means of transportation, they replaced earlier forms of travel, like the stagecoach. Railroads remained the unchallenged leader for a hundred years. Beginning in the early 1900s, railroads faced **competition** from newer forms of transportation.

Today, millions of people have their own automobiles. Buses offer inexpensive travel between cities. Large trucks haul goods across the country. Airplanes provide quick transportation over long distances. The result has been a sharp drop in the use of trains.

Today, nearly all railroads face serious problems that threaten to drive them out of business. But railroads still provide low-cost, fuel-saving transportation that will remain important. One gallon of diesel fuel will haul about four times as much by railroad as by truck. In a time when the world is concerned about saving fuel, this is but one area in which the railroads still have much to offer.

1. What is the main idea of this selection?
   X When railroads became the major means of transportation, they replaced earlier forms of travel.
   ___ Beginning in the early 1900s, railroads have faced competition from newer forms of transportation.
2. Based on the other words in the sentence, what is the correct definition of **competition**?
   X businesses trying to get the same customers
   ___ problems
   ___ support
3. What are four newer forms of transportation that have challenged railroads?
   cars, trucks, buses, airplanes
4. One gallon of diesel fuel will haul about twice as much by railroad as by truck. Yes **No**

Page 168

Reading Comprehension: Printing

Directions: Read the information about printing. Then, answer the questions.

When people talk about printing, they usually mean making exact copies of an original document, such as a newspaper, magazine, or an entire book. The inventions that have allowed us to do this are some of the most important developments in history. Look around you at the many examples of printed materials. Can you imagine life without them?

Until the thirteenth century, all material had to be printed by hand, one copy at a time. To make a copy of a book took much time and effort.

The oldest known example of a printed book was made in China in 848 A.D. by Wang Chieh, who carved each page of a book by hand onto a block of wood. He then put ink on the wood and pressed it on paper. The idea of printing with wood blocks spread to Europe. The letters in these block books were made to look handwritten.

In about 1440, a German goldsmith named Johann Gutenberg developed the idea of movable type. He invented separate letters of metal for printing. The letters could be joined together to make words and sentences. Ink was applied to the letters to print many copies of the same material. Because they were made of metal, the letters could be used over and over. This wonderful invention made it possible to have more printed material at a lower cost.

Gutenberg had other ideas that were important to printing. He developed a special type of ink that would stick to the new metal letters. Gutenberg's ideas were so successful that the process of printing went almost unchanged for more than 300 years.

1. In what country was the oldest known printed book made?
   China
2. Who made the first printed book?
   Wang Chieh
3. What is "movable type"?
   separate letters made of metal for printing
4. Who developed the idea of movable type?
   Johann Gutenberg
5. What was another one of Gutenberg's important inventions?
   He developed a special type of ink that would stick to the new metal letters.

Page 169

Reading Comprehension: Newspapers

Directions: Read the information about newspapers. Then, answer the questions.

1. Why has the number of newspapers published fallen in recent years? As more people have access to the Internet, there are many more ways they can get their news.
2. What services do newspapers provide? They provide information at little cost.
3. What are subscribers? people who pay to have each edition of the paper delivered to them
4. How often are most newspapers published? daily or weekly
5. What do newspapers do to keep the cost to the reader low, but still make money? They sell space to advertisers.
6. What is the name of the newspaper in the town or city where you live? Answers will vary.

Page 170

Reading Comprehension: Newspapers

Directions: Read the information about the first newspapers. Then, answer the questions.

1. How were the earliest newspapers different from today's newspapers? They were handwritten notices posted in towns.
2. In what year and where was the first true newspaper printed? in Germany in 1609
3. What was the name of the first successful newspaper in America? The Boston News-Letter
4. Why was 1833 important in newspaper publishing? The New York Sun became the first penny newspaper.
5. List four ways penny newspapers were like the newspapers of today. printed fresh news; printed ads; sold at newsstands; delivered to homes

Page 171

Reading Comprehension: News Stories

Directions: Read the information about news stories. Then, draw an X on the line to show the correct meaning of the bold word.

1. Based on the other words in the sentence, what is the correct definition of **eyewitness**?
   _ a reporter
   X a person who saw what happened
   _ a lawyer
2. How is the way that reporters send in stories different today than it was in the past? Today, they often write the stories on location and send them in via the Internet.

Page 172

Reading Comprehension: Nellie Bly

Directions: Read the information about Nellie Bly. Then, answer the questions.

1. What does it mean "to give a voice to people who could not speak for themselves"? She wanted to tell the stories of people who did not have a voice in society.
2. Was Around the World in 80 Days a work of fiction or nonfiction? fiction
3. The name of the New York newspaper Bly wrote for was The World.
4. What was the result of Bly's story about the insane asylum? The city investigated the asylum, and treatment of the mentally ill improved.
5. Investigative reporting is no longer a common practice. True **False**

Page 173

Reading Comprehension: Samuel Clemens

Directions: Read the information about Samuel Clemens.

Directions: Check the correct answer.

1. Based on the other words in the sentence, what is the correct definition of **pseudonym**?
   _ book title
   X a made-up name used by an author
   _ a humorous article
2. Based on the other words in the sentence, what is the correct definition of **piloting**?
   _ driving an airplane
   X steering a steamboat on a river
   _ being a train engineer

Directions: Write the answers.

3. Under what name did Samuel Clemens write his books? Mark Twain
4. What do the words **mark twain** mean? two fathoms deep
5. Besides author, list two other jobs held by Mark Twain. Possible answers: printer and gold miner
6. List two of the best-known books written by Mark Twain. The Adventures of Tom Sawyer and The Adventures of Huckleberry Finn

Page 174

Review

Directions: Write the answers.

1. What are two ways newspapers earn money? seeling subscriptions and selling advertising space
2. What was Mark Twain's real name? Samuel Langhorne Clemens
3. Explain how newspaper reporting is different today than it was in the past. Possible answer: Things move more quickly today than they did in the past. Reporters and photographers can submit stories and pictures electronically. Facts can be checked online.
4. How has social media changed the way stories are discovered and reported? Answers will vary.

Directions: Use dates from the articles "Printing" and "Newspapers" to create a time line of the development of newspapers.

848 A.D.	1440	1609	1665	1704	1833
first book printed in China	movable type invented in Germany	first true newspaper printed in Germany	London Gazette first printed in England	first successful American paper, The Boston Herald	first penny newspaper published

Page 175

Comprehensive Curriculum - Grade 5

Recognizing Details: The Coldest Continent

Directions: Read the information about Antarctica. Then, answer the questions.

Antarctica lies at the South Pole and is the coldest continent. It is without sunlight for months at a time. Even when the sun does shine, its angle is so slanted that the land receives little warmth. Temperatures often drop to 100 degrees below zero, and a fierce wind blows almost endlessly. Most of the land is covered by snow heaped thousands of feet deep. The snow is so heavy and tightly packed that it forms a great ice cap covering more than 95 percent of the continent.

Considering the conditions, it is no wonder there are no towns or cities in Antarctica. There is no permanent population at all, only small scientific research stations. Many teams of explorers and scientists have braved the freezing cold since Antarctica was sighted in 1820. Some have died in their effort, but a great deal of information has been learned about the continent.

From fossils, pieces of coal, and bone samples, we know that Antarctica was not always an ice-covered land. Scientists believe that 200 million years ago it was connected to southern Africa, South America, Australia, and India. Forests grew in warm swamps, and insects and reptiles thrived there. Today, there are animals that live in and around the waters that border the continent. In fact, the waters surrounding Antarctica contain more life than oceans in warmer areas of the world.

1. Where is Antarctica? _at the South Pole_
2. How much of the continent is covered by an ice cap? _more than 95 percent_
3. When was Antarctica first sighted by explorers? _1820_
4. What clues indicate that Antarctica was not always an ice-covered land?
   fossils, pieces of coal, and bone samples
5. Is Antarctica another name for the North Pole?   Yes   (No)

Page 176

Reading Comprehension: The Arctic Circle

Directions: Read the article about the Arctic Circle. Then, answer the questions.

On the other side of the globe from Antarctica, at the northernmost part of Earth, is another icy land. This is the Arctic Circle. It includes the North Pole itself and the northern fringes of three continents—Europe, Asia, and North America, including the state of Alaska—as well as Greenland and other islands.

The seasons are opposite at the two ends of Earth. When it is summer in Antarctica, it is winter in the Arctic Circle. In both places, there are very long periods of sunlight in summer and very long nights in the winter. On the poles themselves, there are six full months of sunlight and six full months of darkness each year.

Compared to Antarctica, the summers are surprisingly mild in some areas of the Arctic Circle. Much of the snow cover may melt, and temperatures often reach 50 degrees in July. Antarctica is covered by water—frozen water, of course—so nothing can grow there. Plant growth is limited in the polar regions, not only by the cold, but also by wind, lack of water, and the long winter darkness.

In the far north, willow trees grow but only become a few inches high! The annual rings, the circles within the trunk of a tree that show its age and how fast it grows, are so narrow in those trees that you need a microscope to see them.

A permanently frozen layer of soil, called permafrost, keeps roots from growing deep enough into the ground to anchor a plant. Even if a plant could survive the cold temperatures, it could not grow roots deep enough or strong enough to allow the plant to get very big.

1. What three continents have land included in the Arctic Circle?
   Europe   _Asia_   _North America_
2. Is the Arctic Circle generally warmer or colder than Antarctica?
   warmer
3. What is permafrost? _a permanently frozen layer of soil_
4. Many tall pine trees grow in the Arctic Circle.   Yes   (No)

Page 177

Reading Comprehension: Undersea Harvest

Directions: Read the selection. Then, answer the questions that follow.

A group of Inuit in Arctic Canada are known for an extremely dangerous type of harvesting **expedition**. You may be surprised to learn that what they are looking for are mussels on the seabed floor. The reason that this is so dangerous is that the mussel hunters must go beneath the icy surface of the Arctic Sea. The mussels provide a welcome relief from a diet that consists mostly of seal meat. During extreme low tides, the level of sea ice drops enough to create caverns below the ice. It exposes the seabed floor—and hundreds of mussels.

The brave hunters lower themselves as much as 40 feet below the surface to gather mussels. It is dark and cold in the icy caverns. The thick layer of ice creaks eerily overhead. Without the water to support it, it isn't nearly as stable. The Inuit must work quickly. They have only about an hour before the tide starts to move back in and the water level begins to rise. Imagine how scary it would be to hear the water rushing in around you in an icy undersea cavern!

The locals all know stories of mussel hunter who didn't make it out in time. It's a dangerous **expedition**, but the rewards are sweet: plenty of fresh mussels to eat!

1. What group of people is known for harvesting mussels under the ice?
   the Inuit
2. The seabed floor is only exposed at a certain time. When does this occur?
   during extreme low tides
3. Why are there caverns under the ice? _When there are extreme low tides, the levels of sea ice drop and create caverns_
4. Why is mussel gathering so risky for the Inuit? _The top layer of ice isn't very stable without water to support it, and the tide starts coming back in after about an hour._
5. What does the word **expedition** mean?

☐ harvest   ☐ mussels   ☒ journey

Page 178

Main Idea: The Polar Trail

Directions: Read the information about explorers to Antarctica.

A recorded sighting of Antarctica, the last continent to be discovered, was not made until the early nineteenth century. Since then, many brave explorers and adventurers have sailed south to conquer the icy land. Their achievements once gained as much world attention as those of the first astronauts.

Long before the continent was first spotted, the ancient Greeks suspected there was a continent at the bottom of the world. Over the centuries, legends of the undiscovered land spread. Some of the world's greatest seamen tried to find it, including Captain James Cook in 1772.

Cook was the first to sail all the way to the solid field of ice that surrounds Antarctica every winter. In fact, he sailed all the way around the continent but never saw it. Cook went farther south than anyone had ever gone. His record lasted 50 years.

Forty years after Cook, a new kind of seamen sailed the icy waters. They were hunters of seals and whales. Sailing through unknown waters in search of their prey, they soon became explorers as well as hunters. The first person known to sight Antarctica was an American hunter, 21-year-old Nathaniel Brown Palmer, in 1820.

Directions: Draw an X on the blank for the correct answer.

1. The main idea is:
   ___ Antarctica was not sighted until the early nineteenth century.
   _X_ Many brave explorers and adventurers have sailed south to conquer the icy land.

2. The first person to sail to the ice field that surrounds Antarctica was:
   ___ Nathaniel Brown Palmer.
   _X_ Captain James Cook.
   ___ Neil Armstrong.

3. His record for sailing the farthest south stood for:
   ___ 40 years.
   _X_ 50 years.
   ___ 500 years.

4. The first person known to sight Antarctica was:
   ___ an unknown ancient Greek.
   ___ Captain James Cook.
   _X_ Nathaniel Brown Palmer.

5. His profession was:
   ___ hunter.
   ___ ship captain.
   _X_ explorer.

Page 179

Recognizing Details: The Frozen Continent

Directions: Read the information about explorers. Then, answer the questions.

By the mid-1800s, most of the seals of Antarctica had been killed. The seal hunters no longer sailed the icy waters. The next group of explorers who took an interest in Antarctica were scientists. Of these, the man who took the most daring chances and made the most amazing discoveries was British Captain James Clark Ross.

Ross first made a name for himself sailing to the north. In 1831, he discovered the North Magnetic Pole—one of two places on Earth toward which a compass needle points. In 1840, Ross set out to find the South Magnetic Pole. He made many marvelous discoveries, including the Ross Sea, a great open sea beyond the ice packs that stopped other explorers, and the Ross Ice Shelf, a great floating sheet of ice bigger than all of France!

The next man to make his mark exploring Antarctica was British explorer Robert Falcon Scott. Scott set out in 1902 to find the South Pole. He and his team suffered greatly, but they were able to make it a third of the way to the pole. Back in England, Scott was a great hero. In 1910, he again attempted to become the first man to reach the South Pole. But this time, he had competition: an explorer from Norway, Roald Amundsen, was also leading a team to the South Pole.

It was a brutal race. Both teams faced many hardships, but they pressed on. Finally, on December 14, 1911, Amundsen became the first man to reach the South Pole. Scott arrived on January 17, 1912. He was bitterly disappointed at not being first. The trip back was even more horrible. None of the five men in the Scott expedition survived.

1. After the seal hunters, who were the next group of explorers interested in Antarctica?
   scientists
2. What great discovery did James Ross make before ever sailing to Antarctica?
   He discovered the North Magnetic Pole.
3. What were two other great discoveries made by James Ross?
   the Ross Sea   _the Ross Ice Shelf_
4. How close did Scott and his team come to the South Pole in 1902?
   They made it a third of the way to the pole.
5. Who was the first person to reach the South Pole? _Roald Amundsen_

Page 180

Reading Skills: Research

To learn more about the explorers of Antarctica, reference sources like encyclopedias, CD-ROMs, the Internet, and history books are excellent sources for finding more information.

Directions: Use reference sources to learn more about Captain James Cook and Captain James Clark Ross. Write an informational paragraph about each man.

1. Captain James Cook
   Answers will vary.

2. Captain James Clark Ross

3. What dangers did both of these men and their teams face in their attempts to reach the South Pole?

Page 181

Reading Comprehension: Polar Bears

Directions: Read the information about polar bears. Then, answer the questions by circling **Yes** or **No**.

Some animals are able to survive the cold weather and difficult conditions of the snow and ice fields in the Arctic polar regions. One of the best known is the polar bear.

Polar bears live on the land and in the sea. They may drift hundreds of miles from land on huge sheets of floating ice. They use their great paws to paddle the ice along. Polar bears are excellent swimmers, too. They can cross great distances of open water. While in the water, they feed mostly on fish and seals.

On land, these huge animals, which measure 10 feet long and weigh about 1,000 pounds, can run 25 miles an hour. Surprisingly, polar bears live as plant-eaters rather than hunters while on land. Unlike many kinds of bears, polar bears do not hibernate. They are active the whole year.

Baby polar bears are born during the winter. At birth, they are pink and almost hairless. These helpless cubs weigh only two pounds—less than one-third the size of most human infants. The mother bears raise their young in dens dug in snowbanks. By the time they are 10 weeks old, polar bear cubs are about the size of puppies and have enough white fur to protect them in the open air. The mothers give their cubs swimming, hunting, and fishing lessons. By the time autumn comes, the cubs are left to survive on their own.

1. Polar bears can live on the land and the sea. (Yes) No
2. Polar bears are excellent swimmers. (Yes) No
3. Polar bears hibernate in the winter. Yes (No)
4. A newborn polar bear weighs more than a newborn human baby. Yes (No)
5. Mother polar bears raise their babies in caves. Yes (No)
6. Father polar bears give the cubs swimming lessons. Yes (No)

Page 182

Context Clues: Seals

Directions: Read the information about seals. Use context clues to determine the meaning of the bold words. Check the correct answers.

Seals are **aquatic** mammals that also live on land at times. Some seals stay in the sea for weeks or months at a time, even sleeping in the water. When seals go on land, they usually choose **secluded** spots to avoid people and other animals.

The 31 different kinds of seals belong to a group of animals often called pinnipeds meaning "fin-footed." Their fins, or flippers, make them very good swimmers and divers. Their nostrils close tightly when they dive. They have been known to stay **submerged** for as long as a half-hour at a time!

Seals are warm-blooded animals that can adjust to various temperatures. They live in both **temperate** and cold climates. Besides their fur to keep them warm, seals have a thick layer of fat, called blubber, to protect them against the cold. It is harder for seals to cool themselves in hot weather than to warm themselves in cold weather. They can sometimes become so overheated that they die.

1. Based on other words in the sentence, what is the correct definition of **aquatic**?
   ___ living on the land
   _X_ living in the sea
   ___ living in large groups

2. Based on other words in the sentence, what is the correct definition of **submerged**?
   _X_ under the water
   ___ on top of the water
   ___ in groups

3. Based on other words in the sentence, what is the correct definition of **secluded**?
   ___ rocky
   _X_ private or hidden
   ___ near other animals

4. Based on other words in the sentence, what is the correct definition of **temperate**?
   ___ rainy
   ___ measured on a thermometer
   _X_ warm

Page 183

Reading Comprehension: Walruses

Directions: Read the information about walruses. Then answer the questions.

A walrus is actually a type of seal that lives only in the Arctic Circle. It has two huge upper teeth, or tusks, which it uses to pull itself out of the water or to move over the rocks on land. It also uses its tusks to dig clams, one of its favorite foods, from the bottom of the sea. On an adult male walrus, the tusks may be three and a half feet long!

A walrus has an unusual face. Besides its long tusks, it has a big, bushy mustache made up of hundreds of movable, stiff bristles. These bristles also help the walrus push food into its mouth. Except for small wrinkles in the skin, a walrus has no outer ears.

Like a seal, the walrus uses its flippers to help it swim. Its front flippers serve as paddles, and while swimming, it swings the back of its huge body from side to side. A walrus looks awkward using its flippers to walk on land, but don't be fooled! A walrus can run as fast as a human.

Baby walruses are born in the early spring. They stay with their mothers until they are two years old. There is a good reason for this—they must grow little tusks, at least three or four inches long, before they can catch their own food from the bottom of the sea. Until then, they must stay close to their mothers to eat. A young walrus that is tired from swimming will climb onto its mother's back for a ride, holding onto her with its front flippers.

1. The walrus is a type of seal found only _in the Arctic Circle_
2. List two ways the walrus uses its tusks.
   to _pull itself out of the water_   _to dig clams_
3. A walrus cannot move quickly on land. Yes (No)
4. A walrus has a large, bushy mustache. (Yes) No
5. A baby walrus stays very close to its mother until it is two years old. (Yes) No
6. Baby walruses are born late in fall. Yes (No)

Page 184

Main Idea: Penguins

Directions: Read the information about penguins.

People are amused by the funny, duck-like waddle of penguins and by their appearance, because they seem to be wearing little tuxedos. Penguins are among the best-liked animals on Earth, but they are also a most misunderstood animal. People may have more inaccurate ideas about penguins than any other animal.

For example, many people are surprised to learn that penguins are really birds, not mammals. Penguins do not fly, but they do have feathers, and only birds have feathers. Also, like other birds, penguins build nests and their young hatch from eggs. Because of their unusual looks, though, you would never confuse them with any other bird!

Penguins are also thought of as symbols of the polar regions, but penguins do not live north of the equator, so you would not find a penguin near the North Pole. Penguins don't live at the South Pole, either. Only two of the seventeen **species** of penguins spend all of their lives on the frozen continent of Antarctica. You would be just as likely to see a penguin living on an island in a warm climate as in a cold area.

Directions: Draw an X on the blank for the correct answer.

1. The main idea is:
   ___ Penguins are among the best-liked animals on Earth.
   _X_ The penguin is a much misunderstood animal.

2. Penguins live
   ___ only at the North Pole.
   ___ only at the South Pole.
   _X_ only south of the equator.

3. Based on the other words in the sentence, what is the correct definition of the word **species**?
   ___ number
   ___ bird
   _X_ a distinct kind

Directions: List three ways penguins are like other birds.

They have feathers, build nests, and hatch their young from eggs.

Page 185

Review

Directions: Write your answers on the lines.

1. Which contains the South Pole—the Arctic or Antarctica?
   Antarctica

2. Would you like to live in either the Arctic or Antarctica? Why or why not?
   Answers will vary.

3. What adaptations would people who live (even for a short time) in these areas have to make?
   Possible answers: They would have to be prepared to live in extreme cold and to handle long periods of darkness.

4. What characteristics are common to animals who live in the polar regions?
   thick coat of fur, ability to find food, layer of fat for warmth

5. Name two animals that live in the polar regions. _Possible answers:_
   polar bears   _walruses_

6. Write three facts you learned about one of the animals that live in the polar regions.
   Answers will vary.

7. On each of the poles, there are six months of sunlight and six months of darkness each year. How do you think this would affect you?
   Answers will vary.

8. Write three facts you learned about explorers to the North or South Pole regions.
   Answers will vary.

Page 186

Reading Comprehension: The Desert

Directions: Read the information about the desert. Then, answer the questions by circling **Yes** or **No**.

Deserts are found where there is little rainfall or where the rainfall for a whole year occurs in only a few weeks' time. Ten inches of rain may be enough for many plants to survive if the rain is spread throughout the year. If the 10 inches of rain falls during one or two months and the rest of the year is dry, those plants may not be able to survive, and a desert may form.

When people think of deserts, they may think of long stretches of sand. Sand begins as tiny pieces of rock that get smaller and smaller as wind and weather wear them down. Sand dunes, or hills of drifting sand, are formed as winds move the sand across the desert. Grain by grain, the dunes grow over the years, always shifting with the winds and changing shape. Most dunes are only a few feet tall, but they can grow to be several hundred feet high.

There is, however, much more to a desert than sand. In the deserts of the southwestern United States, cliffs and canyons were formed from thick mud that once lay beneath a sea more than 100 million years ago. Over the centuries, the water drained away. Wind, sand, rain, heat, and cold all wore away at the remaining rocks. The faces of the desert mountains are always changing—very, very slowly—as these forces of nature continue to work on the rock.

Most deserts have a surprising variety of life. There are plants, animals, and insects that have adapted to life in the desert. During the heat of the day, a visitor may see very few signs of living things, but as the air begins to cool in the evening, the desert comes to life. As the moon begins to rise again in the sky, the desert once again becomes quiet and lonely.

1. Deserts are found where there is little rainfall or where the rainfall for a whole year falls in only a few weeks. (Yes) No
2. Sand begins as tiny pieces of rock that get smaller and smaller as wind and weather wear them down. (Yes) No
3. Sand dunes were formed from thick mud that once lay beneath a sea more than 100 million years ago. Yes (No)
4. The faces of the desert mountains can never change. Yes (No)

Page 187

Comprehensive Curriculum - **Grade 5**

ANSWER KEY

Reading Comprehension: Desert Weather

Directions: Read the information about desert weather. Then, answer the questions.

One definition of a desert is an area that has, on average, less than 10 inches of rain a year. Many deserts have far less than that. Death Valley in California and Nevada, for example, averages fewer than 2 inches of rain each year. The driest of all deserts is the Atacama Desert in Chile. This desert averages less than 1 inch of rainfall a year. In some parts, no rain fell for 400 years!

Some deserts have a regular rainy season each year, but usually desert rainfall is totally unpredictable. An area may have no rainfall for many years. Sometimes a passing cloud may look like it will send relief to the waiting land, but only a "ghost rain" falls. This means that the hot, dry air dries up the raindrops long before they ever reach the ground.

The temperature in the desert varies greatly. The daytime temperatures in the desert frequently top 120 degrees. In Death Valley, temperatures have been known to reach 190 degrees! In most parts of the world, moisture in the air works like a blanket to hold the heat of the day close to the earth at night. But, because it has so little moisture, the desert has no such blanket. As a result, nighttime temperatures are very chilly. Temperatures have been known to drop 50 or even 100 degrees at night in the desert.

1. On the average, how much rainfall is there in a year in a desert?
   <u>less than 10 inches</u>
2. Where is the driest desert in the world? <u>Atacama Desert in Chile</u>
3. What is a ghost rain? <u>Hot, dry air dries up the raindrops</u>
   <u>before they reach the ground</u>
4. In other parts of the world, what works as a blanket to hold the heat of the day close to the earth at night? <u>moisture in the air</u>
5. What happens to the temperature in the desert at night?
   <u>Temperatures can drop 50 or even 100 degrees.</u>

Page 188

Review

Directions: Write a three-sentence summary of each of these selections. Include the main idea in your summaries.

1. "The Desert"
   <u>Answers will vary.</u>

2. "Desert Weather"
   <u>Answers will vary.</u>

Directions: Define these words. Then, use them in sentences of your own.
<u>Sentences will vary.</u>
3. dunes
   <u>hills of sand</u>
4. canyon
   <u>a deep valley with very steep sides</u>
5. adapt
   <u>change based on conditions</u>
6. average
   <u>usual, normal</u>
7. unpredictable
   <u>not known in advance</u>

Page 189

Context Clues: Desert Plants

Directions: Read the information about desert plants. Use context clues to determine the meaning of the bold words. Check the correct answers.

Desert plants have special features, or adaptations, that allow them to **survive** the harsh conditions of the desert. A cactus stores water in its tissues when it rains. It then uses this supply of water during the long dry season. The tiny needles on some kinds of **cacti** may number in the tens of thousands. These sharp thorns protect the cactus. They also form tiny shadows in the sunlight that help keep the plant from getting too hot.

Other plants are able to live by dropping their leaves. This cuts down on the **evaporation** of their water supply in the hot sun. Still other plants survive as seeds, protected from the sun and heat by tough seed coats. When it rains, the seeds **sprout** quickly, bloom, and produce more seeds that can **withstand** long dry spells.

Some plants spread their roots close to Earth's surface to quickly gather water when it does rain. Other plants, such as the mesquite, have roots that grow 50 or 60 feet below the ground to reach underground water supplies.

1. Based on the other words in the sentence, what is the correct definition of **survive**?
   <u>X</u> continue to live
   ___ bloom in the desert
   ___ flower

2. Based on the other words in the sentence, what is the correct definition of **evaporation**?
   <u>X</u> water loss from heat
   ___ much-needed rainfall
   ___ boiling

3. Based on the other words in the sentence, what is the correct definition of **withstand**?
   <u>X</u> put up with
   ___ stand with another
   ___ take from

4. Based on the other words in the sentence, what is the correct definition of **cacti**?
   ___ a type of sand dune
   <u>X</u> more than one cactus
   ___ a caravan of camels

5. Based on the other words in the sentence, what is the correct definition of **sprout**?
   ___ a type of bean that grows only in the desert
   <u>X</u> begin to grow
   ___ a small flower

Page 190

Recognizing Details: The Cactus Family

Directions: Read the information about cacti. Pay close attention to details. Answer the questions.

Although cacti are the best-known desert plants, they don't live only in hot, dry places. While cacti are most likely to be found in the desert areas of Mexico and the southwestern United States, they can be seen as far north as Nova Scotia, Canada. Certain types of cacti can live even in the snow!

Desert cacti are particularly good at surviving very long dry spells. Most cacti have a very long root system so they can absorb as much water as possible. Every available drop of water is taken into the cactus and held in its fleshy stem. A cactus stem can hold enough water to last for two years or longer.

A cactus may be best known for its spines. Although a few kinds of cacti don't have spines, the stems of most types are covered with these sharp needles. The spines have many uses for a cactus. They keep animals from eating the cactus. They collect raindrops and dew. The spines also help keep the plant cool by forming shadows in the sun and by trapping a layer of air close to the plant. They break up the desert winds that dry out the cactus.

Cacti come in all sizes and shapes. The biggest type in North America is the saguaro. It can weigh 12,000 to 14,000 pounds and grow to be 50 feet tall. A saguaro can last several years without water, but it will grow only after summer rains. In May and June, white blossoms appear. Many kinds of birds nest in these enormous cacti: white-winged doves, woodpeckers, small owls, thrashers, and wrens all build nests in the saguaro.

1. Where are you most likely to find a cactus growing?
   <u>desert areas of Mexico and the southwestern</u>
   <u>United States</u>
2. How long can most cacti survive without water?
   <u>two years or longer</u>
3. What are two ways the spines help a cactus?
   <u>They protect it, and they collect raindrops and dew.</u>
4. What is the biggest cactus in North America?
   <u>the saguaro</u>
5. What animals live in a saguaro cactus?
   <u>birds such as doves, woodpeckers, small owls,</u>
   <u>thrashers, and wrens</u>

Page 191

Review

Directions: Write a three-sentence summary of these selections. Refer to the reading selections for review if necessary.

1. "Desert Plants"
   <u>Answers will vary.</u>

2. "The Cactus Family"
   <u>Answers will vary.</u>

Possible answers:
Directions: Describe the adaptations these plants have made to survive in the desert.

3. cacti <u>They can survive for long periods</u>
   <u>without rainfall.</u>
4. mesquite <u>It has long roots to reach under-</u>
   <u>ground water.</u>
5. saguaro cactus <u>It stores water and can withstand</u>
   <u>drought.</u>
Directions: Answer these questions.
6. What is the purpose of cactus spines? <u>They collect moisture</u>
   <u>and protect the cactus from animals.</u>
7. Why does the mesquite have long roots? <u>to reach water</u>
   <u>deep underground</u>
Directions: Define these words. Then, use them in sentences of your own.
<u>Sentences will vary.</u>
8. evaporation
   <u>water loss due to heat/wind</u>
9. spine
   <u>sharp, needle-like growths on cacti</u>

Page 192

Reading Comprehension: Lizards

Directions: Read the information about lizards. Then, answer the questions.

Lizards are reptiles, related to snakes, turtles, alligators, and crocodiles. Like other reptiles, lizards are cold-blooded. This means that their body temperature changes with that of their surroundings. However, by changing their behavior throughout the day, they can keep their temperature fairly constant.

Lizards are among the many animals that live in deserts. They usually come out of their burrows early in the morning. Most lizards lie in the sun to get warm before starting their daily activities. In mid-morning, they hunt for food. If it becomes too hot, lizards can raise their tails and bodies off the ground to help them cool off. At midday, they return to their burrows or crawl under rocks for several hours. Late in the day, they again lie in the sun to absorb heat before the chilly desert night falls.

Like all animals, lizards have ways of protecting themselves. Some types of lizards have developed a most unusual defense. If a hawk or other animal grabs one of these lizards by its tail, the tail will break off. The tail will continue to wiggle around to distract the attacker while the lizard runs away. A month or two later, the lizard grows a new tail.

There are about 3,000 kinds of lizards, and all of them can bite, but only two types of lizards are poisonous: the Gila monster of the southwestern United States and the Mexican bearded lizard. Both are short-legged, thick-bodied reptiles with fat tails. These lizards do not attack people and will not bite them unless they are attacked.

1. What can a lizard do if it becomes too hot? <u>They can raise their tails</u>
   <u>and bodies off the ground to help them cool off.</u>
2. What is an unusual defense some lizards have developed to protect themselves?
   <u>The tail will break off and will wiggle around to</u>
   <u>distract the predator.</u>
3. What two types of lizards are poisonous? <u>the Gila monster and the</u>
   <u>Mexican bearded lizard</u>

Page 193

Main Idea: People in the Desert

Directions: Read the information about people in the desert. Then, answer the questions.

Long before Europeans came to live in America, Native Americans had discovered ways of living in the desert. Some of these Native Americans were hunters or belonged to wandering tribes that stayed in the desert for only short periods of time. Others learned to farm and live in villages. They made their houses of trees, clay, and brush.

The desert met all of their needs for life: food, water, skins for clothing, materials for tools, weapons, and shelter. For meat, the desert offered deer, birds, and rabbits for hunting. When these animals were hard to find, the Native Americans would eat mice and lizards. Many desert plants, such as the prickly pear and mesquite, provided moisture, fruit, and seeds that could be eaten.

The first Europeans in the American deserts were searching for furs and metals, like silver and gold. They explored but did not settle in the desert. The early pioneers were usually unsuccessful at desert living. They found the great heat and long dry periods too difficult. When they moved away, they left behind empty mining camps, houses, and sheds that slowly fell apart in the sun and wind.

1. What is the main idea of this selection?

   ☒ Before Europeans came to live in America, Native Americans had discovered ways of successfully living in the desert.

   ___ Some Native Americans were hunters or belonged to wandering tribes who stayed in the desert for only short periods of time.

2. Who were the first people to live in the deserts of North America?
   Native Americans

3. What did the Native Americans use to make their houses in the desert?
   trees, clay, and brush

4. What kinds of food did the Native Americans find in the desert?
   deer, birds, rabbits, prickly pear, mesquite, fruit, and seeds

5. What were the first Europeans who came to the desert looking for?
   furs and metals, like silver and gold

Page 194

Main Idea: Camels

Directions: Read the information about camels. Then, answer the questions.

Camels are well suited to desert life. They can cope with infrequent supplies of food and water, blazing heat during the day, low temperatures at night, and sand blown by high winds.

There are two kinds of camels: the two-humped bactrian and the one-humped dromedary. The dromedary is the larger of the two. It has coarse fur on its back that helps protect it from the sun's rays. The hair on its stomach and legs is short to prevent overheating. When camels **molt** in the spring, their wool can be collected in tufts from the bushes and ground.

The legs of the dromedary are much longer than those of the bactrian. Animals that live in very hot countries tend to have longer legs. This gives them a larger area of body surface from which heat can escape. Bactrian camels live in the deserts of central Asia where winters are bitterly cold, so they are not as tall as dromedaries.

Both kinds of camels have pads on their feet that keep them from sinking into the sand as they walk. A camel's long neck allows it to reach the ground to drink water and eat grass without having to bend its legs. It also can reach up to eat leaves from trees.

Camels do not store water in their humps as many people believe. The hump is for fat storage. When there is plenty of food, the camel's hump swells and feels firm. During the dry season when there is little food, the fat is used up, and the hump shrinks and becomes soft.

1. What is the main idea of this selection?

   ☒ Camels are well suited to desert life.

   ___ There are two kinds of camels.

2. Based on the other words in the sentence, what is the correct definition of **molt**?

   ___ turns into a butterfly

   ☒ sheds its hair

   ___ becomes overheated

3. What are the two kinds of camels? the bactrian and the dromedary

4. Why don't camels sink into the sand when they walk? They have special pads on their feet.

5. What is the purpose of a camel's hump? The hump is for fat storage.

Page 195

Review

Directions: Write your answers in complete sentences.

1. Describe how the cold-blooded lizard regulates its body temperature.
   It lies in the sun to get warm in the morning.
   It raises its tail and body off the ground to cool off.
   It hides in burrows or under rocks to cool off.
   It lies in the sun late in the day to absorb warmth before night.

2. What is the main idea of the selection "Lizards"?
   Lizards have adapted to desert life in many ways.

3. Describe how Native Americans adapted to life in the desert.
   They made homes of available materials. They learned to find food, water, shelter, and clothing.

4. Why do you think early pioneers were unsuccessful at desert living?
   Answers will vary.

5. Describe the adaptations of camels for successful desert habitation.
   They store fat in their humps, cope with little food or water, have longs legs for larger body surface, fur to protect from sun's rays, pads on feet, etc.

Page 196

Reading Comprehension: Desert Lakes

Directions: Read the information about lakes in the desert. Then, answer the questions.

A few deserts have small permanent lakes. While they may be a welcome sight in the desert, the water in them is not fit for drinking. They are salt lakes. Rain from nearby higher land keeps these lakes supplied with water, but the lakes are blocked in with nowhere to drain. Over the years, mineral salts collect in the water and build up to a high level, making the water undrinkable.

Most desert lakes are only temporary. Occasional rains may fill them to depths of several feet, but in a matter of weeks or months, all the water has been dried up by the heat and sun. The dried lake beds that remain are called **playas**. Some playas are simply areas of sun-baked mud; others are covered with a sparkling layer of salt.

Perhaps the most unusual desert lake is in central Australia. It is called Lake Eyre. It is a huge lake—nearly 3,600 square miles in area—but it is almost totally dry most of the time. Since it was discovered in 1840, it has been filled only two times. Both times, the lake completely dried up again within a few years.

1. Why is water in a desert lake not fit for drinking?
   It is salt water.

2. Why are the lakes in the desert salt lakes?
   The lakes are blocked in with nowhere to drain, so over the years, mineral salts collect in the water.

3. Why are most desert lakes only temporary?
   The heat and sun dry up the water quickly.

4. What is a **playa**? a dried lake bed

5. What is the name of the unusual desert lake in central Australia?
   Lake Eyre

6. How big is this desert lake? nearly 3,600 square miles

Page 197

Review

Directions: Write your answers in complete sentences.

1. What is a desert?
   A desert is an area where less than 10 inches of rain falls per year.

2. Name a desert in the United States, and tell where it is.
   Answers will vary.

3. What special characteristics must an animal have to survive in the desert?
   It must be able to tolerate extremes of heat and cold, be able to protect itself from the sun's rays, and be able to find or store food and water.

4. What special characteristics must a plant have to survive in the desert?
   It must have a way to collect or store moisture, withstand long dry periods, and tolerate extremes of heat and cold.

5. What differences exist between animals whose habitat is the polar regions and animals whose habitat is the desert regions?
   Answers may include: Polar animals need warm fur or feathers, a layer of fat, the ability to tolerate cold and find food. Desert animals need to protect themselves from heat and find moisture when little exists.

6. Would you like to visit the desert? Why or why not?
   Answers will vary.

Page 198

Nouns

A **noun** is a word that names a person, place, or thing.

Examples:
person — friend
place — home
thing — desk

Nouns are used many ways in sentences. They can be the subjects of sentences.

Example: Noun as subject: Your high-topped **sneakers** look great with that outfit.

Nouns can be direct objects of a sentence. The **direct object** follows the verb and completes its meaning. It answers the question **who** or **what**.

Example: Noun as direct object: Shelly's family bought a new **car**.

Nouns can be indirect objects. An **indirect object** comes between the verb and the direct object and tells **to whom** or **for whom** something was done.

Example: Noun as indirect object: She gave **Vijay** a big hug.

Directions: Underline all the nouns. Write **S** above the noun if it is a subject, **DO** if it is a direct object, or **IO** if it is an indirect object. The first one has been done for you.

1. Do alligators eat people?
2. James hit a home run, and our team won the game.
3. The famous actor gave Marissa his autograph.
4. Eric loaned Keith his bicycle.
5. The kindergarten children painted cute pictures.
6. Robin sold David a magazine subscription.
7. The neighbors planned a going-away party and bought a gift.
8. The party and gift surprised Kurt and his family.
9. My scout leader told our group a funny joke.
10. Catalina made her little sister a clown costume.

Page 200

Comprehensive Curriculum - **Grade 5**

Page 201

Nouns

Directions: Write 10 nouns for each category. Answers will vary. Possible answers:

People
1. farmer
2. doctor
3. mother
4. baby
5. brother
6. librarian
7. teacher
8. girl
9. coach
10. neighbor

Places
1. school
2. home
3. museum
4. post office
5. park
6. restaurant
7. library
8. gym
9. backyard
10. auditorium

Things
1. desk
2. mug
3. strawberry
4. quilt
5. pool
6. marker
7. movie
8. book
9. sunflower
10. racket

PERSON PLACE THING

Page 202

Proper and Common Nouns

Common nouns name nonspecific people, places, or things.

Examples: man, fortress, dog

Proper nouns name specific people, places, or things.

Examples: Washington, D.C., Thomas Jefferson, Red Sea

Directions: Underline the proper nouns, and circle the common nouns in each sentence.

1. My friend, Josephine, loves to go to the docks to watch the boats sail into the harbor.
2. Josephine is especially interested in the boat named Maiden Voyage.
3. This boat is painted red with yellow stripes and has several large masts.
4. Its sails are white and billow in the wind.
5. At Misty Harbor, many boats are always sailing in and out.
6. The crew on the boats rush from bow to stern working diligently to keep the sailboats moving.
7. Josephine has been invited aboard Maiden Voyage by its captain.
8. Captain Ferdinand knew of her interest in sailboats so he offered a tour.
9. Josephine was amazed at the gear aboard the boat and the skills of the crew.
10. It is Josephine's dream to sail the Atlantic Ocean on a boat similar to Maiden Voyage.
11. Her mother is not sure about this dangerous dream and urges Josephine to consider safer dreams.
12. Josephine thinks of early explorers like Christopher Columbus, Amerigo Vespucci, and Leif Ericson.
13. She thinks these men must have been brave to set out into the unknown waters of the world.
14. Their boats were often small and provided little protection from major ocean storms.
15. Josephine believes that if early explorers could challenge the rough ocean waters, she can, too.

Page 203

Abstract and Concrete Nouns

Concrete nouns name something that can be touched or seen.
Abstract nouns name an idea, a thought, or a feeling that cannot be touched or seen.

Examples:
concrete nouns: house, puppy, chair
abstract nouns: love, happiness, fear

Directions: Write **concrete** or **abstract** in the blank after each noun.

1. loyalty abstract
2. light bulb concrete
3. quarter concrete
4. hope abstract
5. satellite concrete
6. ability abstract
7. patio concrete
8. door concrete
9. allegiance abstract
10. Cuba concrete
11. Michael Jordan concrete
12. friendship abstract
13. telephone concrete
14. computer concrete

Directions: Write eight nouns for each category.

Concrete	Abstract
1. pool	1. respect
2. mockingbird	2. admiration
3. football	3. worry
4. cucumber	4. joy
5. swingset	5. courage
6. monkey	6. grace
7. diary	7. jealousy
8. lantern	8. embarrassment

Page 204

Verbs

A **verb** tells what something does or that something exists.

Examples:
Tim **has shared** his apples with us.
Those apples **were** delicious.
I hope Tim **is bringing** more apples tomorrow.
Tim **picked** the apples himself.

Directions: Underline the verbs.

1. Gene moved here from Philadelphia.
2. Now, he is living in a house on my street.
3. His house is three houses away from mine.
4. I have lived in this house all my life.
5. I hope Gene will like this town.
6. I am helping Gene with his room.
7. He has a lot of stuff!
8. We are painting his walls green.
9. He picked the color himself.
10. His parents are glad we are helping out.

Directions: Write verbs to complete these sentences.
Answers will vary.

11. We _____ some paintbrushes.
12. Gene already _____ the paint.
13. I _____ my old clothes.
14. There _____ no furniture in his room right now.
15. It _____ several hours to paint his whole room.

Page 205

Verbs

A **verb** is the action word in a sentence. It tells what the subject does (**build, laugh, express, fasten**) or that it exists (**is, are, was, were**).

Examples: Randy **raked** the leaves into a pile.
I **was** late to school today. Possible answers:

Directions: In the following sentences, write verbs that make sense.

1. The quarterback threw the ball to the receiver.
2. My mother made some soup yesterday.
3. John delivers newspapers to make extra money.
4. The teacher wrote the instructions on the board.
5. Last summer, our family took a trip to Florida to visit relatives.

Sometimes, a verb can be two or more words. Verbs used to support other verbs are called **helping verbs**.

Examples: We **were** listening to music in my room.
Chris **has been** studying for over 2 hours.

Directions: In the following sentences, write helping verbs along with the correct form of the given verbs. The first one has been done for you.

1. Michelle (write) is writing a letter to her grandmother right now.
2. My brother (have) is having trouble with his math homework.
3. When we arrived, the movie (start) had started already.
4. My aunt (live) has lived in the same house for 30 years.
5. Our football team (go) is going to win the national championship this year.
6. My sister (talk) has been talking on the phone all afternoon!
7. I couldn't sleep last night because the wind (blow) was blowing so hard.
8. Last week, Owen was sick, but now he (feel) is feeling much better.
9. Tomorrow, our class (have) is having a bake sale.
10. Mr. Rivera (collect) has collected stamps for 20 years.

Page 206

Verb Tenses

Verbs have different forms to show whether something already happened, is happening right now, or will happen.

Examples:
Present tense: I walk
Past tense: I walked
Future tense: I will walk

Directions: Write **PAST** if the verb is past tense, **PRES** for present tense, or **FUT** for future tense. The first one has been done for you.

PRES 1. My sister Sara works at the grocery store.
PAST 2. Last year, she worked in an office.
PRES 3. Sara is going to college, too.
FUT 4. She will be a dentist some day.
PRES 5. She says studying is difficult.
PAST 6. Sara studied pretty hard in high school, too.
FUT 7. I will be ready for college in a few years.
PAST 8. Last night, I read my history book for two hours.

Directions: Complete these sentences using verbs in the tenses listed. The first one has been done for you.

9. take: future tense — My friends and I will take a trip.
10. talk: past tense — We talked for a long time about where to go.
11. want: present tense — Brianna wants to go to the lake.
12. want: past tense — Jake wanted to go with us.
13. say: past tense — His parents said no.
14. ride: future tense — We will ride our bikes.
15. pack: past tense — Dante and Jared already packed lunches for us.

Verb Tenses

The past tense of many verbs is formed by adding **ed**.

Examples:
remember + **ed** = remembered
climb + **ed** = climbed

If a verb ends in **e**, drop the **e** before adding **ed**.

Examples:
Present	Past
phone	phoned
arrive	arrived

If a verb ends in **y**, change the **y** to **i** before adding **ed**.

Examples:
Present	Past
carry	carried
try	tried

If a verb ends in a short vowel followed by a single consonant, double the final consonant.

Examples:
Present	Past
trip	tripped
pop	popped

Directions: Circle the misspelled verb in each sentence, and write it correctly in the blank.

1. They stopped at our house and then (hurried) home. _hurried_
2. I (scrubed) and mopped the floor. _scrubbed_
3. The coach (nameed) the five starting players. _named_
4. He popped the potatoes into the oil and (fryed) them. _fried_
5. I accidentally (droped) my papers on the floor. _dropped_
6. I had (hopeed) you could go climbing with me. _hoped_
7. He (triped) on the rug. _tripped_
8. The baby (cryed) and screamed all night. _cried_
9. I (moped) the mess up after the glass dropped on the floor. _mopped_
10. First, she frowned, and then she (smileed) _smiled_

Page 207

Writing: Verb Forms

Present-tense verbs tell what is happening right now. To form present-tense verbs, use the "plain" verbs or use **is** or **are** before the verb and add **ing** to the verb.

Examples: We eat. We are eating.
He **serves.** He **is serving.**

Directions: Complete each sentence with the correct verb form, telling what is happening right now. Read carefully, as some sentences already have **is** or **are**.

Examples: Scott is (loan) loaning Jenny his math book.
Jenny (study) is studying for a big math test.

1. The court is (release) _releasing_ the prisoner early.
2. Jonah and Jill (write) _are writing_ their notes in code.
3. Are you (vote) _voting_ for Baxter?
4. The girls are (coax) _coaxing_ the dog into the bathtub.
5. The leaves (begin) _are beginning_ to fall from the trees.
6. My little brother (stay) _is staying_ at his friend's house tonight.
7. Is she (hide) _hiding_ behind the screen?

To change a verb to the **past tense**, or tell what already happened, add **ed**, or use **was** or **were** and add **ing** to the verb.

Example: I watched. I was watching.

Directions: Complete each sentence with the correct verb form. This time, tell what already happened.

Examples: We (walk) walked there yesterday.
They were (talk) talking.

1. The government was (decrease) _decreasing_ our taxes.
2. Was anyone (cheat) _cheating_ in this game?
3. We were (try) _trying_ to set goals for the project.

Page 208

Writing: Future-Tense Verbs

Future-tense verbs tell about things that will happen in the future. To form future-tense verbs, use **will** before the verb.

Example: Tomorrow, I **will walk** to school.

When you use **will**, you may also have to add a helping verb and the ending **ing**.

Example: Tomorrow, I **will be walking** to school.

Directions: Imagine what the world will be like 100 years from now. Maybe you think robots will be doing our work for us, or that people will be living on the moon. What will our houses look like? What will school be like? Write a paragraph describing what you imagine. Be sure to use future-tense verbs.

Answers will vary.

Page 209

Principal Parts of Verbs

Verbs have three principal parts. They are **present**, **past**, and **past participle**.

Form the past tense of regular verbs by adding **ed** to the present tense.

Form the past participle by using the past tense verb with a helping verb: **has**, **have**, or **had**.

has have had

Directions: Write the correct form of each verb. The first one has been done for you.

Present	Past	Past Participle
1. look	looked	have/has/had looked
2. _plan_	planned	has/have/had planned
3. _close_	closed	has/have/had closed
4. wash	washed	has/have/had washed
5. _prepare_	prepared	has/have/had prepared
6. _provide_	provided	has/have/had provided
7. invite	invited	has/have/had invited
8. _discover_	discovered	has/have/had discovered
9. approve	approved	has/have/had approved
10. _search_	searched	has/have/had searched
11. establish	established	has/have/had established
12. _form_	formed	has/have/had formed
13. _push_	pushed	has/have/had pushed
14. travel	traveled	has/have/had traveled

Page 210

Irregular Verbs

Irregular verbs change completely in the past tense. Unlike regular verbs, the past tense of irregular verbs is not formed by adding **ed**.

Examples:
Chung **eats** the grapes.
Chung **ate** them yesterday.
Chung **has eaten** them for weeks.

Present Tense	Past Tense	Past Participle
begin	began	has/have/had begun
speak	spoke	has/have/had spoken
drink	drank	has/have/had drunk
know	knew	has/have/had known
eat	ate	has/have/had eaten
wear	wore	has/have/had worn

Directions: Rewrite these sentences once using the past tense and again using the past participle of each verb.

1. Todd begins football practice this week.
Todd began football practice this week.
Todd had begun football practice this week.

2. She wears her hair in braids.
She wore her hair in braids.
She had worn her hair in braids.

3. I drink two glasses of milk.
I drank two glasses of milk.
I had drunk two glasses of milk.

4. The man is speaking to us.
The man spoke to us.
The man had spoken to us.

5. The dogs are eating.
The dogs ate.
The dogs had eaten.

Page 211

Irregular Verbs

The past participle form of an irregular verb needs a helping verb.

Examples:
Present	Past	Past Participle
begin	began	has/have/had begun
drive	drove	has/have/had driven

present, past, and past participle

Directions: Write the past and past participle forms of these irregular verbs. Use a dictionary if you need help.

Present	Past	Past Participle
1. speak	spoke	has/have/had spoken
2. break	broke	has/have/had broken
3. beat	beat	has/have/had beaten
4. dream	dreamed	has/have/had dreamed
5. tear	tore	has/have/had torn
6. forget	forgot	has/have/had forgotten
7. lead	led	has/have/had led
8. stand	stood	has/have/had stood
9. sting	stung	has/have/had stung
10. freeze	froze	has/have/had frozen
11. grow	grew	has/have/had grown
12. lose	lost	has/have/had lost
13. run	ran	has/have/had run
14. meet	met	has/have/had met
15. sit	sat	has/have/had sat
16. do	did	has/have/had done

Page 212

Be as a Helping Verb

A **helping verb** tells when the action of a sentence takes place. The helping verb **be** has several forms: **am**, **is**, **are**, **was**, **were**, and **will**. These helping verbs can be used in all three tenses.

Examples:
Past tense: Kenji **was** talking. We **were** eating.
Present tense: I **am** coming. Simon **is** walking. They **are** singing.
Future tense: I **will** work. The puppies **will** eat.

In the present and past tense, many verbs can be written with or without the helping verb **be**. When the verb is written with a form of **be**, add **ing**. **Was** and **is** are used with singular subjects. **Were** and **are** are used with plural subjects.

Examples:
Present tense: Angela **sings**. Angela **is singing**. The children **sing**. They **are singing**.
Past tense: I **studied**. I **was studying**. They **studied**. They **were studying**.

The helping verb **will** is always needed for the future tense, but the **ing** ending is not used with **will**. **Will** is both singular and plural.

Examples:
Future tense: I **will** eat. We **will** watch.

Directions: Underline the helping verbs.

1. Brian <u>is</u> helping me with this project.
2. We <u>are</u> working together on it.
3. Tess <u>was</u> painting the background yesterday.
4. Matt and Malik <u>were</u> cleaning up.
5. Tomorrow, we <u>will</u> present our project to the class.

Directions: Rewrite the verbs using a helping verb. The first one has been done for you.

6. Our neighborhood plans a garage sale. — is planning
7. The sale starts tomorrow. — is starting
8. My brother Doug and I think about things we sell. — are thinking
9. My grandfather cleans out the garage. — is cleaning
10. Doug and I help him. — are helping

Page 213

Be as a Linking Verb

A **linking verb** links a noun or adjective in the predicate to the subject. Forms of the verb **be** are the most common linking verbs. Linking verbs can be used in all three tenses.

Examples:
Present: My father **is** a salesman.
Past: The store **was** very busy last night.
Future: Tomorrow **will be** my birthday.

In the first sentence, **is** links the subject (father) with a noun (salesman). In the second sentence, **was** links the subject (store) with an adjective (busy). In the third sentence, **will be** links the subject (tomorrow) with a noun (birthday).

Directions: Circle the linking verbs. Underline the two words that are linked by the verb. The first one has been done for you.

1. <u>Columbus</u> (is) the <u>capital</u> of Ohio.
2. By bedtime, <u>Nicole</u> (was) <u>bored</u>.
3. <u>Andy</u> (will be) the <u>captain</u> of our team.
4. <u>Tuesday</u> (is) the first <u>day</u> of the month.
5. I hate to say this, but <u>we</u> (are) <u>lost</u>.
6. Ask him if the <u>water</u> (is) <u>cold</u>.
7. By the time I finished my paper, <u>it</u> (was) <u>late</u>.
8. <u>Spaghetti</u> (is) my favorite <u>dinner</u>.
9. The <u>children</u> (were) <u>afraid</u> of the big truck.
10. <u>Aliyah</u> (will be) a good <u>president</u> of our class.
11. These <u>lessons</u> (are) <u>helpful</u>.
12. (Was) that <u>report</u> <u>due</u> today?

Page 214

Be as a Linking or Helping Verb

Directions: Write **H** if the form of **be** is used as a helping verb or **L** if it is used as a linking verb.

<u>H</u> 1. Bella was watching for the mail.
<u>L</u> 2. The mail was late, as usual.
<u>H</u> 3. Her friends were calling her to come to the park.
<u>H</u> 4. "We will be missed by everyone at the park," they said.
<u>L</u> 5. Still, Bella was hopeful as she waited.
<u>H</u> 6. She knew her brother was sending her a letter.
<u>L</u> 7. He was a soldier in the army.
<u>L</u> 8. He was homesick for his family, so he wrote every day.

Directions: Write two sentences using a form of **be** as a helping verb.

9. _____ Answers will vary. _____
10. _____

Directions: Write two sentences using a form of **be** as a linking verb.

11. _____ Answers will vary. _____
12. _____

Page 215

Transitive and Intransitive Verbs

An **intransitive verb** can stand alone in the predicate because its meaning is complete. In the examples below, notice that each short sentence is a complete thought.

Examples: Intransitive verbs: The tree **grows**. The mouse **squeaked**. The deer **will run**.

A **transitive verb** needs a direct object to complete its meaning. The meaning of a sentence with a transitive verb is not complete without a direct object.

Examples: Transitive verbs: The mouse **wants** seeds. The deer **saw** the hunter. The tree **will lose** its leaves.

The direct object **seeds** tells what the mouse wants. **Leaves** tells what the tree will lose and **hunter** tells what the deer saw.

Both transitive and intransitive verbs can be in the past, present, or future tense.

Directions: Underline the verb in each sentence. Write **I** if the sentence has an intransitive verb or **T** if it has a transitive verb.

<u>I</u> 1. The snake <u>slid</u> quietly along the ground.
<u>T</u> 2. The snake <u>scared</u> a rabbit.
<u>I</u> 3. The rabbit <u>hopped</u> quickly back to its hole.
<u>I</u> 4. Safe from the snake, the rabbit <u>shivered</u> with fear.
<u>T</u> 5. In the meantime, the snake <u>caught</u> a frog.
<u>T</u> 6. The frog <u>was watching</u> flies and didn't <u>see</u> the snake.

Directions: Complete these sentences with intransitive verbs.

7. Our friends _____ Answers will vary. _____
8. The movie _____

Directions: Complete these sentences with transitive verbs and direct objects.

9. My family _____ Answers will vary. _____
10. The lightning _____

Page 216

Subjects and Predicates

The **subject** tells who or what a sentence is about. The **predicate** tells what the subject does, did, or is doing. All complete sentences must have a subject and a predicate.

Examples:

Subject	Predicate
Hamsters	are common pets.
Pets	need special care.

Directions: Circle the subjects, and underline the predicates.

1. (Many children) <u>keep hamsters as pets.</u>
2. (Mice) <u>are good pets, too.</u>
3. (Hamsters) <u>collect food in their cheeks.</u>
4. (My sister) <u>sneezes around furry animals.</u>
5. (My brother) <u>wants a dog instead of a hamster.</u>

Directions: Write subjects to complete these sentences.

6. _____ has two pet hamsters.
7. _____ got a new pet last week.
8. _____ keeps forgetting to feed his goldfish.

Answers will vary.

Directions: Write predicates to complete these sentences.

9. Baby hamsters _____
10. Pet mice _____
11. I _____

Answers will vary.

Directions: Write **S** if the group of words is a sentence or **NS** if the group of words is not a sentence.

12. <u>NS</u> A new cage for our hamster.
13. <u>NS</u> Picked the cutest one.
14. <u>S</u> We started out with two.
15. <u>NS</u> Liking every one in the store.

Page 217

Which Noun Is the Subject?

A **noun** is a word that names a person, place, or thing.

Examples: Andy, Mrs. Henderson, doctor, child, house, shirt, dog, freedom, country

Often, a noun is the subject of a sentence. The **subject** tells who or what the sentence is about. In this sentence, the subject is **Sara**: Sara drank some punch. A sentence can have several nouns, but they are not all subjects.

Directions: Underline each noun in the sentences below. Then, circle the noun that is the subject of the sentence.

Example: (Benny) caught a huge <u>fish</u> in a small <u>net</u>.

1. (Anna) bragged about her big <u>brother</u>.
2. The (car) has a <u>dent</u> in the fender.
3. Our (school) won the city spirit <u>award</u>.
4. The (cook) scrubbed the pots and pans.
5. The (quarter) flipped onto the <u>floor</u>.
6. My (sister) rinsed her <u>hair</u> in the sink.
7. Our (neighbor) has 12 <u>pets</u>.
8. The cross country (team) ran 5 <u>miles</u> at practice.
9. (Syd) walked to the store on the <u>corner</u>.
10. A (farmer) stocks this <u>pond</u> with fish.

Directions: Each sentence below has two subjects. Underline all the nouns, as you did above. Then, circle both subjects.

Example: (Joe) and (Peter) walked to <u>school</u>.

1. (Apples) and (peaches) grow in different <u>seasons</u>.
2. The (chair) and (table) matched the other <u>furniture</u>.

Page 218

Which Noun Is the Subject?

Usually, the noun that is the subject will come at the beginning of the sentence.

Examples: The [truck] turned quickly around the corner.
[Kevin] stayed home from school yesterday.

Sometimes, other words will come before the subject. When this happens, remember to look for who or what the sentence is about.

Example: After school, [Katie] usually walks to the library.

I come first!

Noun

The sentence is about Katie, not school.

Directions: In the sentences below, circle the nouns that are subjects. Some sentences have more than one subject, and they will not always be at the beginning of the sentence.

1. [Mark] and [I] helped the teacher clean the classroom.
2. In the morning, my [mother] cooks breakfast for the whole family.
3. To finish the project, [Keiko] had to stay up very late last night.
4. After the storm, [power lines] were down all over the city.
5. [Oranges] and [grapefruits] grow very well in Florida.
6. During the summer, [squirrels] work hard to gather nuts for the winter.
7. While skiing last weekend, my [neighbor] fell and broke his leg.
8. [Pictures] and [posters] cover all the walls of our classroom.
9. To save gas, my [father] takes the bus to work instead of driving.
10. In my opinion, [dogs] and [cats] make the best pets.

Page 219

Subjects and Verbs

Directions: Underline the subject and verb in each sentence below. Write **S** over the subject and **V** over the verb. If the verb is two words, mark them both.

Examples: <u>Dennis</u> <u>was drinking</u> some punch.
The <u>punch</u> <u>was</u> too sweet.

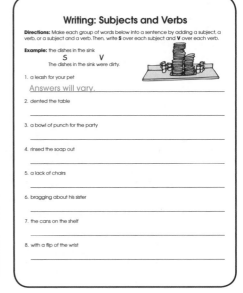

1. <u>Hayley</u> <u>talks</u> about her dog all the time.
2. <u>Mrs. Thomas</u> <u>scrubbed</u> the dirt off her car.
3. Then, her <u>son</u> <u>rinsed</u> off the soap.
4. The <u>teacher</u> <u>was flipping</u> through the cards.
5. Sophia's <u>rabbit</u> <u>was</u> hungry and thirsty.
6. Your science <u>report</u> <u>lacks</u> a little detail.
7. <u>Chris</u> <u>is stocking</u> the shelves with cans of soup.
8. The <u>accident</u> <u>caused</u> a huge dent in our car.

Just as sentences can have two subjects, they can also have two verbs.

Example: <u>Gabriela</u> and <u>Amie</u> <u>fed</u> the dog and <u>gave</u> him clean water.

Directions: Underline all the subjects and verbs in these sentences. Write **S** over the subjects and **V** over the verbs.

1. <u>Mom</u> and <u>Dad</u> <u>scrubbed</u> and <u>rinsed</u> the basement floor.
2. The <u>men</u> <u>came</u> and <u>stocked</u> the lake with fish.
3. <u>Someone</u> <u>broke</u> the window and <u>ran</u> away.
4. <u>Carrie</u> <u>punched</u> a hole in the paper and <u>threaded</u> yarn through the hole.
5. <u>Julie</u> and <u>Ahmad</u> <u>turned</u> their bikes around and <u>went</u> home.

Page 220

Writing: Subjects and Verbs

Directions: Make each group of words below into a sentence by adding a subject, a verb, or a subject and a verb. Then, write **S** over each subject and **V** over each verb.

Example: the dishes in the sink
        S   V
The dishes in the sink were dirty.

1. a leash for your pet
   Answers will vary.
2. dented the table
   _____
3. a bowl of punch for the party
   _____
4. rinsed the soap out
   _____
5. a lack of chairs
   _____
6. bragging about his sister
   _____
7. the cans on the shelf
   _____
8. with a flip of the wrist
   _____

Page 221

Writing: Subjects and Verbs

Directions: Decide which words in the box are subjects (nouns) and which are verbs. Write each word under the correct heading. Then, match each subject with a verb to make a sentence. Use each subject and verb only once. The first one has been done for you.

dog	girls	walked	barked	honked
flew	car	played	neighbor	teacher
wrote	mowed	Marcus	birds	

Subjects	**Verbs**
girls	walked
dog	flew
car	wrote
Marcus	mowed
neighbor	played
birds	barked
teacher	honked

1. The tired girls walked slowly home from school.
2. _____Answers will vary._____
3. _____
4. _____
5. _____
6. _____
7. _____

Page 222

Complete Sentences

A sentence that does not contain both a subject and a predicate is called a **fragment**.

Directions: Write **C** if the sentence is complete or **F** if it is a fragment.

1. __C__ My mother and I hope to go to the mall this afternoon.
2. __F__ To get shoes.
3. __C__ We both need a new pair of tennis shoes.
4. __F__ Maybe blue and white.
5. __C__ Mom wants a pair of white shoes.
6. __C__ That seems rather boring to me.
7. __C__ There are many shoe stores in the mall.
8. __F__ Sure to be a large selection.
9. __C__ Tennis shoes are very expensive.
10. __C__ I wore my last pair almost every day.

Directions: Write the missing subject or predicate for these sentences.

11. _____Answers will vary._____ decided to go for hamburgers.
12. We _____
13. My parents _____
14. One day soon, I _____
15. My favorite subject in school _____
16. _____ went fishing on Sunday.

Page 223

Direct Objects

A **direct object** is a word or words that follow a transitive verb and complete its meaning. It answers the question **whom** or **what**. Direct objects are always nouns or pronouns.

Examples:
We built a **doghouse**. **Doghouse** is the direct object. It tells **what** we built.
I called **Elena**. **Elena** is the direct object. It tells **whom** I called.

Directions: Underline the direct objects.

1. Maggy drew <u>a picture</u> of the doghouse.
2. Then, we bought <u>some wood</u> at the store.
3. Erin measured <u>each board</u>.
4. Who will saw <u>the wood</u> into boards?
5. Thad hammered <u>nails</u> into the boards.
6. He accidentally hit <u>his thumb</u> with the hammer.
7. Kirsten found <u>some paint</u> in the basement.
8. Should we paint <u>the roof</u>?
9. Will you write <u>Sparky's name</u> above the door?
10. Spell <u>his name</u> correctly.

Directions: Write direct objects to complete these sentences.

11. Will Sparky like _____Answers will vary._____?
12. When we were finished, we put away _____
13. We washed out _____
14. We threw away _____
15. Then, to celebrate, we ate _____

Page 224

Comprehensive Curriculum - **Grade 5**

Indirect Objects

An **indirect object** is a word or words that come between the verb and the direct object. An indirect object tells **to whom** or **for whom** something has been done. Indirect objects are always nouns or pronouns.

Examples:
She cooked **me** a great dinner. **Me** is the indirect object. It tells **for whom** something was cooked.
Give the **photographer** a smile. **Photographer** is the indirect object. It tells **to whom** the smile should be given.

Directions: Circle the indirect objects. Underline the direct objects.

1. Grace showed me her drawing.
2. The committee had given her an award for it.
3. The principal offered Grace a special place to put her drawing.
4. While babysitting, I read Xavier a story.
5. He told me the end of the story.
6. Then, I fixed him some hot chocolate.
7. Xavier gave me a funny look.
8. Why didn't his mother tell me?
9. Hot chocolate gives Xavier a rash.
10. Will his mom still pay me for watching him?

Directions: Write indirect objects to complete these sentences.

11. I will write _Answers will vary._ a letter.
12. I'll give _____ part of my lunch.
13. Show _____ your model.
14. Did you send _____ a card?
15. Don't tell _____ my secret.

Page 225

Direct and Indirect Objects

Directions: Underline the direct objects. Circle the indirect objects.

1. Please give him a note card.
2. My father told me a secret.
3. I carefully examined the dinosaur bones.
4. Joseph decorated the banquet hall for the wedding.
5. Every night, I telephone my grandmother.
6. The head of the company offered my father a new position.
7. Too much pizza can give you a stomachache.
8. Will you draw me a picture?
9. This new computer gives me a headache!
10. Thomas discovered a new entrance to the cave.
11. He showed me the rare penny.
12. While watching television, I wrote Maria a letter.
13. Mrs. Fetters will pay me ten dollars for shoveling her sidewalk this winter.
14. The teacher handed her class a surprise quiz.
15. I like to drink iced tea on summer days.
16. Mom bought Josh new school supplies for kindergarten.
17. I had to pay the library a fine for overdue books.
18. My family enjoys playing football.
19. Each night my mom reads me one chapter of a novel.
20. The teacher gave us our report cards.

Page 226

Prepositions

A **preposition** is a word that comes before a noun or pronoun and shows the relationship of that noun or pronoun to other words in the sentence.

The **object of a preposition** is a noun or pronoun that follows a preposition and completes its meaning. A **prepositional phrase** includes a preposition and the object(s) of the preposition.

Examples:
The girl **with red hair** spoke first.
With is the preposition.
Hair is the object of the preposition.
With red hair is a prepositional phrase.

In addition to being subjects, direct objects, and indirect objects, nouns and pronouns can also be objects of prepositions.

	Prepositions					
across	behind	from	near	over	to	on
by	through	in	around	off	with	of
after	before	for	between	beyond	at	into

Directions: Underline the prepositional phrases in these sentences. Circle the prepositions. The first sentence has been done for you.

1. The name of our street is Redsail Court.
2. We have lived in our house for three years.
3. In our family, we eat a lot of hamburgers.
4. We like hamburgers on toasted buns with mustard.
5. Sometimes we eat in the living room in front of the TV.
6. In the summer, we have picnics in the backyard.
7. The ants crawl into our food and into our clothes.
8. Behind our house is a park with swings.
9. Kids from the neighborhood walk through our yard to the park.
10. Sometimes they cut across Mom's garden and stomp on her beans.
11. Mom says we need a tall fence without a gate.
12. With a fence around our yard, we could get a dog!

Page 227

Pronouns

A **pronoun** is a word used in place of a noun. Instead of repeating a noun again and again, use a pronoun.

Examples:
I	you	he	she	them	us
me	your	his	her	they	it
my	our	his	we	their	its

Each pronoun takes the place of a certain noun. If the noun is singular, the pronoun should be singular. If the noun is plural, the pronoun should be plural.

Examples: John told **his** parents **he** would be late.
The girls said **they** would ride **their** bikes.

Directions: In the sentences below, draw an arrow from each pronoun to the noun it replaces.

Example: Addy needs the salt. Please pass it to her.

1. The workers had faith they would finish the house in time.
2. Jana fell and scraped her knees. She put bandages on them.
3. The teacher told the students he wanted to see their papers.

Directions: Cross out some nouns and write pronouns to replace them.

Example: Dan needed a book for ~~Dan's~~ book report. _his_

1. Brian doesn't care about the style of ~~Brian's~~ clothes. _his_
2. Omar dyed ~~Omar's~~ jeans to make ~~the jeans~~ dark blue. _his_ _them_
3. Faith said ~~Faith~~ was tired of sharing a bedroom with ~~Faith's~~ two sisters. ~~Faith~~ wanted a room of ~~Faith's~~ own. _she_ _her_ _She_ _her_
4. Bathe babies carefully so the soap doesn't get in ~~the babies'~~ eyes and make ~~the babies~~ cry. _their_ _them_
5. When the children held up ~~the children's~~ pictures, we could see the pride in ~~the children's~~ eyes. _their_ _their_

Page 228

Singular and Plural Pronouns

Directions: Rewrite the sentences so the pronouns match the nouns they replace in gender and number. Change the verb form if necessary. The first one has been done for you.

1. Canada geese are the best-known geese in North America. It was here when the first settlers came from Europe.
   Canada geese are the best-known geese in North America.
   They were here when the first settlers came from Europe.
2. A Canada goose has a white patch from their chin to a spot behind their eyes.
   A Canada goose has a white patch from its chin
   to a spot behind its eyes.
3. Canada geese can harm farmland when it grazes in fields.
   Canada geese can harm farmland when they
   graze in fields.
4. Geese have favorite fields where it likes to stop and eat.
   Geese have favorite fields where they like to stop
   and eat.
5. While most of the flock eats, some geese stand guard. He warns if there is any danger.
   While most of the flock eats, some geese stand
   guard. They warn if there is any danger.
6. Each guard gets their turn to eat, too.
   Each guard gets its turn to eat, too.
7. Female geese usually lay five or six eggs, but she may lay as many as eleven.
   Female geese usually lay five or six eggs, but they
   may lay as many as eleven.
8. While the female goose sits on the eggs, the male goose guards their mate.
   While the female goose sits on the eggs, the male
   goose guards his mate.

Page 229

Possessive Pronouns

A **possessive pronoun** shows ownership. A possessive pronoun can be used with the name of what is owned or by itself.

Examples:
This is **my** book. The book is **mine**.
This is **your** sandwich. It is **yours**.
This is **our** room. The room is **ours**.

The possessive pronouns are **my, your, our, his, her, their, its, mine, yours, ours, hers,** and **theirs**. Possessive pronouns do not have apostrophes.

Directions: Complete the sentences with the correct possessive pronouns.

1. I entered ___my___ picture in the contest. That farm scene is ___mine___.
2. Shelby entered ___her___ picture, too. Do you see ___hers___?
3. Hal didn't finish ___his___ drawing. He left ___his___ at home.
4. Did you enter ___your___ clay pot? That looks like ___yours___.
5. One picture has fallen off ___its___ stand.
6. Brian and Kendell worked together on a chalk drawing. That sketch by the doorway is ___theirs___.
7. The judges have made ___their___ choices.
8. We both won! They picked both of ___ours___!
9. Here come the judges with our ribbons in ___their___ hands.
10. Your ribbon is the same as ___mine___.

Page 230

Writing: Possessive Pronouns

A **possessive pronoun** shows ownership. Instead of writing "That is Jill's book," write "That is her book" or "That is hers." Instead of "I lost my pencil," write "I lost mine." Use possessive pronouns to name what is owned or possessed.

Examples: my (book) our (car) your (hat) his (leg)
her (hair) their (group) its (team)

Use **mine, ours, yours, his, hers,** and **theirs** when you do not name what is possessed. Notice that possessive pronouns don't use apostrophes.

Directions: Complete these sentences with the correct possessive pronoun.

Example: This book belongs to Jon. It is ___**his**___

1. I brought my lunch. Did you bring ___yours___?
2. I can't do my homework. I wonder if Audrey figured out ___hers___?
3. Deepak saved his pretzels, but I ate ___mine___.
4. Our team finished our project, but the other team didn't finish ___theirs___.
5. They already have their assignment. When will we get ___ours___?

It's easy to confuse the possessive pronoun **its** with the contraction for **it is**, which is spelled **it's**. The apostrophe in **it's** shows that the **i** in **is** has been left out.

Directions: Write **its** or **it's** in each sentence below.

Examples: The book has lost its cover. It's going to rain soon.

1. ___It's___ nearly time to go.
2. The horse hurt ___its___ leg.
3. Every nation has ___its___ share of problems.
4. What is ___its___ name?
5. I think ___it's___ too warm to snow.
6. The teacher said ___it's___ up to us.

Page 231

Indefinite Pronouns

Indefinite pronouns often end with **body, one,** or **thing.**

Examples:
Everybody is going to be there.
No one wants to miss it.

Indefinite pronouns do not change form when used as subjects or objects. They are always singular.

Example:
Incorrect: Everyone must bring **their** own lunches.
Correct: All students must bring **their** own lunch.
Everyone must bring **his or her** own lunch.
Everyone must bring **a** lunch.

Directions: Write twelve indefinite pronouns by matching a word from column A with a word from column B.

Column A	Column B
any	thing
every	one
no	body
some	

1. anything
2. anyone
3. anybody
4. everything
5. everyone
6. everybody
7. nothing
8. no one
9. nobody
10. something
11. someone
12. somebody

Directions: Write all the indefinite pronouns that would make sense in the sentence below.
_____ can come.

13. Anyone, Anybody, Everyone, Everybody, No one, Nobody, Someone, Somebody

Directions: Rewrite this sentence correctly.

14. Everybody has their books.

Everybody has his or her books.

Page 232

Interrogative and Relative Pronouns

An **interrogative pronoun** is used when asking a question. The interrogative pronouns are **who, what,** and **which.** Use **who** when referring to people. Use **what** when referring to things. **Which** can be used to refer to people or things.

Directions: Circle the interrogative pronouns. Write whether the pronoun refers to people or things.

1. (Who) brought this salad for the picnic?
people
2. (Which) car will we drive to the movies?
things
3. (Which) girl asked the question?
people
4. (What) time is it?
things
5. (What) will we do with the leftover food?
things
6. (Who) is going to the swim meet?
people

Relative pronouns refer to the noun or pronoun that comes before them. The noun or pronoun to which it refers is called the **antecedent.** The relative pronouns are **who, whom, which,** and **that. Who** and **whom** refer to people. **Which** refers to things or animals. **That** can refer to people, animals, or things.

Directions: Circle the relative pronouns, and underline the antecedents.

1. My dog, (which) is very well-behaved, never barks.
2. The story was about a girl (who) wanted a horse of her own.
3. The bookcase, (which) was full, toppled over during the night.
4. The man to (whom) I spoke gave me complicated directions.
5. The book (that) I wanted had already been checked out of the library.

Page 233

Gender and Number of Pronouns

Pronouns that identify males are **masculine.** The masculine pronouns are **he, his,** and **him.** Pronouns that identify females are feminine. The **feminine** pronouns are **she, her,** and **hers.** Pronouns that identify something as neither male nor female are **gender-neutral.** The gender-neutral pronouns are **it** and **its.**

The plural pronouns **they** and **them** are used to replace masculine, feminine, or gender-neutral nouns.

Examples: Noun Pronoun Noun Pronoun
boot it woman she
man he John's his
they dog's its

Directions: List four nouns that each pronoun could replace in a sentence. The first one has been done for you. **Possible answers:**

1. she mother doctor girl friend
2. he father runner boy teacher
3. it dog book an apple a pencil
4. they girls athletes cousins mosquitoes
5. hers Ella's Mom's Aunt Lea's Ms. Ruiz's
6. its the goat's the TV's the lamp's the backpack's

Singular pronouns take the place of singular nouns. Plural pronouns take the place of plural nouns. The singular pronouns are **I, me, mine, he, she, it, its, hers, his, him, her, you,** and **yours.** The plural pronouns are **we, you, yours, they, theirs, ours, them,** and **us.**

Directions: Write five sentences. Include a singular and a plural pronoun in each sentence.

1. ___Answers will vary.___
2. _____
3. _____
4. _____
5. _____

Page 234

Writing: Pronouns

Sometimes, matching nouns and pronouns can be difficult.

Example: A **teacher** should always be fair to **their** students.

Teacher is singular, but **their** is plural, so they don't match. Still, we can't say "A teacher should always be fair to his students," because teachers are both men and women. "His or her students" sounds awkward. One easy way to handle this is to make **teacher** plural so it will match **their.**

Example: Teachers should always be fair to **their** students.

Directions: Correct the problems in the following sentences by crossing out the incorrect words and writing in the correct nouns and pronouns. (If you make the noun plural, make the verb plural, too.)

its
Examples: Ron's school won ~~their~~ basketball game.
cats are
You can tell if ~~a cat is~~ angry by watching their tails.

Students its
1. ~~A student~~ should try to praise their friends' strong points.
Parents have
2. The group finished ~~their~~ work on time in spite of the deadline.
3. ~~A parent~~ usually ~~has~~ a lot of faith in their children.
its
4. The company paid ~~their~~ workers once a week.
its
5. The train made ~~their~~ daily run from Chicago to Detroit.
Students
6. ~~Each student~~ should have a title on their papers.

Directions: Complete these sentences with the correct pronouns.

1. Simon fell out of the tree and scraped ___his___ arm.
2. The citizens felt a deep pride in ___their___ community.
3. Abby and Leah wear ___their___ hair in the same style.
4. I dyed some shirts, but ___they___ didn't turn out right.
5. The nurse showed the mother how to bathe ___her___ baby.
6. Our school made $75 from ___its___ carnival.

Page 235

Pronouns as Subjects

A **pronoun** is a word that takes the place of a noun. The pronouns **I, we, he, she, it, you,** and **they** can be the subjects of a sentence.

Examples:
I left the house early.
You need to be more careful.
She dances well.

A pronoun must be singular if the noun it replaces is singular. A pronoun must be plural if the noun it replaces is plural. **He, she,** and **it** are singular pronouns. **We** and **they** are plural pronouns. **You** is both singular and plural.

Examples:
Jazmin practiced playing the piano. **She** plays well.
Andre and I are studying Africa. **We** made a map of it.
The children clapped loudly. **They** liked the clown.

Directions: Write the correct pronouns.

1. Bobcats hunt at night. ___They___ are not seen during the day.
2. The mother bobcat usually has babies during February or March. ___She___ may have two litters a year.
3. The father bobcat stays away when the babies are first born. Later, ___he___ helps find food for them.
4. We have a new assignment. ___It___ is a project about bobcats.
5. My group gathered pictures of bobcats. ___We___ made a display.
6. Stella wrote our report. ___She___ used my notes.

Directions: Circle the pronouns that do not match the nouns they replace. Then, write the correct pronouns on the lines.

7. Two boys saw a bobcat. (He) told us what happened. ___They___
8. Then, we saw a film. (They) showed bobcats climbing trees. ___It___

Page 236

Comprehensive Curriculum - **Grade 5**

Pronouns as Direct Objects

The pronouns **me**, **you**, **him**, **her**, **it**, **us**, and **them** can be used as direct objects.

Examples:
I heard Grant. Grant heard **me**.
We like the teacher. The teacher likes **us**.
He saw the dog. The dog saw **him**.

A pronoun used as a direct object must be plural if the noun is plural and singular if the noun is singular.

Directions: Write the correct pronouns.

1. Goldfish come from China. The Chinese used to eat _____them_____ like trout.
2. The prettiest goldfish were kept as pets. The Chinese put _____them_____ in small bowls and ponds.
3. My sister, brother, and I have goldfish. Grandpa took _____us_____ to the store to get them.
4. They come to the top when I am around. I think they like _____me_____ .
5. My sister's fish was white. She kept _____it_____ for three weeks.
6. She claimed the fish splashed _____her_____ when she fed it.

Directions: Circle pronouns that do not match the nouns they replace. Rewrite the sentences using the correct pronouns. Change the verbs after the pronouns if necessary.

7. Goldfish often die because kids don't feed (it).
Goldfish often die because kids don't feed them.
8. Some goldfish live a long time because (it) well cared for.
Some goldfish live a long time because they are well cared for.
9. A wild goldfish will eat anything (they) think looks good.
A wild goldfish will eat anything it thinks looks good.
10. Birds eat wild goldfish. (It) likes the young ones best.
Birds eat wild goldfish. They like the young ones best.

Page 237

Pronouns as Indirect Objects and Objects of Prepositions

The pronouns **me**, **you**, **him**, **her**, **it**, **us**, and **them** can be used as indirect objects and objects of prepositions.

Examples:
Pronouns as indirect objects: Shawn showed **me** his new bike. The teacher gave **us** two more days to finish our reports.
Pronouns as objects of prepositions: It's your turn after **her**. I can't do it without **them**.

A pronoun used as an indirect object or an object of a preposition must be singular if the noun it replaces is singular and plural if the noun it replaces is plural.

Directions: Write the correct pronouns. Above the pronoun, write **S** if it is the subject, **DO** if it is the direct object, **IO** if it is the indirect object, or **OP** if it is the object of a preposition.

1. Markos is coming to our party. I gave _IO_ him the directions.
2. Janelle and Eldon used to be his friends. Is he still friends with _OP_ them ?
3. Kevin and I like playing soccer, but _S_ we are not on the same team.
4. We listened closely while she told _IO_ us what happened to _OP_ her .
5. My brother hurt his hand, but I took care of _OP_ him .
6. A piece of glass cut him when _S_ he dropped _DO_ it .
7. When Annalisa won the race, the coach gave _IO_ her a trophy.
8. We were hot and sweaty, but a breeze cooled _DO_ us off.

Page 238

Pronouns

Subjects:	he	she	it	you	I	they	we
Objects:	him	her	it	you	me	them	us
Possessive:	his	her	its	your	my	their	our
Possessive:	his	hers	its	yours	mine	theirs	ours
Indefinite:	everyone	nobody	something	(and others)			

Directions: Complete these sentences with the correct pronouns from the box. Above each pronoun, write how it is used: **S** for subject, **DO** for direct object, **IO** for indirect object, **OP** for object of a preposition, **PP** for possessive pronoun, or **IP** for indefinite pronoun.

1. Last week, we had a food drive at _PP_ our church.
2. _S/IP_ Everyone in our Sunday school class helped collect food.
3. I walked down my street and asked _OP_ our neighbors for food.
4. They gave _S_ us cans and boxes of food.
5. Kelly came with _OP_ us and helped _PP_ us carry all of _OP_ it .
6. Tomas had brought his old red wagon from _PP_ his house.
7. When I saw it, _S_ I wished I had brought _PP_ mine .
8. Kelly and _S_ I had to put _PP_ our cans in grocery bags.
9. Those bags were really heavy when _S_ they were full.
10. When I picked one up, _S_ it tore and the cans fell out!
11. Jeremy's sister gave _IO_ us a ride around the neighborhood.
12. Walking made Kelly and _DO_ me hungry.

Page 239

Review

Answers will vary.

Directions: Write a noun for each possessive pronoun.

1. my _____
2. his _____
3. your _____
4. their _____
5. our _____
6. her _____
7. its _____

Directions: Use these indefinite pronouns in sentences.

8. everyone _____
9. nobody _____
10. something _____

Directions: Use these interrogative pronouns in sentences.

11. who _____
12. what _____
13. which _____

Directions: Use these relative pronouns in sentences.

14. who _____
15. whom _____
16. which _____
17. that _____

Page 240

Adjectives

An **adjective** describes a noun or pronoun. There are three types of adjectives. They are **positive**, **comparative**, and **superlative**.

Examples:

Positive	Comparative	Superlative
big	bigger	biggest
beautiful	more beautiful	most beautiful
likely	less likely	least likely

Directions: Write the comparative and superlative forms of these adjectives.

	Positive	Comparative	Superlative
1.	happy	happier	happiest
2.	kind	kinder	kindest
3.	sad	sadder	saddest
4.	slow	slower	slowest
5.	low	lower	lowest
6.	delicious	more delicious	most delicious
7.	strong	stronger	strongest
8.	straight	straighter	straightest
9.	tall	taller	tallest
10.	humble	humbler	humblest
11.	hard	harder	hardest
12.	clear	clearer	clearest
13.	loud	louder	loudest
14.	clever	more clever	most clever

Page 241

Writing: Comparatives

Comparatives are forms of adjectives or adverbs used to compare different things. With adjectives, you usually add **er** to the end to make a comparative. If the adjective ends in **y**, drop the **y** and add **ier**.

Examples:

Adjective	Comparative
tall	taller
easy	easier

With adverbs, you usually add **more** before the word to make a comparative.

Examples:

Adverb	Comparative
quickly	more quickly
softly	more softly

Directions: Using the given adjective or adverb, write a sentence comparing the two nouns.

Answers will vary.

Example: clean   my room   my sister's room
My room is always cleaner than my sister's room.

1. cold   Alaska   Florida
2. neatly   Maria   her brother
3. easy   English   math
4. scary   book   movie
5. loudly   the drummer   the guitarist
6. pretty   autumn   winter

Page 242

Good and Bad

When the adjectives **good** and **bad** are used to compare things, the entire word changes.

Examples:

	Comparative	Superlative
good	better	best
bad	worse	worst

Use the comparative form of an adjective to compare two people or objects. Use the superlative form to compare three or more people or objects.

Examples:
This is a **good** day.
Tomorrow will be **better** than today.
My birthday is the **best** day of the year.

This hamburger tastes **bad**.
Does it taste **worse** than the one your brother cooked?
It's the **worst** hamburger I have ever eaten.

Directions: Write the correct words in the blanks to complete these sentences.

worst	1. Our team just had its bad/worse/worst season ever.
bad	2. Not everything about our team was bad/worse/worst, though.
better	3. Our pitcher was good/better/best than last year.
best	4. Our catcher is the good/better/best in the league.
good	5. We had good/better/best uniforms, like we do every year.
better	6. I think we just needed good/better/best fielders.
better	7. Next season we'll do good/better/best than this one.
worse	8. We can't do bad/worse/worst than we did this year.
bad	9. I guess everyone has one bad/worse/worst year.
better	10. Now that ours is over, we'll get good/better/best.

Page 243

Demonstrative and Indefinite Adjectives

A **demonstrative adjective** identifies a particular person, place, or thing. **This**, **these**, **that**, and **those** are demonstrative adjectives.

Examples:
this pen   **these** earrings
that chair   **those** books

An **indefinite adjective** does not identify a particular person, place, or thing, but rather a group or number. **All**, **any**, **both**, **many**, **another**, **several**, **such**, **some**, **few**, and **more** are indefinite adjectives.

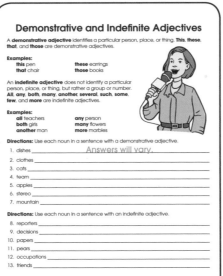

Examples:
all teachers   **any** person
both girls   **many** flowers
another man   **more** marbles

Directions: Use each noun in a sentence with a demonstrative adjective.

1. dishes _____ Answers will vary. _____
2. clothes _____
3. cats _____
4. team _____
5. apples _____
6. stereo _____
7. mountain _____

Directions: Use each noun in a sentence with an indefinite adjective.

8. reporters _____
9. decisions _____
10. papers _____
11. pears _____
12. occupations _____
13. friends _____

Page 244

Interrogative and Possessive Adjectives

An **interrogative adjective** is used when asking a question. The interrogative adjectives are **what** and **which**.

Examples:
What kind of haircut will you get?
Which dog snarled at you?

A **possessive adjective** shows ownership. The possessive adjectives are **our**, **your**, **her**, **his**, **its**, **my**, and **their**.

Examples:
That is **my** dog.
He washed **his** jeans.
Our pictures turned out great.

Directions: Write six sentences containing interrogative adjectives and six sentences containing possessive adjectives.

Interrogative Adjectives

1. _____ Answers will vary. _____
2. _____
3. _____
4. _____
5. _____
6. _____

Possessive Adjectives

1. _____
2. _____
3. _____
4. _____
5. _____
6. _____

Page 245

Prepositional Phrases as Adjectives

An adjective can be one word or an entire prepositional phrase.

Examples:
The **new** boy **with** red hair
The **tall** man **in** the raincoat
The **white** house **with** green shutters

Directions: Underline the prepositional phrases used as adjectives.

1. The boy in the blue cap is the captain.
2. The house across the street is 100 years old.
3. Jo and Ty love muffins with nuts.
4. I lost the book with the green cover.
5. Do you know the girl in the front row?
6. I like the pony with the long tail.
7. The dog in that yard is not friendly.
8. The picture in this magazine looks like you.

Directions: Complete these sentences with prepositional phrases used as adjectives.

9. I'd like a sandwich _____ Answers will vary. _____
10. Did you read the book _____?
11. The dog _____ is my favorite.
12. The woman _____ is calling you.
13. I bought a shirt _____
14. I'm wearing socks _____
15. I found a box _____

Page 246

Adverbs

Adverbs modify verbs. Adverbs tell **when**, **where**, or **how**. Many, but not all adverbs, end in **ly**.

Adverbs of time answer the questions **how often** or **when**.

Examples:
The dog escapes its pen **frequently**.
Smart travelers **eventually** will learn to use travelers' checks.

Adverbs of place answer the question **where**.

Example: The police pushed bystanders **away** from the accident scene.

Adverbs of manner answer the questions **how** or **in what manner**.

Example: He **carefully** replaced the delicate vase.

Directions: Underline the verb in each sentence. Circle the adverb. Write the question each adverb answers on the line.

1. My grandmother walks gingerly to avoid falls.
   how
2. The mice darted everywhere to escape the cat.
   where
3. He decisively moved the chess piece.
   how
4. Our family frequently enjoys a night at the movies.
   when/how often
5. Later we will discuss the consequences of your behavior.
   when
6. The audience glanced up at the balcony where the noise originated.
   where
7. The bleachers are already built for the concert.
   when
8. My friend and I study daily for the upcoming exams.
   how often/when

Page 247

Adverbs

Like adjectives, adverbs have types of comparison. They are positive, comparative, and superlative.

Examples:

Positive	Comparative	Superlative
expertly	more expertly	most expertly
soon	sooner	soonest

Directions: Underline the adverb in each sentence. Then, write the type of comparison on the line.

1. The car easily won the race. positive
2. Our class most eagerly awaited the return of our test. superlative
3. My ice cream melted more quickly than yours. comparative
4. Frances awoke early on the first day of school. positive
5. He knows well the punishment for disobeying his parents. positive
6. There is more work to be done on the stadium project. positive
7. The child played most happily with the building blocks. superlative
8. This article appeared more recently than the other. comparative

Directions: Write the comparative and superlative forms of these adverbs.

Positive	Comparative	Superlative
9. hard	harder	hardest
10. impatiently	more impatiently	most impatiently
11. anxiously	more anxiously	most anxiously
12. suddenly	more suddenly	most suddenly
13. far	farther	farthest
14. long	longer	longest

Page 248

Comprehensive Curriculum - **Grade 5**

Prepositional Phrases as Adverbs

An adverb can be one word or an entire prepositional phrase.

Examples:
They'll be here **tomorrow**.
They always come **on time**.
Move it **down**.
Put it **under the picture**.
Drive **carefully**.
He drove **with care**.

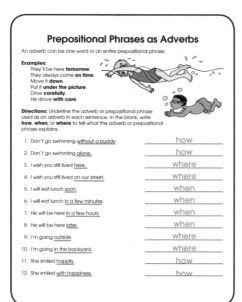

Directions: Underline the adverb or prepositional phrase used as an adverb in each sentence. In the blank, write **how**, **when**, or **where** to tell what the adverb or prepositional phrase explains.

1. Don't go swimming <u>without a buddy</u>. — how
2. Don't go swimming <u>alone</u>. — how
3. I wish you still lived <u>here</u>. — where
4. I wish you still lived <u>on our street</u>. — where
5. I will eat lunch <u>soon</u>. — when
6. I will eat lunch <u>in a few minutes</u>. — when
7. He will be here <u>in a few hours</u>. — when
8. He will be here <u>later</u>. — when
9. I'm going <u>outside</u>. — where
10. I'm going <u>in the backyard</u>. — where
11. She smiled <u>happily</u>. — how
12. She smiled <u>with happiness</u>. — how

Page 249

Writing: Adjectives and Adverbs

An **adjective** is a describing word. It describes nouns. Adjectives can tell:
• Which one or what kind — the dog's **floppy** ears, the **lost** child
• How many — **three** wagons, **four** drawers

An **adverb** is also a describing word. It describes verbs, adjectives, or other adverbs. Adverbs can tell:
• How — ran **quickly**, talked **quietly**
• When — finished **promptly**, came **yesterday**
• Where — lived **there**, drove **backward**
• How often — sneezed **twice**, **always** wins

Directions: The adjectives and adverbs are bold in the sentences below. Above each, write **ADJ** for adjective or **ADV** for adverb. Then, draw an arrow to the noun the adjective describes or to the verb the adverb describes.

Example: A girl in a **green** jacket **quickly** released the birds into the sky.

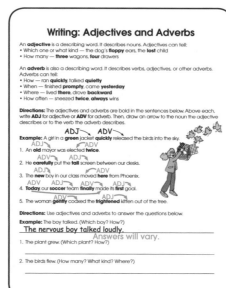

1. An **old** mayor was elected **twice**. (ADJ, ADV)
2. He **carefully** put the **tall** screen between our desks. (ADV, ADJ)
3. The **new** boy in our class moved **here** from Phoenix. (ADJ, ADV)
4. **Today**, our soccer team **finally** made its **first** goal. (ADV, ADV, ADJ)
5. The woman **gently** coaxed the **frightened** kitten out of the tree. (ADV, ADJ)

Directions: Use adjectives and adverbs to answer the questions below.

Example: The boy talked. (Which boy? How?)
The nervous boy talked loudly.

Answers will vary.

1. The plant grew. (Which plant? How?)

2. The birds flew. (How many? What kind? Where?)

Page 250

Writing: Adjectives and Adverbs

Adjectives and adverbs make sentences more interesting. Often, we can make adverbs from adjectives by adding **ly** to the end.

Examples:	**Adjectives**	**Adverbs**
	quick	quickly
	brief	briefly

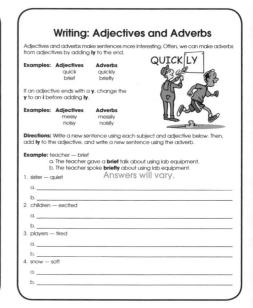

If an adjective ends with a **y**, change the **y** to an **i** before adding **ly**.

Examples:	**Adjectives**	**Adverbs**
	messy	messily
	noisy	noisily

Directions: Write a new sentence using each subject and adjective below. Then, add **ly** to the adjective, and write a new sentence using the adverb.

Example: teacher — brief
a. The teacher gave a **brief** talk about using lab equipment.
b. The teacher spoke **briefly** about using lab equipment.

Answers will vary.

1. sister — quiet
   a. _____
   b. _____
2. children — excited
   a. _____
   b. _____
3. players — tired
   a. _____
   b. _____
4. snow — soft
   a. _____
   b. _____

Page 251

Placement of Adjective and Adverb Phrases

Adjectives and adverbs, including prepositional phrases, should be placed as close as possible to the words they describe to avoid confusion.

Example:
Confusing: The boy under the pile of leaves looked for the ball.
(Is the boy or the ball under the pile of leaves?)
Clear: The boy looked under the pile of leaves for the ball.

Directions: Rewrite each sentence by moving the prepositional phrase closer to the word or words it describes. The first one has been done for you.

1. A bird at the pet store bit me in the mall.
   A bird in the mall bit me.
2. The woman was looking for her dog in the large hat.
   The woman in the large hat was looking for her dog.
3. This yard would be great for a dog with a fence.
   This yard with a fence would be great for a dog.
4. The car hit the stop sign with the silver stripe.
   The car with the silver stripe hit the stop sign.
5. My cousin with a big bow gave me a present.
   My cousin gave me a present with a big bow.
6. The house was near some woods with a pond.
   The house with a pond was near some woods.
7. I'll be back to wash the dishes in a minute.
   I'll be back in a minute to wash the dishes.
8. We like to eat eggs in the morning with toast.
   We like to eat eggs with toast in the morning.
9. He bought a shirt at the new store with short sleeves.
   He bought a shirt with short sleeves at the new store.
10. We live in the house down the street with tall windows.
   We live in the house with tall windows down the street.

Page 252

Writing: Parts of Speech Story

Directions: Play the following game with a partner. In the story below, some of the words are missing. Without letting your partner see the story, ask him or her to provide a word for each blank. Each word should be a noun, verb, adjective, or adverb, as shown. Then, read the story aloud. It might not make sense, but it will make you laugh!

Answers will vary.

Last night, as I was _____ (verb + ing) through the _____ (noun), a _____ (adjective) _____ (noun) fell from the ceiling and landed on my head! "Yikes!" I shrieked. I _____ (past-tense verb) _____ (adverb) through the _____ (noun), trying to get rid of the thing. Finally, it fell off, and it started _____ (verb + ing) around the _____ (noun). I tried to hit it with a _____ (noun), but it was too _____ (adjective). I _____ (adverb) managed to _____ (verb) it out of the house, where it quickly climbed the nearest _____ (noun).

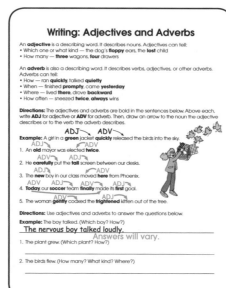

Page 253

Writing: Parts of Speech

Directions: Write each word from the box in the column that names its part of speech. Some words can be listed in two columns.

Example: Smile for the the camera. (VERB) Hanna has a nice **smile**. (NOUN)

code	young	slowly	today	finally	screen
thirsty	praise	loan	broken	decrease	slowly
nearby	twenty	Monday	town	faithful	red
coax	goal	bathe	release	cheat	there

Noun	Verb	Adjective	Adverb
code	coax	thirsty	nearby
goal	praise	young	slowly
loan	cheat	twenty	finally
Monday	bathe	broken	today
screen	release	faithful	anxiously
town	decrease	red	there

Directions: Write four sentences, using at least three words from the box in each one. Mark each word as a noun (**N**), verb (**V**), adjective (**ADJ**), or adverb (**ADV**).

Example: Twenty people **slowly** walked through the **town**. (ADJ, ADV, N)

Answers will vary.

Page 254

Conjunctions

A **conjunction** joins words or groups of words in a sentence. The most commonly used conjunctions are **and**, **but**, and **or**.

Examples: My brother **and** I both want to win the trophy.
Tonight, it will rain **or** sleet.
I wanted to go to the party, **but** I got sick.

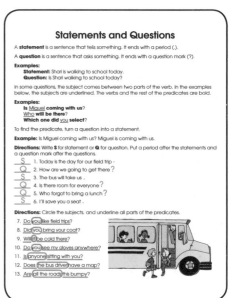

Directions: Circle the conjunctions.

1. Dolphins (and) whales are mammals.
2. They must rise to the surface of the water to breathe (or) they will die.
3. Dolphins resemble fish (but) they are not fish.
4. Sightseeing boats are often entertained by groups of dolphins (or) whales.
5. Whales appear to effortlessly leap out of the water (and) execute flips.
6. Both whale (and) dolphin babies are born alive.
7. The babies are called calves (and) are born in the water (but) they must breathe air within a few minutes of birth.
8. Sometimes an entire pod of whales will help a mother (and) calf reach the surface to breathe.
9. Scientists (and) marine biologists have long been intrigued by these ocean animals.
10. Whales (and) dolphins do not seem to be afraid of humans (or) boats.

Directions: Write six sentences using conjunctions.

11. _____ Answers will vary. _____
12. _____
13. _____
14. _____
15. _____
16. _____

Page 255

Writing: Conjunctions

Too many short sentences make writing seem choppy. Short sentences can be combined to make writing flow better. Words used to combine sentences are called **conjunctions**.

Examples: but, before, after, because, when, or, so, and

Directions: Use **or**, **but**, **before**, **after**, **because**, **when**, **and**, or **so** to combine each pair of sentences. The first one has been done for you.

Possible answers:

1. I was wearing my winter coat. I started to shiver.
   I was wearing my winter coat, but I started to shiver.
2. Animals all need water. They may perish without it.
   Because animals all need water, they may perish without it.
3. The sun came out. The ice began to thaw.
   Because animals all need water, they may perish without it.
4. The sun came out. The day was still chilly.
   The sun came out, but the day was still chilly.
5. Will the flowers perish? Will they thrive?
   Will the flowers perish, or will they thrive?
6. The bear came closer. We began to feel threatened.
   When the bear came closer, we began to feel threatened.
7. Winning was a challenge. Our team didn't have much experience.
   Winning was a challenge because our team didn't have much experience.
8. Winning was a challenge. Our team was up to it.
   Winning was a challenge, but our team was up to it.

Directions: Write three sentences of your own. Use a conjunction in each sentence.
Answers will vary.
_____
_____

Page 256

Statements and Questions

A **statement** is a sentence that tells something. It ends with a period (.).

A **question** is a sentence that asks something. It ends with a question mark (?).

Examples:
Statement: Shari is walking to school today.
Question: Is Shari walking to school today?

In some questions, the subject comes between two parts of the verb. In the examples below, the subjects are underlined. The verbs and the rest of the predicates are bold.

Examples:
Is Miguel **coming with us**?
Who **will be there**?
Which one did you **select**?

To find the predicate, turn a question into a statement.

Example: Is Miguel coming with us? Miguel is coming with us.

Directions: Write **S** for statement or **Q** for question. Put a period after the statements and a question mark after the questions.

__S__ 1. Today is the day for our field trip .
__Q__ 2. How are we going to get there ?
__S__ 3. The bus will take us .
__Q__ 4. Is there room for everyone ?
__Q__ 5. Who forgot to bring a lunch ?
__S__ 6. I'll save you a seat .

Directions: Circle the subjects. and underline all parts of the predicates.

7. Do you like field trips?
8. Did you bring your coat?
9. Will it be cold there?
10. Do you see my gloves anywhere?
11. Is anyone sitting with you?
12. Does the bus driver have a map?
13. Are all the roads this bumpy?

Page 257

Statements and Questions

Directions: Write 10 statements and 10 questions.

Statements

1. _____ Answers will vary. _____
2. _____
3. _____
4. _____
5. _____
6. _____
7. _____
8. _____
9. _____
10. _____

Questions

1. _____
2. _____
3. _____
4. _____
5. _____
6. _____
7. _____
8. _____
9. _____
10. _____

Page 258

Commands, Requests, and Exclamations

A **command** is a sentence that orders someone to do something. It ends with a period or an exclamation mark (!).

A **request** is a sentence that asks someone to do something. It ends with a period or a question mark (?).

An **exclamation** is a sentence that shows strong feeling. It ends with an exclamation mark (!).

Examples:
Command: Stay in your seat.
Request: Would you please pass the salt?
Please pass the salt.
Exclamation: Call the police!

In the first and last two sentences in the examples, the subject is not stated. The subject is understood to be **you**.

Directions: Write **C** if the sentence is a command, **R** if it is a request, and **E** if it is an exclamation. Put the correct punctuation at the end of each sentence.

__C__ 1. Look both ways before you cross the street .
__R__ 2. Please go to the store and buy some bread for us .
__E__ 3. The house is on fire !
__R__ 4. Would you hand me the glue ?
__C__ 5. Don't step there .
__C__ 6. Write your name at the top of the page .
__R__ 7. Please close the door .
__R__ 8. Would you answer the phone ?
__E__ 9. Watch out !
__C__ 10. Take one card from each pile .

Page 259

Commands, Requests, and Exclamations

Directions: Write six sentences for each type listed.

Command

1. _____ Answers will vary. _____
2. _____
3. _____
4. _____
5. _____
6. _____

Request

1. _____ Answers will vary. _____
2. _____
3. _____
4. _____
5. _____
6. _____

Exclamation

1. _____ Answers will vary. _____
2. _____
3. _____
4. _____
5. _____
6. _____

Page 260

Comprehensive Curriculum - **Grade 5**

Writing: Four Kinds of Sentences

There are four kinds of sentences used in writing. Different punctuation is used for different kinds of sentences.

A **statement** tells something. A period is used after statements.

Examples: I jogged five miles yesterday.
We are going to have a spelling test on Friday.

A **question** asks something. A question mark is used after questions.

Examples: What are you wearing to the dance?
Will it ever stop raining?

An **exclamation** shows strong feeling or excitement. An exclamation mark is used after exclamations.

Examples: Boy, am I tired!
What a beautiful painting!

A **command** tells someone to do something. A period or an exclamation mark is used after a command, depending on how strong it is.

Examples: Please hand me that pen. Don't touch the stove!

Directions: Write the correct punctuation mark at the end of each sentence below. Then, write whether the sentence is a statement, question, exclamation, or command.

Example: I didn't have time to finish my homework last night. __statement__

1. Why didn't she come shopping with us __?__ ___question___
2. Somebody call an ambulance __!__ ___exclamation___
3. He's been watching TV all morning __.__ ___statement___
4. How did you do on the quiz __?__ ___question___
5. Go sit in the third row __.__ ___command___
6. I have to go to the dentist tomorrow __.__ ___statement___
7. I've never been so hungry __!__ ___exclamation___
8. Who tracked mud all over the house __?__ ___question___
9. That restaurant is too expensive __.__ ___statement___

Page 261

Compound Subjects/Compound Predicates

A **compound subject** has two or more nouns or pronouns joined by a conjunction. Compound subjects share the same predicate.

Examples:
Suki and Spot walked to the park in the rain.
Cars, buses, and **trucks** splashed water on them.
He and I were glad we had our umbrella.

A **compound predicate** has two or more verbs joined by a conjunction. Compound predicates share the same subject.

Examples:
Suki **went** in the restroom **and wiped** off her shoes.
Chloe **followed** Suki **and waited** for her.

A sentence can have a compound subject and a compound predicate.

Example: Amelia and Maria went to the mall **and shopped** for an hour.

Directions: Circle the compound subjects. Underline the compound predicates.

1. Luke and Kanye went to the store and bought some gum.
2. Police and firefighters worked together and put out the fire.
3. Makayla and Ellie did their homework and checked it twice.
4. In preschool the boys and girls drew pictures and colored them.

Directions: Write compound subjects to go with these predicates.

5. ____Answers will vary.____ ate peanut butter sandwiches.
6. _____ left early.
7. _____ don't make good pets.
8. _____ found their way home.
9. _____ are moving to Denver.

Directions: Write compound predicates to go with these subjects.

10. A scary book ____Answers will vary.____
11. My friend's sister _____
12. The shadow _____
13. The wind _____
14. The runaway car _____

Page 262

Combining Subjects

Too many short sentences make writing sound choppy. Often, we can combine sentences with different subjects and the same predicate to make one sentence with a compound subject.

Example:
Katrina tried out for the play. Austin tried out for the play.
Compound subject: Katrina and Austin tried out for the play.

When sentences have different subjects and different predicates, we cannot combine them this way. Each subject and predicate must stay together. Two short sentences can be combined with a conjunction.

Examples:
Katrina got a part in the play. Austin will help make scenery.
Katrina got a part in the play, and Austin will help make scenery.

Directions: If a pair of sentences share the same predicate, combine them with compound subjects. If the sentences have different subjects and predicates, combine them using **and**.

1. Rachel read a book about explorers. Eric read the same book about explorers.
   Rachel and Eric read a book about explorers.
2. Rachel really liked the book. Eric agreed with her.
   Rachel really liked the book, and Eric agreed with her.
3. Aiko went to the basketball game last night. Dan went to the basketball game, too.
   Aiko and Dan went to the basketball game last night.
4. Aiko lost her coat. Dan missed his ride home.
   Aiko lost her coat, and Dan missed his ride home.
5. My uncle planted corn in the garden. My mother planted corn in the garden.
   My uncle and my mother planted corn in the garden.
6. Isaac helped with the food drive last week. Amy helped with the food drive, too.
   Isaac and Amy helped with the food drive last week.

Page 263

Combining Predicates

If short sentences have the same subject and different predicates, we can combine them into one sentence with a compound predicate.

Example:
Andy got up late this morning.
He nearly missed the school bus.
Compound predicate: Andy got up late this morning and nearly missed the school bus.

The pronoun **he** takes the place of Andy in the second sentence, so the subjects are the same and can be combined.

When two sentences have different subjects and different predicates, we cannot combine them this way. Two short sentences can be combined with a conjunction.

Examples:
Andy got up late this morning. Pilar woke up early.
Andy got up late this morning, but Pilar woke up early.

Directions: If the pair of sentences share the same subject, combine them with compound predicates. If the sentences have different subjects and predicates, combine them using **and** or **but**.

1. Kyle practiced pitching all winter. Kyle became the pitcher for his team.
   Kyle practiced pitching all winter and became the pitcher for his team.
2. Kisha studied for her history test for two hours. Angela watched TV.
   Kisha studied for her history test for two hours, but Angela watched TV.
3. Ethan had an earache. He took medicine four times a day.
   Ethan had an earache and took medicine four times a day.
4. Nikki found a new hairstyle. Lily didn't like that style.
   Nikki found a new hairstyle, but Lily didn't like that style.
5. Kirby buys his lunch every day. Sean brings his lunch from home.
   Kirby buys his lunch every day, and Sean brings his lunch from home.

Page 264

Writing: Using Commas Correctly

A **comma** tells a reader where to pause when reading a sentence. Use commas when combining two or more complete sentences with a joining word.

Examples: We raked the leaves, and **we put them into bags.**
Brian dressed quickly, but **he still missed the school bus.**

Do not use commas if you are not combining complete sentences.

Examples: We raked the leaves and put them into bags.
Brian dressed quickly but still missed the school bus.

If either part of the sentence does not have both a subject and a verb, do not use a comma.

Directions: Read each sentence below, and decide whether or not it needs a comma. If it does, rewrite the sentence, placing the comma correctly. If it doesn't, write **OK** on the line.

1. The cat stretched lazily and walked out of the room.
   OK
2. I could use the money to buy a new shirt or I could go to the movies.
   I could use the money to buy a new shirt, or I could go to the movies.
3. My sister likes pizza but she doesn't like spaghetti.
   My sister likes pizza, but she doesn't like spaghetti.
4. Mom mixed the batter and poured it into the pan.
   OK
5. The teacher passed out the tests and she told us to write our names on them.
   The teacher passed out the tests, and she told us to write our names on them.
6. The car squealed its tires and took off out of the parking lot.
   OK
7. The snow fell heavily and we knew the schools would be closed the next day.
   The snow fell heavily, and we knew the schools would be closed the next day.
8. The batter hit the ball and it flew over the fence.
   The batter hit the ball, and it flew over the fence.

Page 265

Run-On Sentences

A **run-on sentence** occurs when two or more sentences are joined together without the correct punctuation. A run-on sentence must be divided into two or more separate sentences.

Example:
Run-on: On Tuesday my family went to the amusement park but unfortunately it rained and it took hours for our clothes to dry.
Correct: On Tuesday, my family went to the amusement park. Unfortunately, it rained and we got wet. It took hours for our clothes to dry.

Directions: Rewrite these run-on sentences correctly.

1. I have a dog named Boxer and a cat named Phoebe and they are both well-behaved and friendly.
   I have a dog named Boxer and a cat named Phoebe. They are both well-behaved and friendly.
2. Jacob's basketball coach makes the team run for 20 minutes each practice and then he makes them play a full game and afterwards he makes them do 50 push-ups and 100 sit-ups.
   Jacob's basketball coach makes the team run for 20 minutes each practice, and then he makes them play a full game. Afterwards, he makes them do 50 push-ups and 100 sit-ups.
3. My family members each enjoy different hobbies Mom likes to paint Dad likes to read I like to play sports and my younger sister likes to build model airplanes although I think they are too hard.
   My family members each enjoy different hobbies. Mom likes to paint, Dad likes to read, and I like to play sports. My younger sister likes to build model airplanes, although I think they are too hard.

Page 266

Commas

Commas are used to separate items in a series.

Example:
The fruit bowl contains oranges, peaches, pears, and apples.

Commas are also used to separate geographical names and dates.

Examples:
Today's date is January 13, 2015.
My grandfather lives in Tallahassee, Florida.
I would like to visit Paris, France.

Directions: Place commas where needed in these sentences.

1. I was born on September 21, 2006.
2. Mateo's favorite sports include basketball, football, hockey, and soccer.
3. The ship will sail on November 16, 2016.
4. My family and I vacationed in Salt Lake City, Utah.
5. I like to plant beans, beets, corn, and radishes in my garden.
6. Xander's party will be held in Youngstown, Ohio.
7. Periods, commas, colons, and exclamation marks are types of punctuation.
8. Cardinals, juncos, blue jays, finches, and sparrows frequent our birdfeeder.
9. My grandfather graduated from high school on June 4, 1962.
10. The race will take place in Burlington, Vermont.

Directions: Write a sentence using commas to separate words in a series.

11. _____ Answers will vary. _____

Directions: Write a sentence using commas to separate geographical names.

12. _____

Directions: Write a sentence using commas to separate dates.

13. _____

Page 267

Commas

Commas are used to separate a noun or pronoun in a direct address from the rest of the sentence. A noun or pronoun in a **direct address** is one that names or refers to the person addressed.

Examples:
John, this room is a mess!
This room, **John,** is a disgrace!
Your room needs to be more organized, **John.**

Commas are used to separate an appositive from the rest of the sentence. An **appositive** is a word or words that give the reader more information about a previous noun or pronoun.

Examples:
My teacher, **Ms. Wright**, gave us a test.
Thomas Edison, **the inventor of the lightbulb**, was an interesting man.

Directions: Place commas where needed in these sentences. Then, write **appositive** or **direct address** on the line to explain why the commas were used.

1. Li, do you know the answer? **direct address**
2. Jackson, the local football hero, led the parade through town. **appositive**
3. Cancun, a Mexican city, is a favorite vacation destination. **appositive**
4. Please help me move the chair, Isobel. **direct address**
5. My great-grandfather, an octogenarian, has witnessed many events. **appositive**
6. The president of the company, Madison Fagan, addressed his workers. **appositive**
7. My favorite book, Anne of Green Gables, is a joy to read. **appositive**
8. Your painting, Andre, shows great talent. **direct address**

Page 268

Combining Sentences

When the subjects are the same, sentences can be combined by using appositives.

Examples:
Tony likes to play basketball. Tony is my neighbor.
Tony, **my neighbor,** likes to play basketball.

Ms. Herman was sick today. Ms. Herman is our math teacher.
Ms. Herman, **our math teacher,** was sick today.

Appositives are set off from the rest of the sentence with commas.

Directions: Use commas and appositives to combine the pairs of sentences.

1. Julie has play practice today. Julie is my sister.
   Julie, my sister, has play practice today.
2. Greg fixed my bicycle. Greg is my cousin.
   Greg, my cousin, fixed my bicycle.
3. Mr. Cruz told us where to meet. Mr. Cruz is our coach.
   Mr. Cruz, our coach, told us where to meet.
4. Tiffany is moving to Detroit. Tiffany is my neighbor.
   Tiffany, my neighbor, will be moving to Detroit.
5. Kyle has the flu. Kyle is my brother.
   Kyle, my brother, has the flu.
6. My favorite football team is playing tonight. Houston is my favorite team.
   My favorite football team, Houston, is playing tonight.
7. Bonnie Pryor will be at our school next week. Bonnie Pryor is a famous author.
   Bonnie Pryor, a famous author, will be at our school next week.
8. Our neighborhood is having a garage sale. Our neighborhood is the North End.
   Our neighborhood, the North End, is having a garage sale.

Page 269

Combining Sentences

Directions: Combine these sentences. Some of them can be combined using commas and appositives. Some can be combined using compound subjects or predicates. Others can be combined using conjunctions.

1. Alana enjoyed playing on the beach. Ty did not like the sand.
   Alana enjoyed playing on the beach, but Ty did not like the sand.
2. Jelani studied hard for the math test. Kim studied hard for the math test.
   Jelani and Kim studied hard for the math test.
3. Ryan got sick. Ryan had to visit his family doctor.
   Ryan got sick and had to visit his family doctor.
4. Jeni is my study partner. Jeni is always running late for class.
   Jeni, my study partner, is always running late for class.
5. Drake scored the game-winning touchdown. Drake is the team's star quarterback.
   Drake, the team's star quarterback, scored the game-winning touchdown.
6. We were ready to leave. The car wouldn't start.
   We were ready to leave, but the car wouldn't start.
7. Vanessa ran outside. Vanessa rode her bicycle to the park.
   Vanessa ran outside and rode her bicycle to the park.
8. The fierce wind ruined our family picnic. The pouring rain ruined our family picnic.
   The fierce wind and pouring rain ruined our family picnic.
9. Mrs. Raposa handed me a new book about dinosaurs. Mrs. Raposa is the school librarian.
   Mrs. Raposa, the school librarian, handed me a new book about dinosaurs.
10. School was out for the summer. Amira was ready for new adventures.
    School was out for the summer, and Amira was ready for new adventures.

Page 270

Punctuation

Directions: Add commas where needed.
Put the correct punctuation at the end of each sentence.

1. My friend, Jamie, loves to snowboard.
2. Winter sports, such as hockey, skiing, and skating are fun.
3. Oh, what a lovely view!
4. The map shows the continents of Asia, Africa, Australia, and Antarctica.
5. My mother, a ballet dancer, will perform tonight.
6. What will you do tomorrow?
7. When will the plane arrive at the airport?
8. Jason, do you know what time it is?
9. Friends of ours, the Watsons, are coming for dinner.
10. Margo, look out for that falling rock!
11. The young child sat reading a book.
12. Who wrote this letter?
13. My sister, Jill, is very neat.
14. The trampoline is in our backyard.
15. We will have chicken, peas, rice, and salad for dinner.
16. That dog, a Saint Bernard, looks dangerous.

Page 271

Quotation Marks

When a person's exact words are used in a sentence, **quotation marks** (" ") are used to identify those words. Commas are used to set off the quotation from the rest of the sentence. End punctuation is placed inside the final quotation mark.

Examples:
"When are we leaving?**"** Joe asked.
Jada shouted, **"**Go, team!**"**

When a sentence is interrupted by words that are not part of the quotation (he said, she answered, etc.), they are not included in the quotation marks. Note how commas are used in the next example.

Example: "I am sorry,**"** the man announced,
"for my rude behavior.**"**

Directions: Place quotation marks, commas, and other punctuation where needed in the sentences below.

1. "Watch out!" yelled Dad.
2. Angela said, "I don't know how you can eat Brussels sprouts, Ted."
3. "Put on your coats," said Morri, "We'll be leaving in 10 minutes."
4. "Did you hear the assignment?" asked Salima.
5. Dominic shouted, "This game is driving me up the wall!"
6. After examining our dog, the veterinarian said, "He looks healthy and strong."
7. The toddlers both wailed, "We want a snack!"
8. The judge announced to the swimmers, "Take your places."
9. Upon receiving the award, the actor said, "I'd like to thank my friends and family!"
10. "These are my favorite granola bars," said Becca.
11. "This test is too hard," moaned the class.
12. When their relay team came in first place, the runners shouted, "Hooray!"
13. "Where shall we go on vacation this year?" Dad asked.
14. As we walked past the machinery, the noise was deafening. "Cover your ears!" said Mom.
15. "Fire!" yelled the chef as his pan ignited.
16. "I love basketball," my little brother stated.

Page 272

Page 273

Capitalization/Punctuation

Directions: Rewrite the paragraphs below, adding punctuation where it is needed. Capitalize the first word of each sentence and all other words that should be capitalized.

my mom is a geologist so she has the opportunity to travel often for work last year she visited england scotland and ireland dad says that he hopes the whole family can come when she goes to the netherlands next year would you like to have a job where you travel or are you a homebody

My mom is a geologist, so she has the opportunity to travel often for work. Last year, she visited England, Scotland, and Ireland. Dad says that he hopes the whole family can come when she goes to the Netherlands next year. Would you like to have a job where you travel, or are you a homebody?

my cousin jeff is starting college this fall he wants to be a medical doctor so he's going to central university the mayor of our town went there mayor stevens told jeff all about the university our town is so small that everyone knows what everyone else is doing is your town like that

My cousin, Jeff, is starting college this fall. He wants to be a medical doctor, so he's going to Central University. The mayor of our town went there. Mayor Stevens told Jeff all about the university. Our town is so small that everyone knows what everyone else is doing. Is your town like that?

my grandparents took a long vacation last year grandma really likes to go to the atlantic ocean and watch the dolphins my grandfather likes to fish in the ocean my aunt went with them last summer they all had a party on the fourth of july

My grandparents took a long vacation last year. Grandma really likes to go to the Atlantic ocean and watch the dolphins. My grandfather likes to fish in the ocean. My aunt went with them last summer. They all had a party on the Fourth of July.

Page 274

Capitalization

Directions: Write **C** if capital letters are used correctly or **X** if they are used incorrectly.

★★★Vote★★★
TOM JOHNSON
for Mayor

X   1. Who will win the election for Mayor in November?
C   2. Tom Johnson used to be a police officer.
X   3. He announced on monday that he wants to be mayor.
C   4. My father said he would vote for Tom.
C   5. Mom and my sister Mia haven't decided yet.
C   6. They will vote at our school.
X   7. Every Fall and Spring they put up voting booths there.
C   8. I hope the new mayor will do something about our river.
X   9. That River is full of chemicals.
C   10. I'm glad our water doesn't come from Raven River.
X   11. In late Summer, the river actually stinks.
X   12. Is every river in our State so dirty?
C   13. Scientists check the water every so often.
C   14. Some professors from the college even examined it.
X   15. That is getting to be a very educated River!

Directions: Write sentences that include:

16. A person's title that should be capitalized.

Answers will vary.

17. The name of a place that should be capitalized.

18. The name of a time (day, month, holiday) that should be capitalized.

Page 275

Who Clauses

A **clause** is a group of words with a subject and a verb. When the subject of two sentences is the same person or people, the sentences can sometimes be combined with a "who" clause.

Examples:
Layla likes animals. Layla feeds the squirrels.
Layla, **who likes animals**, feeds the squirrels.

A "who" clause is set off from the rest of the sentence with commas.

Directions: Combine the pairs of sentences using "who" clauses.

1. Teddy was late to school. Teddy was sorry later.
   Teddy, who was late to school, was sorry later.
2. Our principal is retiring. Our principal will be 65 this year.
   Our principal, who will be 65 this year, is retiring.
3. Michael won the contest. Michael will receive an award.
   Michael, who won the contest, will receive an award.
4. Aisha lives next door. Aisha has three cats.
   Aisha, who has three cats, lives next door.
5. Devon drew that picture. Devon takes art lessons.
   Devon, who takes art lessons, drew that picture.
6. Marta was elected class president. Marta gave a speech.
   Marta, who was elected class president, gave a speech.
7. Amy broke her arm. Amy has to wear a cast for six weeks.
   Amy, who broke her arm, has to wear a cast for six weeks.
8. Dr. Chandra fixed my tooth. He said it would feel better soon.
   Dr. Chandra, who fixed my tooth, said it would feel better soon.

Page 276

Which Clauses

When the subject of two sentences is the same thing or things, the sentences can sometimes be combined with a "which" clause.

Examples:
The guppy was first called "the millions fish." The guppy was later named after Reverend Robert Guppy in 1866.
The guppy, **which was first called "the millions fish,"** was later named after Reverend Robert Guppy in 1866.

A "which" clause is set off from the rest of the sentence with commas.

Directions: Combine the pairs of sentences using "which" clauses.

1. Guppies also used to be called rainbow fish. Guppies were brought to Germany in 1908.
   Guppies, which were brought to Germany in 1908, also used to be called rainbow fish.
2. The male guppy is about 1 inch long. The male is smaller than the female.
   The male guppy, which is about 1 inch long, is smaller than the female.
3. The guppies' colors range from red to violet. The colors are brighter in the males.
   The guppies' colors, which range from red to violet, are brighter in the males.
4. Baby guppies hatch from eggs inside the mothers' bodies. The babies are born alive.
   Baby guppies, which hatch from eggs inside the mothers' bodies, are born alive.
5. The young are usually born at night. The young are called "fry."
   The young, which are usually born at night, are called "fry."
6. Female guppies have from two to 50 fry at one time. Females sometimes try to eat their fry!
   Female guppies, which have from two to 50 fry at one time, sometimes try to eat their fry!
7. These fish have been studied by scientists. The fish actually like dirty water.
   These fish, which have been studied by scientists, actually like dirty water.
8. Wild guppies eat mosquito eggs. Wild guppies help control the mosquito population.
   Wild guppies, which eat mosquito eggs, help control the mosquito population.

Page 277

Who and Which Clauses

Directions: Combine the pairs of sentences using "who" or "which" clauses.

1. Bullfrogs are rarely found out of the water. They live near ponds and streams.
   Bullfrogs, which are rarely found out of the water, live near ponds and streams.
2. These frogs grow to be about 8 inches long. These frogs can jump 3 feet.
   These frogs, which grow to be about 8 inches long, can jump 3 feet.
3. Mark Twain was a famous writer. He wrote a story about a frog-jumping contest.
   Mark Twain, who was a famous writer, wrote a story about a frog-jumping contest.
4. This story took place in California. This story started an annual frog-jumping contest there.
   This story, which took place in California, started an annual frog-jumping contest there.
5. The contest has rules and judges. The contest allows each frog to make three leaps.
   The contest, which has rules and judges, allows each frog to make three leaps.
6. The judges watch carefully. They measure each frog's leap.
   The judges, who watch carefully, measure each frog's leap.
7. Bullfrogs eat many insects. Bullfrogs also eat small snakes.
   Bullfrogs, which eat many insects, also eat small snakes.
8. Scientists study what frogs eat. Scientists know bullfrogs can catch birds.
   Scientists, who study what frogs eat, know bullfrogs can catch birds.

Page 278

That Clauses

When the subject of two sentences is the same thing or things, the sentences can sometimes be combined with a "that" clause. Use **that** instead of **which** when the clause is very important in the sentence.

Examples:
The store is near our house. The store was closed.
The store **that is near our house** was closed.

The words **that is near our house** are very important in the combined sentence. They tell the reader which store was closed. A "that" clause is not set off from the rest of the sentence with commas.

Examples:
Pete's store is near our house. Pete's store was closed.
Pete's store, which is near our house, was closed.

The words **which is near our house** are not important to the meaning of the combined sentence. The words **Pete's store** already told us which store was closed.

Directions: Combine the pairs of sentences using "that" clauses.

1. The dog lives next door. The dog chased me.
   The dog that lives next door chased me.
2. The bus was taking us to the game. The bus had a flat tire.
   The bus that was taking us to the game had a flat tire.
3. The fence is around the school. The fence is painted yellow.
   The fence that is around the school is painted yellow.
4. The notebook had my homework in it. The notebook is lost.
   The notebook that had my homework in it is lost.
5. A letter came today. The letter was from Mary.
   A letter that came today was from Mary.
6. The lamp was fixed yesterday. The lamp doesn't work today.
   The lamp that was fixed yesterday doesn't work today.
7. The lake is by our cabin. The lake is filled with fish.
   The lake that is by our cabin is filled with fish.

That and Which Clauses

Directions: Combine the pairs of sentences using either a "that" or a "which" clause.

1. The TV show was on at 8:00 last night. The TV show was funny.

   The TV show that was on at 8:00 last night was funny.

2. The Snappy Show was on at 8:00 last night. The Snappy Show was funny.

   The Snappy Show, which was on at 8:00 last night, was funny.

3. The Main Bank is on the corner. The Main Bank is closed today.

   The Main Bank, which is on the corner, is closed today.

4. The bank is on the corner. The bank is closed today.

   The bank that is on the corner is closed today.

5. The bus takes Dad to work. The bus broke down.

   The bus that takes Dad to work broke down.

6. The Broad Street bus takes Dad to work. The Broad Street bus broke down.

   The Broad Street bus, which takes Dad to work, broke down.

Page 279

Combining Sentences

Not every pair of sentences can be combined with "who," "which," or "that" clauses. These sentences can be combined in other ways, either with a conjunction or by renaming the subject.

Examples:
Tim couldn't go to sleep. Todd was sleeping soundly.
Tim couldn't go to sleep, **but** Todd was sleeping soundly.

The zoo keeper fed the baby ape. A crowd gathered to watch.
When the zoo keeper fed the baby ape, a crowd gathered to watch.

Directions: Combine each pair of sentences using "who," "which," or "that" clauses, by using a conjunction, or by renaming the subject.

1. The box slipped off the truck. The box was filled with bottles.

   The box that slipped off the truck was filled with bottles.

2. Carolyn is our scout leader. Carolyn taught us a new game.

   Carolyn, who is our scout leader, taught us a new game.

3. The girl is 8 years old. The girl called the emergency number when her grandmother fell.

   The girl, who is 8 years old, called the emergency number when her grandmother fell.

4. The meatloaf is ready to eat. The salad isn't made yet.

   The meatloaf is ready to eat, but the salad isn't made yet.

5. The rain poured down. The rain canceled our picnic.

   The rain poured down and canceled our picnic.

6. The sixth-grade class went on a field trip. The school was much quieter.

   When the sixth-grade class went on a field trip, the school was much quieter.

Page 280

Who's and Whose

Who's is a contraction for **who is.**

Whose is a possessive pronoun.

Examples:
Who's going to come?
Whose shirt is this?

To know which word to use, substitute the words "who is." If the sentence makes sense, use **who's.**

Directions: Write the correct words to complete these sentences.

who's 1. Do you know who's/whose invited to the party?

whose 2. I don't even know who's/whose house it will be at.

Whose 3. Who's/Whose towel is on the floor?

Who's 4. Who's/Whose going to drive us?

Whose 5. Who's/Whose ice cream is melting?

whose 6. I'm the person who's/whose gloves are lost.

Who's 7. Who's/Whose in your group?

Whose 8. Who's/Whose group is first?

who's 9. Can you tell who's/whose at the door?

Whose 10. Who's/Whose friend are you?

Who's 11. Who's/Whose cooking tonight?

Whose 12. Who's/Whose cooking do you like best?

Page 281

Their, There, and They're

Their is a possessive pronoun meaning "belonging to them."

There is an adverb that indicates place.

They're is a contraction for **they are.**

Examples:
Raj and Kai took **their** dog to the park.
They like to go **there** on Sunday afternoon.
They're probably going back next Sunday, too.

Directions: Write the correct words to complete these sentences.

their 1. All the students should bring their/there/they're books to class.

there 2. I've never been to France, but I hope to travel their/there/they're someday.

their 3. We studied how dolphins care for their/there/they're young.

they're 4. My parents are going on vacation next week, and their/there/they're taking my sister.

There 5. Their/There/They're was a lot of food at the party.

their 6. My favorite baseball team lost their/there/they're star pitcher this year.

they're 7. Those peaches look good, but their/there/they're not ripe yet.

there 8. The book is right their/there/they're on the table.

Page 282

Teach and Learn

Teach is a verb meaning "to explain something." **Teach** is an irregular verb. Its past tense is **taught.**

Learn is a verb meaning "to gain information."

Examples:
Carrie will **teach** me how to play the piano.
Yesterday, she **taught** me "Chopsticks."

I will **learn** a new song every week.
Yesterday, I **learned** to play "Chopsticks."

Directions: Write the correct words to complete these sentences.

taught 1. My brother taught/learned me how to ice skate.

learned 2. With his help, I taught/learned in three days.

learn 3. First, I tried to teach/learn skating from a book.

learn 4. I couldn't teach/learn that way.

learn 5. You have to try it before you can really teach/learn how to do it.

teach 6. Now, I'm going to teach/learn my cousin.

learned 7. My cousin already taught/learned how to roller skate.

teaching 8. I shouldn't have any trouble teaching/learning her how to ice skate.

taught 9. Who taught/learned you how to skate?

taught 10. My brother taught/learned Mom how to skate, too.

learn 11. My mother took longer to teach/learn it than I did.

teach 12. Who will he teach/learn next?

learn 13. Do you know anyone who wants to teach/learn how to ice skate?

teach 14. My brother will teach/learn you for free.

learn 15. You should teach/learn how to ice skate in the wintertime, though. The ice is a little thin in the summer!

Page 283

Lie and Lay

Lie is a verb meaning "to rest." **Lie** is an intransitive verb that doesn't need a direct object.

Lay is a verb meaning "to place or put something down." **Lay** is a transitive verb that requires a direct object.

Examples:
Lie here for a while. (**Lie** has no direct object; **here** is an adverb.)
Lay the book here. (**Lay** has a direct object: **book.**)

Lie and **lay** are especially tricky because they are both irregular verbs. Notice the past tense of **lie** is **lay!**

Present tense	ing form	Past tense	Past participle
lie	lying	lay	has/have/had lain
lay	laying	laid	has/have/had laid

Examples:
I **lie** here today.
I **lay** here yesterday.
I was **lying** there for three hours.

I **lay** the baby in her bed.
I will be **laying** her down in a minute.
I **laid** her in her bed last night, too.

Directions: Write the correct words to complete these sentences.

lays 1. Shelly lies/lays a blanket on the grass.

lies 2. Then, she lies/lays down in the sun.

lies 3. Her dog lies/lays there with her.

lay 4. Yesterday, Shelly lay/laid in the sun for an hour.

laying 5. The workers are lying/laying bricks for a house.

laid 6. Yesterday, they lay/laid a ton of them.

lay 7. They lie/lay one brick on top of the other.

lie 8. The bricks just lie/lay in a pile until the workers are ready for them.

lie 9. At lunchtime, some workers lie/lay down for a nap.

lay 10. Would you like to lie/lay bricks?

laid 11. Last year, my uncle lay/laid bricks for his new house.

lay 12. He was so tired every day that he lay/laid down as soon as he finished.

Page 284

Comprehensive Curriculum - **Grade 5**

Rise and Raise

Rise is a verb meaning "to get up" or "to go up." **Rise** is an intransitive verb that doesn't need a direct object.

Raise is a verb meaning "to lift" or "to grow." **Raise** is a transitive verb that requires a direct object.

Examples:
The curtain **rises**.
The girl **raises** her hand.

Raise is a regular verb. **Rise** is irregular.

Present tense	Past tense	Past participle
rise	rose	has/have/had risen
raise	raised	has/have/had raised

Examples:
The sun **rose** this morning.
The boy **raised** the window higher.

Directions: Write the correct words to complete these sentences.

1. _rises_ This bread dough rises/raises in an hour.
2. _raise_ The landlord will rise/raise the rent.
3. _rose_ The balloon rose/raised into the sky.
4. _raised_ My sister rose/raised the seat on my bike.
5. _raised_ The baby rose/raised the spoon to his mouth.
6. _rose_ The eagle rose/raised out of sight.
7. _raises_ The farmer rises/raises pigs.
8. _raised_ The scouts rose/raised the flag.
9. _rose_ When the fog rose/raised, we could see better.
10. _rose_ The price of gasoline rose/raised again.
11. _raised_ The king rose/raised the glass to his lips.
12. _Raise_ Rise/Raise the picture on that wall higher.

Page 285

All Right, All Ready, and Already

All right means "well enough" or "very well." Sometimes, you may see **all right** spelled **alright**. This is not the preferred spelling and is considered very informal.

Example:
Correct: We'll be all right when the rain stops.
Incorrect: Are you feeling **alright** today?

All ready is an adjective meaning "completely ready."

Already is an adverb meaning "before this time" or "by this time."

Examples:
Are you **all ready** to go?
He was **already** there when I arrived.

Directions: Write the correct words to complete these sentences.

1. _all ready_ The children are all ready/already for the picnic.
2. _already_ Ted was all ready/already late for the show.
3. _all right_ Is your sister going to be all right/alright?
4. _already_ I was all ready/already tired before the race began.
5. _already_ Nadia has all ready/already left for the dance.
6. _all right_ Will you be all right/alright by yourself?
7. _all ready_ We are all ready/already for our talent show.
8. _already_ I all ready/already read that book.
9. _all ready_ I want to be all ready/already when they get here.
10. _all right_ Dad was sick, but he's all right/alright now.
11. _all ready_ The dinner is all ready/already to eat.
12. _already_ Brooklyn all ready/already wrote her report.

Page 286

Accept and Except / Affect and Effect

Accept is a verb meaning "to receive."

Except can be used as a verb or a preposition. As a verb, it means "to leave out." As a preposition, it means "excluding."

Examples:
I will **accept** the invitation to the dinner dance.
No one **except** Robert will receive an award.

Affect is a verb meaning "to impress one's thoughts or feelings."

Effect can be used as a noun or a verb. As a verb, it means "to accomplish." As a noun, it means "the result of an action."

Examples:
Her attitude may **affect** her performance on the test.
He **effected** several changes during his first few months as governor.
The **effects** of the storm will be felt for some time.

Directions: Write the correct words to complete these sentences.

1. _effect_ My partner and I will work to affect/effect attitudes toward rainforest renewal.
2. _accepted_ He courageously accepted/excepted the challenge of a chess duel.
3. _effect_ The affect/effect of the strike by truck drivers was felt nationwide.
4. _effect_ The new CEO of the company sought to affect/effect a change in company morale.
5. _except_ Everyone accept/except Zola will attend the game.
6. _accept_ My grandmother will never accept/except the fact that she can no longer drive.
7. _Except_ Accept/Except for this chewing incident, my puppy has been well-behaved.
8. _affected_ The sights of the war affected/effected soldiers for the rest of their lives.
9. _effect_ What affect/effect will the drop in the stock market have on the average person?
10. _effect_ The affect/effect of the wind was devastating.
11. _affect_ How will cheating on a test affect/effect your reputation?
12. _except_ I would like to go to the park on any day accept/except Monday.

Page 287

Review

Directions: Use each of these words correctly in a sentence of your own.
Answers will vary.

1. good _____
2. bad _____
3. who's _____
4. whose _____
5. their _____
6. there _____
7. they're _____
8. teach _____
9. learn _____
10. lie _____
11. lay _____
12. rise _____
13. raise _____
14. all ready _____
15. already _____
16. all right _____
17. accept _____
18. except _____
19. affect _____
20. effect _____

Page 288

Writing: Topic Sentences

The topic sentence in a paragraph usually comes first. Sometimes, however, the topic sentence can come at the end or even in the middle of a paragraph. When looking for the topic sentence, try to find the one that tells the main idea of a paragraph.

Directions: Read the following paragraphs, and underline the topic sentence in each.

The maple tree sheds its leaves every year. The oak and elm trees shed their leaves, too. Every autumn, the leaves on these trees begin changing color. Then, as the leaves gradually begin to die, they fall from the trees. Trees that shed their leaves annually are called deciduous trees.

When our family goes skiing, my brother enjoys the thrill of going down the steepest hill as fast as he can. Mom and Dad like to ski because it gets them out of the house and into the fresh air. I enjoy looking at the trees and birds and the sun shining on the snow. There is something about skiing that appeals to everyone in my family. Even the dog came along on our last skiing trip!

If you are outdoors at night and there is traffic around, you should always wear bright clothing so that cars can see you. White is a good color to wear at night. If you are riding a bicycle, be sure it has plenty of reflectors, and if possible, headlamps as well. Be especially careful when crossing the street, because sometimes drivers cannot see you in the glare of their headlights. Being outdoors at night can be dangerous, and it is best to be prepared!

Page 290

Writing: Supporting Sentences

A **paragraph** is a group of sentences that tell about one topic. The **topic sentence** in a paragraph usually comes first and tells the main idea of the paragraph. **Supporting sentences** follow the topic sentence and provide details about the topic.

Directions: Write at least three supporting sentences for each topic sentence below.

Example: Topic Sentence: Carly had an accident on her bike.
Supporting Sentences: She was on her way to the store to buy some bread. A car came weaving down the road and scared her. She rode her bike off the road so the car wouldn't hit her. Now, her knee is scraped, but she's all right.
Answers will vary.

1. I've been thinking of ways I could make some more money after school.
_____
_____
_____

2. In my opinion, cats (dogs, fish, etc.) make the best pets.
_____
_____
_____

3. My life would be better if I had a(n) (younger sister, younger brother, older sister, older brother).
_____
_____
_____

4. I'd like to live next door to a (swimming pool, library, movie theater, etc.).
_____
_____
_____

Page 291

Writing: Building Paragraphs

Directions: Read the groups of topic sentences and questions below. On another sheet of paper, write supporting sentences that answer the questions. Use your imagination! Write the supporting sentences in order, and copy them on this page after the topic sentence.

Answers will vary.

1. On her way home from school, Mariko made a difficult decision.

   Questions: What was Mariko's decision? Why did she decide that? Why was the decision hard to make?

2. Suddenly, Conrad thought of a way to clear up all the confusion.

   Questions: What was the confusion about? How was Conrad involved in it? What did he do to clear it up?

3. Bethany used to feel awkward at the school social activities.

   Questions: Why did Bethany feel awkward before? How does she feel now? What happened to change the way she feels?

Page 292

Writing: Sequencing

When writing paragraphs, it is important to write events in the correct order. Think about what happens first, next, later, and last.

Directions: The following sentences tell about Chandra's day, but they are all mixed up. Read the sentences, and number them in the order in which they happened.

_3_ She arrived at school and went to her locker to get her books.

_7_ After dinner, she did the dishes, and then read for a while.

_8_ Chandra brushed her teeth and put on her pajamas.

_5_ She rode the bus home, and then she ate a snack.

_2_ She ate breakfast and went out to wait for the bus.

_1_ Chandra woke up and picked out her clothes for school.

_4_ She met her friend Sarah on the way to the cafeteria.

_6_ She worked on homework and watched TV until her mom called her for dinner.

Directions: Write a short paragraph about what you did today. Use words like **first**, **next**, **then**, **later**, and **finally** to indicate the order in which you did things.

Paragraphs will vary.

Page 293

Sequencing

Sequencing means to place events in order from beginning to end or first to last.

Example:
To send a letter, you must:
Get paper, pencil or pen, an envelope, and a stamp.
Write the letter.
Fold the letter, and put it in the envelope.
Address the envelope correctly.
Put a stamp on the envelope.
Put the envelope in the mailbox or take it to the post office.

Possible answer:

Directions: Write the sequence for making a peanut butter and jelly sandwich.

Get out bread, peanut butter, jelly, and a knife.
Spread jelly on one slice of bread.
Spread peanut butter on the other slice of bread.
Put the two pieces of bread together so peanut butter and jelly sides are together.
Put away knife, peanut butter, and jelly.
Enjoy your sandwich.

Directions: After you finish, try making the sandwich **exactly** the way you wrote the steps. Did you leave out any steps? Which ones?

Answers will vary.

Does a particular section you wrote require a better explanation? Clarify your explanation by adding missing information.

Answers will vary.

Page 294

Author's Purpose

Authors write to fulfill one of three purposes: to **inform**, to **entertain**, or to **persuade**.

Authors who write to inform are providing facts for the reader in an informational context.
Examples: Encyclopedia entries and educational websites

Authors who write to entertain are hoping to provide enjoyment for the reader.
Examples: Funny stories and comics

Authors who write to persuade are trying to convince the reader to believe what they believe.
Examples: Editorials and opinion essays

Directions: Read each paragraph. Write **inform**, **entertain**, or **persuade** on the line to show the author's purpose.

1. The whooping crane is a migratory bird. At one time, this endangered bird was almost extinct. These large white cranes are characterized by red faces and trumpeting calls. Through protection of both the birds and their habitats, the whooping crane is slowly increasing in number.

   inform

2. It is extremely important that all citizens place bird feeders in their yards and keep them full for the winter. Birds that spend the winter in this area are in danger of starving due to lack of food. It is every citizen's responsibility to ensure the survival of the birds.

   persuade

3. Imagine being able to hibernate like a bear each winter! Wouldn't it be great to eat to your heart's content all fall? Then, sometime in late November, inform your teacher that you will not be attending school for the next few months because you'll be resting and living off your fat? Now, that would be the life!

   entertain

4. Bears, woodchucks, and chipmunks are not the only animals that hibernate. The queen bumblebee also hibernates in winter. All the other bees die before winter arrives. The queen hibernates under leaves in a small hole. She is cold-blooded and therefore is able to survive slightly frozen.

   inform

Page 295

Author's Purpose

Directions: Write a paragraph of your own for each purpose. The paragraph can be about any topic.

1. to inform
   Answers will vary.

2. to persuade

3. to entertain

Directions: Reread your paragraphs. Do they make sense? Check for grammar, spelling, and punctuation errors, and make corrections where needed.

Page 296

Descriptive Sentences

Descriptive sentences give readers a vivid image and enable them to imagine a scene clearly.

Example:
Nondescriptive sentence: There were grapes in the bowl.
Descriptive sentence: The plump purple grapes in the bowl looked tantalizing.

Directions: Rewrite these sentences using descriptive language.

Sentences will vary.

1. The dog walked in its pen.

2. The turkey was almost done.

3. I became upset when my computer wouldn't work.

4. Jared and Michelle went to the ice-cream parlor.

5. The telephone kept ringing.

6. I wrote a story.

7. The movie was excellent.

8. Dominique was upset that her friend was ill.

Page 297

Page 298

Writing: Descriptive Details

A writer creates pictures in a reader's mind by telling him/her how something looks, sounds, feels, smells, or tastes. For example, compare **A** and **B** below. Notice how the description in **B** makes you imagine how the heavy door and the cobweb would feel and how the broken glass would look and sound as someone walked on it.

A. I walked into the house.
B. I pushed open the heavy wooden door of the old house. A cobweb brushed my face, and broken glass, sparkling like ice, crackled under my feet.

Directions: Write one or two sentences about each topic below. Add details that will help your reader see, hear, feel, smell, or taste what you are describing.

1. Your favorite dinner cooking *Sentences will vary.*

2. Old furniture

3. Wind blowing in the trees

4. A tired stranger

5. Wearing wet clothes

6. A strange noise somewhere in the house

Page 299

Writing: Descriptive Details

Directions: For each topic sentence below, write three or four supporting sentences. Include details about how things look, sound, smell, taste, or feel. Don't forget to use adjectives, adverbs, similes, and metaphors.

Example: After my dog had his bath, I couldn't believe how much better he looked. His fur, which used to be all matted and dirty, was as clean as new snow. He still felt a little damp when I scratched behind his ears. The smell from rolling in our garbage was gone, too. The shampoo made him smell like apples. *Answers will vary.*

1. My little cousin's birthday party was almost over.

2. I always keep my grandpa company while he bakes bread.

3. By the end of our day at the beach, I was a mess.

4. Early morning is the best time to go for a bike ride.

Page 300

Personal Narratives

A **personal narrative** tells about a person's own experiences.

Directions: Read the example of a personal narrative. Write your answers in complete sentences.

My Worst Year

When I look back on that year, I can hardly believe that one person could have such terrible luck for a whole year. But then again, I should have realized that if things could begin to go wrong in January, it didn't bode well for the rest of the year.

It was the night of January 26. One of my best friends was celebrating her birthday at the local roller-skating rink, and I had been invited. The evening began well enough with pizza and laughs. I admit I have never been an excellent roller skater, but I could hold my own. After a few minutes of skating, I decided to exit the rink to get a drink of water.

Unfortunately, I did not notice the trailing ribbons of carpet that wrapped around the wheel of my skate, yanking my left leg from under me. My leg was broken. It wasn't just broken in one place but in four places! At the hospital, the doctor set the bone and put a cast on my leg. Three months later, I felt like a new person.

Sadly, the happiness wasn't meant to last. Five short months after the final cast was removed, I fell and broke the same leg again. Not only did it rebreak, but it broke in the same four places! We found out later that it hadn't healed correctly. Three months later, it was early December and the end of a year I did not wish to repeat.

1. List the sequence of events in this personal narrative.

   January 26: fell while skating and broke leg in four places.
   Three months later: cast removed.
   Five months later: fell and broke leg again in same four
   places.

2. From reading the personal narrative, what do you think were the author's feelings toward the events that occurred?

   Answers will vary.

Page 301

Personal Narratives

A **narrative** is a spoken or written account of an actual event. A **personal narrative** tells about your own experience. It can be written about any event in your life and may be serious or comical.

When writing a personal narrative, remember to use correct sentence structure and punctuation. Include important dates, sights, sounds, smells, tastes, and feelings to give your reader a clear picture of the event.

Directions: Write a personal narrative about an event in your life that was funny.

Paragraphs will vary.

Page 302

Complete the Story

Directions: Read the beginning of this story. Then, complete the story with your own ideas.

It was a beautiful summer day in June when my family and I set off on vacation. We were headed for Portsmouth, New Hampshire. There, we planned to go on a whale-watching ship and perhaps spy a humpback whale or two. However, there were many miles between our home and Portsmouth.

We camped at many lovely parks along the way to New Hampshire. We stayed in the Adirondack Mountains for a few days and then visited the White Mountains of Vermont before crossing into New Hampshire.

My family enjoys tent camping. My dad says you can't really get a taste of the great outdoors in a pop-up camper or RV. I love sitting by the fire at night, gazing at the stars, and listening to the animal noises.

The trip was going well, and everyone was enjoying our vacation. We made it to Portsmouth and were looking forward to the whale-watching adventure. We arrived at the dock a few minutes early. The ocean looked rough, but we had taken seasickness medication. We thought we were prepared for any kind of weather.

Stories will vary.

Page 303

Writing Fiction

Directions: Use descriptive writing to complete each story. Write at least five sentences.

1. It was a cold, wintry morning in January. Snow had fallen steadily for four days. I was staring out my bedroom window when I saw the bedraggled dog staggering through the snow.

   Paragraphs will vary.

2. Alyssa was home Saturday studying for a big science test. Report cards were due next Friday, and the test on Monday would be on the report card. Alyssa needed to do well on the test to get an A in Science. The phone rang. It was her best friend, Tierra.

3. Martin works every weekend delivering newspapers. He wakes up at 5:30 A.M. and begins his route at 6:00 A.M. He delivers 150 newspapers on his bike. He enjoys his weekend job because he is working toward a goal.

Writing: Point of View

People often have different opinions about the same thing. This is because each of us has a different "point of view." **Point of view** is the attitude someone has about a particular topic as a result of his or her personal experience or knowledge.

Directions: Read the topic sentence below about the outcome of a basketball game. Then, write two short paragraphs, one from the point of view of a player for the Reds and one from the point of view of a player for the Cowboys. Be sure to give each person's opinion of the outcome of the game. Answers will vary.

Topic Sentence: In the last second of the basketball game between the Reds and the Cowboys, the Reds scored and won the game.

Terry, a player for the Reds . . . _____

_____

Chris, a player for the Cowboys . . . _____

_____

Directions: Here's a different situation. Read the topic sentence, and then write three short paragraphs from the points of view of Katie, her dad, and her brother. Answers will vary.
Topic Sentence: Katie's dog had chewed up another one of her father's shoes.

Katie . . . _____

Katie's father . . . _____

Katie's brother, Mark, who would rather have a cat . . . _____

Page 304

Friendly Letters

A **friendly letter** has these parts: return address, date, greeting, body, closing, and signature.

Directions: Read this letter. Then, label the parts of the letter.

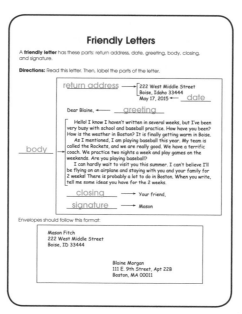

return address → 222 West Middle Street
Boise, Idaho 33444
May 17, 2015 ← date

Dear Blaine, ← greeting

body — Hello! I know I haven't written in several weeks, but I've been very busy with school and baseball practice. How have you been? How is the weather in Boston? It is finally getting warm in Boise.
As I mentioned, I am playing baseball this year. My team is called the Rockets, and we are really good. We have a terrific coach. We practice two nights a week and play games on the weekends. Are you playing baseball?
I can hardly wait to visit you this summer. I can't believe I'll be flying on an airplane and staying with you and your family for 2 weeks! There is probably a lot to do in Boston. When you write, tell me some ideas you have for the 2 weeks.

closing → Your friend,

signature → Mason

Envelopes should follow this format:

Mason Fitch
222 West Middle Street
Boise, ID 33444

Blaine Morgan
111 E. 9th Street, Apt 22B
Boston, MA 00011

Page 305

Friendly Letters

Directions: Write a friendly letter. Then, address the envelope.

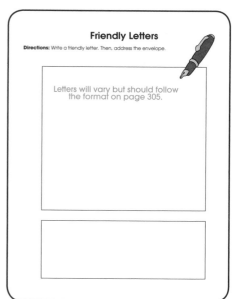

Letters will vary but should follow the format on page 305.

Page 306

Writing: Supporting Your Opinion

Directions: Decide what your opinion is on each topic below. Then, write a paragraph supporting your opinion. Begin with a topic sentence that tells the reader what you think. Add details in the next three or four sentences that show why you are right.

Example: Whether kids should listen to music while they do homework

Kids do a better job on their homework if they listen to music. The music makes the time more enjoyable. It also drowns out the sounds of the rest of the family. If things are too quiet while kids do homework, every little sound distracts them.
Paragraphs will vary.

1. Whether young people should have a choice about going to school, no matter how old they are

_____

_____

2. Whether all parents should give their children the same amount of money for an allowance

_____

_____

3. Whether you should tell someone if you doubt he or she is telling the truth

_____

_____

Page 307

Writing from a Prompt: An Opinion Essay

Directions: Write an opinion essay in response to the prompt.

Writing Prompt: Think about rainforests. What is the importance of preserving the rainforests of the world? What problems could arise if there were no longer any rainforest areas? What problems could arise for humans due to the preservation of rainforests? How do rainforests affect you?

Essays will vary.

_____

_____

_____

_____

_____

_____

_____

_____

Directions: When you finish writing, reread your essay. Use this checklist to help make corrections.

☐ I have used correct spelling, grammar, and punctuation.
☐ I have no sentence fragments.
☐ My essay makes sense.
☐ I wrote complete sentences.
☐ I have no run-on sentences.
☐ I answered the prompt.

Page 308

Writing a Summary

Directions: Read the following selection. Using page 309 as a guide, write a summary of the selection.

First Flights

In the first few years of the 20th century, most people strongly believed that humans would never be able to fly. However, a few daring individuals worked to prove the public wrong.

On December 8, 1903, Samuel Langley attempted to fly his version of an airplane from the roof of a houseboat on the Potomac River. Langley happened to be the secretary of the Smithsonian Institution, so his flight was covered not only by news reporters but also by government officials. Unfortunately, his trip met with sudden disaster when his aircraft did a nose dive into the river.

Nine days later, brothers Orville and Wilbur Wright attempted a flight. They had assembled their aircraft at their home in Dayton, Ohio, and shipped it to Kitty Hawk, North Carolina. On December 17, the Wright brothers made several flights, the longest one lasting an incredible 59 seconds. Since the Wright brothers had kept their flight attempts secret, their miraculous flight was only reported by two newspapers in the United States.

Summaries will vary.

_____

_____

_____

_____

_____

Page 310

ANSWER KEY

Comparing and Contrasting

When writing comparison/contrast essays, it is helpful to write one paragraph which contains all the similarities and another paragraph which contains all the differences.

Directions: Write an essay in response to the prompt.

Writing Prompt: Think of your brother, sister, or a friend. What similarities are there between you and this person? What differences are there?

Essays will vary.

Directions: When you finish writing, reread your essay. Use this checklist to help make corrections.

- [ ] My essay makes sense.
- [ ] I listed at least two similarities and two differences.
- [ ] My sentences are correctly written.
- [ ] I used correct spelling, grammar, and punctuation.

Page 311

Advantages and Disadvantages

As in the comparison/contrast essay, it is easiest to put all of the advantages in one paragraph and the disadvantages in another paragraph.

Directions: Write an essay in response to the prompt.

Writing Prompt: Think about what a society would be like if all people had the same skin tone, hair color, eye color, height, and weight. What would be the benefits of living in such a society be? Would there be any disadvantages? What would they be?

Essays will vary.

Directions: When you finish writing, reread your essay. Use this checklist to help make corrections.

- [ ] My essay makes sense.
- [ ] I used correct spelling, grammar, and punctuation.
- [ ] I answered the writing prompt.
- [ ] I have varied sentence length.

Page 312

Newswriting

Newswriting is a style of writing used by news reporters and other journalists who write for periodicals. **Periodicals** are newspapers, magazines, and newsletters that are published regularly either as hard copies or digitally.

Magazine and news writers organize their ideas and their writing around what is called "the five W's and the H" — who, what, when, where, why, and how. As they conduct research and interview people for articles, journalists keep these questions in mind.

Directions: Read a news article of your choice. Use the information you read to answer the questions.

Answers will vary.

Who Who is involved? _____
Who is affected? _____
Who is responsible? _____

What What is the event or subject? _____
What exactly has happened? _____

When When did this happen? _____

Where Where did it happen? _____

Why Why did it happen? _____
Why will readers care? _____

How How did it happen? _____

Page 313

Newswriting: Inverted Pyramid Style

Reporters organize their news stories in what is called the **inverted pyramid** style. The inverted pyramid places the most important facts at the beginning of the story—called the lead (LEED)—and the least important facts at the end.

There are two practical reasons for this approach:

1) If the story must be shortened by an editor, he or she can simply cut paragraphs from the end of the story rather than rewriting the entire story.

2) Because so much news and information is available to the public, few people read every word of every story. Instead, many readers skim headlines and opening paragraphs. The inverted pyramid style of writing enables readers to quickly get the basics of what the story is about without reading the entire story.

Directions: Read the news story. Then, answer the questions.

Introducing children to peanuts when they are young helps reduce the risk of peanut allergies, a new study has found.

The study, published in *The New England Journal of Medicine*, could change doctors' recommendations to parents of young babies and children. Instead of telling parents to avoid peanuts in their children's diets, doctors may now recommend that peanuts be introduced in small amounts at an early age. This frequent and early exposure has been shown to cut the risk of peanut allergies in children.

Peanut allergies have become more common among children in recent years. Peanuts are banned from many schools and daycare centers, in hopes of preventing severe reactions. Peanuts are a delicious and nutritious source of protein. In addition to being used as a sandwich spread, they make a nice addition to dips and smoothies.

1. What is this news story about? a new recommendation to introduce kids to peanuts earlier
2. Where was the study about peanuts published? The New England Journal of Medicine
3. How have doctors' views about peanuts changed? They used to have young kids avoid peanuts.
4. Name two groups of people who might be interested in reading this article. doctors and parents
5. What two sentences could you cut from this article if you were an editor? the last two sentences

Page 314

Writing: Just the Facts

Some forms of writing, such as reports and essays, contain opinions that are supported by the writer. In other kinds of writing, however, it is important to stick to the facts. News reporters, for example, must use only facts when they write their stories.

Directions: Read the following news story about a fire, and underline the sentences or parts of sentences that are opinions. Then, rewrite the story in your own words, giving only the facts.

At around 10:30 P.M. last night, a fire broke out in a house at 413 Wilshire Boulevard. The house is in a very nice neighborhood, surrounded by beautiful trees. The family of four who lives in the house was alerted by smoke alarms, and they all exited the house safely, although they must have been very frightened. Firefighters arrived on the scene at approximately 10:45 P.M., and it took them over 3 hours to extinguish the blaze. The firefighters were very courageous. The cause of the fire has not yet been determined, although faulty electric wiring is suspected. People should have their electric wiring checked regularly. The family is staying with relatives until repairs to their home can be made, and they are probably very anxious to move back into their house.

Paragraphs will vary.

Page 315

Writing: You're the Reporter

Directions: Now, write your own short news story about an interesting event that occurred at your school or in your neighborhood. Find out who and what the story is about, where and when it happened, and why and how it happened. Take some notes, interview some of the people involved, and write your story. Give your story a title, and remember to stick to the facts! In the box, draw a picture (or "photo") to go with your story.

Answers will vary.

Pictures will vary.

Page 316

Comprehensive Curriculum - **Grade 5**   506

Writing: Personification

Sometimes writers use descriptions such as "The fire engine **screamed** as it rushed down the street," or "The sun **crawled** slowly across the sky." We know that fire engines do not really scream, and the sun does not really crawl. Writers use descriptions like these to make their writing more interesting and vivid. When a writer gives an object or animal human qualities, it is called **personification**.

Directions: For each object below, write a sentence using personification. The first one has been done for you.

1. the barn door
   The old, rusty barn door groaned loudly when I pushed it open.
2. the rain
   Answers will vary.
3. the pickup truck
4. the radiator
5. the leaves
6. the television
7. the kite
8. the river

Page 317

Similes

A **simile** is a comparison of two things that have something in common but are really very different. The words **like** and **as** are used in similes.

Examples:
The baby was **as** happy **as** a lark.
She is **like** a ray of sunshine to my tired eyes.

Directions: Choose a word from the box to complete each comparison. The first one has been done for you.

| tack | grass | fish | mule | ox | rail | hornet | monkey |

1. as stubborn as a **mule**
2. as strong as an **ox**
3. swims like a **fish**
4. as sharp as a **tack**
5. as thin as **rail**
6. as mad as a **hornet**
7. climbs like a **monkey**
8. as green as **grass**

Directions: Use your own words to complete these similes. *Answers will vary.*

9. as _____ as a tack
10. _____ like a bird
11. as hungry as a _____
12. as white as _____
13. as light as _____
14. as _____ as honey
15. _____ like a snake
16. as cold as _____

Directions: Use your own similes to complete these sentences. *Answers will vary.*

17. Our new puppy sounded _____
18. The clouds were _____
19. Our new car is _____
20. The watermelon tasted _____

Page 318

Writing: Common Similes

There are many similes that are used often in the English language. For example, "as frightened as a mouse" is a very common simile. Can you think of others?

Directions: Match the first part of each common simile to the second part. The first one has been done for you.

as slippery as — a mule
as smart as — a statue
as sly as — a rock
as still as — a bee
as quick as — an eel
as slow as — a pancake
as busy as — a whip
as cold as — a turtle
as flat as — a fox
as stubborn as — lightning
as hungry as — ice
as hard as — a bear

Directions: Write sentences using these common similes.
1. eats like a bird *Answers will vary.*
2. fits like a glove
3. sits there like a bump on a log
4. like a bull in a china shop
5. works like a charm

Page 319

Metaphors

A **metaphor** makes a direct comparison between two unlike things. A noun must be used in the comparison. The words **like** and **as** are not used.

Examples:
Correct: The exuberant puppy was a **bundle of energy**.
Incorrect: The dog is **happy**. (**Happy** is an adjective.)

Directions: Circle the two objects being compared.
1. The old truck was a heap of rusty metal.
2. The moon was a silver dollar in the sky.
3. Their vacation was a nightmare.
4. That wasp is a flying menace.
5. The prairie was a carpet of green.
6. The flowers were jewels on stems.
7. This winter, our pond is glass.
8. The clouds were marshmallows.

Directions: Complete the metaphor in each sentence.
9. The ruby was _____ *Answer will vary.*
10. The hospital is _____
11. The car was _____
12. This morning when I awoke, I was _____
13. When my brother is grumpy, he is _____
14. Her fingers on the piano keys were _____

Page 320

Writing: Similes and Metaphors

Using **similes** and **metaphors** to describe things makes writing interesting. Similes are comparisons that use **like** or **as**.

Examples: She looked like a frightened mouse.
She looked as frightened as a mouse.

Metaphors are direct comparisons that do not use **like** or **as**.

Example: She was a frightened mouse.

Directions: Rewrite each sentence two different ways to make it more interesting. In the first sentence (a), add at least one adjective and one adverb. In the second sentence (b), compare something in the sentence to something else, using a simile or metaphor. *Answers will vary.*

Example: The baby cried.
   a. The sick baby cried softly all night.
   b. The baby cried louder and louder, like a storm gaining strength.

1. The stranger arrived.
   a. _____
   b. _____
2. The dog barked.
   a. _____
   b. _____
3. The children danced.
   a. _____
   b. _____
4. The moon rose.
   a. _____
   b. _____

Page 321

Writing: Similes and Metaphors in Poetry

Many poems use similes and metaphors to create a more interesting description of what the poem is about.

Directions: Read the following poems and underline any similes or metaphors you see.

Flint
An emerald is as green as grass,
A ruby red as blood;
A sapphire shines as blue as heaven;
   A flint lies in the mud.

A diamond is a brilliant stone,
   To catch the world's desire;
An opal holds a fiery spark;
   But a flint holds fire.

—Christina Rossetti

The Night Is a Big Black Cat
The night is a big black cat
   The moon is her topaz eye,
The stars are the mice she hunts at night,
   In the field of the sultry sky.

—G. Orr Clark

Directions: Now, write your own poem, using at least one simile and one metaphor.

Poems will vary.

Page 322

Writing: Rhyming Words

Words that share the same vowel sound in their last syllables are **rhyming words**. Rhyming words can have the same number of syllables, like **spike** and **hike**, or different numbers of syllables, like **tent** and **excellent** or **nation** and **conversation**.

Directions: Write words that rhyme with the words below and have the number of syllables shown. The first one has been done for you.

Possible answers:

1. table ___unable___ (3)
2. green ___Halloween___ (3)
3. instead ___red___ (1)
4. store ___ignore___ (2)
5. remember ___December___ (3)
6. concentration ___invitation___ (4)
7. stars ___guitars___ (2)
8. giraffe ___staff___ (1)
9. neighbor ___labor___ (2)
10. berry ___culinary___ (4)
11. vein ___entertain___ (3)
12. bath ___math___ (1)
13. celebration ___admiration___ (4)
14. master ___faster___ (2)
15. baby ___maybe___ (2)

They share the same vowel sound in their last syllables.

spike
hike
like
Mike

Page 323

Writing: Poetry

Directions: For the first group of poems below, both lines should rhyme. The first line is given. Complete each poem, using one of the given rhyming words, or use one of your own. Make sure to add the correct punctuation.

Example: mile, pile, dial   Dylan James has a certain style.
To get his way, he'd walk a mile.

ape, grape, cape   Mindy Lou got a very bad scrape!   Answers will vary.

hide, fried, cried   Sometimes you have to swallow your pride.

Directions: Complete these poems, using one of the given words, or use one of your own. Each poem should have four lines. The second and fourth lines should rhyme.

Example: cape, tape, grape   Kenny skidded on his bike.
And got himself all **scraped**.
Now his bike has a flat tire,
And his whole leg is **taped**.

I, cry, my   I put some water in a bucket
And then threw in some **dye**.
Poems will vary.

file, dial, Nile   Kelly got her hair cut,
But I don't like the **style**.

ride, hide, cried   When Billy Joe didn't win the race,
It really hurt his **pride**.

Page 324

Haiku

Haiku is a form of unrhymed Japanese poetry. Haiku have three lines. The first line has five syllables, the second line has seven syllables, and the third line has five syllables.

Example:

The Fall
Leaves fall from the trees.
Do they want to leave their home?
They float on the breeze.

Directions: Write a haiku about nature. Write the title on the first line. Then, illustrate your haiku.

Haiku will vary but should follow the format.

Nature _____

Page 325

Lantern

Lantern is another type of five-line Japanese poetry. It takes the shape of a Japanese lantern. Each line must contain the following number of syllables:

Line 1:   1 syllable
Line 2:   2 syllables
Line 3:   3 syllables
Line 4:   4 syllables
Line 5:   1 syllable

Example:
Cats—
Stealthy
wild creatures
want to be your
pet.

Poems will vary but should follow the format.

Directions: Write and illustrate your own lantern.

Page 326

Alliterative Poetry

Alliteration is the repetition of a consonant sound in a group of words.

Example: Barney Bear bounced a ball.

Alliterative story poems can be fun to read and write. Any of several rhyming patterns can be used. Possibilities include:
Every two lines rhyme.
Every other line rhymes.
The first line rhymes with the last line, and the two middle lines rhyme with each other.
All four lines rhyme.

Example:
Thomas Tuttle tries to dine,
On turkey, tea, and treats so fine.
Thomas eats tomatoes and tortellini,
He devours tuna and tettrazini.

When tempting tidbits fill the table,
Thomas tastes as much as he is able,
He stuffs himself from top to toes,
Where he puts it, goodness knows!

Directions: Write an alliterative story poem using any rhyming pattern listed above. Your poem should be at least four lines long.

Poems will vary but should follow one of the patterns above.

Page 327

How to Write a Book Report

Writing a book report should not be a chore. Instead, consider it an opportunity to recommend a book you have enjoyed. Simply writing, "I really liked this book. You will, too!" is not enough. You need to explain what makes the book worth reading.

Like other essays, book reports have three parts. An essay is a short report that presents the personal views of the writer. The three parts of an essay (and a book report) are introduction, body, and conclusion.

The **introduction** to a book report should be a full paragraph that will capture the interest of your readers. The **body** paragraphs contain the main substance of your report. Include a brief overview of the plot of your book, along with supporting details that make it interesting. In the **conclusion**, summarize the central ideas of your report. Sum up why you would or would not recommend it to others.

Directions: Answer these questions about writing book reports.

1. Which of these introductory sentences is more interesting?

   ☒ Brian, a thirteen-year-old boy, must survive in the Canadian wilderness after his plane crashes.

   ☐ Hatchet is an interesting book about survival and the wilderness.

2. In a report on a fiction book about a teenage survivor of a plane crash, where would these sentences go?

   "Brian is flying in a plane to visit his father when the plane's pilot dies unexpectedly of a heart attack."

   ☒ introduction
   ☐ conclusion

3. In the same report, where would these sentences go?

   "Author Gary Paulsen has written an exciting adventure story about a boy's patience and courage as he survives alone for two months in the wilderness. I strongly recommend the book to people of all ages."

   ☐ body
   ☒ conclusion

Page 328

Book Report: A Book I Devoured

Directions: Follow the writing prompts to write a short book report on a book you truly enjoyed.

Recently, I read a book I could not put down.

Its title is _____ Reports will vary. _____

One reason I "devoured" this book was _____

_____

_____

If I could be one of the characters, I'd be _____ because _____

_____

_____

_____

_____

My favorite part of the story was when _____

_____

_____

_____

_____

_____

_____

Page 329

Book Report: Comparing Two Books

Directions: Follow the writing prompts to write a short book report comparing two books on the same subject.

Two books I recently read on the same subject

are _____ Reports will vary. _____

by _____

and _____

by _____

I liked _____ better because _____

_____

_____

The best part of this book was when _____

_____

_____

_____

Even though I did not like it as well, one good thing I can say about the other book is

_____

_____

_____

Page 330

Reference Sources: Languages, Social Studies

Reference sources are books and other materials that provide facts and information. Dictionaries, encyclopedias, and nonfiction books are reference books. Magazine and newspaper articles, the Internet, and computer CDs are also reference sources.

There are many other kinds of reference sources on specific topics. Some of these are listed below by the topics covered.

Language:
1. *The American Heritage Dictionary*
2. *Dictionary of American Idioms* by Adam Makkai
3. *Math Dictionary for Kids* by Theresa Fitzgerald
4. *Oxford Dictionary of Foreign Words and Phrases* by Andrew Delahunty
5. *Scholastic Children's Thesaurus*

Social Studies:
1. *Book of Black Heroes from A to Z* by Wade Hudson and Valerie Wilson Wesley
2. *If You Lived When Women Won Their Rights* by Anne Kamma
3. *Understanding Myself: A Kid's Guide to Intense Emotions and Strong Feelings* by Mary C. Lamia
4. *Merriam Webster's Geographical Dictionary*

Directions: Answer the questions.

1. Which book would be the best source for finding the meaning of the Spanish term, *que pasa*?
   Oxford Dictionary of Foreign Words and Phrases

2. Which book would be the best source of information on Martin Luther King, Jr.?
   Book of Black Heroes from A to Z

3. Where would you find information on the average yearly rainfall in the Amazon?
   Merriam Webster's Geographical Dictionary

4. Which book would have information on women getting the right to vote?
   If You Lived When Women Won Their Rights

5. Where would you look for a list of terms that mean the same as **incredible**?
   Scholastic Children's Thesaurus

Page 331

Reference Sources: General, Science, and Technology

These reference sources are listed by the topics covered.

General:
1. How Things Work Encyclopedia
2. Children's Encyclopedia of American History
3. World Book Encyclopedia Kids (online subscription)
4. National Geographic Student World Atlas
5. United States Census Bureau website (www.census.gov)

Science and Technology:
1. A Field Guide to Rocks and Minerals by Frederick H. Pough
2. Encyclopedia of Animals
3. National Wildlife Federation Field Guide to Trees of North America
4. The Universe (Discovery Kids)
5. The Complete Human Body (book and DVD-ROM) by Dr. Alice Roberts

Directions: Answer the questions.

1. Which reference source would you check to find a map of Poland?
   National Geographic Student World Atlas

2. Which source would you consult to find the most recent statistics on the number of single parents in the United States?
   United States Census Bureau website (www.census.gov)

3. Where would you find the most complete information on the Milky Way and other galaxies?
   The Universe (Discovery Kids)

4. Where would you find the most complete information about a rock crystal called quartz?
   A Field Guide to Rocks and Minerals

5. Where would you find the most complete information on the Boston Tea Party?
   Children's Encyclopedia of American History

Page 332

Using the Library Catalog

The **call number** for a book is printed on its spine and also appears in the library catalog. Nonfiction books are shelved in order by call number.

Directions: Use what you learned about library catalogs to answer these questions.

1. What should you type into a library's computerized catalog for a listing of all the books the library has on birds?
   birds

2. What should you type into the library's catalog for a list of all the books by Louisa May Alcott?
   Alcott, Louisa May

3. What should you type into the library's catalog to see if the library owns a book called *Birds of North America*?
   Birds of North America

4. According to the catalog entry shown on the previous page, what company published the book *Unusual Creatures*?
   Chronicle Books

5. Under what subject is *Unusual Creatures* listed?
   Animals—Miscellanea—Juvenile Literature

6. What is the call number for *Unusual Creatures*?
   J590

7. What are three ways to find a book in the library? *Possible answers: title, author, subject*

8. If you don't find the book you were looking for after your first catalog search, what else can you try?
   Try changing the type of search you used.

9. Besides the call number, title, and author, what are three other types of information given for a book in a library catalog?
   Possible answer: the ISBN number, the date of publication, and the place of publication

Page 334

Research

Directions: Read about doing research. Then, answer the questions.

Step 1: Look in a general online encyclopedia, such as Encyclopedia Britannica Kids or Fact Monster (which uses the Columbia Encyclopedia), for background information on your topic. Check for a bibliography at the end of the article for clues to other sources. A **bibliography** lists all the books and magazines used to write the article.

Step 2: Use a special encyclopedia for more specific information or for definitions of special terms. How Things Work Encyclopedia, Children's Encyclopedia of American History, and Human Body: A Visual Encyclopedia are examples of special encyclopedias.

Step 3: Look for a general book on your topic using the subject headings in the library catalog. Be sure to note the copyright date (date published) on all books you select. For current topics, such as medical research or computers, you will want to use only the most recently published and up-to-date sources. You will be most likely to find these using online resources.

Step 4: When using the Internet to research a topic, be sure to use only trustworthy, reliable sites. Choose sites that are run by companies, schools, or organizations you've heard of, such as NASA, the Smithsonian Institution, National Geographic Kids, Time Magazine, PBS, or the National Gallery of Art. If you're not sure whether a site is reliable, ask a parent or a teacher.

1. Name two general encyclopedias. *Encyclopedia Britannica Kids and Columbia Encyclopedia*

2. Name three special encyclopedias. *How Things Work Encyclopedia, Children's Encyclopedia of American History, and Human Body: A Visual Encyclopedia*

3. How can you tell whether a website contains trustworthy, reliable information?
   Choose sites that are run by companies, schools, or organizations that are familiar, or ask a parent or teacher.

Page 335

Research

Directions: Read the following questions. Use the Internet or library resources to answer them.

1. Choose two figures from history. Research them on www.biography.com. Write two facts you found about each person.

   Answers will vary.

2. Use a resource book or online search to find out during what period the dinosaur Diplodocus lived.

   the Jurassic period

3. What were the last three winners of the Newbery Award for best children's books?

   Answers will vary.

4. Name three types of mollusks. List the source of your information.

   Answers will vary.

5. Visit the site www.libraryspot.com. Write three questions that a classmate could answer by using this site.

   Answers will vary.

6. Use a library catalog to search for books about ancient Egypt. List the titles and call numbers of three books you find.

   Answers will vary.

Page 336

Research

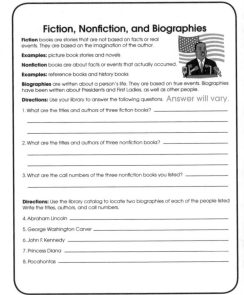

Directions: Read the following questions. Use the Internet or library resources to answer them.

1. Use a print or online children's almanac to find two facts about the weather or weather-related events.

   Answers will vary.

2. What is the world's tallest building? How tall is it?

   the Burj Khalifa in Dubai: 2,717 feet

3. List two sources you could use to find current information about global warming.

   Answers will vary.

4. Use a print or online atlas to find out what African countries and what body of water border Namibia.

   Angola, Zambia, Botswana, South Africa, and the South Atlantic Ocean

5. Use an online encyclopedia to research the Chinese New Year. Briefly describe what it is below.

   Answers will vary.

6. How are hurricanes named? What source did you use to find the answer?

   A list of names are assigned in alphabetical order to tropical storms. If they develop into hurricanes, they keep the name. Sources will vary.

Page 337

Fiction, Nonfiction, and Biographies

Fiction books are stories that are not based on facts or real events. They are based on the imagination of the author.

Examples: picture book stories and novels

Nonfiction books are about facts or events that actually occurred.

Examples: reference books and history books

Biographies are written about a person's life. They are based on true events. Biographies have been written about Presidents and First Ladies, as well as other people.

Directions: Use your library to answer the following questions. Answer will vary.

1. What are the titles and authors of three fiction books?

2. What are the titles and authors of three nonfiction books?

3. What are the call numbers of the three nonfiction books you listed?

Directions: Use the library catalog to locate two biographies of each of the people listed. Write the titles, authors, and call numbers.

4. Abraham Lincoln

5. George Washington Carver

6. John F. Kennedy

7. Princess Diana

8. Pocahontas

Page 338

Book Search: Fiction

 Have you ever been on a scavenger hunt? Usually, when you go on a scavenger hunt, you need to find unusual items on a list. This scavenger hunt will take place at your library. Instead of finding unusual items, you will need to find books.

Directions: Find these books at your library. They will be in alphabetical order by the author's last name in the picture book section of the children's department. Then, answer the questions.

Author: Margaret Wise Brown   **Title:** Goodnight Moon

1. Where is the cow jumping over the moon?   in the picture

2. What is the old lady whispering?   Hush

3. How many kittens are in the story?   three

Author: Audrey Wood   **Title:** Napping House

4. In the beginning, what is everyone in the house doing?   sleeping

5. What kind of flea is in this story?   a wakeful flea

6. What breaks at the end of the story?   the bed

Author: Mo Willems   **Title:** Knuffle Bunny: A Cautionary Tale

7. Who is Knuffle Bunny?   a stuffed bunny

8. How does Trixie explain her problem to her father?   She tries to use baby talk, and then she has a tantrum.

9. How does the story end?   They go back to the laundromat and find Knuffle Bunny there.

Page 339

Book Search: Nonfiction

Directions: Look in your library catalog to find the types of nonfiction books listed. Then, go to the shelf in the nonfiction section, and locate the books. Write the information requested for each book.

A book about gorillas   Answers will vary.

Title: _____

Author: _____

Call number: _____

First sentence in book: _____

A book about the solar system

Title: _____

Author: _____

Call number: _____

Last sentence in book: _____

A book about baseball

Title: _____

Author: _____

Call number: _____

Color of book's cover: _____

A book about flowers

Title: _____

Author: _____

Call number: _____

Name of a flower pictured in book: _____

Page 340

Book Search: Biographies

Biographies may be located in the 920 section in your library or may be filed by call number according to subject.

Directions: Use the library catalog and the actual books to answer these questions.   Answers will vary.

1. How many books can you find about Elizabeth Blackwell?

2. What is the title of one of the books?

3. How many books can you find about Kareem Abdul-Jabar?

4. What are the titles, authors, and call numbers of three books about George Washington?

5. What are the titles, authors, and call numbers of three books about Martin Luther King, Jr.?

6. What are the titles, authors, and call numbers of three books about Eleanor Roosevelt?

7. What are the titles, authors, and call numbers of three books about Marie Curie?

Page 341

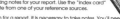

Reports: Choosing a Topic

Directions: Read about how to write a report. Then, answer the questions.

A report is a written paper based on the writer's research. It is logically organized and, if it is a good report, presents information in an interesting way. Reports can focus on many different topics. A social studies report may provide information about a city or state. A science report may explain why the oceans are polluted.

If possible, choose a topic you're interested in. Sometimes a teacher assigns a general topic to the whole class, such as the solar system. This is a very broad topic, so you must first narrow it to a smaller topic about which you can write an interesting four- or five-page report. For example, your report could be on "The Sun, the Center of the Solar System" or "Jupiter, the Jumbo Planet."

A narrower topic gives your paper a better focus. Be careful not to make your topic too narrow, because then you may not be able to find much information about it for your report.

The inverted pyramid on the right shows how to narrow your topic from the general, at the top of the pyramid, to the specific, at the bottom.

The solar system

Planets in the solar system

Jupiter, the jumbo planet

Directions: Select a topic for a paper you will write. You may choose one of these topics or select one of your own. Then, answer the questions.

| American wars | Games | Presidents | States |
| Famous American women | Solar system | Sports heroes | Ecology |

1. What is a report? _A report is a written paper based on the writer's research, and it presents information in an interesting way._

2. Which general topic did you choose? _Answers will vary._

3. What specific topic will you write about? _Answers will vary._

Page 342

Reports: Doing Research

Directions: Review the information on pages 333–335 about doing library research. Then, read about how to do research for a report, and answer the questions.

Before starting your report, locate the most likely places to find relevant information for your research. Ask the librarian for help if necessary. A good report will be based on at least three or four sources, so it's important to find references that provide varied information.

Is the topic a standard one, such as a report on the skeletal system? A children's encyclopedia of the human body is a good place to begin your research. You may also want to look online for some children's websites about the body and how it works.

Does your report require current statistics and/or facts? Specific websites will probably be your best source for information. For example, if you want to know the current population of various endangered animals, you could visit the World Wildlife Fund site. Be sure to use sites that are credible and reliable. If you are not sure whether a site is reliable, ask a parent or teacher.

For current magazine articles, see if your school has a membership to the *Reader's Guide to Periodical Literature*, which lists the names and page numbers of magazine articles related to a variety of topics. If you need geographical information about a country, check an atlas such as the *National Geographic Student World Atlas*.

1. How many reference sources should you consult before writing your report? _3 or 4_

2. What are two references that provide statistics and facts? _encyclopedias and websites_

3. Where will you find a listing of magazine articles? _Reader's Guide to Periodical Literature_

4. Where should you look for geographical information? _an atlas_

5. If you're stumped or don't know where to begin, who can help? _a librarian_

Page 343

Reports: Taking Notes

Directions: Read about taking notes for your report. Use the "index card" below to write a sample note from one of your reference sources.

When gathering information for a report, it is necessary to take notes. You'll need to take notes when you read encyclopedia entries, books, and magazine or news articles related to your topic.

Before you begin gathering information for a report, organize your thoughts around the who, what, when, where, why, and how questions of your topic. This organized approach will help direct you to the references that best answer these questions. It will also help you select and write in your notes only useful information.

There are different ways of taking notes. Some people use notebook paper. If you write on notebook paper, put a heading on each page. Write only notes related to each heading on specific pages. Otherwise, your notes will be disorganized, and it will be difficult to begin writing your paper.

Many people prefer to put their notes on index cards. Index cards can be easily sorted and organized when you begin writing your report and are helpful when preparing an outline. If you use index cards for your notes, put one fact on each card.

Take several notes from each reference source you use. Having too many notes is better than not having enough information when you start to write your report.

Answer will vary.

Page 344

Encyclopedia Skills: Taking Notes

A **biography** is a written report of a person's life. It is based on facts and actual events. To prepare to write a biographical essay, you could look up information about the person in a biographical or online encyclopedia.

Directions: Select one of the people listed below. Read about that person in an encyclopedia. Take notes to prepare for writing a biographical essay. Then, use your notes to answer the questions.

Babe Ruth	Ben Carson
Mikhail Baryshnikov	Steve Jobs
Jane Goodall	Woodrow Wilson
Jesse Owens	Charles Darwin
J.K. Rowling	Marie Curie

Answers will vary.

My Notes:

1. Where and when was he or she born? _____

2. If deceased, when did the person die? _____

3. When and why did he or she first become famous? _____

4. What are some important points about this person's career? _____

Page 345

Reports: Making an Outline

An outline will help you organize your ideas before you begin writing your report.

Title
I. First Main Idea
  A. A supporting idea or fact
  B. Another supporting idea or fact
    1. An example or related fact
    2. An example or related fact
II. Second Main Idea
  A. A supporting idea or fact
  B. Another supporting idea or fact
III. Third Main Idea
  A. A supporting idea or fact
  B. Another supporting idea or fact

Directions: Use information from your notes to write an outline for your report. Follow the above format, but expand your outline to include as many main ideas, facts, and examples as necessary.

Outlines will vary but should follow the format above.

Page 346

Reports: Writing the Paper

Directions: Read more about writing a report. Then, write your report.

Before you begin, be certain you clearly understand what is expected. How long should your report be? Must it be typed? Can it be written in pen? Should it be double-spaced?

Begin the first draft of your report with a general introduction of your topic. In the introduction, briefly mention the main points you will write about. One paragraph is usually enough to introduce your paper.

Next, comes the body of your report. Start a new paragraph for each main point. Include information that supports that point. If you are writing a long report, you may need to write a new paragraph for each supporting idea and/or each example. Follow your outline to be certain you cover all points. Depending on the number of words required to cover your topic, the body of the report will be anywhere from three or four paragraphs to several pages long.

In one or two concluding paragraphs, briefly summarize the main points you wrote about in the body of the report, and state any conclusions you have drawn as a result of your research.

Once you finish the first draft, you will need to edit and rewrite your report to make it read smoothly and correct errors. You may need to rewrite your report more than once to make it the best it can be.

If possible, put the report aside for a day or two before you rewrite it so you can look at it with fresh eyes and a clear mind. Professional writers often write several drafts, so don't be discouraged about rewrites! Rewriting and editing are the keys to good writing—keys that every writer, no matter how old or experienced, relies on.

Directions: Circle the words in the puzzle related to writing a report.

K	K	N	K	T	O	P	I	C	D	T	B
L	D	O	A	T	O	D	P	T	D	O	
I	N	T	R	O	D	U	C	T	I	O	N
E	N	E	R	G	D	E	E	O	O	O	N
D	W	S	R	G	E	Y	C	P	C	X	R
S	A	F	E	A	T	T	E	I	E	Y	O
R	W	A	Q	U	B	W	P	C	D	G	F
L	I	C	O	N	C	L	U	S	I	O	N
O	U	T	L	I	N	E	U	T	T	E	D
R	E	S	E	A	R	C	H	R	E	S	E

topic
facts
outline
introduction
body
conclusion
notes
research
edit

Page 347

Comprehensive Curriculum - **Grade 5**

Page 348

Review

1. Why should you narrow your topic when writing a report?
- [x] So you can include specific, relevant information
- [ ] So you can write a short paper
- [ ] So you can use only one reference book

2. Which of the following is not a reference book?
- [ ] *The American Heritage Children's Thesaurus*
- [ ] *National Geographic Student World Atlas*
- [x] *Flowers for Cosmo*
- [ ] *How Things Work Encyclopedia*

3. Writing an outline for your report will help you
- [ ] narrow your topic.
- [ ] gather many notes.
- [x] get organized and follow a plan.
- [ ] broaden your topic.

4. Which of the following is not a part of a finished report?
- [ ] Introduction
- [ ] Conclusion
- [ ] Body
- [x] Outline

5. When taking notes, index cards will help you
- [ ] check spelling, grammar, and punctuation.
- [x] organize your writing later.
- [ ] find things quickly on the shelves.
- [ ] transfer facts to your notebook.

Page 349

Editing

To **edit** means to revise and correct written work. Learning how to edit your work will help you become a better writer. First you should write a rough draft of your paper, and then edit it to make it better. Remember these things when writing your rough draft:

► **Do not overcrowd your page.** Leave space between every line and at the sides of your pages to make notes and changes.
► **Write so you can read it.** Don't be sloppy just because you're only writing a rough draft.
► **Number your pages.** This will help you keep everything in order.
► **Write on only one side of the page.** This gives you plenty of space if you want to make changes or add information between paragraphs.
► **Use the same size notebook paper for all drafts.** If all pages are the same size, you're less likely to lose any.

Before turning in your report or paper, ask yourself these questions:
► **Have I followed my outline?**
► **Have I told who, what, when, where, why, and how?**
► **Have I provided too much information?** (Good writers are concise. Don't repeat yourself after you have made a point.)
► **Do I still have unanswered questions?** (If you have questions, you can bet your readers will also. Add the missing information.)

It is always a good idea to let a day or so pass before rereading your paper and making final corrections. That way you will see what you actually wrote, instead of what you **think** you wrote.

When you edit your work, look for:
► **Correct grammar.**
► **Correct spelling.** Use the dictionary if you are not 100 percent sure.
► **Correct punctuation.**
► **Complete sentences.** Each should contain a complete thought.

Directions: Answer these questions about editing by writing **T** for true or **F** for false.

T 1. When you are editing, you should look for correct grammar and spelling.
F 2. Editors do not look for complete sentences.
F 3. Editors do not have to read each word of a story.
F 4. It is best to use both sides of a sheet of paper when writing the rough draft of your report.
F 5. It does not matter how neat your first draft is.
T 6. Editors make sure that sentences are punctuated correctly.

Page 350

Editing

Editors and proofreaders use certain marks to note the changes that need to be made. In addition to circling spelling errors and fixing capitalization mistakes, editors and proofreaders also use the following marks to indicate other mistakes that need to be corrected.

the	Delete.	∧	Insert a comma.	is	Insert a word.
a nt	Remove the space.	∨	Insert an apostrophe.	⊙	Insert a period.
in this	Insert a space.	⌄	Insert quotation marks.	sara	Capitalize.

Directions: Use editing marks to correct the errors in these sentences. Then, write the sentences correctly on the lines.

1. Mr. Ramsey was a man who liked to do nothing⊙
Mr. Ramsey was a man who liked to do nothing.

2. Lili, a young hawaiian girl, liked to swim in the sea.
Lili, a young Hawaiian girl, liked to swim in the sea.

3. Youngsters who play baseball always have a favorite player.
Youngsters who play baseball always have a favorite player.

4. Too many people said,⌄That movie was terrible."
Too many people said, "That movie was terrible."

5. I didn't want to go to the movie with jaden⊙
I didn't want to go to the movie with Jaden.

6. Prince charles has two adult sons⊙
Prince Charles has two adult sons.

7. The little boy's name was gilbert leonard longfellow⊙
The little boy's name was Albert Leonard Longfellow.

Page 351

Editing

Directions: Use editing marks to show the changes that need to be made in the following sentences.

1. billy bob branstool was was the biggest bully at our school⊙

2. mr. Ling told my mother that i was a good student⊙

3. I heard your mom say, "give your mother a kiss."

4. david and justin liked reading about dinosaurs,especially tyrannosaurus rex.

5. milton said to to mabel, "maybe we can play tomorrow."

6. gna and Liam knew the answers to the questions,but they would not raise their hands⊙

7. too many people were going to see the movie,so we decided to go get pizza instead⊙

8. tillie's aunt teresa was coming to visit for the month of may⊙

9. we lived in a small town called sophia, north carolina, for 20 days before we decided to move away.

10. we saw the mother fox bringing food to her cubs in the den⊙

11. i was reading the book called,haunting at midnight.

12. kevin and i decided that we would be detective bob and detective joe.

13. there were thirteen questions on the test. kevin missed all but the first one⊙

14. thirty of us were going on a fieldtrip when suddenly the teacher told the bus driver to turn around.

Page 352

Editing

not is	Flip the words around; transpose.
wan l jut	Flip letters around; transpose.
¶ That was when Peter began talking.	Indent the paragraph or start a new paragraph.
with you⌐ The movie we went to see was good.	Move text down to line below.
There were no people there.⌐ Jason thought we should go.	Move text up to line above.

Directions: Use editing marks to edit this story.

The Fallen Log

There was once a log on the floor of a very damp and eerie forest.two men came upon the log and sat down for a rest. these two men, leroy and larry, did not know that someone could hear every word they said.⌐I'm so tired, moaned larry, as he began unlacing his heavy hikingboots. "and my feet hurt, too."

"Quit complaining" friend his said. "We've got miles to walk before we'll find the cave with the hidden treasure. besides, if you think you're tired at look feet/my, with that he kicked off his tennis shoe and discovered a very red big toe. "I think i won't be able to go any farther.

"Sh-h-h, already!" the two men heard a voice. "enough about feet, enough!"Larry and Leroy began looking around them. they couldn't see anyone, though. "I'm in here, the voice said hoarsely.

Page 353

Editing

Directions: Use editing marks to edit the continuing story of Larry and Leroy.

Larry and Leroy

larry and leroy jumped up from the log as soon as they realized that they were sitting on something that had a voice. "Hey, that was fast," said the voice.

"How did you figure out where i was?"

By this time larry and leroy felt a little silly. They certainly didn't want to talk to a log. they looked at each other and then back at the log again. together they turned around and started walking down the path that had brought them to this point in the forest. "Hey, were are you going?" the voice called.

"Well, I-I-I don't know," Larry replied, wondering if he sould be answering a log. "Who are you?"

"I'm a tiny elf who has been lost in this tree for years," said the voice.

"Sure you are," replied lar, with that he and leroy began running for their lives.

Editing

Directions: Draw a line from the editing mark on the left to its meaning on the right.

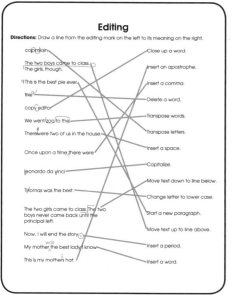

cop̂lain	Close up a word.
The two boys came to class. The girls, though.	Insert an apostrophe.
¶This is the best pie ever.	Insert a comma.
this	Delete a word.
copy editor	Transpose words.
We went zoo to the.	Transpose letters.
There were two of us in the house	Insert a space.
Once upon a time there were	Capitalize.
leonardo da vinci	Move text down to line below.
Thomas was the best.	Change letter to lower case.
The two girls came to class. The two boys never came back until the principal left.	Start a new paragraph.
Now, I will end the story	Move text up to line above.
My mother was the best lady I know	Insert a period.
This is my mothers hat.	Insert a word.

Page 354

Review

Directions: Use editing marks to edit the story. Also watch for and change:
Important details that may have been left out.
Places where the wording could be livelier.
Information that is not related to the story.

Answers may vary.

My friend Annie and I decided to go windsurfing one day. We gathered up our equipment—our windsurfing boards and sails—and headed down to the lake. The air was cool that day so annie and I didn't wear our bathing suits. we were just in cut-off shorts and t-shirts.

It took us a few minutes to get our windsails put together. This was the first time Annie and I had ever did this alone. Usually, our big brothers helped us. They had to be in school, though, and one annie and I don', so we decided to try the sport alone.

Annie's smile was ok. But I was glad the sun was shining brightly. It made it feel like it was warming outside than it really was. "Are you sure we should do this?" said annie, just as I was pulling my windsurf board down to the water. It will be fine, I assured her. I had gum in my mouth.

I put my toe into the lake.

"Wow, is it cold!" I yelled back to Annie. She pulled her windsurf board down beside mine. Hers was orange, blue and yellow. Mine was just purple and green. I finally got into the water with my board. Annie was right beside me. We got onto our boards and finally, both of us were standing up. But our windsails wouldn't move. Then Annie and I realized there was no wind that day!

Page 355

Proofreading

Proofreading, or "proofing," means to carefully look over what has been written, checking for spelling, grammar, punctuation, and other errors. All good writers carefully proofread and correct their own work before turning it into an editor—or a teacher.

Here are three common proofreading marks:
Correct spelling — dog / dol
Replace with lower case letter — A
Replace with capital letter — a

Directions: Carefully read the following paragraphs. Use proofreading marks to mark errors in the second paragraph. Correct all errors. The first sentence has been done for you.

A six-alarm fire at 2121 windsor Terrace on the northeast side awoke apartment residents at 3 A.M. yesterday morning. Eleven people were in the building. No one was hurt in the blaze, which caused $200,000 of property damage.

Property manager Jim Polaski credits a perfectly functioning smoke alarm system for waking residents so they could get out safely. A springkler system were also in place. "There was No panick," Polaski said proudly. "Everyone was calm and Orderly."

Page 356

Proofreading

Directions: Proofread the news article. Mark and correct the 20 errors in capitalization and spelling.

Be Wise When Buying a Car

Each year, about five percent of the U.S. population buys a new car, acprding to J.D. Link and Associates, a New York-based auto industry research company.

"A new car is the second most expensive purchase most people Ever make," says Link. "It's amazing how litle research people do before they enter the car showroom."

Link says research is the most important Thing a new car buyer can do to protect himself or herself. That way, he or she will get the Best car at the best price.

"the salespeople are not trying to get You the best deal," says Link. "they're trying to get themselves the best deal. Bee smart! Read up on new cars online and in magazines like Car and Driver and motortrend before you talk to a salesperson!"

NEW MODELS

Page 357

Editing: Check Your Proofreading Skills

Directions: Read about the things you should remember when you are revising your writing. Then, follow the instructions to revise the paper below.

After you have finished writing your rough draft, you should reread it later to determine what changes you need to make to ensure it's the best possible paper you are capable of writing.

Ask yourself the following questions:
Does my paper stick to the topic?
Have I left out any important details?
Can I make the writing more lively?
Have I made errors in spelling, punctuation, or capitalization?
Is there any information that should be left out?

Directions: Revise the following story by making changes to correct spelling, punctuation, and capitalization; add details; and cross out words or sentences that do not stick to the topic.

Hunting for Treasure

¶No one really believes me when I tell them that I'm a treasure hunter. But really I am. It isn't just any treasure that I like to hunt, though. I like treasures related to coins. Usually, when I go treasure huting I go alone. I always wear my blue coat.

One day, my good friend Jesse wanted to come with me. Why would you want to do that? asked. Because I like coins, too, he replied. What Jesse did not know was that the coins that I dig to find are not the coins that just anyone collects. The coins I like are special. They are coins that have been buried in dirt for years!

Page 358

Ancient Egypt

Have you ever wished you could visit Egypt for a first-hand look at the pyramids and ancient mummies? For most people, learning about Egypt is the closest they will come to visiting these ancient sites.

Directions: Test your knowledge about Egypt by writing as many of the answers as you can.

1. Write a paragraph describing what you already know about Egypt.
   Answers will vary.
   _____
   _____
   _____
   _____

2. Name at least two famous Egyptian kings or queens. _____
   Possible answer: King Tut and Queen Nefertiti

3. What was the purpose of a pyramid? _____
   Possible answer: to bury Egyptian kings in; to worship the gods

4. What was the purpose of mummification? _____
   to preserve bodies after death

5. What major river runs through Egypt? the Nile

Page 359

Comprehensive Curriculum - **Grade 5**

Taking Notes: Egyptian Mummies

Taking notes is the process of writing important points to remember, such as taking notes on material prepared by your teacher, what is discussed in class, or an article you read. Taking notes is useful when preparing for a test or when writing a report. When taking notes, follow these steps:

1. Read the article carefully.
2. Select one or two important points from each paragraph.
3. Write your notes in your own words.
4. Reread your notes to be sure you understand what you have written.
5. Abbreviate words to save time.

Directions: Read about Egyptian mummies. Select one or two important points from each paragraph. Write your notes in your own words.

> After the Egyptians discovered that bodies buried in the hot, dry sand of the desert became mummified, they began searching for ways to improve the mummification process. The use of natron became a vital part of embalming.
> Natron is a type of white powdery salt found in oases throughout Egypt. An oasis is a place in the desert where underground water rises to the surface. This water contains many types of salts, including table salt. It also contained natron. As the water evaporated in the hot sun of the desert, the salts were left behind. Natron was then collected for use in the mummification process.
> The body was dried in natron for up to 40 days. The natron caused the body to shrink and the skin to become leathery. For thousands of years, natron was a vital ingredient in preserving the bodies of kings, queens, and other wealthy Egyptian citizens.

Sample notes:

Paragraph 1 Bodies buried in hot dry sand became mummified. Natron is vital for embalming.

Paragraph 2 Natron is a salt that is found when water from an oasis evaporates, leaving behind salts that were in it.

Paragraph 3 The body was soaked in natron for up to 40 days, causing it to shrink and the skin to become leathery. Natron was used for thousands of years.

Page 360

Outlining

Outlining is a way to organize information before you write an essay or informational paragraph. Outlining helps you understand the information you read.

This sample form will help you get started. When outlining, you can add more main points, more smaller points, and/or more examples.

Title
I. First Main Idea
  A. A smaller idea
    1. An example
    2. An example
  B. Another smaller idea
II. Second Main Idea
  A. A smaller idea
  B. Another smaller idea
    1. An example
    2. An example
III. Third Main Idea
  A. A smaller idea
  B. A smaller idea

Directions: Read about building pyramids. Then, complete the outline on the next page.

> The process of building pyramids began as a way to honor a king or queen. Since the Egyptians believed in an afterlife, they thought it only fitting for their kings and queens to have elaborate burial tombs filled with treasures to enjoy in the afterlife. Thus, the idea of the pyramid was born.
> At first, pyramids were not built as they are known today. In the early stages of the Egyptian dynasty, kings were entombed in a mastaba. Mastabas were tombs made of mud-dried bricks. They formed a rectangular tomb with angled sides and a flat roof.
> Later, as the Egyptian kingdom became more powerful, kings felt they needed grander tombs. The step pyramid was developed. These pyramids were made of stone, rather than mud, and were much taller. A large mastaba was built on the ground. Then, four more mastabas (each smaller than the previous) were stacked on top.
> Finally, the pyramids took the shape that is familiar today. They were constructed with a flat bottom and four slanting sides that ascended to a final point. One of the tallest is over 400 feet high. These pyramids were also built of stone and were finished with an exterior of white limestone.

Page 361

Outlining: Egyptian Pyramids

Directions: Complete the outline. Then, answer the question.

Possible answers:

Egyptian Pyramids
    (title)

I. Mastabas
  A. made of mud-dried bricks
  B. rectangular tomb
  C. angled sides and a flat roof
II. Step pyramids
  A. made of stone
  B. much taller than a mastab
  C. large mastaba with four smaller mastabas stacked on top
III. Pyramids
  A. flat bottom and four slanting sides ascending to a final point
  B. tallest is over 400 feet high
  C. built of stone and finished with white limestone exterior

What do you find is the most interesting aspect about the pyramids of ancient Egypt? Why?
Answers will vary.

Page 362

Summarizing

A **summary** includes the main points from an article, book, or speech.

Example:

> Tomb robbing was an important business in ancient Egypt. Often, entire families participated in the plunder of tombs. These robbers may have been laborers, officials, tomb architects, or guards, but they all probably had one thing in common. They were involved in the building or designing of the tomb, or they wouldn't have had the knowledge necessary to successfully rob the burial sites. Not only did tomb robbing ensure a rich life for the robbers, but it also enabled them to be buried with many riches themselves.

Summary:

> Tomb robbing occurred in ancient Egypt. The robbers stole riches to use in their present lives or in their burials. Tomb robbers usually had some part in the building or design of the tomb. This allowed them to find the burial rooms where the treasures were stored.

Directions: Read about life in ancient Egypt. Then, write a three- to five-sentence summary.

> Egyptologists have learned much from the pyramids and mummies of ancient Egypt from the items left by grave robbers.
> Women of ancient Egypt wore makeup to enhance their features. Dark colored minerals called kohl were used as eyeliner and eye shadow. Men also wore eyeliner. Women used another mineral called ocher on their cheeks and lips to redden them. Henna, a plant which produces an orange dye, tinted the fingernails, the palms of their hands, and the soles of their feet.
> Perfume was also important in ancient Egypt. Small cones made of wax were worn on top of the head. These cones contained perfume oils. The sun slowly melted the wax, and the perfume would scent the hair, head, and shoulders.

Possible answer:

We have learned much from the pyramids and mummies. Women wore makeup made out of the minerals kohl and ocher and a plant called henna. Men wore eyeliner, too. Perfume made out of wax was also important to the ancient Egyptians.

Page 363

Summarizing: King Tut

Directions: Read about King Tut. Then, write a five- to seven-sentence summary.

> King Tutankhamen (TO-TAN-KO-MEN) became king of Egypt when he was only nine years old. Known today as "King Tut," he died in 1355 B.C. when he was 18. Because King Tut died so young, not much is known about what he did while he was king.
> After his death, Tut's body was mummified and buried in a pyramid in the Valley of the Kings in Egypt. Many other kings of ancient Egypt were buried there also.
> In 1922, King Tut became famous when an Englishman named Howard Carter discovered and explored his tomb. The king's mummy, wearing a gold mask decorated with precious stones, was found intact. Amazingly, all King Tut's riches were still in his tomb. His was the only one in the Valley of the Kings that had not been discovered and robbed.
> The king's tomb contained four rooms. One contained his mummy. The other rooms were filled with beautiful furniture, including King Tut's throne. Also found in Tut's tomb were more than 3,000 objects, like clothes, jewelry, wine, food—and a trumpet that could still be played. Obviously, King Tut planned to live royally in the next world!

Possible answer:

King Tut ruled Egypt from age 9 to 18. Because he died so young, not much is known about his life. He was buried in the Valley of the Kings. His tomb was discovered by Howard Carter. All of King Tut's riches were still inside. There were more than 3,000 objects found in the tomb, including his mummy and his throne.

Page 364

Place Value

The place value of a digit or numeral is shown by where it is in the number. In the number 1,234, 1 has the place value of thousands, 2 is hundreds, 3 is tens, and 4 is ones.

Example: 1,250,000,000

Read: One billion, two hundred fifty million

Write: 1,250,000,000

Billions			Millions			Thousands			Ones		
h	t	o	h	t	o	h	t	o	h	t	o
	1,	2	5	0,		0	0	0,		0	0	0

Directions: Read the words. Then, write the numbers.

twenty million, three hundred four thousand   20,304,000

five thousand, four hundred twenty-three   5,423

one billion fifty billion, eight million, one thousand, five hundred   150,008,001,500

sixty billion, seven hundred million, one hundred thousand, three hundred twelve   60,700,100,312

four hundred million, fifteen thousand, seven hundred one   400,015,701

six hundred ninety-nine million, four thousand, nine hundred forty-two   699,004,942

Here's a game to play with a partner.

Write a 10-digit number using each digit, 0 to 9, only once. Do not show the number to your partner. Give clues like: "There is a five in the hundreds place." The clues can be given in any order. See if your partner can write the same number you have written.

Page 366

Place Value

Directions: Draw a line to connect each number to its correct written form.

1. 791,000 — Three hundred fifty thousand
2. 350,000 — Seventeen million, five hundred thousand
3. 17,500,000 — Seven hundred ninety-one thousand
4. 3,500,000 — Seventy thousand, nine hundred ten
5. 70,910 — Three million, five hundred thousand
6. 35,500,000 — Seventeen billion, five hundred thousand
7. 17,000,500,000 — Thirty-five million, five hundred thousand

Directions: Look carefully at this number: 2,071,463,548. Write the numeral for each of the following places.

8. __6__ ten thousands
9. __1__ millions
10. __5__ hundreds
11. __2__ billions
12. __4__ hundred thousands
13. __7__ ten millions
14. __3__ one thousands
15. __0__ hundred millions

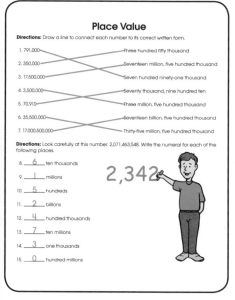

Page 367

Addition

Addition is putting together two or more numbers to find the sum.

Directions: Add. Fill the backpacks with the right answers.

38 + 92 = 130	71 + 48 = 119	43 + 62 = 105	56 + 14 = 70	87 + 13 = 100
24 + 39 = 63	15 + 67 = 82	83 + 47 = 130	35 + 80 = 115	17 + 64 = 81
95 + 25 = 120	54 + 19 = 73	61 + 77 = 138	42 + 89 = 131	37 + 97 = 134
62 + 39 = 101	18 + 43 = 61	27 + 94 = 121	11 + 89 = 100	48 + 58 = 106

Page 368

Addition

Teachers of an Earth science class planned to take 50 students on an overnight hiking and camping experience. After planning the menu, they went to the grocery store for supplies.

Breakfast	**Lunch**	**Dinner**	**Snacks**
bacon	sandwiches	pasta	graham crackers
eggs	apples	sauce	marshmallows
fruit	pretzels	garlic bread	chocolate bars
cereal	juice	salad	
juice	granola bars		
$34.50	$52.15	$47.25	$23.40

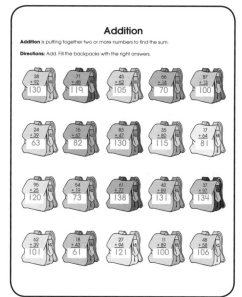

Directions: Answer the questions. Write the total amount spent on food for the trip.

What information do you need to answer the question? __the amount for each meal plus snacks added together__

What is the total? __$157.30__

Directions: Add.

462 + 574 = 1,036	918 + 359 = 1,277	527 + 582 = 1,109	386 + 745 = 1,131	295 + 764 = 1,059
397 + 448 = 845	524 + 725 = 1,249	906 + 337 = 1,243	750 + 643 = 1,393	891 + 419 = 1,310
1,568 + 2,341 = 3,909	3,214 + 2,896 = 6,110	5,147 + 4,285 = 9,432	7,259 + 2,451 = 9,710	9,317 + 3,583 = 12,900

Page 369

Addition

Directions: Add.

1. Tourists travel to national parks to see the many animals that live there. Park rangers estimate 384 buffalo, 282 grizzly bears, and 426 deer are in the park. What is the total number of buffalo, bears, and deer estimated to be in the park?
__1,092 buffalo, bears, and deer__

2. Last August, 2,248 visitors drove motor homes into the campgrounds for overnight camping. 647 set up campsites with tents. How many campsites were there altogether in August?
__2,895 campsites__

3. During a three-week camping trip, Carlos and his family hiked 42 miles, took a 126-mile canoeing trip, and drove their car 853 miles. How many miles did they travel in all?
__1,021 miles__

4. Old Faithful is a geyser that spouts water high into the air. 10,000 gallons of water burst into the air regularly. Two other geysers spout 2,400 gallons of water during each eruption. What is the amount of water thrust into the air during one cycle?
__14,800 gallons__

5. Yellowstone National Park covers approximately 2,221,772 acres of land. Close by, the Grand Tetons cover approximately 310,350 acres. How many acres of land are there in these two parks?
__2,532,122 acres__

6. Hiking trails cover 486 miles, motor routes around the north rim total 376 miles, and another 322 miles of road allow visitors to follow a loop around the southern part of the park. How many miles of trails and roadways are there?
__1,184 miles__

Page 370

Addition

Bob the butcher is popular with the dogs in town. He was making a delivery this morning when he noticed he was being followed by two dogs. Bob tried to climb a ladder to escape from the dogs. Solve the following addition problems, and shade in the answers on the ladder. If all the numbers are shaded when the problems have been solved, Bob made it up the ladder. Some answers may not be on the ladder.

1. 986,145 + 621,332 + 200,008 = 1,807,485
2. 1,873,402 + 925,666 + 4,689 = 2,803,757
3. 506,328 + 886,510 + 342,225 = 1,735,063
4. 43,015 + 2,811,604 + 987,053 = 3,841,672
5. 18,443 + 300,604 + 999,999 = 1,319,046
6. 8,075 + 14,608 + 33,914 = 56,597
7. 9,162 + 7,804 + 755,122 = 772,088
8. 88,714 + 1,986,114 + 5,441,298 = 5,743,665
9. 3,244,662 + 521,387 = 5,752,163
10. 4,581 + 22,983 + 5,618,775 = 5,646,339
11. 818,623 + 926 + 3,260,004 = 4,079,553
12. 80,436 + 9,159 + 3,028,761 = 3,118,356

Ladder: 1,319,046 / 2,803,757 / 5,743,665 / 3,118,356 / 56,597 / 4,079,553 / 1,807,485 / 2,943,230 / 18,344,666 / 1,735,063 / 5,752,163 / 896,316 / 3,841,672 / 5,646,339

Does Bob make it? __no__

Page 371

Subtraction

Subtraction is taking away one number from another to find the difference between the two numbers.

Directions: Subtract.

76 − 23 = 53	93 − 14 = 79	68 − 25 = 43	49 − 17 = 32	88 − 39 = 49	54 − 25 = 29

Brent saved $75.00 of the money he earned delivering the local newspaper in his neighborhood. He wanted to buy a new bicycle that cost $139.00. How much more would he need to save in order to buy the bike?

__$64__

38 − 29 = 9	74 − 25 = 49	67 − 49 = 18	92 − 35 = 57	43 − 26 = 17	85 − 37 = 48

When Brent finally went to buy the bicycle, he saw a light and basket for the bike. He decided to buy them both. The light was $5.95, and the basket was $10.50. He gave the clerk a 20-dollar bill that his grandmother had given him for his birthday. How much change did he get back?

__$3.55__

Page 372

Comprehensive Curriculum - **Grade 5**

Subtraction

When working with larger numbers, it is important to keep the numbers lined up according to place value.

Directions: Subtract.

398	543	491
− 149	− 287	− 311
249	256	180

786	1,825	4,172
− 597	− 495	− 2,785
189	1,330	1,387

8,391	63,852	24,107	52,900
− 5,492	− 34,765	− 19,350	− 43,081
2,899	29,087	4,757	9,819

Eagle Peak is the highest mountain peak at Yellowstone National Park. It is 11,353 feet high. The next highest point at the park is Mount Washburn. It is 10,243 feet tall. How much higher is Eagle Peak?

1,110 feet higher

The highest mountain peak in North America is Mount McKinley, which stretches 20,320 feet toward the sky. Two other mountain ranges in North America have peaks at 10,302 feet and 8,194 feet. What is the greatest difference between the peaks?

12,126 feet

Page 373

Checking Subtraction

You can check your subtraction by using addition.

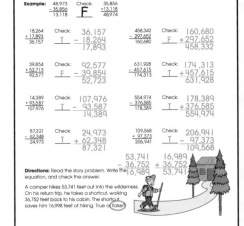

Example: 34,436   Check: 22,172
− 12,264   →   + 12,264
22,172   →   34,436

Directions: Subtract. Then, check your answers by adding.

	Check:			Check:	
15,326		3,794	28,615		3,286
− 11,532		+ 11,532	− 25,329		+ 25,329
3,794		15,326	3,286		28,615

96,521	Check:	49,143	46,496	Check:	10,619
− 47,378		+ 47,378	− 35,877		+ 35,877
49,143		96,521	10,619		46,496

77,911	Check:	14,128	156,901	Check:	44,169
− 63,783		+ 63,783	− 112,732		+ 112,732
14,128		77,911	44,169		156,901

395,638	Check:	208,069	67,002	Check:	13,807
−187,569		+ 187,569	− 53,195		+ 53,195
208,069		395,638	13,807		67,002

16,075	Check:	179	39,678	Check:	19,909
−15,896		+ 15,896	−19,769		+ 19,769
179		16,075	19,909		39,678

84,654	Check:	34,657	12,335	Check:	1,638
− 49,997		+ 49,997	−10,697		+ 10,697
34,657		84,654	1,638		12,335

During the summer, 158,941 people visited Yellowstone National Park. During the fall, there were 52,397 visitors. How many more visitors went to the park during the summer than the fall?

106,544 visitors

Page 374

Addition and Subtraction

Directions: Check the answers. Write **T** if the answer is true and **F** if it is false.

Example: 48,973   Check: 35,856
− 35,856   **F**   +13,118
13,118   48,974

18,264	Check:	36,157	458,342	Check:	160,680
+ 17,893	**T**	− 18,264	− 297,652	**F**	+297,652
36,157		17,893	160,680		458,332

39,854	Check:	92,577	631,928	Check:	174,313
+ 52,713	**F**	− 39,854	− 457,615	**T**	+457,615
92,577		52,723	174,313		631,928

14,389	Check:	107,976	554,974	Check:	178,389
+ 93,587	**T**	− 93,587	− 376,585	**T**	+376,585
107,976		14,389	178,389		554,974

87,321	Check:	24,973	109,568	Check:	206,941
− 62,348	**T**	+ 62,348	+ 97,373	**T**	− 97,373
24,973		87,321	206,941		109,568

53,741	16,989
− 36,752	+ 36,752
16,989	53,741

Directions: Read the story problem. Write the equation, and check the answer.

A camper hikes 53,741 feet out into the wilderness. On his return trip, he takes a shortcut, walking 36,752 feet back to his cabin. The shortcut saves him 16,998 feet of hiking. True or false?

Page 375

Addition and Subtraction

Directions: Add or subtract to find the answers.

Eastland School hosted a field day. Students could sign up for a variety of events. 175 students signed up for individual races. Twenty two-person teams competed in the mile relay, and 36 kids took part in the high jump. How many students participated in the activities?

251 students

Westmore School brought 42 students and 7 adults to the field day event. Northern School brought 84 students and 15 adults. There was a total of 300 students and 45 adults at the event. How many were from other schools?

174 students and 23 adults

The Booster Club sponsored a concession stand during the day. Last year, they made $1,000 at the same event. This year they hoped to earn at least $1,250. They actually raised $1,842. How much more did they make than they had anticipated?

$592.00

Each school was awarded a trophy for participating in the field day's activities. The Booster Club planned to purchase three plaques as awards, but they only wanted to spend $150. The first-place trophy they selected was $68. The second-place award was $59. How much would they be able to spend on the third-place award if they stay within their budgeted amount?

$23.00

The Booster Club decided to spend $1,000 to purchase several items for the school with the money they had earned. Study the list of items suggested, and decide which combination of items they could purchase.

A. Swing set $425   A+B+D

B. Sliding board $263   B+C+D

C. Scoreboard $515   A+C

D. Team uniforms $180

Page 376

Rounding

Rounding a number means to express it to the nearest ten, hundred, thousand, and so on. When rounding a number to the nearest ten, if the number has five or more ones, round up. Round down if the number has four or fewer ones.

Examples:

Round to the nearest ten:	84 → 80	86 → 90
Round to the nearest hundred:	187 → 200	120 → 100
Round to the nearest thousand:	981 → 1,000	5,480 → 5,000

Directions: Round these numbers to the nearest ten.

87 → 90   53 → 50   48 → 50   32 → 30   76 → 80

Directions: Round these numbers to the nearest hundred.

168 → 200   243 → 200   591 → 600   743 → 700   493 → 500

Directions: Round these numbers to the nearest thousand.

895 → 1,000   3,492 → 3,000   7,521 → 8,000   14,904 → 15,000   62,387 → 62,000

City Populations	
City	Population
Cleveland	390,113
Seattle	652,405
Omaha	434,353
Kansas City	467,007
Atlanta	447,841
Austin	885,400

Directions: Use the city population chart to answer the questions.

Which city has a population of about 500,000?

Kansas City

Which city has a population of about 900,000?

Austin

How many cities have a population of about 400,000? 3

Which ones? Cleveland, Omaha, Atlanta

Page 377

Estimating

To **estimate** means to give an approximate rather than an exact answer. Rounding each number first makes it easy to estimate an answer.

Example:

93 → 90	321 → 300	1,859 → 2,000
+ 48 + 50	+ 597 + 600	− 997 − 1,000
140	900	1,000

Directions: Estimate the sums and differences by rounding the numbers first.

68 → 70	12 → 10	89 → 90
+ 34 + 30	+ 98 +100	+ 23 + 20
100	110	110

638 → 600	281 → 300	271 → 300
− 395 − 400	− 69 − 100	− 126 − 100
200	200	200

1,532 → 2,000	8,312 → 8,000	6,341 → 6,000
− 998 − 1,000	− 4,789 − 5,000	+ 9,286 + 9,000
1,000	3,000	15,000

Alejandra has $50 to purchase tennis shoes, a tennis racquet, and tennis balls. Does she have enough money?

yes

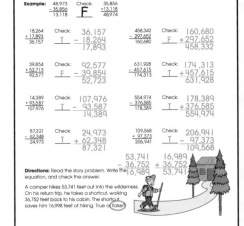

Page 378

Page 379

Rounding and Estimating

Rounding numbers and estimating answers is an easy way of finding the approximate answer without writing out the problem or using a calculator.

Directions: Circle the correct answer.

Round to the nearest **ten**:

73 → (70) / 80   48 → 40 / (50)   65 → 60 / (70)

85 → (80) / 90   92 → (90) / 100   37 → (30) / 40

Round to the nearest **hundred**:

139 → (100) / 200   782 → 700 / (800)   390 → (300) / 400

640 → (600) / 700   525 → (500) / 600   457 → 400 / (500)

Round to the nearest **thousand**:

1,375 → (1,000) / 2,000   21,800 → 21,000 / (22,000)   36,240 → (36,000) / 37,000

Sam wanted to buy a new computer. He knew he had about $1,200 to spend. Which of the following ones could he afford to buy?

$1,165 $1,279   ($1,249)

If Sam spent $39 on software for his new computer, $265 for a printer, and $38 for a cordless mouse, about how much money did he need?

$40 + $300 + $40 = $380.00

Page 380

Prime Numbers

Example: 3 is a prime number because 3 ÷ 1 = 3 and 3 ÷ 3 = 1. Any other divisor will result in a mixed number or fraction.

A **prime number** is any number greater than 1 that can only be divided by itself and the number 1.

A **composite number** is not a prime number. That is, it can be divided evenly by numbers other than itself and 1.

A prime number is a positive whole number that can be divided evenly only by itself or one.

Directions: Write the first 15 prime numbers. Test them by dividing by 2 and by 3.

Prime Numbers:

2   3   5   7   11

13   17   19   23   29

31   37   41   43   47

How many prime numbers are there between 0 and 100? 25

Page 381

Prime Numbers

Directions: Circle the prime numbers.

(71)	(3)	82	20	(43)	69
128	(97)	(23)	111	75	51
(13)	44	(137)	68	171	(83)
(61)	21	77	(101)	34	16
(2)	39	92	(17)	52	(29)
(19)	156	63	99	27	147
121	25	88	12	87	55
57	(7)	(139)	91	9	(37)
(67)	183	(5)	(59)	(11)	95

Page 382

Multiples

A **multiple** is the product of a specific number and any other number. When you multiply two numbers, the answer is called the **product**.

Example:
The multiples of 2 are 2 (2 x 1), 4 (2 x 2), 6, 8, 10, 12, and so on.

The **least common multiple** (LCM) of two or more numbers is the smallest number other than 0 that is a multiple of each number.

Example:
Multiples of 3 are **6**, 9, **12**, 15, **18**, 21, **24**, etc.
Multiples of 6 are **6**, **12**, **18**, **24**, 30, 36, 42, etc.
Multiples that 3 and 6 have in common are 6, 12, 18, 24.
The LCM of 3 and 6 is 6.

Directions: Write the first nine multiples of 3, 4, and 6. Write the LCM.

3: 3, 6, 9, 12, 15, 18, 21, 24, 27
4: 4, 8, 12, 16, 20, 24, 28, 32, 36
6: 6, 12, 18, 24, 30, 36, 42, 48, 54

LCM = 12

Directions: Write the first nine multiples of 2 and 5. Write the LCM.

2: 2, 4, 6, 8, 10, 12, 14, 16, 18
5: 5, 10, 15, 20, 25, 30, 35, 40, 45

LCM = 10

Directions: Find the LCM for each pair of numbers.

7 and 3 21   4 and 6 12   6 and 9 18
5 and 15 15   5 and 4 20   3 and 18 18

Directions: Fill in the missing numbers.

30 has multiples of 5 and 6, of 2 and 15, of 3 and 10.

Page 383

Factors

Factors are the numbers multiplied together to give a product. The **greatest common factor** (GCF) is the largest number for a set of numbers that divides evenly into each number in the set.

Example:
The factors of 12 are 3 x 4, 2 x 6, and 1 x 12.
We can write the factors like this: 3, 4, 2, 6, 12, 1.
The factors of 8 are 2, 4, 8, 1.
The common factors of 12 and 8 are 2 and 4 and 1.
The GCF of 12 and 8 is 4.

Directions: Write the factors of each pair of numbers. Then, write the common factors and the GCF.

1. 12: 1, 2, 3, 4, 6, 12
   15: 1, 3, 5, 15
   The common factors of 12 and 15 are 1, 3.
   The GCF is 3.

2. 20: 1, 2, 4, 5, 10, 20
   10: 1, 2, 5, 10
   The common factors of 10 and 20 are 1, 2, 5, 10.
   The GCF is 10.

3. 32: 1, 2, 4, 8, 16, 32
   24: 1, 2, 3, 4, 6, 8, 12, 24
   The common factors of 24 and 32 are 1, 2, 4, 8.
   The GCF is 8.

Directions: Write the GCF for the following pairs of numbers.

28 and 20 4   42 and 12 6
36 and 12 12   20 and 5 5

Page 384

Factor Trees

A **factor tree** shows the prime factors of a number. The factors for a prime number, such as 7, are only itself and 1.

Example:
30 = 6 x 5 → 6 = 3 x 2
30 = 3 x 2 x 5.
3, 2, and 5 are prime numbers.

Directions: Fill in the numbers in the factor tree.

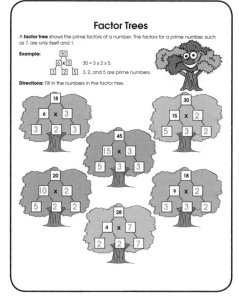

18 = 6 x 3 → 3 x 2, 3
30 = 15 x 2 → 5 x 3, 2
45 = 15 x 3 → 5 x 3, 3
20 = 10 x 2 → 5 x 2, 2
18 = 9 x 2 → 3 x 3, 2
28 = 4 x 7 → 2 x 2, 7

Comprehensive Curriculum - **Grade 5**

Factor Trees

Directions: Fill in the numbers in the factor trees. The first one has been done for you.

Page 385

Greatest Common Factor

Directions: Write the greatest common factor for each set of numbers.

10 and 35   5
2 and 10   2
42 and 63   21
16 and 40   8
25 and 55   5
12 and 20   4
14 and 28   14
8 and 20   4
6 and 27   3
15 and 35   5
18 and 48   6

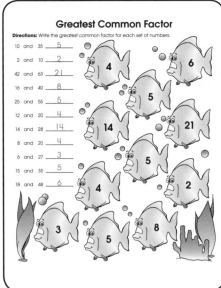

Page 386

Least Common Multiple

Directions: Write the least common multiple for each pair of numbers.

12 and 7   84
2 and 4   4
22 and 4   44
6 and 10   30
3 and 7   21
6 and 8   24
5 and 10   10
8 and 12   24
9 and 15   45
7 and 5   35
3 and 8   24
9 and 4   36

Page 387

Multiplication

Multiplication is a process of quick addition of a number a certain number of times.

Example: 3 x 15 = 45   is the same as adding   15 + 15 + 15 = 45
                                                    15 three times.

Directions: Multiply.

32	48	26	19	63
x 3	x 7	x 5	x 6	x 2
96	336	130	114	126

251	523	915	431	275
x 4	x 8	x 3	x 7	x 3
1,004	4,184	2,745	3,017	825

412	643	526	742
x 21	x 17	x 22	x 35
8,652	10,931	11,572	25,970

256	874	372	951
x 74	x 15	x 45	x 34
18,944	13,110	16,740	32,334

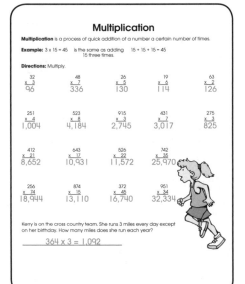

Kerry is on the cross country team. She runs 3 miles every day except on her birthday. How many miles does she run each year?

364 x 3 = 1,092

Page 388

Multiplication

Be certain to keep the proper place value when multiplying by tens and hundreds.

Examples:

143	250
x 262	x 150
286	000
858	1250
286	250
37,466	37,500

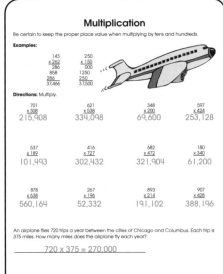

Directions: Multiply.

701	621	348	597
x 308	x 538	x 200	x 424
215,908	334,098	69,600	253,128

537	416	682	180
x 189	x 727	x 472	x 340
101,493	302,432	321,904	61,200

878	267	893	907
x 638	x 196	x 214	x 428
560,164	52,332	191,102	388,196

An airplane flies 720 trips a year between the cities of Chicago and Columbus. Each trip is 375 miles. How many miles does the airplane fly each year?

720 x 375 = 270,000

Page 389

Division

Division is the reverse of multiplication. It is the process of dividing a number into equal groups of smaller numbers.

Directions: Divide.

Greg had 936 marbles to share with his two brothers. If the boys divided them evenly, how many will each one get? 312

The marbles Greg kept were four different colors: blue, green, red, and orange. He had the same number of each color. He divided them into two groups. One group had only orange marbles. The rest of the marbles were in the other group. How many marbles did he have in each group?   orange 78   others 234

The **dividend** is the number to be divided by another number. In the problem 28 ÷ 7 = 4, 28 is the dividend.

The **divisor** is the number by which another number is divided. In the problem 28 ÷ 7 = 4, 7 is the divisor.

The **quotient** is the answer in a division problem. In the problem 28 ÷ 7 = 4, 4 is the quotient.

The **remainder** is the number left over in the quotient of a division problem. In the problem 29 ÷ 7 = 4 r1, 1 is the remainder.

Directions: Write the answers.

In the problem 25 ÷ 8 = 3 r1 . . .

What is the divisor?   8   What is the remainder?   1

What is the quotient?   3   What is the dividend?   25

Directions: Divide.

225	418	75	80	578
9)2,025	6)2,508	3)225	5)400	2)1,156

Page 390

Division

The remainder in a division problem must always be less than the divisor.

Example:

```
      244 r 23
26 ) 6,367
     52
     116
     104
     127
     104
      23
```

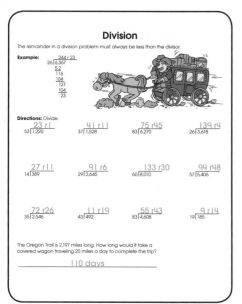

Directions: Divide.

```
     23 r 1          41 r 11         75 r 45         139 r 4
53 ) 1,220      37 ) 1,528      83 ) 6,270      26 ) 3,618

     27 r 11         91 r 6          133 r 30        94 r 48
14 ) 389        29 ) 2,645      60 ) 8,010      57 ) 5,406

     72 r 26         11 r 19         55 r 43         9 r 14
35 ) 2,546      43 ) 492        83 ) 4,608      19 ) 185
```

The Oregon Trail is 2,197 miles long. How long would it take a covered wagon traveling 20 miles a day to complete the trip?

__110 days__

Page 391

Checking Division

Answers in division problems can be checked by multiplying.

Example:

```
      481 r 17                Check:      481
33 ) 15,890                            x  33
     132                                 1443
      269                                1443
      264                               15,873
       50                           +      17
       33                               15,890
       17
```
Add the remainder

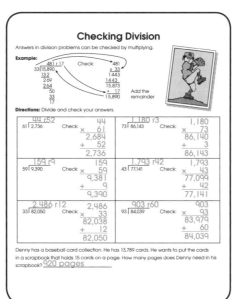

Directions: Divide and check your answers.

```
      44 r 52          Check:    44       |      1,180 r 3      Check:   1,180
61 ) 2,736                    x   61      | 73 ) 86,143              x     73
                              2,684       |                          86,140
                          +      52       |                      +        3
                              2,736       |                          86,143

     159 r 9           Check:   159       |      1,793 r 42      Check:   1,793
59 ) 9,390                    x   59      | 43 ) 77,141              x      43
                              9,381       |                          77,099
                          +       9       |                      +       42
                              9,390       |                          77,141

   2,486 r 12          Check:  2,486      |      903 r 60       Check:     903
33 ) 82,050                   x    33     | 93 ) 84,039              x      93
                             82,038       |                          83,979
                          +      12       |                      +       60
                             82,050       |                          84,039
```

Denny has a baseball card collection. He has 13,789 cards. He wants to put the cards in a scrapbook that holds 15 cards on a page. How many pages does Denny need in his scrapbook? __920 pages__

Page 392

Multiplication and Division

Directions: Multiply or divide to find the answers.

Brianne's summer job is mowing lawns for three of her neighbors. Each lawn takes about 1 hour to mow and needs to be done once every week. At the end of the summer, she will have earned a total of $630. She collected the same amount of money from each job. How much did each neighbor pay for her summer lawn service?

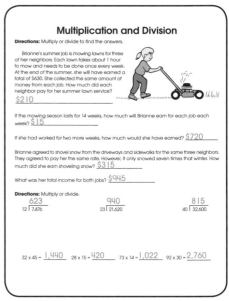

$210

If the mowing season lasts for 14 weeks, how much will Brianne earn for each job each week? __$15__

If she had worked for two more weeks, how much would she have earned? __$720__

Brianne agreed to shovel snow from the driveways and sidewalks for the same three neighbors. They agreed to pay her the same rate. However, it only snowed seven times that winter. How much did she earn shoveling snow? __$315__

What was her total income for both jobs? __$945__

Directions: Multiply or divide.

```
      623              940                 815
12 ) 7,476       23 ) 21,620         40 ) 32,600
```

32 x 45 = __1,440__   28 x 15 = __420__   73 x 14 = __1,022__   92 x 30 = __2,760__

Page 393

Adding and Subtracting Like Fractions

A **fraction** is a number that names part of a whole. Examples of fractions are $\frac{1}{2}$ and $\frac{1}{3}$. **Like fractions** have the same **denominator**, or bottom number. Examples of like fractions are $\frac{1}{4}$ and $\frac{3}{4}$.

To add or subtract fractions, the denominators must be the same. Add or subtract only the **numerators**, the numbers above the line in fractions.

Example:

$$\frac{5}{8} - \frac{1}{8} = \frac{4}{8}$$

numerators / denominators

Directions: Add or subtract these fractions.

$$\frac{6}{12} - \frac{3}{12} = \frac{3}{12} \qquad \frac{4}{9} + \frac{1}{9} = \frac{5}{9} \qquad \frac{1}{3} + \frac{1}{3} = \frac{2}{3} \qquad \frac{5}{11} + \frac{4}{11} = \frac{9}{11}$$

$$\frac{3}{5} - \frac{1}{5} = \frac{2}{5} \qquad \frac{5}{6} - \frac{2}{6} = \frac{3}{6} \qquad \frac{2}{4} + \frac{2}{4} = \frac{4}{4} \qquad \frac{5}{10} + \frac{3}{10} = \frac{8}{10}$$

$$\frac{3}{8} + \frac{2}{8} = \frac{5}{8} \qquad \frac{1}{7} + \frac{4}{7} = \frac{5}{7} \qquad \frac{2}{15} + \frac{15}{15} = \frac{17}{20} \qquad \frac{11}{15} - \frac{9}{15} = \frac{2}{15}$$

Directions: Color the part of each pizza that equals the given fraction.

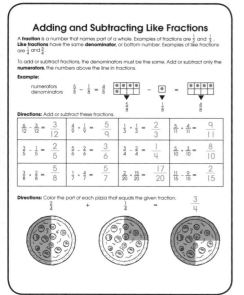

$$\frac{2}{4} \quad + \quad \frac{1}{4} \quad = \quad \frac{3}{4}$$

Page 394

Adding and Subtracting Unlike Fractions

Unlike fractions have different denominators. Examples of unlike fractions are $\frac{1}{4}$ and $\frac{2}{8}$. To add or subtract fractions, the denominators must be the same.

Example:

Step 1: Make the denominators the same by finding the least common denominator. The LCD of a pair of fractions is the same as the least common multiple (LCM) of their denominators.

$$\frac{1}{3} + \frac{1}{4} =$$

Multiples of 3 are 3, 6, 9, **12**, 15.
Multiples of 4 are 4, 8, **12**, 16.
LCM (and LCD) = 12

Step 2: Multiply by a number that will give the LCD. The numerator and denominator must be multiplied by the same number.

A. $\frac{1}{3} \times \frac{4}{4} = \frac{4}{12}$ **B.** $\frac{1}{4} \times \frac{3}{3} = \frac{3}{12}$

Step 3: Add the fractions.

$$\frac{1}{3} + \frac{1}{4} = \frac{4}{12} + \frac{3}{12} = \frac{7}{12}$$

Directions: Follow the above steps to add or subtract unlike fractions. Write the LCM.

$$\frac{2}{4} + \frac{3}{8} = \frac{7}{8} \qquad \frac{3}{2} + \frac{1}{3} = \frac{5}{6} \qquad \frac{4}{5} - \frac{1}{4} = \frac{11}{20}$$
LCM = 8 \qquad LCM = 6 \qquad LCM = 20

$$\frac{2}{3} + \frac{2}{9} = \frac{8}{9} \qquad \frac{4}{7} - \frac{2}{14} = \frac{6}{14} \qquad \frac{7}{12} - \frac{2}{4} = \frac{1}{12}$$
LCM = 9 \qquad LCM = 14 \qquad LCM = 12

The basketball team ordered two pizzas. They left $\frac{1}{3}$ of one and $\frac{1}{4}$ of the other. How much pizza was left?

$\frac{7}{12}$

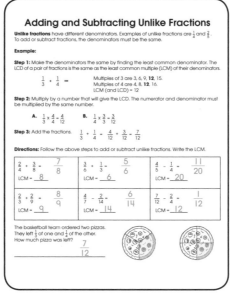

Page 395

Reducing Fractions

A fraction is in lowest terms when the GCF of both the numerator and denominator is 1. These fractions are in lowest possible terms: $\frac{2}{3}$, $\frac{1}{8}$, and $\frac{99}{100}$.

Example: Write $\frac{4}{8}$ in lowest terms.

Step 1: Write the factors of 4 and 8.
Factors of 4 are **4**, 2, 1.
Factors of 8 are 1, 8, 2, **4**.
Step 2: Find the GCF: 4.
Step 3: Divide both the numerator and denominator by 4.

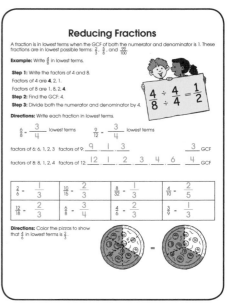

$$\frac{4 \div 4}{8 \div 4} = \frac{1}{2}$$

Directions: Write each fraction in lowest terms.

$$\frac{6}{8} = \frac{3}{4} \text{ lowest terms} \qquad \frac{9}{12} = \frac{3}{4} \text{ lowest terms}$$

factors of 6: 6, 1, 2, 3   factors of 9: __9__, __3__, __1__   __3__ GCF

factors of 8: 8, 1, 2, 4   factors of 12: __12__, __1__, __2__, __3__, __4__, __6__   __4__ GCF

$$\frac{5}{15} = \frac{1}{3} \qquad \frac{10}{15} = \frac{2}{3} \qquad \frac{8}{32} = \frac{1}{3} \qquad \frac{4}{10} = \frac{2}{5}$$

$$\frac{12}{18} = \frac{2}{3} \qquad \frac{6}{9} = \frac{3}{3} \qquad \frac{6}{9} = \frac{2}{3} \qquad \frac{3}{9} = \frac{1}{3}$$

Directions: Color the pizzas to show that $\frac{4}{6}$ in lowest terms is $\frac{2}{3}$.

Page 396

Comprehensive Curriculum - **Grade 5**

Improper Fractions

An **improper fraction** has a numerator that is greater than its denominator. An example of an improper fraction is $\frac{7}{6}$. An improper fraction should be reduced to its lowest terms.

Example: $\frac{5}{4}$ is an improper fraction because its numerator is greater than its denominator.

Step 1: Divide the numerator by the denominator: $5 \div 4 = 1$, r1

Step 2: Write the remainder as a fraction: $\frac{1}{4}$

$\frac{5}{4} = 1\frac{1}{4}$ $1\frac{1}{4}$ is a mixed number—a whole number and a fraction.

Directions: Follow the steps above to change the improper fractions to mixed numbers.

$\frac{9}{8} = 1\frac{1}{8}$	$\frac{11}{5} = 2\frac{1}{5}$	$\frac{5}{3} = 1\frac{2}{3}$	$\frac{7}{6} = 1\frac{1}{6}$	$\frac{8}{7} = 1\frac{1}{7}$	$\frac{4}{3} = 1\frac{1}{3}$
$\frac{21}{5} = 4\frac{1}{5}$	$\frac{9}{4} = 2\frac{1}{4}$	$\frac{3}{2} = 1\frac{1}{2}$	$\frac{9}{6} = 1\frac{3}{6}$	$\frac{25}{4} = 6\frac{1}{4}$	$\frac{8}{3} = 2\frac{2}{3}$

Sara had 29 duplicate stamps in her stamp collection. She decided to give them to four of her friends. If she gave each of them the same number of stamps, how many duplicates will she have left? ___

Name the improper fraction in this problem. $\frac{29}{4}$

What step must you do next to solve the problem? _____

change to a mixed number

Write your answer as a mixed number. $7\frac{1}{4}$

How many stamps could she give each of her friends? 7

Page 397

Mixed Numbers

A **mixed number** is a whole number and a fraction together. An example of a mixed number is $2\frac{3}{4}$. A mixed number can be changed to an improper fraction.

Example: $2\frac{3}{4}$

Step 1: Multiply the denominator by the whole number: $4 \times 2 = 8$

Step 2: Add the numerator: $8 + 3 = 11$

Step 3: Write the sum over the denominator: $\frac{11}{4}$

Directions: Follow the steps above to change the mixed numbers to improper fractions.

$3\frac{2}{3} = \frac{11}{3}$	$6\frac{1}{5} = \frac{31}{5}$	$4\frac{7}{8} = \frac{39}{8}$	$2\frac{1}{2} = \frac{5}{2}$
$1\frac{4}{5} = \frac{9}{5}$	$5\frac{3}{4} = \frac{23}{4}$	$7\frac{1}{8} = \frac{57}{8}$	$9\frac{1}{9} = \frac{82}{9}$
$8\frac{1}{2} = \frac{17}{2}$	$7\frac{1}{6} = \frac{43}{6}$	$5\frac{3}{5} = \frac{28}{5}$	$9\frac{3}{8} = \frac{75}{8}$
$12\frac{1}{5} = \frac{61}{5}$	$25\frac{1}{2} = \frac{51}{2}$	$10\frac{2}{3} = \frac{32}{3}$	$14\frac{3}{8} = \frac{115}{8}$

Page 398

Adding Mixed Numbers

To add mixed numbers, first find the least common denominator.

Always reduce the answer to lowest terms.

Example:
$$5\frac{1}{4} \rightarrow 5\frac{3}{12}$$
$$+ 6\frac{1}{3} \rightarrow + 6\frac{4}{12}$$
$$11\frac{7}{12}$$

Directions: Add. Reduce the answers to lowest terms.

$8\frac{1}{2}$ $+7\frac{1}{4}$ $15\frac{3}{4}$	$5\frac{1}{4}$ $+2\frac{3}{8}$ $7\frac{5}{8}$	$9\frac{3}{10}$ $+7\frac{1}{5}$ $16\frac{1}{2}$	$8\frac{1}{5}$ $+6\frac{7}{10}$ $14\frac{9}{10}$
$4\frac{4}{5}$ $+3\frac{3}{10}$ $8\frac{1}{10}$	$3\frac{1}{2}$ $+7\frac{1}{4}$ $10\frac{3}{4}$	$4\frac{1}{2}$ $+1\frac{1}{3}$ $5\frac{5}{6}$	$6\frac{1}{12}$ $+3\frac{3}{4}$ $9\frac{5}{6}$
$5\frac{1}{3}$ $+2\frac{3}{9}$ $8\frac{2}{3}$	$6\frac{1}{3}$ $+2\frac{1}{5}$ $8\frac{8}{15}$	$2\frac{2}{7}$ $+4\frac{1}{14}$ $6\frac{5}{14}$	$3\frac{1}{2}$ $+3\frac{1}{4}$ $6\frac{3}{4}$

The boys picked $3\frac{1}{2}$ baskets of apples. The girls picked $5\frac{1}{2}$ baskets. How many baskets of apples did the boys and girls pick in all?   9

Page 399

Subtracting Mixed Numbers

To subtract mixed numbers, first find the least common denominator. Reduce the answer to its lowest terms.

Directions: Subtract. Reduce to lowest terms.

Example:
$$6\frac{5}{8} \rightarrow 6\frac{10}{16}$$
$$-3\frac{4}{16} \rightarrow -3\frac{4}{16}$$
$$3\frac{6}{16} = 3\frac{3}{8}$$

$2\frac{3}{7}$ $-1\frac{2}{14}$ $1\frac{5}{14}$	$7\frac{2}{3}$ $-5\frac{1}{8}$ $2\frac{13}{24}$	$6\frac{3}{4}$ $-2\frac{1}{4}$ $4\frac{1}{2}$	$9\frac{5}{12}$ $-5\frac{9}{24}$ $4\frac{1}{24}$
$5\frac{1}{2}$ $-3\frac{1}{3}$ $2\frac{1}{6}$	$7\frac{3}{8}$ $-5\frac{1}{6}$ $2\frac{5}{24}$	$8\frac{1}{4}$ $-6\frac{5}{8}$ $1\frac{23}{24}$	$11\frac{5}{6}$ $-7\frac{1}{12}$ $4\frac{3}{4}$
$9\frac{3}{6}$ $-7\frac{1}{15}$ $2\frac{8}{15}$	$4\frac{4}{5}$ $-2\frac{1}{4}$ $2\frac{11}{20}$	$9\frac{2}{3}$ $-4\frac{1}{6}$ $5\frac{1}{2}$	$14\frac{3}{8}$ $-9\frac{3}{16}$ $5\frac{3}{16}$

The Rodriguez Farm has $9\frac{1}{2}$ acres of corn. The Johnson Farm has $7\frac{1}{3}$ acres of corn. How many more acres of corn does the Rodriguez Farm have? $2\frac{1}{6}$

Page 400

Comparing Fractions

Directions: Use the symbol **>** (greater than), **<** (less than), or **=** (equal to) to show the relationship between each pair of fractions.

$\frac{1}{2}$ **>** $\frac{1}{3}$ $\frac{2}{5}$ **<** $\frac{3}{7}$ $\frac{3}{8}$ **<** $\frac{2}{4}$

$\frac{3}{4}$ **=** $\frac{6}{8}$ $\frac{2}{3}$ **<** $\frac{4}{5}$ $\frac{3}{9}$ **=** $\frac{1}{3}$

$\frac{3}{12}$ **=** $\frac{1}{4}$ $\frac{2}{14}$ **=** $\frac{1}{7}$ $\frac{5}{15}$ **<** $\frac{2}{3}$

If Kelly gave $\frac{1}{3}$ of a pizza to Holly and $\frac{1}{5}$ to Zoe, how much did she have left? $\frac{7}{15}$

Holly decided to share $\frac{1}{2}$ of her share of the pizza with Lila. How much did each of them actually get?

___ $\frac{1}{6}$ ___

Page 401

Ordering Fractions

When putting fractions in order from smallest to largest or largest to smallest, it helps to find a common denominator first.

Example:
$\frac{1}{3}$, $\frac{1}{2}$ changed to $\frac{2}{6}$, $\frac{3}{6}$

Directions: Put the following fractions in order from least to largest value.

				Least				Largest
$\frac{1}{2}$	$\frac{2}{7}$	$\frac{4}{5}$	$\frac{1}{3}$	$\frac{2}{7}$	$\frac{1}{3}$	$\frac{1}{2}$	$\frac{4}{5}$
$\frac{3}{12}$	$\frac{3}{6}$	$\frac{1}{3}$	$\frac{3}{4}$	$\frac{3}{12}$	$\frac{1}{3}$	$\frac{3}{6}$	$\frac{3}{4}$
$\frac{2}{5}$	$\frac{4}{15}$	$\frac{3}{5}$	$\frac{5}{15}$	$\frac{4}{15}$	$\frac{5}{15}$	$\frac{2}{5}$	$\frac{3}{5}$
$3\frac{4}{5}$	$3\frac{2}{5}$	$3\frac{9}{6}$	$3\frac{1}{5}$	$3\frac{1}{5}$	$3\frac{2}{5}$	$3\frac{4}{5}$	$3\frac{9}{6}$
$9\frac{1}{3}$	$9\frac{2}{3}$	$9\frac{9}{12}$	$8\frac{2}{3}$	$8\frac{2}{3}$	$9\frac{1}{3}$	$9\frac{2}{3}$	$9\frac{9}{12}$
$5\frac{8}{12}$	$5\frac{5}{12}$	$5\frac{4}{24}$	$5\frac{4}{3}$	$5\frac{4}{24}$	$5\frac{5}{12}$	$5\frac{8}{12}$	$5\frac{4}{3}$
$4\frac{4}{5}$	$7\frac{7}{15}$	$6\frac{2}{5}$	$5\frac{1}{5}$	$4\frac{3}{5}$	$5\frac{1}{5}$	$7\frac{7}{15}$	$6\frac{2}{5}$

Four dogs were selected as finalists at a dog show. They were judged in four separate categories. One received a perfect score in each area. The dog with a score closest to four is the winner. Their scores are listed below. Which dog won the contest? _Dog A_

Dog A $\left(3\frac{4}{5}\right)$ Dog B $3\frac{2}{3}$ Dog C $3\frac{5}{15}$ Dog D $3\frac{9}{12}$

Page 402

Multiplying Fractions

To multiply fractions, follow these steps:

$\frac{1}{2} \times \frac{3}{4}$ **Step 1:** Multiply the numerators. $1 \times 3 = \frac{3}{8}$
Step 2: Multiply the denominators. $2 \times 4 = 8$

When multiplying a fraction by a whole number, first change the whole number to a fraction.

Example:

$\frac{1}{2} \times 8 = \frac{1}{2} \times \frac{8}{1} = \frac{8}{2} = 4$ reduced to lowest terms

Directions: Multiply. Reduce your answers to lowest terms.

$\frac{3}{4} \times \frac{1}{6} = \frac{1}{8}$	$\frac{1}{2} \times \frac{5}{8} = \frac{5}{16}$	$\frac{2}{3} \times \frac{1}{6} = \frac{1}{9}$	$\frac{2}{3} \times \frac{1}{2} = \frac{1}{3}$
$\frac{5}{6} \times 4 = 3\frac{1}{3}$	$\frac{3}{8} \times \frac{1}{16} = \frac{3}{128}$	$\frac{1}{5} \times 5 = 1$	$\frac{7}{8} \times \frac{3}{4} = \frac{21}{32}$
$\frac{7}{11} \times \frac{1}{3} = \frac{7}{33}$	$\frac{2}{9} \times \frac{9}{4} = \frac{1}{2}$	$\frac{1}{3} \times \frac{1}{3} \times \frac{1}{3} = \frac{1}{27}$	$\frac{1}{8} \times \frac{1}{4} \times \frac{1}{2} = \frac{1}{64}$

Amina has 10 pets. Two-fifths of the pets are cats, one-half are fish, and one-tenth are dogs. How many of each pet does she have?

cats = 4
fish = 5
dogs = 1

Page 403

Multiplying Mixed Numbers

Multiply mixed numbers by first changing them to improper fractions. Always reduce your answers to lowest terms.

Example:

$2\frac{1}{3} \times 1\frac{1}{8} = \frac{7}{3} \times \frac{9}{8} = \frac{63}{24} = 2\frac{15}{24} = 2\frac{5}{8}$

Directions: Multiply. Reduce to lowest terms.

$4\frac{1}{4} \times 2\frac{1}{5} = 9\frac{7}{20}$	$1\frac{1}{3} \times 3\frac{1}{4} = 4\frac{1}{3}$	$1\frac{1}{9} \times 3\frac{3}{5} = 4$
$1\frac{6}{7} \times 4\frac{1}{2} = 8\frac{5}{14}$	$2\frac{3}{4} \times 2\frac{3}{5} = 7\frac{3}{20}$	$4\frac{2}{3} \times 3\frac{1}{7} = 14\frac{2}{3}$
$6\frac{2}{5} \times 2\frac{1}{8} = 13\frac{3}{5}$	$3\frac{1}{7} \times 4\frac{5}{8} = 14\frac{15}{28}$	$7\frac{3}{8} \times 2\frac{1}{9} = 15\frac{41}{72}$

Sunnyside Farm has two barns with 25 stalls in each barn. Cows use $\frac{3}{5}$ of the stalls, and horses use the rest.

How many stalls are for cows? ____30____

How many are for horses? ____20____

(Hint: First, find how many total stalls are in the two barns.)

Page 404

Dividing Fractions

To divide fractions, follow these steps:

$\frac{3}{4} \div \frac{1}{4} =$

Step 1: Invert the divisor. That means to turn it upside down.

$\frac{3}{4} \div \frac{4}{1}$

Step 2: Multiply the two fractions:

$\frac{3}{4} \times \frac{4}{1} = \frac{12}{4}$

Step 3: Reduce the fraction to lowest terms by dividing the denominator into the numerator.

$12 \div 4 = 3$
$\frac{3}{4} \div \frac{1}{4} = 3$

Directions: Follow the above steps to divide fractions.

$\frac{1}{4} \div \frac{1}{5} = 1\frac{1}{4}$	$\frac{1}{3} \div \frac{1}{12} = 4$	$\frac{3}{4} \div \frac{1}{3} = 2\frac{1}{4}$
$\frac{5}{12} \div \frac{1}{3} = 1\frac{1}{4}$	$\frac{3}{4} \div \frac{1}{6} = 4\frac{1}{2}$	$\frac{2}{9} \div \frac{2}{3} = \frac{1}{3}$
$\frac{3}{7} \div \frac{1}{4} = 1\frac{5}{7}$	$\frac{2}{4} \div \frac{1}{6} = 1$	$\frac{1}{8} \div \frac{2}{3} = \frac{3}{16}$
$\frac{4}{5} \div \frac{1}{3} = 2\frac{2}{5}$	$\frac{4}{8} \div \frac{1}{2} = 1$	$\frac{5}{12} \div \frac{6}{8} = \frac{5}{9}$

Page 405

Dividing Whole Numbers by Fractions

Follow these steps to divide a whole number by a fraction:

$8 \div \frac{1}{4} =$

Step 1: Write the whole number as a fraction:

$\frac{8}{1} \div \frac{1}{4} =$

Step 2: Invert the divisor.

$\frac{8}{1} \div \frac{4}{1} =$

Step 3: Multiply the two fractions:

$\frac{8}{1} \times \frac{4}{1} = \frac{32}{1}$

Step 4: Reduce the fraction to lowest terms by dividing the denominator into the numerator: $32 \div 1 = 32$

Directions: Follow the above steps to divide a whole number by a fraction.

$6 \div \frac{1}{3} = 18$	$4 \div \frac{1}{2} = 8$	$21 \div \frac{1}{3} = 63$
$8 \div \frac{1}{2} = 16$	$3 \div \frac{1}{6} = 18$	$15 \div \frac{1}{7} = 105$
$9 \div \frac{1}{5} = 45$	$4 \div \frac{1}{9} = 36$	$12 \div \frac{1}{6} = 72$

Three-fourths of a bag of popcorn fits into one bowl. How many bowls do you need if you have six bags of popcorn? ____8____

Page 406

Decimals

A **decimal** is a number with one or more places to the right of a decimal point.

Examples: 6.5 and 2.25

Fractions with denominators of 10 or 100 can be written as decimals.

Examples:

$\frac{7}{10} = 0.7$

0	.	7	
ones		tenths	hundredths

$1\frac{52}{100} = 1.52$

1	.	5	2
ones		tenths	hundredths

Directions: Write the fractions as decimals.

$\frac{1}{2} = \frac{5}{10} = 0.5$		
$\frac{2}{5} = \frac{4}{10} = 0.4$		
$\frac{1}{5} = \frac{2}{10} = 0.2$		
$\frac{3}{5} = \frac{6}{10} = 0.6$		

		$\frac{1}{4}$	$\frac{1}{5}$	1/10
	$\frac{1}{2}$		$\frac{1}{5}$	1/10
$\frac{1}{2}$		$\frac{1}{4}$		1/10
			$\frac{1}{5}$	1/10

$\frac{63}{100} = 0.63$	$2\frac{8}{10} = 2.8$	$38\frac{4}{100} = 38.04$	$6\frac{13}{100} = 6.13$
$\frac{1}{4} = 0.25$	$\frac{2}{5} = 0.4$	$\frac{1}{50} = 0.02$	$\frac{100}{200} = 0.5$
$5\frac{2}{100} = 5.02$	$\frac{4}{25} = 0.16$	$15\frac{3}{5} = 15.6$	$\frac{3}{100} = 0.03$

Page 407

Decimals and Fractions

Directions: Write the letter of the fraction that is equal to the decimal.

0.25 = __G__
0.5 = __L__
0.7 = __O__
0.8 = __N__
0.37 = __J__
0.2 = __K__
0.65 = __C__
0.75 = __B__
0.6 = __D__
0.12 = __E__
0.33 = __A__
0.95 = __F__
0.24 = __M__
0.3 = __I__
0.4 = __H__

A.	B.	C.
$\frac{33}{100}$	$\frac{3}{4}$	$\frac{13}{20}$

D.	E.	F.
$\frac{3}{5}$	$\frac{3}{25}$	$\frac{19}{20}$

G.	H.	I.
$\frac{1}{4}$	$\frac{2}{5}$	$\frac{3}{10}$

J.	K.	L.
$\frac{37}{100}$	$\frac{1}{5}$	$\frac{1}{2}$

M.	N.	O.
$\frac{6}{25}$	$\frac{4}{5}$	$\frac{7}{10}$

Page 408

Comprehensive Curriculum - **Grade 5**

Adding and Subtracting Decimals

Add and subtract with decimals the same way you do with whole numbers. Keep the decimal points lined up so that you work with hundreths, then tenths, then ones, and so on.

Directions: Add or subtract. Remember to keep the decimal point in the proper place.

| 0.5 + 0.8 = 1.3 | 0.35 + 0.25 = 0.6 | 47.5 − 32.7 = 14.8 | 85.7 − 9.8 = 75.9 |

| 13.90 + 4.23 = 18.13 | 9.53 − 8.16 = 1.37 | 72.8 − 63.9 = 8.9 | 6.43 + 4.58 = 11.01 |

| 638.07 − 19.34 = 618.73 | 811.060 + 78.430 = 889.49 | 521.09 − 148.75 = 372.34 | |

| 916.635 + 172.136 = 1088.771 | 287.768 − 63.951 = 223.817 | 467.05 − 398.19 = 68.86 | |

Sean ran a 1-mile race in 5.58 minutes. Carlos ran it in 6.38 minutes. How much less time did Sean need?

___0.8 minutes___

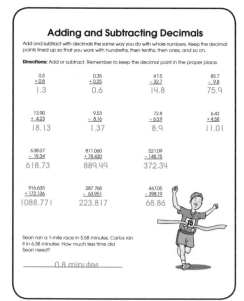

Page 409

Multiplying Decimals

Multiply with decimals the same way you do with whole numbers. The decimal point moves in multiplication. Count the number of decimal places in the problem, and use the same number of decimal places in your answer.

Example:

3.5
x 1.5
175
3 5
5.25

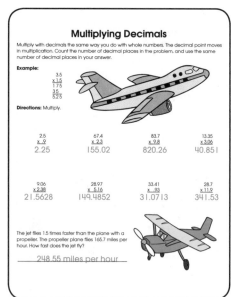

Directions: Multiply.

| 2.5 x .9 = 2.25 | 67.4 x 2.3 = 155.02 | 83.7 x 9.8 = 820.26 | 13.35 x 3.06 = 40.851 |

| 9.06 x 2.38 = 21.5628 | 28.97 x 5.16 = 149.4852 | 33.41 x .93 = 31.0713 | 28.7 x 11.9 = 341.53 |

The jet flies 1.5 times faster than the plane with a propeller. The propeller plane flies 165.7 miles per hour. How fast does the jet fly?

___248.55 miles per hour___

Page 410

Dividing with Decimals

When the dividend has a decimal, place the decimal point for the answer directly above the decimal point in the dividend. The first one has been done for you.

| 12.5 / 3√37.5 −3 07 −6 15 −15 0 | 8.6 / 4√34.4 | 15.8 / 2√31.6 | 43.8 / 3√131.4 |

| 37.5 / 5√187.5 | 25.9 / 7√181.3 | 56.8 / 6√340.8 | 32.7 / 9√294.3 |

| 45.2 / 3√135.6 | 52.9 / 5√264.5 | 67.3 / 2√134.6 | 94.3 / 8√754.4 |

| 7.05 / 5√35.25 | 11.35 / 7√79.45 | 3.19 / 9√28.71 | 5.54 / 36√199.44 |

Page 411

Dividing Decimals by Decimals

When the divisor has a decimal point, you must eliminate it before dividing. You can do this by moving the decimal point to the right to create a whole number. You must also move the decimal point the same number of spaces to the right in the dividend.

Sometimes you need to add zeros to do this.

Example:

0.25√85.50 changes to 342 / 25√8550 −75 105 −100 50 50 0

Directions: Divide.

| 93 / 0.3√27.9 | 71 / 0.6√42.6 | 91 / 0.9√81.9 | 119 / 0.7√83.3 |

| 58 / 0.4√23.2 | 81 / 0.7√56.7 | 9 / 1.2√10.8 | 63 / 2.2√138.6 |

| 450 / 12.6√5,670 | 120 / 4.7√564 | 98 / 8.6√842.8 | 543 / 3.7√2,009.1 |

| 325 / 5.9√1,917.5 | 320 / 4.3√1,376 | 318 / 2.9√922.2 | 2079 / 2.7√5613.3 |

Page 412

Geometry

Geometry is the branch of mathematics that has to do with points, lines, and shapes.

Directions: Write the word from the box that fits each description. Use the glossary on pages 446-455 if you need help.

| triangle | square | cube | angle |
| line | ray | segment | rectangle |

a collection of points on a straight path that goes on and on in opposite directions ___line___

a figure with three sides and three corners ___triangle___

a figure with four equal sides and four corners ___square___

part of a line that has one end point and goes on and on in one direction ___ray___

part of a line having two end points ___segment___

a space figure with six square faces ___cube___

two rays with a common end point ___angle___

a figure with four corners and four sides ___rectangle___

Page 413

Geometry

Review the definitions on the previous page before completing the problems below.

Directions: Identify the labeled section of each of the following diagrams.

AB = ___segment___

ABC = ___angle___

AB = ___segment___

CD = ___line___

AC = ___ray___

AB = ___segment___

EBC = ___angle___

BC = ___ray___

Page 414

Similar, Congruent, and Symmetrical Figures

Similar figures have the same shape but have varying sizes.

Figures that are **congruent** have identical shapes but different orientations. That means they face in different directions.

Symmetrical figures can be divided equally into two identical parts.

Directions: Cross out the shape that does not belong in each group. Label the two remaining shapes as similar, congruent, or symmetrical.

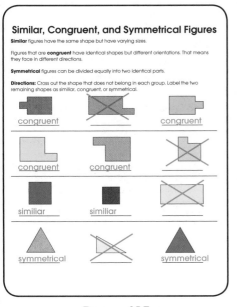

congruent   congruent

congruent   congruent

similiar   similiar

symmetrical   symmetrical

Page 415

Perimeter and Area

The **perimeter (P)** of a figure is the distance around it. To find the perimeter, add the lengths of the sides.

The **area (A)** of a figure is the number of units in a figure. Find the area by multiplying the length of a figure by its width.

Example:

P = 16 units
A = 16 units

Directions: Find the perimeter and area of each figure.

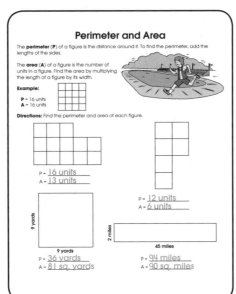

P = 16 units
A = 13 units

P = 12 units
A = 6 units

P = 36 yards
A = 81 sq. yards

P = 94 miles
A = 90 sq. miles

Page 416

Volume

The formula for finding the volume of a box is length times width times height (**L x W x H**). The answer is given in cubic units.

Directions: Solve the problems.

Example:

Height 8 ft.
Length 8 ft.
Width 8 ft.   **L x W x H = volume**
8' x 8' x 8' = 512 cubic ft. or 512 ft.³

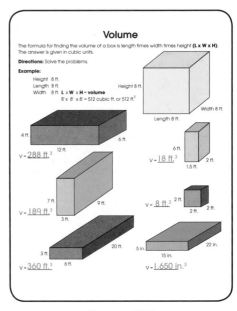

V = 288 ft.³

V = 18 ft.³

V = 189 ft.³

V = 8 ft.³

V = 360 ft.³

V = 1,650 in.³

Page 417

Perimeter and Area

Directions: Use the formulas for finding perimeter and area to solve these problems.

Julie's family moved to a new house. Her parents said she could have the largest bedroom. Julie knew she would need to find the area of each room to find which one was largest.

One rectangular bedroom is 7 feet wide and 12 feet long. Another is 11 feet long and 9 feet wide. The third bedroom is a square. It is 9 feet wide and 9 feet long. Which one should she select to have the largest room?

the 11 x 9 room

The new home also has a swimming pool in the backyard. It is 32 feet long and 18 feet wide. What is the perimeter of the pool?

100 feet

Julie's mother wants to plant flowers on each side of the new house. She will need three plants for every foot of space. The house is 75 feet across the front and back and 37.5 feet along each side. Find the perimeter of the house.

225 feet

How many plants should she buy? 675 plants

The family decided to buy new carpeting for several rooms. Complete the necessary information to determine how much carpeting to buy.

Den: 12 ft. x 14 ft. = 168 sq. ft.

Master bedroom: 20 ft. x 18 ft. = 360 sq. ft.

Family room: 15 ft. x 25 ft. = 375 sq. ft.

Total square feet of carpeting: 903 sq. ft.

Page 418

Perimeter, Area, and Volume

Directions: Find the perimeter and area.

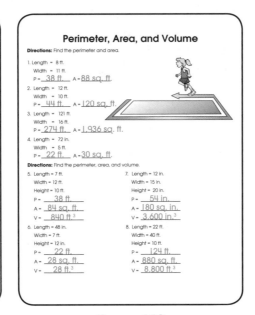

1. Length = 8 ft.
   Width = 11 ft.
   P = 38 ft.   A = 88 sq. ft.

2. Length = 12 ft.
   Width = 10 ft.
   P = 44 ft.   A = 120 sq. ft.

3. Length = 121 ft.
   Width = 16 ft.
   P = 274 ft.   A = 1,936 sq. ft.

4. Length = 72 in.
   Width = 5 ft.
   A = 30 sq. ft.

Directions: Find the perimeter, area, and volume.

5. Length = 7 ft.
   Width = 12 ft.
   Height = 10 ft.
   P = 38 ft.
   A = 84 sq. ft.
   V = 840 ft.³

6. Length = 48 in.
   Width = 7 ft.
   Height = 12 in.
   P = 22 ft.
   A = 28 sq. ft.
   V = 28 ft.³

7. Length = 12 in.
   Width = 15 in.
   Height = 20 in.
   P = 54 in.
   A = 180 sq. in.
   V = 3,600 in.³

8. Length = 22 ft.
   Width = 40 ft.
   Height = 10 ft.
   P = 124 ft.
   A = 880 sq. ft.
   V = 8,800 ft.³

Page 419

Circumference

Circumference is the distance around a circle. The **diameter** is a line segment that passes through the center of a circle and has both end points on the circle.

To find the circumference of any circle, multiply 3.14 times the diameter. The number 3.14 represents **pi** (pronounced *pie*) and is often represented by this Greek symbol, π.

The formula for circumference is C = π x d

C = circumference

d = diameter

π = 3.14

Example:

Circle A
d = 2 in.
C = 3.14 x 2 in.
C = 6.28 in.

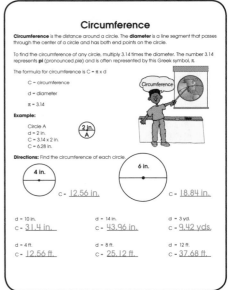

Directions: Find the circumference of each circle.

C = 12.56 in.

C = 18.84 in.

d = 10 in.
C = 31.4 in.

d = 14 in.
C = 43.96 in.

d = 3 yd.
C = 9.42 yds.

d = 4 ft.
C = 12.56 ft.

d = 8 ft.
C = 25.12 ft.

d = 12 ft.
C = 37.68 ft.

Page 420

Comprehensive Curriculum - **Grade 5**

Circumference

The **radius** of a circle is the distance from the center of the circle to its outside edge. The diameter equals two times the radius.

Find the circumference by multiplying π (3.14) times the diameter or by multiplying π (3.14) times 2r (2 times the radius).

$C = \pi \times d$ or $C = \pi \times 2r$

Directions: Write the missing radius, diameter, or circumference.

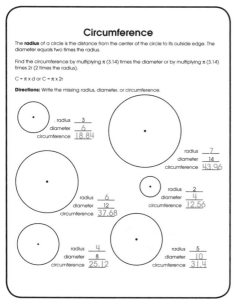

radius __3__
diameter __6__
circumference __18.84__

radius __7__
diameter __14__
circumference __43.96__

radius __6__
diameter __12__
circumference __37.68__

radius __2__
diameter __4__
circumference __12.56__

radius __4__
diameter __8__
circumference __25.12__

radius __5__
diameter __10__
circumference __31.4__

Page 421

Diameter, Radius, and Circumference

$C = \pi \times d$ or $C = \pi \times 2r$

Directions: Write the missing radius, diameter, or circumference.

Katie was asked to draw a circle on the playground for a game during recess. If the radius of the circle needed to be 14 inches, how long is the diameter? __28 inches__

What is the circumference? __87.92 inches__

A friend told her that more kids could play the game if they enlarged the circle. She had a friend help her. They made the diameter of the circle 45 inches long.

What is the radius? __22.5 inches__

What is the circumference? __141.3 inches__

Jamie was creating an art project. He wanted part of it to be a sphere. He measured 24 inches for the diameter.

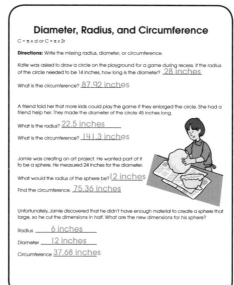

What would the radius of the sphere be? __12 inches__

Find the circumference. __75.36 inches__

Unfortunately, Jamie discovered that he didn't have enough material to create a sphere that large, so he cut the dimensions in half. What are the new dimensions for his sphere?

Radius __6 inches__

Diameter __12 inches__

Circumference __37.68 inches__

Page 422

Triangle Angles

A **triangle** is a figure with three corners and three sides. Every triangle contains three angles. The sum of the angles is always 180°, regardless of the size or shape of the triangle.

If you know two of the angles, you can add them together, and then subtract the total from 180 to find the number of degrees in the third angle.

Directions: Find the number of degrees in the third angle of each triangle.

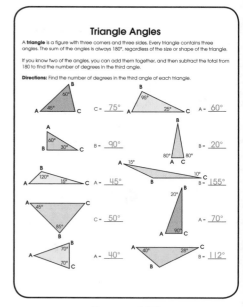

C = __75°__
A = __60°__
B = __90°__
B = __20°__
A = __45°__
B = __155°__
C = __50°__
A = __70°__
A = __40°__
B = __112°__

Page 423

Area of a Triangle

The area of a triangle is found by multiplying $\frac{1}{2}$ times the base times the height.
$A = \frac{1}{2} \times b \times h$

Example:

$\overline{CD}$ is the height.   4 in.

$\overline{AB}$ is the base.   8 in.

Area = $\frac{1}{2} \times 4 \times 8 = \frac{32}{2} = 16$ sq. in.

Directions: Find the area of each triangle.

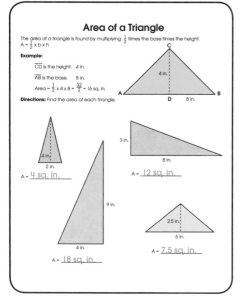

A = __4 sq. in.__

A = __12 sq. in.__

A = __18 sq. in.__

A = __7.5 sq. in.__

Page 424

Space Figures

Space figures are figures whose points are in more than one plane. Cubes and cylinders are space figures.

rectangular prism   cone   cube   cylinder   sphere   pyramid

A **prism** has two identical, parallel bases.

All of the faces on a **rectangular prism** are rectangles.

A **cube** is a prism with six identical, square faces.

A **pyramid** is a space figure whose base is a polygon and whose faces are triangles with a common vertex—the point where two rays meet.

A **cylinder** has a curved surface and two parallel bases that are identical circles.

A **cone** has one circular, flat face and one vertex.

A **sphere** has no flat surface. All points are an equal distance from the center.

Directions: Circle the name of the figure you see in each of these familiar objects

cone   (sphere)   cylinder

cone   sphere   (cylinder)

cube   (rectangular prism)   pyramid

(cone)   pyramid   cylinder

Page 425

Length

Inches, feet, yards, and **miles** are used to measure length in the United States.

12 inches = 1 foot (ft.)
3 feet = 1 yard (yd.)
36 inches = 1 yard
1,760 yards = 1 mile (mi.)

Directions: Circle the best unit to measure each object. The first one has been done for you.

the length of a   (inches)   feet   yards   miles

the height of a   inches   (feet)   yards   miles

the length of a   (inches)   feet   yards   miles

distance to the   inches   feet   yards   (miles)

the height of a   inches   (feet)   (yards)   miles

the length of a ___ field   inches   (feet)   (yards)   miles

Page 426

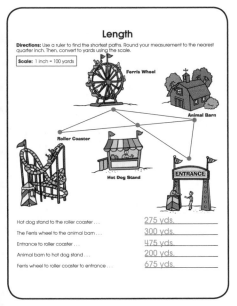

Length

Directions: Use a ruler to find the shortest paths. Round your measurement to the nearest quarter inch. Then, convert to yards using the scale.

Scale: 1 inch = 100 yards

Hot dog stand to the roller coaster . . . 275 yds.
The Ferris wheel to the animal barn . . . 300 yds.
Entrance to roller coaster . . . 475 yds.
Animal barn to hot dog stand . . . 200 yds.
Ferris wheel to roller coaster to entrance . . . 675 yds.

Page 427

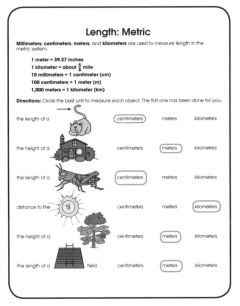

Length: Metric

Millimeters, centimeters, meters, and **kilometers** are used to measure length in the metric system.

1 meter = 39.37 inches
1 kilometer = about ⅝ mile
10 millimeters = 1 centimeter (cm)
100 centimeters = 1 meter (m)
1,000 meters = 1 kilometer (km)

Directions: Circle the best unit to measure each object. The first one has been done for you.

the length of a → (centimeters) / meters / kilometers
the height of a centimeters / (meters) / kilometers
the length of a (centimeters) / meters / kilometers
distance to the centimeters / meters / (kilometers)
the height of a centimeters / (meters) / kilometers
the length of a field centimeters / (meters) / kilometers

Page 428

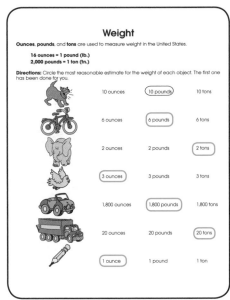

Weight

Ounces, pounds, and **tons** are used to measure weight in the United States.

16 ounces = 1 pound (lb.)
2,000 pounds = 1 ton (tn.)

Directions: Circle the most reasonable estimate for the weight of each object. The first one has been done for you.

10 ounces / (10 pounds) / 10 tons
6 ounces / (6 pounds) / 6 tons
2 ounces / 2 pounds / (2 tons)
(3 ounces) / 3 pounds / 3 tons
1,800 ounces / (1,800 pounds) / 1,800 tons
20 ounces / 20 pounds / (20 tons)
(1 ounce) / 1 pound / 1 ton

Page 429

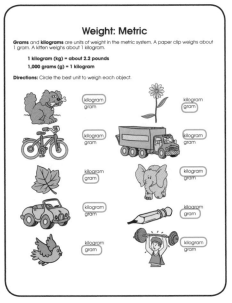

Weight: Metric

Grams and **kilograms** are units of weight in the metric system. A paper clip weighs about 1 gram. A kitten weighs about 1 kilogram.

1 kilogram (kg) = about 2.2 pounds
1,000 grams (g) = 1 kilogram

Directions: Circle the best unit to weigh each object.

(kilogram) / gram
kilogram / (gram)
(kilogram) / gram
kilogram / (gram)
kilogram / (gram)
(kilogram) / gram
kilogram / (gram)
(kilogram) / gram
kilogram / (gram)
(kilogram) / gram

Page 430

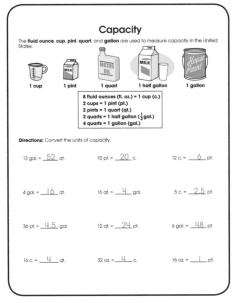

Capacity

The **fluid ounce, cup, pint, quart,** and **gallon** are used to measure capacity in the United States.

1 cup / 1 pint / 1 quart / 1 half gallon / 1 gallon

8 fluid ounces (fl. oz.) = 1 cup (c.)
2 cups = 1 pint (pt.)
2 pints = 1 quart (qt.)
2 quarts = 1 half gallon (½ gal.)
4 quarts = 1 gallon (gal.)

Directions: Convert the units of capacity.

13 gal. = 52 qt.   10 pt. = 20 c.   12 c. = 6 pt.
4 gal. = 16 qt.   16 qt. = 4 gal.   5 c. = 2.5 pt.
36 pt. = 4.5 gal.   12 qt. = 24 pt.   6 gal. = 48 pt.
16 c. = 4 qt.   32 oz. = 4 c.   16 oz. = 1 pt.

Page 431

Capacity: Metric

Milliliters and liters are units of capacity in the metric system. A can of soda contains about 350 milliliters of liquid. A large plastic bottle contains 1 liter of liquid. A liter is about a quart.

1,000 milliliters (mL) = 1 liter (L)

Directions: Circle the best unit to measure each liquid.

(milliliters) / liters   milliliters / (liters)
milliliters / (liters)   milliliters / (liters)
milliliters / (liters)   (milliliters) / liters
(milliliters) / liters   (milliliters) / liters
milliliters / (liters)   milliliters / (liters)

Page 432

ANSWER KEY

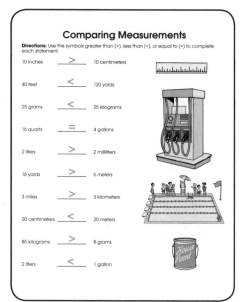

Comparing Measurements

Directions: Use the symbols greater than (>), less than (<), or equal to (=) to complete each statement.

10 inches **>** 10 centimeters

40 feet **<** 120 yards

25 grams **<** 25 kilograms

16 quarts **=** 4 gallons

2 liters **>** 2 milliliters

16 yards **>** 6 meters

3 miles **>** 3 kilometers

20 centimeters **<** 20 meters

85 kilograms **>** 8 grams

2 liters **<** 1 gallon

Page 433

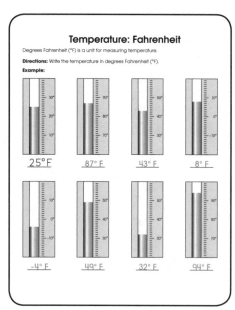

Temperature: Fahrenheit

Degrees Fahrenheit (°F) is a unit for measuring temperature.

Directions: Write the temperature in degrees Fahrenheit (°F).

Example:

25°F   87° F   43° F   8° F

-4° F   49° F   32° F   94° F

Page 434

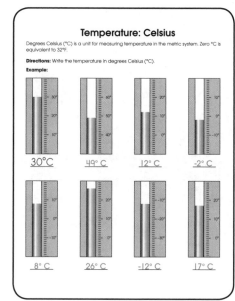

Temperature: Celsius

Degrees Celsius (°C) is a unit for measuring temperature in the metric system. Zero °C is equivalent to 32°F.

Directions: Write the temperature in degrees Celsius (°C).

Example:

30°C   49° C   12° C   -2° C

8° C   26° C   -12° C   17° C

Page 435

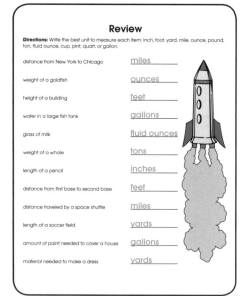

Review

Directions: Write the best unit to measure each item: inch, foot, yard, mile, ounce, pound, ton, fluid ounce, cup, pint, quart, or gallon.

distance from New York to Chicago — miles

weight of a goldfish — ounces

height of a building — feet

water in a large fish tank — gallons

glass of milk — fluid ounces

weight of a whale — tons

length of a pencil — inches

distance from first base to second base — feet

distance traveled by a space shuttle — miles

length of a soccer field — yards

amount of paint needed to cover a house — gallons

material needed to make a dress — yards

Page 436

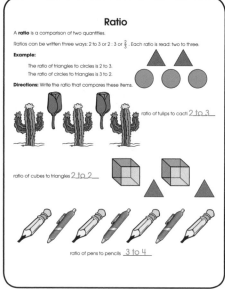

Ratio

A **ratio** is a comparison of two quantities.

Ratios can be written three ways: 2 to 3 or 2 : 3 or $\frac{2}{3}$. Each ratio is read: two to three.

Example:

The ratio of triangles to circles is 2 to 3.
The ratio of circles to triangles is 3 to 2.

Directions: Write the ratio that compares these items.

ratio of tulips to cacti **2 to 3**

ratio of cubes to triangles **2 to 2**

ratio of pens to pencils **3 to 4**

Page 437

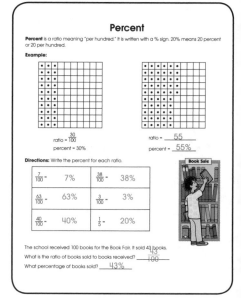

Percent

Percent is a ratio meaning "per hundred." It is written with a % sign. 20% means 20 per hundred or 20 per hundred.

Example:

ratio = $\frac{30}{100}$
percent = 30%

ratio = 55
percent = 55%

Directions: Write the percent for each ratio.

$\frac{7}{100}$ = 7%		$\frac{38}{100}$ = 38%	
$\frac{63}{100}$ = 63%		$\frac{3}{100}$ = 3%	
$\frac{40}{100}$ = 40%		$\frac{1}{5}$ = 20%	

The school received 100 books for the Book Fair. It sold 43 books.

What is the ratio of books sold to books received? $\frac{43}{100}$

What percentage of books sold? **43%**

Page 438

Probability

Probability is the ratio of favorable outcomes to possible outcomes of an experiment.

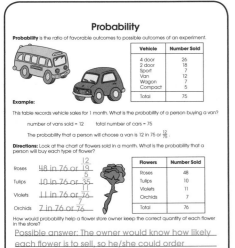

Vehicle	Number Sold
4 door	26
2 door	18
Sport	7
Van	12
Wagon	7
Compact	5
Total	75

Example:

This table records vehicle sales for 1 month. What is the probability of a person buying a van?

number of vans sold = 12   total number of cars = 75

The probability that a person will choose a van is 12 in 75 or $\frac{12}{75}$.

Directions: Look at the chart of flowers sold in a month. What is the probability that a person will buy each type of flower?

Roses   48 in 76 or $\frac{12}{19}$

Tulips   10 in 76 or $\frac{5}{35}$

Violets   11 in 76 or $\frac{11}{76}$

Orchids   7 in 76 or $\frac{7}{76}$

Flowers	Number Sold
Roses	48
Tulips	10
Violets	11
Orchids	7
Total	76

How would probability help a flower store owner keep the correct quantity of each flower in the store?

Possible answer: The owner would know how likely each flower is to sell, so he/she could order quantities based on those numbers.

Page 439

Using Calculators to Find Percent

A **calculator** is a machine that rapidly does addition, subtraction, multiplication, division, and other mathematical functions.

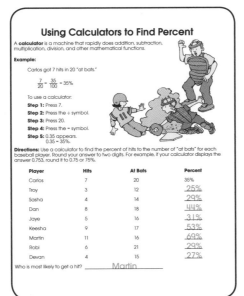

Example:

Carlos got 7 hits in 20 "at bats."

$\frac{7}{20} = \frac{35}{100} = 35\%$

To use a calculator:

Step 1: Press 7.
Step 2: Press the ÷ symbol.
Step 3: Press 20.
Step 4: Press the = symbol.
Step 5: 0.35 appears.
  0.35 = 35%.

Directions: Use a calculator to find the percent of hits to the number of "at bats" for each baseball player. Round your answer to two digits. For example, if your calculator displays the answer 0.753, round it to 0.75 or 75%.

Player	Hits	At Bats	Percent
Carlos	7	20	35%
Troy	3	12	25%
Sasha	4	14	29%
Dan	8	18	44%
Jaye	5	16	31%
Keesha	9	17	53%
Martin	11	16	69%
Robi	6	21	29%
Devan	4	15	27%

Who is most likely to get a hit?   Martin

Page 440

Finding Percents

Find percent by dividing the number you have by the number possible.

Example:

15 out of 20 possible: $\frac{0.75}{20\overline{)15.00}} = 75\%$
  $\underline{-140}$
  100
  $\underline{100}$

Annie has been keeping track of the scores she earned on each spelling test during the grading period.

Directions: Find out each percentage grade she earned. The first one has been done for you.

Week	Number Correct	Total Number of Words	Score in Percent
1	14 (out of)	20	70%
2	16	20	80%
3	18	20	90%
4	12	15	80%
5	16	16	100%
6	17	18	94%
Review Test	51	60	85%

If Carmen scored 5% higher than Annie on the review test, how many words did she get right?   54

Carrie scored 10% lower than Carmen on the review test. How many words did she spell correctly?   48

Of the 24 students in Annie's class, 25% had the same score as Annie. Only 10% had a higher score. What percent had a lower score?   65

Is that answer possible?   no

Why? 65% of 24 is 15.6, and you can't have part of a person

Page 441

Locating Points on a Grid

To locate points on a grid, read the first coordinate, and follow it to the second coordinate.

Example: C, 3

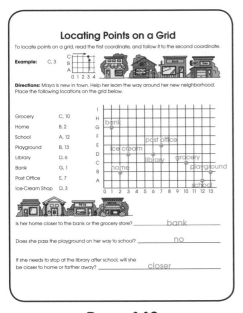

Directions: Maya is new in town. Help her learn the way around her new neighborhood. Place the following locations on the grid below.

Grocery	C, 10
Home	B, 2
School	A, 12
Playground	B, 13
Library	D, 6
Bank	G, 1
Post Office	E, 7
Ice-Cream Shop	D, 3

Is her home closer to the bank or the grocery store?   bank

Does she pass the playground on her way to school?   no

If she needs to stop at the library after school, will she be closer to home or farther away?   closer

Page 442

Graphs

A **graph** is a drawing that shows information about changes in numbers.

Directions: Use the graph to answer the questions.

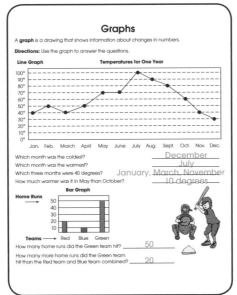

Line Graph — Temperatures for One Year

Which month was the coldest?   December
Which month was the warmest?   July
Which three months were 40 degrees?   January, March, November
How much warmer was it in May than October?   10 degrees

Bar Graph — Home Runs

How many home runs did the Green team hit?   50
How many more home runs did the Green team hit than the Red team and Blue team combined?   20

Page 443

Graphs

Directions: Read each graph, and follow the directions.

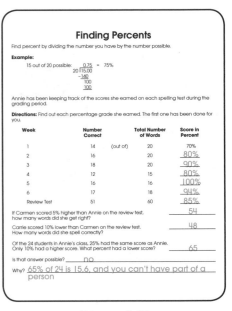

Heights of Students

List the names of the students from the shortest to the tallest.

1. Tiffany   4. Louis
2. Michele   5. Jessie
3. Andy   6. Selena

Lunches Bought

List how many lunches the students bought each day, from the day the most were bought to the least.

1. 92/Friday   4. 78/Thursday
2. 84/Wednesday   5. 72/Tuesday
3. 82/Monday

Days of Outside Recess

List the months in the order of the most number of outside recesses to the least number.

1. June   6. March
2. May   7. November
3. April   8. February
4. September   9. January
5. October   10. December

Page 444

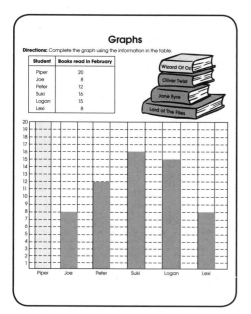

Page 445

Adjectives and Adverbs

Choose a page or two from a book your child is reading. Go through the pages with your child, and underline all the adjectives and adverbs. Then, ask him to rewrite the paragraph, replacing all the adjectives and adverbs with synonyms and/or antonyms.

Basic Math Operations

Addition, subtraction, multiplication, and division are the four basic math functions we use every day. Play counting games, including skip counting by threes, fours, etc. While tossing a ball back and forth, alternate turns counting by a given number. The person catching the ball says the next consecutive number in the sequence.

Make up word problems with addition, subtraction, multiplication, and division at odd moments when you are with your child, such as while traveling in the car, waiting at the doctor's office, or doing the dishes together. Use the situation to add relevance to the word problems. Include your child's name or friends' names in the problems. Examples: 1) It is 375 miles to Grandma's house. We have traveled 217 miles. How much farther do we need to drive? 2) It is 375 miles to Grandma's house. We will take a break about half way there. After how many miles will we take a break?

Each day, post a math question on the refrigerator, and award a point to each family member who answers it correctly. Present a reward to the person who answers the most questions accurately during the week.

Capitalization

Help your child develop listening skills while playing a capitalization game. Have your child listen carefully while you say a sentence. Ask him to tell you which word or words need to be capitalized and why.

Chapter Books

Invite your child to write a different ending or a new chapter to a story. If your child can logically build on previous plot events, you will know that he has grasped the main ideas of the story.

Your child is now reading chapter books. These books usually have very few pictures. Check your child's comprehension by having her draw pictures representing the action or problem for each chapter. Before starting each new chapter, ask your child to predict what will happen.

Fact or Opinion?

Many advertisements are confusing or misleading. Your child should be aware that not everything in an ad may be factual. Cut out ads from magazines and newspapers, or listen to ads on the radio or television. Help your child sort through the information. Ask her to point out the parts that are facts and those that are opinions.

For a period of about 5 minutes, have your child keep a record of sentences she hears friends or family members saying. Then, have your child review the list of sentences and decide which ones are facts, which ones are opinions, and which ones are neither facts nor opinions. Have her explain the reasons for the classification.

Fractions

Let your child cut sandwiches into fractional parts other than one-half or one-quarter. Ask her to cut a pizza into equal parts. Calculate the fraction of the pizza each member of the family can eat.

Homophone Challenge

Homophones are words that are pronounced the same but are spelled differently and have different meanings, such as *to*, *two*, and *too*. Challenge your child to a contest to see who can write the most homophones.

Kitchen Math

Baking and cooking are great opportunities for using math skills like measurement, multiplication, and fractions. Have your child help double or triple a recipe and calculate the ingredients needed.

If your child invents a new recipe, encourage her to write down both the ingredient list and the steps to follow in making the dish. Be sure to share the recipe with family members and friends.

On your shelves or at the grocery store, ask your child to find items labeled in standard or metric units. At home, work together to change a recipe to metric measures.

Measurement

A tape measure is a great learning tool. Let your child measure and compare the size of various objects. Challenge her to find two unlike objects with the same perimeter.

Money

Involve your child in math activities dealing with money. Ask her to estimate prices on a shopping list, calculate change, double check a bill at a restaurant, and calculate tips.

Have your child determine how she spends her money. When your child receives a money gift or allowance, ask her to figure the percent spent on savings, gifts, and items purchased.

Newspaper Activities

On your shelves or at the grocery store, ask your child to find items labeled in standard or metric units. At home, work together to change a recipe to metric measures.

Cut out or print out articles of interest to your child—ones about neighborhood events, people you know, or items relating to school or special hobbies and favorite sports. Some children will find newspaper reading less intimidating and more appealing when they read only one article a day.

Read news articles with your child. Help him find the "who, what, when, where, why, and how" answers to the stories. Each week, help your child write one news article about something that has happened in his life.

Ask other family members to write short articles, too. Combine the articles, and make a family newspaper once a month. Send the articles to family and friends when you write or send cards.

Ask your child, "If a news article were about something that happened to you today, what would the headline say?" Encourage your child to think up short, snappy headlines to summarize an event.

Opinions

Write a thought-provoking question on a piece of paper, and post it on the refrigerator early in the day for all family members to read and think about. At dinner or in the evening, use that topic for a family discussion. Encourage your child to give reasons for his opinions.

You might pose a question about a fad or fashion, a current TV series, or a computer game. Let your child and other family members take turns writing the question of the day.

Use the time you spend taking a walk or riding in the car with your child to discuss the pros and cons of your question of the day. Encourage your child to look at both sides of an issue to see other viewpoints.

Parts of Speech

Copy sentences from a book, newspaper, or magazine article. Ask your child to read the sentences aloud. Then, have him identify the part of speech of each word. If he has trouble, suggest consulting a dictionary. Most dictionaries list the part of speech for each word.

Help your child practice recognizing parts of speech as you travel. Point out billboards, and ask your child to name the part of speech for each word in the advertisements.

Percents

Help your child collect family data on time usage, such as time spent sleeping, driving to work, or in school. Ask him to create a graph showing time usage or to calculate the percent of a day or week spent doing various tasks.

Possessive Adjectives and Apostrophes

Write a story that contains several phrases with possessive adjectives, such as *Mom's keys* or *Joshua's backpack*, and leave out all the apostrophes. Have your child go through the paragraph and insert apostrophes where needed.

Practical Math

If you are planning any project involving measurement and materials, such as planting a garden, building a doghouse, buying new carpeting, or painting a room, involve your child in the process by letting him help measure and calculate expenses. Create a supply list together. Use ads to find prices and calculate the total cost. Explore alternate ways to complete the project at a lower cost.

Prefixes, Suffixes, and Root Words

Write a list of common root words, prefixes, and suffixes. Write the root words on squares of colored construction paper, the prefixes on squares of another color, and the suffixes on squares of a third color. Help your child mix and match the squares, seeing how many different word combinations he can make. Ask your child for the meaning of each new word created.

Proofreading

Help your child proofread letters and reports he writes. Proofreading consists of checking for grammatical errors and correcting spelling, punctuation, and capitalization errors. Make the corrections together until your child is able to handle proofreading on his own. Even when you write using a word processing program, material needs to be read and checked. Spell checkers are helpful but cannot find and correct all types of errors.

Have your child help you with your own writing, whether it is a short report or memo for work or an email to a friend. Ask your child to use her proofreading skills to check for errors before you write the final draft.

Choose a paragraph from a book your child is reading. Rewrite the paragraph, leaving out all punctuation and capitalization. Ask your child to proofread the paragraph, putting in correct punctuation and capitalization without looking back at the book. She can check the book when finished.

Reading Labels

Reading and understanding labels is a skill everyone needs. As you shop, let your child read labels to compare ingredients and other nutritional information. Reading labels will help your child become a better consumer and may encourage her to eat more healthful foods.

Stress the importance of reading labels and following directions, particularly on medications or products that may be hazardous.

Recalling Details

As you read with your child, encourage her to picture what is happening. Forming a mental picture will help your child recall the story using the "mind's eye," as well as the ear. Then, ask her to retell the story, noting details from the beginning, middle, and end.

Sequencing

Print out a newspaper or magazine article. Cut the article into separate paragraphs. Ask your child to arrange the paragraphs in the correct order. (Keep in mind that the final story may not be in the exact order as the original but may still make sense.) Discuss with your child why she chose that particular sequence and why it makes sense to her.

Spelling

Have your child keep a spelling log in which she writes previously misspelled words. Ask your child to write each word several times and also use it in a sentence.

Together with your child, review the writing exercises she has done in this book, looking for spelling errors. Then, have your child correct any misspelled words, using a dictionary if necessary. As an alternative, write short paragraphs or sentences that contain minor spelling and punctuation errors. Invite your child to find the mistakes, and have her rewrite the sentences correctly.

Summarizing and Comparing

Visit the library, and borrow two copies of a book so both you and your child can read and discuss the book together. After each chapter, ask your child to summarize story events. Discuss what you both liked and disliked about the book, the characters, and the plot. Encourage your child to compare and contrast the book with another she has read.

Synonyms and Antonyms

Play a synonym/antonym game when you and your child are together for an extended time, perhaps on a walk or a long car ride. Say a word, and ask your child to name a synonym or antonym for that word. If your child is correct, ask her to take a turn in thinking of a word.

Using Reference Sources

If your child has a question about a topic in a newspaper or magazine article, use various reference sources to find the answer. If you don't have the references you need at home, go to the library with your child and help her find the answer.

Help your child do research on the Internet to find up-to-the-minute information on a variety of topics. Be sure to teach your child Internet safety and closely monitor her use of the Internet.

Select a topic of the month for you and your child to research. Prepare a report together. Select one of the topics below or come up with one of your own.

The history of a sport
A specific 10-year period of American history
The Constitution or Declaration of Independence
The development of computers
Virtual reality

Follow the steps of the writing process as you prepare the report together.

1. Gather information from reference sources.
2. Take notes listing the main points. Summarize what you have read, and write an outline.
3. Write a research paper based on the information you found.
4. Edit your work. Make corrections, and rewrite if necessary.

A good dictionary, along with a thesaurus and access to an online encyclopedia, is a valuable resource. When you and your child come across a word you don't know, look it up together. Check the pronunciation. Use the word in a sentence.

Word Games

Word games, such as crossword puzzles and word scrambles, will expand your child's vocabulary and develop his spelling skills. You can find word games and puzzles online, in the newspaper, or in puzzle books at the library or bookstore.

Writing Experiences

Help your child write friendly letters to relatives and friends. Saying "thank you" in writing is a good habit for your child to learn. Thank-you notes can be sent for gifts and for thoughtful actions, like an invitation from a friend's parents for dinner or an overnight visit.

Read several movie reviews with your child. Then, watch a movie of your child's choice, and invite him to write a movie review. You may want to write one yourself. Compare the two, and discuss why you felt differently/similarly about the movie.

Show your child that writing is important. Make sure he sees you and other family members writing frequently. Invite your child to help you write grocery lists, letters or emails to relatives and friends, holiday cards, and notes to other family members. Let your child see you proofreading and correcting your own writing.

An anthology is a collection of short stories, poems, essays, etc. by one author. As your child completes a writing project or special piece of artwork, save it in a three-ring binder. Date each item. When the binder is full, pack it away and start another. Save the full binders until your child is older. Gift wrap one and give it to your child as a unique present for a special occasion.

Encourage your child to keep a personal journal. You might suggest writing topics, but your child should understand that the journal is his outlet for thoughts and feelings. Make it clear that you will not check or correct the journal and that you will not read it unless he chooses to show it to you. Encourage your child to write every day about anything he wishes. Suggested topics might include a trip to the store, an episode of a favorite TV show, going to the park, favorite things to with friends, or favorite foods.

If you have access to the Internet, have your child write to someone using email. Whether on a computer or with paper and pen, the format of a letter is the same. Stress correct grammar, spelling, punctuation, and sentence structure.

Writing Poetry

Help your child use metaphors, similes and alliteration to create poetry.

Encourage your child to illustrate his poems for greater visual effect or write his best poems with glittery pens on fancy paper. Or, type your child's original poetry and print it out, perhaps with a fancy border. Frame and hang the poems in your home for all to enjoy.

Read favorite poems to your child to give her a better appreciation for this type of writing. Then, write a "tandem poem" with your child. Either you or your child can start by writing a single line or stanza, and then giving the poem to the other to continue. Switch back and forth until the poem is complete. You may want to decide on a length before beginning the poem. You can carry out this exercise over the course of several days. When the poem is finished, ask your child to illustrate it, and display it prominently in your home. Help your child brainstorm topics to write about in a poem. You may want to use one of the following suggestions: All About Me, What If?, A Strange Dream, What I Smelled, The Perfect Day, The One That Got Away, If Wishes Came True, or What I Saw.

Comprehensive Curriculum - **Grade 5**

INDEX